FRONT COVER

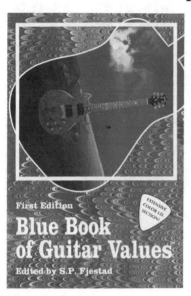

Perhaps many of you have already noticed the 1st Edition cover graphics are a little different than the images you have seen on other guitar publications. The swirl pattern background is a reproduction of a "marbled" paper design that has been classically used to formally separate the hardbound cover from the inside main text on finer quality publications. The different colored inks are literally poured in layers on heavy paper stock, followed by a very precise series of mechanical fingered "combings" that produce the unique and imperfect geometrical patterns and color arrays (some marbled paper designs are so precise and consistent that once the inks dry, the final image can be copyrighted for future reproduction).

The guitar pictured is a rare Moonstone Vulcan Model (ser. no. 7980) manufactured circa 1979 by Moonstone Guitars located in Arcata, California. This manufacturer became famous for almost fanatical craftsmanship in addition to using only the finest and most exotic woods in the construction of its instruments. This particular specimen features a double cutaway, one-piece highly figured spalted maple body, 5-piece laminated birdseye maple/padouk neck with rosewood binding and ebony fretboard featuring multiple diamond/star abalone inlays, gold plated tuners and active Bartolini pickups. Taking off the matching wood back plate cover reveals internal workmanship that resembles the internal movements of a Rolex watch.

Unfortunately, the plant was destroyed by fire in the early '80s (including their stock of exotic woods), and lack of insurance precluded them from building another guitar. Every once in a while, if you are in the Grand Canyon on a blustery day, you may also see a Moonstone ascending out of the lower depths if you look carefully!

Once printed in four-color, the cover sheets were transported onto the next production stop which specialized in high-tech foil stamping/embossing, which made this unique imaging possible. Once the covers were foil stamped (a separate press run requiring perfect die registration), the cover sheets were again transported from Minneapolis back to the printer in Brainerd for laminating (a clear, protective laminate which after heating adheres to the cover paper stock). Once the laminating had been completed, the "2-up" sheets went through the embossing stage, a critical phase where the images are punched up in multi-levels by using state-of-the-art custom dies. Once embossed, it was back to the printer one last time for final trimming, and the final destination - the bindery.

These four separately critical operations allowed the 1st Edition covers to cumulatively put on close to 1,500,000 miles before they ever left our warehouse!

BACK COVER

The guitars pictured on the back cover of this 1st Edition of the *Blue Book of Guitar Values*™ feature several Gibsons and a Fender. The Les Paul pictured on the left (serial number 2-1012) is very unusual in that it is the first 12 string ever manufactured by Gibson's Custom Shop in 1992. It is patterned after the '59 Les Paul Standard configuration utilizing book-matched flame maple top with single binding, one-piece mahogany body, one-piece mahogany neck, rosewood fingerboard with pearl trapezoid inlays, gold (even though nickel was standard) plated hardware, and this instrument was custom ordered sans pickguard. The bridge had to be specially machined to allow the addition of another 6 strings.

The Fender Stratocaster (serial number E333031) pictured in the middle is a 1983 Elite Model in rare Emerald Green with push-button pickup controls and active electronics. An extremely heavy Strat, the body features 3-piece ash construction, maple neck with rosewood fretboard. Note how the bridge with tremolo extension differs from other Stratocasters.

The Gibson Les Paul Custom featured on the right (serial number 81289525) is an above-average example of the Custom Shop's finest. Spectacular book-matched flame maple is highlighted by the uniform Cherry Sunburst finish and 7-lamination body binding. Gold plated metal parts are offset nicely by black mounting hardware and control knobs which further add to this instrument's stunning appearance. Formerly owned by Jimmy Wallace, lead guitar player of the Dallas based Stratoblasters, this instrument has not seen too many smoke-filled bar rooms (yet).

The lucky musician who owns these instruments has just moved into yet another motel room for a gig the following evening. Silk pajamas and this nice variety of premium instruments indicate good times, good tunes, and just a little bit more practicing before bedtime (nocturnally inclined, he's probably on the phone trying to figure out if room service will still deliver).

COVER CREDITS

Cover Design and Final Layout - S.P. Fjestad

Art Director - Doreen Pomije

Front Cover Photography and Imagery Compositing - Tom Farmer and crew from Prism Studios, Inc.

Back Cover Photography - S. P. Fjestad

Color Separations - Leslie, Roger, and Dick from Northwoods Color

Printing - Carol, Sandy, and crew from Bang Printing

Foil Stamping and Embossing - Fraser Company

First Edition

Blue Book of Guitar Values ™

Publisher's Note:

This book is the result of nonstop and continual guitar research obtained by attending guitar shows, communicating with guitar dealers and collectors throughout the country each year, and staying on top of trends as they occur. This book represents an analysis of prices for which both recently manufactured and collectible guitars have actually been selling for during that period at an average retail level.

Although every reasonable effort has been made to compile an accurate and reliable guide, guitar prices may vary significantly depending on such factors as the locality of the sale, the number of sales we were able to consider, famous musician endorsement of certain models, regional economic conditions, and other critical factors.

Accordingly, no representation can be made that the guitars listed may be bought or sold at prices indicated, nor shall the editor or publisher be responsible for any error made in compiling and recording such prices.

Blue Book of Guitar Values™ Order Form
One Appletree Square
Minneapolis, MN 55425 U.S.A.
Phone No. 612-854-5229
-To Order Domestically-

Call : **TOLL FREE 1-800-877-4867** or FAX (612) 853-1486 to use your **VISA, MASTERCARD** or **DISCOVER** charge cards, or send in this order form with payment.

MN residents please include 7% sales tax - $1.40 per book.

OFFICE HOURS: 8:30 AM - 5:00 PM (CST), Monday - Friday. Answering machine services available 5:00 PM - 8:30 AM, Monday - Friday and weekends. FAX service available 24 hours per day. All FAX and phone message orders (if information is complete) will be shipped within 2 business days.

☐ **1st Edition — $24.95** ($19.95 + $5 s/h- 4th class U.S. Mail)

> **Expedited Shipping Costs:** *in the continental U.S.* ; 1st class U.S. Mail or UPS ground service - add $2.00; UPS 2nd day air - add $5.00; Next Day - add $15.00
>
> *Alaska and Hawaii* - 2nd day air - add $10.00; Next Day - add $20.00
>
> **International Shipping** - *Canada and Mexico* - add $5.00
>
> *Europe* - air mail - add $15.00, to *Africa, Asia*, or *Pacific Rim* - add $20.00
>
> *International* Surface Rate - add $5.00

☐ **1st & 2nd Editions — $39.95** (includes 4th class U.S. Mail delivery)
1st edition shipped immediately — 2nd edition will be shipped in 1994.

SORRY, NO C.O.D.'s.
This offer expires March 1, 1994

Company Name _____

Name _____

Address_____

City _____ **State** _____ **Zip** _____

Phone _____

VISA/MASTERCARD/DISCOVER # _____

Expiration Date of Card _____

Signature _____

(Personal or cashier's check, money order, etc. are also considered good funds.
All orders are shipped within 2 working days after receiving good funds).

Or Send Payment To:

Blue Book of Guitar Values™
Department 522
One Appletree Square #1391
Minneapolis, MN 55425 U.S.A.

☐ Please send me more information on other "Blue Book" Products.

Interested In Contributing?

I've always said that once you publish a book, you find out what you don't know. This publication is no different. Fortunately, however, an annual pricing guide should always get better. Accumulating new research is an ongoing process with the results being published in each new edition.

The *Blue Book of Guitar Values*™ has been the result of non-stop and continual guitar research obtained by observing and analyzing market trends, going to guitar shows, utilizing critical and up-to-date information obtained from NAMM's fretted instrument manufacturers/importers/dealers, following major vintage dealer and collector pricing and trends, trying to accurately gauge the current Japanese demand factor, and guestimating the influence of new investment dollars.

If you feel that you can contribute in any way to the materials published herein, I would encourage you to contact me about your potential additions, revisions, corrections, or any other pertinent information that you feel would enhance the benefits this book provides to the readers. No one person can know it all — it takes a combination of many individuals' knowledgeable brain cells before any publication such as this can be truly accurate and complete.

All materials sent in for possible inclusion into the upcoming 2nd Edition of the *Blue Book of Guitar Values*™ should be mailed/FAXed to us no later than March 1, 1994 at the address listed below.

Blue Book Publications, Inc.
Attn: Guitar Contributions
One Appletree Square
Minneapolis, MN 55425 USA
FAX: 612-853-1486

Once you have sent your contributions in, we will contact you at a later date to discuss their possible inclusion in upcoming editions. The last chapter on intelligence can't be written until you accumulate the additional knowledge learned after you start to think that you already know it all.

CONTENTS

Cover Explanation 2-3
Publisher's Note 4
Order Form 5
Interested in Contributing? 6
How to Use the Blue Book 8-11
Acknowledgements 12
Dedication...13
Correspondence Inquiries...14
A Unique Concept 15
Introduction 16-22
Guitars, Suds, and Pork Chops 23-27
An Overview of the Guitar Marketplace 28-31
Explaining/Converting the Photo Percentage Grading System© 32
Foreword of the Photo Percentage Grading System© 33-34
Photo Percentage Grading System© 35-72
Guitar Glossary..73-81
Abbreviations 82
Guitar Inventory Records 83-85
Meet the Staff 86-88
American Guitar Player's Association 89
Periodicals Listing 90
Guitar Book References..91
Guitar Text...93-506
Trademark Index 507-512
Guitar Serialization..513-519
Index..520

How to Use This Book

The prices listed in the 1st Edition of the *Blue Book of Guitar Values*™ are based on national average retail prices for both vintage and modern guitars. This is NOT a wholesale pricing guide (I doubt if there could be such a thing). Nor should you expect to walk into a music store/guitar shop and think that the proprietor will pay you the retail price listed within this text for your instrument(s). **Dealer offers on most models could be 15%-40% less than values listed**. Percentages of original condition (with corresponding prices) are listed between 20%-90% for most vintage guitars (unless configuration, rarity, and age preclude upper conditions) and 60%-100% on modern guitars since condition below 60% is seldom encountered (or purchased). Please consult our 40-page Photo Percentage Grading System© insert (pages 33-72) to learn more about the condition of your guitar. This is the first time, to my knowledge, that color plates have been utilized to accurately illustrate the guitar's percentage grading system. Since condition is the overriding factor in price evaluation, study these photos carefully to learn more about the condition of your specimen(s).

For your convenience, explanations of percentages of condition, older guitar standards, and other grading criteria have been included on page 32 to assist you in learning more about the percentage grading system. This will be especially helpful when evaluating older vintage instruments.

All values within this text assume original condition. Any repairs, alterations, modifications, "enhancements", "improvements", or any other non-factory changes usually detract from an instrument's value. Depending on the seriousness of the modification/alteration, you may have to go down 1-3 condition factors when recomputing price for these changes. Also, knowing how to convert existing grading systems to the Photo Percentage Grading System© is critical when ascertaining value. Please refer to page 32 of this text to learn more about this very important conversion process.

You will note that line-art graphics and black-and-white photos have been provided to assist you with the visual identification of certain models and variations.

When looking up information in this text remember, it reads just like a good *National Enquirer* article — turn the page to see if there is some more juicy info awaiting you.

For sake of simplicity the following organizational framework has been adopted throughout this publication.

1. Trademark manufacturer, brand name, or importer is listed in bold face type alphabetically, i.e.,

FENDER, GIBSON, MARTIN, OVATION

2. Manufacturer information is listed directly beneath the trademark heading, i.e.,

Manufacturer located in Nazareth, PA since 1838.

3. Next classification is a category name (upper-case typeface description inside a shortened gray box) referring mostly to a guitar's primary configuration, i.e.,

ACOUSTIC, BASS, ELECTRIC

4. A sub-classification of the category name (upper/lower-case description inside a page-wide gray box) usually indicates a grouping or series within the definition of the category name, i.e.,

Artist Series, Original Les Paul Series, Solid Bodies

5. Model names appear flush left, are bold faced, and capitalized in alpha-numerical (normally) order grouped under various subheadings, i.e.,

BROADCASTER, D-28, DUO-JET 6128, FLYING V, TL5

6. Model descriptions appear directly under Model names and appear as follows:

— body configuration and identifying features and materials, neck configuration and construction, wood used on fingerboard/headstock and any discernible inlays/features, type and style of pickups (if any), tuner configuration and style, colors and/or finishes and other definitive descriptive data are further categorized adjacent to the model names in this typeface. This is where most of the information is listed for each specific model.

7. Variations within a model appear as sub-models - they are differentiated from model names by an artistic "bullet" prefix, are indented, and in upper and lower case, i.e.,

⚡ Coronado Wildwood II, ES-175D, Nightbird Deluxe, 330/12

8. *Manufacturer and other notes/information appear in smaller type and should be read since they contain both important and other critical, up-to-date information, last manufacturer's suggested retail price (if known), i.e.,*

This guitar had an unusually large headstock, thus giving it the nickname "Hockey Stick". An economy version was produced with an unbound fingerboard with dot inlays.

9. *Extra cost features/special orders and other value added/subtracted items (add-ons for currently manufactured guitars reflect retail) are placed directly under individual price lines and appear bolder than other descriptive typeface, i.e.,*

Add 15% for Brazilian rosewood back/sides - available 1966-69 only.

10. *Grading lines will appear at the top of each page or wherever pricing lines change. The most commonly encountered grading line in this text is from 100%-60%, i.e.,*

Grading	100%	98%	95%	90%	80%	70%	60%

Vintage instrument grading lines (used mostly on Pre-WWII instruments) have values listed for 90%-20% condition factors, i.e.

Grading	90%	80%	70%	60%	50%	40%	20%

11. *The most common price line will appear as follows throughout this text. When the price line shown below is encountered,*

Mfr.'s Sug. Retail	$170	$150	$130	$115	$105	$95	$85	$80

it automatically indicates the guitar is currently manufactured and the manufacturer's retail price is shown left of the 100% column. Following are the 100%-60% values. The 100% price is what you can typically expect to pay for a new, previously unsold instrument that is NIC (new in case, if any) condition (must include EVERYTHING the factory provided with the instrument) with normal discounting (if any). The 98%-60% remaining values represent actual retail selling prices - simply find the correct column and refer to the price listed. Please consult the Photo Percentage Grading System© *located on pages 33-72 to learn more about determining condition or turn to page 32 to convert other grading system terminology to the* Photo Percentage Grading System© *condition factor. The 100% condition factor, when encountered in a currently manufactured guitar, assumes not sold previously at retail. 100% specimens that have played a few licks but are without original cases, warranties, etc., and are currently manufactured must be discounted somewhat (5%-25%, depending on the desirability of make and model). The 98% condition factor used throughout this text when encountered in a currently manufactured guitar means previously sold at retail, even though the instrument may appear new.*

13. A price line with 7 values listed (represented below) indicates a

$715 $660 $605 $550 $440 $385 $330

discontinued, out of production model with values shown for 100%- 60% conditions. Obviously, "Mfr.'s Sug. Retail" will not appear in the left margin, but a model note may appear below the price line indicating what the last Mfr.'s Sug. Retail was. Also, N/A may appear in place of upper condition values for instruments that are not commonly encountered in that condition factor(s).

To find a particular guitar in this book, first look under the name of the manufacturer, importer, or brand name. Next find the correct subdivision (either acoustics, basses, electrics, etc.). When applicable, vintage instruments will appear before modern guitars and are subdivided like other descriptions. Once you find the correct model or sub-model under its respective subheading, determine the guitar's percentage of *original* condition (see the Photo Percentage Grading System on pages 33-72), simply find the corresponding percentage column to ascertain price. Special/limited editions usually appear last under a manufacturer's heading.

Additional sections in this publication that should be of special interest are the Photo Percentage Grading System, Correspondence Inquiries (involving specific research and appraisals), Interest in Contributing, Glossary, References, Periodicals, Trademark Index, and Serialization Charts. When using the Serialization Charts, make sure your model is listed and find the serial number within the yearly range listings. More research and data regarding serialization is being compiled, and will be published in the upcoming 2nd Edition of the *Blue Book of Guitar Values*™.

Acknowledgements

As you would suspect, no single person can possibly assemble a publication with this much data. It is a great responsibility to accurately compile all the information in this text. Remembering and listing everyone who has assisted me in the compilation of the 1st Edition of the *Blue Book of Guitar Values*™ would be impossible, but go ahead and take a bow - you know who you are, and you have earned it. The following people, however, deserve a special thanks, because without them, this publication would not be in your hands:

Dave Rogers and Crew
>from Dave's Guitar Shop in LaCrosse, WI

Nate Westgor and Skip
>from Willie's American Guitars in St. Paul, MN

Pete Wagener
>from LaVonne's Music in Savage, MN

Jimmy Wallace
>from Southwest Music in Dallas, TX

NAMM
>(National Association of Musical Merchants)

and to

Michelle Schroeder and **Lisa Winkels** for editing, correcting, proofing, reproofing, formating, reformating, becoming neurotic, reproofing again, and in the end (thank goodness), flunking their entrance exam for one of the local state hospitals. Ask them sometime if they would like to do it again.

and also to

Mr. Dwight Bode, who originally started the manuscript research and continued to assist our staff throughout the entire production cycle. By now, Dwight fully understands the words "format" and "deadlines". And, by the way, when receiving manuscript revisions made on a floppy from an Iowa pawn shop, make sure that you have some anti-viral medicine in your computer medicine cabinet.

and a special thanks to

Jeff Perkins, who was initially caught in a manuscript cross-fire, but managed to persevere, numb out, and was the first to reach the summit. Tenderizing this manuscript took more than what Adolf's could offer, and Jeff finally overcame a lot of derailments to put this project back on track.

Dedication

The 1st Edition of the *Blue Book of Guitar Values*™ is dedicated to the late Tim Koivisto, a dedicated axe grinder, kind soul, and part-time gun-eria guru. Without Tim, there would be no book. I hope he understands the trade I made - his Anniversary Strat for a newer Custom Shop set-neck edition with a book-matched flame-top.

The Marines have a few good men, but when in LaCrosse, you have to settle for the folks pictured above. From left to right, Dave Rogers, Jimbo, J.P., Tim, and Jeff, the Cereal Killer - the entire crew from Dave's Guitar Shop located in LaCrosse, WI. These guys must be seen in action to be believed (no different from the Marines). The publisher expresses his thanks to Dave and Staff for spending the time, doing a lot of undercover work, and jamming when we needed it most. After the G. Heileman's Brewing Co. tour, make sure you walk over and take a glimpse of their huge shop.

CORRESPONDENCE INQUIRIES

As with any new publication, certain models and variations will not initially be included within the scope of the text. Not believing in ivory towers and one-way traffic, this publisher offers a mechanism for the consumer to get further information about models not listed in these pages. No book can ever be totally complete in a collectible field as broad as this one. For that reason, we are offering correspondence and telephone inquiries to help you obtain additional information on items not listed or even questions on the data and prices provided.

With the addition of new personnel, correspondence under normal circumstances takes us between 10-14 working days, one of the fastest turn-around times in the industry. To make sure we can assist you with any correspondence, please include good quality photos of the specimen in question, any information available about that particular specimen, including manufacturer, model, body style, color/finish, unusual or other discernible features (if any) that will assist us with identifying your guitar. The charge for this comprehensive research program is $20.00 per instrument. In addition to payment, be sure to include both your address and phone number, giving us an option of how to contact you for best service. To keep up with this constant onslaught of mail/FAXes, we have a large network of both dealers and collectors who can assist us (if necessary) to answer most of your questions within this time frame.

Remember, the charge for this research service is $20.00 per guitar and payment must accompany your correspondence. Your letters/FAXes will be answered in a FIFO system (first in — first out). Thank you for your patience.

Because of the flood of mail and phone calls we get annually, we can no longer perform free evaluations. Correspondence sent in without payment will be returned. Phone calls regarding guitar related questions will be taken between 2-5 pm daily (CST), during most weekdays, unless we are absent.

Time permitting, pink slip calls will be returned, but paid correspondence and FAXes will receive first priority. We are hoping our turnaround time for research will allow us to give prompt service, and the only way to achieve this is to limit phone access time. It's a big job! All Correspondence Should be directed to:

Blue Book Publications, Inc.
ATTN: Guitar Research
One Appletree Square
Minneapolis, MN 55425
FAX# 612-853-1486

SORRY - No order or request for research paid by credit card will be processed without a credit card expiration date.

A Unique Concept

The *Blue Book of Guitar Values*™ is the only book that:

✓ *Utilizes the professionals' grading system of percentage of original finish remaining. (Eliminates confusing condition descriptions such as "Good", "Excellent+", "Fair", between "7/8", or "9+").*

✓ *Is updated annually and expeditiously provides the freshest information available!*

✓ *Is based on actual selling prices. (These are the prices you can expect to pay — not artificial list prices or some "expert's" opinion).*

✓ *Offers you personal consultation by mail on special questions you may have! (No book can cover everything).*

Individual appraisals and/or additional research can be performed for $20.00 per guitar (see the "Correspondence Inquiries" section for more information on this service). Please include a detailed description with all pertinent information about the guitar(s) in question in your letter/fax. Good quality photos of the receiver, special markings, etc. would also be appreciated.

BUYING OR SELLING?

Interested in buying or selling a particular guitar(s)? Or maybe hesitating because you are unsure of what a fair market price should be? Depending on what you are interested in, a referral will be made that will enable you to be sure that you are getting what you paid for (or getting paid a fair price). This service is designed to help all those people who are worried or scared about purchasing a potentially "bad guitar" or getting "ripped off" when selling. There is no charge for this referral service - we are simply connecting you with the best person(s) possible within your field of collecting ensuring that you get a fair deal. This hybrid matchmaking can make 25%-50% worth of difference on potentially buying or selling a guitar. Please phone or write the *Blue Book of Guitar Values*™ for both availability and dealer referrals that can be relied upon for both buying and selling. All replies are treated strictly confidential. Replies should be directed to:

Blue Book of Guitar Values™
Attn: Jeff Perkins
One Appletree Square
Minneapolis, MN 55425
Phone No. 612-854-5229
FAX NO. 612-853-1486

If we're not available, please leave a message.

Introduction

How to Start Guitar Collecting

In every part of this country, there are guitar collecting enthusiasts, dealers, and maybe even a few investors. In most major cities, there are regularly scheduled guitar shows where you can buy, sell or swap your guitars and gain insight into general information, including prices. Also, at the larger national shows, you'll find many prominent and reputable dealers who usually have high-quality merchandise for sale.

I personally recommend that you attend at least one major guitar show each year. When you attend, you'll see everything from ultra-rare and expensive vintage instruments to state-of-the-art newer guitars. Hopefully, this will help you to determine where your interest(s) lies. You can also make price comparisons. Shows are a place to meet dealers, collectors, investors, and maybe even a few high-powered guitar slingers from all over the world. Once you have decided what you want to collect, I recommend you talk to everyone who could have any knowledge and provide you with information in your selected area. You must do the homework. Recently, I wrote a dealer friend of mine on what a beginning collector should do to start this fascinating hobby. His comments were: collect what you really like, buy books and read, get out and look with a magnifying glass, be involved in the collecting fraternity, know your dealer(s)— pick them carefully, listen to them and knowledgeable others, avoid speculation, and get a receipt. These are good measures to follow.

For your benefit, we've included a mini-directory of recommended reading material and reference works, as well as trade publications that will further assist you in gathering the knowledge needed for your chosen area(s) of interest.

Starting Tips

My advice would be to pick out an area where knowledge or interest already exists. Once you have found an area that you find interesting and want to collect, formulate a plan on what you would like to purchase for an overall collection. Expand this established base with additional knowledge. Buy the necessary books, magazines, and trade periodicals to make yourself as informed as possible in the niche you've chosen.

Most advanced collectors and dealers have expansive reference libraries for fast, fingertip accessibility. Don't worry about the price for reference material — one book can easily pay for itself in one guitar trade. And, the books themselves become investments as they may go out of print and command increased prices. No one individual can know everything about every guitar — reference works are a must.

Once you're "book trained", the next step is to start looking at — not buying — guitars in the field you've chosen. Attend a few guitar shows or visit dealers that have inventories of items you're looking for. *Don't* get side-tracked by other fascinating merchandise. Pay close attention to the amount and coloration of the finish, possible non-original alterations, any damage or repairs, and the price tag.

In this business, the experience gained by running guitars through your hands has no substitute. I have known people who would quote from memory every special order factory color, fret configuration, options listing, and maybe even the original retail price, yet these same people can't spot a refinished guitar. Knowing the correct factory color, style of wood, finish, production variations, etc., does not come overnight. It takes experience and a well-trained eye. If in doubt about "original finish" someone claims, consult a dealer or collector who does know the difference. Only after you've taken these steps are you ready to become a buyer. Anything less could result in a "long-term" investment.

Where and How to Buy and Sell Guitars

This "Art" has changed drastically over the last 20 years. Dealer showrooms, guitar shows, pawn shops, and local advertising were the only means of buying or selling guitars for many years. Trading was more localized and regional price differences were more evident. Many fine instruments stayed in one locality for long periods of time. With the advent of the 5 second long distance telephone call and overnight express mail, the guitar marketplace is now an international business. All this means increased merchandise exposure, more  universal grading standards, and higher levels of competition when pricing guitars fairly.

It's been said that good guitars are wherever you find them. Nothing could be truer. The following listing will give an idea of where to purchase both new and vintage instruments.

Guitar Show Purchases

Guitar shows have become much bigger business during the past decade and are held throughout the United States on a regular basis. With more and more guitar shows being held yearly (check your music store or trade publications for dates), it is even possible to take in two shows on a single weekend — locations permitting.

Remember — most good guitar show "buys" occur during the show's opening hours, or the night previous to opening before the public is admitted (some shows offer V.I.P. passes enabling you to walk the show during dealer set-up). An apparent bargain found on Sunday afternoon sounds skeptical, although many dealers will "negotiate" a price late in the show, depending on their cash flow and if they can find room in their van to haul it to yet another guitar show. Get to the show at the opening, walk the aisles with orderly precision, avoid back tracking, and when you find a specimen that meets *all* of your criteria *and* is on your shopping list - Buy It. Too many times I've walked back to a booth ready to buy and a guitar stand is all that remains. Truly good guitars that are fairly priced sell fast because dealers are competing with collectors. One last item — don't interrupt an exhibitor engaged in selling (even if it's one you want). It's not in the guitar circuit code of ethics. Be patient.

Advantages include:

1. Physically inspecting potential purchases.
2. Comparing prices against other similar items at the same show.
3. Having a large selection from which to choose.
4. Providing unequaled opportunity to meet fellow collectors and other experts in the field to exchange information.

5. Displaying the broadest base of guitars, accessories, memorabilia, and other related items from which to develop new interests.

6. Listening to your dream riff screaming out of an older, Fender blackface Super Reverb on 9 played by a nationally recognized artist that you would have paid twenty bucks to see.

7. Haggling for better prices, especially for items still unsold late in the show.

8. Offering "trade-in" potential with prices established at the show — rather hard and lengthy to do by mail.

Disadvantages include:

1. A good chance of running into problems including some refinished items, non-factory alterations or conversions, and other riddles that you will have to decode before potentially purchasing. Higher prices over the last 5 years have resulted in many common, lower condition models becoming more expensive.

2. Most sales are final. Once the cash has been transferred, your inspection is over. A collector pays for his "mistakes" in this business. If a sale is contingent on a yet-to-come factory letter, part(s), or additional accessories, make sure the seller includes them in his bill-of-sale. It's simply good business for both parties. When contemplating a purchase, ask the seller what he/she knows about the specimen(s) you are considering, including finish condition (and if original), possible alterations, and how it was obtained. If those answers pass your screening test, then you are ready to ask what the seller would take in payment for the guitar OR if they would be interested in trading. Asking a seller what his/her lowest cash price would be on a 1938 D-45 Martin, and then offering a "pretty good old Silvertone" for trade-in will not put you on the Christmas card list of your average guitar dealer.

3. "Show Pressure" forces you into decisions that have to be made in a few minutes — oftentimes with 2 other people simultaneously bargaining for the same guitar.

4. Being side-tracked into other areas. Know what you want, what you want to pay for it, and don't impulse buy. Keep a level head, and stick to the areas you're familiar with. This is important since merchandise can range from spiked, black leather bracelets to D'Angelico New Yorkers.

5. People-Gawking. Just when you thought you remembered how to get back to that one booth with the blue re-issue Strat, some babe with her blow-up nozzle hidden from sight, in spray-painted leathers generously revealing what there should be another nozzle for. GAZOOKS! What was I looking for and how did I get here?

Guitar Shop/Music Store Purchases

Many modern guitar shops have good selections of collector instruments in stock. Take one guitar at a time here — and make sure that guitar is within your field of expertise. Sometimes dealers selling mostly new guitars get items in on trade that they know very little about — including trade-ins that "aren't right". Be able to know the difference before you buy. Again, don't get sidetracked. While you are likely to get a fair deal at your local guitar shop, you may not find an item in your field as often as you would like.

Mail Order Dealer Purchases

Marketing

This area has really grown in the past 10 years. These dealers send out regular inventory listings to previous customers and much business is out-of-state. It is to the dealer's advantage to accurately grade his guitars very carefully to avoid misrepresentation and eliminate customer fears in not being able to see the guitar. Good mail-order dealers *always* give an inspection period. Returned guitars don't make anyone happy, so the dealer is always faced with selling as good a guitar as possible for a competitive price. Anything less results in stagnating inventory levels. Many of these dealers specialize in specific areas. Their specialization usually ensures the buyer of good condition, original guitars made possible by the dealer's thorough "screening" used before buying. Getting as many dealer inventory listings as possible will give you a chance to "shop" around and check prices. A dealer's reputation is a big factor in this area. Deal with those you're comfortable with and who will listen when you want to trade in something previously purchased.

Auction Purchases

While not as major as guitar shows or guitar shops in the marketplace, auctions can be used to your advantage in buying. Large auction houses such as Christie's and Sotheby's deal in only extremely fine and rare specimens that carry big price tags. Many guitars sold at major auctions are historically significant in that they were played or owned by a famous musician or personality. To date, there has been very little predictability on a price tag for a guitar that Elvis Presley, Jimi Hendrix, Buddy Holly, etc. used to own. Know what you want and your monetary limit before conducting business at this level, since a normal guitar selling for $4,000 might be gavelled off at $115,000 if SOMEONE FAMOUS owned it previously. Some auction guitars are "dogs" with hidden defects that preclude their sale through reputable dealers. Estate, household, and farm auctions can be used with some success if you know previously which guitars will be sold. Frequently, no "guitar" dealers will be in attendance and prices could be quite low. Make sure that condition is at par with your standards. With all auctions, attend the preliminary exhibition and be sure you make a careful inspection of all guitars you might bid on. Mail order bids are sometimes an option to being at the auction. Before bids are submitted, know everything about what you're potentially purchasing.

Collector-to-Collector Purchases

Buying from other collectors is dependent upon how comfortable you are with his/her knowledge, expertise, honesty, and previous dealings. Serious collectors usually sell their finest guitars last. Make sure the guitar you're considering isn't a poor duplicate in the collection or one of his "mistakes". Obviously, it is to a collector's advantage to sell to another collector and thereby avoid the "middleman" dealer markup. Find out if the guitars were carefully chosen originally, part of an estate settlement, or other important past history. Also, big collections don't necessarily guarantee good collections. More than a few "collections" are gathered around poor quality, high quantity odds and ends.

Classified Ad Purchases

Rarely anymore do good quality, collector guitars show up under the "Guitars for Sale" section in the local newspaper. The "steals" of the '60s, '70s, and '80s are mostly gone. Still, keep your eyes open and follow every lead. These wild goose chases can sometimes be very rewarding. An "advertised" older, solid body Fender with 3 pickups for $475 is certainly worth buying if it turns out to be a 1957 Stratocaster. Be fast — don't hesitate when real "buys" do pop up. Also, if the advertiser tells you the caller ten minutes before you bought it, don't consider suicide - there will always be another one.

Buying Through Trade Periodicals

Magazines, such as *Vintage Guitar Player, 20th Century Guitar, National Music Exchange,* and others, contain valuable guitar information. Some listed instruments are good buys — others are out and out rip-offs. Know who you are buying from, insist on an inspection period covering all purchases, and get a receipt. See References/Periodicals Section for addresses and subscription costs.

Selling

Certainly as many considerations confront the potential seller as the potential buyer. Different approaches must be used when selling a single guitar, a few instruments, or an extensive collection. Locality, modern or vintage status, and proper grading all have to be studied. No standard format is applicable to every situation here.

Knowing the market and prices should be an advantage in selling. The collector is familiar with guitar values, knows dealers that handle his type of guitars, and has established contact with fellow collectors of similar merchandise. These potential buyers increase the liquidity base.

When selling more than one guitar and similar items are involved, either the piecemeal or "sold only as a group" method should be determined first. Selling a collection intact is certainly cleaner than taking one-at-a-time. More money can be extracted selling individually — if you have the patience.

When selling, use the same general headings listed under "Buying" as possibilities. Certainly, an obvious place to sell a valuable guitar is to the dealer or individual who might have originally sold you the item. Since he considered it worthy of ownership previously, restocking the guitar should be in his scope of interest. How much will you get? This will depend on length of ownership, any change of condition, the guitar's increased market appeal (if any), and the dealer's current inventory levels. Unless the funds generated in selling a guitar are needed immediately, never be in a rush to sell a nice instrument. Patience will reward you over panic. When that right person shows genuine interest, offer the guitar professionally and stick close to your asking price — you'll probably get it.

Many major trade publications offer national exposure — and larger exposure generally means higher prices. It makes sense that 180,000+ people reading the *Guitar Player* classifieds may generate more interest than 300 tire-kickers at a hometown guitar show. While results may take more time (3-6 weeks), the added dollars on the sale price usually justify the wait.

Trends to be Aware Of

Collecting guitars as a hobby originally started because of the nostalgia and mystique surrounding vintage guitars and their place in music history. While vintage instruments are ruling the roost today, the next generation of guitar players that grew up with an Ibanez or Jackson maybe won't be as interested in a '59 Les Paul Standard or an early '60s Sunburst Stratocaster. Supply-and-demand factors can change very rapidly in the guitar marketplace. Oftentimes, a major  musician that has taken a relatively standard or unknown guitar and performed successfully with it on tour/TV, will make prices rise dramatically - almost overnight!

What to Collect — The Answers Depend on You

Guitars can offer something for everyone. There are different-purpose instruments incorporating many designs and player features. Some have historical value and are quite fascinating.

To a certain extent, there is no right or wrong area in which to collect. Pick the area or category you prefer and then do some studying before you make a choice and begin buying. Be sure you're comfortable with the area you ultimately decide on.

I would suggest that you keep your collection orderly and coherent. Collect one maker or a model and variations (if possible) you have interest in. You could also base a collection on type, such as pre-war mandolins or 12-strings only. This should not stop you from purchasing something outside your collection if you like it — and it is a genuine bargain. When buying for your collection, you will be much better off if you purchase quality items. Owning only one extremely high-quality collector guitar is preferable to owning two or three lesser ones. The greatest demand and appreciation has usually been in the highest-quality pieces. Instruments in poor condition may show smaller increases in value over the years. Current production guitars and those recently discontinued have collector value only if in close to new condition or in the original case. The corresponding ratings shown herein would be 95%, 98% or 100%. Please note the Photo Percentage Grading System© with explanation on pages 32-72 for more information in this area. If a limited edition instrument is no more than the standard issue item with only minor additional embellishments/finish enhancements, its chances of appreciating are low to none, depending on the overall desirability factor. At the other end of the price spectrum, however, a vintage guitar may be found with no remaining finish, and if there is demand because of rarity, it could be an excellent addition to a collection. The main consideration is how they are normally found and collector demand. Study my price value guidelines for a better indication of rarity and values. A shrewd collector may look for a guitar not actively collected but with growing interest.

What Dictates Value — A Combination of Factors

Condition, rarity, demand, special features, historical significance and/or provenance determine current value. All values are based on the premise that the guitar is authentic and original. The value of a collector instrument is always relative to the condition of other examples of the same make, model, and variation. Condition is the amount of overall original finish remaining on all parts of the guitar (please refer to pages 32-72 to learn more about the percentage grading system). The collector is motivated by acquiring better examples of what he/she is interested in. If you find an instrument better than normally encountered and it can be purchased at a fair price, you have had a stroke of luck. Most modern guitars should be in the upper condition factors - 95%-100%, for collector purposes and for maximum price appreciation.

Restoration

Restoration occurs mainly in vintage instruments, but also can be observed in newer instruments. In most cases, a restored or refinished guitar no longer has the same set of desirability factors that an original instrument commands. Once a guitar has been restored, it can never be returned to its original condition. Many dealers polled during the course of this book simply commented, "Even if it's a good refinish, subtract 50%." Unfortunately, as some refinished instruments pass through several owners, the information regarding refinishing tends to get forgotten or isn't mentioned. Replacement or professional repair done with original parts from that period of manufacture (OEM) should not affect values, if the work was high quality.

Modification and Conversion

Many collector guitars have been modified for personal taste or playing, not necessarily with the intent to defraud or fake an original. Often, these modifications were done because a guitar player's individual needs could not be met by factory options. Usually, after-market alterations, modifications, or conversions detract in value from the price of an original instrument in the same condition factor. An exception would be a player (not a collector) who happened to want the same modifications as the instrument for sale. Many older Gibson electrics are known to have had their tuners replaced, and if the holes in the headstock haven't been redrilled (i.e., OEM tuning machines could be put back on with no alterations), values are approximately the same as a 100% original specimen. Knowing how a modification/alteration was made will generally help you in either adding or subtracting these added features from the overall price of the instrument.

An Explorer's Sudsman Meats Pork Chops In Truth Or Consequences Showdown

By a fellow Sudsperson and witness (identity intentionally withheld)

When I finally hook up with Dave, my boss's neighbor, the two 16's had already been dry for over an hour. And you know what that means in Minnesota every night after 10 p.m. - panic buying some 3.2 squaw piss at the local Tom Thumb or take your chances on 'Jack' in the ominous 1.75 liter container within easy arm's length. The next band's getting set up on stage, the garage door is up again (revealing a boisterous crew of 60 outside), and my hearing is finally coming back (it's been '68 Hendrix LOUD).

"So, you're a guitar guy?"

"Yeah," I replied.

"If I want to buy a guitar, how much is it going to cost me?"

"What are you looking for? You looking to invest in something, or are you looking for something to play?"

"Well, I want something I can play that won't sound like anything else."

Pondering this not-so-simple question, I walk over and get another Cajun pork chop on a stick before they're gone. The food's killer. Hmmm.....What are you really looking for in an instrument? First, I imagine you should define what you are looking to get out of that instrument. Is it for play or for show? How much can you afford to spend? Do you want an investment or a classic sound? Do you have a problem with where the instrument was made? How original do you want the instrument? And, probably the most important part of originality is, what type of condition would you like this instrument to be in (or, if it's a potential vintage purchase, would you mind if it was refinished and still get a vintage sound for a lot less money?) His main concern is that he wants to sound completely different from everyone or everything else. Now if you do not feel like inventing a new playing style or trying to make up for lost time - since you didn't take up the instrument playing aspect when you were 5 or 6 - what you might want to look into is some of the new instruments being produced.

By new, I mean instruments produced by companies within the last 10-20 years. There are a lot of people out there trying all sorts of new things, from different body designs on the acoustic side of the coin, to electronic advances that make you wonder how they fit it all into that little body. And we have not begun to talk about the real cutting edge stuff being done with synthetic materials, or the new innovations combining acoustic and electric qualities into a closed system that can be plugged right into digital amplification mediums.

"If you really want it to sound like something new, you should get something new."

"Oh, yeah?"

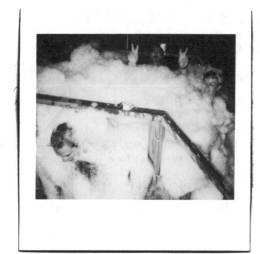

"Yeah. You can go out and pick up something like the Universe from Ibanez, 7 strings, double locking vibrato, state of the art electronics. Or, if you don't like that many strings, try a JS Series from Ibanez, or maybe something from Hamer or Warwick. I mean, these are the instruments people like Steve Vai, Joe Satriani, Living Colour and on and on are using, and they're doing things that sound pretty unique."

Here we are.

The choices are pretty far-ranging since new instruments have new woods, the intonation hasn't had a chance to age and acquire that smoke-filled bar room pitch yet - underline, bold and italicize yet. Also, several companies are trying out different kinds of woods. It's no secret that the world's wood market is getting smaller - when was the last time you walked into a topshelf lumberyard and saw 10 board feet of Brazilian rosewood? People are looking into non-traditional woods to replace traditional and mostly foreign diminishing timbers for instrument construction. New candidates are competing with the older established standards. Performance in playability and musical command are the most sought after qualities in these new instruments. And they are putting these woods together in a lot of different ways. The kind of laminations for bodies, necks and even fingerboards varies widely. What the sound will be like in 10-20 years can be guessed at, but since you're dealing with a natural substance with various growing conditions, you're going to get some neat little tonal changes that may be worth big bucks in 10-15 years after the next generation spends heavy dough on the instruments they wish they could've bought back when they were juniors in high school.

There can be no argument that the electronics of today are much better than 30-40 years ago. The accumulated engineering improvements used in all the manufacturing procedures are much tighter today. The guitar pickups that are coming off today's assembly lines have equal parameters in sound performance and tone. New products and innovations continue to keep today's top-of-the-line instruments very exciting. With the new demand for acoustic instruments to be amplified, while still maintaining their acoustic sound properties, companies have responded by creating new hybrids of both acoustic and electric instrument features, thereby combining the best of both worlds to meet today's more flexible musical demands.

The new razor's edge is the synthetic material world in musical instrument construction. Ned Steinberger broke ground in this area with his epoxy/carbon/glass fibers resin and created a new design in the bass guitar while also defining new manufacturing techniques. Now several companies combine woods, traditional designs and new concepts with synthetic materials to make a whole new world for luthiers to construct in.

And, And, And!...if you don't want or like what is offered by the Big Folks, there are many competent luthiers around the world turning out very high quality products. Most are flexible enough to make highly personalized, truly unique, reasonably delivered-before-you-are-no-longer-excited-about-the-project instruments that should sound very unique and invidualistic. It's also kinda cool to design an instrument and then get to play it.

"Okay, so how much is it going to cost me?"

"Maybe $2,000 to $3,000 should get you what you'd like."

"Is that all?"

"Unless you mean to really trick it out and have some additional inlay work or better materials. Or if you decide to go through somebody's custom shop, then you could option up the cost quite a bit."

"I thought it would be more like $12,000 to $20,000 or more."

"Now, you are talking about collector's items and you're in a new ball game."

And indeed, not only are you in a new ball game, you're in a new ballpark. The vintage market can be a rascal to get a handle on. What's hot and/or What's not? (this month) What's always been hot is still hot, it's just gotten a little bit harder (and a lot more expensive) to acquire. Prices on instruments continue to rise and the availability of some is as limited as the wood it took to build them. It's a finite supply for a growing market that wants the real deal.

When looking to purchase a vintage instrument, highly collectible or not, you need to know what you are looking at. You need to learn what to look for on an instrument. Sometimes you can't depend on the serial number, if you can find one, and if you have access to reliable information. Companies did not always keep a clear record of what happened when. Some companies have been around for over a hundred years and some companies' trademark or brand name have traded hands several times.

You'll probably need to know what year, or unfortunately, what time period, a serial number was used. In the case of the same serial numbers being used multiple times in different years, you will need to know specific changes in an instrument's life. For in-

stance, was the finish used in the year that serial number was issued? Are all the particulars about the design in order? Any changes in binding, body, inlay, logo, peghead or pickguards design, tuners, bridges and tailpieces, pickups, controls and switches all have to be noted to help accurately date an instrument. And if all the proper attributes of the instrument are present, are they in the correct configuration?

Be a little scared of forgery, especially in the higher dollar price ranges. As I stated earlier, there are many competent luthiers out there that can do great work. In addition to intentional fakes, there are still other things such as finishes to consider. A good refinisher can reproduce classic finishes. But a refinished instrument is usually worth 50% of an original's value. You will need to be aware of what finishes were offered when, or make sure you have access to the right people to guide you when making your purchase.

"Bet you think I'm pretty stupid asking all these questions, huh?"

"Not at all."

The biggest consideration when buying a vintage or collectible instrument is the original condition factor. The value of an instrument can increase greatly if found in 95%+ condition. Now, 95% condition has to be used in a relative way of speaking. Is it realistic to consider an instrument made last century, or several centuries ago, (considering how desirable Stradivarious violins are) to look like it was made 10 years ago? There are certain types of instruments that people won't consider a complete original if it has no flaws or wear. As a general rule of thumb, or toe, take your pick - wear on an instrument caused by playing the instrument is negligible. Most instruments do not lose any of their value from playing wear and many times only the most adamant collector will haggle about the few percentage points gained by having a totally unflawed instrument.

"I'm going to go back to my house and bring back a couple of Schmidt's and a weird looking guitar I bought back in high school."

"Oh?"

"Yeah, I'll be right back. I haven't looked at it for a long time."

Originality also extends into the hardware and other parts of instruments. On acoustics, reset necks are one thing, replaced bridges are another matter. Tuners are probably the most replaced part of any instrument, aside from strings. Exact reproductions that require no additional alterations make no

change in value. Replaced parts (i.e. neck, top, fingerboard, etc.) or repairs can cause dramatic drops in value. The strange part is, the difference in value may depend on who did the repair/replacement. I don't think anybody will bitch about a repair done to a D'Angelico that was done by John D'Angelico.

As you can see, going out to buy a guitar can be a little more than getting something just so you can air jam.

Dave returns, decked out in swimming trunks, puts down an interesting looking brown case, heads for the hottub, opens up a sidedoor, and does something with a soap bottle inside.

There can be some pretty serious money involved and there are people out there that are willing to pay serious money for something that - wait a minute, what's that white stuff? Are those suds going over Steve's roof? WOW! What's happening? This is RADICAL!

"What I'm looking for is the next big thing. I want to have the next instrument that will revolutionize the music industry," he tells me, I don't know how much later while I'm standing in the oversized sudsmaker, trying to scan through the white clouds.

"The next big thing in the biz is probably going to look like a ten key. It will be hooked up to a processing unit that will have slide switches to adjust the parameters. It will probably not even look like a guitar, or anything else in the traditional instrument sense. It will probably have a little roller ball to make tonal slides with. I imagine if you want a fingerboard with strings on it to trigger this device, you could get it. But I don't think the Next-Big-Thing will particularly look like a guitar."

That's when he crawled out of the towering suds, walked over and opened up the case, came back and commented:

"Look at this thing - I bought it back in 1959 for 250 bucks."

Someone snapped a couple of polaroids but I hardly noticed since I had gone into shock. It was the cleanest Gibson Korina Explorer I'd ever seen.

"What do you think it's worth?"

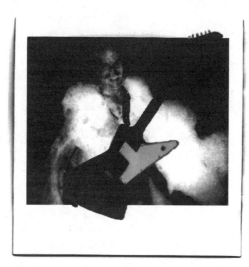

Editor's Note: the conclusion to the sudspeople will be published in the 2nd edition of **Blue Book of Guitar Values**™.

A Publisher's Overview Of The Guitar Marketplace

This final recipe has been brewing for ages, and the final flavoring may taste differently from palate to palate. How are words possibly going to explain all the wierdness that goes on in the guitar business? And besides, what I write today could be real old news by spring. It's hard to explain a roller-coaster ride until you've been on one.

This section is an attempt to provide the reader more information on what really goes on and the supply/demand economics that backdrop the guitar marketplace. And since there are many niches and specialized little pockets of interest that generate unique price tags, knowing the total marketplace is truly the big picture, but perhaps impossible to explain in this language. I've talked to older guitar dealers who have simply told me, "Don't try to figure it out, Steve, just have a new box of price tags ready."

First of all, a few basic concepts of 101 Economics have to be considered. Supply and demand - the only two factors you have to worry about. Really, there's nothing else. In a collectible marketplace, demand usually dictates supply. The guitar marketplace, especially with vintage instruments, can undergo a supply and demand earthquake within a relatively short period of time. Knowing what's hot and what's not is a never-ending ritual for successful guitar dealers. Crystal-balling supply/demand guitar economics is almost a full-time job.

To fully understand what's happened in today's marketplace, it might be best to take a quick peak in the rear view mirror to see what's happened in the guitar marketplace since World War II. During this earlier time period, guitar players (particularly, the well-to-do and advanced musicians) were primarily responsible for the demand half of the formula, since they were the largest part of the sales. With this limited demand factor, prices did not vary much until the late '50s. As the newer musicians (especially rock musicians, once platinum albums and multi-million dollar recording contracts became a way of life) began to purchase both new and vintage instruments, the dollar amount escalated due to both the increase in demand and the disposable dollars available.

As some guitar players acquired the status of "Guitar Gods" (i.e., Eric Clapton, Jimmy Page, Jeff Beck, John Lee Hooker, B.B. King, and others), the models these individuals used became a separate marketplace entity with an international identity. Plug in MTV, major movies, and news print coverage into the overall guitar exposure and identity package in a relatively short period of time, and certain trademark models and variations will become internationally desirable. When was the last time you saw a picture of Stevie Ray Vaughn playing a Gibson?

Suddenly, the artistic status of these Guitars-of-the-Gods also increased dramatically. As fretted instruments became more legitimate and bona fide as serious safe-havens for collector and investment dollars, additional domestic and international demand escalated from both guitar-ists and non-players who could appreciate the meticulous craftsmanship, top-shelf woods and materials, and other art-form mainstays which pulled out additional interest from the pawn-shops and music stores to transform it into the sophisticated and more complex marketplace we have to contend with today.

OK, so let's get into it. Why are mint '54 Tobacco finished Fender Stratocasters selling for $12,000+? Is it model rarity? Not. Is it pure Koolness? Maybe, but I hope not. Is it the virtually impossible to obtain condition factor? Now we're getting someplace. Are these prices legit? We'll find out. Is it because the overall desirability factor of this model, year of manufacture, and condition factor has gone up tremendously? Yes. Fifteen years ago, I doubt anyone would have bet on a five digit common Stratocaster within the next decade. But who could have possibly guesstimated the runaway Japanese demand factors that possibly seeded additional domestic interest (and speculation). In shooting down the rarity argument, remember, there has been more Fender Stratocasters manufactured in the last 40 years than Martin's entire production over the last 160 years! In this whole process, it seems like rarity is usually mistaken for desirability rather than understanding a guitar's rarity factor is only one component when determining overall desirability.

To understand any guitar's desirability factor, one has to understand this word's definition fully. To be desirable is to be demanded, but to be rare does not guarantee anything. Desirability insures demand - rarity does not. In fact, in some cases, the only thing rarer than a particular guitar is the guy who will spend money to own it. Why is this? Ever gone to a garage sale and seen a home brewed painting under the card table that the owner was pumping up for $20? You would have probably pulled out an 'Andy Jackson' rather fast if you would have seen an authentic Picasso signature at the bottom right. Why? Because the demand factor became much larger once the collectible's trademark/status became accurately established.

Let's break down each guitar's desirability into individual elements enabling us to understand both the demand and supply economics one guitar at a time. The following components will always come into play (even though any guitar's unique "mix" of these properties is usually different) when determining a specimen's overall desirability. The key factors when determining a guitar's demand factor (desirability) are as follows:

① **Trademark Recognition/Acceptance/Importance**. How popular or collected is the maker's name? Having a Martin, Fender, D'Angelico, Elvis Presley's 1958 Gibson LG-1, Gretsch, Epiphone, etc. is going to be a lot different than having a Magnatone, Maybell, Harmony, chocolate flavored Danelectro, or any one of the hundreds of trademarks nobody has heard of or really cares about. Most of the instruments manufactured by these lesser known trademarks were manufactured to undercut the competition at the time, and while many were (some still are) fair quality, inexpensively made, utilitarian pieces, their value today must be based on the player utility factor only since, in most cases, there is little or no collector interest. Many of these turn of the century companies (or subcontractors) were in business for only a brief time and little history remains on their shoe-string operations. One of the big reasons that Fender, Martin, Gibson, Epiphone, Guild, and other trademarks have a large collector following today is because these factories are still in business and company records/documents may authenticate their older instruments. In many cases, however, factory information is non-existent or incomplete when linking up a serial number with a specific model complete with description and shipping date.

② **Condition**. In most cases a guitar's original condition is what is rare, not the model itself. Original condition for many collectors is the most important factor in determining a guitar's desirability. Many collectors simply will not purchase a guitar below a certain condition factor, regardless of price (unless, of course, it's an early Stratocaster in a rare Dupont color). Original condition is Polar North for most guitar collectors and investors today. Once condition decreases on most specimens, the "player utility factor" controls the equation more than the "collector's value" on more recently made models. Major trademark older vintage instruments retain collector interest down to a "no finish left" condition factor since they are collectible regardless of their "playability".
Refinished guitars in commonly encountered models in good supply are not as desirable as original condition specimens, and values are generally considered to be 50% less than an original instrument. In other words, a common '70s Guild flat top that has been professionally refinished will never be as desirable as an original specimen, since all things considered, collectors and players would rather concentrate on original condition (if it is available in the marketplace).

③ **Historical Recognition/Notarized Provenance**. In other words, if you can prove by historical documentation that the guitar(s) you own belonged to a Jimi Hendrix, Stevie Ray Vaughn, David Gilmour, Hank Williams, Elvis Presley, President Nixon, etc., the price tag will escalate tremendously. The sale price will be contingent on how well the personality/organization is known. Very few people will care (or pay) for a local personality's "main squeeze". A specimen owned by a regionally famous person will command a regional price. If the guitar belonged to John Lennon and you can prove it in front of a judge and jury, then, in most cases, an auction may be the only way of assessing the correct value. In some cases, whoever presented the guitar as a gift may make at least as much difference as whom the guitar was presented to.

④ **Price**. Any guitar becomes a value at the right price. At some subterranean low price, regardless what kind of fretted instrument is being sold, many of us will buy it (justified by becoming more diversified in our collecting). As you would expect, pricing is more predictable as your sampling ratio increases. In other words, the correct price will be much easier to determine on a 1979 Gibson Les Paul than on an inscribed pre-war Stromberg. While there are literally thousands of Les Pauls that are internationally bought/sold annually, only a very few Strombergs will exchange hands during the same time period.

If the price seems like it's at the summit, see if it can be budged into the price range you are looking for. If not, give it up and wait until the next opportunity. If the price is close to what you would like to pay, perhaps light "chiseling" may be used with some effectiveness. Veterans in this business, however, will tell you to pay a little extra to get something that is a little bit better. The worst feeling at a guitar show is when you walk back to that booth looking for the nice Telecaster Rosewood Re-issue (that you tried to buy a 1/2 hour ago for $75 off a $575 asking price) and all that remains is an empty stand on the table. Does the price make the guitar more desirable or does it detract from it to the point that you can't possibly buy it? These are questions you have to ask yourself on every potential purchase. During the past several years, a new pattern has been established for selling top-shelf trademarks with famous person provenances. Some major auction houses have set new records on many of these historically significant intruments. Recently, an older Martin previously owned by Elvis Presley was gavelled off at over $130,000! This is what can happen to price when you hook up Star notoriety with historical documentation/acceptance, trademark significance, and condition - then let the top dealers, collectors, and investors turbocharge the price tag in the fast and furious atmosphere of an auction house.

My advice on the pricing issue is to do your homework before you get tested under "combat conditions". Map out your area of collecting and buy the necessary pricing guides and reference books that will give you the information that you are going to need. I always chuckle when I hear someone complain about the "high price" of a particular book when it could have saved him/her hundreds of dollars on the non-original guitar he "stole" late Sunday at the last guitar show. In addition, attend a few guitar shows annually (including at least one big show). Get to know a few reputable dealers in your field and make sure you get their inventory listings and pricing information. Last, but certainly not least, BUY SOMETHING! It's good for the economy and your collection.

⑤ **Rarity**. Most guitars are not rare. Rather, their condition and/or scarce features may make them rare. Again, while it is true that many instruments may be relatively hard to find, sometimes the potential purchaser for these off-brand trademarks can be rarer than the guitar. Literally, there are hundreds of trademark/brand names both domestically and internationally that nobody really cares about (or is willing to pay $500 for). In many cases, the configuration of certain makes and models becomes much more important than the headstock markings (i.e., a Danelectro 6-string bass in Coral Green is going to be a lot more desirable than a black standard model). Also remember that because a guitar belonged to a great-uncle or family relative does not make it any rarer (or desirable) in the eyes of the next potential purchaser.

Many people think that some popular guitars are rare. As an example, most Fender Stratocasters are not rare - they have made over 500,000 during the past 40 years! A mint 1954 factory white Stratocaster is rare, however, since the color was never very popular and most saw heavy use (and possibly, some abuse). Sometimes, the most commonly encountered features in a particular model end up being the most desirable. Let's pick on early Strats again. Even though it is rarer to find this model without a tremolo bar, values are the same as a specimen that has a factory tremolo unit, since most advanced collectors and even players prefer this factory option. Be careful when letting the rarity control your pocketbook - the other factors listed in this article are considerably more important. Exercise caution on those unknown specimens commonly described as, "I don't think I've ever seen another one like it." While a fortunate few have been lucky when adding these rarities to their collections, more have "damaged their estates" by basing value on rarity only.

(6) **Special Order Features/Embellishments/Accessories.** Many guitars have been special ordered with optional accessories including non-standard hardware, customized electronics, wood and paint finishes, a variety of tuning machines, inlays and ornamentation, personalization, and other custom/special features that have to be taken into consideration to determine the price of any given instrument. All of these special orders/options act both independently and interdependently to determine the correct value for a particular guitar. On major trademark specimens it is important that these optional features were done at the factory, not by someone outside the factory at a later date.

On modern customized guitars, the resale is hard to predict since a customized guitar was originally created to fit a particular musician's playing style, not someone else's at a later date. Many times on a customized guitar involving resale, "the whole is not the sum of its parts." In other words, the total cost of the guitar and customizing will be more than what it will resell for in the used marketplace. On many rare guitar options/special orders, prices can be very hard to predict accurately, since very few instruments incorporating these special features are bought/sold during the course of each year. Most of the time, a knowledgeable dealer or advanced collector should be consulted on the difference these special orders/options can make on the price of a guitar.

(7) **Supply/Demand Differences.** Some guitars have regional supply and demand economics that affect values. An older Martin flat top with some wear is going to be more desirable in West Virginia and Kentucky than it would be in northern Montana. Also, certain currently manufactured models with a low supply factor can have a short-term effect on pricing. A good example of this is the National Reso-Lectric - this model has had extremely limited manufacture (currently, an 18-month back-order is typical) and because of this, used specimens are selling close to the manufacturer's suggested retail price. As soon as supply can catch demand, this situation could change in a hurry. Short-term economic situations that present potential downside risk factors are solved by dealers watching their inventory levels very closely during these supply/demand cross-overs.

In closing, I would like you to remember that when purchasing guitars for storing value, consider overall desirability first, condition second, price third, and rarity last. Since the supply of most vintage and some recent out-of-production guitars is decreasing (how many more end up overseas each year?), it is the demand side of the marketplace that determines what is desirable, regardless of rarity. Most collectors like trademarks backed by historical provenance having many models/variations (and existing information) from which to choose and build into an orderly collection. Once a guitar's overall desirability factor has been accurately determined, you will have a much better idea if that next potential guitar purchase deserves input number 1 on your twin Marshall stack.

Steven P. Fjestad
Editor and Publisher
Blue Book of Guitar Values™

Explaining/Converting The Photo Percentage Grading System©

As in any other area of collecting, grading standards have a lot to do with the way a collectible is described when buying, selling, or trading. Most fields have at least one or two grading systems which are designed to indicate condition as accurately as possible to those people who are interested. The system that usually wins is the system that is more helpful to everyone interested in that area of collecting.

The Photo Percentage Grading System© has been used successfully in over 175,000 copies of the *Blue Book of Gun Values*™. Since condition has become very important in today's expensive marketplace, we feel the differences between 80% and 100% are so significant, and values must be listed for those extremely important additional condition factors (90%, 95%, 98%, etc.). In the past, guitar grading has utilized terminology such as Exc., Exc.+, VG+ (++), Near Mint, 7 overall, Good condition, and other idioms.

The conversion chart listed below has been provided to help you convert other grading standards into the approximate Photo Percentage Grading System© factors (i.e. in most cases, percentages ranging from 60%-100%). While no grading system can be perfect, we hope that this percentage type of grading system will provide a more accurate and reliable way to describe each guitar's unique condition once it has become used. All percentage descriptions and/or possible conversions made thereof, are based on original condition — alterations, repairs, and any other non-original work that has altered the condition of an instrument must be listed additionally and subtracted from the values based on condition throughout this text.

Condition Factors

100% — New with all factory materials including warranty card, owner's manual, case, and other items that were originally included by the manufacturer. Not previously sold at retail.

Mint Condition — This condition factor, while not included within the pricing structure of this text, refers to an instrument that is one tick away from being new. Refers to as new condition - at or only 100%. To interpolate this condition term when considering value, mint condition typically gets priced right below the 100% value.

98% — Only very slightly used and/or played very little, may have minor "case" wear or light dings on exterior finish only, without finish checking, very close to new condition, also refers to a new instrument that has previously sold at retail with perhaps some slight case wear only, Exc.+, Mint or Near Mint, exceptional, 9+, slight scratch — otherwise as new.

95% — Very light observable wear, perhaps some very light plating deterioration on metal parts, extremely light finish scratching, may have slight neck wear, Exc., close to mint, 9.

90% — Light exterior finish wear with a few minor dings, no paint chips to wood, normal nicks and scratches, light observable neck wear in most cases, excellent, near 9 or 8-9 condition.

80% — Exterior finish wear that may include minor chips that extend down to the base wood, body wear but nothing real serious, Exc.- or near excellent, 8, nice shape, honest player wear.

70% — More serious exterior finish wear that could include some major gouges and nicks, or player arm wear, fret deterioration, Good condition, 7 overall, above average condition, "very nice condition for this year."

60% — Noticeable wear on most areas - normally this consists of some major belt buckle wear and finish deterioration, may include cracking, possible repairs or alterations, 40% of the original finish is gone. When this condition factor is encountered, normally an instrument should have all logos intact, original pickups, minor headstock damage, and perhaps a few non-serious alterations. With or without original case. Good minus (-), 6.

40% — Major features are still discernible, major parts missing, probably refinished, original logo and case may be missing, structurally sound though usually encountered with non-factory alterations, 4, fair minus (-) overall.

20% — Near the end, not much left (and the Governor's not going to call), must still be playable, however, 2, poor overall, no condition+, "the parts are worth this much", bloated road kill, dog meat, etc.

THE **BLUE BOOK OF GUITAR VALUES** ™
PHOTO PERCENTAGE GRADING SYSTEM ©

It usually starts when the person on the other end of the telephone asks, "I have this old Gibson guitar that Uncle Mortimer used to own - what's it worth?" After I tell them to please hold this rare fretted instrument closer to the microphone so that I can "see" it better, their next sentence is usually devoted to establishing the rarity factor since they haven't been able to find out much information about it in any guitar book(s). We all struggle with this problem - how to determine a guitar's condition accurately. Hopefully, this Photo Percentage Grading System© might bring an end to this era.

If there is a harder subject to write about than trying to explain a collectible's unique condition factor via the pen-and-ink mode, I'm glad I haven't had a chance to write about it. As with most other collectibles (including guitars), value is usually determined by a variety of factors, the most critical usually being realistically determining the original condition of the specimen in question. Once the condition question has been answered, monetary evaluation will get much easier.

This problem is not unique to the area of collectible guitars - try calling up a coin, car, stamp, baseball card, or antique furniture dealer and ask him/her what they will pay you in C-notes for your deceased relative's up-to-this-point previously unknown mother-lode stash of "good stuff." Again, the answer is pretty standard, "I'm going to have to see it before I can make a determination on how much it's worth." In other words, talk is cheap because condition is usually either mis-described or over-described. In the end, the merchandise always speaks for itself better than any verbal description. If a good photo is worth a thousand words, an axe-in-hand is worth a million.

The photos on pages 35-72 basically depict three categories of guitars: Solid Body Electrics, Acoustic-Electrics, and Acoustics. Chosen category representative models are as follows: Solid Body Electrics — Fender Stratocasters, Telecasters, Esquires, and the Jazzmaster Bass, in addition to Gibson Les Pauls and related variations, a Paul Reed Smith and a Danelectro; Acoustic-Electrics — miscellaneous Gibsons and a Gretsch; Acoustics — various Martins, Gibsons, Epiphones, and a Guild. Simply compare your guitar(s) against these photos to find the corresponding condition in percentages. If your particular configuration is not pictured, try to interpolate areas of wear to the closest category shown.

It is extremely important when examining wear on a guitar to think about how that wear occurred after a period of normal (and possibly abnormal) use. As a player uses a guitar, certain areas will accumulate finish deterioration more rapidly than others. Note the lower bout wear on photos 15 and 29 caused by arm wear created after strumming a couple million chords (i.e., the Grand Canyon effect). Neck wear, however, seems to be somewhat forgivable in lieu of the rest of the instrument's overall condition. This is evident in photos 17 and 18, which depict a Fender Telecaster in 70% overall condition with rather heavy neck wear. In many instances, advanced collectors and dealers can look at a guitar's specific wear areas and tell you if the player specialized in country-western or Led Zeppelin. Accumulating the knowledge necessary to know the differences simply takes running a lot of instruments through your hands.

Almost of equal importance to player wear is how well the instrument was transported, handled, or stored while it was NOT being played. This "off-stage" wear is demonstrated in photos 7 and 8. Note the chips and dings on the body, while the back of the neck appears almost new with virtually no clear lacquer finish removed. Each older guitar thus becomes a unique, one-of-a-kind item that has to be individually examined to determine its unique condition factor(s).

Guitar alterations also have to be integrated into the overall condition formula per instrument. It is a known fact that many Gibson instruments have replaced tuners. This is normally not a problem unless the back of the headstock has been redrilled to accept a new tuning machine (observe photo 40). Also, replaced pickups or other changes that do not fall within the original equipment specifications from a particular manufacturing period have to be subtracted from the overall value. In most cases, non-original alterations make an instrument worth less.

Remember, for most guitars in good supply, original condition is Polar North to the serious collector or investor. Not even a professionally refinished guitar (compare photo 32 to photo 31) that could otherwise be readily purchased in mint original condition will approach the price of an original. The key to value in situations like this is the desirability factor **after** the restoration in relation to the value of an original. Most guitar collectors frown on a restored instrument (regardless how good the job). Many dealers consulted during this project simply commented, "Subtract 50% of the value if refinished." Knowing how and why these condition factors can override others becomes critical on an accurate price. Pro-rating these condition factors in their proper pecking order is not a job for amateurs and professional advice should be obtained from several sources before the C-notes change hands.

We are lucky that the consistency and uniformity of guitar grading standards have not changed. In the coin business, just when you thought those easy, short-term profits were in your sights, the coin industry changed the grading system making your numismatics fall (not to mention profits) a grade or two. A 90% guitar from 1960 is still a 90% guitar today. Nothing has changed except for the values going up considerably, and the really good stuff has never been harder to find, because guitar collectors usually dispose of their guitars as their last financial alternative. The first thing an investor sells after 4 or 5 years is their worst investment. The last thing a guitar collector will sell is their main squeeze, unless a cash offer gets tendered that can't be refused.

Always try to buy as much original condition as you can afford. Remember, however, that you can overpay for those last couple of percentage points of a guitar's condition. During the past twelve months, some trademarks/models seem to be linked with some very unpredictable, high price tags. Some dealers have recently indicated that if they priced their better merchandise along-side these high asking prices, not only would they get laughed at on the expensive items, but some potential buyers may think the rest of their merchandise is overpriced as well. Don't forget about those crazed investment (non-collector) diamond buyers who purchased 1-Carat, D-Flawless certified stones (the best quality) for over $80,000 in the early 1980's and flushed them down their portfolio toilets several years later for $12,000. As in any other area of collecting, it is typically wise to stay away from a model, area, or category that has gone up faster than an F-15 in an alarmingly short time. While it's true that these short-term boomers may continue to rise and take you with them, chances are you may be dropped off at the summit of Mt. Everest with no oxygen for the way down. Inflationary or non-inflationary domestic economics occurring in the next 3-5 years will have the final say on whether today's price tags constitute a value or a long-term tax loss.

If you have any questions regarding either the photos or accompanying captions, please contact me. While no grading system is perfect, hopefully this Photo Percentage Grading System© will enable you to ascertain the approximate grade of your individual guitars. Only after learning the correct condition of a guitar can you accurately determine its true value.

Sincerely,

Steven P. Fjestad
Editor - *Blue Book of Guitar Values*

P.S. I would like to thank Dave Rogers and Crew from Dave's Guitar Shop in LaCrosse, WI, Nate Westgor of Willie's American Guitars located in St. Paul, MN, and Pete Wagener of LaVonne's Music from Savage, MN for opening up their doors and allowing the photography crew complete access to their inventories. This section could not have happened without their support.

All photos in this section were taken by S. P. Fjestad with the assistance of Jeff Perkins.

Photos 1 & 2 — 1960 Fender Stratocaster - Ser. #60492, 3-Tone Sunburst finish, 95%-98% condition. If you're a Strat player, you'll have a hard time leaving this page. Note factory hanging tag and tremolo cover still intact - definite bonuses on any Fender solid body electric. Original paint exhibits almost no fading and back of body shows no belt buckle wear - but slight ding appears below tremolo cover. Also, close scrutiny reveals slight upper neck wear. Rosewood fingerboard. Notice how the 3-Tone Sunburst finish (Red, Black and Orange) differs from photos 7 and 8 - a 2-Tone Sunburst (Black and Orange). It doesn't get much better than this!

 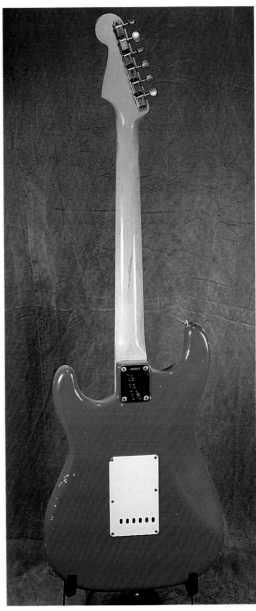

Photos 3 & 4 — 1964 Fender Stratocaster - Ser. #L 64322, Dakota Red finish, 80%-85% overall condition. Again, note original tremolo cover still intact. Careful observation reveals light touching-up on both the front and back of body. Back plate cover has operation ID numbers engraved by previous owner. Backside of body also exhibits light chipping (note white primer coat showing through). Observe wear on back of upper neck (clear lacquer coat has dulled). Technically, the front of this instrument is 85%-90%, while the back is in 80%-85% condition.

 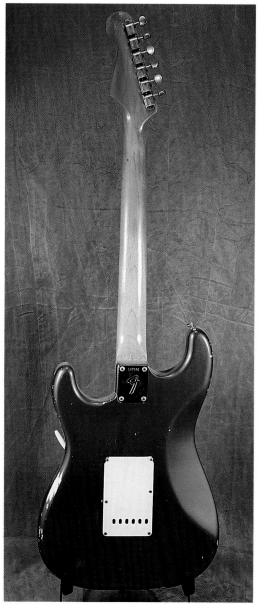

Photos 5 & 6 — 1965 Fender Stratocaster - Ser. #107632, Ocean Turquoise finish, 75%-80% overall condition. Custom color finishes on Fender instruments were done by applying a base coat, followed by the color coat, and finally a clear lacquer coat. Normally, the lacquer coat starts to yellow with age, giving the finish a yellowish tint. Close observation reveals a dark spot on the lower bout that was caused by the player's arm wearing away the lacquer coat, resulting in the color coat becoming more pronounced than the rest of the body color. While appearing to be touched-up, this is a common occurrence on custom color finishes. Again, note chipping on body sides.

Photos 7 & 8 — 1960 Fender Stratocaster - Ser. #49227, 2-Tone Sunburst finish, 70% overall condition. During this particular period of production, Fender used a slab board rosewood fingerboard. Inspecting the back of this instrument reveals serial number on the bottom of the neckplate, differing from the top location found in the previous three instruments. Note back of neck appears almost new - indicating this instrument's wear was accumulated more from handling and transporting than by actual playing. As pictured previously, note base coat finish where chipping has occurred.

 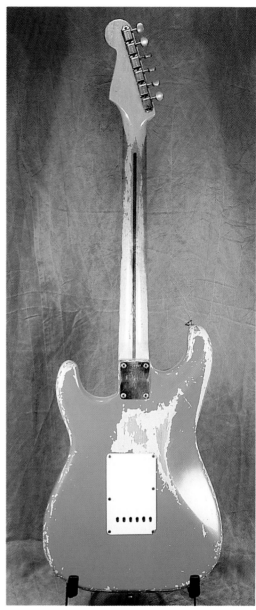

Photos 9 & 10 — 1957 Fender Stratocaster - Ser. #920869, Dupont prototype color, 50%-60% overall condition. Observe how maple fretboard and neck back (with "skunk stripe") have accumulated finish wear down to the raw wood. This much back wear reveals a lot of the original white base coat. You're probably thinking that a guitar with this much finish deterioration is worth $300-$400 - Wrong! Because of the guitar's extreme rarity factor in this special prototype color (one of four known), this instrument's price tag could hit $15,000. It just shows you that, Kool Kustom Kolors in Stratocasters Kan Knock down Kopious Kwantities of Koinage!

 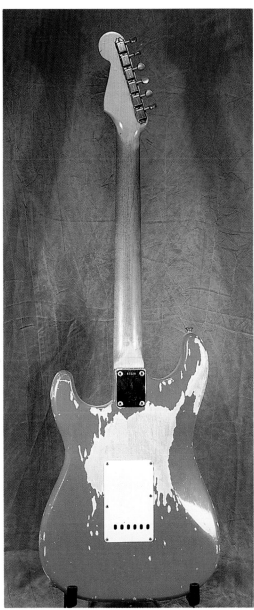

Photos 11 & 12 — 1963 Fender Stratocaster - Ser. #87529, Salmon Pink finish, 50% overall condition. Again, this instrument proves that much player use will remove the color coat where the right arm has rubbed against the body (60% front condition). Back of instrument shows a lot of chipping (40%-45% condition), and dark neck further proves this guitar belted out more than a few licks. Originally retailing for approximately $285, this instrument's current value is in the $7,000 range - mostly due to the tremendous desirability of the rare color.

 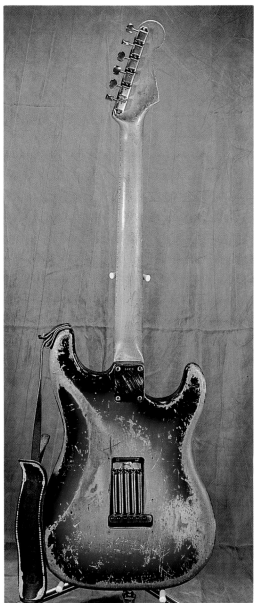

Photos 13 & 14 — 1962 Fender Stratocaster - Ser. #94313, 3-Tone Sunburst finish, 20% overall original condition (and going down every playing job). Realistically, it doesn't get much worse than this, and even if it did, it wouldn't make any difference for value. This is an original left-handed factory second instrument that has literally been dragged through gravel on the way to and from the music store. This instrument belongs to a Serial Killer guitar player from Wisconsin who thinks so much of it, he wouldn't trade it even-up for a rusty axe! (No, he's not from Milwaukee).

 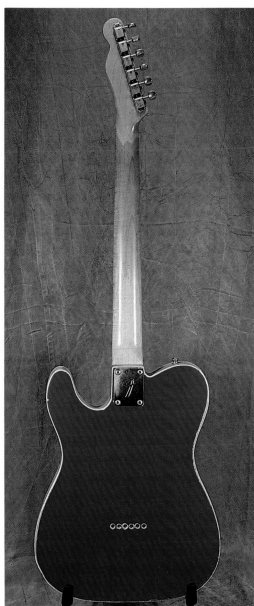

Photos 15 & 16 — 1966 Fender Telecaster Custom - Ser. #173125, Candy Apple Red finish, approximately 75% overall condition. Note maple fingerboard and related wear (not as bad as the Stratocaster pictured in photo 9). A maple fingerboard in this year of Telecaster is ultra-rare and very desirable to Fender collectors. The serious chip on right side of bridge plate and lower bout reduce the front condition to 70%, but relatively clean backside with some neck wear makes it 90% condition.

 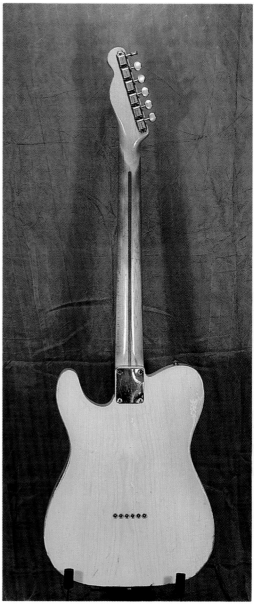

Photos 17 & 18 — 1953 Fender Telecaster - Ser. #3527, Blonde finish, 70% overall condition. Study the wear on the neck and pickguard, indicative of some serious playing. Back of neck (with "skunk stripe") has gone dark on top. Neck wear is forgivable. Neckplate without serial number is correct through 1953 manufacture - Telecaster serialization appears on the bridgeplate during this period. Telecasters are currently hot - a 95% specimen (extremely hard to find since most of these instruments got a blue collar workout) in this year of manufacture would sell for $11,000-$12,000. Even in 70% condition, the going rate is still $6,500-$7,000.

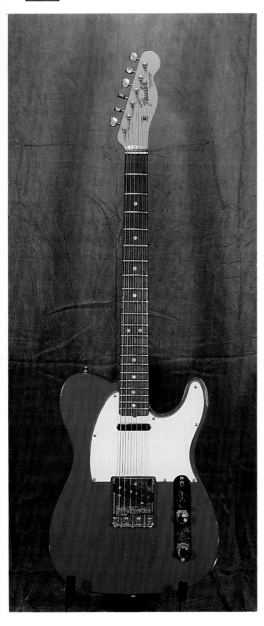
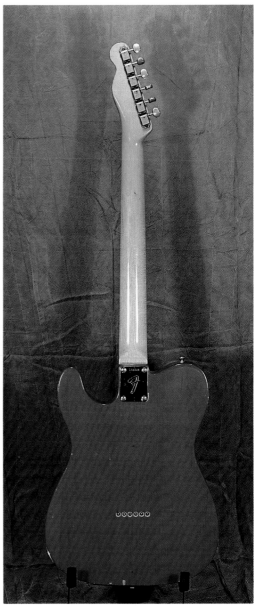

Photos 19 & 20 — 1966 Fender Telecaster - Ser. #132349, Transparent Red prototype finish, 80% overall condition. Most people (even a few Fender dealers) would think that this color was a production finish - it is not. Note the transitional logo - sometimes referred to as a "macaroni" logo instead of the "spaghetti" logo - patent number under name on decal. Single string tree was used until 1972. Rosewood fingerboard is unusual. Also examine recessed ferrules - flush body ferrules became standard after 1967. The top end of this specimen's price is hard to predict due to the extreme rarity factor.

 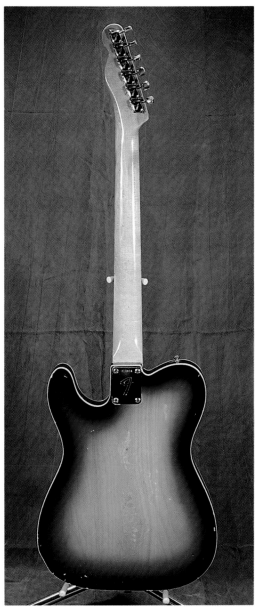

Photos 21 & 22 — 1966 Fender Custom Telecaster - Ser. #215406, 3-Tone Sunburst finish, 70%-75% overall condition. This specimen is unusual with original Bigsby vibrato tailpiece (observe Fender logo on bottom). Note the differences in color of the Sunburst finish between the front and back of the instrument. This Telecaster must have been exposed to sunlight for some duration, as the red has mostly faded from the front Sunburst while remaining mostly intact on the backside. Not much player wear, discernible by the clean back of neck.

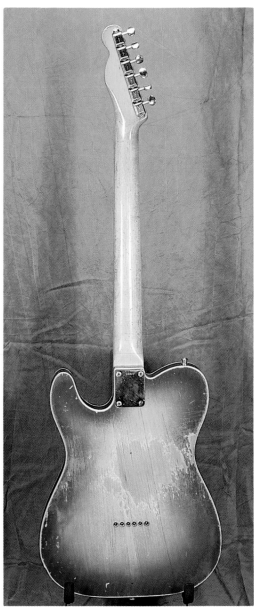

Photos 23 & 24 — 1960 Fender Custom Esquire - Ser. #65882, 3-Tone Sunburst finish, 60% overall condition (due to heavy fading and checking). While appearing to look almost partially refinished, this Esquire is proof that early Sunburst finishes presented some problems to Fender. Color pigmentation would begin to fade with or without light exposure. Custom Esquires were the first Fenders to have a layered pickguard. Double bound Esquires are rare, especially with custom color finishes. 1960s instruments generally do not have a neck date, and a slab board neck will always add a premium.

Photo 25 — 1958 Fender Esquire - Ser. #31373, Natural color, 75% overall condition. Observe that this instrument has a bridge that allows the strings to go through to the back of the body. While hard to see, the pickguard on this model should have counter-sunk screw holes. In today's marketplace, this instrument is in the $3,500-$4,000 range.

Photo 26 — 1959 Fender Esquire? NOT! The neck and body of this impostor were made from new parts and intentionally faked. Close examination will reveal truss rod mark on top of nut is visibly longer than in photo 25. **Buyer Beware** - this instrument was sold to the customer as a refinished Fender Esquire. Bet he didn't get his money back!

Photos 27 & 28 — 1965 Fender Jazzmaster - Ser. #L 51369, Candy Apple Red finish, 85%-90% overall condition. Note the large peghead on this instrument as compared to the Stratocasters pictured in photos 1-14. The Jazzmaster model was never offered with the small, pre-1965 Stratocaster-style headstock. The back of the body has been shown at right so you may get a feel for the horizontal weather checking striations that do occur under natural circumstances. This is caused by temperature fluctuations effecting the clear lacquer finish, and it does not detract from the overall condition. Photographer's fingerprints can be observed in finer post offices throughout the country.

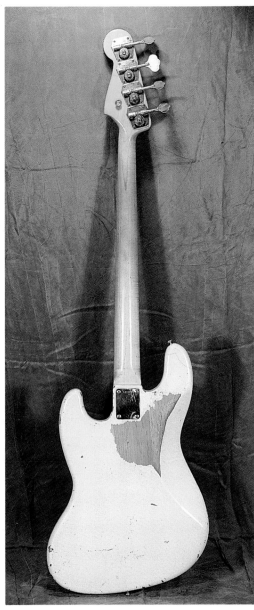

Photos 29 & 30 — 1964 Fender Jazz Bass - Ser. #L 32223, Olympic White finish, 60% overall condition. Lots of bare wood showing, but it's all original. Note the clay dot fingerboard inlays, indicative of pre-CBS features. In late 1964, Fender went to pearl dots, but the real pre-CBS aficionados are looking for these clay dot inlays. Original Olympic White finish with matching color headstock. Notice original strap hook next to tuning machines. Most bass musicians would agree that this continues to be one of Leo's better playing instruments.

Photo 31 — 1952 Gibson Les Paul - without Ser. # (correct), Gold Top finish, approximately 85% overall condition. One of the first LP's produced with trapeze tailpiece, but without neck binding. Examine greenish hue where arm has rubbed off color coat that was mixed with bronze powder, producing a green oxidation. Horizontal weather checking striations normal.

Photo 32 — 1954 Gibson Les Paul - original inked serial number has been restamped, Gold Top finish, 100% refinished condition. Compare the matted color and lack of arch-top dimensionality between this and original finish in photo 31. Also, Gibson dropped the trapeze tailpiece in 1953. Refinishing decreases value 50%, and re-drilled tuner holes knock off an additional 10%.

Photos 33 & 34 — Gibson Les Paul Custom - Ser. #964991, Black finish, 85% overall condition. Note split diamond peghead inlays with multi-binding - always indicative of a Les Paul Custom - Gibson's finest. Photographically presenting wear on a black instrument is always difficult, but close scrutiny reveals light chipping on the body back and front. Gold-plated humbucking pickup covers, tunomatic bridge, and stop tailpiece also exhibit quite a lot of wear.

Photos 35 & 36 — 1974 Gibson Les Paul Deluxe - Ser. #393787, Blue Sparkle finish, 98%+ overall condition. Compare the binding of this instrument to photo 33 - Deluxe models have a single bound front body, and do not have a peghead binding. Also, study the back of this instrument, featuring a 3-piece neck and original tuning machines. Many LPs have had replacement tuners put on - not critical, unless the holes have been re-drilled. Small humbucking pickups are correct for this era. Red Sparkle is even rarer in this model.

 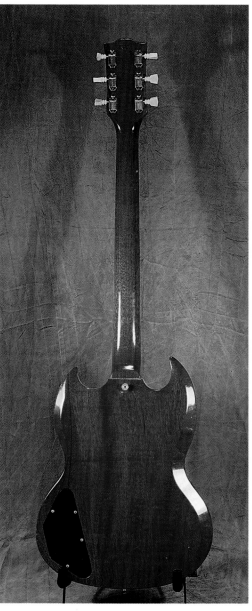

Photos 37 & 38 — 1961 Gibson Les Paul - Ser. #6227, Cherry finish, 90% overall condition. Gibson discontinued the original Les Paul configuration circa 1961 and the new body style (renamed "SG" in late 1963) was produced with Les Paul logos during this brief three-year period. A newly styled "lever action" vibrato unit was standard on this model. Note how the nickel finish is worn off the humbuckers and has faded on the tremolo cover, typical of natural aging. This model retailed for $290 in Gibson's 1962 catalog.

 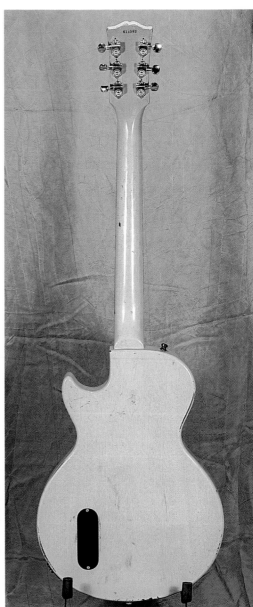

Photos 39 & 40 — 1956 Gibson Les Paul Junior (nicknamed Les Paul TV) - Ser. #611582, TV Yellow finish, 80%-85% overall condition. Finish is so named because this color would match the rest of the wooden props (i.e., furniture, etc.) used during the filming of the black-and-white television programs of that era. Careful scrutiny reveals reproduction tuning machines (used so peghead did not need to be redrilled) do not fit original screw holes.

 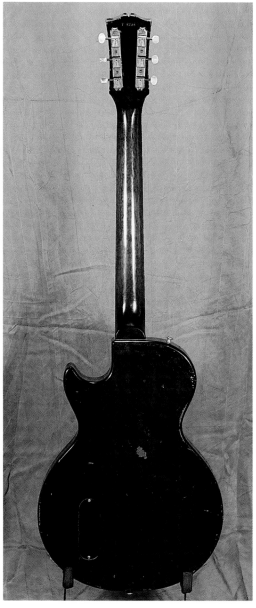

Photos 41 & 42 — 1957 Gibson Les Paul Junior - Ser. #7 8238, Tobacco Sunburst finish, 75% overall condition. This instrument was designed at a price point under the original Les Paul model and differences are immediately discernible: unbound slab board body, single pickup, single volume/tone controls, flat pickguard, and dot neck inlays. Examine belt buckle chipping on back. This model has become popular because of its playability, simplicity, and relative light weight. Note original bridge - rare, since most were replaced.

Photo 43 — 1989 Paul Reed Smith Custom - Ser. #97407, Transparent Burgundy Top finish, new condition (100% overall). This is a newly manufactured PRS Custom that has the dove inlays that are normally found on the Artist Series. A "10" top - it's hard to imagine getting a better quilted maple bookmatched top than pictured here.

Photo 44 — 1958 Danelectro - without Ser. # (correct), rare Green color, 60% overall condition. No real wear spots on this instrument, just lots of little nicks. Knobs are non-original. Most Danelectros are black - rare color makes this one worth 3x normal value (instead of $250-$350, this specimen is $950-$1,000).

 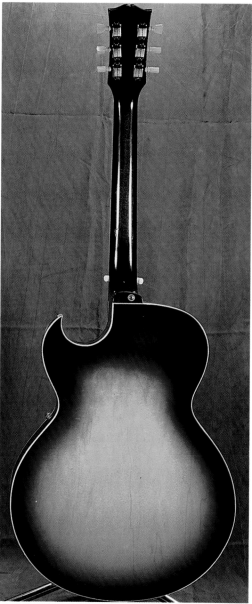

Photos 45 & 46 — 1962 Gibson ES-175D - Ser. #85879, Tobacco Sunburst finish, 98% overall condition. Certainly a mainstay of Gibson acoustic/electrics, this model (and close cousins) are gathering more of a following every year. Observe F holes, lack of binding on headstock, triple bound body front, and nickel plated trapeze tailpiece which has begun to oxidize. Mother-of-Pearl parallelogram fretboard inlays are also a trademark of this model. During this year, Fender Strats were selling for approximately $285, while this ES-175D model retailed at $340.

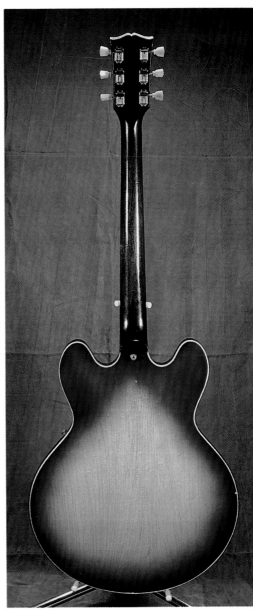

Photo 47 & 48 — 1969 Gibson ES-345 Stereo Ser. #899288, Cherry Sunburst finish, 90%-95% overall condition. The Gibson 335 Series and variations (including 345, 350, etc.) have enjoyed tremendous popularity amongst musicians, including the likes of Chuck Berry, B.B. King, Alvin Lee, Justin Hayward of the Moody Blues, and others. No major wear on front or back of body, but note light finish wear on back of neck and one of the original tuners (upper right) has been replaced with a Kluson.

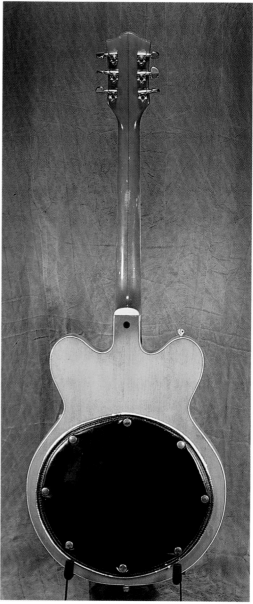

Photos 49 & 50 — 1959 Gretsch Chet Atkins Nashville (Model 6120) - Ser. #33926, Western Orange finish, 90%-95% overall condition. No electric guitar section would be complete without the inclusion of at least one Gretsch instrument. This specimen is very clean, with only light wear on back of 2-piece neck. Note circular protective pad to prevent premature back of body wear. Note bound F holes and thumbnail inlays on neck.

 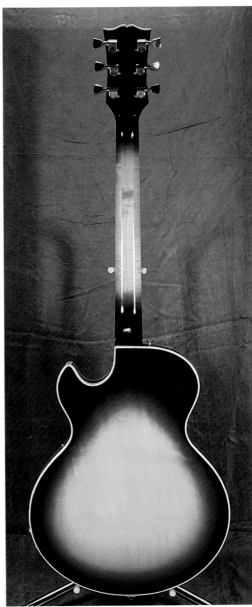

Photos 51 & 52 — 1977 Gibson ES Artist - Ser. #06 195965, 3-Tone Sunburst, mint condition (99% overall). Gibson fan, yet don't recognize this guitar? Don't feel bad, there are only two ES Artists out there. Ultra-rare? Yes. Ultra-expensive? Surprisingly not. In this case, rarity does not dictate desirability. With a $2,500 asking price, compared to $7,000 for the Strat in photos 11 and 12, rarity can sometimes come up last when determining a guitar's overall desirability factor. Note 3-piece neck, headstock and body binding, unusual tunomatic mounts, and Gibson's rarest (and perhaps most distinctive) trapeze tailpiece.

Photos 53 & 54 — 1964 Gibson J-200 - Ser. #62460, Natural Blonde finish, 80%-85% overall condition. Observe wear underneath "mustache" bridge and nicks on back of neck. Observe 3-piece neck, spectacular bookmatched flame maple on back, and extra holes on back of headstock. Also, examine neck inlays and definitive pickguard graphics on this model. The J-200 series has many variations.

Photos 55 & 56 — Guild D3JN.T. - Ser. #180154, Natural finish, 80% overall condition. Notice considerable wear on left side of pickguard below soundhole - the only major area of deterioration on this instrument outside of normal nicks and scratches. This dreadnought features a 2-piece bookmatched spruce top, mahogany back and neck, rosewood fingerboard with dot inlays, and enclosed tuners.

Photos 57 & 58 — Epiphone Texan (FT79N) - Ser. #424923, Natural finish, 75%-80% overall condition. No major wear in any one area, just normal scratches, dings, and handling marks. Two-piece mahogany back with normal horizontal finish weather checking. Astute Epiphone acoustic aficionados will recognize the replaced tuners. Note "E" logo on bell.

Photos 59 & 60 — 1945 Martin D-18 - Ser. #92775, Natural finish, 70%-75% overall condition. Examine wear along the sides of the neck above soundhole and crack on right side. It is not uncommon for Martin's to have cracked tops because of their 1-piece construction. Note scratching on 2-piece bookmatched mahogany back and relative lack of wear on neck. No acoustic guitar is more desirable than a Martin - hence the $2,600 price tag.

Photos 61 & 62 — 1957 Martin D-18 - Ser. #168235, Natural finish, 70% overall condition. An initial observation might conclude that this specimen is in better condition than the D-18 pictured in photos 59 and 60. However, careful inspection reveals a top surface crack running from the bridge to the bottom of the body. This doesn't effect value that much, unless there has been an unprofessional attempt to repair. Eagle-eye readers will note small operation ID numbers between tuning machines.

 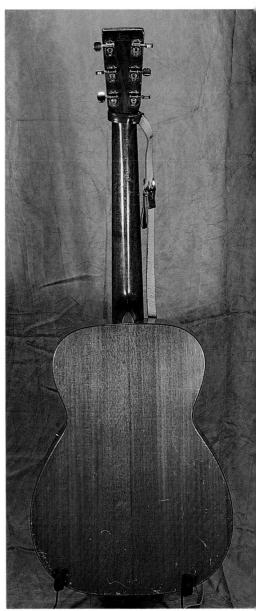

Photos 63 & 64 — 1934 Martin R-18 - Ser. # unknown, Dark Mahogany finish, 75% overall condition. Small arch top body style with round soundhole and trapeze tailpiece. Note finish deterioration around left side of soundhole and neck, and continuing to top of body. Nice back with minimal scratching. Normal neck wear (although upper back has a few scratches and some finish loss). This Martin is all original - not a bad pre-war Martin. Originality is Polar North for Martin collectors.

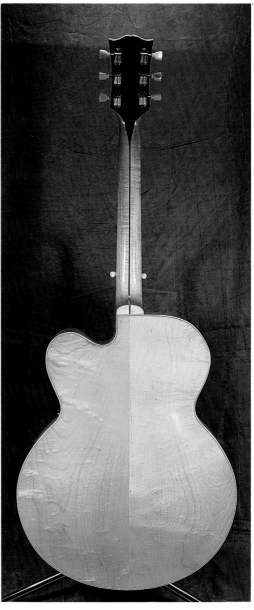

Photos 65 & 66 — 1953 Gibson L-7C - Ser. #A-13933, Natural finish, 85% overall condition. Note this instrument would have been in 95% condition without the nicks and scratches mostly found on the right side of the lower body. Examine exceptionally clean bookmatched back and very little wear on back of 2-piece neck. Trapeze tailpiece shows normal dulling due to oxidation. Parallelogram inlays, rosewood bridge, and layered black pickguard are standard features on this model.

Photos 67 & 68 — 1946 Epiphone Emperor - Ser. #55580, Natural finish, 90%-95% overall condition. In wide bodies, Boeing has the 747, and Epiphone had the 18-inch Emperor. Spectacular bookmatched flame maple multi-bound backside with 7-piece laminate neck. Double inlay blocks on fretboard, tortoise shell multi-layered pickguard, and split trapeze tailpiece are all hallmarks of this model.

Photos 69 & 70 — 1942 Gibson Super 400 - Ser. #97668, Regular finish, 80%-85% overall condition. Examine finish scratches on upper top of front and sides of back. Gibson's top-of-the-line carved top acoustic, like the Emperor pictured on facing page also had an 18-inch body. Bookmatched flame maple back is an equal to the Epiphone pictured on the facing page. Note front and back headstock inlays, marbled celluloid pickguard, and Super 400 logo on heel.

Photos 71 & 72 — 1935 Gibson L7 - Ser. #90980, Regular finish, 60% condition. While this instrument does not exhibit extreme wear in any one area, multiple scratches and nicks on front, in addition to back of neck wear, reduce this specimen's overall condition to 60%. Observe unusual fretboard inlays, small headstock, and flame maple back that has been somewhat covered up by the dark original finish. All original with no major problems.

Photos 73 & 74 — 1950 Epiphone Zenith - Ser. # unknown, Regular finish, 65%-70% overall condition. Back side of this instrument is living proof of what a belt buckle can do to the finish over a period of time. Sunburst finish on back reveals 3-piece laminate neck. Dulling trapeze tailpiece, dot inlays, and adjustable rosewood bridge are all standard features on this model.

Photos 75 & 76 — 1924 Gibson L-4 - Ser. #92109, Regular finish, 50% overall condition. Note nasty cracks on right front side of body in addition to more than normal scratches and dings on back side of body caused by excessive jean rivet damage. Also, note missing pickguard. $795 as is, double that if in 80%, and double again if in 98%+ condition (virtually impossible to find). Note early Gibson script logo on headstock.

GLOSSARY

This glossary is divided into 4 sections: General Glossary; Bridges, Pegs, Tailpieces and Tuners; Pickups and Book Terminology. If you are looking for something and can't find it in one section, please check the others. If you can't find it after you've been through the whole glossary, give us a call. We value your input for future editions.

General Glossary

Abalone — Shellfish material used in instrument ornamentation.

Acoustic — Generic term used for hollow bodied instruments that rely on the body to produce the amplified sound of the instrument, rather than electronic amplification.

Acoustic Electric — A thin hollow bodied instrument that relies on a pickup to amplify its sound.

Action — Everybody wants a piece of it. It is also the height the strings are off of the fingerboard, stretched between the nut and bridge.

Arch/Arched Top — The top of an instrument that has been carved or pressed to have a "rounded" top.

Avoidire — blonde mahogany.

Binding (bound) — Trim that goes along the outer edge of the body, neck or peghead. It is made out of many different materials, natural and synthetic.

Black Beauty — This term is generally used in reference to early (1955-1960) Gibson Les Paul Customs, due to thier glossy black finish.

Body — The main bulk of the instrument, usually. It is where the bridge, tailpiece and pickguard are located. On acoustics, the soundhole, or holes, are located on the body top, usually, and the sound is amplified inside it. On electrics it is where the pickups are routed into and the electronics housing is stored. It is what the player cradles.

Bolt On/Bolt On Neck — Construction technique that involves attaching the neck to the body by means of bolts.

Bound
See BINDING.

Bout/Bouts — The rounded, generally, side/sides on the top and bottom of an instrument's body.

Bridge — Component that touches the top of the instrument and transfers vibrations from string to body. It is usually attached by glue or screws but is also found to be held in place by string tension, the same as a violin.

Carved Top
See ARCH TOP.

Cutaway — An area that has been cut away on the upper bout, or both bouts, to allow access to the higher frets.

Dobro — Slang term for a guitar that has a built-in resonator.

Dreadnought — A generic term used to describe steel string guitar configuration consisting of a boxy body and solid headstock.

Ebonized — It means the wood has been stained dark to appear to be ebony.

Ebonol — A synthetic material that is used as replacement for wood.

Electric — A generic term referencing the fact that the instrument relies on pickups to amplify its sound.

F-Hole — Stylized f shaped soundhole that is carved into the top of various instruments, most commonly acoustic. It usually comes in pairs.

Fingerboard — An area on top of the neck that the string is pressed against to create the desired note (frequency).

Finish — The outer coat of an instrument. The sealant of the wood. The protector of the instrument. Color me a rainbow. How many ways do you say it? It's all of the above, it's the finish.

Flat Top — Term used to describe an acoustic steel stringed instrument whose top is flat.

Fret — A strip of metal that is embedded at specific intervals into the fingerboard.

Fretboard — Another way of saying fingerboard and specifying that it has frets embedded into it.

Fretless Fingerboard — Commonly found on Bass instruments, this fingerboard is smooth, with no frets.

Graphite — Used in various forms of instrument construction because of its rigidity and weight, this type of carbon is used in the body, neck and nut.

Hardware — Generic term for the bridge, tailpiece, tuners or vibrato system.

Headless — This means the instrument has no peghead.

Headstock
See PEGHEAD.

Heel — On the backside of an instrument, at the base of the neck is an area where the neck curves outward, this is the heel, more pronounced and important on acoustic instruments.

Inlay — Decoration or identifying marks on an instrument that are inlaid into one of the surface areas. They are made of a number of materials, though abalone, pearl and wood are the most common.

Locking Tuners — These tuners are manufactured with a locking mechanism built right into them, thus preventing string slippage.

Logo — An identifying feature on an instrument; it could be a symbol or a name, it could be a decal, an inlay or painted on, and it could be missing.

Mother of Pearl — A shellfish (oyster/clam) material used for inlay.

Nato — A lower grade or quality of mahogany, sometimes referred to as lumberyard mahogany.

Neck — The area that the strings of the instrument are stretched along, the peghead sits at the top, the body lies at the bottom.

Octave — Every 12 frets on a stringed instrument is an octave in the musical scale of things.

Pearl — Slang term for Mother of Pearl, a shellfish. See MOTHER OF PEARL.

Pearloid — A synthetic material made of plastic and pearl dust.

Peghead — The area at the top of an instrument where the tuning machines, or pegs, are located.

Phenolic — A synthetic material that is used as fingerboard wood replacement.

Pickguard — A piece of material used to protect the instrument from gouges in the top or finish that are caused by the pick or your fingers.

Pickup — An electronic devise that translates string vibrations into the electronic signal needed for amplification of the sound.
See PICKUP Section.

Pre-CBS — Fender terminology referring to the CBS buy out of Fender Instruments, which occurred in 1965.

Purfling — Decorative trim that is found running along the inside of the binding.

Relief — The upward slope of the fingerboard that keeps the strings off the frets.

Resonator — A metal device located in some instruments that is the means of their amplification.

Reverse Headstock — On this instrument the peghead has been flipped over from the normal configuration and the tuners are all on the highest note side of the instrument (tuners are all located on one side).

Reverse Peghead
See REVERSE HEADSTOCK.

Rosette — A decorative design that is placed around the soundhole.

S/Plate — Slang for Scratch Plate.
See PICKGUARD.

Saddle — The area that a string passes over to create the length needed for an exact note (frequency).

Scale Length — The area between the nut and bridge over which the strings of the instrument are stretched.

Scalloped — This is what the area on the fingerboard between the frets is called when it has been scooped out, creating a dip between the frets.

Scratch Plate
See PICKGUARD.

Semi-Acoustic — term used to describe a shallow bodied instrument that is constructed with a solid piece of wood running the length of the center of the body.

Slotted Peghead — A peghead usually associated with classic style instruments. The peghead has slots running lengthwise that allows access to the tuners.

Soundhole — A hole found in the top of acoustic instruments, mostly, that allows the sound to be projected from the body.

Strings — They are the substance that is stretched between the tuners/pegs and the bridge/tailpiece. The weight of the string is what determines the range of frequencies it will cover.

Sunburst/Sunburst Finish — A finish that is dark at the edge of the instrument's top and gets progressively lighter towards the middle.

Thinline — Original Gibson terminology referring to a hollow bodied instrument that has a shallow depth of body.

Through Body
See THRU BODY.

Thru Body — Type of construction that consists of the neck wood extending through the entire length of the instrument and the pieces of wood that make up the body being attached to the sides of the neck wood.

Tremolo — An increase and decrease in the volume of a continuous sound.

Truss Rod — A rod, or rods, placed in necks made of wood to create stability and a means of adjustment.

Vibrato — The act of physically lengthening or shortening the medium (in this case, it will be strings) to produce a fluctuation in frequency.

Wildwood Finish — A type of finish used by Fender in which beechwood had been injected with dyes during growth. This left different colored streaks in the wood grain, which was then carved into guitar bodies and headstocks and finished in a clear protective material.

BRIDGES, PEGS, TAILPIECES AND TUNERS

Acoustic Bridge — The bridge on an acoustic instrument is usually glued to the top and though pins are usually used there are still numerous ways of holding the strings taut.

Banjo Tuners — tuners that are perpendicular to the peghead and pass through it, as opposed to being mounted on the side of the peghead, ei: classic style peghead tuners.

Bigsby Vibrato — A vibrato system that involves a roller bar with little pegs that run in a perpendicular line, around which you hook the string balls. One end of the bar has an arm coming off of it, a spring is located under the arm, and the entire apparatus is connected to a trapeze tailpiece. The bridge is separate from the vibrato system. This vibrato was designed by Paul Bigsby.

Bridge — Component that touches the top of the instrument and transfers vibrations from string to body. It is usually attached by glue or screws but is also found to be held in place by string tension, the same as a violin.

Bridge Pin — A peg that passes through the bridge anchoring one end of the string for tuning.

Double Locking Vibrato — A vibrato system that locks the strings into place by tightening down screws on each string, thus stopping the string's ability to slip. There is also a clamp at the top of the fingerboard that holds the strings from the tuners. See VIBRATO SYSTEM.

Fixed Bridge — One piece, usually metal, usually on electric instruments, unit that contains the saddles, bridge and tailpiece all in one and is held onto the body by screws.

Friction Pegs — Wooden dowels that rely on the friction created between itself and the wood of the hole it is put in to keep the tension of the strings constant.

Headless — Term meaning that the instrument's headstock is missing. The top of the neck is capped with a piece of hardware that acts like a regular tailpiece on the instrument body.

Locking Tuners — These tuners are manufactured with a locking mechanism built into them, thus preventing string slippage.

Nut — Device located at the top of the fingerboard (opposite from the bridge) that determines the action and spacing of the strings.

Pegs —See FRICTION PEGS.

Pins — Pegs that are used to anchor the strings in place on the bridge.

Roller Bridge — This is a Gretsch trademark feature. It is an adjustable metal bridge that sits on a wooden base, the saddles of this unit sit on a threaded bar and are easily moved back and forth to allow personal string spacing.

Saddle/Saddles — A part of the bridge that holds the string/strings in place, helps transfer vibrations to the instrument body and helps in setting the action.

Sideways Vibrato — Built off the trapeze tailpiece concept, this unit has a lever that pulls the string attachment bar back along a pair of poles that have springs on them to push the bar back into place. This is all covered by a plate with a design on it.

Single Locking Vibrato — A vibrato system that locks the strings on the unit to keep them from going out of tune during heavy arm use. This style of vibrato does not employ a clamping system at the top of the fingerboard.

Standard Vibrato — Usually associated with the Fender Stratocaster, this unit has the saddles on top and an arm off to one side. The arm allows you to bend the strings, making the frequencies (notes) rise or drop. All of this sits on a metal plate that rocks back and forth. Strings may have an area to attach to on top or they may pass through the body and have holding cups on the back side. A block of metal, usually called the Inertia Block, is generally located under the saddles to allow for increased sustain. The block travels through the instrument's body and has springs attached to it to create the tension necessary to keep the strings in tune. See VIBRATO SYSTEM.

Steinberger Bridge — A bridge designed by Ned Steinberger, it combines the instrument bridge and tuners all in one unit. It is used with headless instruments.

Steinberger Vibrato — A vibrato system that has the instrument's bridge, vibrato and tuners all in one unit. Like the Steinberger Tailpiece, this was also designed by Ned Steinberger. It is also used with headless instruments.

Stop Tailpiece — This piece of hardware is attached to the top of an instrument by screws and has slots in it to hold the string balls. Generally used with a tunomatic bridge.

Strings Thru Anchoring — A tailpiece that involves the strings passing through an instrument's body and the string balls are held in place by cups.

Stud Tailpiece — See STOP TAILPIECE.

Tailpiece — The device that holds the strings at the body end of the scale. It may be all in one unit that contains the saddle/saddles also, or stands alone.

Tied Bridge — Style of bridge usually associated with "classical" style instruments that have the strings secured by tying them around the bridge.

Trapeze Tailpiece — A type of tailpiece that is hinged, has one end attached to the bottom bout of the instrument and the other end has grooves in it to hold the string balls.

Trem/Tremolo/Tremolo Arm — Terms inaccurately used to mean Vibrato System.
See VIBRATO SYSTEM.

Tuner/Tuners — Mechanical device that is used to stretch the string/strings. These are located on the peghead.

Tunable Stop Tailpiece — A taipiece that rests on a pair of posts and has small fine tuning machines mounted on top of it.

Tunomatic Bridge — A bridge that is attached to the instrument's top by two metal posts and has adjustable saddles on the topside.

Vibrato — Generic term used to describe Vibrato System.

Vibrato System — A device that stretches or slackens the strings by the means of a lever, the arm or bar, and a fulcrum, the pivot pins or blades.

Vibrola — Another way of saying Vibrato.

Wang Bar — Slang term used for Vibrato System.

Whammy/Whammy Bar — Slang terms used for Vibrato System.

Wrapover Bridge — A self contained bridge/tailpiece bar device that is attached to the body, with the strings wrapping over the bar.

Wrapunder Bridge — The same as above except the strings wrap under the bar.

PICKUPS

The Pickup Principle follows this idea: your instrument's pickup is composed of a magnetic core that has wire wrapped about it. This creates a magnetic field that the strings pass through. As the string is plucked it vibrates in this field and creates fluctuations. These fluctuations are then translated into electronic pulses by induction; the magic of having electrons excited into activity by being wrapped next to each other via the wire coils. Once the fluctuations are in electron form they move along the wires in groups called waveforms, which move to an amplifier and get enlarged. The rest is up to you.

Active Electronics — A form of electronic circuitry that involves some power source, usually a 9 volt battery. Most of the time the circuit is an amplification circuit, though it may also be onboard effects circuitry.

Alnico — An alloy commonly used in the construction of pickup magnets. It consists of aluminum, nickel and cobalt.

Amplify/Amplification — To increase, in this case to increase the volume of the instrument.

Blade — A pickup that uses a blade or rail instead of polepieces.

Bobbin — The structure, usually plastic, that the coil wires are wound around. See COILS.

Ceramic — A substance used in pickup magnets that consists of magnetic particles mixed with a clay-like base.

Coils — Insulated wire wrapped around a nonconductive material.

Coil Split — A switch and a term that means you are splitting the coils in a humbucker and turning it into two single coil pickups. See SPLIT PICKUP.

Coil Tap — A term and a switch that refers to accessing a coil tap in a pickup. See TAPPED.

Control/Controls
See POT and POTENTIOMETERS

Crystal
See PIEZO.

Dirty Fingers — Coverless humbucker pickups that have black and white bobbins.

Equalizer — An effect that allows you to boost or cut certain frequencies.

Hex Pickup — A device that has six individual pickups, one for each string, housed in a single unit. This unit is used to provide the signals for synth (synthesizer) instruments.

Humbucker — Consists of two single coil pickups being placed side by side and wired together in such a fashion that the hum is canceled out of the single coils.

J-Style — A single coil pickup, though some are humbucker pickups, designed for electric bass and usually placed near the bridge. It is largely associated with the Fender Jazz Bass.

Lace Sensor — A pickup developed by Don Lace that Fender Instruments currently licenses, this pickup takes a single bobbin and windings and places it inside a magnetic housing with an open top. This creates an electromagnetic shielding effect and allows only the area directly over the pickup to sense string vibration. Pretty Trekkish.

Onboard — Usually referencing effects, it means built into the instrument.

Out Of Phase — When a signal from two pickups are run through a switch that puts their respective signals 180 degrees out of phase with each other.

P-Style — An offset pickup with two magnets per half. They are usually located near the neck and are associated with the Fender Precision Bass.

P.A.F. (Patent Applied For) — Common term used to mean the pickup that Seth Lover designed for Gibson in 1955. The patent was not awarded till 1959.

Parametric Equalizer — An equalizer that allows you to specifically choose which range of frequencies you wish to affect.

Passive Electronics — Electronic circuitry that has no power supply. Usually it consists of filter circuitry.

Phase Switch — A switch used to accomplish the feat of putting the signal out of phase. See OUT OF PHASE.

Piezo (piezoelectric) — A crystalline substance that induces an electrical current caused by pressure or vibrations.

Polepiece/Polepieces — Small magnetic rods that are found inside the pickup coils and, usually, situated under the instrument's strings. Some of these polepieces are adjustable.

Pot — What the knobs are connected to.

Potentiometer — A variable resistor that is used to make adjustments.

Preamp — An electronic circuit that amplifies the signal from the pickup/s and preps it for the amplifier.

Pre-post Switch — A switch on instruments with active electronics, that allows you to bypass the active electronics and go with a raw signal.

Rail Pickup
See BLADE.

Shielding — Term used to describe materials, usually copper or a spray applicant, used to protect the signal in electronic instruments from outside electrical interference.

Single Coil — See opening paragraph for this section, it applies to this term.

Soap Bar — Term used to describe a specific Gibson single coil pickup, model number: P-90.

Soundhole — An opening in the instrument's top, usually, that allows the amplified sound out of the body cavity.

Split Pickup — A humbucker that has been wired so it has the capability of being split into two single coil pickups.

Stacked Coil — A form of humbucker pickup that is in a stacked configuration so it can be installed as a replacement for a single coil.

Tapped — The process of taking a wire out of the midst of the windings in a pickup and leaving it open for hookup to a switch. This can be done a number of times in one pickup.

Transducer/Transducer Pickup — A device that converts energy from one form to another, in this instance it is the vibrations caused by the strings, moving along the wood and being converted into electrical energy for amplification.

Book Terms

This glossary section should help you understand the jargon that we use in our model descriptions of the instruments in this text.

3 Per Side — To the number of tuners on the sides of the peghead.

3/2 Per Side — This is in reference to a 5 string instrument with three tuners on one side of the peghead and two tuners on the other.

335 Style — refers to an instrument that has a body style that is similar to that of the Gibson 335.

4 On One Side — Four tuners on one side of the peghead.

4 Per Side — Four tuners on each side of the peghead an eight string instrument.

4/1 Per Side — On an instrument with five strings this would mean four tuners are on one side of the peghead, and one is on the other.

4/2 Per Side — Four tuners on one side and two on the other side of a peghead.

4/3 Per Side — This instrument has seven strings with four of the tuners located on one side of the peghead and three on the other side.

5 On One Side — All the tuners on one side of the peghead a five string instrument.

6 On One Side — All six tuners on one side of the peghead.

6 Per Side — Talking about a twelve string instrument here and the term means the number of tuners on each side of the peghead.

6/1 Per Side — A seven string instrument with six tuners on one side and one on the other.

7 On One Side — A term referring to a seven string instrument with all the tuners on the peghead are on one side.

12/14 Fret — Term in which the first number describes the fret at which the neck joins the body, and the second number is the total number of frets on the fingerboard.

Dreadnought Style — This term refers to steel string instruments that are fashioned after the traditional build of a Martin instrument, a boxy type instrument with squared top and bottom bouts, approximately 14 inches across the top bouts, 16 inches across the bottom bouts, there is not much of a waist and the depth of instrument is about 4-5 inches.

Explorer style — The instrument's body shape is similar to a Gibson Explorer model.

Jazz Style — A body shape similar to that of a Fender Jazz Bass.

Les Paul Style — Shaped like a Gibson Les Paul.

Point Fingerboard — A fingerboard that has a "V-ed" section on it at the body end of the fingerboard.

Precision Style — Instrument body's looks like a Fender Precision Bass.

Strat Style — Shaped like a Fender Stratocaster.

Tele Style — Shaped like a Fender Telecaster.

Thru Body — Type of construction that consists of the neck wood extending through the entire length of the instrument and the pieces of wood that make up the body being attached to the sides of the neck wood.

Tunomatic Stop Tailpiece — This unit is a combination bridge/taipiece that has adjustable (tunomatic) saddles mounted on a wrap around tailpiece.

V Style — Body style like the Gibson Flying V.

Volume/Tone Control — The instrument has a volume and a tone control. If a two (2) precedes the term then there are two volume and two tone controls.

Common Abbreviations

These abbrreviations are used as prefixes and suffixes. They are also just a guide, nothing should be viewed as being the definitive list. A lot of companies will have their own letters or numbers which are that instrument's company code.

A - Ash

B - Bass or Brazilian Rosewood

C - Cutaway

D - Dreadnought or Double

DC - Double Cutaway

E - Electric

ES - Electric (Electro) Spanish

F - Fretless or Florentine

H - Herringbone

J - Jumbo

K - Koa

L - Left Handed

LE - Limited Edition

M - Mahogany or Maple

OM - Orchestra Model

S - Spanish, Solid Body, Special or Super

SG - Solid Guitar

T - Tremolo or Thinline

V - V shaped Neck, Venetian, Vibrato or Vintage Series

W - Walnut

Guitar Inventory Records

The following pages have been provided so that your may keep an active and accurate inventory record of guitars you may buy, sell, trade and/or keep. Keeping these kinds of records will assist you when dealing with matters like insurance, inventory control, and enable you to *know* what you have at a glance. If you need additional copies for your mother-lode, feel free to copy page 85.

1. Mfr. _____ Model (if any) _____ Ser No. _____

   Configuration: ❐ Acoustic ❐ Acoustic-Electric ❐ Acoustic Bass ❐ Electric ❐ Electric Bass ❐ Other

   Finish/ Color _____

   Hardware: _____

   Overall Condition: _____ Options/Special Orders: _____

   Special/Identifying Features: _____

   Remarks: _____

   Date Purchased: _____ Purchase Price: _____ Purchased from: _____

   Current Value: $ _____ 1994: _____ 1995: _____ 1996: _____

2. Mfr. _____ Model (if any) _____ Ser No. _____

   Configuration: ❐ Acoustic ❐ Acoustic-Electric ❐ Acoustic Bass ❐ Electric ❐ Electric Bass ❐ Other

   Finish/ Color _____

   Hardware: _____

   Overall Condition: _____ Options/Special Orders: _____

   Special/Identifying Features: _____

   Remarks: _____

   Date Purchased: _____ Purchase Price: _____ Purchased from: _____

   Current Value: $ _____ 1994: _____ 1995: _____ 1996: _____

3. Mfr. _____ Model (if any) _____ Ser No. _____

   Configuration: ❐ Acoustic ❐ Acoustic-Electric ❐ Acoustic Bass ❐ Electric ❐ Electric Bass ❐ Other

   Finish/ Color _____

   Hardware: _____

   Overall Condition: _____ Options/Special Orders: _____

   Special/Identifying Features: _____

   Remarks: _____

   Date Purchased: _____ Purchase Price: _____ Purchased from: _____

   Current Value: $ _____ 1994: _____ 1995: _____ 1996: _____

Guitar Inventory Records

4. Mfr. _____ Model (if any)_____ Ser No. _____

   Configuration: ❐ Acoustic ❐ Acoustic-Electric ❐ Acoustic Bass ❐ Electric ❐ Electric Bass ❐ Other

   Finish/ Color _____

   Hardware:_____

   Overall Condition: _____ Options/Special Orders: _____

   Special/Identifying Features: _____

   Remarks: _____

   Date Purchased: _____ Purchase Price: _____ Purchased from: _____

   Current Value: $ _____ 1994:_____ 1995:_____ 1996:_____

5. Mfr. _____ Model (if any)_____ Ser No. _____

   Configuration: ❐ Acoustic ❐ Acoustic-Electric ❐ Acoustic Bass ❐ Electric ❐ Electric Bass ❐ Other

   Finish/ Color _____

   Hardware:_____

   Overall Condition: _____ Options/Special Orders: _____

   Special/Identifying Features:_____

   Remarks: _____

   Date Purchased: _____ Purchase Price: _____ Purchased from: _____

   Current Value: $ _____ 1994:_____ 1995:_____ 1996:_____

6. Mfr. _____ Model (if any)_____ Ser No. _____

   Configuration: ❐ Acoustic ❐ Acoustic-Electric ❐ Acoustic Bass ❐ Electric ❐ Electric Bass ❐ Other

   Finish/ Color _____

   Hardware:_____

   Overall Condition: _____ Options/Special Orders: _____

   Special/Identifying Features:_____

   Remarks: _____

   Date Purchased: _____ Purchase Price: _____ Purchased from: _____

   Current Value: $ _____ 1994:_____ 1995:_____ 1996:_____

Guitar Inventory Records

___. Mfr. _____ Model (if any)_____ Ser No. _____

Configuration: ❏ Acoustic ❏ Acoustic-Electric ❏ Acoustic Bass ❏ Electric ❏ Electric Bass ❏ Other

Finish/ Color _____

Hardware:_____

Overall Condition: _____ Options/Special Orders: _____

Special/Identifying Features: _____

Remarks: _____

Date Purchased: _____Purchase Price: _____ Purchased from: _____

Current Value: $ _____ 1994:_____ 1995:_____ 1996:_____

___. Mfr. _____ Model (if any)_____ Ser No. _____

Configuration: ❏ Acoustic ❏ Acoustic-Electric ❏ Acoustic Bass ❏ Electric ❏ Electric Bass ❏ Other

Finish/ Color _____

Hardware:_____

Overall Condition: _____ Options/Special Orders: _____

Special/Identifying Features: _____

Remarks: _____

Date Purchased: _____Purchase Price: _____ Purchased from: _____

Current Value: $ _____ 1994:_____ 1995:_____ 1996:_____

___. Mfr. _____ Model (if any)_____ Ser No. _____

Configuration: ❏ Acoustic ❏ Acoustic-Electric ❏ Acoustic Bass ❏ Electric ❏ Electric Bass ❏ Other

Finish/ Color _____

Hardware:_____

Overall Condition: _____ Options/Special Orders: _____

Special/Identifying Features: _____

Remarks: _____

Date Purchased: _____Purchase Price: _____ Purchased from: _____

Current Value: $ _____ 1994:_____ 1995:_____ 1996:_____

MEET THE STAFF

"May, we help you?"

1993 has turned out to be the busiest year ever for the staff at Blue Book Publications, Inc. From the original "Hey, what a great idea - let's do a guitar book", to the unspeakable and hopefully, unforgettable amount of staff time it has consumed to put this publication in your hands, the following people (or what's left of them) have made the difference.

The people below keep the One Appletree Square blender always set at "liquify", while trying to deal with eight black AT&T boxes ringing concurrently, attempting to get to the bottom of Bernoe's mailbag, and other tasks that have proven to raise blood pressure levels significantly.

Our office hours remain the same - 8:30 a.m. to 5:00 p.m. CST, Monday through Friday or leave a message. FAXing is possible 24 hours a day. U.S. mail delivers 6 days a week. UPS, Federal Express, Express Mail, and other expedited shipping services deliver to our location with consistency. *Our goal is simple - to give you the best products and services available within the industry.*

S.P. Fjestad
- Editor and Publisher

A thin line, jumbo Les Paul Gibson, a little white frozen water to help keep the mosquitos down, and a grizzly bear coat enabling porch practicing - now it doesn't get any better than this! The editor can also be observed cloning himself above, very helpful during turbo-charged periods of productivity.

Tom Gagnon - *Controller*

As you can see, Tom's musical abilities become one of his greatest assets when working in the complaint department. After 2 or 3 soothing licks, Tom is usually able to make most people stay in tune with him. Being controller, Tom's musical score sheet usually ends up with a fortissimo high C!

Jeff Perkins - *Associate Editor*

The rector of Abalone Abbey - Temple of guitar Madness. Jeff put the words down on paper, coalesced a large smorgasboard of research into a single plateful containing millions of orderly bytes. In brief, he organized a manuscript and made it happen. No one hits the keyboard harder, and that's meant both figuratively and literally. Nice half-court hook shot, Jeff!

Paul G. Wichtendahl
- *Production Manager*

All of it somehow comes together, and Paul is the one who keeps the various menacing mechanical monsters melding and mashing. Note his neck/string bending techniques and Paul's way of getting even with a guitar that won't tune.

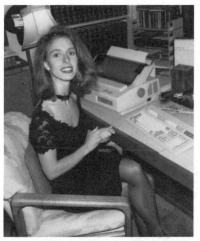

Michelle Schroeder

Michelle Schroeder - *Manuscript Supervisor*

The Wizard of Wordstar, Michelle is responsible for both the typing input and proofing of Blue Book Publications' ever-increasing list of projects. Michelle has helped us on and off for the past 8 years. Makes the keyboard rattle!

Lisa Winkels

Lisa Winkels -
Operations Manager

Reality Central! Lisa is in charge of everything that no one else can do - which is a lot. Somewhat of a Polar North factor at One Appletree Square, Lisa is the last word in operations, customer service, billing, and maintaining.

Kathy Cariveau - *Everyone's Assistant*

Kathy came to us late in this project, and after being with us for a month, seems to know everything except which state hospital she wants to commit herself to. Kathy's middle name has to be flexibility.

Doreen Pomije

Doreen Pomije
- Art Director

Doreen pumps it out! Have you ever tried to layout a guitar ad, look for Smith and Wesson Model 27 graphics, repair caption layouts on a Colt book, perform half-tone beheading in the name of honesty, and put together an auction flyer - all in four hours? You know the rest.

Kathy Cariveau

John Allen

John Allen -
The M&M
Dispenser

While John didn't have a lot to do with the production of this publication, he took the pressure off the ringy-dingies enabling what was left of the rest of the staff to charge forward into another fretted instrument black hole.

AMERICAN GUITAR PLAYERS ASSOCIATION
FOR PEOPLE WHO LOVE TO PLAY GUITARS

- **For people who play all kinds and styles of Guitars:** Acoustic, Electric, Classical, Jazz, Blues, Country.
- **For people in their first year of playing or their 51st year of playing and everyone in between, including music store owners, collectors and manufacturers.**

COMMUNICATE FREE IN THE AGPA NEWSLETTER

The AGPA links together guitarists from around the country who love to play and collect guitars. As an AGPA member, you will be able, free of charge, to communicate with other guitarists through our regular newsletter.

- ☞ Trade your guitar with members.
- ☞ Exchange tips on playing.
- ☞ Play other members' guitars before you buy, or ask members about the quality of new products.
- ☞ Get guitar repair tips from members.
- ☞ Let members help you find the music you want.
- ☞ Meet other players in your area, or when you travel, meet other players in another part of the country.
- ☞ Collectors and traders — see who has what and where.
- ☞ Whatever your needs, send your message all over the country.

Free entry in the newsletter within allowed space limitation, additional entries at very nominal charges.

THE ANNUAL CONVENTION— PLAY, SWAP, LEARN

AGPA members get an invitation to the annual convention. Bring your favorite guitar, or a guitar you want to trade and spend three days jamming, swapping and learning about guitars, styles and techniques from all over the country. Make new friends who love the instrument the way you do. This will be the guitar playing party of your life and the only convention for the guitar-playing public.

PROTECT YOUR GUITAR AGAINST THEFT WITH THE NATIONAL GUITAR REGISTRY

Register your guitar **FREE** with the AGPA. If your guitar is stolen, you can alert music stores and other musicians nationwide, through the newsletter's stolen instrument hotline. Whether it's a rare vintage of just your favorite production number, if it has a serial number, register it, and mark it with free **AGPA theft-guard decals.**

PARTICIPATE IN AGPA FIELD TRIPS AND REGIONAL SOCIAL EVENTS

The AGPA organizes field trips to guitar factories and other places of interest to guitar enthusiasts. It also sponsors special interest section programs in your region. Send us your wish list and we'll set it up.

JOIN SPECIAL INTEREST SECTIONS

Volunteer to be a Director for your region, or nominate your local guitar expert. Join a special interest section, such as classical, jazz etc. Music stores and Manufacturers— contact us to become corporate sponsors.

FREE AGPA COLLECTOR'S PIN WITH MEMBERSHIP

CALL, WRITE, OR FAX US TO SEE HOW YOU CAN PARTICIPATE
American Guitar Players Association • 617 W. 46th Street • Miami Beach, FL 33140
TEL: 305-531-9440 • FAX: 305-672-9177

❑ Here's my $25.00. Send me a membership package.* (***Add 25% Canada, 100% Foreign.**) BB

Included is a ❑ check ❑ Visa ❑ Mastercard

Card # _____   Exp. Date _____

Signature _____

Name _____

Street _____ City _____ State _____

ZIP_____ TEL ( )_____ FAX ( )_____

Return to: American Guitar Players Association • 617 W. 46th Street • Miami Beach, FL 33140

PERIODICALS

You've bought this book so you're obviously interested in stringed instruments. Being knowledgeable about any subject is a good idea and having the up-to-the-minute-news is the best form of knowledge. We recommend the following publications for instrument information, collecting news, updates and show announcements, luthier and artist insights and loads of other information that might interest you.

Acoustic Guitar The String Letter Press Publishers, Inc., 412 Red Hill Avenue #15, San Anselmo, CA 94960; phone no.: 415-485-6946; FAX no.: 415-485-0831.

Published bimonthly. 12 month subscription is $23.95 in USA.

Bass Player Miller Freeman, Inc., 600 Harrison Street, San Francisco, CA 94107; phone no.: 415-905-2200; FAX no.: 415-905-2233.

Published monthly. 12 month subscription is $29.95 in USA.

Guitar for the Practicing Musician Cherry Lane Music Company, Inc., 10 Midland Avenue, Port Chester, NY 10573-1490.

Published monthly. 12 month subscription is $27.95 in USA.

Guitar Player Miller Freeman Publications, 600 Harrison Street, San Francisco, CA 94107; phone no.: 415-905-2200; FAX no.: 415-905-2233.

Published monthly. 12 month subscription is $29.95 in USA.

Guitar World Harris Publications, Inc., 1115 Broadway, New York, NY 10010; phone no.: 212-807-7100; FAX no.: 212-627-4678.

Published monthly. 12 month subscription is $19.94 in USA.

Musician 33 Commercial Street, Gloucester, MA 01930; phone no.: 800-347-6969 or 508-281-3110.

Published monthly. 12 month subscription is $19.97 in USA.

National Instrument Exchange John B. Kinnemeyer, 11115 Sand Run, Harrison, OH 45030: phone/FAX no. 513-353-3320.

Published monthly. Guitar Buy/Sell Newsletter. 12 month subscription is $15.00 in USA.

Vintage Guitar Magazine Alan J. Greenwood, 105 Sioux Avenue, P.O. Box 7301, Bismarck, ND 58507; phone no.: 701-255-1197; FAX no.: 701-255-0250.

Published monthly. 12 month subscription is $17.95 in USA.

20th Century Guitar Seventh String Press, Inc., 135 Oser Avenue, Hauppauge, NY 11788; phone no.: 516-273-1674; FAX no.: 516-435-1805.

Published bimonthly. 12 month subscription is $18.00 in USA.

In addition to the regular publications put out by these publishers, most offer "Special Edition" (i.e., yearly buyers' guides, new product reviews, market overviews, etc.) magazines that are released annually, irregularly or whimsically.

References

Achard, Ken, *The Fender Guitar*, The Bold Strummer, Ltd., Westport CT, 1990

Bacon and Day, *The Fender Book*, Miller Freeman Inc., San Francisco CA, 1992

Bacon and Day, *The Guru's Guitar Guide*, Track Record Publishing, London ENGLAND, 1990

Bacon, Tony, *The Ultimate Guitar Book*, Alfred A. Knopf, Inc., New York NY, 1991

Bishop, Ian C., *The Gibson Guitar*, The Bold Strummer, Ltd., Westport CT, 1990

Bishop, Ian C., *The Gibson Guitar From 1950 Vol. 2*, The Bold Strummer, Ltd., Westport NY 1990

Blasquiz, Klaus, *The Fender Bass*, Hal Leonard Publishing Corp., Milwaukee WI, 1990

Briggs, Brinkman and Crocker, *Guitars, Guitars, Guitars*, All American Music Publishers, Neosho MO, 1988

Brozeman, Bob, *The History & Artistry of National Resonator Instruments*, Centerstream Publishing, Fullerton, CA, 1993

Duchossoir, A.R., *Gibson Electrics*, Hal Leonard Publishing Corp., Milwaukee WI, 1981

Duchossoir, A.R., *Guitar Identification*, Hal Leonard Publishing Corp., Milwaukee WI, 1983

Duchossoir, A.R., *The Fender Stratocaster*, Hal Leonard Publishing Corp., Milwaukee WI, 1989

Duchossoir, A.R., *The Fender Telecaster*, Hal Leonard Publishing Corp., Milwaukee WI, 1991

Gruhn and Carter, *Gruhn's Guide to Vintage Guitars*, Miller Freeman Inc., San Francisco CA, 1991

Longworth, Mike, *Martin Guitars, a History*, 4 Maples Press Inc., Minisink Hills PA, 1987

Moseley, Willie G., *Classic Guitars U.S.A.*, Centerstream Publishing, Fullerton CA, 1992

Schmidt, Paul William, *Aquired of the Angels: The lives and works of master guitar makers John D'Angelico and James L. D'Aquisto*, The Scarecrow Press, Inc., Metuchen, NJ, 1991

Scott, Jay, *The Guitars of the Fred Gretsch Company*, Centerstream Publishing, Fullerton CA, 1992

Smith, Richard R., *The History of Rickenbacker Guitars*, Centerstream Publishing, Fullerton CA, 1989

Van Hoose, Thomas A., *The Gibson Super 400*, Miller Freeman, Inc., San Francisco, 1991

Wheeler, Tom, *American Guitars*, HarperCollins Publishers, New York NY, 1990

ALEMBIC

Manufacturer and distributor located in Santa Rosa, CA. Previously manufactured in San Francisco.

This company was founded in 1969 by Ron and Susan Wickersham, who worked closely with the Grateful Dead during the company's infancy. Alembic continues to turn out a small number of instruments annually, mostly special ordered.

ELECTRIC

Grading	100%	98%	95%	90%	80%	70%	60%

CALIFORNIA SPECIAL — strat style maple body, thru body maple neck, 24 fret ebony fingerboard with pearl oval inlay, double locking vibrato, brass nut, 6 on one side tuners, chrome hardware, 2 single coil/1 humbucker Alembic pickups, volume/tone control, 3 mini switches. Available in Metal Ruby Red, Metal Sapphire Blue, Transparent Ruby Red and Transparent Sapphire Blue finish. Curr. mfr.

Mfr.'s Sug. Retail	$3,120	$2,185	$1,870	$1,560	$1,250	$1,125	$1,030	$935

Series I — similar to California Special, except has treble/bass volume/tone control, treble Q/bass Q/pickup switch, 5 pin stereo output jack. Curr. mfr.

Mfr.'s Sug. Retail	$5,700	$3,990	$3,420	$2,850	$2,280	$2,050	$1,880	$1,710

Series II — similar to California Special, except has master/treble/bass volume control, treble/bass tone control, treble CVQ/bass CVQ/pickup switch, 5 pin Stereo output jack. Curr. mfr.

Mfr.'s Sug. Retail	$7,055	$4,940	$4,235	$3,530	$2,820	$2,540	$2,330	$2,115

ELECTRIC BASS

All models have thru body maple, or maple/mahogany laminate neck construction, dual truss rods, 24 fret ebony fingerboard with pearl oval inlay (unless otherwise listed), brass saddles/bridge/tailpiece/nut (these items may be chrome or gold plated), active electronics, ebony fingerboard and clear gloss finish. A lot of the earlier instruments were custom ordered so there are a number of options that may be found on these guitars that are not standard items.

The tops of these instruments are bookmatched and the wood types vary widely, though the most common are as follows: Bocate, Bubinga, Burl Rosewood, Coco

Grading	100%	98%	95%	90%	80%	70%	60%

Bolo, Figured Maple, Figured Walnut, Flame Koa, Lacewood, Rosewood, Tulip-wood, Vermillion or Zebrawood. Also, the body style, peghead style and electronic/hardware configurations and combinations may vary from instrument to instrument due to the custom order nature of the company's early days.

ELAN — offset double cutaway asymmetrical body, Honduras mahogany back, body wood matching veneer and bronze logo design on peghead, gold Alembic-Gotoh tuners, 2 P-style Alembic pickups, volume/tone/balance control, active electronics switch. Curr. mfr.

꒳ **4 String** — 4 on one side tuners.

	100%	98%	95%	90%	80%	70%	60%
Mfr.'s Sug. Retail $2,770	$1,940	$1,660	$1,385	$1,110	$1,000	$915	$830

꒳ **5 String** — 4/1 per side tuners.

Mfr.'s Sug. Retail $3,090	$2,165	$1,855	$1,545	$1,230	$1,110	$1,020	$930

꒳ **6 String** — 3 per side tuners.

Mfr.'s Sug. Retail $3,415	$2,390	$2,050	$1,710	$1,430	$1,230	$1,125	$1,025

꒳ **7 String** — 4/3 per side tuners.

Mfr.'s Sug. Retail $5,220	$3,655	$3,130	$2,610	$2,040	$1,880	$1,720	$1,565

꒳ **8 String** — 4 per side tuners.

Mfr.'s Sug. Retail $3,570	$2,500	$2,140	$1,785	$1,430	$1,285	$1,175	$1,070

꒳ **10 String** — 5 per side tuners.

Mfr.'s Sug. Retail $4,675	$3,275	$1,965	$2,340	$1,870	$1,685	$1,540	$1,400

ESSENCE — offset double cutaway body, Rock maple back, flame maple top, no fingerboard inlay, body matching veneer and bronze logo design on peghead, chrome Alembic-Gotoh tuners, 2 humbucker Alembic pickups, volume/tone/balance control. Curr. mfr.

꒳ **4 String** — 2 per side tuners.

Mfr.'s Sug. Retail $1,950	$1,365	$1,170	$975	$780	$700	$640	$585

꒳ **5 String** — 3/2 per side tuners.

Mfr.'s Sug. Retail $2,175	$1,525	$1,305	$1,090	$870	$785	$720	$655

꒳ **6 String** — 3 per side tuners.

Mfr.'s Sug. Retail $2,550	$1,785	$1,530	$1,275	$1,020	$920	$840	$765

Grading	100%	98%	95%	90%	80%	70%	60%

EUROPA — offset double cutaway asymmetrical body, Honduras mahogany back, body matching veneer and bronze logo design on peghead, gold Alembic-Gotoh tuners, 2 J-style Alembic pickups, volume/tone/balance control, bass/treble/Q switches. Curr. mfr.

4 String — 4 on one side tuners.

Mfr.'s Sug. Retail	$3,215	$2,250	$1,930	$1,610	$1,290	$1,160	$1,060	$965

5 String — 4/1 per side tuners.

Mfr.'s Sug. Retail	$3,420	$2,395	$2,050	$1,710	$1,370	$1,230	$1,130	$1,025

6 String — 3 per side tuners.

Mfr.'s Sug. Retail	$3,730	$2,610	$2,240	$1,865	$1,490	$1,345	$1,230	$1,120

7 String — 4/3 per side tuners.

Mfr.'s Sug. Retail	$5,325	$3,730	$3,195	$2,665	$2,130	$1,915	$1,755	$1,600

8 String — 4 per side tuners.

Mfr.'s Sug. Retail	$3,855	$2,700	$2,315	$1,930	$1,540	$1,390	$1,270	$1,155

10 String — 5 per side tuners.

Mfr.'s Sug. Retail	$4,590	$3,215	$2,755	$2,295	$1,835	$1,650	$1,510	$1,375

SERIES I — offset double cutaway mahogany core body with bottom bout point, figured wood top/back, body matching veneer and sterling silver logo design on peghead, chrome Schaller tuners, chrome plated hardware, single coil/dummy humbucker/single coil pickups, treble/bass volume/tone control, treble Q/bass Q/pickup switch, 5 pin stereo output jack. Curr. mfr.

4 String — 2 per side tuners.

Mfr.'s Sug. Retail	$5,700	$3,990	$3,420	$2,850	$2,280	$2,050	$1,880	$1,710

5 String — 3/2 per side tuners.

Mfr.'s Sug. Retail	$6,120	$4,285	$3,670	$3,060	$2,450	$2,205	$2,020	$1,835

6 String — 3 per side tuners.

Mfr.'s Sug. Retail	$6,425	$4,500	$3,855	$3,215	$2,570	$2,315	$2,120	$1,930

7 String — 4/3 per side tuners.

Mfr.'s Sug. Retail	$8,245	$5,770	$4,945	$4,125	$3,300	$2,970	$2,720	$2,475

8 String — 4 per side tuners.

Mfr.'s Sug. Retail	$6,640	$4,650	$3,985	$3,320	$2,655	$2,390	$2,190	$1,990

10 String — 5 per side tuners.

Mfr.'s Sug. Retail	$7,225	$5,060	$4,335	$3,615	$2,890	$2,600	$2,385	$2,170

Grading	100%	98%	95%	90%	80%	70%	60%

SERIES II — offset double cutaway mahogany core body with bottom bout point, figured wood top/back, book matched body matching veneer and gold plated sterling silver logo on peghead, gold Schaller tuners, gold plated hardware, single coil/dummy humbucker/single coil pickups, master/treble/bass volume control, treble/bass tone control, treble CVQ/bass CVQ/pickup switch, 5 pin stereo output jack. Curr. mfr.

☌ **4 String** — 2 per side tuners.

Mfr.'s Sug. Retail	$7,055	$4,940	$4,235	$3,530	$2,820	$2,540	$2,330	$2,115

☌ **5 String** — 3/2 per side tuners.

Mfr.'s Sug. Retail	$7,565	$5,295	$3,175	$3,785	$3,330	$2,725	$2,495	$2,270

☌ **6 String** — 3 per side tuners.

Mfr.'s Sug. Retail	$7,865	$5,505	$4,720	$3,935	$3,145	$2,830	$2,595	$2,360

☌ **7 String** — 4/3 per side tuners.

Mfr.'s Sug. Retail	$9,675	$6,775	$5,805	$4,840	$3,870	$3,485	$3,195	$2,900

☌ **8 String** — 4 per side tuners.

Mfr.'s Sug. Retail	$8,085	$5,660	$4,850	$4,095	$3,235	$2,910	$2,665	$2,425

☌ **10 String** — 5 per side tuners.

Mfr.'s Sug. Retail	$9,085	$6,360	$5,450	$4,545	$3,635	$3,270	$2,995	$2,725

SIGNATURE SERIES — similar to Series I, except has gold logo on peghead, 2 humbucker pickups, volume/2 tone/balance controls, 2 Q switches. Curr. mfr.

☌ **Mark King** — long scale length, Mark King signature on peghead, 2 per side gold Alembic-Gotoh tuners.

Mfr.'s Sug. Retail	$2,815	$1,970	$1,690	$1,410	$1,125	$1,015	$930	$895

☌ **Stanley Clarke** — short scale length, Stanley Clarke signature on peghead, 2 per side gold Alembic-Gotoh tuners.

Mfr.'s Sug. Retail	$2,815	$1,970	$1,690	$1,410	$1,125	$1,015	$930	$895

SPOILER — offset double cutaway body, Honduras mahogany back, body matching veneer and bronze logo on peghead, chrome Alembic-Gotoh tuners, 2 humbucker pickups, volume/tone control, pickup/Q switch. Curr. mfr.

☌ **4 String** — 2 per side tuners.

Mfr.'s Sug. Retail	$2,635	$1,845	$1,580	$1,320	$1,055	$950	$870	$790

☌ **5 String** — 3/2 per side tuners.

Mfr.'s Sug. Retail	$2,815	$1,970	$1,690	$1,410	$1,125	$1,015	$930	$895

ALVAREZ

Trademark established in approximately 1967 and currently owned by St. Louis Music (established 1922) located in St. Louis, MO. Alvarez instruments are designed in St. Louis and manufactured in either Japan or Korea.

ACOUSTIC

All Alvarez acoustic steel string guitars (except the 5212, 5214 and 5216) have a stylized double A abalone inlay on their pegheads.

Artist Series

Grading	100%	98%	95%	90%	80%	70%	60%

5002 — classic style, spruce top, round soundhole, bound body, wooden inlay rosette, mahogany back/sides, nato neck, 12/19 fret rosewood fingerboard, rosewood bridge, rosewood veneer on peghead, 3 per side gold tuners. Available in Natural finish. Mfd. 1991 to date.

Mfr.'s Sug. Retail	$325	$230	$195	$165	$130	$120	$110	$100

5004 — similar to 5002, except has rosewood back/sides.

Mfr.'s Sug. Retail	$375	$265	$225	$190	$150	$135	$125	$115

5019 — dreadnought style, spruce top, round soundhole, 5 stripe body binding abalone inlay and rosette, black pickguard, mahogany back/sides, nato neck, 14/20 fret rosewood fingerboard with pearl dot inlay, 12th fret has stylized bird wings inlay, rosewood bridge with white pearl dot pins, 3 per side chrome tuners. Available in Black finish. Mfd. 1991 to date.

Mfr.'s Sug. Retail	$460	$320	$275	$230	$185	$165	$150	$140

5020 — dreadnought style, spruce top, round soundhole, bound body, 5 stripe rosette, black pickguard, mahogany back/sides, 14/20 fret rosewood fingerboard with pearl dot inlay, 12th fret has stylized bird wings inlay, rosewood bridge with black pearl dot pins, rosewood veneer on peghead, 3 per side chrome tuners. Available in Natural and Sunburst finish. Mfd. 1991 to date.

Mfr.'s Sug. Retail	$285	$200	$170	$145	$115	$105	$95	$85

5021 — similar to 5020, except has 12 strings.

Mfr.'s Sug. Retail	$425	$300	$255	$215	$170	$155	$140	$130

5040 — dreadnought style, koa top, round soundhole, 3 stripe bound body and rosette, brown pickguard, koa back/sides, nato neck, 14/20 fret rosewood fingerboard with pearl dot inlay, 12th fret has stylized bird wings inlay, rosewood bridge with black pearl dot pins, koa veneer on peghead, 3 per side chrome tuners. Available in Natural finish. Mfd. 1991 to date.

Mfr.'s Sug. Retail	$400	$280	$240	$200	$160	$145	$130	$120

Grading	100%	98%	95%	90%	80%	70%	60%

5220C — single cutaway dreadnought style, spruce top, round soundhole, 3 stripe bound body and rosette, black pickguard, mahogany back/sides, nato neck, 20 fret rosewood fingerboard with pearl dot inlay, rosewood bridge with black pearl dot pins, 3 per side chrome tuners. Available in Natural finish. Mfd. 1991 to date.

Mfr.'s Sug. Retail	$300	$210	$180	$150	$120	$110	$100	$90

5237 — dreadnought style, spruce top, round soundhole, 5 stripe bound body and rosette, curly maple back/sides, nato neck, 14/20 fret rosewood fingerboard with pearl dot inlay, 12th fret has stylized bird wings inlay, rosewood bridge with white pearl dot pins, 3 per side chrome tuners. Available in Sunburst finish. Mfd. 1991 to date.

Mfr.'s Sug. Retail	$400	$280	$240	$200	$160	$145	$130	$120

Professional Series

5009 — classical style, solid spruce top, round soundhole, bound body, wooden inlay rosette, rosewood back/sides, nato neck, 19 fret rosewood fingerboard, rosewood bridge, rosewood veneer on peghead, 3 per side gold tuners. Available in Natural finish. Mfd. 1991 to date.

Mfr.'s Sug. Retail	$460	$320	$275	$230	$185	$165	$150	$140

5022 — dreadnought style, solid spruce top, round soundhole, herringbone bound body and rosette, tortoise shell pickguard, rosewood back/sides, nato neck, 14/20 fret rosewood fingerboard with pearl dot inlay, 12th fret has stylized bird wings inlay, rosewood bridge with white pearl dot pins, rosewood veneer on peghead, 3 per side chrome tuners. Available in Natural finish. Mfd. 1991 to date.

Mfr.'s Sug. Retail	$525	$370	$315	$260	$210	$190	$170	$160

5054 — similar to 5022, except has 12 strings.

Mfr.'s Sug. Retail	$600	$420	$360	$300	$240	$215	$195	$180

5202 — similar to 5009, except has African mahogany back/sides.

Mfr.'s Sug. Retail	$425	$295	$250	$210	$170	$150	$135	$125

5224 — dreadnought style, solid spruce top, round soundhole, 3 stripe bound body and rosette, black pickguard, mahogany back/sides, nato neck, 14/20 fret rosewood fingerboard with pearl dot inlay, rosewood bridge with black dot pins, rosewood veneer on peghead, 3 per side chrome tuners. Available in Natural finish. Mfd. 1991 to date.

Mfr.'s Sug. Retail	$370	$260	$220	$185	$150	$135	$120	$110

Grading	100%	98%	95%	90%	80%	70%	60%

5225 — similar to 5224, except has tiger rosewood back/sides, bound fingerboard and peghead.

Mfr.'s Sug. Retail	$460	$320	$275	$230	$185	$165	$150	$140

Regent Series

5212 — dreadnought style, spruce top, round soundhole, bound body, 3 stripe rosette, tortoise shell pickguard, mahogany back/sides, nato neck, 14/20 fret rosewood fingerboard with pearl dot inlay, rosewood bridge with white pins, 3 per side chrome tuners. Available in Natural finish. Mfd. 1991 to date.

Mfr.'s Sug. Retail	$200	$140	$120	$100	$80	$70	$65	$60

5314 — similar to 5212, except has black pickguard and black with white dot pins.

Mfr.'s Sug. Retail	$250	$175	$150	$125	$100	$90	$80	$75

5216 — similar to 5212, except is parlor style.

Mfr.'s Sug. Retail	$275	$195	$165	$140	$110	$100	$90	$80

Silver Anniversary Series

2551 — dreadnought style, solid spruce top, round soundhole, 5 stripe bound body, abalone rosette, rosewood back/sides, mahogany neck, 14/20 fret rosewood fingerboard with pearl diamond inlay, rosewood bridge with white black dot pins, rosewood veneer on bound peghead with Silver Anniversary inlay, 3 per side chrome tuners. Available in Natural finish. Mfd. 1991 to date.

Mfr.'s Sug. Retail	$600	$420	$360	$300	$240	$215	$195	$180

255112 — similar to 2551, except has 12 strings.

Mfr.'s Sug. Retail	$700	$490	$420	$350	$280	$250	$230	$210

2552 — dreadnought style, spruce top, round soundhole, 5 stripe bound body, abalone rosette, mahogany back/sides/neck, 14/20 fret rosewood fingerboard with pearl dot inlay, rosewood bridge with black white dot pins, rosewood veneer on peghead, 3 per side chrome tuners. Available in Natural finish. Mfd. 1991 to date.

Mfr.'s Sug. Retail	$400	$280	$240	$200	$160	$145	$130	$120

2555 — single sharp cutaway jumbo style, spruce top, round soundhole, 5 stripe bound body, abalone flake rosette, mahogany back/sides/neck, 21 fret rosewood fingerboard with abalone offset bar inlay, rosewood bridge with black white pins, rosewood veneer on bound peghead with Silver Anniversary inlay, 3 per side chrome tuners, bi-phonic pickup system and controls. Available in Natural and Sunburst finish. Mfd. 1991 to date.

Mfr.'s Sug. Retail	$800	$560	$480	$400	$320	$290	$265	$240

Grading	100%	98%	95%	90%	80%	70%	60%

Wildwood Series

5037 — dreadnought style, cedar top, round soundhole, 5 stripe bound body and rosette, mahogany back/sides, nato neck, 14/20 fret rosewood fingerboard with pearl dot inlay, 12th fret has stylized bird wings inlay, rosewood bridge with white black dot pins, rosewood veneer on peghead, 6 per side gold tuners with amber buttons. Available in Stained finish. Mfd. 1991 to date.

Mfr.'s Sug. Retail	$600	$420	$360	$300	$240	$215	$195	$180

5062 — dreadnought style, spruce top, round soundhole, 5 stripe bound body and rosette, mahogany back/sides, nato neck, 14/20 fret rosewood fingerboard with pearl dot inlay, 12th fret has stylized bird wings inlay, rosewood bridge with white black dot pins, 3 per side chrome tuners. Available in Natural finish. Mfd. 1991 to date.

Mfr.'s Sug. Retail	$430	$300	$260	$215	$175	$155	$140	$130

5063 — similar to 5062, except has gold tuners with amber buttons. Available in Stained finish.

Mfr.'s Sug. Retail	$430	$300	$260	$215	$175	$155	$140	$130

5086 — similar to 5063, except has single cutaway and bi-phonic pickup system and controls.

Mfr.'s Sug. Retail	$750	$525	$450	$375	$300	$270	$245	$225

ACOUSTIC ELECTRIC

Fusion Series

5080N — venetian cutaway dreadnought style, spruce top, round soundhole, 3 stripe bound body, abalone rosette, mahogany back/sides, nato neck, 20 fret rosewood fingerboard with pearl dot inlay, 12th fret has stylized bird wings inlay, rosewood bridge with black pearl dot pins, 3 per side chrome tuners, 6 piezo pickups, volume/tone control. Available in Natural finish. Mfd. 1991 to date.

Mfr.'s Sug. Retail	$650	$455	$390	$325	$260	$235	$215	$195

5081N/5082N/5083N — similar to 5080N, except has curly maple back/sides. Available in Transparent Blue, Transparent Violin and Transparent Red finish respectively. Mfd. 1991 to date.

Mfr.'s Sug. Retail	$650	$455	$390	$325	$260	$235	$215	$195

ELECTRIC

Dana Signature Series

This series was designed by Dana Sutcliffe.

Grading	100%	98%	95%	90%	80%	70%	60%

AE600 — strat style maple body with the "scoop" cutaway, bolt on maple neck, 22 fret rosewood fingerboard with pearl block inlay, double locking vibrato, 6 on one side tuners, black hardware, single coil/humbucker pickups, volume/tone control, 3 position switch. Available in Dark Metallic Blue and Fire Red finish. Mfd. 1991 to date.

Mfr.'s Sug. Retail	$850	$595	$510	$425	$340	$305	$280	$255

AE6001 — similar to AE600, except has Modulus Graphite neck/fingerboard. Available in Black finish.

Mfr.'s Sug. Retail	$900	$630	$540	$450	$360	$325	$300	$275

AED100 — strat style alder body, bolt-on maple neck, 22 fret rosewood fingerboard with pearl block inlay, tunomatic bridge/stop tailpiece, 6 on one side tuners, chrome hardware, 2 DSR humbucker pickups, volume/2 tone controls, 3 position and coil tap switches. Available in Black finish. Mfd. 1991 to date.

Mfr.'s Sug. Retail	$950	$665	$570	$475	$380	$345	$315	$285

AED300 — similar to AED100, except has pearl dot inlay, double locking vibrato, black hardware, 2 single coil/1 humbucker DSR pickups and 5 position switch. Available in Fire Red finish.

Mfr.'s Sug. Retail	$650	$455	$390	$325	$260	$235	$215	$195

Regulator Series

AE100 — strat style, alder body, black pickguard, bolt-on maple neck, 22 fret maple fingerboard with black dot inlay, standard vibrato, 6 on one side tuners, chrome hardware, 2 single coil/1 humbucker EMG pickups, volume/2 tone controls, 5 position switch. Available in Transparent Blue and Transparent Red finish. Mfd. 1991 to date.

Mfr.'s Sug. Retail	$450	$315	$270	$225	$180	$160	$150	$135

AE200 — similar to AE100, except has maple body, rosewood fingerboard with pearl dot inlay, gold hardware and humbucker/single coil/humbucker EMG pickups. Available in Cherry Sunburst finish.

Mfr.'s Sug. Retail	$650	$455	$390	$325	$260	$235	$215	$195

AE300 — similar to AE200, except has Modulus Graphite neck/fingerboard. Available in Black finish.

Mfr.'s Sug. Retail	$500	$350	$300	$250	$200	$180	$165	$150

Grading		100%	98%	95%	90%	80%	70%	60%

Trevor Rabin Signature Series

This series was designed by Trevor Rabin.

AER100 — strat style maple body, arched top, concave back, set in maple neck, 24 fret ebony fingerboard with slanted abalone inlay, double locking, Kahler vibrato, 6 on one side tuners, black hardware, 2 humbucker Alnico pickups, volume/2 tone controls, 3 position switch. Available in Black finish. Curr. mfr.

Mfr.'s Sug. Retail	$1,500	$1,050	$900	$750	$600	$540	$495	$450

AER200 — similar to AER100, except has fixed bridge, gold hardware and 1 tone control. Available in White finish.

Mfr.'s Sug. Retail	$1,300	$910	$780	$650	$520	$470	$430	$390

AER300 — similar to AER100, except has bolt-on maple neck, rosewood fingerboard with pearl dot inlay, standard vibrato, chrome hardware, 2 single coil/1 humbucker pickups and 5 position switch. Available in Red finish.

Mfr.'s Sug. Retail	$1,000	$700	$600	$500	$400	$360	$330	$300

Villain Series

AEV410 — strat style alder body, bolt-on maple neck, 22 fret rosewood fingerboard with pearl dot inlay, double locking Kahler vibrato, 6 on one side tuners, chrome hardware, 2 single coil/1 humbucker Dan Armstrong pickups, volume/tone controls, 5 position switch. Available in Black, Red and White finish. Curr. mfr.

Mfr.'s Sug. Retail	$650	$455	$390	$325	$260	$235	$215	$195

AEV425 — similar to AEV410, except has Modulus Graphite neck/fingerboard and black hardware. Available in Dark Grey Metallic and Red Pearl finish.

Mfr.'s Sug. Retail	$800	$560	$480	$400	$320	$290	$265	$240

AEV520 — similar to AEV410, except has maple body, black hardware and humbucker/single coil/humbucker Dan Armstrong pickups. Available in Cherry Sunburst finish.

Mfr.'s Sug. Retail	$900	$630	$540	$450	$360	$325	$300	$275

ELECTRIC BASS

Dana Signature Series

This series was designed by Dana Sutcliffe.

AE700 — jazz offset alder body, bolt-on maple neck, 24 fret rosewood fingerboard with pearl block inlay, fixed bridge, 4 on one side tuners, black hardware, P-style/J-style pickups, volume/2 tone controls, 3 position switch. Available in Dark Blue Metallic and Black finish. Mfd. 1991 to date.

Mfr.'s Sug. Retail	$700	$490	$420	$350	$280	$250	$230	$210

Grading	100%	98%	95%	90%	80%	70%	60%

Pantera Series

AEBP1 — offset double cutaway alder body, bolt-on maple neck, 24 fret ebony fingerboard with abalone slant inlay, fixed bridge, 2 side tuners, gold hardware, 2 bass pickups, volume/2 tone controls, 3 position switch. Available in White finish. Mfd. 1991 to date.

Mfr.'s Sug. Retail	$1,600	$1,120	$960	$800	$640	$575	$530	$480

AEBP2 — similar to AEBP1, except has rosewood fingerboard with pearl dot inlay and chrome hardware. Available in Black finish.

Mfr.'s Sug. Retail	$900	$630	$540	$450	$360	$325	$300	$275

Villain Series

AE800 — precision style alder body, bolt-on maple neck, 24 fret rosewood fingerboard with pearl dot inlay, 2 per side tuners, black hardware, EMG P-style/J-style pickups, volume/tone/EQ controls, 2 position switch, active electronics with LED. Available in Black and Red Pearl finish. Mfd. 1991 to date.

Mfr.'s Sug. Retail	$600	$420	$360	$300	$240	$215	$195	$180

Add $150 for maple body with Cherry Sunburst finish (AE800CS).

AE900 — similar to AE800, except has 5 strings.

Mfr.'s Sug. Retail	$650	$455	$390	$325	$260	$235	$215	$195

ALVAREZ YAIRI

Trademark established in approximately 1967 and currently owned by St. Louis Music (established 1922) located in St. Louis, MO. Alvarez Yairi instruments are a division of Alvarez and are designed by both Mr. Yairi in Japan and St. Louis Music. Currently, Alvarez Yairi instruments are manufactured in Japan.

Alvarez·Yairi

ACOUSTIC

All Alvarez Yairi acoustic steel string guitars have a stylized A/Y abalone or pearl inlay on their pegheads.

All Alvarez Yairi models may be purchased with Alvarez Natural Response pickups.

Add $110 for installed pickup without volume/tone control.

Add $135 for installed pickup with volume/tone control.

Grading	100%	98%	95%	90%	80%	70%	60%

Classic Series

All classical guitars have rosewood veneer on their pegheads.

CY116 — classical style, solid cedar top, round soundhole, 3 stripe bound body, wooden inlay rosette, mahogany back/sides/neck, 12/19 fret ebony fingerboard, ebony bridge, 3 per side gold tuners with pearloid buttons. Available in Natural finish. Mfd. 1991 to date.

Mfr.'s Sug. Retail	$850	$595	$510	$425	$340	$305	$280	$255

CY118 — similar to CY116, except has jacaranda back/sides.

Mfr.'s Sug. Retail	$900	$630	$540	$450	$360	$325	$300	$275

CY127CE — similar to CY116, except has thin line body style, venetian cutaway, rosewood back/sides, Alvarez Natural Response pickup system and volume/tone control.

Mfr.'s Sug. Retail	$975	$685	$585	$485	$390	$355	$325	$295

CY140 — classical style, cedar top, round soundhole, wooden inlay bound body and rosette, jacaranda back/sides, mahogany neck, 12/19 fret ebony fingerboard, rosewood bridge, 3 per side gold tuners with pearl buttons. Available in Natural finish. Mfd. 1991 to date.

Mfr.'s Sug. Retail	$1,200	$840	$720	$600	$480	$430	$395	$360

Dreadnought Series

DY38 — dreadnought style, spruce top, round soundhole, 3 stripe bound body, 5 stripe rosette, black pickguard, mahogany back/sides/neck, 14/20 fret rosewood fingerboard with pearl dot inlay, 12th fret has pearl snowflake inlay, rosewood bridge with black white dot pins, 3 per side chrome tuners. Available in Natural finish. Mfd. 1991 to date.

Mfr.'s Sug. Retail	$700	$490	$420	$350	$280	$250	$230	$210

DY45 — dreadnought style, spruce top, round soundhole, 3 stripe bound body, 5 stripe rosette, black pickguard, mahogany back/sides/neck, 14/20 fret rosewood fingerboard with pearl dot inlay, 12th fret has pearl snowflake inlay, ebony bridge with black white dot pins, 3 per side chrome tuners. Available in Dark Satin Antique finish. Mfd. 1991 to date.

Mfr.'s Sug. Retail	$700	$490	$420	$350	$280	$250	$230	$210

DY50N — dreadnought style, cedar top, round soundhole, 3 stripe bound body, abalone rosette, tortoise shell pickguard, jacaranda back/sides, mahogany neck, 14/20 fret bound rosewood fingerboard with abalone diamond inlay, rosewood bridge with white pearl dot pins, rosewood veneer on bound peghead, 3 per side gold tuners. Available in Natural finish. Mfd. 1991 to date.

Mfr.'s Sug. Retail	$1,000	$700	$600	$500	$400	$360	$330	$300

Grading	100%	98%	95%	90%	80%	70%	60%

DY52 — dreadnought style, spruce top, round soundhole, 3 stripe bound body, abalone rosette, tortoise shell pickguard, rosewood back/sides, mahogany neck, 14/20 fret rosewood fingerboard with pearl dot inlay, 12th fret has pearl snowflake inlay, rosewood patented Direct Coupled bridge with black pearl dot pins, rosewood veneer on peghead, 3 per side chrome tuners. Available in Natural finish. Mfd. 1991 to date.

Mfr.'s Sug. Retail	$800	$560	$480	$400	$320	$290	$265	$240

DY53N — jumbo style, spruce top, round soundhole, 5 stripe bound body and rosette, tortoise shell pickguard, rosewood back/sides, mahogany neck, 14/20 fret bound rosewood fingerboard with pearl block inlay, rosewood bridge with white pearl dot pins, rosewood veneer on bound peghead, 3 per side chrome tuners. Available in Natural finish. Mfd. 1991 to date.

Mfr.'s Sug. Retail	$900	$630	$540	$450	$360	$325	$300	$275

DY74 — dreadnought style, solid spruce top, round soundhole, 5 stripe bound body and rosette, tortoise shell pickguard, rosewood back/sides, mahogany neck, 14/20 fret rosewood fingerboard with varying pearl inlay, rosewood bridge with white pearl dot pins, rosewood veneer on peghead, 3 per side chrome tuners. Available in Natural finish. Mfd. 1991 to date.

Mfr.'s Sug. Retail	$900	$630	$540	$450	$360	$325	$300	$275

Add $50 for single rounded cutaway (DY74C).

DY75 — dreadnought style, spruce top, round soundhole, wooden inlay bound body and rosette, tortoise shell pickguard, rosewood back/sides, mahogany neck, 14/20 fret rosewood fingerboard with pearl dot inlay, rosewood Direct Coupled bridge, rosewood veneer on bound peghead, 3 per side chrome tuners. Available in Natural finish. Mfd. 1991 to date.

Mfr.'s Sug. Retail	$1,050	$735	$630	$525	$420	$380	$345	$315

DY77N — similar to DY75, except has solid spruce top, herringbone bound body and rosette, ebony fingerboard with abalone diamond inlay and ebony fingerboard with white pearl dot pins.

Mfr.'s Sug. Retail	$1,000	$700	$600	$500	$400	$360	$330	$300

DY80 — similar to DY52, except has 12 strings.

Mfr.'s Sug. Retail	$925	$650	$555	$465	$370	$335	$305	$280

DY90 — dreadnought style, solid spruce top, round soundhole, abalone bound body and rosette, black pickguard with Alvarez Yairi logo, rosewood back/sides, mahogany neck, 14/20 fret bound ebony fingerboard with abalone diamond inlay, abalone bound ebony bridge with black pearl dot pins, rosewood veneer on bound peghead, 3 per side gold tuners. Available in Natural finish. Mfd. 1991 to date.

Mfr.'s Sug. Retail	$1,200	$840	$720	$600	$480	$430	$395	$360

Grading	100%	98%	95%	90%	80%	70%	60%

DY92 — dreadnought style, spruce top, round soundhole, herringbone bound body and rosette, mahogany/rosewood/maple lute style back, 14/20 fret bound ebony fingerboard with pearl dot inlay, ebony bridge with black pearl dot pins, 3 per side gold tuners. Available in Natural finish. Mfd. 1991 to date.

Mfr.'s Sug. Retail	$2,775	$1,945	$1,665	$1,390	$1,110	$1,000	$915	$830

Signature Series

All Signature models have Kazuo Yairi's signature on them.

DY61 — dreadnought style, solid cedar top, round soundhole, 5 stripe wooden bound body, abalone rosette, mahogany back/sides/neck, 14/20 fret rosewood fingerboard, 12th fret has pearl diamond/abalone slash inlay, rosewood bridge with black abalone dot pins, burl mahogany veneer on peghead with abalone and wooden strip inlays, 3 per side gold tuners with amber buttons. Available in Natural finish. Mfd. 1991 to date.

Mfr.'s Sug. Retail	$950	$665	$570	$475	$380	$345	$315	$285

DY62 — similar to DY61, except has venetian cutaway, Alvarez Bi-phonic system, 2 volume/tone controls and selector switch.

Mfr.'s Sug. Retail	$1,225	$860	$735	$615	$490	$440	$405	$370

DY72 — similar to DY61, except has 12 strings and rosewood veneer on peghead.

Mfr.'s Sug. Retail	$1,000	$700	$600	$500	$400	$360	$330	$300

Virtuoso Series

GY1 — venetian cutaway dreadnought style, solid spruce top, round soundhole, 5 stripe bound body and rosette, tortoise shell pickguard, rosewood back/sides, mahogany neck, 20 fret bound ebony fingerboard with varied abalone inlay, rosewood bridge with white abalone dot pins, rosewood veneer on bound peghead with pearl tulip inlay, 3 per side gold tuners, bridge pickup, 3 band EQ. Available in Natural finish. Mfd. 1991 to date.

Mfr.'s Sug. Retail	$1,250	$875	$750	$625	$500	$450	$415	$375

This model was designed for Jerry Garcia.

WY1 — venetian cutaway jumbo style, solid cedar top, round soundhole, herringbone bound body, abalone rosette, rosewood back/sides, mahogany neck, 20 fret rosewood fingerboard, 12th fret has pearl diamond/abalone slash inlay, rosewood Direct Coupled bridge with black abalone dot pins, rosewood veneer on peghead with abalone and wooden strip inlays, 3 per side gold tuners, bridge pickups, 3 band EQ. Available in Natural finish. Mfd. 1991 to date.

Mfr.'s Sug. Retail	$1,250	$875	$750	$625	$500	$450	$415	$375

This model was designed for Bob Weir.

Grading	100%	98%	95%	90%	80%	70%	60%

ACOUSTIC ELECTRIC

Express Series

DY87 — venetian cutaway dreadnought style, curly maple top, round soundhole, 5 stripe bound body and rosette, maple back/sides, mahogany neck, 21 fret ebony fingerboard with pearl dot inlay, 12th fret has pearl snowflake inlay, ebony bridge with white abalone dot pins, 3 per side chrome tuners, bridge pickup, 3 band EQ. Available in Transparent Black finish. Mfd. 1991 to date.

Mfr.'s Sug. Retail	$1,100	$770	$660	$550	$440	$395	$365	$330

DY8712 — similar to DY87, except has 12 strings. Available in Violin Sunburst finish.

Mfr.'s Sug. Retail	$1,200	$840	$720	$600	$480	$430	$395	$360

DY88 — similar to DY87, except has no soundhole, abalone bound body, 23 fret fingerboard with pearl dot pyramid inlay and gold hardware. Available in Black finish.

Mfr.'s Sug. Retail	$1,200	$840	$720	$600	$480	$430	$395	$360

ANDERSON, TOM GUITARS

Manufactured and distributed by Tom Anderson Guitarworks, located in Newbury Park, CA since 1984.

TOM ANDERSON GUITARWORKS

ELECTRIC

All models in this series are available in these finishes: 6120 Orange, Baby Blue, Black, Blonde, Bora Bora Blue, Candy Apple Red, Cherry Burst, Electric Blue, Honey Burst, Metallic Purple, Natural, Seafoam Green, Three-Color Burst, Tobacco Burst, Transparent Amber/Blonde/Blue/Green/Magenta/Purple/Red/White/Yellow, White and White Pearl.

COBRA — tele style basswood or mahogany body, bound figured maple top, bolt-on mahogany or maple neck, 22 fret rosewood fingerboard with pearl dot inlay, fixed bridge, 6 on one side locking tuners, gold hardware, 2 humbucker pickups, volume/tone control, 5 position switch. Curr. mfr.

Mfr.'s Sug. Retail	$2,300	$1,610	$1,380	$1,150	$920	$830	$760	$690

DROP TOP — strat style basswood body, bound figured maple top, bolt-on maple neck, 22 fret maple fingerboard with black dot inlay, standard vibrato, 6 on one side locking tuners, gold hardware, 2 single coil/1 humbucker pickups, volume/tone control, 4 mini switches. Curr. mfr.

Mfr.'s Sug. Retail	$2,300	$1,610	$1,380	$1,150	$920	$830	$760	$690

This model is also available with the following options: alder body, figured koa top, pau ferro, palisander or rosewood fingerboard, fixed bridge, double locking vibrato, chrome hardware, various pickup configurations and left handed.

Grading	100%	98%	95%	90%	80%	70%	60%

🙟 **Drop Top Classic** — similar to Drop Top, except has pearloid or black satin pickguard.

Mfr.'s Sug. Retail	$2,300	$1,610	$1,380	$1,150	$920	$830	$760	$690

🙟 **Drop Top T** — similar to Drop Top, except has tele style body.

Mfr.'s Sug. Retail	$2,300	$1,610	$1,380	$1,150	$920	$830	$760	$690

GRAND AM — strat style lacewood body, bolt-on maple neck, 22 fret maple fingerboard with black dot inlay, double locking vibrato, 6 on one side tuners, gold hardware, 2 single coil/1 humbucker pickups, volume/tone control, 4 mini switches. Curr. mfr.

Mfr.'s Sug. Retail	$2,300	$1,610	$1,380	$1,150	$920	$830	$760	$690

This model is also available with the following options: alder body, figured koa top, palisander, pau ferro or rosewood fingerboard with pearl dot inlay, fixed bridge, double locking vibrato, chrome hardware, various pickup configurations and left handed.

HOLLOW T — tele style swamp ash body with two hollow sound chambers, bolt-on maple neck, 22 fret maple fingerboard with black dot inlay, fixed bridge, 6 on one side locking tuners, chrome hardware, humbucker/single coil/humbucker pickups, volume/tone control, 4 mini switches. Curr. mfr.

Mfr.'s Sug. Retail	$2,180	$1,530	$1,310	$1,090	$870	$785	$720	$655

This model is available with these options: pau ferro, palisander or rosewood fingerboard with pearl dot inlay, standard or double locking vibrato, gold hardware, various pickup and electronic configurations and left handed.

🙟 **Hollow T Classic** — similar to Hollow T, except has pearloid pickguard, 2 single coil pickups, 5 position switch.

Mfr.'s Sug. Retail	$2,180	$1,530	$1,310	$1,090	$870	$785	$720	$655

No options are available on this model.

PRO AM — strat style swamp ash body, bolt-on maple neck, 22 fret pau ferro fingerboard with pearl dot inlay, double locking vibrato, 6 on one side tuners, chrome hardware, volume/tone control, 4 mini switches. Curr. mfr.

Mfr.'s Sug. Retail	$1,900	$1,330	$1,140	$950	$760	$685	$625	$570

This model is also available with the following options: alder or basswood body, maple, palisander or rosewood fingerboard, fixed bridge, standard vibrato, locking tuners, gold hardware, various pickup and electronic configurations and left handed.

Grading	100%	98%	95%	90%	80%	70%	60%

THE CLASSIC — strat style swamp ash body, pearloid pickguard, bolt-on maple neck, 22 fret maple fingerboard with black dot inlay, standard vibrato, 6 on one side locking tuners, chrome hardware, 3 single coil pickups, volume/tone control, 4 mini switches. Curr. mfr.

Mfr.'s Sug. Retail	$1,900	$1,330	$1,140	$950	$760	$685	$625	$570

> This model is also available with the following options: alder or basswood body, black satin pickguard, palisander, pau ferro or rosewood fingerboard with pearl dot inlay, fixed bridge, double locking vibrato, gold hardware, various pickup and electronic configurations and left handed.

ARIA

Started by the Japanese Aria company in the early 1960's. Currently, instruments are manufactured in Korea. Distributed in USA by BBE Sound, Inc. located in Huntington Beach, CA.

ACOUSTIC

AK-70 — classic style, mahogany top, round soundhole, bound body, wooden inlay rosette, mahogany back/sides/neck, 12/19 fret rosewood fingerboard/bridge, 3 per side nickel tuners. Available in Natural finish. Mfd. 1991 to date.

Mfr.'s Sug. Retail	$200	$140	$120	$100	$80	$70	$65	$60

AK-75 — similar to AK-70, except has spruce top.

Mfr.'s Sug. Retail	$230	$160	$135	$115	$90	$80	$70	$65

AK-100 — similar to AK-75, except has different rosette and rosewood veneer on peghead.

Mfr.'s Sug. Retail	$240	$170	$145	$120	$95	$85	$80	$75

AK-200 3/4 — similar to AK-75, except is three-quarter body size.

Mfr.'s Sug. Retail	$240	$170	$145	$120	$95	$85	$80	$75

AK-200 — similar to AK-75, except has different rosette and rosewood veneer on peghead.

Mfr.'s Sug. Retail	$240	$170	$145	$120	$95	$85	$80	$75

AK-600 — classical style, solid spruce top, round soundhole, 5 stripe bound body, wooden inlay rosette, rosewood back/sides, mahogany neck, 12/19 fret rosewood fingerboard/bridge, rosewood veneer on peghead, 3 per side gold tuners. Available in Natural finish. Mfd. 1991 to date.

Mfr.'s Sug. Retail	$380	$265	$225	$190	$150	$135	$120	$110

Grading	100%	98%	95%	90%	80%	70%	60%

AK-900 — similar to AK-600, except has solid cedar top.

Mfr.'s Sug. Retail	$460	$320	$275	$230	$185	$165	$150	$140

AK-1000 — similar to AK-100.

Mfr.'s Sug. Retail	$700	$490	$420	$350	$280	$250	$230	$210

AW-70 — dreadnought style, mahogany top, round soundhole, black pickguard, bound body, 5 stripe rosette, black pickguard, mahogany back/sides/neck, 14/20 fret rosewood fingerboard with pearl dot inlay, rosewood bridge with black pins, 3 per side nickel tuners. Available in Walnut finish. Mfd. 1991 to date.

Mfr.'s Sug. Retail	$200	$140	$120	$100	$80	$70	$65	$60

AW-75 — similar to AW-70, except has spruce top. Available in Black, Brown Sunburst and Natural finish.

Mfr.'s Sug. Retail	$210	$145	$125	$100	$80	$70	$65	$60

AW-100 — dreadnought style, spruce top, round soundhole, black pickguard, bound body, 3 stripe rosette, black pickguard, mahogany back/sides/neck, 14/20 fret rosewood fingerboard with pearl dot inlay, rosewood bridge with black white dot pins, 3 per side chrome tuners. Available in Natural finish. Mfd. 1991 only.

Mfr.'s Sug. Retail	$275	$195	$165	$140	$110	$100	$90	$80

⚔ **AW-100C** — similar to AW-100, except has single rounded cutaway.

Mfr.'s Sug. Retail	$300	$210	$180	$150	$120	$110	$100	$90

AW-110 — similar to AW-100, except has cedar top.

Mfr.'s Sug. Retail	$250	$175	$150	$125	$100	$90	$80	$75

⚔ **AW-110C** — similar to AW-110, except has single rounded cutaway.

Mfr.'s Sug. Retail	$290	$205	$175	$145	$115	$105	$95	$85

⚔ **AW-110CT** — similar to AW-110C, except has 12 strings.

Mfr.'s Sug. Retail	$350	$245	$210	$175	$140	$125	$115	$105

⚔ **AW-110T** — similar to AW-110, except has 12 strings.

Mfr.'s Sug. Retail	$300	$210	$180	$150	$120	$110	$100	$90

AW-200 — similar to AW-100, except has white black dot bridge pins and chrome die cast tuners. Available in Antique Violin, Black, Brown Sunburst and Natural finish. Mfd. 1991 to date.

Mfr.'s Sug. Retail	$300	$210	$180	$150	$120	$110	$100	$90

This model is also available in a folk style body (AW-200F).

⚔ **AW-200C** — similar to AW-200, except has single rounded cutaway.

Mfr.'s Sug. Retail	$350	$245	$210	$175	$140	$125	$115	$105

Grading	100%	98%	95%	90%	80%	70%	60%

AW-200E — similar to AW-200, except has piezo pickup and 3 band EQ. Available in Black and Natural finish.

Mfr.'s Sug. Retail	$410	$285	$245	$205	$165	$145	$135	$125

AW-200CE — similar to AW-200E, except has single rounded cutaway.

Mfr.'s Sug. Retail	$420	$295	$250	$210	$170	$150	$135	$125

AW-200T — similar to AW-200, except has 12 strings.

Mfr.'s Sug. Retail	$300	$210	$180	$150	$120	$110	$100	$90

AW-310 — dreadnought style, cedar top, round soundhole, herringbone bound body/rosette, ovankol back/sides, mahogany neck, 14/20 fret rosewood fingerboard with pearl dot inlay, rosewood bridge with white black dot pins, 3 per side chrome die cast tuners. Available in Natural finish. Mfd. 1991 to 1992.

	$335	$235	$200	$170	$135	$125	$115

AW-310C — similar to AW-310, except has single rounded cutaway.

	$400	$280	$240	$200	$160	$145	$130

AW-310CE — similar to AW-310C, except has piezo pickup and 3 band EQ.

	$470	$330	$280	$235	$190	$170	$155

AW-310T — similar to AW-310, except has 12 strings.

	$350	$245	$210	$175	$140	$125	$115

AW-410 — jumbo style, cedar top, round soundhole, herringbone bound body/rosette, black pickguard, ovankol back/sides, mahogany neck, 14/20 fret rosewood fingerboard with pearl dot inlay, rosewood bridge with white black dot pins, 3 per side chrome die cast tuners. Available in Natural finish. Mfd. 1991 to 1992.

	$360	$250	$215	$180	$145	$130	$120

AW-600 — dreadnought style, spruce top, round soundhole, black pickguard, 3 stripe bound body/rosette, rosewood back/sides, mahogany neck, 14/20 fret bound rosewood fingerboard with pearl dot inlay, rosewood bridge with white black dot pins, rosewood veneer on bound peghead, 3 per side chrome die cast tuners. Available in Natural finish. Mfd. 1991 only.

	$380	$265	$225	$190	$150	$135	$120

AW-700 — dreadnought style, solid spruce top, round soundhole, black pickguard, 3 stripe bound body/rosette, rosewood back/sides, mahogany neck, 14/20 fret rosewood fingerboard with pearl diamond inlay, rosewood bridge with white black dot pins, rosewood veneer peghead, 3 per side gold diecast tuners. Available in Natural finish. Mfd. 1991.

	$390	$275	$235	$195	$155	$140	$125

Grading	100%	98%	95%	90%	80%	70%	60%

AW-800 — dreadnought style, solid spruce top, round soundhole, tortoise shell pickguard, herringbone bound body/rosette, rosewood back/sides, mahogany neck, 14/20 fret rosewood fingerboard with pearl diamond inlay, rosewood bridge with white black dot pins, rosewood veneer on peghead, 3 per side gold die cast tuners. Available in Natural finish. Mfd. 1991 to date.

Mfr.'s Sug. Retail	$470	$330	$280	$235	$190	$170	$155	$140

LW-10 — dreadnought style, spruce top, round soundhole, 3 stripe bound body/rosette, black pickguard, mahogany back/sides/neck, 14/20 fret rosewood fingerboard with pearl dot inlay, ebonized maple bridge with white black dot pins, 3 per side chrome die cast tuners. Available in Black, Natural, Tobacco Brown and Wine Red finish. Mfd. 1991 to 1992.

	$560	$390	$335	$280	$225	$205	$190

Add $15 for 12 string version (LW-10T).

LW-12 — dreadnought style, cedar top, round soundhole, herringbone bound body/rosette, tortoise shell pickguard, walnut back/sides, mahogany neck, 14/20 fret rosewood fingerboard with pearl dot inlay, ebonized maple bridge with white black dot pins, rosewood veneer on peghead, 3 per side chrome die cast tuners. Available in Black and Natural finish. Mfd. 1991 to 1992.

	$540	$380	$325	$270	$215	$195	$180

Add $35 for 12 string version of this model (LW-12T).

LW-14 — dreadnought style, sycamore top, round soundhole, herringbone bound body/rosette, black pickguard, walnut back/sides, mahogany neck, 14/20 fret rosewood fingerboard with pearl dot inlay, ebonized maple bridge with white black dot pins, sycamore veneer on peghead, 3 per side chrome die cast tuners. Available in Tobacco Brown finish. Mfd. 1991 to date.

Mfr.'s Sug. Retail	$575	$405	$345	$285	$230	$205	$190	$175

LW-18 — dreadnought style, spruce top, round soundhole, 5 stripe bound body/rosette, rosewood back/sides, mahogany neck, 14/20 fret rosewood fingerboard with pearl dot inlay, ebonized maple bridge with white black dot pins, rosewood veneer on peghead, 3 per side chrome die cast tuners. Available in Natural finish. Mfd. 1991 to date.

Mfr.'s Sug. Retail	$600	$420	$360	$300	$240	$215	$195	$180

LW-18T — similar to LW-18, except has 12 strings.

Mfr.'s Sug. Retail	$640	$450	$385	$320	$255	$230	$210	$195

SW-8 — dreadnought style, solid cedar top, round soundhole, tortoise shell bound body/rosette/pickguard, mahogany back/sides/neck, 14/20 fret rosewood fingerboard with pearl dot inlay, ebonized maple bridge with white black dot pins, rosewood veneer on peghead, 3 per side chrome die cast tuners. Available in Natural finish. Mfd. 1991 to date.

Mfr.'s Sug. Retail	$640	$450	$385	$320	$255	$230	$210	$195

Grading	100%	98%	95%	90%	80%	70%	60%

≠ **SW-8C** — similar to SW-8, except has single rounded cutaway.

Mfr.'s Sug. Retail	$715	$500	$430	$360	$290	$260	$240	$220

≠ **SW-8CT** — similar to SW-8, except has single rounded cutaway and 12 strings.

Mfr.'s Sug. Retail	$750	$525	$450	$375	$300	$270	$245	$225

≠ **SW-8T** — similar to SW-8, except has 12 strings.

Mfr.'s Sug. Retail	$670	$470	$400	$335	$265	$240	$220	$200

ACOUSTIC ELECTRIC

CES-50 — single rounded cutaway classical style, spruce top, bound body, wooden inlay rosette, mahogany body/neck, 22 fret extended rosewood fingerboard, rosewood bridge, 3 per side gold tuners, piezo pickups, volume/tone control. Available in Black, Natural and White finish. Mfd. 1992 to date.

Mfr.'s Sug. Retail	$600	$420	$360	$300	$240	$215	$195	$180

This model is a solid body with a routed out soundhole and installed plastic dish for resonance.

CE-60 — single rounded cutaway classical style, spruce top, round soundhole, bound body, wooden inlay rosette, mahogany back/sides/neck, 19 fret rosewood fingerboard/bridge, rosewood veneer on peghead, 3 per side gold tuners, piezo pickups with 3 band EQ. Available in Natural finish. Mfd. 1991 to date.

Mfr.'s Sug. Retail	$700	$490	$420	$350	$280	$250	$230	$210

≠ **CE-60S** — similar to CE-60, except has 22 fret extended fingerboard with pearl dot inlay, steel strings with white black dot bridge pins.

Mfr.'s Sug. Retail	$700	$490	$420	$350	$280	$250	$230	$210

≠ **CE-60/14** — similar to CE-60, except has 22 fret extended fingerboard.

Mfr.'s Sug. Retail	$700	$490	$420	$350	$280	$250	$230	$210

FEA-10 — single rounded cutaway dreadnought style, cedar top, round soundhole, bound body, wooden inlay rosette, mahogany back/sides/neck, 22 fret rosewood fingerboard with pearl dot inlay, rosewood bridge with black pearl dot pins, 3 per side die cast tuners, piezo pickup, 3 band EQ. Available in Natural and Walnut finish. Mfd. 1992 to date.

Mfr.'s Sug. Retail	$830	$580	$500	$415	$330	$300	$275	$250

FEA-15 — similar to FEA-10, except has spruce top. Available in Brown Sunburst, Natural and Transparent Black finish.

Mfr.'s Sug. Retail	$950	$665	$570	$475	$380	$345	$315	$285

Grading	100%	98%	95%	90%	80%	70%	60%

FEA-20 — single rounded cutaway dreadnought style, sycamore top, round soundhole, bound body, abalone designed rosette, sycamore back/sides, mahogany neck, 22 fret bound rosewood fingerboard with pearl dot inlay, rosewood bridge with black pearl dot pins, 3 per side gold die cast tuners, piezo pickup, 3 band EQ. Available in Transparent Black and Transparent Blue finish. Mfd. 1991 to 1992.

	$805	$690	$575	$460	$415	$380	$345

Last Mfr.'s Sug. Retail was $1,150.

FET-85 — venetian cutaway jumbo style, arched spruce top, oval soundhole, 5 stripe bound body and rosette, rosewood arched or chestnut back/sides, mahogany neck, 21 fret bound rosewood fingerboard with pearl diamond inlay, rosewood bridge with black pearl dot pins and pearl diamond inlay, bound peghead with chestnut veneer, 3 per side gold die cast tuners, piezo pickup, 3 band EQ. Available in Amber Natural and Antique Sunburst finish. Mfd. 1991 to 1992.

	$980	$840	$700	$560	$505	$460	$420

Last Mfr.'s Sug. Retail was $1,400.

FET-100 — cutaway jumbo style, arched chestnut/spruce laminated top, oval soundhole, 3 stripe bound body and rosette, chestnut arched back/sides, maple neck, 21 fret bound ebony fingerboard with abalone/pearl split block inlay, rosewood bridge with white pearl dot pins and pearl diamond inlay, bound peghead, 3 per side gold die cast tuners, piezo pickup, 3 band EQ. Available in Amber Natural, Blue Shade and Red Shade finish. Mfd. 1991 to 1992.

	$1,050	$900	$750	$600	$540	$495	$450

Last Mfr.'s Sug. Retail was $1,500.

FET-500 (formerly the FET-SPL) — venetian cutaway jumbo style, spruce top, oval soundhole, 5 stripe bound body and rosette, mahogany arched back/sides/neck, 21 fret rosewood bound fingerboard with pearl dot inlay, rosewood bridge with white pearl dot pins, bound peghead, 3 per side die cast tuners, piezo pickup, volume/tone control. Available in Antique Sunburst, Black Sunburst and Transparent Red finish. Mfd. 1991 to 1992.

	$405	$345	$285	$230	$205	$190	$175

Last Mfr.'s Sug. Retail was $575.

FET-600 (formerly the FET-DLX) — cutaway jumbo style, arched sycamore top, oval soundhole, 5 stripe bound body and rosette, sycamore arched back/sides, mahogany neck, 21 fret bound rosewood fingerboard with pearl diamond inlay, rosewood bridge with white pearl dot pins, bound peghead, 3 per side die cast tuners, piezo pickup, 3 band EQ. Available in Amber Natural and Antique Sunburst finish. Mfd. 1991 to 1992.

	$535	$460	$380	$305	$275	$250	$230

Last Mfr.'s Sug. Retail was $765.
This model also available in 12 string version (FET-600/12).

Grading	100%	98%	95%	90%	80%	70%	60%

ELECTRIC

Aquanote Series

CR-60 — strat style alder body, bolt-on maple neck, 24 fret rosewood fingerboard with pearl dot inlay, standard vibrato, 6 on one side locking tuners, chrome hardware, 2 single coil/1 humbucker pickups, volume/tone control, 5 position switch, coil split on tone control. Available in Black, Midnight Cherry, Navy Blue and Pearl White finish. Mfd. 1991 to date.

Mfr.'s Sug. Retail	$850	$595	$510	$425	$340	$305	$280	$255

CR-65 — similar to CR-60, except has sen body, black hardware, single coil/humbucker pickups, 3 position and separate coil split switches. Available in Amber Natural, Dark Red Shade and Purple Shade finish.

Mfr.'s Sug. Retail	$950	$665	$570	$475	$380	$345	$315	$285

CR-65/12 — similar to CR-60, except has 12 strings, fixed bridge.

Mfr.'s Sug. Retail	$850	$595	$510	$425	$340	$305	$280	$255

CR-100 — strat style ash body, set in maple neck, 24 fret rosewood fingerboard with pearl oval inlay, standard vibrato, 6 on one side locking tuners, silver black hardware, Seymour Duncan single coil/humbucker pickups, volume/tone control, 3 position switch, coil split in tone control. Available in Blue Shade, Dark Red Shade, Purple Shade and Vintage Sunburst. Mfd. 1991 to date.

Mfr.'s Sug. Retail	$1,500	$1,050	$900	$750	$600	$540	$495	$450

Full Acoustic Series

FA-70 — single rounded cutaway hollow style, arched maple top/back/sides, bound body/f holes, raised black pickguard, maple neck, 20 fret bound rosewood fingerboard with pearl split block inlay, rosewood bridge, trapeze tailpiece, bound peghead with pearl Aria Pro II logo and dove inlay, 3 per side tuners, gold hardware, 2 humbucker pickups, 2 volume/tone controls, 3 position switch. Available in Brown Sunburst and Vintage Sunburst finish. Mfd. 1991 to date.

Mfr.'s Sug. Retail	$725	$505	$435	$360	$290	$260	$240	$220

FA-70TR — similar to FA-70, except has rosewood/metal bridge, vibrato tailpiece.

Mfr.'s Sug. Retail	$800	$560	$480	$400	$320	$290	$265	$240

Magna Series

MA-10 — strat style alder body, bolt-on maple neck, 22 fret rosewood fingerboard with pearl dot inlay, standard vibrato, roller nut 6 on one side tuners, black hardware, 2 single coil/1 humbucker pickups, volume/tone control, 5 position switch, coil split in tone control. Available in Black, Fiero Red and White finish. Mfd. 1991 only.

Mfr.'s Sug. Retail	$400	$280	$240	$200	$160	$145	$130	$120

Grading	100%	98%	95%	90%	80%	70%	60%

MA-20 — similar to MA-10, except has double locking vibrato.

Mfr.'s Sug. Retail	$500	$350	$300	$250	$200	$180	$165	$150

MA-28 — similar to MA-20, except has smaller strat style body. Available in Transparent finishes. Curr. mfr.

Mfr.'s Sug. Retail	$550	$385	$330	$275	$220	$200	$180	$165

MA-30 — similar to MA-20, except has 24 frets. Available in Black, Navy Blue, Purple Cherry and Pearl White finish. Curr. mfr.

Mfr.'s Sug. Retail	$750	$525	$450	$375	$300	$270	$245	$225

MA-35 — similar to MA-30, except has single coil/humbucker pickups, 3 position switch. Available in Metallic Blue, Metallic Burgundy and Metallic Violet finish. Mfd. 1991 only.

Mfr.'s Sug. Retail	$900	$630	$540	$450	$360	$325	$300	$275

MA-40 — similar to MA-30, except has volume/2 EQ controls, 3 position and 2 EQ switches, active electronics. Available in Black, Metallic Blue, Metallic Burgundy, Metallic Violet, Navy Blue, Pearl White and Purple Cherry finish. Mfd. 1991 only.

Mfr.'s Sug. Retail	$960	$670	$575	$480	$385	$350	$320	$290

MA-45 — similar to MA-40, except has bound fingerboard with pearl oval inlay, tunomatic bridge/stop tailpiece, gold hardware.

Mfr.'s Sug. Retail	$1,025	$720	$615	$510	$410	$370	$340	$310

MA-50 — similar to MA-30, except has gold hardware, three 3 position switches. Available in Black, Metallic Blue, Metallic Burgundy, Metallic Violet, Navy Blue, Pearl White and Purple Cherry finish.

Mfr.'s Sug. Retail	$1,000	$700	$600	$500	$400	$360	$330	$300

MA-55 — strat style sen body, bolt-on maple neck, 24 fret rosewood fingerboard with pearl dot inlay, standard vibrato, roller nut 6 on one side locking tuners, 2 single coil/1 humbucker pickups, volume/tone control, 5 position and coil split switches. Available in Amber Natural, Blue Shade and Dark Red Shade finish. Mfd. 1992 only.

	$735	$630	$525	$420	$380	$345	$315

Last Mfr.'s Sug. Retail was $1,050.

MA-60 — similar to MA-40, except has set neck, bound fingerboard with pearl oval inlay, gold hardware. Mfd. 1991 to date.

Mfr.'s Sug. Retail	$1,100	$770	$660	$550	$440	$395	$365	$330

Grading	100%	98%	95%	90%	80%	70%	60%

MA-75 — strat style sen body, bolt-on maple neck, 22 fret rosewood fingerboard with pearl oval inlay, double locking vibrato, 6 on one side tuners, gold hardware, humbucker/single coil/humbucker pickups, volume/tone control, 5 position and coil split switches. Available in Amber Natural, Cherry Sunburst, Purple Shade and Vintage Sunburst finish. Mfd. 1992 only.

	$805	$690	$575	$460	$415	$380	$345

Last Mfr.'s Sug. Retail was $1,150.

MA-90 — strat style alder body, bolt-on maple neck, 24 fret bound rosewood neck with pearl oval inlay, double locking vibrato, 6 on one side tuners, silver black hardware, 2 single coil/1 Seymour Duncan humbucker pickups, volume/tone control, 5 position switch, coil split in tone control. Available in Emerald Green Sunburst, Gunmetal Grey, Navy Blue Sunburst and Rose Red Sunburst finish. Mfd. 1991 to 1992.

	$905	$775	$645	$515	$465	$425	$385

Last Mfr.'s Sug. Retail was $1,295.

MA-100 — similar to MA-90, except set neck. Available in Gunmetal Grey finish. Mfd. 1991 only.

	$980	$840	$700	$560	$505	$460	$420

Last Mfr.'s Sug. Retail was $1,400.

Pro Electric Series

PE-JR600 — Les Paul style maple body, bolt-on maple neck, 22 fret rosewood fingerboard with pearl dot inlay, tunomatic bridge/stop tailpiece, 3 per side tuners, chrome hardware, 2 single coil pickups, 2 volume/tone controls, 3 position switch. Available in Black, Metallic Blue Shade and Metallic Violet Shade finish. Disc. 1991.

	$540	$460	$385	$310	$280	$255	$230

Last Mfr.'s Sug. Retail was $775.

PE-JR750 — similar to PE-JR600, except has bound body, vibrato tailpiece, gold hardware, volume/tone control. Available in Cherry Sunburst, Pearl White and Vintage Sunburst finish. Disc. 1991.

	$700	$600	$500	$400	$360	$330	$300

Last Mfr.'s Sug. Retail was $1,000.

PE-1000TR — Les Paul style bound mahogany body, bound maple top, set in maple neck, 22 fret bound rosewood fingerboard with abalone/pearl split block inlay, standard vibrato, 3 per side locking tuners, gold hardware, 2 humbucker pickups, volume/tone control. Available in Blondy Natural, Transparent Scarlet and Twilight Black finish. Mfd. 1991 to 1992.

	$910	$780	$650	$520	$470	$430	$390

Last Mfr.'s Sug. Retail was $1,300.

Grading	100%	98%	95%	90%	80%	70%	60%

Thin Acoustic Series

TA-40 — double rounded cutaway semi-hollow style, mahogany arched top/back/sides, bound body and f holes, raised black pickguard, mahogany neck, 22 fret bound rosewood fingerboard with pearl dot inlay, tunomatic bridge/stop tailpiece, 3 per side tuners, chrome hardware, 2 humbucker pickups, 2 volume/tone controls, 3 position switch. Available in Walnut and Wine Red finish. Mfd. 1991 only.

	$315	$270	$225	$180	$160	$150	$135

Last Mfr.'s Sug. Retail was $450.

TA-60 — similar to TA-40, except has white pickguard, block inlay, gold hardware. Available in Pearl Black, Walnut and Wine Red finish.

	$370	$315	$260	$210	$190	$170	$160

Last Mfr.'s Sug. Retail was $525.

TA-61 — similar to TA-60, except has maple top/back/sides, transparent pickguard, bound peghead, tone selector switch. Available in Amber Natural, Cherry and Vintage Sunburst finish.

	$420	$360	$300	$240	$215	$195	$180

Last Mfr.'s Sug. Retail was $600.

TA-65TR — similar to TA-60, except has vibrato tailpiece. Available in Amber Natural, Cherry, Vintage Sunburst, Walnut and Wine Red finish.

	$490	$420	$350	$280	$250	$230	$210

Last Mfr.'s Sug. Retail was $700.

TA-900 (formerly the TA-STD) — double cutaway semi-hollow body, maple arched top/back/sides, f holes, bound body, raised black pickguard, mahogany neck, 22 fret bound rosewood fingerboard with pearl dot inlay, bridge/stop tailpiece, unbound peghead, 3 per side tuners, chrome hardware, 2 humbucker pickups, 2 volume/tone controls, 3 position switch. Available in Black, Brown Sunburst and Transparent Red finish. Mfd. 1991 to 1992.

	$875	$750	$625	$500	$450	$415	$375

Last Mfr.'s Sug. Retail was $1,250.

TA-1300 (formerly the TA-DLX) — double rounded cutaway semi-hollow style, sycamore top/back/sides, bound body and f holes, raised bound tortoise shell pickguard, mahogany neck, 22 fret bound ebony fingerboard with abalone/pearl split block inlay, tunomatic bridge/stop tailpiece, bound peghead with pearl Aria Pro II logo and dove inlay, 3 per side tuners, gold hardware, 2 humbucker pickups, 2 volume/tone controls, 3 position switch. Available in Brown Sunburst and Vintage Sunburst finish. Mfd. 1991 to 1992.

	$1,225	$1,050	$875	$700	$630	$575	$525

Last Mfr.'s Sug. Retail was $1,750.

Grading	100%	98%	95%	90%	80%	70%	60%

Viper Series

VP-30 — strat style maple body , bolt-on maple neck, 22 fret rosewood neck with pearl dot inlay, standard vibrato, roller nut 6 on one side tuners, chrome hardware, 2 single coil/1 humbucker pickups, volume/tone control, 5 position switch. Available in Black, Fiero Red and White finish. Mfd. 1991 only.

	$275	$235	$195	$155	$140	$125	$115

Last Mfr.'s Sug. Retail was $390.

VP-40 — strat style alder body, pearloid pickguard, bolt-on maple neck, 22 fret rosewood fingerboard with pearl wedge inlay, locking vibrato, 6 on one side tuners, black hardware, 2 single coil/1 humbucker pickups, volume/tone control, 5 position switch. Available in Black, Fiero Red, Navy Blue, Pearl White and White finish. Mfd. 1991 only.

	$350	$300	$250	$200	$180	$165	$150

Last Mfr.'s Sug. Retail was $500.

VP-50 — similar to VP-40, except has coil split switch. Available in Black, Candy Apple, Navy Blue, Midnight Cherry and Pearl White finish. Mfd. 1991 only.

	$525	$450	$375	$300	$270	$245	$225

Last Mfr.'s Sug. Retail was $750.

VP-65 — similar to VP-50, except has pearloid pickguard, humbucker/single coil/humbucker pickups. Available in Black, Metallic Lavender Shade and Pearl Blue finish. Mfd. 1992 to date.

Mfr.'s Sug. Retail	$995	$695	$595	$500	$400	$360	$330	$300

VP-90 — semi-solid strat style maple body, bird's eye or curly maple top, wedge soundhole, bound body and soundhole, maple neck, 22 fret bound rosewood fingerboard with pearl dot inlay, standard vibrato, 6 on one side locking tuners, chrome hardware, volume/tone control, 3 position and coil split switch. Available in Cherry Sunburst and Natural finish. Mfd. 1992 to date.

Mfr.'s Sug. Retail	$240	$170	$145	$120	$95	$85	$80	$75

Excel Series

XL-STD-3 — strat style hardwood body, bolt-on maple neck, 22 fret bound rosewood fingerboard with pearl wedge inlay, standard vibrato, 6 on one side tuners, black hardware, 2 single coil/1 humbucker pickups, volume/tone control, 5 position switch, coil split in tone control. Available in Black, Candy Apple, Midnight Blue and White finish. Mfd. 1991 only.

	$280	$240	$200	$160	$145	$130	$120

Last Mfr.'s Sug. Retail was $400.

XL-SPT-3 — similar to XL-STD-3, except has double locking vibrato.

	$350	$300	$250	$200	$180	$165	$150

Last Mfr.'s Sug. Retail was $500.

Grading	100%	98%	95%	90%	80%	70%	60%

XL-DLX-3 — similar to XL-STD-3, except has double locking vibrato.

	$385	$330	$275	$220	$200	$180	$165

Last Mfr.'s Sug. Retail was $550.

XL-CST-3 — similar to XL-DLX-3, except has curly maple top/back, gold hardware. Available in Transparent Black, Transparent Blue and Transparent Red finish.

	$450	$385	$320	$255	$230	$210	$195

Last Mfr.'s Sug. Retail was $640.

ELECTRIC BASS

Avante Bass Series

AVB-50 — jazz style alder body, bolt-on maple neck, 24 fret rosewood fingerboard with pearl dot inlay, fixed bridge, 4 on one side tuners, chrome hardware, P-style/J-style pickups, 2 volume/1 tone controls. Available in Black, Fiero Red and White finish. Mfd. 1991 only.

	$345	$295	$245	$195	$175	$160	$150

Last Mfr.'s Sug. Retail was $490.

AVB-55 — similar to AVB-50, except has carved top and black hardware. Available in Alsace Red, Black, Navy Blue and Pearl White finish. Mfd. 1991 to date.

Mfr.'s Sug. Retail	$850	$595	$510	$425	$340	$305	$280	$255

AVB-80 — similar to AVB-55, except has gold hardware and active electronics. Available in Black, Navy Blue Sunburst, Pearl White and Rose Red Sunburst.

Mfr.'s Sug. Retail	$1,100	$770	$660	$550	$440	$395	$365	$330

AVB-95 — jazz style sen body, carved top/back, bolt-on maple neck, 24 fret rosewood fingerboard with pearl dot inlay, fixed bridge, 4 on one side tuners, silver black hardware, P-style/J-style Seymour Duncan pickups, volume/bass/treble and mixed controls, bypass switch. Available in Blue Shade, Dark Red Shade, Natural and Purple Shade finish. Mfd. 1991 to date.

Mfr.'s Sug. Retail	$1,400	$980	$840	$700	$560	$505	$460	$420

Integra Bass Series

IGB-SPT — jazz style maple body, bolt-on maple neck, 24 fret rosewood fingerboard with pearl dot inlay, fixed bridge, 2 per side tuners, black hardware, P-style/J-style pickups, 2 volume/1 tone controls. Available in Alsace Red, Black, Navy Blue and White finish. Mfd. 1991 only.

	$440	$380	$315	$250	$225	$205	$190

Last Mfr.'s Sug. Retail was $630.

IGB-STD — similar to IGB-SPT, except has chrome hardware. Mfd. 1991 to date.

Mfr.'s Sug. Retail	$800	$560	$480	$400	$320	$290	$265	$240

Grading	100%	98%	95%	90%	80%	70%	60%

IGB-DLX — similar to IGB-STD, except has black hardware and volume/bass/treble and mixed controls.

Mfr.'s Sug. Retail	$900	$630	$540	$450	$360	$325	$300	$275

IGB-CST — similar to IGB-DLX, except has sen body and gold hardware. Available in Blue Shade, Dark Red Shade, Transparent Black and Transparent White finish. Mfd. 1991 to date.

Mfr.'s Sug. Retail	$1,000	$700	$600	$500	$400	$360	$330	$300

IGB-DLX/5 — jazz style alder body, bolt-on maple neck, 24 fret ebony fingerboard with pearl dot inlay, fixed bridge, 3/2 per side tuners, black hardware, 2 single coil pickups, volume/bass/treble and mixed controls. Available in Alsace Red, Black, Navy Blue and Pearl White finish. Mfd. 1991 to date.

Mfr.'s Sug. Retail	$1,100	$770	$660	$550	$440	$395	$365	$330

Magna Bass Series

MAB-20 — precision style alder body, bolt-on maple neck, 22 fret rosewood fingerboard with pearl dot inlay, fixed bridge, 4 on one side tuners, black hardware, P-style/J-style pickups, 2 volume/1 tone controls. Available in Apple Red, Black, Midnight Blue and White finish. Mfd. 1991 only.

		$350	$300	$250	$200	$180	$165	$150

Last Mfr.'s Sug. Retail was $500.

MAB-20/5 — similar to MAB-20, except has 5 strings, 24 frets and 2 J-style pickups. Available in Apple Red, Black and White finish.

		$350	$300	$250	$200	$180	$165	$150

Last Mfr.'s Sug. Retail was $500.

MAB-40 — similar to MAB-20, except has active EQ in tone control, 3 position and bypass switch. Available in Black, Midnight Cherry, Navy Blue, Pearl Black, Pearl White and White finish.

		$420	$360	$300	$240	$215	$195	$180

Last Mfr.'s Sug. Retail was $600.

MAB-50 — similar to MAB-20, except has 24 frets, gold hardware, volume/bass/treble and mixed controls, active electronics. Available in Midnight Cherry, Pearl Black and Pearl White finish.

		$695	$595	$500	$400	$360	$330	$300

Last Mfr.'s Sug. Retail was $995.

MAB-60 — similar to MAB-50, except has sen body, 2 J-style pickups and no active electronics. Available in Blue Shade, Dark Red Shade, Purple Shade and Vintage Sunburst finish.

		$835	$715	$600	$480	$430	$395	$360

Last Mfr.'s Sug. Retail was $1,195.

MAB-60/5 — similar to MAB-50, except has 5 strings, ebony fingerboard, black hardware and 2 double coil pickups. Available in Midnight Cherry, Navy Blue, Pearl Black and Pearl White finish.

$835	$715	$600	$480	$430	$395	$360

Last Mfr.'s Sug. Retail was $1,195.

Super Bass Series

SB-JR600 — jazz style alder body, bolt-on maple neck, 24 fret rosewood fingerboard with pearl dot inlay, fixed bridge, 2 per side tuners, black hardware, P-style/J-style pickup, 2 volume/1 tone controls. Available in Midnight Cherry, Navy Blue, Pearl Black and Pearl White finish. Mfd. 1991 only.

$595	$510	$425	$340	$305	$280	$255

Last Mfr.'s Sug. Retail was $850.

SB-JR750 — similar to SB-JR600, except has maple/walnut/sen body, gold hardware and volume/bass/treble and mixed controls. Available in Amber Natural, Deep Blue and Dark Cherry Shade finish.

$770	$660	$550	$440	$395	$365	$330

Last Mfr.'s Sug. Retail was $1,100.

SB-1000 — jazz style sen body, maple/walnut thru body neck, 24 fret rosewood fingerboard with pearl dot inlay, fixed bridge, 2 per side tuners, gold hardware, 2 humbucker pickups, 2 volume/1 tone controls, active electronics in tone control. Available in Black, Light Oak, Transparent Black and Transparent Red finish. Mfd. 1991 to date.

$980	$840	$700	$560	$505	$460	$420

Last Mfr.'s Sug. Retail was $1,400.

SB-LTD — similar to SB-1000, except has ebony fingerboard with pearl oval inlay and Alembic pickups. Available in Transparent Black and Transparent Red finish.

Mfr.'s Sug. Retail	$1,800	$1,260	$1,080	$900	$720	$650	$595	$540

B

BASS COLLECTION

Manufactured in Japan since 1985. Distributed by Meisel Music Inc., located in Springfield, NJ.

BASS COLLECTION

ELECTRIC BASS

300 Series

Grading	100%	98%	95%	90%	80%	70%	60%

SB301 — offset double cutaway alder body, bolt-on maple neck, 24 fret rosewood fingerboard, fixed bridge, 2 per side Gotoh tuners, black hardware, P-style/J-style pickups, 2 volume/2 tone controls. Available in Black, Magenta, Metallic Grey and Sunburst finish. Curr. mfr.

Mfr.'s Sug. Retail	$660	$460	$395	$330	$265	$240	$220	$200

This model is also available with ash body and Transparent Red finish.

SB302 — similar to SB301, except has fretless fingerboard. Available in Black, Magenta and Metallic Grey finish.

Mfr.'s Sug. Retail	$660	$460	$395	$330	$265	$240	$220	$200

This model is also available with ash body and Transparent Red finish.

SB305 — similar to SB301, except has 5 strings and 2 J-style pickups.

Mfr.'s Sug. Retail	$760	$530	$455	$380	$305	$275	$250	$230

This model is also available with ash body and Transparent Red finish.

400 Series

SB401 — offset double cutaway basswood body, bolt-on maple neck, 24 fret rosewood fingerboard, fixed bridge, 2 per side Gotoh tuners, black hardware, P-style/J-style pickups, 2 volume/2 tone controls, active electronics, 2 band EQ. Available in Black, Metallic Red and Pearl White finish. Curr. mfr.

Mfr.'s Sug. Retail	$995	$695	$595	$500	$400	$360	$330	$300

SB402 — similar to SB401, except has fretless fingerboard.

Mfr.'s Sug. Retail	$995	$695	$595	$500	$400	$360	$330	$300

SB405 — similar to SB401, except has 5 strings and 2 J-style pickups.

Mfr.'s Sug. Retail	$1,195	$835	$715	$600	$480	$430	$395	$360

Grading	100%	98%	95%	90%	80%	70%	60%

500 Series

SB501 — offset double cutaway alder body, bolt-on 3 piece maple neck, 24 fret ebony fingerboard, fixed bridge, 2 per side tuners, black hardware, P-style/J-style pickups, 2 volume/2 tone controls, active electronics with 2 band EQ. Available in Black, Natural and Pearl White finish. Curr. mfr.

Mfr.'s Sug. Retail	$1,195	$835	$715	$600	$480	$430	$395	$360

Add $100 for left handed version.

SB502 — similar to SB501, except has fretless fingerboard.

Mfr.'s Sug. Retail	$995	$695	$595	$500	$400	$360	$330	$300

Add $200 for left handed version.

SB505 — similar to SB501, except has 5 strings.

Mfr.'s Sug. Retail	$1,395	$975	$835	$700	$560	$505	$460	$420

This model is also available with ash body and Transparent Red finish.

600 Series

SB611 — offset double cutaway asymmetrical maple body with padauk or walnut top, bolt-on maple neck, 24 fret ebony fingerboard, fixed bridge, 2 per side Gotoh tuners, gold hardware, P-style/J-style pickups, 2 volume/2 tone controls, active electronics with 2 band EQ. Available in oiled finishes. Curr. mfr.

Mfr.'s Sug. Retail	$1,495	$1,045	$895	$750	$600	$540	$495	$450

SB612 — similar to SB611, except has fretless fingerboard.

Mfr.'s Sug. Retail	$1,495	$1,045	$895	$750	$600	$540	$495	$450

SB615 — similar to SB611, except has 5 strings.

Mfr.'s Sug. Retail	$1,650	$1,155	$990	$825	$660	$595	$545	$495

DB Series

DB41R — asymmetrical double cutaway ash body, bolt-on maple neck, 24 fret rosewood fingerboard with abalone dot inlay, fixed bridge, 2 per side tuners, chrome hardware, 2 J-style pickups, 2 volume/2 tone controls. Available in Transparent Black and Transparent Red finish. Curr. mfr.

Mfr.'s Sug. Retail	$1,200	$840	$720	$600	$480	$430	$395	$360

DB43E — similar to DB41R, except has padauk/maple/mahogany laminated or walnut/maple/mahogany laminated body, ebony fingerboard, gold hardware, 2 humbucker pickups. Available in oil finishes. Curr. mfr.

Mfr.'s Sug. Retail	$1,630	$1,140	$980	$815	$650	$585	$535	$490

Grading	100%	98%	95%	90%	80%	70%	60%

DB51R — similar to DB41R, except has 5 strings.

Mfr.'s Sug. Retail	$1,560	$1,090	$935	$780	$625	$560	$515	$470

DB53E — similar to DB43E, except has 5 strings. Mfd. 1991-1992.

Mfr.'s Sug. Retail	$2,000	$1,400	$1,200	$1,000	$800	$720	$660	$600

BENEDICT GUITARS

Manufactured and distributed by Music Design, located in Blaine, MN.

All instruments are designed by Roger Benedict.

ELECTRIC

BENELECTRO — single rounded cutaway mahogany body, black pickguard, bolt on maple neck, 21 fret maple fingerboard with black dot inlay, string thru bridge, 6 on one side Kluson style tuners, chrome hardware, 2 humbucker Seymour Duncan pickups, 2 volume/1 tone control. Available in Natural finish. New 1993.

Mfr.'s Sug. Retail	$695	$485	$415	$350	$280	$250	$230	$210

This model is also available with walnut body, rosewood fingerboard with pearl dot inlay or Chandler lipstick tube pickups.

Groovemaster Series

CUSTOM — semi hollow strat style spruce body, f hole by lower bout, white pickguard, bolt-on maple neck, 21 fret rosewood fingerboard with pearl dot inlay, string thru bridge, 6 on one side Kluson style vintage tuners, chrome hardware, 3 single coil Seymour Duncan pickups, volume/2 tone controls, 5 position switch. Available in Black, Ivory, Seafoam Green or Sunburst finish. Curr. mfr.

Mfr.'s Sug. Retail	$1,895	$1,325	$1,135	$950	$760	$685	$625	$570

Deluxe — similar to Custom, except is available with alder body and maple fingerboard.

Mfr.'s Sug. Retail	$1,395	$975	$835	$700	$560	$505	$460	$420

Standard — similar to Custom, except has alder body. Available in Black, Ivory, Seafoam Green or Surf Green finish.

Mfr.'s Sug. Retail	$1,195	$835	$715	$600	$480	$430	$395	$360

This model also available with a maple fingerboard with black dot inlay.

Grading		100%	98%	95%	90%	80%	70%	60%

ELECTRIC BASS

Groovemaster Series

CUSTOM — semi hollow precision style alder body, f hole by lower bout, tortoise shell pickguard, thru body maple neck, 20 fret rosewood fingerboard with pearl dot inlay, fixed Schaller bridge, 4 on one side mini tuners, P-style/J-style Bartolini pickups, volume/tone control, 3 position switch. Available in Black, Ivory, Seafoam Green or Sunburst finish. Curr. mfr.

Mfr.'s Sug. Retail	$2,295	$1,605	$1,375	$1,150	$920	$825	$755	$690

This model is also available with curly maple top, ebony and/or fretless fingerboard.

✁ **Deluxe** — similar to Custom, except has bolt-on maple neck, maple fingerboard, vintage Schaller tuners, Seymour Duncan pickups.

Mfr.'s Sug. Retail	$1,495	$1,045	$895	$750	$600	$540	$495	$450

This model may also have a rosewood fingerboard with pearl dot inlay.

✁ **5 String Bass** — similar to Custom, except has 5 strings.

Mfr.'s Sug. Retail	$2,495	$1,745	$1,495	$1,250	$1,000	$900	$825	$750

BLADE

Manufactured and designed by Gary Levinson in Switzerland since approximately 1987. Exclusively distributed by Solo Professional Products, located in Rochester Hills, MI.

ELECTRIC

R3-MB — strat style maple body, white pickguard, bolt-on maple neck, 22 fret maple fingerboard with black dot inlay, standard vibrato, graphite nut 6 on one side Sperzel locking tuners, chrome hardware, 3 stacked coil pickups, volume/tone control, 5 position switch, Variable Spectrum Control electronics, VSC switch. Available in Black, Ice Blue, Iridescent White and Purple Rain finish. Mfd. 1991 only.

			$1,170	$1,000	$835	$670	$600	$550	$500

Add $75 for ebony fingerboard with pearl dot inlay (R3-EB).
Last Mfr.'s Sug. Retail was $1,675.

RH3-MB — similar to R3-MB, except has 2 stacked coil/1 humbucker pickups.

			$1,190	$1,020	$850	$680	$610	$560	$510

Add $100 for ebony fingerboard with pearl dot inlay (RH3-EB).
Last Mfr.'s Sug. Retail was $1,700.

Grading	100%	98%	95%	90%	80%	70%	60%

R4-MB — strat style ash body, black pickguard, bolt-on maple neck, 22 fret maple fingerboard with black dot inlay, standard vibrato, graphite nut 6 per side Sperzel locking tuners, black hardware, 3 stacked coil pickups, volume/tone control, 5 position switch, Variable Spectrum Control electronics, VSC switch. Available in Ocean Blue and Transparent Red finish. Mfd. 1991 only.

		$1,260	$1,080	$900	$720	$650	$595	$540

Add $100 for ebony fingerboard with pearl dot inlay (R4-EB).
Last Mfr.'s Sug. Retail was $1,800.

⚉ **R4-MG** — similar to R4-MB, except has gold hardware. Available in Honey, Misty Violet, Nightwood and Twotone Sunburst finish.

		$1,310	$1,120	$935	$745	$675	$615	$560

Add $90 for ebony fingerboard with pearl dot inlay (R4-EG).
Last Mfr.'s Sug. Retail was $1,870.

RH4-MB — similar to R4-MB, except has 2 stacked coil/1 humbucker pickups. Available in Nightwood, Ocean Blue and Transparent Red finish.

		$1,295	$1,110	$925	$740	$670	$610	$555

Add $100 for ebony fingerboard with pearl dot inlay (RH4-EB).
Last Mfr.'s Sug. Retail was $1,850.

⚉ **RH4-MG** — similar to RH4-MB, except has gold hardware. Available in Honey and Misty Violet finish.

		$1,330	$1,140	$950	$760	$685	$625	$570

Add $100 for ebony fingerboard with pearl dot inlay (RH4-EG).
Last Mfr.'s Sug. Retail was $1,900.

T2-MG — tele style ash body, bolt-on maple neck, 22 fret maple fingerboard with black dot inlay, fixed bridge, graphite nut 6 on one side tuners, gold hardware, 2 single coil pickups, volume/tone control, 3 position switch, Variable Spectrum Control electronics, VSC switch. Available in Harvest Gold, Misty Violet, Ocean Blue and Transparent Red finish. Mfd. 1991 only.

		$905	$775	$645	$515	$465	$425	$385

Add $40 for rosewood fingerboard with pearl dot inlay (T2-RG).
Last Mfr.'s Sug. Retail was $1,290.

ELECTRIC BASS

B3 — jazz style maple body, bolt-on maple neck, 20 fret ebony fingerboard with pearl dot inlay, fixed bridge, 4 on one side Gotoh tuners, 2 J-style pickups, volume/tone and mixed controls, Variable Spectrum Control electronics, VSC switch. Available in Black, Ice Blue, Purple Rain and Snow White finish. Mfd. 1991 only.

		$1,215	$1,045	$870	$695	$625	$570	$520

Last Mfr.'s Sug. Retail was $1,740.

Grading	100%	98%	95%	90%	80%	70%	60%

B4 — similar to B3, except has gold hardware. Available in Honey, Misty Violet, Ocean Blue and Transparent Red finish.

	$1,380	$1,180	$985	$790	$710	$650	$590

Last Mfr.'s Sug. Retail was $1,970.

BREEDLOVE

Manufactured and distributed by Breedlove Guitar Company located in Tumalo, OR since 1990.

Having spent time luthiering with Bob Taylor and his company, Steve Henderson and Larry Breedlove moved to the Pacific Northwest and formed the Breedlove Guitar Company in approximately 1992.
Using high quality woods and original designs, they offer 4 different models of flat top steel string instruments, ranging in price from $1,900 to $3,250, and also produce an acoustic bass ($2,500). Various options are also available at an additional cost.

BUSCARINO

Manufactured and distributed by Buscarino Guitar, Co. located in Largo, FL.

Founder John Buscarino apprenticed with Bob Benedetto of archtop lutherie fame. Approximately 1980, John formed Nova U.S.A., which eventually became Buscarino Guitar Co., who builds limited production, custom instruments. Buscarino offers an innovative line of instruments, both acoustic electric and solid body electric guitars and basses, that are priced between $995 to $1,895.

C

CARVIN

Current manufacturer located in Escondido, CA since 1969. Previously located in Covina, CA from circa 1950-1969. Established in 1946 by Lowell Kiesel in Los Angeles, CA.

Carvin originally manufactured lap steel guitars, small tube amps and pickups and has always been a mail-order only company.

ELECTRIC

Unless otherwise listed, all models in this series are available in the following standard colors: Classic White, Electric Green, Ferrari Red, Jet Black, Pearl Blue, Pearl Red and Pearl White.

In 1992, Carvin made a production change from double locking Carvin/Floyd Rose vibratos to locking Carvin/Floyd Rose vibratos with locking Sperzel tuners. In 1993, Carvin changed to a standard Carvin/Wilkinson vibrato and locking Sperzel tuners combination.

grading	100%	98%	95%	90%	80%	70%	60%

DC120 — strat style poplar body, thru-body maple neck, 24 fret ebony fingerboard with pearl block inlay, fixed bridge, graphite nut, 6 per side locking Sperzel tuners, chrome hardware, 2 humbucker Carvin pickups, volume/treble/bass and mix controls, bright boost, phase and coil split switches, active electronics, built-in headphone amp. Curr. mfr.

Mfr.'s Sug. Retail	$1,630	$1,140	$980	$815	$650	$585	$535	$490

DC125 — strat style poplar body, thru-body maple neck, 24 fret ebony fingerboard with pearl dot inlay, fixed bridge, graphite nut, 6 on one side locking Sperzel tuners, chrome hardware, 1 humbucker Carvin pickup, volume control, one coil split switch. Mfd. 1991 to date.

Mfr.'s Sug. Retail	$1,050	$735	$630	$525	$420	$380	$345	$315

Add $150 for standard vibrato (DC125T).

DC127 — similar to DC125, except has 2 humbucker Carvin pickups, tone control and 3 position switch.

Mfr.'s Sug. Retail	$1,200	$840	$720	$600	$480	$430	$395	$360

Add $150 for standard vibrato (DC127T).

Grading	100%	98%	95%	90%	80%	70%	60%

DC135 — similar to DC 125, except has 2 single coil/1 Carvin humbucker pickups, tone control, 3 pickup switches.

Mfr.'s Sug. Retail	$1,240	$870	$745	$620	$495	$445	$410	$370

Add $160 for standard vibrato (DC135T).

DC145 — similar to DC 125, except has reverse headstock, humbucker/single coil/humbucker Carvin pickups, tone control, 5 position switch.

Mfr.'s Sug. Retail	$1,200	$840	$720	$600	$480	$430	$395	$360

Add $170 for locking vibrato (DC145T).

DC150 — double cutaway maple body, thru-body maple neck, 24 fret ebony fingerboard with pearl dot inlay, tunomatic bridge/stop tailpiece, 3 per side tuners, chrome hardware, 2 humbucker Carvin pickups, volume/tone control, 3 position switch. Available in Classic White, Clear Maple, Ferrari Red, Jet Black, Pearl Blue, Pearl Red and Pearl White finish. Mfd. 1991 only.

		$700	$600	$500	$400	$360	$330	$300

Add $200 for double locking vibrato (DC150C).
Last Mfr.'s Sug. Retail was $999.

DC200 — strat style poplar body, thru-body maple neck, 24 fret ebony fingerboard with pearl block inlay, fixed bridge, graphite nut, 6 on one side locking Sperzel tuners, chrome hardware, 2 humbucker Carvin pickups, volume/treble/bass and mix controls, bright boost, phase and coil split switches, active electronics, built-in headphone amp. Curr. mfr.

Mfr.'s Sug. Retail	$1,450	$1,015	$870	$725	$580	$520	$475	$435

Add $180 for standard vibrato (DC200T).

DC400 — strat style koa body, flame maple top, koa thru-body neck, 24 fret ebony fingerboard with abalone block inlay, fixed bridge, body matching headstock, graphite nut, 6 on one side locking Sperzel tuners, chrome hardware, 2 humbucker Carvin pickups, volume/treble/bass and mix controls, bright boost, phase and coil split switches, built-in headphone amp. Available in Cherry Sunburst, Emerald Green, Sapphire Blue, Tobacco Sunburst and Vintage Yellow finish. Curr. mfr.

Mfr.'s Sug. Retail	$2,050	$1,435	$1,230	$1,025	$820	$745	$675	$615

Add $150 for standard vibrato (DC400T).
This model is also available with quilted maple top and black or gold hardware.

Grading	100%	98%	95%	90%	80%	70%	60%

DN612 — double offset sharp cutaway doubleneck construct, poplar body, maple thru-body necks, 24 fret ebony fingerboards with pearl dot inlays, fixed bridges, graphite nut, 6 per side on 12 string neck, 3 per side on 6 string neck, locking Sperzel tuners, chrome hardware, 2 humbucker Carvin pickups, volume/tone control, 3 position switch per neck, neck selector switch, 2 output jacks. Curr. mfr.

Mfr.'s Sug. Retail	$3,200	$2,240	$1,920	$1,600	$1,280	$1,150	$1,055	$960

This model is also available with bass instead of 12 string (DN640) and double bass (DN440).

TL60 — tele style poplar body, thru body maple neck, 24 fret ebony fingerboard with pearl dot inlay, fixed bridge, graphite nut, 6 per side locking Sperzel tuners, chrome hardware, 2 stacked coil pickups, volume/tone control, 3 position switch. New 1993.

Mfr.'s Sug. Retail	$1,240	$870	$745	$620	$495	$445	$410	$370

Add $140 for standard vibrato (TL60T).

ULTRA V — V style poplar body, maple thru-body neck, 24 fret ebony fingerboard with pearl dot inlay, fixed bridge, graphite nut, 6 on one side locking Sperzel tuners, chrome hardware, 2 humbucker pickups, volume/tone control, 3-way switch. Mfd. 1991 to date.

Mfr.'s Sug. Retail	$1,060	$740	$635	$530	$425	$385	$350	$320

Add $160 for locking vibrato (Ultra VT).

X220 — similar to Ultra V, except has offset double cutaway and 2 coil split switches. Mfd. 1991-1992.

	$800	$685	$570	$460	$410	$375	$340

Add $200 for locking vibrato (X220C).
Last Mfr.'s Sug. Retail was $1,140.

ELECTRIC BASS

All models in this series are also available fretless and come with standard colors: Classic White, Electric Green, Ferrari Red, Jet Black, Pearl Blue, Pearl Red and Pearl White.

BB75 LIMITED — offset double cutaway poplar body, thru body maple neck, 24 fret ebony fingerboard with offset pearl dot inlay, fixed bridge, graphite nut, 3/2 per side tuners, chrome hardware, 2 J-style pickups, volume/treble/bass and mix controls, active electronics. Curr. mfr.

Mfr.'s Sug. Retail	$1,700	$1,190	$1,020	$850	$680	$610	$560	$510

This model available with fretless fingerboard (BB75F Limited).

Grading	100%	98%	95%	90%	80%	70%	60%

LB20 — precision style poplar body, maple thru-body neck, 24 fret ebony fingerboard with pearl dot inlay, fixed bridge, graphite nut, 4 on one side locking Sperzel tuners, chrome hardware, 2 J-style pickups, 2 volume/1 tone controls. Mfd. 1991 to date.

Mfr.'s Sug. Retail	$1,200	$840	$720	$600	$480	$430	$395	$360

This model available with fretless fingerboard (LB20F).

LB70 — precision style poplar body, maple thru-body neck, 24 fret ebony fingerboard with pearl dot inlay, fixed bridge, graphite nut, 4 on one side locking Sperzel tuners, chrome hardware, 2 J-style pickups, volume/bass/treble/mix controls, active electronics. Mfd. 1991 to date.

Mfr.'s Sug. Retail	$1,300	$910	$780	$650	$520	$470	$430	$390

This model available with fretless fingerboard (LB70F).

LB75 — similar to LB70, except has 5 strings, built-in headphone amp.

Mfr.'s Sug. Retail	$1,500	$1,050	$900	$750	$600	$540	$495	$450

This model available with fretless fingerboard (LB75F).

LB76 — similar to LB70, except has 6 strings, built-in headphone amp. Mfd. 1992 to date.

Mfr.'s Sug. Retail	$1,800	$1,260	$1,080	$900	$720	$650	$595	$540

This model available with fretless fingerboard (LB76F).

CHANDLER

Manufacturer located in Burlingame, CA since 1980. Chandler also offers a line of guitar accessories and other related individual components.

ELECTRIC

AUSTIN SPECIAL — single sharp cutaway asymmetrical bound alder body, bolt-on maple neck, 22 fret rosewood fingerboard with pearl dot inlay, fixed bridge, 6 on one side tuners, chrome hardware, 3 single coil lipstick pickups, volume/tone control, 3 position switch. Available in Black finish. Mfd. 1992 to date.

Mfr.'s Sug. Retail	$1,200	$840	$720	$600	$480	$430	$395	$360

Grading	100%	98%	95%	90%	80%	70%	60%

⚡ **Austin Special 5** — similar to Austin Special, except has 5 strings. Mfd. 1993 to date.

Mfr.'s Sug. Retail	$1,700	$1,190	$1,020	$850	$680	$610	$560	$510

"555" — double sharp cutaway alder body, set in maple neck, white pickguard, 22 fret rosewood fingerboard with pearl dot inlay, fixed bridge, classical peghead, 3 per side tuners, chrome hardware, 3 mini humbucker Chandler pickups, volume/tone control, 5 position switch. Available in Black, Transparent Vintage Blonde and Transparent Wine Red finish. Mfd. 1992 to date.

Mfr.'s Sug. Retail	$1,200	$840	$720	$600	$480	$430	$395	$360

CHARVEL

Trademark established in 1978 by Jackson/Charvel Guitar Company. Currently manufactured and distributed by Jackson/Charvel Guitar Co. located in Fort Worth, TX. Originally located in California.

Releasing its first instruments in 1978, Charvel rapidly acquired a reputation for making instruments specifically built for aggressive modern music. Beginning with a two-man shop in California, Charvel has continued to expand, proven by adding the Jackson line of instruments.

ACOUSTIC

525 — single rounded cutaway dreadnought style, spruce top, round soundhole, 5 stripe bound body and rosette, mahogany arched back/sides/neck, 22 fret bound rosewood fingerboard with pearl dot inlay, rosewood bridge with white black dot pins, bound peghead with abalone Charvel logo inlay, 3 per side chrome tuners. Available in Cherry Sunburst, Metallic Black, Natural and Tobacco Sunburst. Curr. mfr.

Mfr.'s Sug. Retail	$400	$280	$240	$200	$160	$145	$130	$120

⚡ **525D** — similar to 525, except has transducer bridge pickup with 3 band EQ. Available in Metallic Black, Natural and Tobacco Sunburst finish.

Mfr.'s Sug. Retail	$500	$350	$300	$250	$200	$180	$165	$150

625 — single rounded cutaway jumbo style, spruce top, round soundhole, 5 stripe bound body and rosette, nato back/sides, mahogany neck, 20 fret rosewood fingerboard with abalone dot inlay, rosewood bridge with white black dot pins, rosewood veneer on peghead with abalone Charvel logo inlay, 3 per side gold tuners. Available in Black, Cherry Sunburst and Tobacco Sunburst finish. Mfd. 1992 to date.

Mfr.'s Sug. Retail	$330	$230	$195	$165	$130	$120	$110	$100

Grading	100%	98%	95%	90%	80%	70%	60%

⚮ **625C** — similar to 625, except has abalone bound body and rosette, rosewood back/sides, 24 fret bound extended fingerboard, abalone dot pins, bound peghead, transducer bridge pickup, 3 band EQ, active electronics.

Mfr.'s Sug. Retail	$450	$315	$270	$225	$180	$160	$150	$135

⚮ **625D** — similar to 625, except has transducer bridge pickup, 3 band EQ, active electronics.

Mfr.'s Sug. Retail	$400	$280	$240	$200	$160	$145	$130	$120

ACOUSTIC ELECTRIC

325SL — double offset cutaway asymmetrical style, spruce top, offset wedge soundhole, bound body and soundhole, nato back/sides/neck, 22 fret rosewood fingerboard with offset abalone dot inlay, rosewood bridge with white pearl dot pins, rosewood veneer with abalone Charvel logo, 3 per side chrome tuners, transducer bridge pickup, 3 band EQ, active electronics. Available in Black, Bright Red and Turquoise finish. Mfd. 1992 to date.

Mfr.'s Sug. Retail	$500	$350	$300	$250	$200	$180	$165	$150

⚮ **325SLX** — similar to 325SL, except has figured maple top, rosewood back/sides, bound fingerboard with shark fin inlay, bound peghead, active electronics with built-in chorus. Available in Cherry Sunburst, Tobacco Sunburst and Transparent Red finish.

Mfr.'s Sug. Retail	$600	$420	$360	$300	$240	$215	$195	$180

ATX — tele style hollow mahogany body, bound maple top, maple neck, 24 fret rosewood fingerboard with offset pearl dot inlay, thru strings rosewood bridge, six on one chrome tuners, Fishman transducer bridge pickup, volume/3 band EQ controls. Available in Black, Deep Metallic Blue and Deep Metallic Violet finish. New 1993.

Mfr.'s Sug. Retail	$895	$625	$535	$445	$360	$325	$300	$275

⚮ **ATX (Trans)** — similar to ATX, except has figured maple top. Available in Tobacco Sunburst, Transparent Black and Transparent Violet finish.

Mfr.'s Sug. Retail	$995	$695	$595	$500	$400	$360	$330	$300

Surfcaster Series

SURFCASTER — double offset rounded cutaway asymmetrical, basswood body, offset wedge soundhole, bound body and soundhole, pearloid pickguard, bolt-on maple neck, 24 fret bound rosewood fingerboard with pearl shark fin inlay, standard vibrato, bound peghead, roller nut, 3 per side tuners, chrome hardware, 2 single coil lipstick pickups, volume/tone control, 3 position switch, phase reversal in tone control. Available in Black, Magenta and Turquoise finish. Mfd. 1992 to date.

Mfr.'s Sug. Retail	$995	$695	$595	$500	$400	$360	$330	$300

Grading	100%	98%	95%	90%	80%	70%	60%

Surfcaster (Trans) — similar to Surfcaster, except has figured maple top/mahogany body. Available in Star Glo, Transparent Orange and Transparent Red finish.

Mfr.'s Sug. Retail	$1,095	$765	$655	$545	$435	$395	$360	$330

SURFCASTER HT — similar to Surfcaster, except has bridge/trapeze tailpiece, graphite nut.

Mfr.'s Sug. Retail	$995	$695	$595	$500	$400	$360	$330	$300

Surfcaster HT (Trans) — similar to Surfcaster (Trans), except has bridge/trapeze tailpiece, graphite nut.

Mfr.'s Sug. Retail	$1,095	$765	$655	$545	$435	$395	$360	$330

SURFCASTER 12 — similar to Surfcaster, except has 12 strings, ebony bound fingerboard, fixed bridge.

Mfr.'s Sug. Retail	$1,195	$835	$715	$600	$480	$430	$395	$360

Surfcaster 12 (Trans) — similar to Surfcaster (Trans), except has 12 strings, ebony bound fingerboard and fixed bridge.

Mfr.'s Sug. Retail	$1,295	$905	$775	$645	$515	$465	$425	$385

ACOUSTIC ELECTRIC BASS

425SL — double offset rounded cutaway asymmetrical style, spruce top, offset wedge soundhole, bound body and soundhole, nato back/sides/neck, 22 fret rosewood fingerboard with offset abalone inlay, rosewood bridge with abalone dot inlay, abalone Charvel logo peghead inlay, 2 per side chrome tuners, transducer bridge pickup, 3 band EQ, active electronics. Available in Bright Red, Metallic Black and Turquoise finish. Mfd. 1992 to date.

Mfr.'s Sug. Retail	$550	$385	$330	$275	$220	$200	$180	$165

425SLX — similar to 425SL, except has figured maple top, rosewood back/sides, bound fingerboard/peghead, active electronics with built-in chorus. Available in Cherry Sunburst, Tobacco Sunburst and Transparent Red finish.

Mfr.'s Sug. Retail	$650	$455	$390	$325	$260	$235	$215	$195

ATX BASS — tele style hollow mahogany body, bound maple top, maple neck, 22 fret rosewood fingerboard with offset pearl dot inlay, thru strings rosewood bridge, 4 on one side chrome tuners, volume/3 band EQ controls. Available in Black, Deep Metallic Blue and deep Metallic Violet finish. New 1993.

Mfr.'s Sug. Retail	$995	$695	$595	$500	$400	$360	$330	$300

ATX Bass (Trans) — similar to ATX Bass, except has figured maple top. Available in Tobacco Sunburst, Transparent Black and Transparent Violet finish.

Mfr.'s Sug. Retail	$1,095	$765	$655	$545	$435	$395	$360	$330

Grading	100%	98%	95%	90%	80%	70%	60%

SURFCASTER BASS — double offset rounded cutaway asymmetrical, basswood body, pearloid pickguard, bolt-on maple neck, 21 fret bound rosewood fingerboard with offset pearl inlay, fixed bridge, bound peghead, 2 per side tuners, chrome hardware, 2 single coil lipstick pickups, volume/tone control, 3 position switch, phase reversal in tone control. Available in Black, Magenta and Turquoise finish. Mfd. 1992 to date.

Mfr.'s Sug. Retail	$995	$695	$595	$500	$400	$360	$330	$300

✕ **Surfcaster Bass (Trans)** — similar to Surfcaster Bass, except has figured maple top/mahogany body. Available in Star Glo, Transparent Orange and Transparent Red finish.

Mfr.'s Sug. Retail	$1,095	$765	$655	$545	$435	$395	$360	$330

ELECTRIC

Contemporary Series

275 DELUXE — strat style hardwood body, bolt-on maple neck, 22 fret rosewood fingerboard with white dot inlay, double locking vibrato, 6 on one side tuners, black hardware, 3 stacked coil pickups (2 side by side at the bridge), volume control, 5-position switch. Available in Candy Blue, Ferrari Red, Midnite Black and Snow White finish. Mfd. 1991 only.

		$485	$415	$350	$280	$250	$230	$210

Last Mfr.'s Sug. Retail was $695.

375 DELUXE — similar to 275 Deluxe, except has 2 single coil/1 Jackson humbucker pickups and tone control. Available in Candy Red, Magenta, Metallic Black, Pearl Blue and Pearl White finish.

		$555	$475	$395	$315	$280	$260	$235

Add $100 for exotic wood body with Cherry Sunburst, Transparent Amber, Transparent Red and Transparent Violet finish.
This model is also available with a maple fingerboard with black dot inlay.
Last Mfr.'s Sug. Retail was $795.

475 DELUXE — strat style hardwood body, bolt-on maple neck, 22 fret bound rosewood fingerboard with pearl sharkfin inlay, double locking vibrato, bound peghead, 6 on one side tuners, black hardware, 2 stacked coil/1 Jackson humbucker, volume/2 tone controls, 5-position switch, active electronics. Available in Candy Red, Magenta, Metallic Black, Pearl Blue and Pearl White finish. Mfd. 1991 only.

		$695	$595	$500	$400	$360	$330	$300

Add $100 for exotic wood body with Cherry Sunburst, Transparent Amber, Transparent Red and Transparent Violet finish.
Add 10% for left handed version.
Last Mfr.'s Sug. Retail was $995.

Grading	100%	98%	95%	90%	80%	70%	60%

650 XL — similar to 475 Deluxe, except has thru body neck. Available in Candy Red, Metallic Black, Pearl White and Snow White finish.

	$905	$775	$645	$515	$465	$425	$385

Last Mfr.'s Sug. Retail was $1,295.

AVENGER — sharkfin style hardwood body, bolt-on maple neck, 22 fret rosewood fingerboard with white dot inlay, double locking vibrato, 6 on one side Gotoh tuners, black hardware, 3 stacked coil Charvel pickups (2 side by side at the bridge), volume control, 5-position switch. Available in Candy Blue, Ferrari Red, Midnite Black and Snow White finish. Mfd. 1991 only.

	$485	$415	$350	$280	$250	$230	$210

Last Mfr.'s Sug. Retail was $695.

PREDATOR — strat style hardwood body, bolt-on maple neck, 22 fret rosewood fingerboard with white dot inlay, double locking vibrato, reverse headstock, 6 on one side tuners, black hardware, blade stacked coil/humbucker Jackson pickups, volume control, 5-position switch. Available in Candy Blue, Candy Red, Magenta, Midnite Black and Pearl White finish. Mfd. 1991 only.

	$555	$475	$395	$315	$280	$260	$235

Last Mfr.'s Sug. Retail was $795.

SPECTRUM — similar to Predator, except has white pickguard, chrome hardware, 3 stacked coil Jackson pickups, active electronics with switch. Available in Candy Red, Midnite Black, Sea Green and Tobacco Sunburst finish.

	$625	$535	$445	$360	$325	$300	$275

This model is also available with maple fingerboard with black dot inlay.
Last Mfr.'s Sug. Retail was $895.

CX Series

CX290 — strat style, basswood body, white pickguard, bolt-on maple neck, 22 fret rosewood fingerboard with pearl dot inlay, standard vibrato, 6 per side tuners, chrome hardware, 3 single coil Jackson pickups, volume/tone control, 5 position switch. Available in Black, Bright Red, Deep Metallic Blue and Snow White finish. Mfd. 1992 to date.

Mfr.'s Sug. Retail	$395	$275	$235	$195	$155	$140	$125	$115

This model also available with 2 single coil/1 humbucker pickup configuration (CX291).

CX390 — strat style, basswood body, black pickguard, bolt-on maple neck, 22 fret rosewood fingerboard with pearl dot inlay, double locking vibrato, 6 on one side tuners, chrome hardware, 2 single coil/ 1 Jackson humbucker pickups, volume/tone control, 5 position switch. Available in Black, Bright Red, Deep Metallic Blue and Snow White finish. Mfd. 1992 to date.

Mfr.'s Sug. Retail	$495	$345	$295	$245	$195	$175	$160	$150

This model also available with humbucker/single coil/humbucker pickup configuration (CX391).

Charvel , cont.

Fusion Series

FUSION CUSTOM — strat style poplar body, bolt-on maple neck, 24 fret rosewood fingerboard with white dot inlay, double locking vibrato, 6 on one side tuners, black hardware, 2 rail stacked coil/1 Jackson humbucker pickups, volume/tone control, 5-position switch. Available in Candy Blue, Candy Red, Metallic Black and Snow White finish. Mfd. 1991 only.

$625	$535	$445	$360	$325	$300	$275

Last Mfr.'s Sug. Retail was $895.

FUSION DELUXE — similar to Fusion Custom, except has chrome hardware, rail stacked coil/humbucker Jackson pickups, volume control.

$555	$475	$395	$315	$280	$260	$235

This model is also available with maple fingerboard with black dot inlay.
Last Mfr.'s Sug. Retail was $795.

FUSION PLUS — strat style ash body, bolt-on maple neck, 24 fret rosewood fingerboard with offset white dot inlay, double locking vibrato, 6 on one side tuners, black hardware, 2 humbucker Jackson pickups, volume/tone control, 5-position switch with coil split. Available in Tobacco Sunburst, Transparent Amber, Transparent Red, Transparent Violet and Transparent White finish. Disc. 1992.

$625	$535	$445	$360	$325	$300	$275

Last Mfr.'s Sug. Retail was $895.

FUSION SPECIAL — strat style poplar body, thru body maple neck, 24 fret rosewood fingerboard with white dot inlay, double locking vibrato, 6 on one side tuners, black hardware, 3 stacked coil Charvel pickups (2 side by side at the bridge), volume control, 5-position switch. Available in Candy Blue, Ferrari Red, Midnite Black and Snow White finish. Mfd. 1991 only.

$485	$415	$350	$280	$250	$230	$210

Last Mfr.'s Sug. Retail was $695.

LS-1 Series

LS-1 — offset double cutaway asymmetrical bound mahogany body, mahogany neck, 22 fret bound rosewood fingerboard with pearl dot inlay, tunomatic bridge, string thru body tailpiece, 3 per side tuners, chrome hardware, 2 humbucker Jackson pickups, volume/tone control, 3 position switch. Available in Black, Deep Metallic Blue and Gold finish. New 1993.

Mfr.'s Sug. Retail	$995	$695	$595	$500	$400	$360	$330	$300

Grading	100%	98%	95%	90%	80%	70%	60%

Classic Series

STX CUSTOM — strat style, basswood body, pearloid pickguard, bolt-on maple neck, 22 fret rosewood fingerboard with pearl dot inlay, double locking vibrato, 6 on one side tuners, chrome hardware, 2 single coil/1 humbucker Jackson pickups, volume/tone control, 5 position switch. Available in Black and Deep Metallic Blue. Mfd. 1991 to date.

Mfr.'s Sug. Retail	$895	$625	$535	$445	$360	$325	$300	$275

STX Custom (Trans) — similar to STX Custom, except has ash body. Available in Tobacco Sunburst, Transparent Blue and Transparent Red.

Mfr.'s Sug. Retail	$995	$695	$595	$500	$400	$360	$330	$300

STX DELUXE — similar to STX Custom, except has standard vibrato. Available in Black, Deep Metallic Blue, Dark Metallic Red, Pearl White and Turquoise finish.

Mfr.'s Sug. Retail	$695	$485	$415	$350	$280	$250	$230	$210

TX CUSTOM (formerly TE Custom) — tele style basswood body, pearloid pickguard, bolt-on maple neck, 22 fret maple fingerboard with black dot inlay, fixed bridge, 6 on one side tuners, chrome hardware, volume/tone control, 5 position switch. Available in Black, Dark Metallic Red and Turquoise finish. Mfd. 1992 to date.

Mfr.'s Sug. Retail	$695	$485	$415	$350	$280	$250	$230	$210

The fingerboard is also available in rosewood with pearl dot inlay.

TTX — tele style basswood body, pearloid pickguard, bolt-on maple neck, 24 fret maple fingerboard with black dot inlay, standard vibrato, 6 on one side locking tuners, chrome hardware, single coil/humbucker Jackson pickup, 3 position/mini switches. Available in Black, Deep Metallic Blue, Deep Metallic Red and Metallic Purple finish. New 1993.

Mfr.'s Sug. Retail	$595	$415	$360	$300	$240	$215	$195	$180

TTX (Trans) — similar to TTX, except has ash body. Available in Transparent Black, Transparent Blue and Transparent Red finish.

Mfr.'s Sug. Retail	$645	$450	$385	$320	$260	$235	$215	$195

TX Custom (Trans) — similar to TX Custom, except has ash body. Available in Tobacco Sunburst finish.

Mfr.'s Sug. Retail	$795	$555	$475	$395	$315	$280	$260	$235

The fingerboard is also available in rosewood with pearl dot inlay.

Grading	100%	98%	95%	90%	80%	70%	60%

ELECTRIC BASS

575 DELUXE — precision style hardwood body, bolt-on maple neck, 21 fret rosewood fingerboard with white dot inlay, fixed bridge, 4 on one side Gotoh tuners, black hardware, P-style/J-style Jackson pickups, volume/tone control, 3-position switch. Available in Candy Blue, Candy Red, Metallic Black and Snow White finish. Mfd. 1991 only.

	$485	$415	$350	$280	$250	$230	$210

Last Mfr.'s Sug. Retail was $695.

CX490 — precision style poplar body, bolt-on maple neck, 22 fret rosewood fingerboard with pearl dot inlay, fixed bridge, 4 on one side tuners, chrome hardware, P-style/J-style Jackson pickups, volume/tone and mix controls. Available in Black, Bright Red, Deep Metallic Blue and Snow White finish. Mfd. 1992 to date.

Mfr.'s Sug. Retail	$495	$345	$295	$245	$195	$175	$160	$150

ELIMINATOR — offset double cutaway hardwood body, bolt-on maple neck, 24 fret rosewood fingerboard with white dot inlay, fixed bridge, 4 on one side tuners, black hardware, P-style/J-style Charvel pickups, volume/treble/bass and mix controls, active electronics. Available in Candy Blue, Ferrari Red, Midnite Black and Snow White finish. Mfd. 1991 only.

	$485	$415	$350	$280	$250	$230	$210

Last Mfr.'s Sug. Retail was $695.

FUSION IV — offset double cutaway hardwood body, bolt-on maple neck, 24 fret rosewood fingerboard with offset pearl dot inlay, pearl Charvel block inlay at 12th fret, fixed bridge, 4 on one side tuners, black hardware, P-style/J-style Charvel pickups, volume/treble/bass and mix controls, active electronics. Available in Candy Blue, Ferrari Red, Magenta, Metallic Black and Pearl White finish. Mfd. 1991 only.

	$555	$475	$395	$315	$280	$260	$235

Last Mfr.'s Sug. Retail was $795.

Fusion V — similar to Fusion IV, except has 5 strings.

	$695	$595	$500	$400	$360	$330	$300

Last Mfr.'s Sug. Retail was $995.

JX BASS — similar to CX490, except has jazz style body. Available in Black, Deep Metallic Blue, Dark Metallic Red, Snow White and Turquoise finish. Mfd. 1992 to date.

Mfr.'s Sug. Retail	$695	$485	$415	$350	$280	$250	$230	$210

Grading	100%	98%	95%	90%	80%	70%	60%

LS-1 — offset double cutaway asymmetrical bound mahogany body, mahogany neck, 21 fret bound rosewood fingerboard with pearl dot inlay, tunomatic bridge, thru body ring and ball holder tailpiece, 2 humbucker Jackson pickups, volume/treble/bass/mix control. Available in Black, Deep Metallic Blue and Gold finish. New 1993.

	100%	98%	95%	90%	80%	70%	60%
Mfr.'s Sug. Retail	$1,195	$835	$715	$600	$480	$430	$395	$360

CHARVETTE

Trademark previously manufactured by the Charvel/Jackson Guitar Company located in Forth Worth, TX in 1991 only.

All models in this series were available in Ferrari Red, Midnite Black, Royal Blue, Snow White and Splatter finish, unless otherwise listed.

ELECTRIC

100 — strat style hardwood body, bolt-on maple neck, 22 fret rosewood fingerboard with white dot inlay, standard vibrato, reverse headstock, 6 on one side tuners, black hardware, stacked coil/humbucker Charvel pickup, volume/tone control, 3-position switch.

Mfr.'s Sug. Retail	$365	$260	$220	$180	$145	$130	$120	$110

150 — similar to 100, except has locking vibrato.

Mfr.'s Sug. Retail	$395	$275	$235	$195	$155	$140	$125	$115

170 — similar to 100, except has double locking vibrato.

Mfr.'s Sug. Retail	$495	$345	$295	$245	$195	$175	$160	$150

200 — similar to 100, except has 2 single coil/1 humbucker Charvel pickups.

Mfr.'s Sug. Retail	$375	$260	$220	$185	$150	$135	$120	$110

250 — similar to 100, except has locking vibrato and stacked coil/single coil/humbucker Charvel pickups.

Mfr.'s Sug. Retail	$425	$295	$250	$210	$170	$150	$135	$125

270 — similar to 100, except has double locking vibrato and stacked coil/single coil/humbucker Charvel pickups.

Mfr.'s Sug. Retail	$525	$370	$315	$260	$210	$190	$170	$160

300 — similar to 100, except has 3 single coil Charvel pickups.

Mfr.'s Sug. Retail	$495	$345	$295	$245	$195	$175	$160	$150

Grading	100%	98%	95%	90%	80%	70%	60%

ELECTRIC BASS

400 — precision style hardwood body, bolt-on maple neck, 21 fret rosewood fingerboard with pearl dot inlay, fixed bridge, 4 on one side tuners, chrome hardware, P-style Charvel pickup, volume/tone control.

Mfr.'s Sug. Retail	$425	$295	$250	$210	$170	$150	$135	$125

COLLINGS

Manufacturer and distributor located in Austin, TX since approximately 1989.

Collings produces two types of archtop guitars in addition to their flattops. These models start at $8,500 and increase in price.

ACOUSTIC

All models are available with the following options:
Add $150 for abalone rosette.
Add $425 for 12 string version.
Add $400 for rounded single cutaway.

C Series

C-10 — folk style, spruce top, round soundhole, pearloid pickguard, ivoroid bound body/rosette, mahogany back/sides/neck, 14/20 fret bound ebony fingerboard, ebony bridge with white black dot pins, pearloid veneer on bound peghead with inscribed logo, 3 per side gold Kluson tuners. Available in Black, Blue, Natural and Red finish. Curr. mfr.

Mfr.'s Sug. Retail	$2,050	$1,435	$1,230	$1,025	$820	$745	$675	$615

C-10 Deluxe — similar to C-10, except has tortoise shell pickguard, Indian rosewood back/sides, pearl dot fingerboard inlay, ebony peghead veneer with pearl logo inlay, gold Schaller mini tuners. Available in Natural finish.

Mfr.'s Sug. Retail	$2,495	$1,745	$1,495	$1,250	$1,000	$900	$825	$750

C-100 — similar to C-10, except has dreadnought style body.

Mfr.'s Sug. Retail	$2,100	$1,475	$1,260	$1,050	$840	$755	$690	$630

C-100 Deluxe — similar to C-10, except has small jumbo style body.

Mfr.'s Sug. Retail	$2,545	$1,780	$1,530	$1,275	$1,020	$915	$840	$765

Grading	100%	98%	95%	90%	80%	70%	60%

D Series

D-1 — dreadnought style, spruce top, round soundhole, tortoise shell pickguard, 3 stripe bound body/rosette, mahogany back/sides/neck, 14/20 fret bound ebony fingerboard, ebony bridge with white black dot pins, ebony or rosewood veneer on bound peghead with pearl logo inlay, 3 per side chrome Gotoh tuners. Available in Natural finish. Curr. mfr.

Mfr.'s Sug. Retail	$1,980	$1,385	$1,190	$990	$790	$715	$655	$595

D-2 — similar to D-1, except has Indian rosewood back/sides, pearl diamond/square headstock inlay.

Mfr.'s Sug. Retail	$2,250	$1,575	$1,345	$1,125	$900	$810	$740	$675

This model may also have herringbone purfling (D-2H).

D-3 — similar to D-1, except has abalone purfling/rosette, Indian rosewood back/sides.

Mfr.'s Sug. Retail	$2,575	$1,805	$1,545	$1,290	$1,030	$925	$850	$775

OM Series

OM-1 — grand concert style, spruce top, round soundhole, tortoise shell pickguard, 3 stripe bound body/rosette, mahogany back/sides/neck, 14/20 fret bound ebony fingerboard, ebony bridge with white black dot pins, ebony or rosewood veneer on bound peghead with pearl logo inlay, 3 per side chrome Gotoh tuners. Available in Natural finish. Curr. mfr.

Mfr.'s Sug. Retail	$1,980	$1,385	$1,190	$990	$790	$715	$655	$595

OM-2H — similar to OM-1, except has herringbone purfling, Indian rosewood back/sides, pearl diamond/square headstock inlay.

Mfr.'s Sug. Retail	$2,250	$1,575	$1,345	$1,125	$900	$810	$740	$675

OOO-2H 12-FRET — similar to OM-2H, except has slightly larger body, 12/20 fret fingerboard.

Mfr.'s Sug. Retail	$2,650	$1,855	$1,590	$1,325	$1,060	$955	$875	$795

OM-3 — similar to OM-1, except has abalone purfling/rosette, Indian rosewood back/sides.

Mfr.'s Sug. Retail	$2,575	$1,805	$1,545	$1,290	$1,030	$925	$850	$775

SJ Series

SJ — small jumbo style, spruce top, round soundhole, tortoise shell pickguard, 3 stripe bound body/rosette, maple back/sides/neck, 14/20 fret bound ebony fingerboard with pearl diamond inlay, ebony bridge with white black dot pins, ebony veneer on bound peghead with pearl diamond and logo inlay, 3 per side gold Schaller mini tuners. Available in Natural finish. Curr. mfr.

Mfr.'s Sug. Retail	$2,650	$1,855	$1,590	$1,325	$1,060	$955	$875	$795

CORAL

Trademark established 1967-1968 by MCA. Manufactured by Danelectro Corp. located in Neptune City, NJ.

The Coral Trademark has not retained the desirability factor that the Danelectro instruments have acquired to date. Perhaps this is because there are simply not the number of configurations or custom colors available during the short period in which they were manufactured.

DANELECTRO

Manufactured and distributed by Danelectro Corp., located in Red Bank, NJ, 1956-1959. Danelectro Corp.'s factory and offices relocated to Neptune City, NJ in 1960. Manufacture and distribution continued at this location until the company's demise in 1968. The majority of instruments were distributed by Sears & Roebuck, Co. circa 1956-1967. Also distributed by MCA Corp. circa 1967-1968.

Danelectro Corp. was founded in 1948 by Nathan Daniel, who at the time had been contracted by Epiphone to build amplifiers for them. In 1955, the Sears & Roebuck, Co. contacted Mr. Daniel about manufacturing guitars, to which he agreed. The Danelectro Co. was sold to the MCA Corp. in 1967 and MCA closed the Danelectro Corp. division in 1968.

Danelectro instrument designs were always innovative. They have a wooden shell construction with a Masonite top and back. There are several different styles, but the most popular ones were the Sears Silvertones, with some models having a case with built-in amplifiers. They generally sold from $39 (single pickup standard) to $145 (3 pickup deluxe model). Today, these instruments will generally range from $225 to $350 depending on condition and rarity. In recent years, Custom Colors and rare features have become a lot more desirable (and expensive). A rare color or model can increase the value between 150%-250%.

D'ANGELICO

Master luthier located in New York City, NY 1932-approx. 1961.

John D'Angelico started manufacturing arch top guitars at his Kenmare Street address in 1932 after an apprenticeship that included both Italian style flat top guitars and mandolins. Early manufacture instruments did not have model names, but by 1936, D'Angelico had settled on five basic styles - the A, A-1, Style B, Excel, and New Yorker. The A, B, and Excel were 17 inch instruments differing mostly in ornamentation while the New Yorker featured an 18 inch body. Styling was similar to Gibson, and most of these instruments were custom ordered. During his close to 30 years as a master luthier, D'Angelico produced slightly over 1,150 instruments - many of which were special orders by prominent jazz/big band musicians of that time. Arguably the most sought after trademark in today's vintage marketplace, these instruments have become very expensive within the past decade. Because each guitar was normally custom built per individual specifications, there is very little standardized pricing structure within the variations. The price range of a D'Angelico guitar can get as low as $10,000-$15,000, while the high can be in excess of $100,000 - depending on the condition, rarity, and even previous owner *premium in some cases. It is highly recommended that several professional appraisals be secured before buying/selling/trading any D'Angelico guitar.*

D'AQUISTO

Manufactured and distributed by James L. D'Aquisto, 1965 to date.

In 1952, James D'Aquisto became an apprentice of master luthier John D'Angelico. He worked with D'Angelico until the time of John's death in 1964. After that, D'Aquisto continued to work in D'Angelico's shop repairing instruments at the new address - 37 Kenmare Street, New York City, NY. In 1965, D'Aquisto moved his shop to Huntington, NY, and sold his first instrument, styled after a D'Angelico New Yorker. Most of D'Aquisto's instruments are styled after John D'Angelico's Excel and New Yorker, with D'Aquisto adding refinements and improvements. In 1973, D'Aquisto relocated his business once again, this time setting up shop in Farmingdale, NY. In the late 1980's, D'Aquisto moved his shop to Greenport, NY and continues to produce instruments from that location. To date, James D'Aquisto has built hundreds of instruments, from archtops to flat tops to solid body electrics. Prices generally start at $7,000, with the model configuration and special order embellishments adding considerably to the base price.

DEAN

Manufactured and distributed by Dean Guitars, located in Chicago, IL, late 1970's to mid 1980's.

As this edition of the Blue Book of Guitar Values goes to press, more research is being done on this line of instruments. The company was founded by Dean Zelinsky, after he had experienced some success in the collecting and repairing field. He began manufacturing electric solid body instruments of popular existing designs and eventually started developing his own designs. The M.L., Belle Star and The E'Lite were all successful models. Dean Guitars ran out of gas in the mid-80's, though the trademark has resurfaced again with current instruments being manufactured overseas and distributes in the U.S. by The Heartland Group, Indianapolis, IN.

DOBRO

As this edition went to press, more research is under way on this trademark and the results will be published in the 2nd edition of the Blue Book of Guitar Values.

EGGLE

Manufactured by the Patrick Eggle Music Company, located in Coventry, UK. Distributed in the USA by Seymour Duncan, located in California.

ELECTRIC

All models listed below are available in left handed versions free of charge.

BERLIN SERIES

Grading	100%	98%	95%	90%	80%	70%	60%

DELUXE — offset double cutaway maple body, carved figured maple top, mahogany neck, 24 fret ebony fingerboard with abalone dot inlay, abalone maple leaf inlay on 12th fret, locking Wilkinson vibrato, 3 per side locking Sperzel tuners, gold hardware, 2 humbucker Eggle pickups, volume/coil tap control, 3 position switch. Available in Antique Gold, Bahamian Blue, Burny Amber, Burgundy Burst, Chardonnay Rouge, Chardonnay Rouge Burst, Cherry, Cherry Burst, Citrus Green, Citrus Green Burst, Deep Sea Blue, Emerald Isle Blue, Pink Glow, Pink Glow Burst, Purple Haze, Shamu Blue, Shamu Blue Burst, Tobacco Burst, Vintage Gold Burst, and Walnut finish. Curr. mfr.

Mfr.'s Sug. Retail	$1,400	$980	$840	$700	$560	$505	$460	$420

⚁ **Plus** — similar to Deluxe, except has mahogany body, abalone dot inlay at 12th fret, tunomatic bridge/stop tailpiece, body matching peghead, chrome hardware, tone control with coil tap. Available in Antique Gold, Bahamian Blue, Chardonnay Rouge, Cherry, Pink Glow, and Walnut finish.

Mfr.'s Sug. Retail	$800	$560	$480	$400	$320	$290	$265	$240

    Add $60 for gold hardware.

⚁ **Pro** — similar to Deluxe, except has mahogany body, abalone dot inlay at 12th fret, body matching peghead, chrome hardware. Available in Antique Gold, Bahamian Blue, Burgundy Burst, Chardonnay Rouge, Chardonnay Rouge Burst, Cherry, Cherry Burst, Deep Sea Blue, Emerald Isle Blue, Pink Glow, Pink Glow Burst, Purple Haze, Tobacco Burst, Vintage Gold Burst, and Walnut finish.

Mfr.'s Sug. Retail	$1,050	$735	$630	$525	$420	$380	$345	$315

    Add $120 for gold hardware.

Grading	100%	98%	95%	90%	80%	70%	60%

⚞ **Standard** — similar to Deluxe, except has mahogany back, abalone dot inlay at 12th fret, tunomatic bridge/stop tailpiece, chrome hardware, tone control. Available in Black, Natural and White finish.

Mfr.'s Sug. Retail	$600	$420	$360	$300	$240	$215	$195	$180

Add $60 for gold hardware.

LEGEND SERIES

JS — offset double cutaway, maple body, carved figured maple top, figured maple neck, 24 fret ebony fingerboard with pearl maple leaf inlay, locking Wilkinson vibrato, ebony veneer on peghead, 3 per side locking Sperzel tuners, 2 active humbucker Reflex pickups, volume/tone control, 3 position switch, coil tap in volume control, active electronics. Available in Antique Gold, Bahamian Blue, Burny Amber, Burgundy Burst, Chardonnay Rouge, Chardonnay Rouge Burst, Cherry, Cherry Burst, Citrus Green, Citrus Green Burst, Deep Sea Blue, Emerald Isle Blue, Natural, Pink Glow, Pink Glow Burst, Purple Haze, Shamu Blue, Shamu Blue Burst, Tobacco Burst, Vintage Gold Burst, and Walnut finish. Curr. mfr.

Mfr.'s Sug. Retail	$1,750	$1,225	$1,050	$875	$700	$630	$575	$525

This instrument was designed for Big Jim Sullivan.
Also available with black hardware.

LOS ANGELES SERIES

PLUS — strat style maple body, bolt-on maple neck, 24 fret maple fingerboard with black pearl dot inlay, locking Wilkinson vibrato, 3 per side locking Sperzel tuners, chrome hardware, 3 dual rail pickups, volume/tone/5 position control, mini switch, active electronics. Available in Antique Gold, Cherry, Cherry Burst, Citrus Green, Pink Glow, Purple Haze, Shamu Blue and Shamu Blue Burst finish. Curr. mfr.

Mfr.'s Sug. Retail	$850	$595	$510	$425	$340	$305	$280	$255

⚞ **Pro** — similar to Plus, except has ebony veneer on peghead, gold hardware, 3 stacked coil Reflex pickups, no mini switch. Available in Antique Gold, Burgundy Burst, Chardonnay Rouge, Chardonnay Rouge Burst, Cherry, Cherry Burst, Citrus Green, Citrus Green Burst, Pink Glow, Pink Glow Burst, Purple Haze, Shamu Blue, Shamu Blue Burst and Vintage Gold Burst finish.

Mfr.'s Sug. Retail	$1,100	$770	$660	$550	$440	$395	$365	$330

⚞ **Standard** — similar to Plus, except available in rubbed finishes. Available in Black, Natural, USA Blue, USA Pink, USA Red and USA Yellow finish.

Mfr.'s Sug. Retail	$650	$455	$390	$325	$260	$235	$215	$195

Grading	100%	98%	95%	90%	80%	70%	60%

NEW YORK SERIES

DELUXE — offset double cutaway semi-hollow mahogany body, carved bound figured maple top, maple/rosewood neck, 22 fret ebony fingerboard with pearl NY inlay at 12th fret, tunomatic bridge, string thru body tailpiece, 3 per side Sperzel tuners, gold hardware, 2 humbucker pickups, volume/tone control, 3 position switch, coil tap in tone control. Available in Antique Gold, Bahamian Blue, Burny Amber, Burgundy Burst, Chardonnay Rouge, Chardonnay Rouge Burst, Cherry, Cherry Burst, Citrus Green, Citrus Green Burst, Deep Sea Blue, Emerald Isle Blue, Pink Glow, Pink Glow Burst, Purple Haze, Shamu Blue, Shamu Blue Burst, Tobacco Burst, Vintage Gold Burst, and Walnut finish. Curr. mfr.

Mfr.'s Sug. Retail	$600	$420	$360	$300	$240	$215	$195	$180

‡ **Plus** — offset double cutaway mahogany body, pearloid pickguard, bolt-on maple neck, 22 fret rosewood fingerboard with offset pearl dot inlay, tunomatic bridge, string thru body tailpiece, 3 per side Sperzel tuners, chrome hardware, single coil/humbucker pickups, volume/tone control, mini switch, coil tap in tone control. Available in Antique Gold, Burny Amber, Cherry, Citrus Green and Deep Sea Blue. Curr. mfr.

Mfr.'s Sug. Retail	$675	$475	$405	$340	$270	$245	$225	$205

Add $60 for gold hardware.

‡ **Standard** — similar to Plus, except available in rubbed finishes. Available in Black, Natural, USA Blue, USA Pink, USA Red and USA Yellow finish.

Mfr.'s Sug. Retail	$500	$350	$300	$250	$200	$180	$165	$150

EPIPHONE

The Epiphone Company became established out of the House of Stathopoulo, circa 1873 in New York, NY. The company president, Mr. Epi Stathopoulo, began using the "Epiphone" trademark on a few House of Stathopoulo models, so named after his surname, Epaminondas. During 1928, the House of Stathopoulo changed names to Epiphone Banjo Corporation. In 1935, this new upcoming company moved from Long Island City to West 14th Street, thus doubling its floor space. During this time period, the Epiphone Trademark was perhaps the most famous in America with few competitors matching the overall quality, status, and musician endorsements. In 1952, the company address for Epiphone was 130 West 3rd Street in New York City, but the factory address was listed as Philadelphia, PA, circa 1953-1955. By 1957, Epiphone had become a wholly owned subsidiary of Gibson. Currently, Epiphone instruments are manufactured both in the U.S. and overseas.

Grading	100%	98%	95%	90%	80%	70%	60%

ACOUSTIC

C70-CE — rounded cutaway classic style, spruce top, round soundhole, bound body, wooden inlay rosette, rosewood back/sides, mahogany neck, 19 fret rosewood fingerboard, rosewood tied bridge, rosewood peghead veneer with circles/star design, 3 per side chrome tuners with pearl buttons, piezo pickup, volume/3 band EQ. Available in Natural finish. Curr. mfr.

Mfr.'s Sug. Retail	$500	$350	$300	$250	$200	$180	$165	$150

EO-1 — rounded cutaway folk style, spruce top, round soundhole, 3 stripe bound body/rosette, mahogany back/sides/neck, 21 fret bound rosewood fingerboard with pearl dot inlay, rosewood bridge with white black dot pins, rosewood veneer on bound peghead with star/crescent inlay, 3 per side chrome tuners. Available in Natural finish. Curr. mfr.

Mfr.'s Sug. Retail	$500	$350	$300	$250	$200	$180	$165	$150

PR-775S — dreadnought style, solid spruce top, round soundhole, tortoise shell pickguard, abalone bound body/rosette, rosewood back/sides, mahogany neck, 14/20 fret bound rosewood fingerboard with abalone pearl block/triangle inlay, rosewood bridge with white black dot pins, rosewood veneer on bound peghead with crescent/star/logo inlay, 3 per side chrome tuners. Available in Natural finish. Curr. mfr.

Mfr.'s Sug. Retail	$500	$350	$300	$250	$200	$180	$165	$150

This model also available in 12 string version (PR-775-12).

ELECTRIC

All instruments in this section are available in Black, Red and White finish, unless otherwise listed.

EM-1 — offset sweeping double cutaway basswood body, bolt on maple neck, 24 fret rosewood fingerboard with pearl trapezoid inlay, standard vibrato, reverse peghead, 6 on one side tuners, gold hardware, humbucker/single coil/humbucker covered pickups, volume/tone control, 5 position/mini switches. Curr. mfr.

Mfr.'s Sug. Retail	$450	$315	$270	$225	$180	$160	$150	$135

EM-2 — similar to EM-1, except has double locking Floyd Rose vibrato.

Mfr.'s Sug. Retail	$550	$385	$330	$275	$220	$200	$180	$165

Grading	100%	98%	95%	90%	80%	70%	60%

EMPEROR — single rounded cutaway hollow style, arched bound maple top, f holes, bound tortoise shell pickguard with stylized E logo and Joe Pass' signature, maple back/sides/neck, 20 fret bound rosewood fingerboard with pearl block inlay, adjustable rosewood bridge/stylized trapeze tailpiece, bound peghead wtih pearl vine/logo inlay, 3 per side tuners, gold hardware, 2 humbucker covered pickups with exposed screws, 2 volume/tone controls, 3 position switch. Available in Sunburst finish. Curr. mfr.

Mfr.'s Sug. Retail	$730	$510	$440	$365	$290	$260	$240	$220

This model has laminated body and neck wood.

G-310 — double sharp cutaway mahogany body, black pickguard, mahognay neck, 22 fret rosewood fingerboard with pearl dot inlay, tunomatic bridge/stop tailpiece, black face peghead with pearl logo inlay, 3 per side tuners, chrome hardware, 2 humbucker covered pickups, 2 volume/tone controls, 3 postion switch. Curr. mfr.

Mfr.'s Sug. Retail	$340	$235	$200	$170	$135	$125	$115	$105

G-400 — similar to G-310, except has smaller pickguard, exposed pickups.

Mfr.'s Sug. Retail	$450	$315	$270	$225	$180	$160	$150	$135

LES PAUL CUSTOM — Les Paul style mahogany body, arched bound maple top, raised black pickguard, mahogany neck, 22 fret bound rosewood fingerboard with pearl block inlay, tunomatic bridge/stop tailpiece, bound peghead with pearl split diamond/logo inlay, 3 per side tuners, gold hardware, 2 humbucker pickups, 2 volume/tone controls, 3 position switch. Available in Black and White finish. Mfd. 1990 to date.

Mfr.'s Sug. Retail	$730	$510	$440	$365	$290	$260	$240	$220

This is a Gibson authorized version of the Gibson Les Paul Custom.

Les Paul Standard — similar to Les Paul Custom, except has figured maple top, white pickguard, trapezoid fingerboard inlay, unbound peghead with with model name and logo inlay, pearl tuner buttons, chrome hardware. Available in Sunburst finish. Mfd. 1991 to date.

Mfr.'s Sug. Retail	$630	$440	$380	$315	$250	$225	$205	$190

This is a Gibson authorized version of the Gibson Les Paul Standard.

S-310 — strat style maple body, black pickguard, bolt on maple neck, 22 fret maple fingerboard with black dot inlay, standard vibrato, 6 on one side tuners, chrome hardware, 3 single coil exposed pickups, volume/2 tone controls, 5 position switch. Available in Black, Red and White finish. Mfd. 1991 to date.

Mfr.'s Sug. Retail	$290	$205	$175	$145	$115	$105	$95	$85

Epiphone , cont.

Grading	100%	98%	95%	90%	80%	70%	60%

SHERATON — double rounded cutaway, arched bound maple top, f holes, raised bound tortoise shell pickguard with stylized E logo, maple back/sides, thru body maple neck, 22 fret bound rosewood fingerboard with pearl/abalone block/triangle inlay, tunomatic bridge/stop tailpiece, bound peghead with pearl vine/logo inlay, 3 per side tuners, gold hardware, 2 humbucker covered pickups with exposed screws, 2 volume/tone controls, 3 position switch. Curr. mfr.

Mfr.'s Sug. Retail	$650	$455	$390	$325	$260	$235	$215	$195

This model has laminated body and neck wood.

USA CORONET — offset double cutaway mahogany body, white pickguard, mahognay neck, 24 fret bound rosewood finger-board with pearl block inlay, tunomatic bridge/stop tailpiece, black face reverse peghead with logo/USA inscription, 6 on one side tuners, gold hardware, single coil/humbucker exposed pickups, volume/tone control, 5 position switch control, active electronics. Available in Black, California Coral, Cherry, Pacific Blue, Sunburst, Sunset Yellow and White finish. Mfd. 1991 to date.

Mfr.'s Sug. Retail	$900	$630	$540	$450	$360	$325	$300	$275

Add $100 for double locking Floyd Rose vibrato, black hardware.
This model is made in the USA.

USA PRO — strat style poplar body, bolt on maple neck, 24 fret extended ebony fingerboard with offset pearl dot inlay, "pro" inscribed pearl block inlay at 24th fret, double locking Floyd Rose vibrato, black face peghead with logo/USA inscription, 6 on one side tuners, black hardware, single coil/humbucker exposed pickups, volume/tone control, 3 position switch. Available in Black, California Coral, Cherry, Pacific Blue, Sunburst, Sunset Yellow and White finish. Mfd. 1991 to date.

Mfr.'s Sug. Retail	$600	$420	$360	$300	$240	$215	$195	$180

This model is made in the USA.

ELECTRIC BASS

All instruments in this section are available in Black, Red and White finish, unless otherwise listed.

ACCU BASS — offset double cutaway maple body, black pickguard with thumb rest, bolt on maple neck, 20 fret maple fingerboard with black dot inlay, fixed bridge, body matching peghead with logo inscription, 4 on one side tuners, chrome hardware, P-style exposed pickup, volume/tone control. Curr. mfr.

Mfr.'s Sug. Retail	$370	$260	$220	$185	$150	$135	$120	$110

Grading	100%	98%	95%	90%	80%	70%	60%

EBM-4 — offset sweeping double cutaway basswood body, bolt on maple neck, 24 fret rosewood fingerboard with pearl offset dot inlay, fixed bridge, black face reverse peghead, 4 on one side tuners, chrome hardware, P-style/J-style covered pickups, 2 volume/tone controls. Mfd. 1992 to date.

Mfr.'s Sug. Retail	$580	$405	$350	$290	$230	$205	$190	$175

EBM-5 — similar to EBM-4, except has 5 strings, 5 on one side tuners.

Mfr.'s Sug. Retail	$620	$435	$370	$310	$250	$225	$205	$190

POWER BASS — offset double cutaway maple body, bolt on maple neck, 20 fret rosewood fingerboard with pearl dot inlay, fixed bridge, body matching peghead with logo inscription, 4 on one side tuners, black hardware, P-style/J-style exposed pickups, 2 volume/1 tone controls. Curr. mfr.

Mfr.'s Sug. Retail	$420	$295	$250	$210	$170	$150	$135	$125

ROCK BASS — similar to Power Bass, except has black pickguard with thumb rest and chrome controls cover, chrome hardware, 2 P-style exposed pickups.

Mfr.'s Sug. Retail	$380	$265	$225	$190	$150	$135	$120	$110

ERNIE BALL/MUSIC MAN

Trademark currently owned by Ernie Ball/Music Man, since 1984. Instruments manufactured and distributed by Ernie Ball/Music Man, located in San Luis Obispo, CA.

Having started his career in the music business by becoming one of the first to offer sets of steel strings for fretted instruments, Ernie Ball eventually started manufacturing his own instruments (the Earthwood acoustic bass being among the first).

ELECTRIC

EDWARD VAN HALEN — single cutaway basswood body, bound figured maple top, bolt on maple neck, 22 fret maple fingerboard with black dot inlay, strings thru bridge, 4/2 per side Schaller tuners with pearl buttons, chrome hardware, 2 humbucker Di-Marzio pickups, volume control, 3 position switch. Available in Translucent Gold, Translucent Purple and Translucent Red finish. Curr. mfr.

Mfr.'s Sug. Retail	$1,600	$1,120	$960	$800	$640	$575	$530	$480

Grading	100%	98%	95%	90%	80%	70%	60%

Edward Van Halen Tremolo — similar to Edward Van Halen, except has Floyd Rose double locking vibrato. Available in Black, Metallic Gold, Natural, Sunburst, Transparent Black, Transparent Blue, Transparent Gold, Transparent Pink, Transparent Purple and Transparent Red finish.

Mfr.'s Sug. Retail	$1,750	$1,225	$1,050	$875	$700	$630	$575	$525

SILHOUETTE — offset double cutaway alder, ash or poplar body, white pickguard, bolt on maple neck, 24 fret maple fingerboard with black dot inlay, strings thru bridge, 4/2 per side Schaller tuners, chrome hardware, 2 humbucker or 3 single coil DiMarzio pickups, volume/tone control, 3 or 5 position switch. Available in Black, Natural, Sunburst, Transparent Blueburst, Transparent Teal, Transparent Red and White finish. Curr. mfr.

Mfr.'s Sug. Retail	$925	$650	$555	$465	$370	$335	$305	$280

Add $200 for double locking vibrato.
Add $50 for 2 single coil/1 humbucker pickups.
Add $75 for humbucker/single coil/humbucker pickups.

STEVE MORSE — offset double cutaway poplar body, black pickguard, bolt-on maple neck, 22 fret rosewood fingerboard with pearl dot inlay, tunomatic bridge/stop tailpiece, 4/2 per side Schaller tuners, chrome hardware, humbucker/2 single coil/humbucker DiMarzio pickups, volume/tone control, 3 position and 2 mini switches. Available in Transparent Blueburst finish. Curr. mfr.

Mfr.'s Sug. Retail	$1,500	$1,050	$900	$750	$600	$540	$495	$450

Add $150 for double locking vibrato.

ELECTRIC BASS

SILHOUETTE BASS GUITAR — offset double cutaway poplar body, bolt-on maple neck, 22 fret maple fingerboard with black dot inlay, strings thru bridge, 4/2 per side Schaller tuners, chrome hardware, 2 humbucker DiMarzio pickups, volume/tone/series-parallel control, 5 way position switch. Available in Black finish. Curr. mfr.

Mfr.'s Sug. Retail	$1,800	$1,260	$1,080	$900	$720	$650	$595	$540

STING RAY — offset double cutaway alder, ash or poplar body, white pickguard, bolt-on maple neck, 21 fret maple fingerboard with black dot inlay, fixed bridge, 3/1 per side Schaller tuners, chrome hardware, humbucker alnico pickup, volume/treble/bass control, active electronics. Available in Black, Natural, Sunburst, Transparent Blueburst, Transparent Teal, Transparent Red and White finish. Curr. mfr.

Mfr.'s Sug. Retail	$1,100	$770	$660	$550	$440	$395	$365	$330

Add $50 for treble/mid/bass control.
This model also available with rosewood fingerboard with pearl dot inlay or pau ferro fretless fingerboard.

Grading	100%	98%	95%	90%	80%	70%	60%

⚡ **Sting Ray 5** — similar to Sting Ray, except has 5 strings, 4/1 per side tuners, treble/mid/bass control, 3 position switch.

Mfr.'s Sug. Retail	$1,500	$1,050	$900	$750	$600	$540	$495	$450

ESP

Manufactured by the ESP Factory 21 in Tokyo, Japan. Importation began in the U.S. during 1985. Currently distributed by The ESP Guitar Company, Inc. located in New York, NY.

ELECTRIC

HORIZON CUSTOM — strat style arched top ash body, thru-body maple neck, 24 fret bound ebony fingerboard with pearl ESP block inlay at 12th fret, double locking vibrato, bound peghead, 3 per side tuners, black hardware, single coil/humbucker EMG pickups, volume/tone control, 3 position switch. Available in Black, Candy Apple Red, Gunmetal Blue, Metallic Green, Metallic Purple and Pearl White finish. Mfd. 1991 to date.

Mfr.'s Sug. Retail	$2,195	$1,540	$1,320	$1,100	$880	$790	$725	$660

⚡ **Horizon Deluxe** — similar to Horizon Custom, except has bolt-on neck and gold hardware. Available in Black, Pearl White, Transparent Blue, Transparent Green, Transparent Purple and Transparent Red finish.

Mfr.'s Sug. Retail	$1,895	$1,325	$1,135	$950	$760	$685	$625	$570

Subtract $200 for model with tunomatic bridge/stop tailpiece.

M-II CUSTOM — strat style alder body, thru body maple neck, 24 fret rosewood bound fingerboard with pearl offset block inlay, pearl ESP block inlay at 12th fret, double locking vibrato, reverse bound peghead, 6 on one side tuners, black hardware, single coil/humbucker ESP pickups, volume control, 3 position switch. Available in Black, Candy Apple Red, Gunmetal Blue, Metallic Green, Metallic Purple and Pearl White finish. Mfd. 1991 to date.

Mfr.'s Sug. Retail	$2,095	$1,465	$1,255	$1,045	$840	$755	$685	$625

⚡ **M-II Deluxe** — similar to M-II Custom, except has bolt-on neck, unbound fingerboard with pearl dot inlay and unbound peghead.

Mfr.'s Sug. Retail	$1,295	$905	$775	$645	$515	$465	$425	$385

This model is also available with a maple fingerboard.

Grading	100%	98%	95%	90%	80%	70%	60%

S-500 — strat style ash body, bolt-on maple neck, 22 fret rosewood fingerboard with pearl dot inlay, vintage vibrato, graphite nut 6 on one side locking Sperzel tuners, gold hardware, 2 single coil/1 humbucker ESP pickups, volume/tone control, 5 position switch. Available in Black, Pearl White, Transparent Blue, Transparent Green, Transparent Purple and Transparent Red finish. Mfd. 1991 to date.

Mfr.'s Sug. Retail	$1,495	$1,045	$895	$750	$600	$540	$495	$450

Add $200 for locking vibrato.

ELECTRIC BASS

HORIZON-4 — offset double cutaway alder body, thru body maple neck, 24 fret bound ebony fingerboard with offset pearl inlay, pearl Horizon block inlay at 12th fret, fixed bridge, bound peghead, 2 per side tuners, black hardware, P-style/J-style EMG pickups, volume/bass/treble and mix controls, active electronics. Available in Black, Candy Apple Red, Gunmetal Blue, Metallic Green, Metallic Purple and Pearl White finish. Mfd. 1991 to date.

Mfr.'s Sug. Retail	$2,195	$1,540	$1,320	$1,100	$880	$790	$725	$660

Horizon-5 — similar to Horizon-4, except has 5 strings.

Mfr.'s Sug. Retail	$2,395	$1,675	$1,435	$1,195	$955	$855	$785	$715

FENDER

Trademark established circa 1946. Currently manufactured in the U.S., Korea, and Mexico, and distrib-
uted by Fender Musical Instruments Corporation located in Scottsdale, AZ.

Originally started as the K & F company in 1945, Leo Fender began modestly building small amplifiers and electric guitars with his partner, Doc Kaufman. Leo then formed the Fender Instrument Co. in 1946, located on South Pomona Avenue in Fullerton, California. The company sales expanded rapidly and soon, Fender's inventive genius began both designing and marketing new models through the early 1950s and early 1960s. By 1964, Fender's line of products included electric guitars, basses, steel guitars, effects units, acoustic guitars, electric pianos and a variety of accessories. Leo's failing health forced him to put the company up for sale, and it was purchased by CBS in early 1965. Later, he worked for the Music Man company, and in 1980, he formed the G & L company with George Fullerton, where he continued to produce innovative designs until his death in March of 1991.

In the early 1980's, the Fender guitar empire began to crumble. Many cost-cutting factors and management problems forced CBS to try various last ditch efforts to salvage the instrument line. CBS finally sold the company in January 1985 to an investment group headed by Fender executives. Because the sale did not include factory buildings, USA guitar production ceased in 1985 (with the exception of some custom instruments). Only models built by Fender of Japan were featured in the 1985 Fender catalog. Soon after, a new factory was built in Corona, California, and USA production was restored in 1986 and continues to this day. Also, in 1990, the Fender company built a Mexican assembly facility to offset rising costs of oriental production due to the weakening of the American dollar in the international market. The Fender company currently manufactures instruments in the United States, Mexico, Japan and Korea.

Visual Identification Features

When trying to determine the date of an instrument's production, it is useful to know a few things about feature changes that have occurred over the years. The following information may help you to determine the approximate date of manufacture of a Fender instrument by visual observation, without having to handle (or disassemble) the instrument for serial number varification.

Fingerboard Construction

From 1950 to 1959, all necks were made out of a solid piece of maple with the frets being driven right into the neck, this is the standard design for maple necks.

Grading	100%	98%	95%	90%	80%	70%	60%

From 1959 to 1962, the maple neck was planed flat and a rosewood fingerboard with frets and inlay was glued to the top of the neck. This is known as the "slab top" fingerboard.

From 1962 to 1983, the maple necks were rounded to the neck's radius and a thinner piece of rosewood being glued to the neck area. This design is called the "veneer" fingerboard.

From 1983 to date, Fender returned to the "slab top" fingerboard design of the 1959 to 1962 era.

Neckplate Identification

From 1950 to 1971, the neck was attached to the body by means of a 4 screw neckplate.

From 1971 to 1981, the neckplate was changed to 3 screws, with a micro neck adjustment device being added.

In 1981, a transition from the 3 screw design back to the 4 screw design began to occur.

By 1983, the 4 screw neckplate was back in standard production, with the micro neck adjuster remaining.

ACOUSTIC

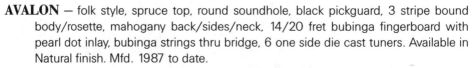

Korean Production Flat Tops

These instruments have strat style headstocks and set necks, unless otherwise listed.

AVALON — folk style, spruce top, round soundhole, black pickguard, 3 stripe bound body/rosette, mahogany back/sides/neck, 14/20 fret bubinga fingerboard with pearl dot inlay, bubinga strings thru bridge, 6 one side die cast tuners. Available in Natural finish. Mfd. 1987 to date.

Mfr.'s Sug. Retail	$370	$260	$220	$185	$150	$135	$120	$110

CATALINA —dreadnought style, spruce top, round soundhole, black pickguard, 3 stripe bound body/rosette, mahogany back/sides/neck, 14/20 fret rosewood fingerboard with pearl dot inlay, rosewood bridge with white black dot pins, 6 on one side diecast tuners. Available in Black finish. Mfd. 1987 to date.

Mfr.'s Sug. Retail	$440	$310	$265	$220	$175	$160	$145	$135

CONCORD — similar to Catalina, except has bubinga fingerboard/bridge. Available in Natural finish. Mfd. 1987 to date.

Mfr.'s Sug. Retail	$370	$260	$220	$185	$150	$135	$120	$110

Grading	100%	98%	95%	90%	80%	70%	60%

MALIBU — dreadnought style, sycamore top, round soundhole, black pickguard, sycamore back/sides, mahogany neck, 14/20 fret rosewood fingerboard with pearl dot inlay, rosewood bridge with white black dot inlay, 6 on one side diecast tuners. Available in Dark Violin Sunburst finish. Mfd. 1987 to date.

Mfr.'s Sug. Retail	$450	$315	$270	$225	$180	$160	$150	$135

NEWPORTER — dreadnought style, mahogany top, round soundhole, black pickguard, 3 stripe bound body/rosette, mahogany back/sides/neck, 14/20 fret rosewood fingerboard with pearl dot inlay, rosewood bridge with white black dot pins, 6 on one side diecast tuners. Available in Natural finish. Curr. mfr.

Mfr.'s Sug. Retail	$380	$265	$225	$190	$150	$135	$120	$110

REDONDO — dreadnought style, spruce top, round soundhole, black pickguard, 3 stripe bound body/rosette, mahogany back/sides/neck, 14/20 fret rosewood fingerboard with pearl dot inlay, rosewood bridge with white black dot pins, 6 on one side diecast tuners. Available in Natural finish. Curr. mfr.

Mfr.'s Sug. Retail	$390	$275	$235	$195	$155	$140	$125	$115

SAN LUIS REY — dreadnought style, solid spruce top, round soundhole, black pickguard, rosewood back/sides, mahogany neck, 14/20 fret rosewood fingerboard with pearl snowflake inlay, 6 on one side chrome tuners. Available in Natural finish. Mfd. 1990 to date.

Mfr.'s Sug. Retail	$525	$370	$315	$260	$210	$190	$170	$160

SANTA MARIA — dreadnought style, spruce top, round soundhole, tortoise shell pickguard, 3 stripe bound body/rosette, mahogany back/sides/neck, 14/20 fret rosewood fingerboard with pearl dot inlay, rosewood bridge with white black dot pins, 6 per side diecast tuners. Available in Natural finish. Mfd. 1989 to date.

Mfr.'s Sug. Retail	$410	$285	$245	$205	$165	$145	$135	$125

SAN MARINO — dreadnought style, solid spruce top, round soundhole, black pickguard, 3 stripe bound body/rosette, mahogany back/sides/neck, 14/20 fret rosewood fingerboard with pearl dot inlay, rosewood bridge with white black dot pins, 6 on one side chrome tuners. Available in Natural finish. Mfd. 1989 to date.

Mfr.'s Sug. Retail	$435	$305	$260	$215	$175	$155	$140	$130

SAN MIGUEL — single round cutaway dreadnought style, spruce top, round soundhole, black pickguard, 3 stripe bound body/rosette, mahogany back/sides/neck, 14/20 fret rosewood fingerboard with pearl dot inlay, rosewood bridge with white black dot pins, 6 on one side tuners. Available in Natural finish. Curr. mfr.

Mfr.'s Sug. Retail	$430	$300	$260	$215	$175	$155	$140	$130

This model also available in left handed version.

Fender, cont.

Grading	100%	98%	95%	90%	80%	70%	60%

SX Series

This series is manufactured in Korea.

1000SX — dreadnought style, solid spruce top, round soundhole, 3 stripe bound body/rosette, mahogany back/sides/neck, 14/20 fret rosewood fingerboard with pearl dot inlay, strings thru rosewood bridge, bound rosewood veneered peghead with pearl logo inlay, 3 per side chrome tuners. Available in Natural finish. New 1993.

Mfr.'s Sug. Retail	$630	$440	$380	$315	$250	$225	$205	$190

1100SX — similar to 1000SX, except has rosewood back/sides, ebony fingerboard/bridge, gold tuners.

Mfr.'s Sug. Retail	$765	$535	$460	$385	$305	$275	$250	$230

1105SXE — similar to 1000SX, except has rosewood back/sides, ebony fingerboard/bridge, gold tuners, piezo pickup, volume/treble/bass/mix controls.

Mfr.'s Sug. Retail	$865	$605	$520	$435	$345	$310	$285	$260

1200SX — dreadnought style, solid spruce top, round soundhole, 3 stripe bound body/rosette, mahogany back/sides/neck, 14/20 fret rosewood fingerboard with pearl dot inlay, strings thru rosewood bridge, bound rosewood veneered peghead with pearl logo inlay, 3 per side chrome tuners. Available in Natural finish. New 1993.

Mfr.'s Sug. Retail	$945	$665	$570	$475	$375	$340	$310	$280

1300SX — similar to 1200SX, except has rosewood back/sides, ebony fingerboard with pearl snowflake inlay, ebony bridge, gold tuners.

Mfr.'s Sug. Retail	$1,150	$805	$690	$575	$460	$415	$380	$345

1500SX — jumbo style, solid spruce top, round soundhole, black pickguard, rosewood back/sides, mahogany neck, 14/20 fret rosewood fingerboard with pearl block inlay, strings thru rosewood bridge, bound rosewood veneered peghead with pearl logo inlay, 3 per side gold tuners. Available in Natural finish. New 1993.

Mfr.'s Sug. Retail	$945	$665	$570	$475	$375	$340	$310	$280

1505SX — similar to 1500SX, except has sycamore back/sides. Available in Sunburst top finish.

Mfr.'s Sug. Retail	$995	$695	$595	$500	$400	$360	$330	$300

1600SXE — similar to 1500SX, except has piezo pickup, volume/treble/back/mix controls.

Mfr.'s Sug. Retail	$1,045	$735	$630	$525	$415	$375	$340	$310

Grading	100%	98%	95%	90%	80%	70%	60%

LA BREA — single round cutaway dreadnought style, spruce top, round soundhole, black pickguard, 3 stripe bound body/rosette, mahogany back/sides/neck, 21 fret rosewood fingerboard with pearl dot inlay, rosewood bridge with white black dot pins, strat style peghead, 6 on one side chrome tuners, acoustic pickup, volume/tone control. Available in Black, Natural and Sunburst finish. Mfd. 1987 to date.

Mfr.'s Sug. Retail	$580	$405	$350	$290	$230	$205	$190	$175

 Add $40 for flame maple top/back/sides/neck.

MONTARA — single round cutaway dreadnought style, spruce top, oval soundhole, bound body, multi-ring rosette, mahogany back/sides/neck, convex back, 21 fret rosewood fingerboard with pearl dot inlay, rosewood bridge with white pins, strat style peghead, 6 on one side die cast tuners with pearl buttons, acoustic pickup, volume/treble/mid/bass controls. Available in Black, Natural and Sunburst finish. Mfd. 1990 to date.

Mfr.'s Sug. Retail	$775	$540	$460	$385	$310	$280	$255	$230

 Add $95 for flame maple top/back/sides/neck.

TELECOUSTIC STANDARD — single rounded cutaway style, spruce top, oval soundhole, basswood back/sides, maple neck, 22 fret rosewood fingerboard, rosewood bridge with white pins, 6 on one side chrome tuners with plastic buttons, piezo bridge pickup, volume/treble/bass slide controls. Available in Antique Burst, Black and Natural finish. New 1993.

Mfr.'s Sug. Retail	$960	$670	$575	$480	$385	$350	$320	$290

Telecoustic Custom — similar to Telecoustic Standard, except has bound solid spruce top, mahogany back/sides/neck, pao ferro fingerboard, pau ferro/ebony laminate bridge, Schaller tuners with pearl buttons, active electronics. Available in Antique Burst and Natural finish.

Mfr.'s Sug. Retail	$2,100	$1,475	$1,260	$1,050	$840	$755	$690	$630

Telecoustic Deluxe — similar to Telecoustic Standard, except has mahogany back/sides/neck, rosewood/ebony laminate bridge, pearl tuner buttons.

Mfr.'s Sug. Retail	$2,100	$1,475	$1,260	$1,050	$840	$755	$690	$630

ELECTRIC

Add 100% to 200% for Custom Colors finishes on models listed below.
Instruments with Custom Colors finishes are more desirable than instruments with standard finishes. The rarer the finish, the higher the price you can expect to pay for that instrument.

ARROW — Refer to the "Swinger" model.

BRONCO — offset double cutaway poplar body, white pickguard, bolt on maple neck, 22 fret rosewood fingerboard with pearl dot inlay, standard vibrato, covered single coil pickup, volume/tone control. Available in Black, Red and White finish. Mfd. 1967-1980.

	$275	$195	$165	$140	$110	$100	$90

Grading	100%	98%	95%	90%	80%	70%	60%

CUSTOM — offset double cutaway asymmetrical body with point on bottom bout, tortoise shell pickguard, bolt-on maple neck, 21 fret bound rosewood fingerboard with pearl block inlay, floating bridge/vibrato with bridge cover, droopy peghead, 3 per side tuners, chrome hardware, 2 split covered pickups, volume/tone control, 4 position rotary switch. Available in Sunburst top/Black back finish. Mfd. 1969-1970.

	$1,000	$700	$600	$500	$400	$360	$330

This instrument was also named the Maverick which appears on the peghead. It was designed primarily to use up Electric XII parts.

CORONADO — double rounded cutaway semi hollow bound beech body, arched top, f holes, raised white pickguard, bolt-on maple neck, 21 fret rosewood fingerboard with pearl dot inlay, adjustable rosewood bridge/trapeze tailpiece, 6 on one side tuners, chrome hardware, single coil covered pickup, volume/tone control. Available in Cherry, Custom Colors and Sunburst finish. Mfd. 1966-1970.

	$425	$295	$250	$210	$170	$150	$135

This model was also offered with checkered binding, gold pickguard and tunomatic bridge/vibrato tailpiece.

Coronado II Wildwood — similar to Coronado, except has dye-injected beechwood body, bound f holes, white pickguard with engraved Wildwood/I-VI, bound fingerboard with block inlay, tunomatic bridge/vibrato trapeze tailpiece, pearl tuner buttons, 2 single coil covered pickups, 2 volume/2 tone controls, 3 position switch. Available in Natural finish. Mfd. 1967-1970.

	$625	$440	$375	$310	$250	$225	$205

Wildwood models were offered with 6 different types of dye applied to the wood. Pickguard numbers (I-VI) refer to the dye color and finish of the instrument.

Coronado XII Wildwood — similar to Coronado, except has 12 strings, dye-injected beechwood body, bound f holes, white pickguard with engraved Wildwood/I-VI, bound fingerboard with block inlay, tunomatic bridge/trapeze tailpiece, ebony tailpiece insert with pearl F inlay, 6 per side tuners with pearl buttons, 2 single coil covered pickups, 2 volume/2 tone controls, 3 position switch. Available in Natural finish. Mfd. 1967-1970.

	$625	$440	$375	$310	$250	$225	$205

Wildwood models were offered with 6 different types of dye applied to the wood. Pickguard numbers (I-VI) refer to the dye color and finish of instrument.

Grading	100%	98%	95%	90%	80%	70%	60%

DUO-SONIC — offset double cutaway hardwood $\frac{3}{4}$ size body, metal pickguard, bolt-on maple neck, 21 fret rosewood fingerboard with pearl dot inlay, fixed bridge with cover, 6 on one side tuners with plastic buttons, chrome hardware, 2 single coil covered pickups, volume/tone control, 3 position switch. Available in Blond, Custom Colors and Sunburst finish. Mfd. 1956-1964.

	$375	$260	$220	$185	$150	$135	$120

This model was released as a student model.

In 1960, tortoise shell or white plastic pickguard replaced metal pickguard.

Duo-Sonic II— similar to Duo-Sonic, except has asymmetrical waist body, restyled plastic/metal pickguard, 22 fret fingerboard, enlarged peghead, 2 pickup selector slide switches. Available in Blue, Red and White finish. Mfd. 1964-1969.

	$400	$280	$240	$200	$160	$145	$130

This instrument has a longer scale length than its predecessor.

ELECTRIC XII — offset double cutaway asymmetrical body, tortoise shell pickguard, bolt-on maple neck, 21 fret rosewood fingerboard with pearl dot inlay, strings thru bridge, droopy peghead, 6 per side tuners, chrome hardware, 2 split covered pickups, volume/tone controls, 4 position rotary switch. Available in Custom Colors and Sunburst finish. Mfd. 1965-1968.

	$950	$665	$570	$475	$380	$345	$315

In 1965, the fingerboard was bound.

In 1966, block fingerboard inlay replaced dot inlay.

ESQUIRE — single cutaway ash body, black pickguard, bolt-on maple neck, 21 fret maple fingerboard with black dot inlay, strings thru bridge with cover, 6 on one side tuners, chrome hardware, single coil pickup, volume/tone control, 3 position switch, controls mounted on metal plate. Available in Butterscotch Blond finish. Mfd. 1950-1969.

1950-1954	$6,500	$4,550	$3,900	$3,250	$2,600	$2,340	$2,145
1955-1959	$4,500	$3,150	$2,700	$2,250	$1,800	$1,620	$1,485
1960-1964	$3,000	$2,095	$1,800	$1,500	$1,200	$1,080	$990
1965-1969	$1,750	$1,225	$1,050	$875	$700	$630	$575

A few early models of this instrument were produced with 2 single coil pickups. First runs on this series were sparse and no instruments were made in the latter part of 1950.

In 1955, white pickguard replaced black pickguard.

In 1958, fixed bridge replaced original item.

In 1959, rosewood fingerboard with pearl dot inlay replaced original item.

In 1960, a strings thru bridge was re-instated as standard.

In 1967, maple fingerboard was optionally available.

In 1969, maple fingerboard became standard.

Grading	100%	98%	95%	90%	80%	70%	60%

⚵ **Esquire Custom** — similar to Esquire, except has bound body, white pickguard, rosewood fingerboard with pearl dot inlay. Available in Sunburst finish. Mfd. 1960-1970.

	100%	98%	95%	90%	80%	70%	60%
1960-1964	$5,000	$3,500	$3,000	$2,500	$2,000	$1,800	$1,650
1965-1970	$2,400	$1,680	$1,440	$1,200	$960	$860	$790

JAGUAR — offset double cutaway asymmetrical alder body, metal/plastic pickguard, bolt-on maple neck, 22 fret rosewood fingerboard with pearl dot inlay, string mute, floating bridge/vibrato, bridge cover plate, 6 on one side tuners, chrome hardware, 2 single coil exposed pickups, volume/tone control, volume/tone roller control, preset slide switch, 3 preset slide switches. Available in Custom Colors and Sunburst finish. Mfd. 1962-1975.

	100%	98%	95%	90%	80%	70%	60%
1962-1964	$1,150	$805	$690	$575	$460	$415	$380
1965-1975	$750	$525	$450	$375	$300	$270	$245

Add 20% for ash body with gold hardware and Blonde finish.
In 1965, the fingerboard was bound.
In 1966, block fingerboard inlay replaced dot inlay.

JAZZMASTER — offset double cutaway asymmetrical alder body, gold metal pickguard, bolt-on maple neck, 21 fret rosewood fingerboard with pearl dot inlay, floating bridge/vibrato, bridge cover plate, 6 on one side tuners, chrome hardware, 2 single coil exposed pickups, volume/tone control, volume/tone roller control, 3 position switch, preset selector slide switch. Available in Custom Colors and Sunburst finish. Mfd. 1958-1980.

	100%	98%	95%	90%	80%	70%	60%
1958-1959	$2,500	$1,750	$1,500	$1,250	$1,000	$900	$825
1960-1964	$1,500	$1,050	$900	$750	$600	$540	$495
1965-1980	$750	$525	$450	$375	$300	$270	$245

Add 20% for ash body with gold hardware and Blonde finish.
In 1960, tortoise shell pickguard replaced metal pickguard.
In 1965, the fingerboard was bound.
In 1966, block fingerboard inlay replaced dot inlay.
In 1976, black pickguard replaced tortoise shell pickguard.

LEAD I — offset double cutaway alder body, black pickguard, bolt on maple neck, 21 fret maple fingerboard with black dot inlay, strings thru bridge, 6 on one side tuners, chrome hardware, humbucker exposed pickup, 2 two position switches. Available in Black and Brown finish. Mfd. 1979-1982.

	100%	98%	95%	90%	80%	70%	60%
	$325	$225	$195	$160	$130	$115	$105

In 1981, Custom Colors became optional.

Grading	100%	98%	95%	90%	80%	70%	60%

Lead II — similar to Lead I, except has 2 single coil exposed pickups.

| | $350 | $245 | $210 | $175 | $140 | $125 | $115 |

Lead III — similar to Lead I, except has 2 humbuckers. Mfd. 1981-1982.

| | $350 | $245 | $210 | $175 | $140 | $125 | $115 |

LTD — single rounded cutaway hollow figured maple body, arched bound spruce top, f holes, raised tortoise shell pickguard, bolt-on maple neck, 20 fret bound ebony fingerboard with pearl "diamond-in-block" inlay, adjustable ebony bridge/metal trapeze tailpiece, ebony tailpiece insert with pearl F inlay, bound peghead with pearl "mirrored F"/logo inlay, 3 per side tuners with pearl buttons, gold hardware, covered humbucker pickup, volume/tone control. Available in Sunburst finish. Mfd. 1968-1974.

| | $2,800 | $1,960 | $1,680 | $1,400 | $1,120 | $1,010 | $925 |

MAVERICK — Refer to the "Custom" Model.

MONTEGO I— single rounded cutaway hollow figured maple body, arched bound spruce top, bound f holes, raised black pickguard, bolt-on maple neck, 20 fret bound ebony fingerboard with pearl "diamond-in-block" inlay, adjustable ebony bridge/metal trapeze tailpiece, ebony tailpiece insert with pearl F inlay, bound peghead with pearl fan/logo inlay, 3 per side tuners with pearl buttons, chrome hardware, covered humbucker pickup, volume/tone control. Available in Natural and Sunburst finish. Mfd. 1968-1974.

| | $800 | $560 | $480 | $400 | $320 | $290 | $265 |

Montego II — similar to Montego I, except has 2 humbucker pickups, 2 volume/2 tone controls, 3 position switch.

| | $1,000 | $700 | $600 | $500 | $400 | $360 | $330 |

MUSICLANDER — Refer to the "Swinger" Model.

MUSICMASTER —offset double cutaway poplar body, metal pickguard, bolt on maple neck, 21 fret maple fingerboard with black dot inlay, fixed bridge with cover, 6 on one side tuners, chrome hardware, single coil covered pickup, volume/tone control. Available in Blonde, Custom Colors and Sunburst finish. Mfd. 1956-1964.

| | $450 | $315 | $270 | $225 | $180 | $160 | $150 |

In 1959, rosewood fingerboard with pearl dot inlay replaced maple fingerboard.
In 1960, pickguard was changed to plastic: tortoise shell or white.

Fender , cont.

Grading	100%	98%	95%	90%	80%	70%	60%

≼ **Musicmaster II** — similar to Musicmaster, except has asymmetrical body, restyled pearloid pickguard, control mounted metal plate, enlarged peghead. Available in Blue, Red and White finish. Mfd. 1964-1975.

	100%	98%	95%	90%	80%	70%	60%
	$350	$245	$210	$175	$140	$125	$115

In 1969, 24 fret fingerboard replaced 21 fret fingerboard.

≼ **Musicmaster, Later Mfr.** — similar to Musicmaster, except has asymmetrical body, black pickguard, 22 fret fingerboard. Available in Black and White finish. Mfd. 1975-1980.

	100%	98%	95%	90%	80%	70%	60%
	$275	$195	$165	$140	$110	$100	$90

This model also available with alder or ash body.

MUSTANG — offset double cutaway asymmetrical ash body, pearloid or shell pickguard, bolt-on maple neck, 21 or 22 fret rosewood fingerboard with pearl dot inlay, floating bridge/vibrato with bridge cover, 6 on one side tuners with plastic buttons, chrome hardware, 2 single coil covered pickups, volume/tone control, 2 selector slide switches. Available in Black, Blonde, Blue, Natural, Sunburst, Red, Walnut and White finish. Mfd. 1964-1981.

	100%	98%	95%	90%	80%	70%	60%
	$275	$195	$165	$140	$110	$100	$90

In 1969, 22 fret fingerboard became standard.

In the 1970's, Black, Blonde, Natural, Sunburst and Walnut were the standard finishes.

In 1975, tuners buttons became metal; black pickguard replaced original item.

≼ **Competition Mustang** — similar to Mustang, except has Competition finishes (finishes with 3 racing stripes). Available in Blue, Burgundy, Orange and Red finish. Mfd. 1968-1973.

	100%	98%	95%	90%	80%	70%	60%
	$300	$210	$180	$150	$120	$110	$100

D'AQUISTO — single rounded cutaway hollow figured maple body, arched bound spruce top, bound f holes, maple neck, raised bound ebony pickguard, 20 fret bound ebony fingerboard with pearl block inlay, adjustable ebony bridge/ebony trapeze tailpiece, bound peghead with pearl vase/logo inlay, 3 per side tuners with ebony buttons, gold hardware, exposed humbucker pickup, volume/tone control. Available in Natural finish. Mfd. 1984, 1989 to date.

Mfr.'s Sug. Retail	100%	98%	95%	90%	80%	70%	60%
	$2,000	$1,400	$1,200	$1,000	$800	$720	$660	$600

This model was designed by master luthier James D'Aquisto.

Grading	100%	98%	95%	90%	80%	70%	60%

ROBBEN FORD — double cutaway alder body, hollowed tone chambers, arched bound spruce top, maple neck, 22 jumbo fret bound ebony fingerboard with pearl split block inlay, tunomatic bridge/stop tailpiece, bound peghead with pearl stylized fan/logo inlay, 3 per side tuners with ebony buttons gold hardware, 2 exposed humbucker pickups, 2 volume/tone controls, 3 position/coil tap switches. Available in Antique Burst, Autumn Gold and Black finish. Mfd. 1989 to date.

Mfr.'s Sug. Retail	$1,750	$1,225	$1,050	$875	$700	$630	$575	$525

This model has Robben Ford's signature on the truss rod cover.

STARCASTER — offset double cutaway asymmetrical semi hollow maple body, bound arched top, f holes, raised black pickguard, bolt-on maple neck, 22 fret maple fingerboard with black dot inlay, fixed bridge, 6 on one side tuners, chrome hardware, 2 covered humbucker pickups, master volume/2 volume/2 tone controls, 3 position switch. Available in Black, Blond, Natural, Tobacco Sunburst, Walnut and White finish. Mfd. 1976-1980.

	$850	$595	$510	$425	$340	$305	$280

SWINGER — offset double cutaway asymmetrical alder body with cutaway on bottom bout, pearloid pickguard, bolt-on maple neck, 21 fret rosewood fingerboard with pearl dot inlay, fixed bridge, pointed peghead, 6 on one side tuners, chrome hardware, single coil covered pickup, volume/tone control. Available in Black, Blue, Green and Red finish. Mfd. 1969 only.

	$1,025	$720	$615	$510	$410	$370	$340

This model was also known as the Arrow and/or the Musiclander.

U.S. PRODIGY — offset double cutaway asymmetrical poplar body, black pickguard, bolt-on maple neck, 22 fret rosewood fingerboard with pearl dot inlay, standard vibrato, 6 on one side tuners, 2 single coil/1 humbucker exposed pickups, volume/tone controls, 5 position switch. Available in Arctic White, Black, Crimson Red Metallic and Lake Placid Blue finish. Mfd. 1991 to date.

Mfr.'s Sug. Retail	$570	$400	$340	$285	$230	$205	$190	$170

This model is also available with maple fingerboard with black dot inlay.

Bullet Series

Models in this series have strat style alder body, white pickguard, bolt-on maple neck, 22 fret maple fingerboard with black dot inlay, fixed bridge, telecaster style peghead, 6 on one side tuners, chrome hardware, fixed bridge, volume/tone control, unless otherwise listed. Available in Ivory, Red, Metallic Red, Sunburst, Walnut and White finish.

Grading	100%	98%	95%	90%	80%	70%	60%

BULLET — tele style body, 22 fret rosewood fingerboard with pearl dot inlay, 2 single coil covered pickups, 3 position switch. Mfd. 1981-1983.

| | $150 | $105 | $90 | $75 | $60 | $55 | $50 |

This model also available with black pickguard.

In 1983, the body was changed to strat style alder body, known as the second version of the Bullet.

Bullet Deluxe — tele style mahogany body, 22 fret rosewood fingerboard with pearl dot inlay, strings thru bridge, 2 single coil covered pickups, 3 position switch.

| | $175 | $120 | $105 | $90 | $70 | $65 | $60 |

This model also available with black pickguard.

Bullet H-1 — covered humbucker pickup, push button coil split switch. Mfd. 1983 only.

| | $215 | $150 | $130 | $105 | $85 | $75 | $70 |

Bullet H-2 — strings thru bridge, 2 covered humbucker pickups, 3 position switch, 2 push button coil split switches. Mfd. 1983 only.

| | $230 | $160 | $135 | $115 | $90 | $80 | $70 |

Bullet S-2 — laminated plastic pickguard, strings thru bridge, 2 single coil covered pickups, 3 position switch. Mfd. 1983 only.

| | $225 | $160 | $135 | $115 | $90 | $80 | $70 |

Bullet S-3 — strings thru bridge, 3 single coil covered pickups, 5 position switch. Mfd. 1983 only.

| | $250 | $175 | $150 | $125 | $100 | $90 | $80 |

Limited Edition Series

All instruments in this series are custom order, limited edition instruments.

'62 JAGUAR — offset double cutaway asymmetrical alder body, metal/plastic pickguard, bolt-on maple neck, 22 fret rosewood fingerboard with pearl dot inlay, string mute, floating bridge/vibrato, bridge cover plate, 6 on one side tuners, chrome hardware, 2 single coil exposed pickups, volume/tone control, volume/tone roller control, preset slide switch, 3 preset slide switches. Available in Candy Apple Red, Vintage White and 3 Tone Sunburst finish. Curr. mfr.

| Mfr.'s Sug. Retail | $750 | $525 | $450 | $375 | $300 | $270 | $245 | $225 |

Grading	100%	98%	95%	90%	80%	70%	60%

'62 JAZZMASTER — offset double cutaway asymmetrical alder body, gold metal pickguard, bolt-on maple neck, 21 fret rosewood fingerboard with pearl dot inlay, floating bridge/vibrato, bridge cover plate, 6 on one side tuners, chrome hardware, 2 single coil exposed pickups, volume/tone control, volume/tone roller control, 3 position switch, preset selector slide switch. Available in Candy Apple Red, vintage White and 3 Tone Sunburst finish. Curr. mfr.

Mfr.'s Sug. Retail	$750	$525	$450	$375	$300	$270	$245	$225

'68 STRATOCASTER — offset double cutaway ash body, white pickguard, bolt-on maple neck, 21 fret maple fingerboard with black dot inlay, standard vibrato, 6 on one side tuners, chrome hardware, 3 single coil pickups, 2 volume/1 tone controls, 5 position switch. Available in Vintage White and 3 Tone Sunburst finish. Curr. mfr.

Mfr.'s Sug. Retail	$620	$435	$370	$310	$250	$225	$205	$190

Add $60 for left handed version of this model.

PAISLEY STRAT — similar to '68 Stratocaster, except has Paisley pickguard/finish.

Mfr.'s Sug. Retail	$720	$500	$430	$360	$290	$260	$240	$220

BLUE FLOWER STRAT — similar to '68 Stratocaster, except has Blue Flower pickguard/finish.

Mfr.'s Sug. Retail	$720	$500	$430	$360	$290	$260	$240	$220

'72 STRATOCASTER — offset double cutaway ash body, white pickguard, bolt-on maple neck, 21 fret maple fingerboard with black dot inlay, standard vibrato, 6 on one side tuners, chrome hardware, 3 single coil pickups, volume/2 tone controls, 5 position switch. Available in Natural and Vintage White finish. Curr. mfr.

Mfr.'s Sug. Retail	$660	$460	$395	$330	$265	$240	$220	$200

STRAT XII — offset double cutaway alder body, white pickguard, bolt-on maple neck, 22 fret rosewood fingerboard with pearl dot inlay, strings thru bridge, 6 per side tuners, chrome hardware, 3 single coil exposed pickups, volume/2 tone controls, 5 position switch. Available in 3 Tone Sunburst finish. Curr. mfr.

Mfr.'s Sug. Retail	$800	$560	$480	$400	$320	$290	$265	$240

"SHORT SCALE" STRAT — offset double cutaway ash body, white pickguard, bolt-on maple neck, 22 fret maple fingerboard with black dot inlay, standard vibrato, 6 on one side tuners, chrome hardware, 3 single coil pickups, volume/2 tone controls, 5 position switch. Available in Arctic White, Black, Frost Red and 3 Tone Sunburst finish. Curr. mfr.

Mfr.'s Sug. Retail	$550	$385	$330	$275	$220	$200	$180	$165

This instrument also available with rosewood fingerboard with pearl dot inlay.

Grading	100%	98%	95%	90%	80%	70%	60%

J.D. TELECASTER — single cutaway bound ash body, black pickguard, bolt-on maple neck, 21 fret maple fingerboard with black dot inlay, strings thru bridge, Jerry Donahue's signature on peghead, 6 on one side tuners, gold hardware, 2 single coil pickups, volume/tone controls, 5 position switch, controls mounted metal plate. Available in Transparent Crimson and 3 Tone Sunburst finish. Mfd. 1992 to date.

Mfr.'s Sug. Retail	$720	$500	$430	$360	$290	$260	$240	$220

ROSEWOOD TELECASTER — single cutaway rosewood body, black pickguard, bolt-on rosewood neck, 21 fret rosewood fingerboard with pearl dot inlay, strings thru bridge with cover, chrome hardware, 2 single coil pickups, volume/tone control, 3 position switch, controls mounted metal plate. Available in Natural finish. Curr. mfr.

Mfr.'s Sug. Retail	$1,000	$700	$600	$500	$400	$360	$330	$300

'72 TELECASTER THINLINE — single cutaway ash body with hollowed bass side, f hole, pearloid pickguard, bolt-on maple neck, 21 fret maple fingerboard with black dot inlay, strings thru bridge with cover, chrome hardware, 2 humbucker pickups, volume/tone control, 3 position switch. Available in Natural finish. Curr. mfr.

Mfr.'s Sug. Retail	$790	$555	$475	$395	$315	$280	$260	$235

PAISLEY TELE — single cutaway ash body, paisley pickguard, bolt-on maple neck, 21 fret maple fingerboard with black dot inlay, strings thru bridge, 6 on one side tuners, chrome hardware, 2 single coil pickups, volume/tone controls, 3 position switch, controls mounted metal plate. Available in Paisley finish. Curr. mfr.

Mfr.'s Sug. Retail	$720	$500	$430	$360	$290	$260	$240	$220

BLUE FLOWER TELE — similar to Paisley Tele, except has Blue Floral pickguard/finish.

Mfr.'s Sug. Retail	$720	$500	$430	$360	$290	$260	$240	$220

'72 TELECASTER CUSTOM — single cutaway ash body, black pickguard, bolt-on maple neck, 21 fret maple fingerboard with black dot inlay, strings thru bridge, chrome hardware, humbucker/single coil pickups, volume/tone control, 3 position switch. Available in Black and 3 Tone Sunburst finish. Curr. mfr.

Mfr.'s Sug. Retail	$660	$460	$395	$330	$265	$240	$220	$200

'54 ESQUIRE — single cutaway ash body, black pickguard, bolt-on maple neck, 21 fret maple fingerboard with black dot inlay, strings thru bridge with cover, 6 on one side tuners, chrome hardware, single coil pickup, volume/tone control, 3 position switch, controls mounted metal plate. Available in Blonde and 2 Tone Sunburst finish. Curr. mfr.

Mfr.'s Sug. Retail	$570	$400	$340	$285	$230	$205	$190	$170

'62 Esquire Custom — similar to '54 Esquire, except has bound body, white pickguard, rosewood fingerboard with pearl dot inlay. Available in Candy Apple Red and 3 Tone Sunburst finish. Curr. mfr.

Mfr.'s Sug. Retail	$580	$405	$350	$290	$230	$205	$190	$175

Grading	100%	98%	95%	90%	80%	70%	60%

'69 MUSTANG — offset double cutaway asymmetrical ash body, pickguard, bolt-on maple neck, 22 fret rosewood fingerboard with pearl dot inlay, floating bridge/vibrato with bridge cover, 6 on one side tuners with plastic buttons, chrome hardware, 2 single coil covered pickups, volume/tone control, 2 selector slide switches. Available in Sonic Blue and Vintage White finish. Curr. mfr.

Mfr.'s Sug. Retail	$600	$420	$360	$300	$240	$215	$195	$180

STRATOCASTER SERIES

This series has an offset double cutaway body, bolt-on maple neck, 6 on one side tuners, unless otherwise listed.

STRATOCASTER - STANDARD (PRE-CBS MFR.) — ash

body, white pickguard, 4 screw bolt-on maple neck, 21 fret maple fingerboard with black dot inlay, strings thru bridge, nickel hardware, 3 single coil exposed pickups, 1 volume/2 tone controls, 3 position switch. Available in 3 Tone Sunburst finish. Mfd. 1954-1959.

	100%	98%	95%	90%	80%	70%	60%
Mfd. 1954	$14,650	$10,255	$8,790	$7,325	$5,860	$5,275	$4,835
Mfd. 1955	$10,950	$7,665	$6,570	$5,475	$4,380	$3,940	$3,615
Mfd. 1956-1957	$10,000	$7,000	$6,000	$5,000	$4,000	$3,600	$3,300
Mfd. 1958	$8,500	$5,950	$5,100	$4,250	$3,400	$3,060	$2,805
Mfd. 1959	$7,500	$5,250	$4,500	$3,750	$3,000	$2,700	$2,475

Add $150 for standard vibrato with cover.
During 1954, the standard vibrato back cover had round string holes.
During 1955, the standard vibrato back cover had oval string holes.
From 1954-1958, some models have aluminum pickguards - Black and Blond finishes are special order items.
In 1956, gold hardware became an option.
In 1958, Black, Dakota Red, Desert Sand, Fiesta Red, Lake Placid Blue, Olympic White, Shoreline Gold and 3 Tone Sunburst finishes became standard items.
In 1959, 3 layer pickguard replaced the original item.

STRATOCASTER WITH ROSEWOOD FINGERBOARD (PRE-CBS MFR.)

— similar to Stratocaster-Standard, except has rosewood fingerboard with pearl dot inlay. Mfd. 1960-1964.

	100%	98%	95%	90%	80%	70%	60%
Mfd. 1960	$5,025	$3,520	$3,015	$2,515	$2,010	$1,810	$1,660
Mfd. 1961	$4,500	$3,150	$2,700	$2,250	$1,800	$1,620	$1,485
Mfd. 1962	$4,250	$2,975	$2,550	$2,125	$1,700	$1,530	$1,400
Mfd. 1963	$4,000	$2,800	$2,400	$2,000	$1,600	$1,440	$1,320
Mfd. 1964	$3,750	$2,625	$2,250	$1,875	$1,500	$1,350	$1,235

In 1960, some models were issued with tortoise shell pickguards, this was not a standard practice.
In 1960, Burgundy Mist, Candy Apple Red, Daphne Blue, Foam Green, Inca Silver, Shell Pink, Sonic Blue and Surf Green finishes also became standard items.

Grading	100%	98%	95%	90%	80%	70%	60%

STRATOCASTER WITHOUT TILTED NECK (CBS MFR.) — similar to Strato-
caster-Standard, except has smaller body contours, large headstock. Mfd. 1965-1971 (referred to as CBS Mfr. because of the sale of Fender Musical Instruments Corp. to the CBS Broadcasting Co. in early 1965).

	100%	98%	95%	90%	80%	70%	60%
Mfd. 1965	$3,500	$2,450	$2,100	$1,750	$1,400	$1,260	$1,150
Mfd. 1966	$3,250	$2,275	$1,950	$1,625	$1,300	$1,170	$1,070
Mfd. 1967	$3,000	$2,095	$1,800	$1,500	$1,200	$1,080	$990
Mfd. 1968	$2,750	$1,925	$1,650	$1,375	$1,100	$990	$905
Mfd. 1969	$2,500	$1,750	$1,500	$1,250	$1,000	$900	$825
Mfd. 1970	$2,250	$1,575	$1,345	$1,125	$900	$810	$740
Mfd. 1971	$2,000	$1,400	$1,200	$1,000	$800	$720	$660

This guitar was also available with rosewood fingerboard with pearl dot inlay.

In 1965, enlarged peghead became standard.

In 1965, Blue Ice, Charcoal Frost, Firemist Gold, Firemist Silver, Ocean Turquoise and Teal Green finishes became standard items.

In 1970, Blond, Black, Candy Apple Red, Firemist Gold, Firemist Silver, Lake Placid Blue, Ocean Turquoise, Olympic White and Sonic Blue finishes became standard items.

STRATOCASTER WITH TILTED NECK AND BULLET HEADSTOCK —
similar to Stratocaster-Standard, except has even smaller body contours, 3 bolt tilted neck with micro adjustment, large headstock with truss rod adjustment, black logo. Mfd. 1972-1980.

	100%	98%	95%	90%	80%	70%	60%
Mfd. 1972-1974	$1,200	$840	$720	$600	$480	$430	$395
Mfd. 1975	$750	$525	$450	$375	$300	$270	$245
Mfd. 1976-1977	$650	$455	$390	$325	$260	$235	$215
Mfd. 1978-1980	$550	$385	$330	$275	$220	$200	$180

This model was also offered with a rosewood fingerboard with pearl dot inlay.

In 1972, Natural finish became a standard item.

In 1975, pickups were installed that had flat pole pieces along the bobbin top.

From the mid to late 70's these instruments became heavier and are less desirable.

☆ Stratocaster, Mfd. 1983-1984 — alder body, white pickguard, 21 fret maple
fingerboard with black dot inlay, strings thru bridge, chrome hardware, 3 single coil exposed pickups, volume/tone control, 3 position switch. Available in Black, Brown Sunburst, Ivory and Sienna Sunburst finish. Mfd. 1983-1984.

	100%	98%	95%	90%	80%	70%	60%
	$675	$475	$405	$340	$270	$245	$225

This model had a vibrato system that was almost surface mounted and without a vibrato back cavity. Also, the cord receptor was mounted through the pickguard at a right angle.

Grading	100%	98%	95%	90%	80%	70%	60%

⚡ **Smith Strat** — similar to original Stratocaster, except has an alder body, small headstock with black logo, 4 bolt neck, 21 fret rosewood fingerboard with pearl dot inlay. Mfd. 1981-1982.

		100%	98%	95%	90%	80%	70%	60%
		$750	$525	$450	$375	$300	$270	$245

AMERICAN STANDARD STRATOCASTER — alder body, white pickguard, 22 fret maple fingerboard with black dot inlay, standard vibrato, chrome hardware, 3 single coil exposed pickups, 5 position switch. Available in Arctic White, Black, Brown Sunburst, Caribbean Mist, Lipstick Red, Midnight Blue and Midnight Wine finish. Mfd. 1984 to date.

		100%	98%	95%	90%	80%	70%	60%
1986-1992		$575	$405	$345	$285	$230	$205	$190
Mfr.'s Sug. Retail	$870	$610	$520	$435	$350	$315	$290	$265

Add $100 for left hand version of this model.

This model is also available with rosewood fingerboard with pearl dot inlay.

These were the first Stratocasters of the post-CBS era to be made in the U.S., at the Corona, California production facility.

⚡ **American Classic Strat** — similar to American Standard Stratocaster, except has pearloid pickguard, reverse wound middle pickup, active electronics. Available in Black Holo-flake and Olympic White finish.

		100%	98%	95%	90%	80%	70%	60%
Mfr.'s Sug. Retail	$1,500	$1,050	$900	$750	$600	$540	$495	$450

Instruments with Olympic White finish have tortoise shell pickguard.

This instrument is a Custom Shop model.

STRATOCASTER (CONTEMPORARY) — alder body, white pickguard, 22 fret rosewood fingerboard with pearl dot inlay, double locking vibrato, black face peghead, chrome hardware, humbucker exposed pickup, volume control. Mfd. in Japan, 1985-1987.

		100%	98%	95%	90%	80%	70%	60%
		$375	$260	$220	$185	$150	$135	$120

This model is also available with black pickguard, 2 humbucker pickups, volume/tone control, 3 position switch, coil tap configuration or 2 single coil/1 humbucker pickups, volume/tone control, 5 position switch, coil tap configuration.

STRATOCASTER GOLD — hardwood body, white pickguard, 21 fret maple fingerboard with black dot inlay, standard brass vibrato, brass tuners, gold hardware, 3 single coil exposed pickups, volume/2 tone controls, 5 position switch. Available in Gold finish. Mfd. 1981-1983.

	100%	98%	95%	90%	80%	70%	60%
	$1,025	$720	$615	$510	$410	$370	$340

This model has been nicknamed the "Gold/Gold" Stratocaster.

FLOYD ROSE CLASSIC STRATOCASTER — alder body, 22 fret rosewood fingerboard with pearl dot inlay, double locking Floyd Rose vibrato system, chrome hardware, 2 single coil/1 humbucker pickups, volume/2 tone controls, 5 position switch. Available in Black, Candy Apple Red, 3 Tone Sunburst and Vintage White finish. Mfd. 1992 to date.

		100%	98%	95%	90%	80%	70%	60%
Mfr.'s Sug. Retail	$1,160	$810	$695	$580	$465	$420	$385	$350

This model also available with maple fingerboard with black dot inlay.

Grading	100%	98%	95%	90%	80%	70%	60%

H.M. STRAT — basswood body, 24 fret maple fingerboard with black dot inlay, double locking Floyd Rose vibrato, black face peghead with Strat logo, black hardware, humbucker exposed pickup, volume/tone control, coil tap. Available in Black, Blue, Red and White finish. Mfd. 1988-1992.

	$1,015	$870	$725	$580	$520	$475	$435

Last Mfr. Sug. Retail price was $1,449.

This instrument is also available with rosewood fingerboard with pearl dot inlay and the following pickup configurations: 1 single coil/1 humbucker, 2 humbucker, 2 single coil/1 humbucker exposed pickups with volume/2 tone controls, pickup selector switch, coil tap.

H.M. Strat Ultra — similar to H.M. Strat, except has figured maple top/back, ebony fingerboard with pearl triangle inlay, mother of pearl headstock logo, 4 single coil covered Lace Sensor pickups (2 pickups in humbucker configuration by the vibrato), volume/2 tone controls, 5 position/mini switches. Mfd. 1990-1992.

	$950	$665	$570	$475	$380	$345	$315

"HRR" 50'S STRATOCASTER — basswood body, 22 fret maple fingerboard with black dot inlay, double locking Floyd Rose vibrato, 2 single coil/1 humbucker pickups, volume/2 tone controls, 5 position/coil split switches. Available in Black, Blue Foto Flame, Crimson Foto Flame, Olympic White and 2 Tone Sunburst finish. Mfd. in Japan, 1990 to date.

Mfr.'s Sug. Retail	$900	$630	$540	$450	$360	$325	$300	$275

"HRR" 60's Stratocaster — similar to "HRR" 50's Stratocaster, except has rosewood fingerboard with pearl dot inlay. Available in Black, Blue Foto Flame, Crimson Foto Flame, Olympic White and 3 Tone Sunburst finish. Mfd. in Japan, 1990 to date.

Mfr.'s Sug. Retail	$900	$630	$540	$450	$360	$325	$300	$275

25TH ANNIVERSARY STRATOCASTER — alder body, black pickguard, "Anniversary" logo on bass cutaway, 21 fret maple fingerboard with black dot inlay, standard vibrato, chrome hardware, 3 single coil pickups, volume/2 tone controls, 5 position switch. Available in Metallic Silver finish. Mfd. 1979-1980.

	$850	$595	$510	$425	$340	$305	$280

Approximately 10,000 of these instruments were produced.

Early models of this series were finished in a Pearl White finish, which checked and cracked very badly. Most models were returned to the factory to be refinished.

ELITE STRATOCASTER — hardwood body, white pickguard, 21 fret maple fingerboard with black dot inlay, Freeflyte vibrato, chrome hardware, 3 single coil covered pickups, volume/2 tone controls, 3 push button pickup selectors, active electronics. Available in Aztec Gold, Candy Apple Green, Emerald Green, Mocha Brown, Pewter, Ruby Red, Sapphire Blue and Stratoburst finish. Mfd. 1983-1984.

	$650	$455	$390	$325	$260	$235	$215

This instrument was also available with rosewood fingerboard with pearl dot inlay.

Grading	100%	98%	95%	90%	80%	70%	60%

⚉ **Gold Elite Stratocaster** — similar to Elite Stratocaster, except has pearloid tuner buttons, gold hardware.

	$600	$420	$360	$300	$240	$215	$195

⚉ **Walnut Elite Stratocaster** — similar to Elite Stratocaster, except has walnut body/neck, ebony fingerboard, pearloid tuner buttons, gold hardware.

	$750	$525	$450	$375	$300	$270	$245

SET NECK STRATOCASTER — mahogany body, figured maple top, 22 fret ebony fingerboard with pearl dot inlay, standard vibrato, chrome hardware, 4 single coil Lace Sensor pickups (2 in humbucker configuration), volume/2 tone controls, 5 position/mini switches, active electronics. Available in Antique Burst, Natural, Transparent Crimson and Transparent Ebony finish. Mfd. 1992 to date.

Mfr.'s Sug. Retail	$2,100	$1,475	$1,260	$1,050	$840	$755	$690	$630

This model also available with gold hardware in Brite White finish.

⚉ **Set Neck Floyd Rose Strat** — similar to Set Neck Stratocaster, except has double locking Floyd Rose vibrato, 2 single coil/1 humbucker pickups. Mfd. 1992 to date.

Mfr.'s Sug. Retail	$2,100	$1,475	$1,260	$1,050	$840	$755	$690	$630

STANDARD STRATOCASTER — poplar body, white pickguard, 22 fret maple fingerboard with black dot inlay, standard bridge, chrome hardware, 3 single coil pickups, 5 position switch. Available in Arctic White, Black, Crimson Red Metallic and Lake Placid Blue finish. Curr. Mfr.

Mfr.'s Sug. Retail	$430	$300	$260	$215	$175	$155	$140	$130

This model also available with rosewood fingerboard with pearl dot inlay.

⚉ **Standard Stratocaster-Left Handed** — similar to Standard Stratocaster, except has rosewood fingerboard with pearl dot inlay. Available in Arctic White and Black finish.

Mfr.'s Sug. Retail	$600	$420	$360	$300	$240	$215	$195	$180

U.S. CONTEMPORARY STRATOCASTER — alder body, white pickguard, 22 fret rosewood fingerboard with pearl dot inlay, double locking vibrato, chrome hardware, 2 single coil/1 humbucker exposed pickups, 5 position switch. Available in Arctic White, Black, Brown Sunburst, Gun Metal Blue, Pewter and Torino Red finish. Mfd. 1989-1991.

	$475	$330	$280	$235	$190	$170	$155

U.S. STRAT PLUS — alder body, 22 fret maple fingerboard with black dot inlay, standard vibrato, roller nut, locking tuners, chrome hardware, 3 single coil Lace Sensor pickups, volume/2 tone controls, 5 position switch. Available in Arctic White, Black, Black Pearl Dust, Blue Pearl Dust, Brown Sunburst, Caribbean Mist, Lipstick Red, Midnight Blue and Midnight Wine finish. Mfd. 1987 to date.

Mfr.'s Sug. Retail	$1,000	$700	$600	$500	$400	$360	$330	$300

This model also available with rosewood fingerboard with pearl dot inlay.

Grading	100%	98%	95%	90%	80%	70%	60%

⚮ **U.S. Deluxe Strat Plus** — similar to U.S. Strat Plus, except has ash top/back. Available in Antique Burst, Blue Burst, Crimson Burst, Mystic Black and Natural finish.

Mfr.'s Sug. Retail	$1,100	$770	$660	$550	$440	$395	$365	$330

⚮ **U.S. Strat Ultra** — similar to U.S. Strat Plus, except has figured maple top/back, ebony fingerboard with pearl dot inlay, locking vibrato, 4 single coil covered Lace Sensor pickups (2 in humbucker configuration), mini switch. Available in Antique Burst, Blue Burst, Crimson Burst and Mystic Black finish. Mfd. 1990 to date.

Mfr.'s Sug. Retail	$1,550	$1,085	$930	$775	$620	$560	$515	$465

U.S. VINTAGE '57 STRATOCASTER

— alder body, white pickguard, 21 fret maple fingerboard with black dot inlay, standard vibrato, nickel hardware, 3 single coil exposed pickups, volume/2 tone controls, 3 position switch. Available in Black, Candy Apple Red, Fiesta Red, Ocean Turquoise, 2 Tone Sunburst and Vintage White finish. Mfd. 1982 to date.

Mfr.'s Sug. Retail	$1,300	$910	$780	$650	$520	$470	$430	$390

This is a replica of the Stratocaster as it appeared in 1957.

⚮ **Custom Shop '57 Stratocaster** — similar to U.S. Vintage '57 Stratocaster, except is left hand model. Available in Black and Olympic White finish. Curr. mfr.

Mfr.'s Sug. Retail	$2,200	$1,540	$1,320	$1,100	$880	$790	$725	$660

U.S. VINTAGE '62 STRATOCASTER

— alder body, white pickguard, 21 fret rosewood fingerboard with pearl dot inlay, standard vibrato, nickel hardware, 3 single coil exposed pickups, volume/2 tone controls, 3 position switch. Available in Black, Candy Apple Red, Fiesta Red, Ocean Turquoise, 3 Tone Sunburst and Vintage White finish. Mfd. 1982 to date.

Mfr.'s Sug. Retail	$1,300	$910	$780	$650	$520	$470	$430	$390

This is a replica of the Stratocaster as it appeared in 1962.

⚮ **Custom Shop '62 Stratocaster** — similar to U.S. Vintage '57 Stratocaster, except is left hand model. Available in Black and Olympic White finish. Curr. mfr.

Mfr.'s Sug. Retail	$2,200	$1,540	$1,320	$1,100	$880	$790	$725	$660

THE STRAT

— alder body, white pickguard, 21 fret maple fingerboard with black dot inlay, standard brass vibrato, body matching peghead with Strat logo, brass tuners, gold hardware, 3 single coil pickups, volume/tone/rotary controls, 5 position switch. Available in Arctic White, Candy Apple Red and Lake Placid Blue finish. Mfd. 1980-1983.

		$650	$455	$390	$325	$260	$235	$215

⚮ **Walnut Strat** — similar to The Strat, except has walnut body/neck, black pickguard, gold hardware. Available in Natural finish. Mfd. 1981-1983.

		$725	$505	$435	$360	$290	$260	$240

A few of these instruments have ebony fingerboards.

Grading	100%	98%	95%	90%	80%	70%	60%

STRATOCASTER XII — alder body, white pickguard, 22 fret rosewood fingerboard with pearl dot inlay, strings thru bridge, 6 per side tuners, chrome hardware, 3 single coil exposed pickups, volume/2 tone controls, 5 position switch. Available in Candy Apple Red finish. Mfd. in Japan, 1988-1990.

	100%	98%	95%	90%	80%	70%	60%
	$600	$420	$360	$300	$240	$215	$195

'54 STRATOCASTER — ash body, white pickguard, figured maple neck, 21 fret maple fingerboard with black dot inlay, strings thru bridge, chrome hardware, 3 single coil pickups, volume/2 tone controls, 3 position switch. Available in 2 Tone Sunburst and Vintage Blond finish. Curr. mfr.

Mfr.'s Sug. Retail	$2,100	$1,475	$1,260	$1,050	$840	$755	$690	$630

    This guitar is a custom order instrument.

'60 STRATOCASTER — similar to '54 Stratocaster, except has alder body, rosewood fingerboard with pearl dot inlay. Available in Olympic White and 3 Tone Sunburst finish.

Mfr.'s Sug. Retail	$2,100	$1,475	$1,260	$1,050	$840	$755	$690	$630

    The pickguard, pickups, controls and finish are aged on this instrument.
    Instruments with Olympic White finish have tortoise shell pickguards and body matching pegheads.
    This guitar is a custom order instrument.

Stratocaster Signature Series

All instruments in this series have strat style body, white pickguard, bolt-on maple neck, 6 on one side tuners, volume/2 tone controls, 5 position switch, unless otherwise listed.

ERIC CLAPTON — alder body, 22 fret maple fingerboard with black dot inlay, standard vibrato, Eric Clapton's signature on headstock, chrome hardware, 3 single coil Lace Sensor pickups, active electronics. Available in Black, Candy Green, Pewter and Torino Red finish. Mfd. 1988 to date.

Mfr.'s Sug. Retail	$1,500	$1,050	$900	$750	$600	$540	$495	$450

HENDRIX LIMITED EDITION — ash body, 21 fret maple fingerboard with black dot inlay, standard vibrato, reverse headstock, chrome hardware, 3 single coil pickups. Available in White finish. Mfd. 1980 only.

Mfr.'s Sug. Retail	$1,500	$1,050	$900	$750	$600	$540	$495	$450

JEFF BECK — alder body, 22 fret rosewood fingerboard with pearl dot inlay, standard vibrato, roller nut, Jeff Beck's signature on peghead, locking tuners, chrome hardware, 4 single coil Lace Sensor pickups (2 in humbucker configuration), coil tap switch. Available in Midnight Purple, Surf Green and Vintage White finish. Mfd. 1991 to date.

Mfr.'s Sug. Retail	$1,400	$980	$840	$700	$560	$505	$460	$420

Grading	100%	98%	95%	90%	80%	70%	60%

RICHIE SAMBORA

— alder body, 22 fret maple fingerboard with abalone star inlay, double locking vibrato, Richie Sambora's signature on peghead, pearl tuner buttons, chrome hardware, 2 single coil/1 humbucker pickups, active electronics. Available in Arctic White and Cherry Sunburst finish. New 1993.

Mfr.'s Sug. Retail	$1,600	$1,120	$960	$800	$640	$575	$530	$480

ROBERT CRAY

— alder body, 21 fret rosewood fingerboard with pearl dot inlay, strings thru bridge, Robert Cray's signature on peghead, chrome hardware, 3 single coil exposed pickups. Available in Inca Silver, 3 Tone Sunburst and Violet finish. Mfd. 1991 to date.

Mfr.'s Sug. Retail	$1,950	$1,365	$1,170	$975	$780	$700	$645	$580

This guitar is available on custom order only.

STEVIE RAY VAUGHN

— alder body, black pickguard with "SRV" logo, 21 fret rosewood fingerboard with pearl dot inlay, left-handed standard vibrato, Stevie Ray Vaughn's signature on peghead, gold hardware, 3 single coil pickups, volume/2 tone controls, 5 position switch. Available in 3 Tone Sunburst finish. Mfd. 1992 to date.

Mfr.'s Sug. Retail	$1,400	$980	$840	$700	$560	$505	$460	$420

YNGWIE MALMSTEEN

— alder body, 21 fret scalloped maple fingerboard with black dot inlay, standard vibrato, brass nut, Yngwie Malmsteen's signature on peghead, chrome hardware, 3 single coil pickups, active electronics. Available in Candy Apple Red, Sonic Blue and Vintage White finish. Mfd. in USA, 1988 to date.

Mfr.'s Sug. Retail	$1,500	$1,050	$900	$750	$600	$540	$495	$450

This model is also available with rosewood fingerboard and pearl dot inlays.

Yngwie Malmsteen Standard

— similar to Yngwie Malmsteen, except has basswood body, 70's style headstock, no active electronics. Available in Black, Sonic Blue and Vintage White finish. Mfd. in Japan, 1991 to date.

Mfr.'s Sug. Retail	$960	$670	$575	$480	$385	$350	$320	$290

Stratocaster Re-Issue Series

This series has strat style basswood body, white pickguard, bolt on maple neck, 21 fret fingerboard, standard vibrato, 6 on one side tuners, nickel hardware, 3 single coil pickups, volume/2 tone controls, 5 position switch, unless otherwise listed.

50'S STRATOCASTER

— maple fingerboard with black dot inlay, strings thru bridge. Available in Black, Olympic White, and 2 Tone Sunburst finish. Mfd. 1992 to date.

Mfr.'s Sug. Retail	$550	$385	$330	$275	$220	$200	$180	$165

50's Stratocaster-Vibrato

— maple fingerboard with black dot inlay. Available in Black, Blue Foto Flame, Crimson Foto Flame, Olympic White, and 2 Tone Sunburst finish.

Mfr.'s Sug. Retail	$640	$450	$385	$320	$255	$230	$210	$195

Grading	100%	98%	95%	90%	80%	70%	60%

60'S STRATOCASTER — rosewood fingerboard with pearl dot inlay. Available in Black, Blue Foto Flame, Crimson Foto Flame, Olympic White, and 3 Tone Sunburst finish. Mfd. 1992 to date.

Mfr.'s Sug. Retail	$640	$450	$385	$320	$255	$230	$210	$195

TELECASTER SERIES

All instruments in this series have a single cutaway body, bolt-on maple neck, 6 on one side tuners, unless otherwise listed.

BROADCASTER — ash body, black pickguard, 21 fret maple fingerboard with black dot inlay, fixed bridge with cover, chrome hardware, 2 single coil pickups, 3 position switch, volume/tone control. Available in Translucent Butterscotch finish. Mfd. 1950.

$13,500	$9,450	$8,100	$6,750	$5,400	$4,860	$4,455

Prototypes and custom models did exist before 1948.

By 1951, the Broadcaster name was changed to Telecaster due to the use of the original name by Gretsch.

"NO"CASTER — similar to Broadcaster, except has Fender name only on headstock.

$10,500	$7,350	$6,300	$5,250	$4,200	$3,780	$3,465

Add $200 for original case.

The "No"Caster was the result of dropping the Broadcaster name because of previous use of the name by the Gretsch company.

TELECASTER (ORIGINAL FENDER MFR.) — ash body, black pickguard, 21 fret maple fingerboard with black dot inlay, strings thru bridge, chrome hardware, 2 single coil pickups, volume/tone controls, 3 position switch, controls mounted metal plate. Available in Blond finish. Mfd. 1951-1964.

1951-1954	$8,500	$5,950	$5,100	$4,250	$3,400	$3,060	$2,805
1955-1959	$5,500	$3,850	$3,300	$2,750	$2,200	$1,980	$1,815
1960-1964	$3,500	$2,450	$2,100	$1,750	$1,400	$1,260	$1,150

In 1955, white pickguard replaced original item.
In 1958, fixed bridge replaced original item.
In 1959, rosewood fingerboard with pearl dot inlay replaced maple fingerboard.
In 1960, strings thru bridge replaced fixed bridge.

TELECASTER (CBS MFR.) — similar to original Telecaster, except has F stamp on back of neck plates. Mfd. 1965-1983 (referred to as CBS Mfr. because of the sale of Fender Musical Instruments Corp. to the CBS Broadcasting Co. in early 1965.)

1965-1969	$1,750	$1,225	$1,050	$875	$700	$630	$575
1970-1975	$1,000	$700	$600	$500	$400	$360	$330
1976-1979	$750	$525	$450	$375	$300	$270	$245
1980-1983	$525	$370	$315	$260	$210	$190	$170

In 1967, Bigsby vibrato tailpiece was optionally available.
From 1967-1969, maple fingerboard was optionally available.

(More information on the following page)

In 1969, maple fingerboard with black dot inlay replaced original item.
In 1975, black pickguard replaced respective item.

TELECASTER WITH BIGSBY VIBRATO — similar to original Telecaster, except has Bigsby vibrato unit. Mfd. 1967-1975.

	100%	98%	95%	90%	80%	70%	60%
	$2,100	$1,475	$1,260	$1,050	$840	$755	$690

TELECASTER CUSTOM — bound alder body, white pickguard, 21 fret maple fingerboard with pearl dot inlay, strings thru bridge, chrome hardware, 2 single coil pickups, volume/tone controls, 3 position switch, controls mounted metal plate. Available in Custom Colors finish. Mfd. 1959-1972.

	100%	98%	95%	90%	80%	70%	60%
1959-1964	$4,500	$3,150	$2,700	$2,250	$1,800	$1,620	$1,485
1965-1972	$1,500	$1,050	$900	$750	$600	$540	$495

This model is also found with an ash body.

ACOUSTIC/ELECTRIC TELECASTER — single rounded cutaway semi hollow basswood body, bound solid spruce top, f hole, 22 fret rosewood fingerboard with pearl triangle inlay, double locking vibrato, 6 on one side tuners, black hardware, single coil Lace Sensor/piezo bridge pickups, volume/pan control, mini boost switch. Available in Black, Natural, Transparent Crimson and 3 Color Sunburst finish. Curr. mfr.

	100%	98%	95%	90%	80%	70%	60%
Mfr.'s Sug. Retail	$900	$630	$540	$450	$360	$325	$300	$275

AMERICAN STANDARD TELECASTER — alder body, white pickguard, 22 fret maple fingerboard with black dot inlay, fixed bridge, chrome hardware, volume/tone control, 3 position switch. Available in Black, Caribbean Mist, Lipstick Red, Midnight Blue, Midnight Wine, Sunburst and Vintage White finish. Mfd. 1988 to date.

	100%	98%	95%	90%	80%	70%	60%
1988-1992		$575	$405	$345	$285	$230	$205	$190
Mfr.'s Sug. Retail	$860	$600	$515	$430	$345	$310	$285	$260

This model also available with rosewood fingerboard with pearl dot inlay.
Only vintage Telecasters were available in 1986 and 1987.
These were the first Telecasters of the post-CBS era to be made in the U.S., at the Corona, California production facility.

BLACK & GOLD TELECASTER — hardwood body, black pickguard, 21 fret maple fingerboard with black dot inlay, brass strings thru bridge, black face peghead with logo, gold hardware, 2 single coil pickups, volume/tone control, 3 position switch, controls mounted metal plate. Available in Black finish. Mfd. 1981-1983.

	100%	98%	95%	90%	80%	70%	60%
	$750	$525	$450	$375	$300	$270	$245

This model is also available with rosewood fingerboard with pearl dot inlay.

Grading	100%	98%	95%	90%	80%	70%	60%

CONTEMPORARY TELECASTER — hardwood body, 22 fret rosewood fingerboard with pearl dot inlay, standard vibrato, black hardware, 2 single coil/1 humbucker pickup, volume/tone controls, 3 mini switches. Mfd. in Japan, 1985-1987.

	$300	$210	$180	$150	$120	$110	$100

This model was also available with 2 humbucker pickups, 3 position/coil tap switches.

CUSTOM TELECASTER — ash body, black pickguard, 21 fret maple fingerboard with black dot inlay, strings thru bridge with cover, chrome hardware, humbucker/single coil pickups, 2 volume/2 tone controls, 3 position switch. Available in Natural and Sunburst finish. Mfd. 1972-1981.

	$750	$525	$450	$375	$300	$270	$245

Bigsby vibrato and maple fingerboard were optional.

DELUXE TELECASTER — poplar body, black pickguard, 21 fret maple fingerboard with black dot inlay, strings thru bridge with cover, strat style peghead, chrome hardware, 2 humbucker pickups, 2 volume/2 tone controls, 3 position switch. Available in Blonde, Custom Colors, Natural and 3 Tone Sunburst finish. Mfd. 1973-1981.

	$750	$525	$450	$375	$300	$270	$245

From 1977-1979, Antigua finish available with matching pickguard.

ELITE TELECASTER — bound alder body, 21 fret fingerboard with black dot inlay, fixed bridge, chrome hardware, 2 covered humbuckers, 2 volume/2 tone controls, 3 position switch, active electronics. Available in Natural and Sunburst finish. Mfd. 1983-1985.

	$450	$315	$270	$225	$180	$160	$150

This model came with an adhesive applicable white pickguard.
This model is also available with rosewood fingerboard with pearl dot inlay.

⚄ Elite Telecaster Gold — similar to Elite Telecaster, except has pearloid button tuners, gold hardware.

	$550	$385	$330	$275	$220	$200	$180

⚄ Elite Telecaster Walnut— similar to Telecaster Elite, except has walnut body/neck, ebony fingerboard with pearl dot inlay, pearloid button tuners, gold hardware. Available in Natural finish.

	$650	$455	$390	$325	$260	$235	$215

FLORAL/PAISLEY TELECASTER — ash body, floral/paisley pickguard, 21 fret maple fingerboard with black dot inlay, strings thru bridge, chrome hardware, 2 single coil pickups, volume/tone controls, 3 position switch, controls mounted metal plate. Available in Blue Floral and Pink Paisley finish. Mfd. 1968-1970.

	$2,500	$1,750	$1,500	$1,250	$1,000	$900	$825

Fender, cont.

FORTIETH ANNIVERSARY TELECASTER — ash body, bound figured maple top, cream pickguard, 22 fret maple fingerboard with black dot inlay, fixed bridge, pearl tuner buttons, gold hardware, 2 single coil pickups, volume/tone control, 3 position switch. Available in Antique Two-Tone, Natural and Transparent Red finish. Mfd. 1988-1990.

		$2,750	$1,925	$1,650	$1,375	$1,100	$990	$905

Approximately 300 of these instruments were mfd.

ROSEWOOD TELECASTER — rosewood body, black pickguard, bolt-on rosewood neck, 21 fret rosewood fingerboard with pearl dot inlay, strings thru bridge with cover, chrome hardware, 2 single coil pickups, volume/tone control, 3 position switch, controls mounted metal plate. Available in Natural finish. Mfd. 1969-1972.

		$2,200	$1,540	$1,320	$1,100	$880	$790	$725

SET NECK TELECASTER — mahogany body, bound figured maple top, mahogany neck, 22 fret rosewood fingerboard with pearl dot inlay, strings thru bridge, locking tuners, 2 humbucker DiMarzio pickups, volume/tone control, 3 position/coil tap switches. Available in Antique Burst, Autumn Gold, Transparent Crimson, Transparent Ebony and Transparent Sapphire Blue finish. Mfd. 1990 to date.

Mfr.'s Sug. Retail	$2,100		$1,475	$1,260	$1,050	$840	$755	$690	$630

This model is also available with double locking Floyd Rose vibrato, roller nut.
In 1993, pau ferro fingerboard became standard.

⚔ **Set Neck Telecaster C/A** — similar to Set Neck Telecaster, except has tortoise shell pickguard, pau ferro fingerboard, gold hardware, humbucker/single coil pickups. Available in Gold Sparkle, Natural, Silver Sparkle and Transparent Sunset Orange finish. Mfd. 1991 to date.

Mfr.'s Sug. Retail	$2,100		$1,475	$1,260	$1,050	$840	$755	$690	$630

STANDARD TELECASTER — poplar body, white pickguard, 21 fret maple fingerboard with black dot inlay, strings thru bridge, chrome hardware, 2 single coil pickups, volume/tone control, 3 position switch. Available in Arctic White, Black, Crimson Red Metallic and Lake Placid Blue finish. Curr. mfr.

Mfr.'s Sug. Retail	$420		$295	$250	$210	$170	$150	$135	$125

THINLINE TELECASTER — ash body with hollowed bass side, f hole, pearloid pickguard, 21 fret maple fingerboard with black dot inlay, strings thru bridge with cover, chrome hardware, 2 single coil pickups, volume/tone control, 3 position switch. Available in Custom Colors, Natural and Sunburst finish. Mfd. 1968-1971.

		$1,800	$1,260	$1,080	$900	$720	$650	$595

Add $300 for Sunburst or custom color finish.
In 1969, rosewood fingerboard with pearl dot inlay became an option.

⚔ **Telecaster Thinline II** — similar to Thinline Telecaster, except has 2 humbucker pickups. Mfd. 1972-1978.

		$750	$525	$450	$375	$300	$270	$245

Add $100 for Sunburst or custom color finish.

Grading	100%	98%	95%	90%	80%	70%	60%

TELE PLUS — alder body, ash top/back, 22 fret rosewood fingerboard with pearl dot inlay, fixed bridge, chrome hardware, 3 single coil Lace Sensor pickups (2 in humbucker position by bridge), volume/tone control, 3 position/mini switch. Available in Antique Burst, Blue Burst, Crimson Burst and Mystic Blue finish. Mfd. 1990 to date.

Mfr.'s Sug. Retail	$1,000	$700	$600	$500	$400	$360	$330	$300

Add $100 for solid ash body with Natural finish.
This model also available with maple fingerboard with black dot inlay.

Telecaster Custom Classic Series Solid Bodies

BAJO SEXTO TELECASTER — ash body, black pickguard, 24 fret maple fingerboard with black dot inlay, strings thru bridge with brass saddles, nickel hardware, 2 single coil pickups, volume/tone control, 3 position switch. Available in Honey Blond and 2 Tone Sunburst finish. New 1993.

Mfr.'s Sug. Retail	$1,900	$1,330	$1,140	$950	$760	$685	$625	$570

This instrument is a longer scaled (baritone) instrument and custom order only.

SPARKLE TELECASTER — poplar body, white pickguard, figured maple neck, 21 fret maple fingerboard with black dot inlay, strings thru bridge with brass saddles, nickel hardware, 2 single coil pickups, volume/tone control, 3 position switch. Available in Gold Sparkle and Silver Sparkle finish. New 1993.

Mfr.'s Sug. Retail	$2,100	$1,475	$1,260	$1,050	$840	$755	$690	$630

This guitar is custom order only.

Telecaster Signature Series

This series has tele style bodies and the artist's signature on their namesake instrument's peghead.

ALBERT COLLINS — bound ash body, white pickguard, bolt-on maple neck, 21 fret maple fingerboard with black dot inlay, strings thru bridge with cover, 6 on one side tuners, chrome hardware, humbucker/single coil pickups, volume/tone control, 3 position switch, controls mounted metal plate. Available in Natural finish. Mfd. 1990 to date.

Mfr.'s Sug. Retail	$2,500	$1,750	$1,500	$1,250	$1,000	$900	$825	$750

This guitar is custom order only.

DANNY GATTON — ash body, black pickguard, bolt-on maple neck, 22 fret maple fingerboard with black dot inlay, strings thru bridge, 2 single coil Barden pickups, volume/tone control, 3 position switch. Available in Frost Gold and Honey Blond finish. Mfd. 1990 to date.

Mfr.'s Sug. Retail	$2,500	$1,750	$1,500	$1,250	$1,000	$900	$825	$750

This guitar is custom order only.

Grading	100%	98%	95%	90%	80%	70%	60%

JAMES BURTON — light ash body, bolt-on maple neck, 21 fret maple fingerboard with black dot inlay, strings thru bridge, 6 on one side tuners, gold hardware, 3 single coil Lace Sensor pickups, volume/tone control, 5 position switch. Available in Black with Candy Red Paisley, Black with Gold Paisley, Frost Red and Pearl White finish. Mfd. 1990 to date.

Mfr.'s Sug. Retail	$1,500	$1,050	$900	$750	$600	$540	$495	$450

This model is also available with black hardware, depending on finish.

JERRY DONAHUE — ash body, bird's eye maple top/back, black pickguard, bolt on bird's eye maple neck, 21 fret maple fingerboard with black dot inlay, strings thru bridge, 6 on one side tuners, gold hardware, 2 single coil pickups, volume/tone control, 3 position switch. Available in 3 Tone Sunburst and Transparent Crimson finish. Mfd. 1992 to date.

Mfr.'s Sug. Retail	$2,100	$1,475	$1,260	$1,050	$840	$755	$690	$630

This guitar is custom order only.

Telecaster Re-Issue Series Solid Bodies

U.S. VINTAGE/'52 TELECASTER — ash body, black pickguard, 21 fret maple fingerboard with black dot inlay, fixed bridge with brass saddles, nickel hardware, 2 single coil pickups, volume/tone control, 3 position switch. Available in Butterscotch Blonde finish. Mfd. 1982-1984, 1986 to date.

1982-1984		$750	$525	$450	$375	$300	$270	$245
Mfr.'s Sug. Retail	$1,300	$910	$780	$650	$520	$470	$430	$390

This model is based upon the instrument as it appeared in 1952.

'52 Telecaster-Left Hand Model — similar to U.S. Vintage/'52 Telecaster, except is left handed. Available in Honey Burst and 2 Color Sunburst finish.

Mfr.'s Sug. Retail	$2,200	$1,540	$1,320	$1,100	$880	$790	$725	$660

50'S TELECASTER — basswood body, white pickguard, 21 fret maple fingerboard with black dot inlay, fixed bridge with brass saddles, nickel hardware, 2 single coil pickups, volume/tone control, 3 position switch. Available in Blonde, Candy Apple Red and 2 Color Sunburst finish. Mfd. 1990 to date.

Mfr.'s Sug. Retail	$630	$440	$380	$315	$250	$225	$205	$190

'62 CUSTOM TELECASTER — bound basswood body, 3 ply white pickguard, 21 fret rosewood fingerboard with pearl dot inlay, fixed bridge, chrome hardware, 2 single coil pickups, volume/tone control, 3 position switch. Available in Candy Apple Red and 3 Color Sunburst finish. Curr. Mfr.

Mfr.'s Sug. Retail	$690	$485	$415	$350	$280	$250	$230	$210

Add $70 for left handed version of this model.

Grading	100%	98%	95%	90%	80%	70%	60%

'69 THINLINE TELECASTER — semi hollow mahogany body, f hole, white pick-guard, 21 fret maple fingerboard with black dot inlay, fixed bridge, nickel hardware, 2 single coil pickups, volume/tone control, 3 position switch. Available in Natural finish. Curr. mfr.

Mfr.'s Sug. Retail	$790	$555	$475	$395	$315	$280	$260	$235

ELECTRIC BASS

BASS V — offset double cutaway elongated ash body, white plastic/metal pickguard, thumb rest, bolt-on maple neck, 15 fret rosewood fingerboard with pearl dot inlay, strings thru bridge, coverplate with F logo, 5 on one side tuners, chrome hardware, single coil split covered pickup, pickup coverplate, volume/tone control. Available in Custom Colors and Sunburst finish. Mfd. 1965-1970.

	$1,450	$1,015	$870	$725	$580	$520	$475

Add $100 for left-hand version.

In 1966, bound fingerboard with black inlay became standard.

BASS VI — offset double cutaway asymmetrical ash body, tortoise shell/metal or white pickguard, bolt-on maple neck, 21 fret rosewood fingerboard with pearl dot inlay, floating bridge/vibrato with bridge cover, 6 on one side tuners, chrome hardware, 3 single coil exposed pickups with metal rings, volume/tone control, 3 two position switches. Available in Custom Color and Sunburst finish. Mfd. 1961-1975.

1962-1964	$3,750	$2,625	$2,250	$1,875	$1,500	$1,350	$1,235
1965-1975	$2,500	$1,750	$1,500	$1,250	$1,000	$900	$825

In 1963, strings mute and another 2 position switch were added, a maple fingerboard with black dot inlay was made available.

In 1966, bound fingerboard with block inlay became standard.

In 1969, Fender locking vibrato was offered as an option.

In 1974, a black pickguard became standard.

BULLET B30 — offset double cutaway alder body, white pickguard, bolt on maple neck, 19 fret maple fingerboard with black dot inlay, fixed bridge, tele-style peghead, chrome hardware, 1 split covered pickup, volume/tone control. Available in Brown Sunburst, Custom Colors, Ivory, Red and Walnut finish. Mfd. 1982-1983.

	$325	$225	$195	$160	$130	$115	$105

BULLET B34 — similar to Bullet B30, except has a long scale length.

	$350	$245	$210	$175	$140	$125	$115

BULLET B40 — similar to Bullet B30, except has 20 fret fingerboard.

	$375	$260	$220	$185	$150	$135	$120

Grading	100%	98%	95%	90%	80%	70%	60%

CORONADO BASS I — double rounded cutaway semi hollow bound maple body, arched top, f holes, 2 finger rests, bolt-on maple neck, 21 fret rosewood fingerboard with pearl dot inlay, adjustable aluminum bridge/trapeze tailpiece, ebony tailpiece insert with pearl F inlay, 4 on one side tuners, chrome hardware, single coil covered pickup, volume/tone control. Available in Cherry and Sunburst finish. Mfd. 1966-1970.

	$450	$315	$270	$225	$180	$160	$150

A wide variety of bridge styles was available on this model.

⚵ **Coronado Bass II** — similar to Coronado Bass I, except has bound f holes/fingerboard with block inlay, tunomatic bridge, string mutes, 2 single coil covered pickups, 2 volume/2 tone controls, 3 position switch. Mfd. 1967-1970.

	$600	$420	$360	$300	$240	$215	$195

Wildwood finishes were optionally available.

⚵ **Coronado Bass II Antigua** — similar to Coronado Bass II, except has Antigua (black to silver sunburst) finish. Mfd. 1970-1972.

	$650	$455	$390	$325	$260	$235	$215

JP-90 — offset double cutaway asymmetrical poplar body, black pickguard, bolt-on maple neck, 20 fret rosewood fingerboard with pearl dot inlay, fixed bridge, 4 on one side tuners, chrome hardware, P-style/J-style pickups, volume/tone control, 3 position switch. Available in Arctic White, Black and Torino Red finish. Mfd. 1990 to date.

Mfr.'s Sug. Retail	$530	$370	$320	$265	$210	$190	$175	$160

MUSICMASTER — offset double cutaway asymmetrical ash body, black pickguard, thumb rest, bolt-on maple neck, 19 fret rosewood fingerboard with pearl dot inlay, fixed bridge, 4 on one side tuners, chrome hardware, single coil covered pickup, volume/tone control. Available in Black, Blue, Red and White finish. Mfd. 1970-1983.

	$225	$160	$135	$115	$90	$80	$70

MUSTANG — offset double cutaway poplar body, plastic/metal pickguard, thumb rest, bolt-on maple neck, 19 fret rosewood fingerboard with pearl dot inlay, fixed bridge, 4 on one side tuners, chrome hardware, P-style pickup, volume/tone control. Available in Antigua, Black, Blond, Blue, Natural, Red, Sunburst, Walnut, White and Wine finish. Mfd. 1966-1983.

	$275	$195	$165	$140	$110	$100	$90

Add $45 for left-hand version.

In 1969, Competition finishes were introduced. These finishes consist of solid colors (blue, burgundy, orange and red) with racing stripes. The instrument was also referred to as Competition Mustang Bass with these finishes.

Grading	100%	98%	95%	90%	80%	70%	60%

PERFORMER — offset dual cutaway asymmetrical hardwood body, white pickguard, bolt-on maple neck, 24 fret rosewood fingerboard with pearl dot inlay, fixed bridge, 4 on one side tuners, chrome hardware, 2 single coil covered pickups, 2 volume/1 tone controls, active electronics. Available in Sunburst finish. Mfd. 1987-1988.

	$400	$280	$240	$200	$160	$145	$130

PRODIGY ACTIVE BASS — offset double cutaway poplar body, bolt-on maple neck, 20 fret rosewood fingerboard with pearl dot inlay, fixed bridge, 4 on one side tuners, chrome hardware, P-style/J-style pickups, concentric volume-pan/treble-bass controls, active electronics. Available in Arctic White, Black, Crimson Red Metallic and Lake Placid Blue finish. Mfd. 1992 to date.

Mfr.'s Sug. Retail	$600	$420	$360	$300	$240	$215	$195	$180

TELCASTER-1st VERSION — offset double cutaway ash body, white pickguard, finger rest, bolt-on maple neck, 20 fret maple fingerboard with black dot inlay, fixed bridge with cover, tele style peghead, 4 on one side tuners, chrome hardware, single coil exposed pickup with cover, volume/tone control. Available in Blond or Custom Colors finish. Mfd. 1968-1972.

	$1,500	$1,050	$900	$750	$600	$540	$495

In 1970, a fretless fingerboard became an option.

✦ **Telecaster-2nd Version** — similar to Telecaster, except has redesigned pickguard, thumb rest, 2 section bridge, covered humbucker pickup with no separate cover. Available in Blond and Sunburst finish. Mfd. 1972-1979.

	$1,000	$700	$600	$500	$400	$360	$330

A 4 section single string groove bridge was available 1977-1979.

✦ **Telecaster Paisley/Floral** — similar to Telecaster, except available in Blue Floral and Pink Paisley finish. Mfd. 1968-1970.

	$3,000	$2,095	$1,800	$1,500	$1,200	$1,080	$990

URGE BASS — offset double cutaway alder body, pearloid pickguard, bolt on maple neck, 24 fret pau ferro fingerboard, strings thru gold bridge, Stu Hamm's signature on peghead, 4 on one side black chrome tuners, J-style/P-style/J-style pickups, concentric volume-pan/treble-bass controls, 3 position mini/rotary switches. Available in Burgundy Mist, Lake Placid Blue, Montego Black and Sherwood Metallic finish. New 1993.

Mfr.'s Sug. Retail	$1,400	$980	$840	$700	$560	$505	$460	$420

This instrument was designed by Stu Hamm.

Grading	100%	98%	95%	90%	80%	70%	60%

Jazz Series

Instruments in this series have an offset double cutaway asymmetrical body, bolt-on maple neck, 4 on one side tuners, unless otherwise listed.

JAZZ — ash body, white/metal pickguard with finger rest, 20 fret rosewood fingerboard with pearl dot inlay, fixed bridge with string mutes, F logo bridge cover, chrome hardware, 2 J-style pickups, 2 concentric (volume/tone) controls. Available in Blond, Custom Colors and 3 Tone Sunburst finish. Mfd. 1960-1974.

1960-1964	$4,200	$2,940	$2,520	$2,100	$1,680	$1,510	$1,385
1965-1974	$2,100	$1,475	$1,260	$1,050	$840	$755	$690

In 1962, Blonde and Custom Colors finish became available, 2 volume/1 tone controls replace concentric controls.

In 1963, string mutes were removed.

In 1965, bound fingerboard was added.

In 1966, block fingerboard inlay replaced dot inlay.

In 1969, black bound maple fingerboard with black block inlay was made optional.

Jazz 3 Bolt Neck — similar to Jazz, except has a 3 bolt neck. Mfd. 1975-1980.

$725	$505	$435	$360	$290	$260	$240

AMERICAN STANDARD JAZZ — alder body, white/metal pickguard, 22 fret rosewood fingerboard with pearl dot inlay, fixed bridge, chrome hardware, 2 J-style pickups, 2 volume/1 tone controls. Available in Arctic White, Black, Brown Sunburst, Caribbean Mist, Lipstick Red, Midnight Blue and Midnight Wine finish. Made in USA. Curr. mfr.

Mfr.'s Sug. Retail	$900	$630	$540	$450	$360	$325	$300	$275

JAZZ CONTEMPORARY — ash body, 20 fret rosewood fingerboard with pearl dot inlay, fixed bridge, chrome hardware, P-style/J-style pickups, volume/tone controls. Mfd. 1987.

$350	$245	$210	$175	$140	$125	$115

This model also available without frets.

Jazz Gold — similar to Jazz, except has gold hardware. Available in Gold finish. Mfd. 1981-1984.

$750	$525	$450	$375	$300	$270	$245

JAZZ SPECIAL — P-style basswood body, no pickguard, J-bass style neck, graphite nut, black hardware, P/J pickup configuration.

$450	$315	$270	$225	$180	$160	$150

Jazz "Power" Special — similar to Jazz Special, except has triple laminated maple, graphite and rosewood neck, active circuitry.

$525	$370	$315	$260	$210	$190	$170

Grading	100%	98%	95%	90%	80%	70%	60%

JAZZ PLUS — alder body, 22 fret rosewood fingerboard with pearl dot inlay, fixed bridge, chrome hardware, 2 J-style Lace Sensor pickups, volume/pan control, concentric treble/bass control, active electronics. Available in Arctic White, Black, Black Pearl Burst, Blue Pearl Burst, Brown Sunburst, Caribbean Mist, Lipstick Red, Midnight Blue, Midnight Wine and Natural finish. Mfd. in USA. Curr. mfr.

Mfr.'s Sug. Retail	$1,100	$770	$660	$550	$440	$395	$365	$330

Add $100 for ash body.

This model is also available with a maple fingerboard.

⚞ **Jazz Plus V** — similar to Jazz Plus, except has 5 strings, 5 on one side tuners.

Mfr.'s Sug. Retail	$1,160	$810	$695	$580	$465	$420	$385	$350

JAZZ STANDARD — poplar body, white/metal pickguard, 20 fret rosewood fingerboard with pearl dot inlay, fixed bridge, chrome hardware, 2 J-style pickups, 2 volume/1 tone controls. Available in Arctic White, Black, Crimson Red Metallic and Lake Placid Blue finish. Mfd. in Japan. Curr. mfr.

Mfr.'s Sug. Retail	$430	$300	$260	$215	$175	$155	$140	$130

⚞ **Jazz Standard Fretless** — similar to Jazz Standard, except has basswood body, fretless fingerboard. Available in Arctic White and Black finish.

Mfr.'s Sug. Retail	$550	$385	$330	$275	$220	$200	$180	$165

⚞ **Jazz Standard Left Hand** — similar to Jazz Standard, except has basswood body, left handed configuration. Available in 3-Color Sunburst and Vintage White finish.

Mfr.'s Sug. Retail	$780	$545	$470	$390	$315	$280	$260	$235

JAZZ RE-ISSUE SIXTIES — basswood body, white/metal pickguard with finger rest, 20 fret rosewood fingerboard with pearl dot inlay, fixed bridge, chrome hardware, 2 J-style pickups, 2 volume/1 tone controls. Available in Black, Candy Apple Red, Olympic White, Sonic Blue and 3-Color Sunburst finish. Curr. mfr.

Mfr.'s Sug. Retail	$680	$475	$405	$340	$270	$245	$225	$205

This model is also referred to as the '60's Jazz Bass.

JAZZ U.S. VINTAGE '62 — alder body, white/metal pickguard with finger rest, 20 fret rosewood fingerboard with pearl dot inlay, fixed bridge, chrome hardware, 2 J-style pickups, 2 concentric (volume/tone) controls. Available in Black, 3-Color Sunburst and Vintage White finish. Curr. mfr.

Mfr.'s Sug. Retail	$1,400	$980	$840	$700	$560	$505	$460	$420

This model is also referred to as the '62 Jazz Bass.

This model is also available with black and tortoise shell pickguards.

Grading	100%	98%	95%	90%	80%	70%	60%

Limited Edition Series

All instruments in this series are custom order, limited edition instruments.

'51 PRECISION — offset double cutaway ash body, black pickguard, bolt-on maple neck, 20 fret maple fingerboard with black dot inlay, strings thru bridge, tele style peghead, chrome hardware, single coil exposed pickup, pickup cover, volume/tone controls on metal plate. Available in Blonde and 2 Tone Sunburst finish. Curr. mfr.

Mfr.'s Sug. Retail	$700	$490	$420	$350	$280	$250	$230	$210

'75 PRECISION — similar to '51 Precision, except has P-style pickup. Available in Natural finish.

Mfr.'s Sug. Retail	$720	$500	$430	$360	$290	$260	$240	$220

This model also available with rosewood fingerboard with pearl dot inlay.

'75 JAZZ — offset double cutaway asymmetrical ash body, white/metal pickguard with finger rest, 20 fret rosewood fingerboard with pearl dot inlay, fixed bridge with string mutes, F logo bridge cover, chrome hardware, 2 J-style pickups, 2 volume/1 tone controls. Available in Natural and 3 Tone Sunburst finish. Curr. mfr.

Mfr.'s Sug. Retail	$770	$540	$460	$385	$310	$280	$255	$230

This model also available with maple fingerboard with black dot inlay.

Precision Series

All instruments in this series have an offset double cutaway body, bolt-on maple neck, 4 on one side tuners, unless otherwise listed.

PRECISION, EARLY DESIGN — ash body, black pickguard, 20 fret maple fingerboard with black dot inlay, strings thru bridge with cover, tele style peghead, chrome hardware, single coil exposed pickup, pickup cover, volume/tone controls on metal plate. Available in Blond finish. Mfd. 1951-1954.

	$3,250	$2,275	$1,950	$1,625	$1,300	$1,170	$1,070

Precision, Mfd. 1954-1964 — similar to original design Precision, except has white pickguard. Available in Blond, Custom Colors, 2 Tone Sunburst and 3 Tone Sunburst finish. Mfd. 1954 to date.

1954-1964	$4,500	$3,150	$2,700	$2,250	$1,800	$1,620	$1,485
1965-1969	$1,500	$1,050	$900	$750	$600	$540	$495
1970-1979	$750	$525	$450	$375	$300	$270	$245

Black pickguard with Blond finish was an option on this instrument.

In 1957, redesigned aluminum pickguard, fixed bridge, strat style peghead and split pickup replaced original items.

In 1959, rosewood fingerboard with pearl dot inlay replaced maple.

In 1968, maple fingerboard was optionally available.

In 1970, fretless fingerboard was optionally available.

By 1976, thumbrest on pickguard was standard.

Grading	100%	98%	95%	90%	80%	70%	60%

PRECISION ACOUSTIC/ELECTRIC — hollowed basswood body, bound solid spruce top, f hole, fretless rosewood fingerboard, strings thru acoustic style rosewood bridge, chrome hardware, P-style Lace Sensor/piezo bridge pickups, volume/tone/pan controls, active electronics. Available in Antique Burst and Natural finish. Curr. mfr.

Mfr.'s Sug. Retail	$1,100	$770	$660	$550	$440	$395	$365	$330

This model is also available with 20 fret fingerboard.

Precision Contemporary — similar to Precision, except has no pickguard and a rosewood fingerboard. Mfd. 1987.

	$350	$245	$210	$175	$140	$125	$115

PRECISION CONTEMPORARY "LYTE" — basswood body, 22 fret rosewood fingerboard with pearl dot inlay, fixed bridge, gold hardware, P-style/J-style Lace Sensor covered pickups, volume/treble/bass/pan controls, active electronics. Available in Blue Foto Flame, Crimson Foto Flame, Frost White, Montego Black and Violin Burst finish. Curr. mfr.

Mfr.'s Sug. Retail	$730	$510	$440	$365	$290	$260	$240	$220

PRECISION ELITE I — ash body, white pickguard, 20 fret maple fingerboard with black dot inlay, fixed bridge with tuners, die cast tuners, chrome hardware, P-style covered pickup, volume/tone control, active electronics. Mfd. 1983-1985.

	$525	$370	$315	$260	$210	$190	$170

Precision Elite II — similar to Precision Elite I, except has 2 P-style pickups, 2 volume/1 tone controls, 3 position mini switch.

	$750	$525	$450	$375	$300	$270	$245

Precision Gold Elite I — similar to Precision Elite I, except has gold hardware.

	$725	$505	$435	$360	$290	$260	$240

Precision Gold Elite II — similar to Precision Elite I, except has gold hardware, 2 P-style pickups, 2 volume/1 tone controls, 3 position mini switch.

	$800	$560	$480	$400	$320	$290	$265

Precision Walnut Elite I — similar to Precision Elite I, except has walnut body/neck, black pickguard, ebony fingerboard with pearl dot inlay, strings thru bridge, gold hardware, P-style exposed pickup, volume/treble/bass controls, series/parallel switch. Available in Natural finish.

	$775	$540	$460	$385	$310	$280	$255

Precision Walnut Elite II — similar to Precision Elite I, except has walnut body/neck, black pickguard, ebony fingerboard with pearl dot inlay, strings thru bridge, gold hardware, 2 P-style exposed pickups, volume/treble/bass controls, series/parallel switch. Available in Natural finish.

	$825	$580	$495	$415	$330	$300	$275

Grading	100%	98%	95%	90%	80%	70%	60%

PRECISION PLUS — alder body, 22 fret rosewood fingerboard with pearl dot inlay, fixed bridge with tuners, chrome hardware, P-style/J-style Lace Sensor pickups, volume/tone control, 3 position switch, series/parallel pushbutton, active electronics. Available in Arctic White, Black, Black Pearl Burst, Blue Pearl Burst, Brown Sunburst, Caribbean Mist, Lipstick Red, Midnight Blue, Midnight Wine and Natural finish. Mfd. 1990 to date.

Mfr.'s Sug. Retail	$1,000	$700	$600	$500	$400	$360	$330	$300

Add $100 for ash body with Natural finish.

This model also available with maple fingerboard with black dot inlay.

↯ **Precision Deluxe Plus** — similar to Precision Plus, except has down-sized body style, volume/treble/bass/pan controls, redesigned active electronics.

Mfr.'s Sug. Retail	$1,100	$770	$660	$550	$440	$395	$365	$330

↯ **Precision Re-issue '50's** — basswood body, white pickguard, 20 fret maple fingerboard with black dot inlay, fixed bridge, chrome hardware, P-style exposed pickup, volume/tone control. Available in Black, Candy Apple Red, Olympic White, Sonic Blue and 3 Tone Sunburst finish. Curr. mfr.

Mfr.'s Sug. Retail	$670	$470	$400	$335	$265	$240	$220	$200

↯ **Precision Re-Issue '60's** — similar to Precision Re-issue 50's, except has tortoise shell pickguard, rosewood fingerboard with pearl dot inlay.

Mfr.'s Sug. Retail	$670	$470	$400	$335	$265	$240	$220	$200

This model also available with white pickguard.

PRECISION SPECIAL — alder body, white pickguard, 22 fret maple fingerboard with black dot inlay, fixed bridge, brass hardware, P-style exposed pickup, volume/treble/bass controls, active electronics. Available in Candy Apple Red and Lake Placid Blue finish. Mfd. 1982-1983.

		$675	$475	$405	$340	$270	$245	$225

↯ **Precision Special Walnut** — similar to Precision Special, except has walnut body/neck. Available in Natural finish. Mfd. 1982-1983.

		$550	$385	$330	$275	$220	$200	$180

STANDARD PRECISION — poplar body, white pickguard, 20 fret rosewood fingerboard with pearl dot inlay, fixed bridge, chrome hardware, P-style pickup, volume/tone control. Available in Arctic White, Black, Crimson Red, and Lake Placid Blue finish. Mfd. 1987 to date.

Mfr.'s Sug. Retail	$430	$300	$260	$215	$175	$155	$140	$130

U.S. VINTAGE '57 PRECISION — ash body, gold aluminum pickguard with thumbrest, 20 fret maple fingerboard with black dot inlay, fixed bridge, gold hardware, P-style pickup, volume/tone control. Available in Blond, Black, 2 Tone Sunburst and Vintage White finish. Mfd. 1982 to date.

Mfr.'s Sug. Retail	$1,300	$910	$780	$650	$520	$470	$430	$390

This model is a replica of the Precision Bass as it appeared in 1957.

In 1989, alder body and nickel plated hardware replaced original items.

Grading	100%	98%	95%	90%	80%	70%	60%

⚔ **U.S. Vintage '57 Precision-Left Hand Model** — similar to U.S. Vintage '57 Precision, except is left handed. Available in Black and Olympic white finish. Curr. mfr.

Mfr.'s Sug. Retail	$2,200	$1,540	$1,320	$1,100	$880	$790	$725	$660

U.S. VINTAGE '62 PRECISION — ash body, tortoise shell pickguard with thumbrest, 20 fret rosewood fingerboard with pearl dot inlay, fixed bridge, chrome hardware, P-style pickup, volume/tone control. Available in Blond, Black, 3 Tone Sunburst and Vintage White finish. Mfd. 1982 to date.

Mfr.'s Sug. Retail	$1,300	$910	$780	$650	$520	$470	$430	$390

This model is a replica of the Precision Bass as it appeared in 1962.

⚔ **U.S. Vintage '62 Precision-Left Hand Model** — similar to U.S. Vintage '62 Precision, except is left handed. Available in Black and Olympic white finish. Curr. mfr.

Mfr.'s Sug. Retail	$2,200	$1,540	$1,320	$1,100	$880	$790	$725	$660

VINTAGE PRECISION CUSTOM — ash body, 20 fret maple fingerboard with black dot inlay, fixed bridge, tele style peghead, nickel hardware, P-style/J-style pickups, 2 volume/2 tone controls. Available in Honey Blond and 2 Tone Sunburst finish. New 1993.

Mfr.'s Sug. Retail	$2,100	$1,475	$1,260	$1,050	$840	$755	$690	$630

FERNANDES

These instruments are produced by the Fernandes Company, Ltd., located in Tokyo, JAPAN. USA distribution is done by Fernandes Guitars U.S.A. Inc. in Van Nuys, CA.

ELECTRIC

AFR-80 — strat style maple body, bolt-on maple neck, 24 fret rosewood fingerboard with pearl dot inlay, double locking vibrato, 6 on one side tuners, black hardware, 2 stacked coil/1 humbucker pickups, volume/tone control, 5 position switch. Available in Candy Apple Red, Metallic Blue, Pearl Black and Pearl White finish. Mfd. 1991-1992.

		$525	$450	$375	$300	$270	$245	$225

This model is also available with an ash body.
Last Mfr.'s Sug. Retail was $750.

⚔ **AFR-85** — similar to AFR-80, except has humbucker/stacked coil/humbucker pickups.

		$560	$480	$400	$320	$290	$265	$240

Last Mfr.'s Sug. Retail was $800.

Grading	100%	98%	95%	90%	80%	70%	60%

AMG-60 — double cutaway basswood body, set in maple neck, 24 fret maple fingerboard with black dot inlay, standard vibrato, 3 per side tuners, gold hardware, 2 humbucker pickups, volume/tone control, 3 position switch. Available in Fire Red, Navy Blue, Screaming Yellow and Snow White finish. Mfd. 1991-1992.

			$510	$440	$365	$290	$260	$240	$220

Last Mfr.'s Sug. Retail was $730.

� **AMG-70** — similar to AMG-60, except has ash body, rosewood fingerboard with white dot inlay, black hardware, 2 stacked coil/1 humbucker pickups. Available in Transparent Black, Transparent Green, Transparent Purple and Transparent Red finish. Mfd. 1991 to date.

Mfr.'s Sug. Retail	$750	$525	$450	$375	$300	$270	$245	$225

APG-80 — double cutaway bound mahogany body, maple top, set in maple neck, 24 fret rosewood fingerboard with pearl dot inlay, double locking vibrato, bound peghead, 3 per side tuners, gold hardware, stacked coil/humbucker pickups, volume/tone control, 3 position switch. Available in Lemon Drop, Transparent Blue, Transparent Purple and Transparent Red finish. Mfd. 1991-1992.

			$630	$540	$450	$360	$325	$300	$275

Last Mfr.'s Sug. Retail was $900.

✁ **APG-90FS** — similar to APG-80, except has arched maple top, tunomatic bridge/stop tailpiece, 2 humbucker pickups, mini switch, active electronics. Available in Lemon Drop, Transparent Black and Transparent Red finish. New 1993.

Mfr.'s Sug. Retail	$1,200	$840	$720	$600	$480	$430	$395	$360

✁ **APG-100** — similar to APG-80, except has arched maple top, tunomatic bridge/stop tailpiece and 2 humbucker pickups. Available in Cherry Sunburst, Lemon Drop, Transparent Black and Transparent Red finish. Mfd. 1991 to date.

Mfr.'s Sug. Retail	$1,000	$700	$600	$500	$400	$360	$330	$300

FSG-60 — strat style basswood body, bolt-on maple neck, 22 fret rosewood fingerboard with pearl dot inlay, standard vibrato, 6 on one side tuners, black hardware, 2 single coil/1 humbucker pickups, 2 volume/1 tone control, 3 position switch, 2 mini switches, active electronics. Available in Black, Cobalt Blue and Cream White finish. New 1993.

Mfr.'s Sug. Retail	$800	$560	$480	$400	$320	$290	$265	$240

✁ **FSG-100** — similar to FSG-60, except has ash body, double locking vibrato, gold hardware. Available in Transparent Black, Transparent Purple, Transparent Red and Tobacco Sunburst finish.

Mfr.'s Sug. Retail	$1,100	$770	$660	$550	$440	$395	$365	$330

Grading	100%	98%	95%	90%	80%	70%	60%

LE-1 — strat style basswood body, white pickguard, bolt-on maple neck, 21 fret maple fingerboard with black dot inlay, standard vibrato, 6 on one side tuners, chrome hardware, 3 single coil pickups, volume/2 tone controls, 5 position switch. Available in Black, Cream White and Red finish. New 1993.

Mfr.'s Sug. Retail	$400	$280	$240	$200	$160	$145	$130	$120

This model is available with rosewood fingerboard with pearl dot inlay.

LE-2 — similar to LE-1, except has vintage finish neck. Available in Black, Candy Apple Red, Cream, Sonic Blue, Two Tone Sunburst and Three Tone Sunburst finish. Mfd. 1991 to date.

Mfr.'s Sug. Retail	$470	$330	$280	$235	$190	$170	$155	$140

Add $70 for left handed version of this model (LE-2LH).
This model is also found with alder body.

LE-2FS — similar to LE-2, except has active electronics. New 1993.

Mfr.'s Sug. Retail	$710	$495	$425	$355	$285	$255	$235	$215

LE-2G — similar to LE-2, except has gold hardware. Available in Candy Apple Red, Cream White, Gold, Vintage Metallic Blue and 3 Tone Sunburst finish.

Mfr.'s Sug. Retail	$500	$350	$300	$250	$200	$180	$165	$150

LE-2X — similar to LE-2, except has double locking vibrato, 2 single coil/1 humbucker pickups. Available in Black, Candy Apple Red, Cream, Sonic Blue and Three Tone Sunburst finish.

Mfr.'s Sug. Retail	$600	$420	$360	$300	$240	$215	$195	$180

Add $30 for gold hardware (LE-2GX).
Add $20 for reverse headstock (LE-2XR).

LE-3 — strat style basswood body, white pickguard, bolt-on maple neck, 21 fret maple fingerboard with black dot inlay, standard vibrato, roller nut, 6 on one side tuners, chrome hardware, 3 single coil pickups, volume/2 tone controls, 5 position switch. Available in Black, Cream White and Red finish. New 1993.

Mfr.'s Sug. Retail	$700	$490	$420	$350	$280	$250	$230	$210

LE-3FS — similar to LE-3, except has active electronics.

Mfr.'s Sug. Retail	$1,000	$700	$600	$500	$400	$360	$330	$300

TE-1 — tele style basswood body, white pickguard, bolt-on maple neck, 21 fret maple fingerboard with black dot inlay, thru strings bridge, 6 on one side tuners, chrome hardware, 2 single coil pickups, volume/tone control, 3 position switch. Available in Black, Candy Apple Red, Cream White and 3 Tone Sunburst finish. New 1993.

Mfr.'s Sug. Retail	$470	$330	$280	$235	$190	$170	$155	$140

Add $30 for ash body (TE-1N).
This model also available with rosewood fingerboard with pearl dot inlay.

TE-2 — similar to TE-1, except has bound body. Available in Black, Candy Apple Red, Vintage Metallic Blue and 3 Tone Sunburst finish.

Mfr.'s Sug. Retail	$500	$350	$300	$250	$200	$180	$165	$150

Grading	100%	98%	95%	90%	80%	70%	60%

⚡ TE-3 — similar to TE-1, except has semi hollow ash body, restyled pearloid pickguard. Available in Black, Candy Apple Red, Natural and 3 Tone Sunburst finish.

Mfr.'s Sug. Retail	$700	$490	$420	$350	$280	$250	$230	$210

ELECTRIC BASS

AMB-40 — offset double cutaway basswood body, bolt-on maple neck, 24 fret rosewood fingerboard with pearl dot inlay, fixed bridge, 2 per side tuners, chrome hardware, P-style/J-style Fernandes pickups, 2 volume/1 tone control. Available in Black, Blue Sunburst, Fire Red and Snow White finish. Mfd. 1991 to date.

Mfr.'s Sug. Retail	$570	$400	$340	$285	$230	$205	$190	$170

Available in left handed style only.

⚡ AMB-60 — similar to AMB-40, except has black hardware.

Mfr.'s Sug. Retail	$600	$420	$360	$300	$240	$215	$195	$180

Available in right handed style only.

AMB-70 — similar to AMB-40, except has ash body, active pickups and gold hardware. Available in Transparent Black, Transparent Purple, Transparent White and Vintage Natural finish. Disc. 1992.

		$560	$480	$400	$320	$290	$265	$240

Last Mfr.'s Sug. Retail was $800.

APB-80 — offset double cutaway ash body, bolt-on maple neck, 24 fret rosewood fingerboard with pearl dot inlay, fixed bridge, 2 per side tuners, gold hardware, P-style/J-style pickups, 2 volume/1 tone control. Available in Black, Fire Red, Metallic Blue and Snow White finish. Curr. Mfr.

Mfr.'s Sug. Retail	$700	$490	$420	$350	$280	$250	$230	$210

APB-90 — similar to APB-80, except has active pickups, volume/treble/bass/mix controls. Available in Transparent Blue, Transparent Purple, Transparent Red and Transparent White finish.

Mfr.'s Sug. Retail	$900	$630	$540	$450	$360	$325	$300	$275

This model also available with maple fingerboard with black dot inlay, 2 J-style pickups (APB-90M).

This model also available with fretless fingerboard.

APB-100 — similar to APB-80, except has 5 strings, 3/2 per side tuners, 2 active J-style pickups. Available in Transparent Black, Transparent Purple, Transparent White and Vintage Natural finish.

Mfr.'s Sug. Retail	$1,000	$700	$600	$500	$400	$360	$330	$300

This model also available with fretless fingerboard.

Grading	100%	98%	95%	90%	80%	70%	60%

TEB-1 — tele style basswood body, black pickguard, bolt-on maple neck, 21 fret maple fingerboard with black dot inlay, fixed bridge, 4 on one side tuners, gold hardware, P-style/J-style pickups, 2 volume/1 tone control. Available in Black and Cream White finish. New 1993.

Mfr.'s Sug. Retail	$700	$490	$420	$350	$280	$250	$230	$210

G

G & L

Manufacturer located in Fullerton, CA. Distributed by G & L Musical Products located in Huntington Beach, CA.

This was the last company founded by legendary guitar innovator Leo Fender, who continued to bring new ideas and high standards to the fretted instrument industry.

ELECTRIC

Unless otherwise listed, all models in this series are available with 22 fret maple fingerboard with black dot inlay or rosewood fingerboard with pearl dot inlay and in the following finishes: Belair Green, Black, Black Swirl, Blueburst, Blue Emerald, Blue Swirl, Candy Apple Red, Cherryburst, Gold Metallic, Lake Placid Blue, Natural, Red Swirl, Silver Metallic, Sparkle Purple, Sparkle Red, Sunburst, Tobacco Sunburst, Transparent Blonde, Transparent Blue, Transparent Forest Green, Transparent Red and White.

ASAT — tele style alder body, black pickguard, bolt-on maple neck, fixed bridge with locking saddles, 6 on one side tuners, black hardware, 2 single coil pickups, volume/tone control, 3 position switch. Mfd. 1986 to date.

Mfr.'s Sug. Retail	$900	$630	$540	$450	$360	$325	$300	$275

ASAT Classic — similar to ASAT, except has ash body, white pickguard, standard fixed bridge, chrome hardware. Mfd. 1990 to date.

Mfr.'s Sug. Retail	$1,200	$840	$720	$600	$480	$430	$395	$360

ASAT Special — similar to ASAT, except has ash body, white pickguard.

Mfr.'s Sug. Retail	$900	$630	$540	$450	$360	$325	$300	$275

BROADCASTER — tele style alder body, black pickguard, bolt-on maple neck, fixed bridge with locking saddles, body color matching peghead, 6 on one side tuners, black hardware, 2 single coil pickups, volume/tone control, 3 position switch. Available in Black finish. Mfd. 1985-1986.

maple fingerboard	$1,800	$1,260	$1,080	$900	$720	$650	$595
ebony fingerboard	$1,200	$840	$720	$600	$480	$430	$395

Last Mfr.'s Sug. Retail was $706.

This model also available with ebony fingerboard with pearl dot inlay.

A Certificate of Authenticity was also issued with each instrument.

(more information on the next page)

Grading	100%	98%	95%	90%	80%	70%	60%

These instruments return to Leo Fender's original Telecaster design, and once again Gretsch notified Leo that it already had rights to the name. Leo produced this instrument for one year, with all instruments being signed and dated by Leo in the neck pocket of the body.

G & L decided to manufacture a limited number of instruments, the total number being 869. The following year, the Broadcaster was renamed the ASAT.

CLIMAX — strat style ash body, bolt-on maple neck, double locking vibrato, 6 on one side tuners, black hardware, 2 single coil/1 humbucker pickups, volume/tone control, 5 position switch. Curr. mfr.

Mfr.'s Sug. Retail	$950	$665	$570	$475	$380	$345	$315	$285

⚱ **Climax Plus** — similar to Climax, except has humbucker/single coil/humbucker pickups.

Mfr.'s Sug. Retail	$1,050	$735	$630	$525	$420	$380	$345	$315

⚱ **Climax XL** — similar to Climax, except has 2 humbucker pickups, 3 position switch.

Mfr.'s Sug. Retail	$980	$685	$585	$485	$390	$355	$325	$295

COMMANCHE V — offset double cutaway ash body, black pickguard, bolt-on maple neck, 22 fret maple fingerboard with black dot inlay, standard vibrato, 6 on one side tuners, chrome hardware, 3 "split-coil" pickups, volume/2 tone controls, 5 position/mini switches. Available in Black, Blonde, Cherryburst and Natural finish. Mfd. 1990-1991.

	$930	$795	$660	$530	$475	$435	$395

Add $60 for Leo Fender vibrato.
Last Mfr.'s Sug. Retail was $1,325.

⚱ **Commanche VI** — similar to Commanche V, except has 6 mini switches, no 5 position switch.

	$930	$795	$660	$530	$475	$435	$395

Add $60 for Leo Fender vibrato.
Last Mfr.'s Sug. Retail was $1,325.

LEGACY — strat style alder body, white pickguard, bolt-on maple neck, standard vibrato, 6 on one side tuners, chrome hardware, 3 single coil pickups, volume/treble/bass controls, 5 position switch. Curr. mfr.

Mfr.'s Sug. Retail	$850	$595	$510	$425	$340	$305	$280	$255

Grading	100%	98%	95%	90%	80%	70%	60%

✠ **Legacy Special** — similar to Legacy, except has ash body, graphite nut, locking Sperzel tuners, 3 single coil blade pickups.

Mfr.'s Sug. Retail	$1,100	$770	$660	$550	$440	$395	$365	$330

S-500 — strat style ash body, white pickguard, bolt-on maple neck, standard vibrato, 6 on one side locking Sperzel tuners, chrome hardware, 3 single coil pickups, volume/treble/bass control, 5 position/mini switch. Mfd. 1985 to date.

Mfr.'s Sug. Retail	$1,250	$875	$750	$625	$500	$450	$415	$375

ELECTRIC BASS

All models in this series are available with 21 fret maple fingerboard with black dot inlay or rosewood fingerboard with pearl dot inlay, fixed bridge with locking saddles and in the following finishes: Belair Green, Black, Black Swirl, Blueburst, Blue Emerald, Blue Swirl, Candy Apple Red, Cherryburst, Gold Metallic, Lake Placid Blue, Natural, Red Swirl, Silver Metallic, Sparkle Purple, Sparkle Red, Sunburst, Tobacco Sunburst, Transparent Blonde, Transparent Blue, Transparent Forest Green, Transparent Red and White.

ASAT BASS — tele style ash body, bolt-on maple neck, 4 on one side tuners, chrome hardware, 2 humbucker pickups, volume/treble/bass controls, pickup/series-parallel/preamp switches, active electronics. Curr. mfr.

Mfr.'s Sug. Retail	$1,200	$840	$720	$600	$480	$430	$395	$360

CLIMAX BASS — precision style ash body, bolt-on maple neck, 4 on one side tuners, chrome hardware, humbucker pickup, volume/treble/bass controls, bypass/preamp switches. Curr. mfr.

Mfr.'s Sug. Retail	$1,100	$770	$660	$550	$440	$395	$365	$330

LEGACY BASS — precision style alder body, white pickguard, bolt-on maple neck, 4 on one side tuners, chrome hardware, P-style pickup, volume/tone control. Curr. mfr.

Mfr.'s Sug. Retail	$900	$630	$540	$450	$360	$325	$300	$275

L1000 — precision style ash body, bolt-on maple neck, 4 on one side tuners, humbucker pickup, volume/treble/bass controls, series-parallel switch. Curr. mfr.

Mfr.'s Sug. Retail	$950	$665	$570	$475	$380	$345	$315	$285

Available with ebony fingerboard with pearl dot inlay.

✠ **L2000** — similar to L1000, except has 2 humbucker pickups, pickup/series-parallel/preamp/treble boost switches, active electronics.

Mfr.'s Sug. Retail	$1,200	$840	$720	$600	$480	$430	$395	$360

✠ **L5000** — similar to L1000, except has 5 strings, alder body, black pickguard, 4/1 per side tuners, volume/tone control.

Mfr.'s Sug. Retail	$950	$665	$570	$475	$380	$345	$315	$285

 , cont.

Grading	100%	98%	95%	90%	80%	70%	60%

SB1 — strat style alder body, black pickguard, 4 on one side tuners, chrome hardware, P-style pickup, volume/tone control. Curr. mfr.

Mfr.'s Sug. Retail	$700	$490	$420	$350	$280	$250	$230	$210

SB2 — similar to SB1, except has P-style/J-style pickups, 2 volume controls.

Mfr.'s Sug. Retail	$800	$560	$480	$400	$320	$290	$265	$240

GIBSON

Current manufacturer located in Nashville, TN and Bozeman, MT. Previously manufactured in Kalamazoo, MI until the early 80's. This company was originally founded by Orville Gibson in 1902. Gibson instruments continue to offer musicians a wide array of models and features—not to mention Gibson's trademark quality.

Identifying Features on Gibson Musical Instruments

The most consistent and easily found feature that goes across all models of Gibson production is the logo, or lack of one, found on the peghead. The very earliest instruments made are generally found with a star inside a crescent design, or a blank peghead. This lasted until approximately 1902. From 1902 to the late 1920's, "The Gibson", inlaid in pearl and placed at a slant, is found on the peghead. In the late 1920's, this style of logo was changed to having "The Gibson" read straight across the peghead as opposed to being slanted. Flat top acoustics production began at approximately this time and these instruments generally do not have "The" on the inlay, it just has "Gibson" in script writing. By 1933, this was the established peghead logo for Gibson. Just before WWII, Gibson began making the lettering on the logo thicker and this became standard on most prewar instruments. Right after WWII, the styling of the logo remained but it became slanted once again. In 1947, the logo that is still in use today made its debut. This logo has a block styling with the "G" having a tail, the "i" dot is touching the "G", the "b" and "o" are open and the "n" is connected at the bottom. The logo is still slanted. By 1951, the dot on the "i" is no longer connected to the "G". In 1967, the logo styling became even more squared (pentographed) with the "b" and "o" becoming closed and the "i" dot being removed. In 1970, Gibson replaced the black tinted piece of wood that had been used on peghead face with a black fiber that the logo and other peghead inlay were placed into. With the change in peghead facing came a slightly smaller logo lettering. In 1972, the "i" dot reappeared on the peghead logo. In 1981, the "n" is connected at the top to the "o". There are a few models through the years that do not follow this timeline, ie: reissues and limited editions, but most of the production instruments can be found with the above feature changes. The figuration of the Kluson tuners used on Gibson instruments can be used to date an instrument. Before 1959, all Kluson tuners with plastic buttons had a single ring around the stem end of the button. In 1960, this was changed to a double ring configuration. Another dating feature of Gibsons are the use of a headstock volute found on instruments between 1970 and 1973. Also in 1965, Gibson switched from the 17 degrees to 14 degrees on the tilt

Grading	100%	98%	95%	90%	80%	70%	60%

of the peghead. Before 1950, peghead thickness varied, getting narrower towards the top of the peghead. After 1950, pegheads all became one uniform thickness, from bottom to top.

Common Gibson Abbreviations

C - Cutaway

D - Dreadnought or Double

E - Electric

ES - Electric (Electro) Spanish

J - Jumbo

LE - Limited Edition

S - Spanish, Solid Body, Special or Super

SG - Solid Guitar

T - Tremolo or Thinline

V - V shaped Neck, Venetian, Vibrato or Vintage Series

ACOUSTIC

DOVE — dreadnought style, spruce top, round soundhole, tortoise shell pickguard with dove inlay, 3 stripe bound body/rosette, figured maple back/sides/neck, 14/20 fret bound rosewood fingerboard with pearl parallelogram inlay, enlarged rosewood bridge with black pearl dot pins, pearl dove inlay on bridge wings, blackface peghead with pearl plant/logo inlay, 3 per side gold tuners with pearl buttons. Available in Antique Cherry finish. Mfd. 1962 to date.

	100%	98%	95%	90%	80%	70%	60%
1962-1968		$1,200	$840	$720	$600	$480	$430	$395
1969-1975		$1,000	$700	$600	$500	$400	$360	$330
1976-1982		$900	$630	$540	$450	$360	$325	$300
Mfr.'s Sug. Retail	$2,400	$1,680	$1,440	$1,200	$960	$860	$790	$720

In 1969, adjustable bridge replaced original item.

In 1970, non-adjustable bridge replaced respective item.

In 1975, ebony fingerboard replaced original item.

Current model features rosewood fingerboard.

HUMMINGBIRD — dreadnought style, spruce top, round soundhole, tortoise shell pickguard with engraved floral/hummingbird pattern, 3 stripe bound body/rosette, mahogany back/sides/neck, 14/20 fret bound rosewood fingerboard with pearl parallelogram inlay, rosewood bridge with black pearl dot pins, blackface peghead with pearl plant/logo inlay, 3 per side nickel tuners with pearl buttons. Available in Vintage Cherry Sunburst finish. Mfd. 1960 to date.

	100%	98%	95%	90%	80%	70%	60%
1960-1968		$1,500	$1,050	$900	$750	$600	$540	$495
1969-1975		$750	$525	$450	$375	$300	$270	$245
1976-1982		$1,100	$770	$660	$550	$440	$395	$365
Mfr.'s Sug. Retail	$1,900	$1,330	$1,140	$950	$760	$685	$625	$570

In 1962-1963, some models found with maple back/sides.

In 1969, adjustable saddle replaced original item.

In 1970, non-adjustable saddle replaced respective item.

In 1973, block fingerboard inlay replaced original item.

In 1984, parallelogram fingerboard inlay replaced respective item.

Gibson USA , cont.

Grading	100%	98%	95%	90%	80%	70%	60%

JUBILEE — ¾ size dreadnought style, spruce top, round soundhole, black pickguard, bound body/rosette, mahogany back/sides/neck, 14/20 fret rosewood fingerboard with pearl dot inlay, adjustable rosewood bridge, 3 per side tuners. Available in Natural finish. Mfd. 1970-1971.

	$625	$440	$375	$310	$250	$225	$205

Jubilee 12 String — similar to Jubilee, except has 12 strings, 6 per side tuners.

	$600	$420	$360	$300	$240	$215	$195

Jubilee Deluxe — similar to Jubilee, except has multi-wooden binding/purfling, rosewood back/sides.

	$750	$525	$450	$375	$300	$270	$245

SUPER 300 — grand auditorium style body, arched spruce top, f holes, raised multi-ply black pickguard, figured maple back/sides, multiple bound body, 3 piece figured maple/mahogany neck, 14/20 fret bound Brazilian rosewood fingerboard with pearl parallelogram inlay, adjustable rosewood bridge/nickel trapeze tailpiece, multi-bound blackface peghead with pearl crown/logo inlay, 3 per side nickel tuners. Available in Golden Sunburst finish. Mfd. 1948-1955.

	$2,500	$1,750	$1,500	$1,250	$1,000	$900	$825

Super 300 C — similar to Super 300, except has a single round cutaway. Mfd. 1957-1958.

	$1,525	$1,070	$915	$765	$610	$550	$505

SUPER 400 — grand auditorium style body, arched spruce top, bound f holes, raised multi-bound mottled plastic pickguard, figured maple back/sides, multiple bound body, 3 piece figured maple/mahogany neck, model name engraved into heel cap, 14/20 fret bound ebony fingerboard with point on bottom, pearl split block fingerboard inlay, adjustable rosewood bridge with pearl triangle wings inlay, gold trapeze tailpiece with engraved model name, multi-bound blackface peghead with pearl 5 piece split diamond/logo inlay, pearl 3 piece split diamond inlay on back of peghead, 3 per side engraved gold Grover tuners. Available in Brown Sunburst finish. Mfd. 1934 -1955.

	$5,500	$3,850	$3,300	$2,750	$2,200	$1,980	$1,815

In 1936, upper bouts were widened.

In 1937, sealed tuners became optional.

In 1938, Grover Imperial tuners replaced original item.

Super 400 Premier (400C) — similar to Super 400, except has a single round cutaway, multi-bound pearloid pickguard, unhinged "PAF" trapeze tailpiece. Available in Brown Sunburst and Natural finish. Mfd. 1937-1983.

	$8,000	$5,600	$4,800	$3,400	$3,200	$2,880	$2,640

Some early models are found with solid metal tuners.

In 1942, no model name is found on heel cap.

In 1949, rosewood fingerboard replaced original item.

In 1953, ebony fingerboard replaced respective item.

By 1957, metal tuners replaced original item.

Grading	100%	98%	95%	90%	80%	70%	60%

J Series

J-30 — dreadnought style, spruce top, round soundhole, tortoise shell pickguard, 3 stripe bound body/rosette, mahogany back/sides/neck, 14/20 fret rosewood fingerboard with pearl dot inlay, rosewood bridge with black pins, 3 per side nickel tuners with pearl buttons. Available in Antique Walnut and Vintage Sunburst finish. Curr. mfr.

	100%	98%	95%	90%	80%	70%	60%
Mfr.'s Sug. Retail	$1,300	$910	$780	$650	$520	$470	$430	$390

J-45 — vintage dreadnought style, spruce top, round soundhole, tortoise shell pickguard, 3 stripe bound body/rosette, mahogany back/sides/neck, 14/20 fret rosewood fingerboard with pearl dot inlay, rosewood bridge with black pins, 3 per side nickel tuners with pearl buttons. Available in Sunburst finish. Mfd. 1942-1982.

	100%	98%	95%	90%	80%	70%	60%
1942-1945	$1,675	$1,170	$1,000	$835	$670	$600	$550
1946-1950	$1,400	$980	$840	$700	$560	$505	$460
1951-1959	$1,325	$930	$795	$660	$530	$475	$435
1960-1964	$1,250	$875	$750	$625	$500	$450	$415
1965-1968	$850	$595	$510	$425	$340	$305	$280
1969-1974	$750	$525	$450	$375	$300	$270	$245
1975-1982	$700	$490	$420	$350	$280	$250	$230

This model was originally released with one stripe body binding.

In 1947, Natural finish version of this instrument was introduced (J-50).

In 1950, upper belly on bridge and 3 stripe body binding replaced original items.

In 1955, redesigned pickguard replaced original item.

In 1956, adjustable bridge became optional.

In 1962, Cherry Sunburst finish was offered.

In 1968, belly under bridge replaced respective item.

In 1969, redesigned body/pickguard replaced respective items.

In 1971, non-adjustable saddle became standard.

In 1975, redesigned pickguard, 4 stripe top purfling and tortoise shell body binding replaced respective items.

In 1981, 3 stripe top purfling replaced respective item.

J-45 Celebrity — similar to J-45, except has rosewood back/sides, fern peghead inlay. Mfd. 1985 only.

	100%	98%	95%	90%	80%	70%	60%
	$1,000	$700	$600	$500	$400	$360	$330

J-45 Re-Issue — similar to J-45, except has vintage style dreadnought body. Available in Ebony, Natural and Sunburst finish. Mfd. 1984 to date.

	100%	98%	95%	90%	80%	70%	60%
Mfr.'s Sug. Retail	$1,400	$980	$840	$700	$560	$505	$460	$420

J-60 — similar to J-30, except has rosewood back/sides. Available in Antique Natural and Vintage Sunburst finish. Curr. mfr.

	100%	98%	95%	90%	80%	70%	60%
Mfr.'s Sug. Retail	$1,700	$1,190	$1,020	$850	$680	$610	$560	$510

Grading		100%	98%	95%	90%	80%	70%	60%

J-100 — jumbo style, spruce top, round soundhole, black pickguard, 2 stripe bound body/rosette, maple back/sides/neck, 14/20 fret rosewood fingerboard with pearl dot inlay, rosewood bridge with black pins, 3 per side nickel tuners with pearl buttons. Available in Natural finish. Mfd. 1985-1991.

			$900	$630	$540	$450	$360	$325	$300

This model is also found with cedar top.

J-100 XTRA — jumbo style, spruce top, round soundhole, black pickguard, 2 stripe bound body/rosette, mahogany back/sides/neck, 14/20 fret rosewood fingerboard with pearl dot inlay, rosewood bridge with black pins, 3 per side nickel tuners with pearl buttons. Available in Antique Walnut and Vintage Sunburst finish. Curr. mfr.

Mfr.'s Sug. Retail	$1,400	$980	$840	$700	$560	$505	$460	$420

J-185 — jumbo style, spruce top, round soundhole, tortoise shell pickguard, 2 stripe bound body/rosette, figured maple back/sides, mahogany neck, 14/20 fret rosewood fingerboard with pearl parallelogram inlay, upper belly rosewood bridge with white pins, pearl cross bridge wings inlay, blackface peghead with pearl crown/logo inlay, 3 per side nickel tuners. Available in Cremona Brown Burst and Natural finish. Mfd. 1951-1958.

	$4,200	$2,940	$2,520	$2,100	$1,680	$1,510	$1,385

J-200 — jumbo style, spruce top, round soundhole, black pickguard with engraved floral pattern, figured maple back/sides/neck, 14/20 bound rosewood fingerboard with pearl crown inlay, rosewood mustache bridge with pearl block inlay, black pearl dot pins, bound peghead with pearl plant/logo inlay, 3 per side gold tuners with pearl buttons. Available in Antique Walnut, Natural and Vintage Sunburst finish. Mfd. 1937 to date.

		100%	98%	95%	90%	80%	70%	60%
1937-1941		N/A	N/A	N/A	N/A	N/A	N/A	N/A
1942-1945		N/A	N/A	N/A	N/A	N/A	N/A	N/A
1946-1950		$5,250	$3,675	$3,150	$2,625	$2,100	$1,890	$1,730
1951-1959		$4,250	$2,975	$2,550	$2,125	$1,700	$1,530	$1,400
1960-1964		$3,450	$2,415	$2,070	$1,725	$1,380	$1,240	$1,140
1965-1968		$2,650	$1,855	$1,590	$1,325	$1,060	$955	$875
1969-1974		$1,500	$1,050	$900	$750	$600	$540	$495
1975-1982		$1,000	$700	$600	$500	$400	$360	$330
Mfr.'s Sug. Retail	$2,550	$1,785	$1,530	$1,275	$1,020	$920	$840	$765

This model was known as the Super Jumbo (SJ-200) from 1936-1945.

Original release of this instrument had single peghead binding.

In 1948, Natural finish became optional.

In 1960, adjustable saddle bridge became optional.

In 1961, Tune-O-Matic bridge with pearl block inlay replaced original items.

In 1969, adjustable saddle became standard.

In 1971, ebony fingerboard replaced original item, non-adjustable bridge replaced respective item.

In 1979, rosewood fingerboard replaced respective item.

In 1985, mustache bridge with pearl block inlay replaced respective item, multi-bound peghead replaced original item.

Grading	100%	98%	95%	90%	80%	70%	60%

J-200 Jr. — similar to J-200, except has smaller body, nickel tuners. Curr. mfr.

Mfr.'s Sug. Retail	$1,800	$1,260	$1,080	$900	$720	$650	$595	$540

J-2000/CUSTOM — single round cutaway jumbo style, spruce top, round soundhole, abalone bound body/rosette, rosewood back/sides, mahogany neck, 20 fret bound ebony point fingerboard with abalone crown inlay, ebony bridge with white abalone dot pins, stylized wing abalone bridge wings inlay, bound peghead with stylized wing/logo inlay, 3 per side gold tuners with pearl buttons, piezo bridge pickup, endpin pickup jack. Available in Antique Natural and Vintage Sunburst finish. Curr. mfr.

Mfr.'s Sug. Retail	$4,010	$2,800	$2,400	$2,000	$1,600	$1,440	$1,320	$1,200

SJ (SOUTHERNER JUMBO) — vintage dreadnought style, spruce top, round soundhole, black pickguard, 2 stripe bound body/rosette, mahogany back/sides/neck, 14/20 fret bound rosewood fingerboard with pearl parallelogram inlays, rosewood bridge with white pins, blackface peghead with pearl banner logo inlay, 3 per side nickel tuners. Available in Sunburst finish. Mfd. 1942-1978.

	100%	98%	95%	90%	80%	70%	60%
1942-1945	$1,725	$1,210	$1,040	$865	$690	$620	$570
1946-1950	$1,500	$1,050	$900	$750	$600	$540	$495
1951-1959	$1,300	$910	$780	$650	$520	$470	$430
1960-1964	$1,125	$790	$675	$565	$455	$405	$370
1965-1968	$800	$560	$480	$400	$320	$290	$265
1969-1978	$700	$490	$420	$350	$280	$250	$230

A few early models are found with rosewood back/sides.
In 1946, no peghead logo appeared.
In 1949, upper belly bridge replaced original item.
In 1954, Natural finish became an option.
In 1955, redesigned pickguard replaced original item.
In 1961, adjustable saddle replaced original item.
In 1963, redesigned body/pickguard replaced respective items.
In 1969, standard style bridge replaced respective item.
In 1970, non-adjustable saddle replaced respective item.
In 1974, 4 stripe body/2 stripe neck binding replaced original items.

SJN (Country Western) — similar to SJ (Southern Jumbo), except has tortoise shell pickguard. Available in Natural finish. Mfd. 1956-1978.

	100%	98%	95%	90%	80%	70%	60%
1956-1964	$950	$665	$570	$475	$380	$345	$315
1965-1968	$700	$490	$420	$350	$280	$250	$230
1969-1978	$500	$350	$300	$250	$200	$180	$165

L Series

L-00 — folk style, spruce top, round soundhole, 2 stripe bound body/rosette, mahogany back/sides/neck, 14/19 fret bound rosewood fingerboard with pearl dot inlay, rosewood bridge with white pins, 3 per side nickel tuners with plastic buttons. Available in Antique Walnut and Vintage Sunburst finish. Curr. mfr.

Mfr.'s Sug. Retail	$1,300	$910	$780	$650	$520	$470	$430	$390

L-1 — similar to L-OO, except has Vintage Cherry Sunburst finish.

Mfr.'s Sug. Retail	$1,400	$980	$840	$700	$560	$505	$460	$420

L-20 SPECIAL — similar to L-OO, except has rosewood back/sides, gold tuners, piezo bridge pickup, endpin pickup jack. Available in Antique Natural and Vintage Sunburst finish.

Mfr.'s Sug. Retail	$2,000	$1,400	$1,200	$1,000	$800	$720	$660	$600

Mark Series

All of the following guitars have dreadnought style bodies, round soundholes, removable pickguards, bound body, mahogany neck, 14/20 fret fingerboard, fan shaped bridges pointing toward the treble side, 3 different replaceable saddles, blackface snakehead shaped peghead, 3 per side tuners. Available in Natural and Sunburst finish, unless otherwise noted. Mfd. 1975-1979.

MK-35 — spruce top, 2 stripe rosewood soundhole cap, mahogany back/sides, rosewood fingerboard with pearl dot inlay, nickel tuners.

$550	$385	$330	$275	$220	$200	$180

MK-35-12 — similar to MK-35, except has 12 strings. Mfd. 1977 only.

$600	$420	$360	$300	$240	$215	$195

MK-72 — spruce top, 3 stripe rosette, rosewood back/sides, 3 piece ebony/rosewood/ebony fingerboard with pearl dot inlay, nickel tuners.

$700	$490	$420	$350	$280	$250	$230

MK-81 — spruce top, 3 stripe rosewood rosette cap, multi-bound body, rosewood back/sides, ebony fingerboard with block abalone inlays, gold tuners.

$750	$525	$450	$375	$300	$270	$245

ACOUSTIC ELECTRIC

BOSSA NOVA — single round cutaway dreadnought style, spruce top, round soundhole, 2 stripe bound body/rosette, rosewood back/sides, mahogany neck, 20 fret rosewood fingerboard, rosewood tied bridge, classical style slotted peghead, 3 per side nickel tuners with plastic buttons, ceramic bridge pickup. Available in Natural finish. Mfd. 1971-1973.

$1,050	$735	$630	$525	$420	$380	$345

This model is a nylon strings instrument.

J-160 E — vintage dreadnought style, spruce top, round soundhole, tortoise shell pickguard, 2 stripe bound body/rosette, mahogany back/sides/neck, 15/19 fret bound rosewood fingerboard with pearl block inlay, rosewood bridge with white pins, blackface peghead with pearl plant/logo inlay, 3 per side nickel tuners, single coil pickup, volume/tone control. Available in Vintage Sunburst finish. Curr. mfr.

Mfr.'s Sug. Retail	$1,800	$1,260	$1,080	$900	$720	$650	$595	$540

Grading	100%	98%	95%	90%	80%	70%	60%

LES PAUL JUMBO — single round cutaway dreadnought style, spruce top, round soundhole, tortoise shell pickguard, 2 stripe bound body/rosette, rosewood back/sides, mahogany neck, 19 fret rosewood fingerboard with pearl dot inlay, rosewood bridge with black white dot pins, 3 per side chrome tuners, single coil pickup, volume/treble/mid/bass controls, 2 position switch. Available in Natural finish. Mfd. 1970 only.

	$1,200	$840	$720	$600	$480	$430	$395

Chet Atkins Series

CHET ATKINS CE/CEC — classical style single round cutaway mahogany body with hollow sound chambers, solid spruce top, round soundhole with plastic bowl insert, 2 stripe bound body, wood inlay rosette, mahogany neck, 19 fret rosewood fingerboard, tied rosewood bridge, rosewood veneer on slotted peghead, 3 per side gold tuners with pearl buttons, Gibson piezo bridge pickups, volume/tone control, active electronics. Available in Alpine White, Ebony and Wine Red finish. Curr. mfr.

Mfr.'s Sug. Retail	$1,350	$945	$810	$675	$540	$485	$445	$405

Add $150 for Antique Natural finish.

CHET ATKINS SST — single round cutaway mahogany body with hollow sound chamber, 5 stripe bound solid spruce top with Chet Atkins' signature, mahogany neck, 21 fret ebony fingerboard with pearl star inlay, ebony bridge with black pearl dot pins, pearl star bridge wings inlay, blackface peghead with pearl star/logo inlay, 3 per side gold tuners, transducer bridge pickup, volume/treble/bass controls, active electronics. Available in Alpine White, Ebony and Wine Red finish. Mfd. 1987 to date.

Mfr.'s Sug. Retail	$1,250	$875	$750	$625	$500	$450	$415	$375

Add $200 for Antique Natural, Heritage Cherry Sunburst and Translucent Red finish.

Chet Atkins SST Flame Top — similar to Chet Atkins SST, except has figured maple top. Available in Antique Natural, Heritage Cherry Sunburst and Translucent Red finish.

Mfr.'s Sug. Retail	$1,600	$1,120	$960	$800	$640	$575	$530	$480

Chet Atkins SST 12 — similar to Chet Atkins SST, except has 12 string configuration, 6 per side tuners. Available in Ebony and Wine Red finish. Curr. mfr.

Mfr.'s Sug. Retail	$1,250	$875	$750	$625	$500	$450	$415	$375

Add $250 for Antique Natural finish.

Chet Atkins SST 12 Flame Top — similar to Chet Atkins SST, except has 12 string configuration, flame maple top, 6 per side tuners. Available in Antique Natural, Heritage Cherry Sunburst and Translucent Red finish. Curr. mfr.

Mfr.'s Sug. Retail	$1,600	$1,120	$960	$800	$640	$575	$530	$480

Grading	100%	98%	95%	90%	80%	70%	60%

ELECTRIC

BYRDLAND — single round cutaway multi-bound hollow body, solid spruce top, raised bound black pickguard, f holes, figured maple back/sides/neck, 22 fret multi-bound ebony pointed fingerboard with pearl block inlay, Tune-O-Matic bridge with ebony base, trapeze tailpiece, multi-bound blackface peghead with pearl torch/logo inlay, 3 per side tuners, gold hardware, 2 single coil pickups, 2 volume/2 tone controls, 3 position switch. Available in Natural and Sunburst finish. Mfd. 1956 to 1981.

	100%	98%	95%	90%	80%	70%	60%
	$2,025	$1,420	$1,215	$1,015	$810	$730	$670

CHALLENGER I — Les Paul style mahogany body, black pickguard, bolt-on maple neck, 22 fret rosewood fingerboard with pearl dot inlay, Tune-O-Matic stud tailpiece, 3 per side tuners, chrome hardware, humbucker pickup, volume/tone control. No finish information available at this time. Mfd. 1983-1985.

	$275	$195	$165	$140	$110	$100	$90

⚄ **Challenger II** — similar to Challenger I, except has 2 humbucker pickups, 2 volume controls.

	$300	$210	$180	$150	$120	$110	$100

CHET ATKINS TENNESSEAN — single round cutaway semi hollow bound maple body, f holes, raised pickguard with engraved "Tennessean", arm rest on bottom bass bout, 3 piece maple neck, 22 fret rosewood fingerboard with offset pearl dot inlay, Tune-O-Matic bridge/stop tailpiece, blackface peghead with signature/pearl logo inlay, 3 per side tuners with pearl buttons, chrome hardware, 2 covered humbucker pickups, master volume on upper treble bout, 2 volume/1 tone controls, 3 position switch. Available in Ebony finish. Curr. mfr.

Mfr.'s Sug. Retail	$1,050	$735	$630	$525	$420	$380	$345	$315

Add $100 for Country Gentleman Brown, Sunrise Orange and Wine Red finish.

CORVUS I — can opener style hardwood body, black pickguard, bolt-on maple neck, 22 fret rosewood fingerboard with white dot inlay, Tune-O-Matic stud tailpiece, 6 on one side tuners, chrome hardware, covered humbucker pickup, volume/tone control. Available in Silver finish. Mfd. 1983-1985.

	$200	$140	$120	$100	$80	$70	$65

⚄ **Corvus II** — similar to Corvus I, except has 2 covered humbucker pickups, 3 position switch.

	$225	$160	$135	$115	$90	$80	$70

⚄ **Corvus III** — similar to Corvus I, except has 3 exposed single coil pickups, 5 position switch.

	$250	$175	$150	$125	$100	$90	$80

Grading	100%	98%	95%	90%	80%	70%	60%

FUTURA — can opener style hardwood body, black tri-lam pickguard, thru body maple neck, 22 fret rosewood fingerboard with white dot inlay, Tune-O-Matic bridge/stop tailpiece, 6 on one side tuners, chrome hardware, 2 covered humbucker pickups, 2 volume/1 tone controls, 3 position switch. Available in Ebony, Ultraviolet and White finish. Mfd. 1983-1985.

	$225	$160	$135	$115	$90	$80	$70

GK-55 — Les Paul style mahogany body, bolt-on mahogany neck, 22 fret rosewood fingerboard with pearl dot inlay, Tune-O-Matic bridge/stop tailpiece, 3 per side tuners, chrome hardware, 2 exposed humbucker pickups, 2 volume/2 tone controls, 3 position switch. Available in Tobacco Sunburst finish. Mfd. 1979 only.

	$300	$210	$180	$150	$120	$110	$100

INVADER — Les Paul style mahogany body/neck, 22 fret ebony fingerboard with dot inlay, double locking vibrato, 6 on one side tuners, black hardware, 2 exposed "dirty finger" humbucker pickups, 2 volume/2 tone controls, 3 position switch. Available in Black finish. Mfd. 1983-1989.

	$350	$245	$210	$175	$140	$125	$115

L-5CES — single round cutaway bound hollow body, carved spruce top, layered tortoise shell pickguard, bound f holes, maple back/sides/neck, 20 fret bound pointed ebony fingerboard with pearl block inlay, ebony bridge with pearl inlay on wings, model name engraved trapeze tailpiece with chrome insert, multi-bound blackface peghead with pearl flame/logo inlay, 3 per side tuners, gold hardware, 2 single coil pickups, 2 volume/2 tone controls, 3 position switch. Available in Natural finish. Mfd. 1969 to date.

	100%	98%	95%	90%	80%	70%	60%
1951-1959	$3,750	$2,625	$2,250	$1,875	$1,500	$1,350	$1,235
1960-1964	$3,250	$2,275	$1,950	$1,625	$1,300	$1,170	$1,070
1965-1968	$5,000	$3,500	$3,000	$2,500	$2,000	$1,800	$1,650
1969-1974	$2,250	$1,575	$1,345	$1,125	$900	$810	$740
1975-1981	$4,000	$2,800	$2,400	$2,000	$1,600	$1,440	$1,320

> Curr. mfr. instruments are part of the Historic Collection Series, found at the end of this section.
> In 1957, humbucker pickups replaced original item.
> In 1960, sharp cutaway replaced original item.
> In 1969, round cutaway replaced respective item.

L-5S — single sharp cutaway multi bound maple body, carved figured maple top, maple neck, 22 fret bound ebony pointed-end fingerboard with abalone block inlay, Tune-O-Matic bridge/trapeze tailpiece, silver center tailpiece insert with engraved model name, multi bound blackface peghead vase/logo inlay, 3 per side tuners, gold hardware, 2 covered single coil pickups, 2 volume/2 tone controls, 3 position switch. Available in Cherry Sunburst finish. Mfd. 1972-1985.

	$2,250	$1,575	$1,345	$1,125	$900	$810	$740

> In 1974, covered humbucker pickups replaced original items.
> In 1975, stop tailpiece replaced original item.
> In 1976, tunable stop tailpiece replaced respective item.

Grading	100%	98%	95%	90%	80%	70%	60%

L-6S — single sharp cutaway maple body, black pickguard, maple neck, 24 fret maple fingerboard with pearl block inlay, tunable bridge/stop tailpiece, blackface peghead, 3 per side tuners, chrome hardware, 2 covered humbucker pickups, 2 volume/1 tone controls, rotary switch. Available in Cherry and Natural finish. Mfd. 1973-1980.

	$400	$280	$240	$200	$160	$145	$130

This model available with ebony fingerboard in Tobacco Sunburst finish.

In 1975, pearl dot inlay replaced block inlay, instrument renamed L-6S Custom.

✠ **L-6S Deluxe** — similar to L6-S, except has bolt-on maple neck, strings thru anchoring, volume/tone control, 3 position switch. Mfd. 1975-1980.

	$450	$315	$270	$225	$180	$160	$150

A few of these instruments have set necks.

This instrument is also available with rosewood fingerboard.

MAP — United States shaped mahogany body, 3 piece maple neck, 22 fret bound rosewood fingerboard with pearl dot inlay, Tune-O-Matic bridge/stop tailpiece, blackface peghead with pearl logo inlay, chrome hardware, 2 covered humbucker pickups, 2 volume/2 tone controls, 3 position switch. Available in Natural finish. Mfd. 1983 only.

	$1,000	$700	$600	$500	$400	$360	$330

MARAUDER — Les Paul style alder body, white pickguard, bolt-on maple neck, 22 fret rosewood fingerboard with pearl dot inlay, Tune-O-Matic bridge/stop tailpiece, 3 per side tuners, chrome hardware, humbucker/single coil pickups, volume/tone control, rotary switch. Available in Black and Natural finish. Mfd. 1975-1980.

	$400	$280	$240	$200	$160	$145	$130

Black pickguards were also available on this instrument.

In 1978, maple fingerboard replaced original item.

✠ **Marauder Custom** — similar to Marauder, except has bound fingerboard with block inlay, 3 position switch, no rotary switch. Available in Sunburst finish. Mfd. 1976-1977.

	$450	$315	$270	$225	$180	$160	$150

MODERNE — seldom has more ink and type been potentially wasted on a guitar that no one has ever observed. Originally designed as a Gibson modernistic concept guitar, this instrument was blue-printed in 1958. Speculation on this model won't stop until someone actually has a real one in their hands. Enough said - if you have one, please call us or send in a picture.

MODERNE HERITAGE — single cutaway sharkfin style korina body, black pickguard, korina neck, 22 fret rosewood fingerboard with pearl dot inlay, Tune-O-Matic bridge/stop tailpiece, tulip blackface peghead with pearl logo inlay, inked serial number on peghead, 3 per side tuners with plastic single ring buttons, gold hardware, 2 humbucker pickups, 2 volume/1 tone controls, 3 position switch. Available in Natural finish. Mfd. 1982.

	$1,500	$1,050	$900	$750	$600	$540	$495

This is a re-issue of a 1958 Moderne blueprint, an actual specimen has never been observed.

Grading	100%	98%	95%	90%	80%	70%	60%

NIGHTHAWK CUSTOM — single cutaway mahogany body, bound figured maple top, mahogany neck, 22 fret bound ebony fingerboard with pearl crown inlay, strings thru bridge, bound blackface peghead with pearl plant/logo inlay, 3 per side tuners with pearl buttons, gold hardware, 2 humbucker pickups, volume/tone control, 5 position switch, push/pull tone control for tone variation. Available in Antique Natural, Dark Wineburst, Fireburst, Translucent Red and Vintage Sunburst finish. Curr. mfr.

Mfr.'s Sug. Retail	$1,500	$1,050	$900	$750	$600	$540	$495	$450

　　Add $100 for 3 humbucker pickup configuration.

Nighthawk Special — single cutaway mahogany body, bound maple top, mahogany neck, 22 fret rosewood fingerboard with pearl dot inlay, strings thru bridge, blackface peghead with pearl logo inlay, 3 per side tuners, gold hardware, 2 humbucker pickups, volume/tone control, 5 position switch, push/pull tone control for tone variation. Available in Ebony, Heritage Cherry and Vintage Sunburst finish. Curr. mfr.

Mfr.'s Sug. Retail	$800	$560	$480	$400	$320	$290	$265	$240

　　Add $100 for 3 humbucker pickup configuration.

Nighthawk Standard — single cutaway mahogany body, bound figured maple top, mahogany neck, 22 fret bound rosewood fingerboard with pearl parallelogram inlay, strings thru bridge, bound blackface peghead with pearl plant/logo inlay, 3 per side tuners with pearl buttons, gold hardware, 2 humbucker pickups, volume/tone control, 5 position switch, push/pull tone control for tone variation. Available in Fireburst, Translucent Amber, Translucent Red and Vintage Sunburst finish. Curr mfr.

Mfr.'s Sug. Retail	$1,100	$770	$660	$550	$440	$395	$365	$330

　　Add $100 for 3 humbucker pickup configuration.

RD STANDARD — single cutaway asymmetrical hour glass style maple body, black pickguard, maple neck, 22 fret rosewood fingerboard with pearl dot inlay, Tune-O-Matic bridge/stop tailpiece, blackface peghead with logo decal, 3 per side tuners, nickel hardware, 2 covered humbucker pickups, 2 volume/2 tone controls, 3 position switch. Available in Cherry Sunburst, Ebony, Natural and Tobacco Sunburst finish. Mfd. 1977-1979.

		$500	$350	$300	$250	$200	$180	$165

RD Artist — similar to RD Standard, except has an ebony fingerboard with block inlay, multi bound peghead with pearl stylized f hole/logo inlay, gold hardware, mini switch, active electronics.

		$750	$525	$450	$375	$300	$270	$245

　　In 1978, tunable stop tailpiece replaced original item.

RD Custom — similar to RD Standard, except has maple fingerboard, active electronics, mini switch.

		$600	$420	$360	$300	$240	$215	$195

S-1 — Les Paul style ash body, black tri-lam pickguard, bolt-on maple neck, 22 fret rosewood fingerboard with pearl dot inlay, Tune-O-Matic bridge/stop tailpiece, 3 per side tuners, chrome hardware, 3 single coil bar pickups, volume/tone control, 3 position/rotary switches. Available in Blonde finish. Mfd. 1976-1980.

		$400	$280	$240	$200	$160	$145	$130

Grading	100%	98%	95%	90%	80%	70%	60%

SONEX-180 CUSTOM — Les Paul style composite body, black pickguard, bolt-on maple neck, 22 fret ebony fingerboard with dot inlay, Tune-O-Matic bridge/stop tailpiece, blackface peghead with decal logo, 3 per side tuners, chrome hardware, 2 "dirty fingers" humbucker pickups, 2 volume/2 tone controls, 3 position switch. Available in Ebony and White finish. Mfd. 1981-1982.

		100%	98%	95%	90%	80%	70%	60%
		$325	$225	$195	$160	$130	$115	$105

Sonex-180 Deluxe — similar to Sonex-180 Custom, except has 2 ply pickguard, rosewood fingerboard. Available in Ebony finish. Mfd. 1981-1984.

		$325	$225	$195	$160	$130	$115	$105

In 1982, left handed version of this instrument became available.

Sonex Artist — similar to Sonex-180 Custom, except has rosewood fingerboard, tunable stop tailpiece, 3 mini switches, active electronics. Available in Candy Apple Red and Ivory finish. Mfd. 1981-1984.

		$375	$260	$220	$185	$150	$135	$120

SUPER 400 CES — single round cutaway grand auditorium style body, arched spruce top, bound f holes, raised multi-bound mottled plastic pickguard, figured maple back/sides, multiple bound body, 3 piece figured maple/mahogany neck, model name engraved into heel cap, 14/20 fret bound ebony fingerboard with point on bottom, pearl split block fingerboard inlay, adjustable rosewood bridge with pearl triangle wings inlay, gold trapeze tailpiece with engraved model name, multi-bound blackface peghead with pearl split diamond/logo inlay, pearl split diamond inlay on back of peghead, 3 per side tuners, gold hardware, 2 single coil pickups, 2 volume/2 tone controls, 3 position switch. Available in Ebony, Natural, Sunburst and Wine Red finish. Mfd. 1951 to date.

		100%	98%	95%	90%	80%	70%	60%
1951-1954		$6,500	$4,550	$3,900	$3,250	$2,600	$2,340	$2,145
1954-1959		$6,250	$4,375	$3,750	$3,125	$2,500	$2,250	$2,060
1960-1969		$8,500	$5,950	$5,100	$4,250	$3,400	$3,060	$2,805
1970-1974		$5,500	$3,850	$3,300	$2,750	$2,200	$1,980	$1,815
1975-1981		$4,000	$2,800	$2,400	$2,000	$1,600	$1,440	$1,320
Mfr.'s Sug. Retail	$5,000	$3,500	$3,000	$2,500	$2,000	$1,800	$1,650	$1,500

Curr. mfr. instruments are limited run instruments.
In 1957, humbucker pickups replaced original item.
In 1960, sharp cutaway replaced original item.
In 1969, round cutaway replaced respective item.

Super 400 CES — Curr. mfr. with Vintage Sunburst finish.

Mfr.'s Sug. Retail	$7,000	$4,900	$4,200	$3,500	$2,800	$2,520	$2,310	$2,100

Super 400 CES — Curr. mfr. with Natural finish.

Mfr.'s Sug. Retail	$9,000	$6,300	$5,400	$4,500	$3,600	$3,240	$2,970	$2,700

Grading	100%	98%	95%	90%	80%	70%	60%

ES Series

ES-5 (CES) — single round cutaway hollow body, arched figured maple top, bound f holes, raised layered black pickguard, 3 stripe bound body, figured maple back/sides/neck, 20 fret multi-bound pointed fingerboard with pearl block inlay, adjustable ebony bridge/trapeze tailpiece, bound blackface peghead with pearl crown/logo inlay, 3 per side tuners with plastic buttons, gold hardware, 3 single coil pickups, tone control on cutaway bout, 3 volume controls. Available in Natural and Sunburst finish. Mfd. 1949-1962.

	100%	98%	95%	90%	80%	70%	60%
1949-1955	$2,250	$1,575	$1,345	$1,125	$900	$810	$740
1956-1962	$6,525	$4,565	$3,915	$3,255	$2,605	$2,345	$2,150

Add $1,200 for Natural finish.
Subtract $750 for 2 pickup versions.
A few early models can be found with unbound f holes.
In 1955, model renamed "ES-5 Switchmaster", Tune-O-Matic bridge, 3 volume/3 tone controls, 4 position switch replaced respective items.
In 1957, humbucker pickups replaced original items.
In 1960, sharp cutaway replaced original item.

Grading	90%	80%	70%	60%	50%	40%	20%

ES-100 — folk style body, arched maple top, f holes, raised black pickguard, bound body, maple back, mahogany sides/neck, 14/20 fret rosewood fingerboard with pearl dot inlay, adjustable rosewood bridge/trapeze tailpiece, blackface peghead with pearl logo inlay, 3 per side tuners, nickel hardware, single coil pickup, volume/tone control. Available in Sunburst finish. Mfd. 1938-1941.

	90%	80%	70%	60%	50%	40%	20%
1938-1939	$1,000	$700	$600	$500	$400	$360	$330
1940-1941	$650	$455	$390	$325	$260	$235	$215

Grading	100%	98%	95%	90%	80%	70%	60%

ES-120T — dreadnought style thin body, arched maple top, molded black pickguard, f hole, maple back, mahogany sides/neck, 14/20 fret rosewood fingerboard with pearl dot inlay, adjustable rosewood bridge/trapeze tailpiece, 3 per side tuners with plastic buttons, chrome hardware, single coil pickup, volume/tone control. Available in Sunburst finish. Mfd. 1962-1971.

	100%	98%	95%	90%	80%	70%	60%
	$375	$260	$220	$185	$150	$135	$120

Add $100 for 2 pickup versions (ES-120 TD).

ES-125 — folk style body, arched maple top, f holes, raised black pickguard, bound body, maple back, mahogany sides/neck, 14/20 fret rosewood fingerboard with pearl dot inlay, adjustable rosewood bridge/trapeze tailpiece, blackface peghead with pearl logo inlay, 3 per side tuners, nickel hardware, single coil pickup, volume/tone control. Available in Sunburst finish. Mfd. 1946-1970.

	100%	98%	95%	90%	80%	70%	60%
	$1,250	$875	$750	$625	$500	$450	$415

Some models found to be produced in 1941, though most production done after WWII.
In 1946, a few models found with all mahogany body.

ES-125 T — similar to ES-125, except has a thin body. Mfd. 1956-1969.

	100%	98%	95%	90%	80%	70%	60%
	$950	$665	$570	$475	$380	$345	$315

Grading	100%	98%	95%	90%	80%	70%	60%

ES-125 T ¾ — similar to ES-125 T, except has a ¾ size body. Mfd. 1957-1969.

	$450	$315	$270	$225	$180	$160	$150

ES-135 — dreadnought style thin body, arched maple top, layered black pickguard, f hole, maple back, mahogany sides/neck, 14/20 fret bound rosewood fingerboard with pearl block inlay, adjustable rosewood bridge/trapeze tailpiece, 3 per side tuners with plastic buttons, nickel hardware, single coil pickup, volume/tone control. Available in Sunburst finish. Mfd. 1954-1958.

	$800	$560	$480	$400	$320	$290	$265

Add $200 for 2 pick-up version.

ES-135, CURR. MFR. — single sharp cutaway semi hollow bound maple body, f holes, raised black pickguard, maple neck, 22 fret rosewood fingerboard with pearl dot inlay, Tune-O-Matic bridge/trapeze tailpiece, 3 per side tuners with pearl buttons, chrome hardware, 2 single coil pickups, 2 volume/2 tone controls, 3 position switch. Available in Ebony finish. Curr. mfr.

Mfr.'s Sug. Retail	$1,000	$700	$600	$500	$400	$360	$330	$300

Add $100 for Cherry and Vintage Sunburst finish.

ES-140 ¾ — single sharp cutaway folk style, arched maple top, raised black pickguard, f holes, bound body, maple back/sides, mahogany neck, 19 fret rosewood fingerboard with pearl dot inlay, adjustable rosewood bridge/trapeze tailpiece, 3 per side tuners with plastic buttons, nickel hardware, single coil pickup, volume/tone control. Available in Natural and Sunburst finish. Mfd. 1950-1957.

	$825	$580	$495	$415	$330	$300	$275

ES-140 T ¾ — similar to ES-140 ¾, except has a thin body. Mfd. 1957-1968.

	$675	$475	$405	$340	$270	$245	$225

Grading	90%	80%	70%	60%	50%	40%	20%

ES-150, PREWAR — folk style body, spruce top, f holes, bound black pickguard, bound body, maple back, mahogany sides/neck, 14/19 fret bound rosewood fingerboard with pearl dot inlay, adjustable rosewood bridge/trapeze tailpiece, pearl peghead logo inlay, 3 per side tuners, nickel hardware, single coil pickup, volume/tone control. Available in Sunburst finish. Mfd. 1936-1942.

	$1,950	$1,365	$1,170	$975	$780	$700	$645

This guitar was known as the "Charlie Christian" model.
In 1940, arched back and unbound fingerboard replaced original items.

Grading	100%	98%	95%	90%	80%	70%	60%

ES-150, POST-WAR — similar to ES-150, prewar, except has slightly larger body, layered black pickguard, silkscreen peghead logo. Mfd. 1946-1956.

	$1,950	$1,365	$1,170	$975	$780	$700	$645

In 1950, bound fingerboard with trapezoid inlay replaced original item.

Grading	100%	98%	95%	90%	80%	70%	60%

⚞ **ES-150DC** — double cutaway semi-hollow style, arched maple top, f holes, raised layered black pickguard, bound body, maple back/sides, mahogany neck, 22 fret rosewood fingerboard with pearl block inlay, Tune-O-Matic bridge/trapeze tailpiece, 3 per side tuners, chrome hardware, 2 covered humbucker pickups, master volume control on upper treble bout, 2 volume/2 tone controls, 3 position switch. Available in Cherry, Natural and Walnut finish. Mfd. 1969-1975.

	100%	98%	95%	90%	80%	70%	60%
	$825	$580	$495	$415	$330	$300	$275

ES-175 — single sharp cutaway dreadnought style, arched maple top, f holes, raised layered black pickguard, bound body, maple back/sides, mahogany neck, 20 fret bound rosewood fingerboard with pearl parallelogram inlay, adjustable rosewood bridge/trapeze tailpiece, black face peghead with pearl crown/logo inlay, single coil pickup, volume/tone control. Available in Natural and Sunburst finish. Mfd. 1949-1971.

	100%	98%	95%	90%	80%	70%	60%
	$2,750	$1,925	$1,650	$1,375	$1,100	$990	$905

In 1957, humbucker pickup replaced original item.

⚞ **ES-175D** — similar to ES-175, except has 2 single coil pickups, 2 volume/2 tone controls, 3 position switch. Mfd. 1953 to date.

		100%	98%	95%	90%	80%	70%	60%
1953-1987		$4,025	$2,815	$2,415	$2,010	$1,610	$1,450	$1,330
Mfr.'s Sug. Retail	$2,300	$1,610	$1,380	$1,150	$920	$830	$760	$690

Currently mfd. instruments are produced on a limited run basis.
In 1957, humbucker pickups replaced original item.
By 1977, Tune-O-Matic bridge replaced original item.
In 1983, mahogany back/sides replaced original items.
In 1990, maple back/sides replaced respective items.

ES-225T — single sharp cutaway thin body style, arched maple top, f holes, raised layered black pickguard, bound body, maple back/sides, mahogany neck, 20 fret bound rosewood fingerboard with pearl dot inlay, trapeze wrapover tailpiece, blackface peghead with pearl logo inlay, single coil pickup, volume/tone control. Available in Sunburst finish. Mfd. 1955-1959.

	100%	98%	95%	90%	80%	70%	60%
	$1,250	$875	$750	$625	$500	$450	$415

⚞ **ES-225TD** — similar to ES-225T, except has 2 pickups, 2 volume/2 tone controls. Mfd. 1956-1959.

	100%	98%	95%	90%	80%	70%	60%
	$1,250	$875	$750	$625	$500	$450	$415

Grading	90%	80%	70%	60%	50%	40%	20%

ES-250 — jumbo style, spruce top, multi-bound black pickguard, multi-bound body, maple back/sides/neck, 14/20 fret bound rosewood fingerboard with pearl block inlay, adjustable rosewood bridge/trapeze tailpiece, bound stairstep peghead with pearl logo inlay, 3 per side tuners, nickel hardware, single coil pickup, volume/tone control. Available in Natural and Sunburst finish. Mfd. 1938-1940.

	90%	80%	70%	60%	50%	40%	20%
	$5,250	$3,675	$3,150	$2,625	$2,100	$1,890	$1,730

, cont.

ES-295 — single sharp cutaway hollow body, multi-bound maple top, f holes, raised white pickguard with etched flowers, maple back/sides/neck, 19 fret bound rosewood fingerboard with pearl parallelogram inlay, trapeze wrapover tailpiece, blackface peghead with pearl plant/logo inlay, 3 per side tuners with pearl buttons, gold hardware, 2 single coil pickups, 2 volume/2 tone controls, 3 position switch. Available in Gold finish. Mfd. 1952-1959.

	100%	98%	95%	90%	80%	70%	60%
	$3,450	$2,415	$2,070	$1,725	$1,380	$1,240	$1,140

In 1955, 20 fret fingerboard replaced original item.
In 1958, humbucker pickups replaced original items.

	90%	80%	70%	60%	50%	40%	20%

ES-300, PRE-WAR — jumbo style, spruce top, bound black pickguard, multi-bound body, maple back/sides/neck, 14/20 fret rosewood fingerboard with pearl parallelogram inlay, adjustable rosewood bridge/trapeze tailpiece, bound peghead with pearl crown/logo inlay, 3 per side tuners, nickel hardware, single coil pickup, volume/tone control. Available in Natural and Sunburst finish. Mfd. 1940-1942.

	90%	80%	70%	60%	50%	40%	20%
	$3,750	$2,625	$2,250	$1,875	$1,500	$1,350	$1,235

This model is also found with split diamond peghead inlay.

ES-300, post-war — similar to ES-300, prewar, except has layered black pickguard, bound fingerboard. Mfd. 1946-1952.

	100%	98%	95%	90%	80%	70%	60%
	$3,750	$2,625	$2,250	$1,875	$1,500	$1,350	$1,235

In 1948, 2 single coil pickups, 2 volume controls replaced original items. Tone control moved to upper treble bout.

ES-320TD — double round cutaway semi-hollow bound body, arched maple top, f holes, raised black pickguard, maple back/sides/neck, 22 fret rosewood fingerboard with pearl dot inlay, fixed Tune-O-Matic bridge with logo engraved cover, 3 per side tuners, nickel hardware, 2 single coil pickups, volume/tone control, 2 slide switches. Available in Cherry, Natural and Walnut finish. Mfd. 1971-1975.

	100%	98%	95%	90%	80%	70%	60%
	$500	$350	$300	$250	$200	$180	$165

ES-325TD — double round cutaway semi-hollow bound body, arched maple top, f hole, raised layered black pickguard, maple back/sides/neck, 22 fret rosewood fingerboard with pearl dot inlay, Tune-O-Matic bridge/trapeze tailpiece, 3 per side tuners with plastic buttons, nickel hardware, 2 mini humbucker pickups, 2 volume/2 tone controls, 3 position switch, control mounted on black plastic plate. Available in Cherry, Walnut and Wine Red finish. Mfd. 1972-1979.

	100%	98%	95%	90%	80%	70%	60%
	$650	$455	$390	$325	$260	$235	$215

Grading	100%	98%	95%	90%	80%	70%	60%

ES-330T — double round cutaway semi-hollow bound body, arched maple top, f holes, raised layered black pickguard, maple back/sides, mahogany neck, 22 fret rosewood fingerboard with pearl dot inlay, Tune-O-Matic bridge/trapeze tailpiece, 3 per side tuners with plastic buttons, nickel hardware, single coil pickup, volume/tone control. Available in Cherry and Sunburst finish. Mfd. 1959-1972.

	$850	$595	$510	$425	$340	$305	$280

ES-330TD — similar to ES-330, except has 2 single coil pickups, 2 volume/2 tone controls, 3 position switch.

	$2,025	$1,420	$1,215	$1,015	$810	$730	$670

ES-335T — double round cutaway semi-hollow bound body, arched maple top, f holes, raised layered black pickguard, maple back/sides, mahogany neck, 22 fret rosewood fingerboard with pearl dot inlay, Tune-O-Matic bridge/stop tailpiece, blackface peghead with pearl crown/logo inlay, 3 per side tuners, nickel hardware, 2 covered humbucker PAF pickups, 2 volume/2 tone controls, 3 position switch. Available in Cherry, Blonde and Sunburst finish. Mfd. 1958-1982.

	100%	98%	95%	90%	80%	70%	60%
1958-1959	$13,500	$9,450	$8,100	$6,750	$5,400	$4,860	$4,450
1960-1961	$10,000	$7,000	$6,000	$5,000	$4,000	$3,600	$3,300
1962-1964	$5,500	$3,850	$3,300	$2,750	$2,200	$1,980	$1,815
1965-1968	$1,525	$1,070	$915	$765	$610	$550	$505
1969-1974	$850	$595	$510	$425	$340	$305	$280
1975-1982	$1,025	$720	$615	$510	$410	$370	$340

Add 20%-30% for Blonde finish.

In 1958, some models were found unbound.

In 1959, Cherry finish became an option.

In 1960, the name changed to ES-335 TD, smaller pickguard replaced original item.

In 1962, block fingerboard inlay, Pat. No. pickups replaced original items.

In 1964, trapeze tailpiece replaced original item.

In 1969, Walnut finish became an option, some models with slanted block fingerboard inlay.

From 1969 to 1970, neck volute was available.

In 1977, coil tap switch was added.

ES-335 Studio — similar to ES-335T, except has no f holes. Mfd. 1987 to date.

Mfr.'s Sug. Retail	$900	$630	$540	$450	$360	$325	$300	$275

ES-335 RE-ISSUE — double round cutaway semi hollow bound maple body, f holes, raised black pickguard, mahogany neck, 22 fret bound rosewood fingerboard with pearl dot inlay, Tune-O-Matic bridge/stop tailpiece, blackface peghead with pearl plant/logo inlay, 3 per side tuners, nickel hardware, 2 covered humbucker pickups, 2 volume/2 tone controls, 3 position switch. Available in Ebony finish. Curr. mfr.

Mfr.'s Sug. Retail	$1,800	$1,260	$1,080	$900	$720	$650	$595	$540

Add $260 for Cherry and Vintage Sunburst finish.

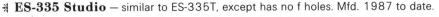

Grading	100%	98%	95%	90%	80%	70%	60%

ES-340TD — double round cutaway semi-hollow bound body, arched maple top, f holes, raised layered black pickguard, maple back/sides/neck, 22 fret rosewood fingerboard with pearl dot inlay, Tune-O-Matic bridge/stop tailpiece, blackface peghead with pearl crown/logo inlay, 3 per side tuners, nickel hardware, 2 covered humbucker pickups, volume/mixer/2 tone controls, 3 position switch. Available in Natural and Walnut finish. Mfd. 1969-1974.

	$1,750	$1,225	$1,050	$875	$700	$630	$575

ES-345TD — double round cutaway semi-hollow bound body, arched maple top, f holes, raised layered black pickguard, maple back/sides, mahogany neck, 22 fret bound rosewood fingerboard with pearl parallelogram inlay, Tune-O-Matic bridge/trapeze tailpiece, blackface peghead with pearl crown/logo inlay, 3 per side tuners with plastic buttons, gold hardware, 2 covered humbucker pickups, 2 volume/2 tone controls, 3 position/Vari-tone switches, stereo output. Available in Cherry, Natural, Sunburst and Walnut finish. Mfd. 1959-1982.

1959-1974	$2,750	$1,925	$1,650	$1,375	$1,100	$990	$905
1975-1982	$1,050	$735	$630	$525	$420	$380	$345

In 1959, Cherry finish became an option.
In 1969, Walnut finish became an option.
In 1982, stop tailpiece replaced original item.

ES-347TD — double round cutaway semi-hollow bound body, arched figured maple top, f holes, raised layered black pickguard, maple back/sides/neck, 22 fret bound ebony fingerboard with pearl block inlay, Tune-O-Matic bridge/tunable stop tailpiece, bound blackface peghead with pearl crown/logo inlay, 3 per side tuners, gold hardware, 2 covered humbucker pickups, 2 volume/2 tone controls, 3 position/coil tap switches. Available in Sunburst finish. Mfd. 1978-1991.

	$1,800	$1,260	$1,080	$900	$720	$650	$595

ES-350TD — single round cutaway hollow bound body, arched figured maple top, bound f holes, raised layered black pickguard, maple back/sides/neck, 22 fret bound rosewood fingerboard with pearl parallelogram inlay, adjustable rosewood bridge/trapeze tailpiece, bound blackface peghead with pearl crown/logo inlay, 3 per side tuners with plastic buttons, gold hardware, 2 covered humbucker pickups, 2 volume/2 tone controls, 3 position switch. Available in Natural and Sunburst finish. Mfd. 1947-1956.

1947-1949	$2,650	$1,855	$1,590	$1,325	$1,060	$955	$875
1950-1956	$1,750	$1,225	$1,050	$875	$700	$630	$575

In 1948, 2 single coil pickups, tone control on cutaway bout, 2 volume controls replaced original items.
In 1952, 2 volume/2 tone controls 3 position switch replaced respective items.
In 1956, Tune-O-Matic bridge replaced original item.

Grading	100%	98%	95%	90%	80%	70%	60%

ES-350 T — similar to ES-350TD, except has a thin body. Mfd. 1955-1963.

	$2,725	$1,895	$1,635	$1,360	$1,085	$975	$895

In 1957, Humbucker pickups replaced original items.
In 1960, sharp cutaway replaced original item.

ES-355TD-SV — double round cutaway semi-hollow bound body, arched maple top, bound f holes, raised layered black pickguard, maple back/sides, mahogany neck, 22 fret bound rosewood fingerboard with pearl block inlay, Tune-O-Matic bridge/Bigsby vibrato tailpiece, bound blackface peghead with pearl split diamond/logo inlay, 3 per side tuners, gold hardware, 2 covered humbucker pickups, 2 volume/2 tone controls, 3 position/Vari-tone switches, stereo output. Available in Cherry and Walnut finish. Mfd. 1958-1982.

	100%	98%	95%	90%	80%	70%	60%
1958-1968	$2,850	$1,995	$1,710	$1,425	$1,140	$1,025	$940
1969-1974	$1,250	$875	$750	$625	$500	$450	$415
1975-1982	$1,000	$700	$600	$500	$400	$360	$330

In 1961, side-pull vibrato replaced original item.
In 1963, Vibrola tailpiece with engraved lyre/logo replaced respective item.
In 1969, Bigsby vibrato replaced respective item, Walnut finish became an option.

ES-369 — double round cutaway semi-hollow bound body, arched maple top, f holes, raised cream pickguard, maple back/sides, mahogany neck, 22 fret bound rosewood fingerboard with pearl trapezoid inlay, Tune-O-Matic bridge/tunable stop tailpiece, blackface peghead with pearl logo inlay, 3 per side tuners, chrome hardware, 2 exposed humbucker pickups, 2 volume/2 tone controls, 3 position/coil tap switches. Available in Cherry, Natural, Sunburst and Walnut finish. Mfd. 1982 only.

	$750	$525	$450	$375	$300	$270	$245

ES-775 — single sharp cutaway hollow bound maple body, f holes, raised bound black pickguard, 3 piece figured maple neck, 20 fret bound ebony fingerboard with pearl block inlay, Tune-O-Matic metal/ebony bridge/trapeze tailpiece, ebony block tailpiece insert, bound peghead with pearl stylized bird/logo inlay, 3 per side Grover Imperial tuners, gold hardware, 2 covered humbucker pickups, 2 volume/2 tone controls, 3 position switch. Available in Ebony finish. Curr. mfr.

Mfr.'s Sug. Retail	$2,400	$1,680	$1,440	$1,200	$960	$860	$790	$720

Add $400 for Antique Natural and Vintage Sunburst finish.

ES ARTIST ACTIVE — double round cutaway semi-hollow bound body, arched maple top, raised layered black pickguard, maple back/sides, mahogany neck, 22 fret bound ebony fingerboard with pearl offset dot inlay, Tune-O-Matic bridge/tunable stop tailpiece, blackface peghead with pearl winged-f/logo inlay, 3 per side tuners, gold hardware, 2 covered humbucker pickups, 2 volume/1 tone controls, 3 position switch, 3 mini switches, active electronics, stereo output. Available in Cherry, Natural, Sunburst and Walnut finish. Mfd. 1979-1986.

	$915	$640	$550	$460	$365	$330	$300

Grading	100%	98%	95%	90%	80%	70%	60%

Explorer Series

EXPLORER (KORINA) — radical offset hour glass korina body, white pickguard, korina neck, 22 fret rosewood fingerboard with pearl dot inlay, Tune-O-Matic bridge/stop tailpiece, blackface peghead with pearl logo inlay, 6 on one side tuners, gold (1958-59) or nickel (1962-63) hardware, 2 PAF (1958-59) or patent number (1962-63) humbucker pickups, 2 volume/1 tone controls, 3 position switch. Available in Natural finish, brown case 1958-59, black case 1962-63. Mfd. 1958-1959 and 1962-1963.

> A few early specimens are found with a V-shaped headstock and a raised plastic logo.
> **The Explorer model was introduced shortly after the Flying V and had a 1958 retail price of $247.50. A modernistic concept guitar from Gibson, this model had very limited manufacture (guestimated to be under 100 instruments). If the original Les Paul Standard flame top is Gibson's Koolest instrument, the original Explorer and Flying V models have certainly become the holy grail of this trademark. Original Explorers exhibiting some wear and no problems are currently priced in the $45,000-$55,000 range. Even though the 1962-1963 period of manufacture was mostly a clean-up of earlier bodies and related parts that were never finished, values seem to be the same for both periods. Until someone finds a Moderne, the Explorer (Korina) will continue to be Gibson's most desirable and rarest electric instrument.**

Explorer Re-issue — similar to Explorer (Korina), except has mahogany body/neck, Available in Black, Natural and White finish. Mfd. 1975-1980.

	$1,500	$1,050	$900	$750	$600	$540	$495

Explorer II — similar to Explorer (Korina), except has 5 piece laminated walnut/maple body, maple neck, ebony fingerboard with dot inlay, tunable stop tailpiece, gold hardware, 2 exposed humbucker pickups. Available in Natural finish. Mfd. 1979-1984.

	$400	$280	$240	$200	$160	$145	$130

> This model also available with maple neck.
> Body woods on this model were interchangeable (ie. walnut or maple used on top).

EXPLORER KORINA RE-ISSUE — radical offset hour glass korina body, white pickguard, korina neck, 22 fret rosewood fingerboard with pearl dot inlay, Tune-O-Matic bridge/stop tailpiece, blackface peghead with pearl logo inlay, stamped serial number on peghead, 6 on one side Schaller tuners, gold hardware, 2 humbucker pickups, 2 volume/1 tone golden controls, 3 position switch. Available in Antique Natural, Candy Apple Red, Ebony and Ivory finish. Mfd. 1983 only.

	$2,000	$1,400	$1,200	$1,000	$800	$720	$660

> This was Gibson's first Explorer Korina re-issue. Limited Edition re-issue of 1958 Explorer.

Explorer Heritage — similar to Explorer Korina Re-issue, except has inked serial number on peghead, plastic single ring tuner buttons, black control knobs. Available in Antique Natural, Ebony and Ivory finish. Mfd. 1983 only.

	$2,000	$1,400	$1,200	$1,000	$800	$720	$660

Grading	100%	98%	95%	90%	80%	70%	60%

EXPLORER III — radical offset hour glass alder body, white pickguard, korina neck, 22 fret rosewood fingerboard with pearl dot inlay, Tune-O-Matic bridge/stop tailpiece, blackface peghead with pearl logo inlay, 6 on one side tuners, chrome hardware, 3 single coil pickups, volume/tone controls, 3 position switch. Available in Natural finish. Mfd. 1984-1985.

	$275	$195	$165	$140	$110	$100	$90

This model was also available with black hardware in 1985 only.

EXPLORER 425 — radical offset hour glass mahogany body/neck, white pickguard, 22 fret ebony fingerboard with pearl dot inlay, double locking vibrato, blackface peghead with pearl logo inlay, 6 on one side tuners, black hardware, 2 single coil/1 humbucker pickups, volume/tone controls, 3 mini switch. Available in Natural finish. Mfd. 1986 only.

	$750	$525	$450	$375	$300	$270	$245

EXPLORER '76 — radical offset hour glass mahogany body/neck, white pickguard, 22 fret rosewood fingerboard with pearl dot inlay, Tune-O-Matic bridge/stop tailpiece, blackface peghead with pearl logo inlay, 6 on one side tuners, chrome hardware, 2 exposed humbucker pickups, 2 volume/1 tone controls, 3 position switch. Available in Cherry, Classic White, Ebony and Vintage Sunburst finish. Curr. mfr.

Mfr.'s Sug. Retail	$1,000	$700	$600	$500	$400	$360	$330	$300

EXPLORER 90 DOUBLE — radical offset hour glass mahogany body/neck, white pickguard, 22 fret rosewood fingerboard with pearl dot inlay, Tune-O-Matic bridge/stop tailpiece, blackface peghead with pearl split diamond/logo inlay, 6 on one side tuners, gold hardware, 2 humbucker pickups, 2 volume/1 tone controls, 3 position switch. Available in Natural finish. Mfd. 1989-1991.

	$950	$665	$570	$475	$380	$345	$315

Firebird Reverse Series

These Custom Colors were available: Amber Red, Cardinal Red, Frost Blue, Golden Mist, Heather, Inverness Green, Kelly Green, Pelham Blue, Polaris Blue, and Silver Mist finish.

FIREBIRD I — asymmetrical hour glass style mahogany body, layered white pickguard, thru body mahogany neck, 22 fret Brazilian rosewood fingerboard with pearl dot inlay, wrapover stop tailpiece, partial blackface reverse peghead with pearl logo inlay, 6 on one side banjo tuners, nickel hardware, covered humbucker pickup, volume/tone control. Available in Sunburst finish. Mfd. 1963-1965.

	$3,250	$2,275	$1,950	$1,625	$1,300	$1,170	$1,070

A few of these guitars are found with vibratos.

In 1965, peghead design changed to bass side tuner array.

In 1965, some models found with perpendicular to peghead tuners, single coil pickups.

Grading	100%	98%	95%	90%	80%	70%	60%

FIREBIRD III — similar to Firebird, except has bound fingerboard, Tune-O-Matic bridge/vibrato tailpiece, 2 humbucker pickups, 2 volume/2 tone controls, 3 position switch.

		$3,675	$2,570	$2,000	$1,830	$1,465	$1,320	$1,210

In 1965, peghead design changed to bass side tuner array.

In 1965, some models found with perpendicular to peghead tuners, single coil pickups.

FIREBIRD V — similar to Firebird, except has bound fingerboard with trapezoid inlay, Tune-O-Matic bridge/vibrato with engraved cover, 2 humbucker pickups, 2 volume/2 tone controls, 3 position switch.

		$5,000	$3,500	$3,000	$2,500	$2,000	$1,800	$1,650

In 1965, peghead design changed to bass side tuner array.

FIREBIRD V RE-ISSUE — asymmetrical hour glass style mahogany body, white pickguard with engraved Firebird symbol, thru body 9 piece mahogany/walnut neck, 22 fret rosewood fingerboard with pearl trapezoid inlay, Tune-O-Matic bridge/stop tailpiece, partial blackface peghead with pearl logo inlay, 6 on one side banjo tuners, chrome hardware , 2 covered pickups, 2 volume/2 tone controls, 3 position switch. Available in Cardinal Red, Classic White, Ebony, Heritage Cherry and Vintage Sunburst. Mfd. 1990 to date.

Mfr.'s Sug. Retail	$1,400	$980	$840	$700	$560	$505	$460	$420

FIREBIRD VII — asymmetrical hour glass style mahogany body, layered white pickguard, thru body mahogany neck, 22 fret bound ebony fingerboard with pearl block inlay, Tune-O-Matic bridge/vibrato tailpiece with engraved cover, partial blackface reverse peghead with pearl logo inlay, 6 on one side banjo tuners, gold hardware, 3 covered humbucker pickups, 2 volume/2 tone controls, 3 position switch. Available in Sunburst finish. Mfd. 1963-1965.

		$10,000	$7,000	$6,000	$5,000	$4,000	$3,600	$3,300

In 1965, peghead design changed to bass side tuner array.

FIREBIRD '76 — similar to Firebird VII, except has red/white/blue Firebird emblem on pickguard, pearl dot fingerboard inlay, 2 humbucker pickups. Available in Black, Mahogany, Sunburst and White finish. Mfd. 1976 only.

		$750	$525	$450	$375	$300	$270	$245

Firebird Non-Reverse Series Solid Bodies

FIREBIRD I — asymmetrical hour glass style mahogany body, layered white pickguard with engraved Firebird logo, mahogany neck, 22 fret Brazilian rosewood fingerboard with pearl dot inlay, compensated bridge/vibrato tailpiece, 6 on one side tuners, chrome hardware, 2 single coil pickups, 2 volume/2 tone controls, 3 position switch. Available in Custom Color and Sunburst finish. Mfd. 1965-1969.

		$1,900	$1,330	$1,140	$950	$760	$685	$625

Grading	100%	98%	95%	90%	80%	70%	60%

FIREBIRD III — similar to Firebird I, except has 3 pickups.

	$2,250	$1,575	$1,345	$1,125	$900	$810	$740

FIREBIRD V — similar to Firebird I, except has Tune-O-Matic bridge/vibrato tailpiece with engraved cover, 2 covered humbucker pickups.

	$1,500	$1,050	$900	$750	$600	$540	$495

⚰ **Firebird V 12** — similar to Firebird I, except has 12 strings, blackface peghead with pearl split diamond inlay, Tune-O-Matic bridge/fixed tailpiece, 6 on one side tuners. Mfd. 1966-1967.

	$1,100	$770	$660	$550	$440	$395	$365

FIREBIRD VII — similar to Firebird I, except has Tune-O-Matic bridge/vibrato tailpiece with engraved cover, gold hardware, 3 humbucker pickups.

	$1,700	$1,190	$1,020	$850	$680	$610	$560

Flying V Series

FLYING V (KORINA) — V shaped korina body, layered white pickguard, rubber strip on treble side of body, korina neck, 22 fret rosewood fingerboard with pearl dot inlay, Tune-O-Matic bridge, strings thru anchoring with V shaped metal plate, raised plastic lettering on peghead, 3 per side tuners with amber buttons, gold (1958-59) or nickel (1962-63) hardware, 2 PAF (1958-59) or patent number (1962-63) humbucker pickups, 2 volume/1 tone controls. Available in Natural finish, brown case 1958-59, black case 1962-63. Mfd. 1958-1959 and 1962-1963.

A few models have black pickguards.

The Flying V model was introduced in 1958 and had an original retail price of $247.50 plus $75 for the case. A modernistic concept guitar (along with the Explorer) from Gibson, this model had very limited manufacture (guesti- mated to be under 100 instruments). If the original Les Paul Standard flame top is Gibson's Koolest instrument, the original Explorer and Flying V models have certainly become the holy grail of this trademark. Original Flying V's exhibiting some wear and no problems are currently priced in the $35,000-$45,000 range. Even though the 1962-1963 period of manufacture was mostly a clean-up of earlier bodies and related parts that were never finished, values seem to be the same for both periods.

⚰ **Flying V Re-issue** — similar to Flying V, except has mahogany body/neck, no rubber strip on body, stop tailpiece, redesigned peghead. Available in Cherry and Sunburst finish. Mfd. 1966-1970.

	$4,500	$3,150	$2,700	$2,250	$1,800	$1,620	$1,485	$1,350

⚰ **Flying V Medallion** — similar to Flying V Reissue, except has Limited Edition medallion on top, redesigned peghead. Mfd. 1971 only.

	$3,000	$2,095	$1,800	$1,500	$1,200	$1,080	$990

Grading	100%	98%	95%	90%	80%	70%	60%

Flying V 2nd Re-issue — similar to Flying V Re-issue, except has Black, Natural, Tobacco Sunburst and White finish. Mfd. 1975-1980.

	$1,000	$700	$600	$500	$400	$360	$330

FLYING V II — V shaped 5 piece laminated walnut/maple body, layered black pickguard, walnut neck, 22 fret ebony fingerboard with pearl dot inlay, Tune-O-Matic bridge, strings thru anchoring with V shaped metal plate, blackface peghead with pearl logo, 3 per side tuners, gold hardware, 2 V shaped humbucker pickups, 2 volume/1 tone controls, 3 position switch. Available in Natural finish. Mfd. 1979-1982.

	$650	$455	$390	$325	$260	$235	$215

This model also available with maple neck.
Body woods on this model were interchangeable, ie. walnut or maple used on top.

FLYING V HERITAGE — V shaped korina body, layered white pickguard, rubber strip on treble side of body, korina neck, 22 fret rosewood fingerboard with pearl dot inlay, Tune-O-Matic bridge, strings thru anchoring with V shaped metal plate, raised plastic lettering on peghead, 3 per side tuners with plastic single ring buttons, gold hardware, 2 humbucker PAF pickups, 2 volume/1 tone gold controls. Available in Antique Natural, Candy Apple Red, Ebony and White finish. Mfd. 1981-1984.

	$2,000	$1,400	$1,200	$1,000	$800	$720	$660

In 1983, renamed Flying V (Reissue), black control knobs replaced original item.

FLYING V XPL — V shaped mahogany body, layered white pickguard, mahogany neck, 22 fret rosewood fingerboard with pearl dot inlay, Tune-O-Matic bridge/stop tailpiece, 6 on one side tuners, black hardware, 2 humbucker pickups, 2 volume/1 tone controls. Available in Night Violet and Plum Wineburst finish. Mfd. 1984-1987.

	$500	$350	$300	$250	$200	$180	$165

This model was also available with double locking vibrato.

FLYING V 90 DOUBLE — similar to Flying V XPL, except has 24 fret ebony fingerboard with pearl split diamond inlay, strings thru anchoring with V shaped metal plate, blackface peghead with pearl logo inlay, single coil/humbucker pickups, volume/tone control, 3 position switch. Available in Black finish. Mfd. 1989-1992.

	$790	$555	$475	$395	$315	$280	$260

FLYING V '67 — "V" style mahogany body, white pickguard, mahogany neck, 22 fret rosewood fingerboard with pearl dot inlay, Tune-O-Matic bridge/stop tailpiece, arrow style peghead, 3 per side tuners with pearl buttons, chrome hardware, 2 exposed humbucker pickups, 2 volume/1 tone controls, 3 position switch. Available in Cherry, Classic White, Ebony and Vintage Sunburst finish. Curr. mfr.

Mfr.'s Sug. Retail	$1,000	$700	$600	$500	$400	$360	$330	$300

Grading	100%	98%	95%	90%	80%	70%	60%

LES PAUL SERIES

Original Les Paul Series

LES PAUL MODEL — single sharp cutaway solid mahogany body, bound carved maple top, raised cream pickguard, one piece mahogany neck, 22 fret bound rosewood fingerboard with pearl trapezoid inlays, trapeze wrapunder bridge, blackface peghead with holly veneer/pearl logo inlay, silkscreen model name on peghead, 3 per side Kluson tuners with plastic single ring buttons, nickel hardware, 2 single coil P-90 pickups, 2 volume/2 tone controls, 3 position switch. Available in Gold Top/Natural back finish. Mfd. 1952-1958.

	100%	98%	95%	90%	80%	70%	60%
1952	$3,250	$2,275	$1,950	$1,625	$1,300	$1,170	$1,070
1953-1954	$4,725	$3,000	$2,835	$2,360	$1,885	$1,695	$1,555
1955-1956	$6,225	$4,355	$3,735	$3,110	$2,485	$2,235	$2,050
1957-1958	$14,500	$10,150	$8,700	$7,250	$5,800	$5,220	$4,780

This was Gibson's first production solid body. Early models are without binding around the fingerboard and do not have a plastic ring around the selector switch. Some models are noted to have Gold finish on sides and back in addition to the top. Original finish on the Gold Top models can usually be determined by a greenish hue around the lower bouts of the instrument where the player's arm(s) has rubbed off the clear and/or color coat (the color coat was originally mixed with bronze powder), producing a green oxidation that can even be noticed on the metal parts occasionally. Horizontal weather checking striations are also normal on original Gold Top finishes.

Special order instruments have Dark Brown back finish.

In 1952, these models were not serialized.

In 1953, serial numbers that were ink stamped were added on back of headstock, and stop wrapover bridge replaced original item.

In 1955, the Tune-O-Matic bridge/stop tailpiece replaced the earlier configuration.

In 1957, humbucker PAF pickups replaced original P-90s.

LES PAUL STANDARD — single sharp cutaway mahogany body, bound carved flame maple top, raised cream pickguard, one piece mahogany neck, 22 fret rosewood fingerboard with pearl trapezoid inlay, Tune-O-Matic bridge/stop tailpiece, blackface peghead with holly veneer/pearl logo inlay, 3 per side Kluson tuners with single ring plastic buttons, nickel hardware, 2 covered humbucker PAF pickups, 2 volume/2 tone controls, 3 position switch. Available in Cherry Sunburst finish. Mfd. 1958-1960.

This model has achieved virtual cult status among guitar collectors (and investors) throughout the world. Perhaps Gibson's Koolest instrument, this flametop's popularity and stratospheric price appreciation have launched a wave of vintage nostalgia and re-issues that have created an independent, significant marketplace. But really, how much are they worth? It depends on two factors - how much flame maple and what kind of original condition. It's hard to believe that two killer bookmatched pieces of flame maple that no one paid much attention to in 1959 will cost you $35,000 EXTRA today. These instruments in average (60%-80%) original condition without much flame start in the $20,000-$25,000 area. 80%-90% condition with nicely flamed tops weigh in at the $40,000-$50,000 range. And a really mint, spectacular flamed instrument in original condition could cost you more than the roof over your head. This model, more than any other, proves what turbo-charged desirability can do to an instrument's price tag. In 1959, they retailed for $279 - if you had a new one in the case today and advertised it as best-offer, you would soon have to change your phone number to unlisted. Several professional appraisals should be secured before you place a second mortgage on your home. Certainly, a cornerstone of any guitar collection.

(more information on the next page)

Grading	100%	98%	95%	90%	80%	70%	60%

In 1959, large frets replaced original item.

In 1960, thin neck, double ring tuner buttons replaced original items.

Les Paul (SG Body Style) — double sharp cutaway mahogany body, layered black pickguard, mahogany neck, 22 fret bound rosewood fingerboard with pearl trapezoid inlay, Tune-O-Matic bridge/side-pull vibrato, blackface peghead with pearl logo inlay, 3 per side Kluson tuners with double ring plastic tuners, nickel hardware, 2 covered humbucker pickups, 2 volume/2 tone controls, 3 position switch. Available in Cherry finish. Mfd. late 1960-1963.

	$2,250	$1,575	$1,345	$1,125	$900	$810	$740

In late 1960, the body style was changed to what is now known as the "SG" body style. Les Paul logo still found on headstock (see submodel description directly below).

In 1961, the Les Paul name was put on truss rod cover, and did not have a model name on the peghead. Pearl crown peghead inlay.

In 1962, some models were found with ebony tailblock and pearl inlay.

In 1963, renamed SG Standard. See SG Series later in text.

Les Paul Standard (1968-1969 Mfr.) — single sharp cutaway solid mahogany body, deeper cutaway binding, bound carved maple top, raised cream pickguard, mahogany neck, 22 fret bound rosewood fingerboard with pearl trapezoid inlay, Tune-O-Matic bridge/stop tailpiece, blackface peghead with pearl logo inlay, 3 per side Kluson tuners with double ring plastic buttons, nickel hardware, 2 single coil P-90 pickups, 2 volume/2 tone controls, 3 position switch. Available in Gold Top/Natural Back finish. Mfd. 1968-1969.

1968	$2,000	$1,400	$1,200	$1,000	$800	$720	$660
1969	$1,400	$980	$840	$700	$560	$505	$460

This was Gibson's first Gold Top re-issue.

Les Paul Standard (1971 Mfr.) — single sharp cutaway solid mahogany body, bound carved maple top, raised cream pickguard, mahogany neck, 22 fret bound rosewood fingerboard with pearl trapezoid inlay, wrapover bridge tailpiece, blackface peghead with pearl logo inlay, 3 per side Kluson tuners with plastic double ring buttons, nickel hardware, 2 single coil P-90 pickups, 2 volume/2 tone controls, 3 position switch. Available in Gold Top finish. Mfd. 1971-1973.

	$1,700	$1,190	$1,020	$850	$680	$610	$560

This model is without neck volute.

This model is a re-issue of the 1954 Les Paul.

Les Paul Standard (Curr. Mfr.) — single sharp cutaway 3 piece mahogany/maple body, deeper cutaway binding, bound carved 3 piece maple top, cream pickguard, 22 fret bound rosewood fingerboard with pearl trapezoid inlay, Tune-O-Matic bridge/stop tailpiece, blackface peghead with pearl logo inlay, "Standard" engraved on truss rod cover, 3 per side tuners with pearloid buttons, chrome hardware, 2 covered humbucker pickups, 2 volume/2 tone controls, 3 position switch. Available in Cherry Sunburst, Dark Sunburst, Ebony, Gold Top, Heritage Sunburst, Honey Burst, Natural, Tobacco Sunburst, TV Yellow, Vintage Sunburst and Wine Red finish. Mfd. 1976 to date.

Mfr.'s Sug. Retail	$1,600	$1,120	$960	$800	$640	$575	$530	$480

In 1978, a one-piece body replaced original item.

In 1990, the TV Yellow finish became standard.

Grading	100%	98%	95%	90%	80%	70%	60%

Les Paul Standard Birdseye — similar to Les Paul Standard, except has birdseye maple top. Available in Heritage Sunburst, Honey Burst and Vintage Sunburst finish. New 1993.

Mfr.'s Sug. Retail	$2,150	$1,500	$1,290	$1,075	$860	$775	$710	$645

LES PAUL DELUXE

— single sharp cutaway 3 piece mahogany/maple body, deeper cutaway binding, bound carved maple top, raised cream pickguard, mahogany neck, 22 fret bound rosewood fingerboard with pearl trapezoid inlay, Tune-O-Matic bridge/stop tailpiece, widened blackface peghead with pearl logo inlay, 3 per side Kluson tuners with plastic double ring buttons, nickel hardware, 2 mini humbucker pickups, 2 volume/2 tone controls, 3 position switch. Available in Blue Sparkle Top, Cherry, Cherry Sunburst, Gold Top, Red Sparkle Top, Tobacco Sunburst, Walnut and Wine Red finish. Mfd. 1969-1985.

1969-1974	$1,200	$840	$720	$600	$480	$430	$395
1975-1985	$850	$595	$510	$425	$340	$305	$280

A few of these models are found with 2 single coil P-90 pickups.

In 1971, the Cherry, Cherry Sunburst and Walnut finishes became standard.

In 1972, the Walnut finish was discontinued, and the Tobacco Sunburst finish became standard.

In 1975, Natural and Wine Red finishes became options.

In 1977, a 2-piece mahogany body replaced original item.

Les Paul Pro-Deluxe — similar to Les Paul Deluxe, except has ebony fingerboard, chrome hardware. Available in Black, Cherry Sunburst, Gold Top and Tobacco Sunburst finish. Mfd. 1978-1982.

	$750	$525	$450	$375	$300	$270	$245

KALAMAZOO CUSTOM ORDER '59 RE-ISSUE LES PAULS

— circa 1978-79, a few companies including Leo's in CA, Guitar Trader in NJ, and Jimmy Wallace through Arnold and Morgan Music in TX, custom ordered Les Paul's that were patterned exactly after Gibson's original 1959 Standard Model (and feature individualized truss rod covers). These guitars are noted for their ebonized holly veneered pegheads, original inked serialization, highly figured (flame or quilted) maple tops and other '59 Standard features.

These instruments are very desirable because they duplicated the original 1959 Les Paul Standard almost exactly. Because of this and limited manufacture (less than 250 exist), asking prices today are in the $5,000- $6,000 range.

LES PAUL KALAMAZOO

— single sharp cutaway solid mahogany body, bound carved maple top, raised cream pickguard, mahogany neck, 22 fret bound rosewood fingerboard with pearl trapezoid inlay, Nashville Tune-O-Matic bridge/stop tailpiece, large blackface peghead with pearl logo inlay, "Les Paul K.M." engraved on truss cover, 3 per side Grover tuners, nickel hardware, 2 cream colored covered humbucker pickups, 2 volume/2 tone controls, 3 position switch. Available in Antique Sunburst, Cherry Sunburst and Natural finish. Mfd. 1979 only.

	$1,200	$840	$720	$600	$480	$430	$395

This was Gibson's first nationally distributed flame top re-issue.

The first production run of these instruments exhibits a metal plate with engraved "Custom Made" logo below the tailpiece. Approximately 1,500 of this model were manufactured in Gibson's Kalamazoo plant.

Grading	100%	98%	95%	90%	80%	70%	60%

LES PAUL HERITAGE 80 — single sharp cutaway mahogany body, bound carved flame maple top, raised cream pickguard, 3 piece mahogany neck, 22 fret rosewood fingerboard with pearl trapezoid inlay, Tune-O-Matic bridge/stop tailpiece, blackface peghead with pearl logo inlay, "Heritage 80" on truss cover, 3 per side Grover tuners, nickel hardware, 2 covered humbucker pickups, 2 volume/2 tone controls, 3 position switch. Available in Cherry Sunburst and Honey Sunburst finish. Mfd. 1980-1982.

	$3,000	$2,095	$1,800	$1,500	$1,200	$1,080	$990

A few of these instruments are found with Ebony finish and are very rare.

꙳ **Les Paul Heritage 80 Elite** — similar to Les Paul Heritage 80, except has quilted maple top, one piece neck, ebony fingerboard.

	$3,000	$2,095	$1,800	$1,500	$1,200	$1,080	$990

LES PAUL SPOTLIGHT SPECIAL — single sharp cutaway mahogany body, bound carved 3 piece maple/mahogany/maple top, raised cream pickguard, mahogany neck, 22 fret rosewood fingerboard with pearl trapezoid inlay, Tune-O-Matic bridge/stop tailpiece, blackface peghead with pearl logo inlay, 3 per side tuners with plastic buttons, chrome hardware, 2 covered humbucker pickups, 2 volume/2 tone controls, 3 position switch. Available in Natural finish. Mfd. 1980-1985.

	$2,250	$1,575	$1,345	$1,125	$900	$810	$740

LES PAUL 1985 RE-ISSUE — similar specifications to the current Gibson Historic Collection Les Paul '59 Flametop Re-issue, this was Gibson's first authorized 1959 Les Paul re-issue.

	$5,060	$3,540	$3,035	$2,530	$2,025	$1,825	$1,670

LES PAUL CMT — similar to Les Paul Spotlight Special, except has maple/walnut/maple body, curly maple top. Mfd. 1986-1989.

	$2,500	$1,750	$1,500	$1,250	$1,000	$900	$825

LES PAUL STANDARD THIRTIETH ANNIVERSARY — single sharp cutaway mahogany body, bound carved maple top, raised cream pickguard, mahogany neck, 22 fret rosewood fingerboard with pearl trapezoid inlay, pearl "Thirtieth Anniversary" inlay at 15th fret, Tune-O-Matic bridge/stop tailpiece, blackface peghead with pearl logo inlay, 3 per side tuners with plastic buttons, nickel hardware, 2 covered humbucker pickups, 2 volume/2 tone controls, 3 position switch. Available in Gold Top finish. Mfd. 1982-1984.

	$1,500	$1,050	$900	$750	$600	$540	$495

꙳ **Les Paul Standard Fortieth Anniversary** — similar to Les Paul Standard Thirtieth Anniversary, except has ebony fingerboard, gold hardware, 2 stacked humbucker pickups. Mfd. 1992 only.

	$1,500	$1,050	$900	$750	$600	$540	$495

Grading	100%	98%	95%	90%	80%	70%	60%

LES PAUL LP-XPL

— single sharp cutaway solid mahogany body, bound carved maple top, raised cream pickguard, mahogany neck, 22 fret bound ebony fingerboard with pearl dot inlay, Tune-O-Matic bridge/stop tailpiece, blackface peghead with pearl logo inlay, 6 on one side tuners, chrome hardware, 2 single coil pickups, 2 volume/2 tone controls, 3 position switch. Available in Cherry Sunburst finish. Mfd. 1984-1987.

	$500	$350	$300	$250	$200	$180	$165

This model was also available with double cutaway body.

This model was also available with 2 single coil/1 humbucker pickups configuration.

Les Paul Re-issue Gold Top

— similar to original Les Paul, except has 2 stacked coil (P-100) pickups. Mfd. 1990 to date.

	$2,550	$1,785	$1,530	$1,275	$1,020	$920	$840

LES PAUL CLASSIC

— single sharp cutaway mahogany body, bound carved maple top, cream pickguard with engraved "1960", bound rosewood fingerboard with pearl trapezoid inlay, Tune-O-Matic bridge/stop tailpiece, blackface peghead with pearl logo inlay, pearloid button tuners, nickel hardware, 2 exposed humbucker pickups. Available in Bullion Gold, Ebony, Honey Burst, Heritage Cherry Sunburst and Vintage Sunburst finish. Mfd. 1990 to date.

Mfr.'s Sug. Retail	$2,200	$1,540	$1,320	$1,100	$880	$790	$725	$660

Les Paul Classic Plus

— similar to Les Paul Classic, except has curly maple top. Available in Honey Burst, Heritage Cherry Sunburst, Translucent Amber, Translucent Purple, Translucent Red and Vintage Sunburst finish. Curr. mfr.

Mfr.'s Sug. Retail	$2,250	$1,575	$1,345	$1,125	$900	$810	$740	$675

Les Paul Classic Premium Plus

— similar to Les Paul Classic, except has highest quality curly maple top. Available in Honey Burst, Heritage Cherry Sunburst, Translucent Amber, Translucent Purple, Translucent Red and Vintage Sunburst finish. Curr. mfr.

Mfr.'s Sug. Retail	$2,750	$1,925	$1,650	$1,375	$1,100	$990	$905	$825

Les Paul Classic Birdseye

— similar to Les Paul Classic, except has birdseye maple top. Available in Honey Burst, Heritage Cherry Sunburst, Translucent Amber, Translucent Purple, Translucent Red and Vintage Sunburst finish. Curr. mfr.

Mfr.'s Sug. Retail	$2,600	$1,820	$1,560	$1,300	$1,040	$935	$860	$780

Les Paul Classic Premium Birdseye

— similar to Les Paul Classic, except has highest quality birdseye maple top. Available in Honey Burst, Heritage Cherry Sunburst, Translucent Amber, Translucent Purple, Translucent Red and Vintage Sunburst finish. Curr. mfr.

Mfr.'s Sug. Retail	$4,700	$3,290	$2,820	$2,350	$1,880	$1,690	$1,550	$1,410

All instruments in this series have a single cutaway mahogany body, raised pickguard, mahogany neck, 22 fret fingerboard, Tune-O-Matic bridge/stop tailpiece, 3 per side tuners, 2 humbucker pickups, 2 volume/2 tone controls, 3 position switch, unless otherwise listed.

Grading	100%	98%	95%	90%	80%	70%	60%

LES PAUL XR-I — single cutaway mahogany body, carved maple top, 22 fret rosewood fingerboard with pearl dot inlay, Tune-O-Matic bridge/stop tailpiece, 3 per side tuners with pearloid buttons, chrome hardware, 2 exposed humbucker pickups, 2 volume/2 tone controls, 3 position/coil tap switches. Available in Cherry Sunburst, Goldburst and Tobacco Sunburst finish. Mfd. 1981-1983.

	$600	$420	$360	$300	$240	$215	$195

⚔ **Les Paul XR-II** — similar to Les Paul XR-I, except has bound figured maple top, "Gibson" embossed pickup covers. Available in Honey Sunburst finish.

	$750	$525	$450	$375	$300	$270	$245

Les Paul Custom Series

LES PAUL CUSTOM — single sharp cutaway multi-bound mahogany body with carved top, raised bound black pickguard, mahogany neck, 22 fret bound ebony fingerboard with pearl block inlay, Tune-O-Matic bridge/stop tailpiece, multi-bound peghead with pearl split diamond/logo inlay, 3 per side Deluxe Kluson tuners with plastic single ring buttons, gold hardware, 2 single coil pickups, 2 volume/2 tone controls, 3 position switch. Available in Black finish. Mfd. 1954-1960.

1954-1957	$5,500	$3,850	$3,300	$2,750	$2,200	$1,980	$1,815
1958-1960	$8,500	$5,950	$5,100	$4,250	$3,400	$3,060	$2,805

This guitar was nicknamed the "Black Beauty" and also the "Fretless Wonder".

In 1957, 3 humbucker PAF pickups replaced 2 pickup configuration. A few models found with 2 humbucker pickups.

In 1959, Grover tuners replaced original item.

⚔ **Les Paul Custom (SG Body Style)** — double sharp cutaway mahogany body, white layered pickguard, mahogany neck, 22 fret bound ebony fingerboard with pearl block inlay, Tune-O-Matic bridge/side-pull vibrato, multi-bound peghead with pearl split diamond inlay, 3 per side tuners, gold hardware, 3 covered humbucker pickups, 2 volume/2 tone controls, 3 position switch. Available in Black, Cherry, Tobacco Sunburst, Walnut, White and Wine Red finish. Mfd. 1961-1963.

	$3,250	$2,275	$1,950	$1,625	$1,300	$1,170	$1,070

In 1962, some models found with pearl inlaid ebony tailpiece insert.

In 1963, renamed SG Custom. See SG Series later in text.

LES PAUL CUSTOM 1968 RE-ISSUE — single sharp cutaway mahogany body, multi-bound carved maple top, raised bound black pickguard, one piece mahogany neck, 22 small fret bound ebony fingerboard with pearl block inlay, Tune-O-Matic bridge/stop tailpiece, multi-bound peghead with pearl split diamond/logo inlay, no neck volute, 3 per side Grover tuners, gold hardware, 2 humbucker Pat. No. pickups, 2 volume/2 tone controls, 3 position switch. Available in Black finish. Mfd. 1968 only.

	$2,750	$1,925	$1,650	$1,375	$1,100	$990	$905

This instrument was a re-issue of 1957 version of the Les Paul Custom.

Grading		100%	98%	95%	90%	80%	70%	60%

⚅ **Les Paul Custom 1969 Re-issue** — similar to Les Paul Custom 1968 Re-issue, except has 3 piece mahogany/maple body, 3 piece neck. Available in Alpine White, Black, Cherry, Cherry Sunburst, Heritage Sunburst, Honeyburst, Tobacco Sunburst, Vintage Sunburst, Walnut, White, and Wine Red finish. Mfd. 1969 to date.

		100%	98%	95%	90%	80%	70%	60%
1969		$2,000	$1,400	$1,200	$1,000	$800	$720	$660
1970		$1,400	$980	$840	$700	$560	$505	$460
1971-1992		$1,200	$840	$720	$600	$480	$430	$395
Mfr.'s Sug. Retail	$2,200	$1,540	$1,320	$1,100	$880	$790	$725	$660

> In 1970, peghead volute was made standard.
> In 1971, Cherry and Cherry Sunburst finish became an option.
> From 1971-1973, 3 humbucker pickup configuration became an option.
> In 1972, Tobacco Sunburst became an option.
> In 1975, jumbo frets replaced original item, Natural and White finish became an option.
> In 1976, Wine Red finish became available.
> In 1977, piece mahogany body replaced original item, Walnut finish became available.
> By 1980, neck volute was no longer available.
> In 1988, Apline White, Ebony, Heritage Sunburst and Vintage Sunburst finish became available.
> In 1990, Honey Burst finish became available.

⚅ **Les Paul Custom Plus** — similar to Les Paul Custom, except has bound figured maple top. Available in Dark Wineburst, Honeyburst, Heritage Cherry Sunburst and Vintage Sunburst finish. Curr. mfr.

		100%	98%	95%	90%	80%	70%	60%
Mfr.'s Sug. Retail	$2,500	$1,750	$1,500	$1,250	$1,000	$900	$825	$750

⚅ **Les Paul Custom Premium Plus** — similar to Les Paul Custom, except has highest quality bound figured maple top. Available in Dark Wineburst, Honey Burst, Heritage Cherry Sunburst and Vintage Sunburst finish. Curr. mfr.

		100%	98%	95%	90%	80%	70%	60%
Mfr.'s Sug. Retail	$3,000	$2,095	$1,800	$1,500	$1,200	$1,080	$990	$900

LES PAUL CUSTOM TWENTIETH ANNIVERSARY — single sharp cutaway multi-bound mahogany body with carved top, raised bound black pickguard, mahogany neck, 22 fret bound ebony fingerboard with pearl block inlay, "Twentieth Anniversary" engraved into block inlay at 15th fret, Tune-O-Matic bridge/stop tailpiece, multi-bound peghead with pearl split diamond/logo inlay, 3 per side tuners with plastic buttons, gold hardware, 2 single coil pickups, 2 volume/2 tone controls, 3 position switch. Available in Black and White finish. Mfd. 1974 only.

		100%	98%	95%	90%	80%	70%	60%
		$1,800	$1,260	$1,080	$900	$720	$650	$595

⚅ **Les Paul Custom Thirty-fifth Anniversary** — similar to original Les Paul Custom Twentieth Anniversary, except has "Thirty-fifth Anniversary" etched on peghead inlay, 3 humbucker pickups. Mfd. 1989 only.

		100%	98%	95%	90%	80%	70%	60%
		$1,600	$1,120	$960	$800	$640	$575	$530

Gibson USA , cont.

THE LES PAUL — single sharp cutaway flame maple body, rosewood bound carved 2 piece bookmatched flame maple top, raised rosewood pickguard, maple neck, 22 fret bound 3 piece rosewood/ebony/rosewood fingerboard with abalone block inlay, Tune-O-Matic bridge/stop tailpiece, pearl split diamond/logo peghead inlay, 3 per side Schaller tuners with mother of pearl buttons, serial number engraved pearl plate on peghead back, gold hardware, 2 Super humbucker pickups with rosewood covers, 2 volume/2 tone rosewood control knobs, 3 position switch, rosewood control plate on back. Available in Natural and Rosewood finish. Mfd. 1976-1980.

> Due to extreme rarity (less than 50 are believed to be produced), accurate price evaluation is difficult for this model. Since this variation was perhaps Gibson's most elaborate and ornate (not to mention most expensive) L.P., most of these instruments were not played. As a result, remaining specimens are usually in 95%+ original condition. Current asking prices for this condition factor are presently in the $11,000-$13,500 price range.
>
> In 1978, Schaller Tune-O-Matic bridge/tunable stop tailpiece replaced original items.
>
> In 1979, Rosewood finish was discontinued.

LES PAUL ARTISAN — single sharp cutaway mahogany body, multi-bound carved maple top, raised bound black pickguard, mahogany neck, 22 fret bound ebony fingerboard with pearl flowers/heart inlay, Tune-O-Matic bridge/tunable stop tailpiece, multi-bound peghead with pearl split flowers/heart/logo inlay, 3 per side tuners, gold hardware, 2 single coil pickups, 2 volume/2 tone controls, 3 position switch. Available in Ebony, Tobacco Sunburst and Walnut finish. Mfd. 1976-1982.

	$1,525	$1,070	$915	$765	$610	$550	$505

> Originally offered with 3 humbuckers pickups optional.
>
> In 1979, 3 humbucker pickup configuration replaced original item.
>
> In 1980, larger Tune-O-Matic bridge replaced original item.

LES PAUL CUSTOM LITE — single sharp cutaway multi-bound mahogany body with carved top, raised bound black pickguard, mahogany neck, 22 fret bound ebony fingerboard with pearl block inlay, Tune-O-Matic bridge/stop tailpiece, multi-bound peghead with pearl split diamond/logo inlay, 3 per side tuners with chrome buttons, gold hardware, 2 covered humbucker pickups, volume/tone control, 3 position switch, mini coil tap switch. Available in Black finish. Mfd. 1987-1990.

	$900	$630	$540	$450	$360	$325	$300

> This model is also available with double locking vibrato.

Les Paul Studio Series

LES PAUL STUDIO — single sharp cutaway mahogany body, carved maple top, raised black pickguard, 22 fret rosewood fingerboard with pearl dot inlay, Tune-O-Matic bridge/stop tailpiece, 3 per side tuners, gold hardware, 2 covered humbucker pickups, 2 volume/2 tone controls, 3 position switch. Available in Ebony, White and Wine Red finish. Mfd. 1984 to date.

Mfr.'s Sug. Retail	$900	$630	$540	$450	$360	$325	$300	$275

> **Add $50 for gold hardware with Alpine White finish.**
>
> In 1987, ebony fingerboard replaced rosewood fingerboard.
>
> In 1990, trapezoid fingerboard inlay replaced dot inlay.

Grading	100%	98%	95%	90%	80%	70%	60%

Les Paul Studio Custom — similar to Les Paul Studio, except has multi-bound body, bound fingerboard, multi-bound peghead. Available in Cherry Sunburst, Ebony and Sunburst finish. Mfd. 1984-1987.

	100%	98%	95%	90%	80%	70%	60%
	$675	$475	$405	$340	$270	$245	$225

Les Paul Studio Standard — similar to Les Paul Studio, except has bound body. Available in Cherry Sunburst, Sunburst and White finish. Mfd. 1984-1987.

	100%	98%	95%	90%	80%	70%	60%
	$675	$475	$405	$340	$270	$245	$225

Les Paul Studio Lite — similar to Les Paul Studio, except has no pickguard, ebony fingerboard with trapezoid inlay, black chrome hardware, exposed pickups. Available in Translucent Black, Translucent Blue and Translucent Red finish. Curr. mfr.

Mfr.'s Sug. Retail	$1,100	$770	$660	$550	$440	$395	$365	$330

Add $100 for gold hardware with Heritage Cherry Sunburst and Vintage Sunburst finish.

Les Paul Studio Lite/M III — similar to Les Paul Studio, except has no pickguard, exposed humbucker/single coil/humbucker pickups, volume/tone control, 5 position switch. Curr. mfr.

Mfr.'s Sug. Retail	$1,200	$840	$720	$600	$480	$430	$395	$360

Les Paul Junior Series

LES PAUL JUNIOR — single cutaway mahogany body, black pickguard, mahogany neck, 22 fret rosewood fingerboard with dot inlay, wrapover stop tailpiece, 3 per side tuners with plastic buttons, nickel hardware, single coil pickup, volume/tone control. Available in Brown Sunburst and Cherry finish. Mfd. 1954-1963.

	$1,500	$1,050	$900	$750	$600	$540	$495

In 1958, double round cutaway body and multi-layer pickguard replaced original items, Cherry finish became available, Sunburst finish was discontinued.

Les Paul Junior (SG Body Style) — double cutaway mahogany body, black pickguard, mahogany neck, 22 fret rosewood fingerboard with pearl dot inlay, Tune-O-Matic bridge/stop tailpiece, silkscreened model name on peghead, 3 per side tuners with plastic buttons, nickel hardware, single coil pickup, volume/tone control. Available in Cherry finish. Mfd. 1961-1963.

In 1962, Maestro vibrato became an option.

In 1963, renamed SG Junior. See SG Series later in text.

Les Paul Junior TV — similar to Les Paul Junior, except has Limed Mahogany finish. Mfd. 1954-1959.

	$2,100	$1,475	$1,260	$1,050	$840	$755	$690

A few of these guitars were made with a ¾ size body.

In 1958, double round cutaway body and multi-layer pickguard replaced original items.

Grading	100%	98%	95%	90%	80%	70%	60%

Les Paul Junior TV (SG Body Style) — double cutaway mahogany body, black pickguard, mahogany neck, 22 fret rosewood fingerboard with pearl dot inlay, Tune-O-Matic bridge/stop tailpiece, silkscreened model name on peghead, 3 per side tuners with plastic buttons, nickel hardware, single coil pickup, volume/tone control. Available in Cherry finish. Mfd. 1959-1963.

	$3,000	$2,095	$1,800	$1,500	$1,200	$1,080	$990

In 1962, Maestro vibrato became an option.

In 1963, renamed SG TV. See SG Series later in text.

Les Paul Junior ¾ — similar to Les Paul Junior, except has ¾ size body, shorter neck. Mfd. 1956-1961.

	$1,100	$770	$660	$550	$440	$395	$365

Les Paul Junior II — similar to Les Paul Junior, except has 2 P-100 pickups. Mfd. 1989 only.

	$800	$560	$480	$400	$320	$290	$265

This model is also available in a dual cutaway version.

Les Paul Junior Re-issue — similar to Les Paul Junior. Available in Cherry, Tobacco Sunburst, TV Yellow or White finish. Mfd. 1986 to date.

	$900	$630	$540	$450	$360	$325	$300

Les Paul Special Series

LES PAUL SPECIAL — single cutaway mahogany body, multi-layer black pickguard, mahogany neck, 22 fret rosewood fingerboard with dot inlay, wrapover stop tailpiece, 3 per side tuners with plastic buttons, nickel hardware, 2 single coil pickups, 2 volume/2 tone controls, 3 position switch. Available in Limed Mahogany finish. Mfd. 1955-1959.

1955-1958	$2,250	$1,575	$1,345	$1,125	$900	$810	$740
1959	$2,000	$1,400	$1,200	$1,000	$800	$720	$660

In 1959, double round cutaway body replaced original item, Cherry finish became available.

Les Paul Special (SG Body Style) — double cutaway mahogany body, black pickguard, mahogany neck, 22 fret rosewood fingerboard with pearl dot inlay, Tune-O-Matic bridge/stop tailpiece, silkscreened model name on peghead, 3 per side tuners with plastic buttons, nickel hardware, single coil pickup, volume/tone control. Available in Cherry finish. Mfd. 1959-1963.

In 1962, Maestro vibrato became an option.

In 1963, renamed SG Specail. See SG Series later in text.

Les Paul Special ¾ — similar to Les Paul Special, except has a ¾ size body, shorter neck. Available in Cherry Red finish. Mfd. 1959-1961.

	$575	$405	$345	$285	$230	$205	$190

Grading	100%	98%	95%	90%	80%	70%	60%

LES PAUL SPECIAL RE-ISSUE — similar to Les Paul Special, except has bound fingerboard, Tune-O-Matic bridge/stop tailpiece, stacked humbucker pickups. Available in Ebony, Heritage Cherry, Tobacco Sunburst and TV Yellow finish. Mfd. 1989 to date.

Mfr.'s Sug. Retail	$950	$665	$570	$475	$380	$345	$315	$285

Low-Impedance Les Paul Series

LES PAUL PERSONAL — single cutaway multi-bound mahogany body, carved top, raised bound pickguard, mahogany neck, 22 fret bound ebony fingerboard with pearl block inlay, Tune-O-Matic bridge/stop tailpiece, multi-bound blackface peghead with pearl diamond/logo inlay, 3 per side tuners with plastic buttons, gold hardware, 2 low impedance pickups, mic volume control on upper bass bout, volume/decade/treble/bass controls, two 3 position switches, phase slide switch. Available in Walnut finish. Mfd. 1969-1971.

	$1,250	$875	$750	$625	$500	$450	$415

This instrument had Bigsby vibrato as an option.

LES PAUL PROFESSIONAL — single cutaway bound mahogany body, raised black pickguard, mahogany neck, 22 fret rosewood fingerboard with pearl trapezoid inlay, Tune-O-Matic bridge/stop tailpiece, blackface peghead with pearl logo inlay, 3 per side tuners, nickel hardware, 2 low impedance pickups, volume/decade/treble/bass controls, two 3 position switches, phase slide switch. Available in Walnut finish. Mfd. 1969-1971.

	$900	$630	$540	$450	$360	$325	$300

This instrument had Bigsby vibrato optionally available.

LES PAUL RECORDING — single cutaway bound mahogany body, carved top, raised multi-layer pickguard, mahogany neck, 22 fret bound rosewood fingerboard with pearl block inlay, Tune-O-Matic bridge/stop tailpiece, multi-bound peghead with pearl split diamond/logo inlay, 2 covered low impedance pickups, "Gibson" formed on pickup covers, volume/decade/treble/bass controls, two 3 position switches, impedance/phase slide switches, built-in transformer. Available in Walnut finish. Mfd. 1971-1980.

	$750	$525	$450	$375	$300	$270	$245

In 1975, White finish became an option.
In 1978, Ebony and Cherry Sunburst finish became an option.

LES PAUL SIGNATURE — offset double cutaway, arched maple top, raised cream pickguard, f holes, maple back/sides, mahogany neck, 22 fret bound rosewood fingerboard with pearl trapezoid inlay, Tune-O-Matic bridge/stop tailpiece, blackface peghead with pearl logo inlay, 3 per side tuners with plastic buttons, chrome hardware, 2 low impedance humbucker pickups, plastic pickup covers with stamped logo, volume/tone control, 3 position/phase/level switches. Available in Gold Top and Sunburst finish. Mfd. 1973-1978.

	$950	$665	$570	$475	$380	$345	$315

This model has walnut back/sides with Gold Top finish.
After 1976, high and low impedance humbuckers became available.

Grading	100%	98%	95%	90%	80%	70%	60%

The Paul Series

THE PAUL STANDARD — single sharp cutaway walnut body/neck, 22 fret ebony fingerboard with pearl dot inlay, Tune-O-Matic bridge/stop tailpiece, 3 per side tuners, chrome hardware, 2 exposed humbucker pickups, 2 volume/2 tone controls, 3 position switch. Available in Natural finish. Mfd. 1978-1982.

	$425	$295	$250	$210	$170	$150	$135

In 1980, this guitar was renamed Firebrand, with the Firebrand logo burned into the peghead.

The Paul Deluxe — similar to original The Paul Standard, except has mahogany body/neck. Available in Antique Natural, Ebony, Natural and Wine Red finish. Mfd. 1980-1986.

	$450	$315	$270	$225	$180	$160	$150

In 1985, Ebony and Wine Red finishes replaced original items.

Melody Maker Series

All notes on original Melody Maker apply to all instruments in this section, unless otherwise noted.

MELODY MAKER — single cutaway mahogany body, black pickguard with model name stamp, mahogany neck, 22 fret rosewood fingerboard with pearl dot inlay, wrapover stop tailpiece, 3 per side tuners with plastic buttons, nickel hardware, covered humbucker pickup, volume/tone control. Available in Sunburst finish. Mfd. 1959-1971.

	100%	98%	95%	90%	80%	70%	60%
1959-1960	$600	$420	$360	$300	$240	$215	$195
1961-1965	$500	$350	$300	$250	$200	$180	$165
1966-1969	$450	$315	$270	$225	$180	$160	$150
1970-1971	$400	$280	$240	$200	$160	$145	$130

In 1961, double round cutaway body replaced original item.
In 1962, Maestro vibrato became an option.
In 1963, Cherry finish became available.
In 1966, double sharp cutaway body, white pickguard, vibrato tailpiece, Fire Engine Red and Pelham Blue finish replaced respective items.
In 1967, Sparkling Burgundy finish became an option.
In 1970, only Walnut finish was available.

Melody Maker ¾ — similar to Melody Maker, except has ¾ size body. Available in Golden Sunburst finish. Mfd. 1959-1970.

	100%	98%	95%	90%	80%	70%	60%
1959-1960	$800	$560	$480	$400	$320	$290	$265
1961-1970	$400	$280	$240	$200	$160	$145	$130

Melody Maker-D — similar to Melody Maker, except has 2 mini humbucker pickups. Available in Golden Sunburst finish. Mfd. 1960-1971.

	$425	$295	$250	$210	$170	$150	$135

Melody Maker III — similar to Melody Maker, except has 3 mini humbucker pickups. Available in Pelham Blue and Sparkling Burgundy finish. Mfd. 1968-1971.

	$525	$370	$315	$260	$210	$190	$170

Grading	100%	98%	95%	90%	80%	70%	60%

Melody Maker-12 — similar to original Melody Maker, except has twelve strings, 6 per side tuners, 2 mini humbucker tuners. Mfd. 1967-1971.

	100%	98%	95%	90%	80%	70%	60%
	$400	$280	$240	$200	$160	$145	$130

In 1970, Pelham Blue and Sparkling Burgundy finish only.

MELODY MAKER, CURR. MFR. — single cutaway mahogany body, black pickguard, mahogany neck, 22 fret rosewood fingerboard with pearl dot inlay, Tune-O-Matic bridge/stop tailpiece, 3 per side tuners with pearloid buttons, chrome hardware, covered humbucker pickup, volume/tone control. Available in Alpine White, Ebony and Frost Blue finish. Curr. mfr.

Mfr.'s Sug. Retail	$750	$525	$450	$375	$300	$270	$245	$225

M Series

M III DELUXE — offset double cutaway poplar/maple/walnut body, tortoise shell pickguard with engraved "M III" logo, maple neck, 24 fret maple fingerboard with wood arrow inlay, double locking Floyd Rose vibrato, reverse peghead, 6 on one side tuners, black chrome hardware, exposed humbucker/single coil/humbucker pickups, volume/tone control, 5 position/tone selector switches. Available in Antique Natural finish. Curr. mfr.

Mfr.'s Sug. Retail	$1,300	$910	$780	$650	$520	$470	$430	$390

M III Standard — similar to M III Deluxe, except has solid poplar body. Available in Alpine White, Candy Apple Red and Ebony finish. Curr. mfr.

Mfr.'s Sug. Retail	$1,000	$700	$600	$500	$400	$360	$330	$300

Add $150 for Translucent Amber and Translucent Red finish, no pickguard.

SG Series

In 1961, these instruments were originally intended to bring a new style to the Les Paul line, but without Les Paul's approval they were renamed the "SG", in 1963. The first two years of instruments in this series have "Les Paul" logos on their pegheads or the area below the fingerboard.

SG STANDARD — double sharp cutaway mahogany body, layered black pickguard, one piece mahogany neck, 22 fret bound rosewood fingerboard with pearl trapezoid inlay, Tune-O-Matic bridge/side-pull vibrato, blackface peghead with pearl logo inlay, 3 per side tuners, nickel hardware, 2 covered humbucker pickups, 2 volume/2 tone controls, 3 position switch. Available in Cherry finish. Mfd. 1963-1971.

	100%	98%	95%	90%	80%	70%	60%
1963-1966	$2,025	$1,420	$1,215	$1,015	$810	$730	$670
1966-1971	$1,200	$840	$720	$600	$480	$430	$395

In 1962, some models were found with ebony tailblock with pearl inlay.

Grading	100%	98%	95%	90%	80%	70%	60%

SG Standard Re-issue — similar to SG Standard, except has pearl block fingerboard inlay, stop tailpiece, pearl crown peghead inlay, chrome hardware. Available in Cherry finish. Mfd. 1972-1981.

		$575	$405	$345	$285	$230	$205	$190

In 1976, Bigsby vibrato became standard, stop tailpiece optionally available, Cherry, Tobacco Sunburst and White finish became available.

In 1977, stop tailpiece became standard, Bigsby vibrato became an option.

SG Standard Re-issue No. II — same as SG Standard Re-issue. Available in Cherry and Sunburst finish. Mfd. 1983-1987.

		$525	$370	$315	$260	$210	$190	$170

SG Standard Re-issue No. III — similar to SG Standard Re-issue No. I, except has trapezoid fingerboard inlay. Available in Ebony and Wine Red finish. Mfd. 1989-1990.

		$500	$350	$300	$250	$200	$180	$165

SG STANDARD, CURR. MFR. — double cutaway mahogany body, layered black pickguard, mahogany neck, 22 fret bound rosewood fingerboard with pearl trapezoid inlay, Tune-O-Matic bridge/stop tailpiece, blackface peghead with pearl crown/logo inlay, 3 per side tuners with plastic buttons, chrome hardware, 2 covered humbucker pickups, 2 volume/2 tone controls, 3 position switch. Available in Candy Apple Blue, Candy Apple Red, Ebony, Heritage Cherry and TV Yellow finish. Curr. mfr.

Mfr.'s Sug. Retail	$1,050	$735	$630	$525	$420	$380	$345	$315

SG Deluxe — double cutaway mahogany body, raised layered black pickguard, mahogany neck, 22 fret bound rosewood fingerboard with pearl block inlay, Tune-O-Matic bridge/Bigsby vibrato tailpiece, blackface peghead with pearl crown/logo inlay, 3 per side tuners, chrome hardware, 2 covered humbucker pickups, 2 volume/2 tone controls mounted on layered black plate, 3 position switch. Available in Cherry, Natural and Walnut finish. Mfd. 1971-1974.

		$450	$315	$270	$225	$180	$160	$150

THE SG (STANDARD) — double cutaway walnut body, layered black pickguard, walnut neck, 22 fret ebony fingerboard with pearl dot inlay, Tune-O-Matic bridge/stop tailpiece, blackface peghead with pearl crown/logo inlay, 3 per side tuners, chrome hardware, 2 covered humbucker pickups, 2 volume/2 tone controls, 3 position switch. Available in Natural finish. Mfd. 1979-1981.

		$450	$315	$270	$225	$180	$160	$150

In 1980, renamed "Firebrand" with new name burned into top.

The SG (Deluxe) — similar to The SG (Standard), except has mahogany body/neck. Available in Antique Mahogany, Ebony, Natural and Wine Red finish. Mfd. 1979-1985.

		$450	$315	$270	$225	$180	$160	$150

In 1980, renamed "Firebrand" with new name burned into top.

Grading	100%	98%	95%	90%	80%	70%	60%

SG CUSTOM — double sharp cutaway mahogany body, white layered pickguard, mahogany neck, 22 fret bound ebony fingerboard with pearl block inlay, Tune-O-Matic bridge/side-pull vibrato, multi-bound peghead with pearl split diamond inlay, 3 per side tuners, gold hardware, 3 covered humbucker pickups, 2 volume/2 tone controls, 3 position switch. Available in Black, Cherry, Tobacco Sunburst, Walnut, White and Wine Red finish. Mfd. 1963-1980.

	100%	98%	95%	90%	80%	70%	60%
1963-1966	$1,750	$1,225	$1,050	$875	$700	$630	$575
1967-1972	$1,250	$875	$750	$625	$500	$450	$415
1973-1975	$1,000	$700	$600	$500	$400	$360	$330
1976-1980	$800	$560	$480	$400	$320	$290	$265

In 1963, Maestro vibrato replaced original item.
In 1972, stop tailpiece replaced respective item.
In 1976, Bigsby vibrato replaced respective item.

SG SPECIAL — double sharp cutaway mahogany body, black pickguard, maple neck, 22 fret rosewood fingerboard with pearl dot inlay, Tune-O-Matic bridge/stop tailpiece, blackface peghead with pearl logo inlay, 3 per side tuners, chrome hardware, 2 covered humbucker pickups, 2 volume/2 tone controls, 3 position switch. Available in Alpine White, Ebony, Ferrari Red and TV Yellow finish. Curr. mfr.

Mfr.'s Sug. Retail	$750	$525	$450	$375	$300	$270	$245	$225

'62 SG RE-ISSUE — double cutaway mahogany body, layered black pickguard, mahogany neck, 22 fret bound rosewood fingerboard with pearl trapezoid inlay, Tune-O-Matic bridge/stop tailpiece, blackface peghead with pearl plant/logo inlay, 3 per side tuner with pearl buttons, nickel hardware, 2 covered humbucker pickups, 2 volume/2 tone controls, 3 position switch. Available in Heritage Cherry finish. Mfd. 1986 to date.

Mfr.'s Sug. Retail	$1,600	$1,120	$960	$800	$640	$575	$530	$480

SG-100 — double cutaway mahogany body, black pickguard, mahogany neck, 22 fret rosewood fingerboard with dot inlay, tunable stop tailpiece, 3 per side tuners, nickel hardware, single coil pickup, volume/tone control. Available in Cherry and Walnut finish. Mfd. 1971-1972.

		$250	$175	$150	$125	$100	$90	$80

SG-200 — similar to SG-100, except has 2 single coil pickups, slide switch.

		$275	$195	$165	$140	$110	$100	$90

SG-250 — similar to SG 100, except has 2 single coil pickups, 2 slide switches. Available in Cherry Sunburst finish.

		$300	$210	$180	$150	$120	$110	$100

SG I — double cutaway mahogany body, black pickguard, mahogany neck, 22 fret rosewood fingerboard with dot inlay, tunable stop tailpiece, 3 per side tuners, nickel hardware, single coil pickup, volume/tone control. Available in Cherry and Walnut finish. Mfd. 1972-1979.

		$250	$175	$150	$125	$100	$90	$80

Grading	100%	98%	95%	90%	80%	70%	60%

SG II — similar to SG-100, except has 2 single coil pickups, slide switch.

	$275	$195	$165	$140	$110	$100	$90

SG III — similar to SG 100, except has 2 single coil pickups, 2 slide switches. Available in Cherry Sunburst finish.

	$300	$210	$180	$150	$120	$110	$100

SG JUNIOR — double cutaway mahogany body, black pickguard, mahogany neck, 22 fret rosewood fingerboard with pearl dot inlay, Tune-O-Matic bridge/stop tailpiece, 3 per side tuners with plastic buttons, nickel hardware, single coil pickup, volume/tone control. Available in Cherry finish. Mfd. 1963-1971.

1963-1965	$475	$330	$280	$235	$190	$170	$155
1966-1971	$400	$280	$240	$200	$160	$145	$130

This model had optionally available vibrato.
In 1965, vibrato became standard.

SG TV — double round cutaway mahogany body, black pickguard, mahogany neck, 22 fret rosewood fingerboard with pearl dot inlay, Tune-O-Matic bridge/stop tailpiece, 3 per side tuners with plastic buttons, nickel hardware, single coil pickup, volume/tone control. Available in Lime Mahogany and White finish. Mfd. 1963-1968.

	$650	$455	$390	$325	$260	$235	$215

SG SPECIAL — double cutaway mahogany body, layered black pickguard, mahogany neck, 22 fret rosewood fingerboard with pearl dot inlay, Tune-O-Matic bridge/stop tailpiece, blackface peghead with pearl logo inlay, 3 per side tuners with plastic buttons, nickel hardware, 2 single coil pickups, 2 volume/2 tone control, 3 position switch. Available in Cherry and White finish. Mfd. 1963-1971.

1963-1965	$800	$560	$480	$400	$320	$290	$265
1966-1971	$575	$405	$345	$285	$230	$205	$190

This model had optionally available vibrato.
In 1965, vibrato became standard.

SG Special $3/4$ — similar to SG Special, except has $3/4$ size body, 19 fret fingerboard. Available in Cherry Red finish. Mfd. 1959-1961.

	$650	$455	$390	$325	$260	$235	$215

SG Professional — similar to SG Special, except has a pearl logo, 2 black soap bar P-90 pickups. Available in Cherry, Natural and Walnut finish. Mfd. 1971-1974.

	$475	$330	$280	$235	$190	$170	$155

SG Studio — similar to SG Special, except has no pickguard, 2 humbucker pickups, 2 volume/1 tone controls. Available in Natural finish. Mfd. 1978 only.

	$450	$315	$270	$225	$180	$160	$150

Grading	100%	98%	95%	90%	80%	70%	60%

SG '90 SINGLE — double sharp cutaway mahogany body, pearloid pickguard, maple neck, 24 fret bound ebony fingerboard with pearl split diamond inlay, strings thru anchoring, blackface peghead with pearl crown/logo inlay, 3 per side tuners, black chrome hardware, humbucker pickups, volume/tone control, 3 position switch. Available in Alpine White, Heritage Cherry and Metallic Turquoise finish. Mfd. 1989-1990.

	$725	$505	$435	$360	$290	$260	$240

This model had double locking vibrato as an option.

⚄ **SG '90 Double** — similar to SG '90 Single, except has single coil/humbucker pickups. Mfd. 1989-1992.

	$675	$475	$405	$340	$270	$245	$225

DOUBLE TWELVE — double cutaway hollow maple body, carved spruce top, 2 stripe bound body, double neck configuration, 2 bound black pickguards, 3 position neck selector switch, each mahogany neck has 20 fret bound rosewood fingerboard with pearl parallelogram inlay, Tune-O-Matic bridge/fixed tailpiece, 6 per side/3 per side tuners with pearl buttons, chrome hardware, 2 covered humbucker pickups, volume/tone control, 3 position switch. Available in Black, Sunburst and White finish. Mfd. 1958-1962.

	$5,500	$3,850	$3,300	$2,750	$2,200	$1,980	$1,815

EDS 1275 — double cutaway mahogany body, double neck configuration, 2 black tri-lam pickguards, 3 position neck/pickup selector switches, 2 volume/2 tone controls, each mahogany neck has 20 fret bound rosewood fingerboard with pearl parallelogram inlay, Tune-O-Matic bridge/fixed tailpiece, 6 per side/3 per side tuners with pearl buttons, chrome hardware, 2 covered humbucker pickups. Available in Black, Sunburst and White finish. Mfd. 1963-1968.

1963-1968	$2,450	$1,715	$1,470	$1,225	$980	$875	$805

⚄ **EDS-1275 Re-issue** — similar to EDS-1275, except available in Alpine White, Cherry, Heritage Cherry, Cherry Sunburst, Sunburst, Walnut and White finish. Mfd. 1977 to date.

1977-1981		$1,250	$875	$750	$625	$500	$450	$415
Mfr.'s Sug. Retail	$2,350	$1,645	$1,410	$1,175	$940	$845	$775	$705

Add $100 for Alpine White finish.
In 1984, Cherry Sunburst, Walnut and White finish became standard items.
In 1987, Cherry finish was an option.
In 1990, Alpine White and Heritage Cherry finish became standard items.

Professional Series

B.B. KING STANDARD — double round cutaway semi-hollow bound body, arched maple top, raised layered black pickguard, maple back/sides/neck, 22 fret bound rosewood fingerboard with pearl dot inlay, Tune-O-Matic bridge/tunable stop tailpiece, blackface peghead with pearl "Lucille"/logo inlay, 3 per side tuners, chrome hardware, 2 covered humbucker pickups, 2 volume/2 tone controls, 3 position switch, stereo output. Available in Cherry and Ebony finish. Mfd. 1980-1985.

	$1,200	$840	$720	$600	$480	$430	$395

Grading	100%	98%	95%	90%	80%	70%	60%

⛌ **B.B. King Custom** — similar to B.B. King Standard, except has bound pickguard, bound ebony fingerboard with pearl block inlay, bound peghead, gold hardware, Vari-tone switch. Mfd. 1980 to date.

Mfr.'s Sug. Retail	$1,400	$980	$840	$700	$560	$505	$460	$420

In 1988, model was renamed B.B. King Lucille.

BARNEY KESSEL REGULAR — double sharp cutaway semi-hollow bound body, arched maple top, bound f holes, raised layered black pickguard, maple back/sides, mahogany neck, 22 fret bound rosewood fingerboard with pearl block inlay, adjustable rosewood bridge/trapeze tailpiece, wood tailpiece insert with pearl model name inlay, bound blackface peghead with pearl crown/logo inlay, 3 per side tuners, nickel hardware, 2 covered humbucker pickups, 2 volume/2 tone controls, 3 position switch. Available in Cherry Sunburst finish. Mfd. 1961-1974.

$2,250	$1,575	$1,345	$1,125	$900	$810	$740

⛌ **Barney Kessel Custom** — similar to Barney Kessel Regular, except has bowtie fingerboard inlay, musical note peghead inlay, gold hardware.

$2,500	$1,750	$1,500	$1,250	$1,000	$900	$825

CHET ATKINS COUNTRY GENTLEMAN — single round cutaway semi-hollow bound maple body, bound f holes, raised bound tortoise shell pickguard, bound arm rest on bottom bass bout, 3 piece maple neck, 22 fret rosewood fingerboard with offset red block inlay, Tune-O-Matic bridge/Bigsby vibrato tailpiece, blackface peghead with pearl plant/logo inlay, 3 per side tuners, gold hardware, 2 covered humbucker pickups, master volume on upper treble bout, 2 volume/1 tone controls, 3 position switch. Available in Ebony finish. Mfd. 1987 to date.

Mfr.'s Sug. Retail	$1,700	$1,190	$1,020	$850	$680	$610	$560	$510

Add $260 for Country Gentleman Brown, Sunrise Orange and Wine Red finish.

ES-165 HERB ELLIS — single sharp cutaway hollow bound maple body, f holes, raised black pickguard, mahogany neck, 20 fret bound rosewood fingerboard with pearl parallelogram inlay, Tune-O-Matic metal/rosewood bridge/trapeze tailpiece, peghead with pearl plant/logo inlay, 3 per side tuners with pearl buttons, gold hardware, 2 covered humbucker pickups, 2 volume/2 tone controls, 3 position switch. Available in Ebony finish. Curr. mfr.

Mfr.'s Sug. Retail	$1,400	$980	$840	$700	$560	$505	$460	$420

Add $350 for Cherry and Vintage Sunburst finish.

Grading	100%	98%	95%	90%	80%	70%	60%

HOWARD ROBERTS ARTIST — single sharp cutaway dreadnought style, arched maple top, oval soundhole, raised multi-bound tortoise shell pickguard, 3 stripe bound body/rosette, maple back/sides/neck, 22 fret bound ebony fingerboard with pearl slot block inlay, adjustable ebony bridge/trapeze tailpiece, wood tailpiece insert with pearl model name inlay, bound peghead with pearl flower/logo inlay, 3 per side tuners, gold hardware, humbucker pickup, volume/treble/mid controls. Available in Natural, Red Wine and Sunburst finish. Mfd. 1976-1981.

	$1,025	$720	$615	$510	$410	$370	$340

In 1979, 2 pickups became available.

Howard Roberts Custom — similar to Howard Roberts Artist, except has rosewood fingerboard, chrome hardware. Available in Cherry, Sunburst and Wine Red finish. Mfd. 1974-1981.

	$1,000	$700	$600	$500	$400	$360	$330

Howard Roberts Fusion III — single sharp cutaway semi-hollow bound maple body, f holes, raised black pickguard, maple neck, 20 fret bound rosewood fingerboard with pearl dot inlay, Tune-O-Matic bridge/adjustable tailpiece, peghead with pearl plant/logo inlay, 3 per side tuners, gold hardware, 2 covered humbucker pickups, 2 volume/2 tone controls, 3 position switch. Available in Ebony and Fireburst finish. Mfd. 1979 to date.

Mfr.'s Sug. Retail	$1,200	$840	$720	$600	$480	$430	$395	$360

Add $350 for Cherry and Vintage Sunburst finish.
In 1990, 6 finger tailpiece replaced original item.

JOHNNY SMITH — single round cutaway bound hollow body, carved spruce top, bound f holes, raised bound tortoise shell pickguard, figured maple back/sides/neck, 20 fret bound ebony fingerboard with pearl split block inlay, adjustable rosewood bridge/trapeze tailpiece, multi-bound peghead with split diamond/logo inlay, 3 per side tuners, gold hardware, mini humbucker pickup, pickguard mounted volume control. Available in Natural and Sunburst finish. Mfd. 1961-1989.

	$3,025	$2,125	$1,815	$1,510	$1,200	$1,080	$995

Add $500 for Blond finish.
In 1963, 2 pickup model was introduced.
By 1979, 6 finger tailpiece replaced original item.

TAL FARLOW — single round cutaway bound hollow body, arched figured maple top, bound f holes, scroll style inlay on cutaway, raised black bound pickguard, maple back/sides/neck, 20 bound rosewood fingerboard with pearl reverse crown inlay, Tune-O-Matic bridge/trapeze tailpiece, rosewood tailpiece insert with pearl engraved block inlay, bound peghead with pearl crown/logo inlay, 3 per side tuners, chrome hardware, 2 covered humbucker pickups, 2 volume/2 tone controls, 3 position switch. Available in Sunburst finish. Mfd. 1962-1971.

	$6,000	$4,200	$3,600	$3,000	$2,400	$2,160	$1,980

Grading	100%	98%	95%	90%	80%	70%	60%

TRINI LOPEZ STANDARD — double round cutaway semi-hollow bound body, arched maple top, bound diamond holes, raised layered black pickguard, maple back/sides, mahogany neck, 22 fret bound rosewood fingerboard with pearl split diamond inlay, Tune-O-Matic bridge/trapeze tailpiece, ebony tailpiece insert with pearl model name inlay, 6 on one side tuners, chrome hardware, 2 covered humbucker pickups, 2 volume/2 tone controls, 3 position switch. Available in Cherry finish. Mfd. 1964-1971.

		$750	$525	$450	$375	$300	$270	$245

Trini Lopez Deluxe — similar to Trini Lopez Standard, except has sharp cutaway, tortoise shell pickguard, 20 fret ebony fingerboard. Available in Cherry Sunburst finish.

	$1,025	$720	$615	$510	$410	$370	$340

ELECTRIC BASS

EB 650 — single sharp cutaway semi-hollow bound maple body, arched top, diamond soundholes, maple neck, 21 fret rosewood fingerboard with pearl dot inlay, adjustable rosewood bridge/trapeze tailpiece, blackface peghead with pearl vase/logo inlay, 2 per side tuners, chrome hardware, 2 covered humbucker pickups, 2 volume/2 tone controls. Available in Translucent Amber, Translucent Black, Translucent Blue, Translucent Purple and Translucent Red finish. Curr. mfr.

Mfr.'s Sug. Retail	$2,100	$1,475	$1,260	$1,050	$840	$755	$690	$630

EB 750 — similar to EB 650, except has deeper body, f holes, figured maple back/sides, abalone inlay, gold hardware, 2 Bartolini pickups, volume/treble/bass/pan controls, active electronics. Available in Ebony finish. Curr mfr.

Mfr.'s Sug. Retail	$2,200	$1,540	$1,320	$1,100	$880	$790	$725	$660

Add $400 for Antique Natural and Vintage Sunburst finish.

LES PAUL SIGNATURE — offset double cutaway, arched maple top, raised cream pickguard, f holes, maple back/sides, mahogany neck, 22 fret rosewood fingerboard with pearl trapezoid inlay, fixed bridge with cover, 2 per side tuners, chrome hardware, humbucker pickup, plastic pickup cover with stamped logo, volume/tone controls, level switch. Available in Gold Top and Sunburst finish. Mfd. 1973-1979.

		$825	$580	$495	$415	$330	$300	$275

This model has walnut back/sides with Gold Top finish.

LPB-1 — single cutaway mahogany body/neck, 20 fret ebony fingerboard with pearl dot inlay, fixed bridge, blackface peghead with pearl logo inlay, 2 per side tuners, black hardware, 2 covered humbucker pickups, volume/treble/bass/pan controls, active electronics. Available in Ebony, Classic White, Heritage Cherry and Translucent Amber finish. Curr. mfr.

Mfr.'s Sug. Retail	$1,050	$735	$630	$525	$420	$380	$345	$315

This model is available with 5 strings, 2/3 per side tuners (LPB-15).

Grading	100%	98%	95%	90%	80%	70%	60%

LPB-2 — similar to LPB-1, except has figured maple top, trapezoid fingerboard inlay, Bartolini pickups. Available in Heritage Cherry Sunburst, Translucent Amber, Translucent Black, Translucent Blue and Translucent Red finish. Curr. mfr.

Mfr.'s Sug. Retail	$1,600	$1,120	$960	$800	$640	$575	$530	$480

☆ **LPB-2 Premium** — similar to LPB-1, except has figured maple top, trapezoid fingerboard inlay, Bartolini pickups. Available in Heritage Cherry Sunburst, Honey Burst, Translucent Amber and Vintage Sunburst finish. Curr. mfr.

Mfr.'s Sug. Retail	$1,700	$1,190	$1,020	$850	$680	$610	$560	$510

This model is available with 5 strings, 2/3 per side tuners (LPB-25).

LPB-3 — similar to LPB-1, except has bound maple top, abalone trapezoid fingerboard inlay, chrome hardware. Available in Ebony finish. Curr. mfr.

Mfr.'s Sug. Retail	$1,650	$1,155	$990	$825	$660	$595	$545	$495

Add $200 for Heritage Cherry Sunburst, Honey Burst and Vintage Sunburst finish.

☆ **LPB-3 Plus** — similar to LPB-1, except has bound figured maple top, abalone trapezoid fingerboard inlay, chrome hardware. Available in Heritage Cherry Sunburst, Honey Burst, Translucent Amber and Vintage Sunburst finish. Curr. mfr.

Mfr.'s Sug. Retail	$2,150	$1,500	$1,290	$1,075	$860	$775	$710	$645

☆ **LPB-3 Premium Plus** — similar to LPB-1, except has bound highest quality figured maple top, abalone trapezoid fingerboard inlay, chrome hardware. Available in Heritage Cherry Sunburst, Honey Burst, Translucent Amber and Vintage Sunburst finish. Curr. mfr.

Mfr.'s Sug. Retail	$2,400	$1,680	$1,440	$1,200	$960	$860	$790	$720

This model is available with 5 strings, 2/3 per side tuners (LPB-35).

RD STANDARD BASS — radical hour glass maple body, layered black pickguard, maple neck, 20 fret maple fingerboard with pearl dot inlay, Tune-O-Matic bridge/strings thru anchoring, blackface peghead with pearl logo inlay, 2 per side tuners, nickel hardware, 2 pickups, 2 volume/2 tone controls. Available in Ebony and Natural finish. Mfd. 1979-1980.

		$375	$260	$220	$185	$150	$135	$120

This model has ebony fingerboard with Ebony finish only.

☆ **RD Artist Bass** — similar to RD Standard Bass, except has winged "f" peghead inlay, 3 mini switches, active electronics. Available in Ebony, Fireburst, Natural and Sunburst finish. Mfd. 1979-1982.

		$475	$330	$280	$235	$190	$170	$155

Grading	100%	98%	95%	90%	80%	70%	60%

THUNDERBIRD II — asymmetrical hour glass style mahogany body, layered white pickguard with engraved Thunderbird logo, thumb rest, thru body mahogany neck, 20 fret rosewood fingerboard with pearl dot inlay, Tune-O-Matic bridge/stop tailpiece, 4 on one side tuners, chrome hardware, single coil pickups with cover, volume/tone controls. Available in Custom Color and Sunburst finish. Mfd. 1963-1969.

	100%	98%	95%	90%	80%	70%	60%
1963-1965	$2,250	$1,575	$1,345	$1,125	$900	$810	$740
1966-1969	$1,000	$700	$600	$500	$400	$360	$330

In 1965, body/neck were redesigned and replaced original items.

Thunderbird IV — similar to Thunderbird II, except has 2 pickups.

	100%	98%	95%	90%	80%	70%	60%
1963-1965	$2,500	$1,750	$1,500	$1,250	$1,000	$900	$825
1966-1969	$1,250	$875	$750	$625	$500	$450	$415

In 1965, body/neck were redesigned and replaced original items.

Thunderbird 1976 Bicentennial — similar to Thunderbird, except has a red/white/blue engraved logo on white pickguard. Available in Black, Natural and Sunburst finish. Mfd. 1976 only.

100%	98%	95%	90%	80%	70%	60%
$1,500	$1,050	$900	$750	$600	$540	$495

THUNDERBIRD IV RE-ISSUE — asymmetrical hour glass style mahogany body, white pickguard with engraved Thunderbird symbol, thru body 9 piece mahogany/walnut neck, 20 fret ebony fingerboard with pearl dot inlay, fixed bridge, partial blackface peghead with pearl logo inlay, 4 on one side tuners, black hardware, 2 covered pickups, 2 volume/1 tone controls. Available in Cardinal Red, Classic White, Ebony and Vintage Sunburst. Curr. mfr.

	100%	98%	95%	90%	80%	70%	60%
Mfr.'s Sug. Retail	$1,400	$980	$840	$700	$560	$505	$460	$420

GIBSON HISTORICAL COLLECTION

The instruments in this series are exacting reproductions of Gibson classics. The instruments are manufactured to the exact specifications of their original release and in several cases, use the same tooling when available.

ACOUSTIC

CITATION — single round cutaway hollow multi-bound body, carved spruce top, bound f holes, raised multi-bound flamed maple pickguard, figured maple back/sides/neck, 20 fret multi-bound pointed fingerboard with pearl cloud inlay, adjustable ebony bridge with pearl fleur-de-lis inlay on wings, gold trapeze tailpiece with engraved model name, multi-bound ebony veneered peghead with abalone fleur-de-lis/logo inlay, abalone fleur-de-lis inlay on back of peghead, 3 per side gold engraved tuners. Available in Faded Cherry Sunburst, Honeyburst and Natural. Curr. mfr.

	100%	98%	95%	90%	80%	70%	60%
Mfr.'s Sug. Retail	$17,000	$17,000	$11,900	$10,200	$8,500	$6,800	$6,120	$5,610

Grading	100%	98%	95%	90%	80%	70%	60%

1934 L-5CES — multi-bound grand auditorium style body, carved spruce top, layered tortoise shell pickguard, bound f holes, maple back/sides/neck, 20 fret bound pointed ebony fingerboard with pearl block inlay, ebony bridge with pearl inlay on wings, model name engraved trapeze tailpiece with chrome insert, multi-bound blackface peghead with pearl flame/logo inlay, 3 per side gold tuners. Available in Cremona Brown Sunburst finish. Curr. mfr.

Mfr.'s Sug. Retail	$3,800	$3,800	$2,660	$2,280	$1,900	$1,520	$1,365	$1,255

1939 SUPER 400 — grand auditorium style body, arched spruce top, bound f holes, raised multi-bound mottled plastic pickguard, figured maple back/sides, multiple bound body, 3 piece figured maple/mahogany neck, model name engraved into heel cap, 14/20 fret bound ebony fingerboard with point on bottom, pearl split block fingerboard inlay, adjustable rosewood bridge with pearl triangle wings inlay, gold trapeze tailpiece with engraved model name, multi-bound blackface peghead with pearl 5 piece split diamond/logo inlay, pearl 3 piece split diamond inlay on back of peghead, 3 per side gold Grover Imperial tuners. Available in Natural finish. Curr. mfr.

Mfr.'s Sug. Retail	$14,000	$14,000	$9,800	$8,400	$7,000	$5,600	$5,040	$4,620

❧ **1939 Super 400** — With Cremona Brown Burst finish.

Mfr.'s Sug. Retail	$13,000	$13,000	$9,100	$7,800	$6,500	$5,200	$4,680	$4,290

1939 SUPER 400 PREMIER — single round cutaway grand auditorium style body, arched spruce top, bound f holes, raised multi-bound pearloid pickguard, figured maple back/sides, multiple bound body, 3 piece figured maple/mahogany neck, model name engraved into heel cap, 14/20 fret bound ebony fingerboard with point on bottom, pearl split block fingerboard inlay, adjustable rosewood bridge with pearl triangle wings inlay, gold unhinged "PAF" trapeze tailpiece with engraved model name, multi-bound blackface peghead with pearl 5 piece split diamond/logo inlay, pearl 3 piece split diamond inlay on back of peghead, 3 per side gold Grover Imperial tuners. Available in Natural finish. Curr. mfr.

Mfr.'s Sug. Retail	$14,000	$14,000	$9,800	$8,400	$7,000	$5,600	$5,040	$4,620

❧ **1939 Super 400 Premier** — With Cremona Brown Burst finish.

Mfr.'s Sug. Retail	$13,000	$13,000	$9,100	$7,800	$6,500	$5,200	$4,680	$4,290

ELECTRIC

ES-295 — single sharp cutaway hollow bound maple body, f holes, raised white pickguard with etched flowers, maple neck, 20 fret bound rosewood fingerboard with pearl parallelogram inlay, Tune-O-Matic metal/rosewood bridge/Bigsby vibrato tailpiece, blackface peghead with pearl plant/logo inlay, 3 per side tuners with pearl buttons, chrome hardware, 2 covered stacked humbucker pickups, 2 volume/2 tone controls, 3 position switch. Available in Bullion Gold finish. Curr. mfr.

Mfr.'s Sug. Retail	$2,000	$2,000	$1,400	$1,200	$1,000	$800	$720	$660

Grading	100%	98%	95%	90%	80%	70%	60%

1958 KORINA EXPLORER — radical offset hour glass korina body, white pickguard, korina neck, 22 fret rosewood fingerboard with pearl dot inlay, Tune-O-Matic bridge/trapeze tailpiece, 6 on one side tuners, gold hardware, 2 humbucker pickups, 2 volume/1 tone controls, 3 position switch. Available in Natural finish. Curr. mfr.

Mfr.'s Sug. Retail	$10,000	$10,000	$7,000	$6,000	$5,000	$4,000	$3,600	$3,300

1958 KORINA FLYING V — V shaped korina body, white pickguard, korina neck, 22 fret rosewood fingerboard with pearl dot inlay, korina neck, Tune-O-Matic bridge/stop tailpiece, 3 per side tuners with plastic buttons, gold hardware, 2 humbucker pickups, 2 volume/1 tone controls, 3 position switch. Available in Natural finish. Curr. mfr.

Mfr.'s Sug. Retail	$10,000	$10,000	$7,000	$6,000	$5,000	$4,000	$3,600	$3,300

LES PAUL CUSTOM BLACK BEAUTY '54 RE-ISSUE — single sharp cutaway multi-bound mahogany body with carved top, raised bound black pickguard, mahogany neck, 22 fret bound ebony fingerboard with pearl block inlay, Tune-O-Matic bridge/stop tailpiece, multi-bound peghead with pearl split diamond/logo inlay, 3 per side tuners with plastic buttons, gold hardware, 2 single coil pickups, 2 volume/2 tone controls, 3 position switch. Available in Ebony finish. Curr. mfr.

Mfr.'s Sug. Retail	$2,400	$2,400	$1,680	$1,440	$1,200	$960	$860	$790

LES PAUL CUSTOM BLACK BEAUTY '57 RE-ISSUE — single sharp cutaway multi-bound mahogany body with carved top, raised bound black pickguard, mahogany neck, 22 fret bound ebony fingerboard with pearl block inlay, Tune-O-Matic bridge/stop tailpiece, multi-bound peghead with pearl split diamond/logo inlay, 3 per side tuners with plastic buttons, gold hardware, 2 humbucker pickups, 2 volume/2 tone controls, 3 position switch. Available in Ebony finish. Curr. mfr.

Mfr.'s Sug. Retail	$2,400	$2,400	$1,680	$1,440	$1,200	$960	$860	$790

This model also available with 3 humbucker pickups configuration.

LES PAUL '56 GOLD TOP RE-ISSUE — single sharp cutaway solid mahogany body, bound carved maple top, raised cream pickguard, mahogany neck, 22 fret bound rosewood fingerboard with pearl trapezoid inlays, Tune-O-Matic bridge/trapeze tailpiece, blackface peghead with pearl logo inlay, 3 per side tuners with plastic buttons, nickel hardware, 2 single coil pickups, 2 volume/2 tone controls, 3 position switch. Available in Antique Gold Top finish. Curr. mfr.

Mfr.'s Sug. Retail	$2,550	$2,550	$1,785	$1,530	$1,275	$1,020	$920	$840

LES PAUL '57 GOLD TOP RE-ISSUE — single sharp cutaway solid mahogany body, bound carved maple top, raised cream pickguard, mahogany neck, 22 fret bound rosewood fingerboard with pearl trapezoid inlays, Tune-O-Matic bridge/stop tailpiece, blackface peghead with pearl logo inlay, 3 per side tuners with plastic buttons, nickel hardware, 2 humbucker pickups, 2 volume/2 tone controls, 3 position switch.

Mfr.'s Sug. Retail	$2,550	$2,550	$1,785	$1,530	$1,275	$1,020	$920	$840

Grading	100%	98%	95%	90%	80%	70%	60%

LES PAUL '59 FLAMETOP RE-ISSUE — single sharp cutaway solid mahogany body, bound carved curly maple top, raised cream pickguard, mahogany neck, 22 fret bound rosewood fingerboard with pearl trapezoid inlays, Tune-O-Matic bridge/stop tailpiece, blackface peghead with pearl logo inlay, 3 per side tuners with plastic buttons, nickel hardware, 2 humbucker pickups, 2 volume/2 tone controls, 3 position switch. Available in Heritage Darkburst and Heritage Cherry Sunburst finish. Curr. mfr.

Mfr.'s Sug. Retail	$5,060	$5,060	$3,540	$3,035	$2,530	$2,025	$1,825	$1,670

LES PAUL '60 FLAMETOP RE-ISSUE — single sharp cutaway mahogany body, bound carved flame maple top, raised cream pickguard, mahogany neck, 22 fret rosewood fingerboard with pearl trapezoid inlay, Tune-O-Matic bridge/stop tailpiece, blackface peghead with pearl logo inlay, 3 per side tuners with plastic buttons, nickel hardware, 2 covered humbucker pickups, 2 volume/2 tone controls, 3 position switch. Available in Heritage Darkburst and Heritage Cherry Sunburst finish. Curr. mfr.

Mfr.'s Sug. Retail	$5,060	$5,060	$3,540	$3,035	$2,530	$2,025	$1,825	$1,670

L-4CES — single sharp cutaway bound hollow body, carved spruce top, layered black pickguard, f holes, mahogany back/sides/neck, 20 fret bound ebony fingerboard with pearl parallelogram inlay, Tune-O-Matic bridge on ebony base with pearl inlay on wings, trapeze tailpiece, blackface peghead with pearl crown/logo inlay, 3 per side tuners with plastic buttons, gold hardware, 2 covered humbucker pickups, 2 volume/2 tone controls, 3 position switch. Available in Natural finish. Mfd. 1987 to date.

Mfr.'s Sug. Retail	$3,700	$3,700	$2,590	$2,220	$1,850	$1,480	$1,330	$1,220

L-4CES — With Vintage Sunburst finish.

Mfr.'s Sug. Retail	$2,650	$2,650	$1,855	$1,590	$1,325	$1,060	$955	$875

L-4CES — With Ebony and Wine Red finish.

Mfr.'s Sug. Retail	$2,100	$2,100	$1,475	$1,260	$1,050	$840	$755	$690

L-5CES — single round cutaway bound hollow body, carved spruce top, layered tortoise shell pickguard, bound f holes, maple back/sides/neck, 20 fret bound pointed ebony fingerboard with pearl block inlay, ebony bridge with pearl inlay on wings, model name engraved trapeze tailpiece with chrome insert, multi-bound blackface peghead with pearl flame/logo inlay, 3 per side tuners, gold hardware, 2 covered humbucker pickups, 2 volume/2 tone controls, 3 position switch. Available in Natural finish. Curr. mfr.

Mfr.'s Sug. Retail	$9,500	$9,500	$6,650	$5,700	$4,750	$3,800	$3,420	$3,135

L-5CES — With Vintage Sunburst finish.

Mfr.'s Sug. Retail	$7,400	$7,400	$5,180	$4,440	$3,700	$2,960	$2,665	$2,440

L-5CES — With Ebony and Wine Red finish.

Mfr.'s Sug. Retail	$5,300	$5,300	$3,710	$3,180	$2,650	$2,120	$1,910	$1,750

Grading	100%	98%	95%	90%	80%	70%	60%

SG LES PAUL CUSTOM — double sharp cutaway mahogany body, white layered pickguard, mahogany neck, 22 fret bound ebony fingerboard with pearl block inlay, model Tune-O-Matic bridge/stop tailpiece, multi-bound peghead with pearl split diamond inlay, 3 per side tuners, gold hardware, 3 covered humbucker pickups, 2 volume/2 tone controls, 3 position switch. Available in Classic White finish. Curr. mfr.

Mfr.'s Sug. Retail	$1,900	$1,900	$1,330	$1,140	$950	$760	$685	$625

TAL FARLOW — single round cutaway bound hollow body, arched figured maple top, bound f holes, scroll style inlay on cutaway, raised black bound pickguard, maple back/sides/neck, 20 fret bound rosewood fingerboard with pearl reverse crown inlay, Tune-O-Matic bridge/trapeze tailpiece, rosewood tailpiece insert with pearl engraved block inlay, bound peghead with pearl crown/logo inlay, 3 per side tuners, chrome hardware, 2 covered humbucker pickups, 2 volume/2 tone controls, 3 position switch. Available in Vintage Sunburst finish. Curr. mfr.

Mfr.'s Sug. Retail	$2,995	$2,995	$2,095	$1,795	$1,495	$1,195	$1,075	$985

Tal Farlow — With Wine Red finish. Curr. mfr.

Mfr.'s Sug. Retail	$2,295	$2,295	$1,605	$1,375	$1,150	$920	$825	$755

SUPER 400 CES — single sharp cutaway grand auditorium style body, arched spruce top, bound f holes, raised multi-bound mottled plastic pickguard, figured maple back/sides, multiple bound body, 3 piece figured maple/mahogany neck, model name engraved into heel cap, 14/20 fret bound ebony fingerboard with point on bottom, pearl split block fingerboard inlay, adjustable rosewood bridge with pearl triangle wings inlay, gold trapeze tailpiece with engraved model name, multi-bound blackface peghead with pearl 5 piece split diamond/logo inlay, pearl 3 piece split diamond inlay on back of peghead, 3 per side tuners, gold hardware, 2 pickups, 2 volume/2 tone controls, 3 position switch. Available in Natural finish. Curr. mfr.

Mfr.'s Sug. Retail	$12,000	$12,000	$8,400	$7,200	$6,000	$4,800	$4,320	$3,960

Super 400 CES — With Vintage Sunburst finish.

Mfr.'s Sug. Retail	$9,550	$9,550	$6,685	$5,730	$4,775	$3,820	$3,440	$3,150

Super 400 CES — With Ebony and Wine Red finish.

Mfr.'s Sug. Retail	$6,350	$6,350	$4,445	$3,810	$3,175	$2,540	$2,285	$2,095

GRETSCH - ORIGINAL U.S. PRODUCTION

Manufacturer located in Savannah, GA, dealer sales only.

The Fred Gretsch Company began manufacturing instruments in 1883. Beginning with percussion, ukeleles, and banjos, Gretsch introduced guitars in the early 1930's, developing a well respected line of archtop orchestra models. During the 1950's, the majority of Gretsch's guitar line was

focused on electric six string Spanish instruments. With the endorsement of Chet Atkins and George Harrison, Gretsch electrics became very popular with both country and rock-n-roll musicians through the 1960's. In 1967, Gretsch was sold to the Baldwin Piano & Organ Co. After a series of mergers, fires and factory changes, production ceased in 1981.

Fred Gretsch Jr. re-established Gretsch guitars in 1989 with a line of Japanese manufactured guitars. These were re-issues of the company's most collectible models. In 1992, Gretsch introduced a new model to the line, completely made in the USA.

ACOUSTIC

American Orchestra/Synchromatic Arch Tops

Grading	90%	80%	70%	60%	50%	40%	20%

35 — auditorium style, carved spruce top, f holes, raised bound black pickguard, bound body, maple back/sides, 3 piece maple/rosewood neck, 14/20 fret ebony fingerboard with pearloid dot inlay, ebony bridge/trapeze tailpiece, rosewood peghead veneer with pearl logo inlay, 3 per side die cast tuners. Available in Dark Red Sunburst finish. Mfd. 1933-1949.

	90%	80%	70%	60%	50%	40%	20%
	$400	$280	$240	$200	$160	$145	$130

> In 1936, adjustable maple bridge and black plastic peghead veneer replaced original items.
> By 1939, 3 stripe body binding, rosewood fingerboard, tortoise shell tuner buttons, nickel plated hardware, and Brown Sunburst finish became standard.

50 — auditorium style, carved spruce top, f holes, raised black pickguard, bound body, avoidire back, figured maple sides/neck, 14/20 fret bound ebony pointed end fingerboard with pearloid diamond inlay, adjustable maple bridge/trapeze tailpiece, black face peghead with pearl scroll inlay, 3 per side nickel tuners with tortoise shell buttons. Available in Brown Sunburst finish. Mfd. 1936-1949.

	90%	80%	70%	60%	50%	40%	20%
	$425	$295	$250	$210	$170	$150	$135

> This model also available with round soundhole (50R), which was discontinued by 1940.
> By 1940, rosewood fingerboard with dot inlay replaced ebony fingerboard with diamond inlay.

75 — auditorium style, arched spruce top, f holes, raised bound tortoise shell pickguard, bound body, figured maple back/sides, 3 piece maple neck, 14/20 fret bound rosewood pointed end fingerboard with pearloid block inlay, adjustable rosewood stairstep bridge/nickel trapeze tailpiece, black face peghead with large floral/logo inlay, 3 per side nickel tuners. Available in Brown Sunburst finish. Mfd. 1939-1949.

	90%	80%	70%	60%	50%	40%	20%
	$550	$385	$330	$275	$220	$200	$180

> Early models had bound pegheads.
> By 1940, 3 stripe bound pickguard/body replaced original items, pickguard was also enlarged.

Grading	100%	98%	95%	90%	80%	70%	60%

CONSTELLATION — single round cutaway hollow style, arched spruce top, 2 stripe bound f holes, raised bound tortoise shell pickguard, 2 stripe bound body, laminated maple back/sides, 3 piece maple/rosewood neck, 19 fret bound rosewood fingerboard with pearloid block inlay, adjustable rosewood stairstep bridge/gold trapeze tailpiece, bound black face peghead with pearl logo inlay, 3 per side gold tuners. Available in Natural and Sunburst finish. Mfd. 1951-1960.

	$1,750	$1,225	$1,050	$875	$700	$630	$575

Originally released as the Synchromatic. It was better known as the Constellation, which it had been renamed by 1955.

By 1955, hump top block fingerboard inlay and ebony bridge/G logo trapeze tailpiece replaced original items.

ELDORADO — single round cutaway hollow style, arched spruce top, f holes, raised pickguard, 3 stripe bound body, maple back/sides/neck, 21 fret bound ebony fingerboard with pearloid humptop block inlay, adjustable ebony stairstep bridge/gold G logo trapeze tailpiece, bound black face peghead with logo inlay, 3 per side gold tuners. Available in Natural and Sunburst finish. Mfd. 1955-1970.

	$1,750	$1,225	$1,050	$875	$700	$630	$575

By 1968, Natural finish was discontinued.

FLEETWOOD — similar to Eldorado, except has smaller body, Synchromatic/logo on peghead. Available in Natural and Sunburst finish. Mfd. 1955-1968.

	$1,950	$1,365	$1,170	$975	$780	$700	$645

In 1959, thumbnail fingerboard inlay replaced block inlay and logo only on peghead.

Flat Tops

BURL IVES — folk style, spruce top, round soundhole, tortoise shell pickguard, 2 stripe bound body/rosette, mahogany back/sides/neck, 14/19 fret rosewood fingerboard with pearloid dot inlay, rosewood bridge with black pins, black peghead face with Burl Ives/logo, 3 per side tuners with plastic buttons. Available in Natural finish. Mfd. 1952-1955.

	$525	$370	$315	$260	$210	$190	$170

FOLK — folk style, spruce top, round soundhole, tortoise shell pickguard, 3 stripe bound body/rosette, mahogany back/sides/neck, 14/19 fret rosewood fingerboard with pearloid dot inlay, rosewood bridge with black pins, black peghead face with logo, 3 per side tuners with plastic buttons. Available in Natural finish. Mfd. 1951-1975.

	$375	$260	$220	$185	$150	$135	$120

By 1955, this model was named Grand Concert and had slanted peghead logo.

In 1959, this was renamed Jimmy Rogers Model.

In 1963, this was renamed Folk Singing Model.

In 1965, this was renamed Folk Model.

In 1967, straight across peghead logo was added.

In 1969, mahogany top and Sunburst finish became optional.

Grading	100%	98%	95%	90%	80%	70%	60%

RANCHER — jumbo style, spruce top with stylized G brand, triangle soundhole, tortoise shell pickguard with engraved longhorn steer head, 3 stripe bound body/rosette, maple arched back/sides/neck, 14/21 fret bound rosewood fingerboard with pearloid block inlay, adjustable rosewood bridge/stop tailpiece mounted on triangular rosewood base, black face bound peghead with pearl steer head/logo inlay, 3 per side gold tuners. Available in Golden Red finish. Mfd. 1954-1973, re-introduced 1975-1980.

	100%	98%	95%	90%	80%	70%	60%
1954-1959	$2,575	$1,805	$1,545	$1,290	$1,030	$925	$850
1960-1964	$2,010	$1,410	$1,205	$1,005	$800	$720	$660
1965-1969	$1,650	$1,155	$990	$825	$660	$595	$545
1970-1980	$950	$665	$570	$475	$380	$345	$315

G brand was on bass side of top, fingerboard inlay was inscribed with cows and cactus.

By 1957, gold pickguard and hump top fingerboard inlay with no engraving replaced original items.

In 1959, tan pickguard, thumbnail fingerboard inlay replaced 1957 updates.

In 1961, no G brand on top, and horseshoe peghead inlay replaced original items.

In 1975, this model was re-introduced but had G brand on treble side of top, block fingerboard inlay with engraved cows and cactus, rosewood bridge with white pins, horseshoe peghead inlay.

In 1978, tri-saddle bridge with white pins replaced respective item.

SUN VALLEY — dreadnought style, spruce top, round soundhole, tortoise shell pickguard, 3 stripe bound body/rosette, mahogany back/sides/neck, 14/20 fret bound rosewood fingerboard with dot inlay, rosewood bridge with black pins, bound peghead, 3 per side chrome tuners. Available in Natural and Sunburst finish. Mfd. 1959-1977.

	100%	98%	95%	90%	80%	70%	60%
1959-1964	$750	$525	$450	$375	$300	$270	$245
1965-1969	$625	$440	$375	$310	$250	$225	$205
1970-1977	$550	$385	$330	$275	$220	$200	$180

By 1973, Sunburst finish was optional.

SYNCHROMATIC JUMBO 125F — jumbo style, arched spruce top, triangle soundhole, tortoise shell pickguard, 2 stripe bound body/rosette, figured maple back/sides/neck, 14/21 fret bound rosewood fingerboard with pearloid block inlay, adjustable rosewood bridge/stop tailpiece mounted on triangular rosewood base, black face peghead with pearl logo inlay, 3 per side die cast tuners. Available in Natural top, Sunburst back/side finish. Mfd. 1947-1954.

	100%	98%	95%	90%	80%	70%	60%
	$1,250	$875	$750	$625	$500	$450	$415

Some models had tortoise shell binding all around, other models came with Transparent White finish.

Grading	100%	98%	95%	90%	80%	70%	60%

SYNCHROMATIC 300F — jumbo style, spruce top, triangle soundhole, raised pickguard, 3 stripe body/rosette, maple arched back/sides/neck, 14/21 fret bound rosewood fingerboard with pearloid slashed humptop block inlay, adjustable rosewood stairstep bridge/gold trapeze tailpiece, bound cloud peghead with silkscreened Synchromatic/logo, 3 per side gold tuners. Available in Natural top, Dark back/side finish. Mfd. 1947-1955.

	$1,750	$1,225	$1,050	$875	$700	$630	$575

⚹ **Synchromatic 400F** — similar to Synchromatic 300F. Available in Sunburst back/side finish.

	$3,250	$2,275	$1,950	$1,625	$1,300	$1,170	$1,070

WAYFARER JUMBO — dreadnought style, spruce top, round soundhole, lucite pickguard with engraved sailboat/logos, 3 stripe bound body/rosette, red maple back/sides/neck, 14/21 fret bound rosewood fingerboard with pearl split block inlay, rosewood bridge with white pins, black face peghead with logo inlay, 3 per side Grover chrome tuners. Available in Natural finish. Mfd. 1969-1972.

	$525	$370	$315	$260	$210	$190	$170

ELECTRIC

ANNIVERSARY — single round cutaway semi hollow maple body, arched top, bound body, f holes, raised white pickguard with logo, mahogany neck, 21 fret ebony fingerboard with pearloid thumbnail inlay, roller bridge/G logo trapeze tailpiece, blackface peghead with logo inlay, peghead mounted nameplate with engraved diamond, 3 per side tuners, chrome hardware, covered pickup, volume control on cutaway bout, 3 position tone switch. Available in Sunburst, 2 Tone Green and 2 Tone Tan finish. Mfd. 1958-1972.

1958-1964	$750	$525	$450	$375	$300	$270	$245
1965-1972	$600	$420	$360	$300	$240	$215	$195

In 1960, rosewood fingerboards replaced ebony fingerboards.

⚹ **Double Anniversary** — similar to Anniversary, except has 2 covered pickups, 2 volume controls, 3 position selector switch. Mfd. 1958-1975.

1958-1964	$1,500	$1,050	$900	$750	$600	$540	$495
1965-1975	$750	$525	$450	$375	$300	$270	$245

In 1961, stereo output was optional.

In 1963, bound fingerboard was added, palm vibrato optional, stereo output was discontinued.

In 1972, f holes were made smaller, adjustable bridge replaced roller bridge, peghead nameplate was removed.

In 1974, block fingerboard inlay replaced thumbnail inlay.

Grading	100%	98%	95%	90%	80%	70%	60%

ASTRO-JET — offset double cutaway asymmetrical hardwood body, black pickguard, metal rectangle plate with model name/serial number on bass side cutaway, maple neck, 21 fret bound ebony fingerboard with thumbnail inlay, tunomatic bridge/Burns vibrato, asymmetrical black face peghead with silkscreen logo, 4/2 per side tuners, chrome hardware, 2 exposed pickups, 3 controls, 3 switches. Available in Red top/Black back/side finish. Mfd. 1965-1968.

	$1,025	$720	$615	$510	$410	$370	$340

ATKINS AXE — single sharp cutaway bound hardwood body, white pickguard with logo, maple neck, 22 fret bound ebony fingerboard with white block inlay, tunomatic stop bridge, bound black face peghead with logo, 3 per side tuners, chrome hardware, 2 covered humbucker pickups, 2 volume/2 tone controls, 3 position switch. Available in Ebony Stain and Rosewood Stain finish. Mfd. 1976-1981.

	$1,025	$720	$615	$510	$410	$370	$340

⚜ **Atkins Super Axe** — similar to Atkins Axe, except has black plate with mounted controls, volume/3 effects controls, 2 effects switches, active electronics.

	$1,075	$750	$645	$535	$430	$390	$355

BIKINI — double cutaway slide-and-lock poplar body with detachable poplar center block, raised white pickguard with logo, bolt-on maple neck, 22 fret maple fingerboard with black dot inlay, adjustable ebony bridge/trapeze tailpiece, black face peghead with logo, 3 per side tuners, chrome hardware, exposed pickup, volume/tone control. Available in Black finish. Mfd. 1961-1963.

	$700	$490	$420	$350	$280	$250	$230

The slide-and-lock body is named a "Butterfly" back and is interchangeable with 6 string or bass shafts. There is also a "double Butterfly", able to accommodate both necks. Controls for this instrument are located on top of detachable center block.

BLACKHAWK — double round cutaway bound maple body, f holes, raised silver pickguard with logo, maple neck, 22 fret bound fingerboard with thumbnail inlay, dot inlay above the 12th fret, tuning fork bridge, roller bridge/G logo Bigsby vibrato tailpiece, black face peghead with logo inlay, peghead mounted nameplate, 3 per side tuners, chrome hardware, 2 covered pickups, volume control on upper bout, 2 volume controls, two 3 position switches. Available in Black and Sunburst finish. Mfd. 1967-1972.

	$1,250	$875	$750	$625	$500	$450	$415

BROADKASTER HOLLOW BODY — double round cutaway semi hollow bound maple body, f holes, raised black pickguard with logo, maple neck, 22 fret rosewood fingerboard with white dot inlay, adjustable bridge/G logo trapeze tailpiece, black-face peghead with logo, 3 per side tuners, chrome hardware, 2 covered pickups, master volume control on cutaway bout, 2 volume/2 tone controls, 3 position switch. Available in Natural, Red and Sunburst finish. Mfd. 1975-1980.

	$725	$505	$435	$360	$290	$260	$240

This model is also available with Bigsby vibrato tailpiece.

In 1976, tunomatic stop tailpiece, 2 covered humbucker DiMarzio pickups replaced respective items.

Grading	100%	98%	95%	90%	80%	70%	60%

BROADKASTER SOLID BODY — strat style maple body, white pickguard, bolt-on maple neck, 22 fret maple fingerboard with black dot inlay, fixed bridge, 3 per side tuners, chrome hardware, 2 exposed pickups, 2 volume controls, pickup selector/tone switch. Available in Natural and Sunburst finish. Mfd. 1975-1980.

	100%	98%	95%	90%	80%	70%	60%
	$550	$385	$330	$275	$220	$200	$180

CHET ATKINS COUNTRY GENTLEMAN — single round cutaway hollow bound maple body, simulated f holes, gold pickguard with logo, maple neck, 22 fret bound ebony fingerboard with pearl thumbnail inlay, adjustable bridge/Bigsby vibrato tailpiece, bound blackface peghead with logo inlay, peghead mounted nameplate, 3 per side tuners, gold hardware, 2 covered humbucker pickups, master volume on cutaway bout, 2 volume controls, two 3 position switches. Available in Mahogany and Walnut finish. Mfd. 1957-1981.

	100%	98%	95%	90%	80%	70%	60%
1957-1959	$3,225	$2,260	$1,935	$1,615	$1,295	$1,165	$1,065
1960-1969	$1,525	$1,070	$915	$765	$610	$550	$505
1970-1981	$1,050	$735	$630	$525	$420	$380	$345

A few of the early models have the Chet Aktins signpost signature on the pickguard, but this was not a standard feature.

The f holes on this model were inlaid in early production years, then they were painted on, sometimes being painted as if they were bound. A few models produced during 1960-1961 did have actual f holes in them, probably special order items.

The Bigsby vibato tailpiece was not gold plated originally.

In 1961, double round cutaway body, bridge mute, stand by switch and padded back became available.

By 1962, gold plated vibrato was standard.

In 1972, this model became available with open f holes.

In 1975, a tubular arm was added to the Bigsby vibrato.

In 1979, vibrato arm was returned to a flat bar.

CHET ATKINS HOLLOW BODY/NASHVILLE — single round cutaway bound maple body, arched top with stylized G brand, bound f holes, raised gold pickguard with Chet Atkins' sign post signature/logo, maple neck, 22 fret bound rosewood fingerboard with pearl Western motif engraved block inlay, adjustable bridge/Bigsby vibrato tailpiece, bound blackface peghead with steershead/logo inlay, 3 per side tuners, gold hardware, 2 exposed DeArmond pickups, volume control on cutaway bout, 2 volume/tone controls, 3 position switch. Available in Red, Red Amber and Western Orange finish. Mfd. 1954-1980.

	100%	98%	95%	90%	80%	70%	60%
1954-1959	$7,500	$5,250	$4,500	$3,750	$3,000	$2,700	$2,475
1960-1964	$4,050	$2,835	$2,430	$2,025	$1,620	$1,460	$1,335
1965-1969	$1,500	$1,050	$900	$750	$600	$540	$495
1970-1980	$800	$560	$480	$400	$320	$290	$265

Some models are available with body matching pegheads.

In 1956, engraved fingerboard inlay was discontinued, horseshoe peghead inlay replaced steershead, vibrato unit was nickel plated.

In 1957, G brand on top discontinued, humptop fingerboard inlay replaced original item.

In 1958, ebony fingerboard with thumbnail inlay and adjustable bar bridge replaced respective items. The tone control changed to a 3 position switch and placed next to the pickup selector switch.

(more information on the next page)

Grading	100%	98%	95%	90%	80%	70%	60%

In 1961, body was changed to a double round cutaway semi hollow style with painted f holes, pickguard had no signpost around Chet Atkins' signature, string mute, mute/standby switches (a few models were produced with a mute control) and back pad were added.

In 1967, this model was renamed the Nashville, with Chet Atkins Nashville on pickguard and peghead mounted nameplate.

In 1972, tunomatic bridge and elongated peghead were added, string mute and switch, nameplate were removed.

In 1973, real f holes were added.

In 1975, tubular arm added to vibrato, hardware became chrome plated and the standby switch was removed.

In 1979, flat vibrato arm replaced tubular arm.

CHET ATKINS TENNESSEAN — single round cutaway hollow bound maple body, arched top, f holes, raised black pickguard with Chet Atkins' sign post signature/logo, maple neck, 22 fret ebony fingerboard with pearl thumbnail inlay, adjustable bar bridge/Bigsby vibrato tailpiece, 3 per side tuners, chrome hardware, exposed pickup, volume control, 3 position switch. Available in Cherry, Dark Cherry Stain, Mahogany and Walnut finish. Mfd. 1958-1980.

	100%	98%	95%	90%	80%	70%	60%
1958-1959	$3,850	$2,695	$2,310	$1,925	$1,540	$1,385	$1,270
1960-1964	$2,500	$1,750	$1,500	$1,250	$1,000	$900	$825
1965-1969	$1,250	$875	$750	$625	$500	$450	$415
1970-1980	$1,000	$700	$600	$500	$400	$360	$330

In 1961, solid maple top with painted f holes, grey pickguard with logo, bound rosewood fingerboard, tuners with plastic buttons replaced respective items; exposed pickup, 2 volume controls, tone switch were added.

In 1962, Chet Atkins signature on pickguard, standby switch were added.

In 1963, painted bound f holes, padded back were added.

In 1964, peghead nameplate became available.

In 1970, real f holes were added.

In 1972, tunomatic bridge replaced bar bridge, peghead nameplate was removed.

CLIPPER — single round cutaway bound maple body, arched top, f holes, raised pickguard with logo, maple neck, 21 fret ebony fingerboard with white dot inlay, adjustable ebony bridge/trapeze tailpiece, blackface peghead with logo, 3 per side tuners with plastic buttons, chrome hardware, exposed DeArmond pickup, volume/tone control. Available in Natural and Sunburst finish. Mfd. 1958-1975.

	100%	98%	95%	90%	80%	70%	60%
	$650	$455	$390	$325	$260	$235	$215

The original release of this model had a deep, full body. By 1958, the body had a thinner, 335 style thickness to it.

In 1963, a palm vibrato was offered as standard, though few models are found with one.

In 1968, vibrato was no longer offered.

In 1972, 2 pickup models became available.

COMMITTEE — double cutaway walnut body, clear pickguard, thru body maple/walnut neck, 22 fret rosewood fingerboard with pearl dot inlay, fixed bridge, bound peghead with burl walnut veneer and pearl logo inlay, 3 per side tuners, chrome hardware, 2 covered humbucker pickups, 2 volume/2 controls, 3 position switch. Available in Natural finish. Mfd. 1975-1981.

	100%	98%	95%	90%	80%	70%	60%
	$425	$295	$250	$210	$170	$150	$135

Grading	100%	98%	95%	90%	80%	70%	60%

CONVERTIBLE — single round cutaway hollow maple body, spruce top, gold pickguard with logo, bound body/f holes, maple neck, 21 fret bound rosewood fingerboard with pearl humptop block inlay, adjustable rosewoood bridge/G logo trapeze tailpiece, bound blackface peghead with logo inlay, 3 per side Grover Imperial tuners, gold hardware, 1 exposed DeArmond pickup, volume/tone control. Available in Bamboo Yellow and Ivory top with Copper Mist and Sunburst body/neck finish. Mfd. 1955-1968.

	100%	98%	95%	90%	80%	70%	60%
1955-1959	$2,750	$1,925	$1,650	$1,375	$1,100	$990	$905
1960-1968	$1,750	$1,225	$1,050	$875	$700	$630	$575

The pickup and controls are pickguard mounted on this instrument.

In 1957, ebony fingerboard with thumbnail inlay replaced original fingerboard/inlay.

In 1958, this model was renamed Sal Salvador.

In 1965, block fingerboard inlay replaced thumbnail fingerboard inlay, controls were mounted into the instrument's top.

CORVETTE — offset double cutaway mahogany body, 2 piece pickguard, mahogany neck, 21 fret rosewood fingerboard with pearl dot inlay, adjustable rosewood bridge/trapeze tailpiece, black face peghead with logo, 3 per side tuners with plastic buttons, chrome hardware, exposed pickup, volume/tone control. Available in Natural and Platinum Grey finish. Mfd. 1961-1978.

		100%	98%	95%	90%	80%	70%	60%
		$525	$370	$315	$260	$210	$190	$170

In 1963, cutaways were sharpened and changed, pickguard styling changed, metal bridge replaced ebony bridge, 1 pickup with vibrato or 2 pickups (extra tone control and 3 position switch) with vibrato became optional, Cherry finish added, and Platinum Grey finish discontinued.

In 1964, peghead shape became rounded with 2/4 tuners per side.

In 1966, Silver Duke with Silver Glitter finish and Gold Duke with Gold Glitter finish were offered. Few of these models exist.

COUNTRY ROC — Les Paul style routed mahogany body, bound arched maple top, raised pickguard with logo, G brand on lower bout, tooled leather side trim, maple neck, 22 fret bound ebony fingerboard with pearl block inlay with engraved western motif, tunomatic bridge/G logo trapeze tailpiece with western motif belt buckle, bound peghead with figured maple veneer and pearl horseshoe logo/inlay, 3 per side tuners, gold hardware, 2 exposed pickups, master volume control on cutaway bout, 2 volume/2 tone controls, 3 position switch. Available in Red Stain finish. Mfd. 1974-1979.

		100%	98%	95%	90%	80%	70%	60%
		$1,350	$945	$810	$675	$540	$485	$445

DELUXE CHET — single round cutaway semi hollow bound maple body, bound f holes, raised black pickguard with model name/logo, 3 piece maple neck, 22 fret bound ebony fingerboard with pearl thumbnail inlay, tunomatic bridge/Bigsby vibrato tailpiece, bound black face peghead with pearl logo inlay, 3 per side tuners, chrome hardware, 2 exposed pickups, master volume control, 2 volume/2 tone controls, 3 position switch. Available in Red and Walnut finish. Mfd. 1973-1975.

		100%	98%	95%	90%	80%	70%	60%
		$950	$665	$570	$475	$380	$345	$315

In 1976, this model was renamed the Super Axe, and was discontinued in 1980.

Grading	100%	98%	95%	90%	80%	70%	60%

ELECTROMATIC — hollow bound maple body, arched spruce top, f holes, raised tortoise shell pickguard, maple neck, 14/20 fret rosewood fingerboard with white dot inlay, adjustable rosewood bridge/trapeze tailpiece, blackface peghead with engraved logo, Electromatic vertically engraved onto peghead, 3 per side tuners with plastic buttons, chrome hardware, exposed DeArmond pickup, volume/tone control. Available in Jaguar Tan, Natural and Sunburst finish. Mfd. 1940-1959.

	$350	$245	$210	$175	$140	$125	$115

Add $150 for 2 pickup version (6189).

The original (1940) version of this model had a larger body style. By 1949, the body style was 16 inches across the bottom bouts.

In 1955, this model was renamed Corvette, with a new peghead design.

In 1957, a single round cutaway body became available.

MONKEES' ROCK-N-ROLL MODEL — double round cutaway bound maple body, arched top, bound f holes, raised white pickguard with Monkees/logo, maple neck, 22 fret bound rosewood fingerboard with pearl double thumbnail inlay, adjustable bridge/Bigsby vibrato tailpiece, blackface peghead with pearl logo inlay, peghead mounted nameplate, 3 per side tuners, chrome hardware, 2 covered pickups, volume control on cutaway bout, 2 volume controls, pickup selector/2 tone switches. Available in Red finish. Mfd. 1966-1968.

	$1,295	$905	$775	$645	$515	$465	$425

The Monkees' name appears on the truss rod cover and pickguard.

PRINCESS — offset double cutaway mahogany body, pickguard with "Princess" logo, mahogany neck, 21 fret rosewood fingerboard with pearl dot inlay, adjustable bridge/trapeze tailpiece, Tone Twister vibrato, body matching peghead with logo, 3 per side tuners with plastic buttons, gold hardware, exposed pickup, volume/tone control. Available in Blue, Pink and White finish. Mfd. 1962-1964.

	$2,200	$1,540	$1,320	$1,100	$880	$790	$725

Pickguard color on this model is dependent on body color.

RALLY — double round cutaway bound maple body, arched top, f holes, raised pickguard with sportstripes/logo, maple neck, 22 fret bound rosewood fingerboard with pearl thumbnail inlay, dot inlay above 12th fret, adjustable bar bridge/Bigsby vibrato tailpiece, blackface peghead with logo inlay, 3 per side tuners, chrome hardware, 2 exposed pickups, volume control on cutaway bout, 2 volume/tone controls, pickup selector/treble boost/standby switches. Available in Bamboo Yellow top/Copper Mist back/side and Rally Green finish. Mfd. 1967-1970.

	$950	$665	$570	$475	$380	$345	$315

Grading	100%	98%	95%	90%	80%	70%	60%

RAMBLER — single sharp cutaway ¾ size hollow bound maple body, f holes, raised black pickguard with logo, maple neck, 20 fret rosewood fingerboard with white dot inlay, adjustable rosewood bridge/G logo trapeze tailpiece, bound blackface peghead with logo inlay, 3 per side tuners with plastic buttons, chrome hardware, 1 exposed DeArmond pickup, volume/tone control. Available in Ivory top/Black body/neck finish. Mfd. 1957-1961.

	$550	$385	$330	$275	$220	$200	$180

In 1960, a round cutaway replaced original style cutaway.

STREAMLINER — double round cutaway bound maple body, arched top, f holes, maple neck, 22 fret bound rosewood fingerboard with pearl thumbnail inlay, dot inlay above 12th fret, roller bridge/G logo trapeze tailpiece, blackface peghead with nameplate, 3 per side tuners with plastic buttons, chrome hardware, 2 covered pickups, master volume control on cutaway bout, 2 volume controls, pickup selector/treble boost/standby switches. Available in Cherry Red and Golden Sunburst finish. Mfd. 1969-1975.

	$950	$665	$570	$475	$380	$345	$315

In 1972, dot fingerboard inlay and nameplate were removed, tunomatic bridge replaced roller bridge.

SUPER CHET — single round cutaway hollow bound maple body, bound f holes, raised black pickguard with engraved model name/logo, maple neck, 22 fret bound ebony fingerboard with abalone floral inlay, tunomatic bridge/trapeze tailpiece with ebony insert with abalone floral inlay, bound blackface peghead with abalone floral/logo inlay, 3 per side tuners, gold hardware, 2 exposed humbucker pickups, master volume/2 volume/2 tone controls all mounted on the pickguard. Available in Red and Walnut finish. Mfd. 1972-1980.

	$2,200	$1,540	$1,320	$1,100	$880	$790	$725

This model was also available with Bigsby vibrato tailpiece.

VAN EPS — single round cutaway hollow bound maple body, bound f holes, raised white pickguard with logo, maple neck, 21 fret bound ebony fingerboard with pearl thumbnail inlay, tuning fork bridge, roller bridge/G logo trapeze tailpiece, bound blackface asymmetrical peghead with pearl logo inlay, peghead mounted nameplate, 4/3 per side tuners, gold hardware, 2 covered humbucker pickups, master volume control on cutaway bout, 2 volume controls, pickup selector/tone/standby switches. Available in Sunburst and Walnut finish. Mfd. 1968-1979.

	$1,950	$1,365	$1,170	$975	$780	$700	$645

The above model is a 7 string version. A six string version was also offered with 3 per side tuners, though it was discontinued in 1972.

In 1972, peghead nameplate, tuning fork bridge and standby switch were removed, ebony bridge and chrome hardware replaced respective items.

Grading	100%	98%	95%	90%	80%	70%	60%

VIKING — double round cutaway hollow bound maple body, f holes, raised pickguard with Viking/logo, 21 fret bound ebony fingerboard with pearl thumbnail inlay, offset dot inlay above 12th fret, string mute, roller bridge/Bigsby vibrato tailpiece with telescoping arm, bound blackface peghead with pearl logo inlay, peghead mounted nameplate, 3 per side tuners, gold hardware, 2 covered humbucker rail pickups, master volume control on cutaway bout, 2 volume controls, pickup selector/tone/mute/standby switches, leatherette back pad. Available in Cadillac Green, Natural and Sunburst finish. Mfd. 1964-1974.

	$1,250	$875	$750	$625	$500	$450	$415

Early models have a Viking ship on the pickguard as well as the logos.

In 1966, tuning fork bridge was added.

In 1968, flat arm vibrato unit replaced original item.

In 1972, string mute, tuning fork and back pad were removed.

WHITE FALCON — single round cutaway hollow bound maple body, arched spruce top, bound f holes, raised gold pickguard with falcon/logo, maple neck, 21 fret bound ebony fingerboard with pearl "feather engraved" humptop block inlay, adjustable bridge/G logo tubular trapeze tailpiece, bound V styled whiteface peghead with vertical Gold Sparkle wings/logo, 3 per side Grover Imperial tuners, gold hardware, 2 exposed DeArmond pickups, master volume on cutaway bout, 2 volume/1 tone control, 3 position switch. Available in White finish. Mfd. 1955-1963.

1955-1958	$13,000	$9,100	$7,800	$6,500	$4,680	$4,290	$3,950
1959-1961	$17,000	$11,900	$10,200	$8,500	$6,120	$5,610	$5,150
1962-1963	$5,750	$4,025	$3,450	$2,875	$2,300	$2,070	$1,850
1964 only	$4,000	$2,800	$2,400	$2,000	$1,600	$1,440	$1,300
1973-1981	$2,300	$1,610	$1,380	$1,150	$920	$830	$750

This instrument has Gold Sparkle binding and jewelled control knobs. The Gold Sparkle binding was not on all bound edges on the earliest models and it was sometimes omitted during this instruments production run.

In 1958, arched maple top, thumbnail fingerboard inlay, horizontal peghead logo, roller bridge and tone switch (placed by pickup selector control) replaced original items, peghead mounted nameplate was added, though it was not placed on all instruments produced. Stereo output became an option.

In 1959, second version of stereo output offered with 3 tone switches placed by pickup selector switch.

In 1960, double mute with 2 controls and back pad were added.

In 1962, double round cutaway body and Bigsby vibrato tailpiece became standard, it was offered as an option up to this time. Some models still have G logo tubular trapeze tailpiece. Stereo models have master volume control removed and pickup selector switch put in its place.

In 1963, mute controls were changed to switches.

In 1964, Gretsch G logo vibrato trapeze tailpiece and oval button tuners replaced respective items.

In 1965, offset dot fingerboard inlay above 12th fret was added, stereo tone switches were moved to lower bout and controls/switches were reconfigured.

In 1966, tuning fork bridge was added.

In early 1970's, single round cutaway body style was re-introduced with original design format.

In 1972, Bigsby vibrato unit replaced Gretsch vibrato unit.

In 1980, non-stereo models were discontinued, double round cutaway stereo model available as special order item.

Grading	100%	98%	95%	90%	80%	70%	60%

Duo-Jet Series

These guitars have a single cutaway Les Paul style body, unless otherwise noted. The body is constructed by placing a top on a highly routed body made of pine, maple, mahogany, spruce or plastic drum material, with rosewood fingerboard, mahogany neck and 2 DeArmond Dynasonic pickups, unless noted otherwise.

CHET ATKINS — Les Paul style routed mahogany body, bound maple top, raised gold pickguard with signature/logo, G brand on lower bout, tooled leather side trim, maple neck, 22 fret bound rosewood fingerboard with pearl block inlay with engraved western motif, adjustable bridge/Bigsby vibrato tailpiece, bound peghead with maple veneer and pearl steershead/logo inlay, 3 per side tuners, gold hardware, 2 exposed DeArmond pickups, control on cutaway bout, 2 volume/tone controls, 3 position switch. Available in Red Orange finish. Mfd. 1955-1963.

	100%	98%	95%	90%	80%	70%	60%
	$4,500	$3,150	$2,700	$2,250	$1,800	$1,620	$1,485

The Bigsby vibrato is available with or without gold plating.

This model was originally issued with a jewelled Western styled strap.

In 1957, G brand and tooled leather side trim were removed, ebony fingerboard with humptop block inlay was added.

In 1958, thumbnail fingerboard inlay replaced block inlay, steershead peghead inlay replaced with horseshoe inlay, tone control replaced by 3 position switch and placed by the pickup selector switch.

In 1961, body was changed to double cutaway style.

In 1962, a standby switch was added.

DUO-JET — Les Paul style routed mahogany body, bound maple top, raised white pickguard with logo, mahogany neck, 22 fret bound rosewood fingerboard with pearloid block inlay, adjustable bridge/G logo trapeze tailpiece, bound black face peghead with logo, 3 per side tuners, chrome hardware, 2 exposed DeArmond pickups, master volume on cutaway bout, 2 volume/1 tone control, 3 position switch. Available in Black and Sparkles finish. Mfd. 1953-1971.

	100%	98%	95%	90%	80%	70%	60%
1953-1959	$2,850	$1,995	$1,710	$1,425	$1,140	$1,025	$940
1960-1964	$1,550	$1,085	$930	$775	$620	$560	$515
1965-1971	$1,025	$720	$615	$510	$410	$370	$340

This model was available as a custom order instrument with Green finish and gold hardware.

In 1956, humptop fingerboard inlay replaced the block inlay.

In 1958, thumbnail fingerboard inlay and roller bridge replaced the respective items, 3 position switch replaced tone control and placed by the other switch.

In 1961, double cutaway body became available.

In 1962, gold pickguard, Burns vibrato, gold hardware and standby switch replaced, or were added, items.

From 1963-1966, Sparkle finishes were offered.

In 1968, Bigsby vibrato replaced existing vibrato/tailpiece, treble boost switch added.

Grading	100%	98%	95%	90%	80%	70%	60%

JET FIREBIRD — similar to Duo Jet, except has black pickguard with logo, 22 fret bound rosewood fingerboard with pearloid block inlay, adjustable bridge/G logo trapeze tailpiece, bound black face peghead with logo, 3 per side tuners, chrome hardware, 2 exposed pickups, master volume on cutaway bout, 2 volume/1 tone control, 3 position switch. Available in Red top/Black back/sides/neck finish. Mfd. 1955-1971.

	100%	98%	95%	90%	80%	70%	60%
1955-1959	$2,250	$1,575	$1,345	$1,125	$900	$810	$740
1960-1964	$1,750	$1,225	$1,050	$875	$700	$630	$575
1965-1971	$1,500	$1,050	$900	$750	$600	$540	$495

A few models were produced without the logo on the pickguard.

ROC JET — Les Paul style mahogany body, arched bound top, raised silver pickguard with logo, mahogany neck, 22 fret bound rosewood fingerboard with pearloid thumbnail inlay, adjustable bridge/G logo trapeze tailpiece, bound black face peghead with logo, nameplate with serial number attached to peghead, 3 per side tuners, chrome hardware, 2 exposed pickups, master volume on cutaway bout, 2 volume/2 tone controls, 3 position switch. Available in Black, Porsche Pumpkin, Red and Walnut Stain finish. Mfd. 1970-1980.

	$950	$665	$570	$475	$380	$345	$315

In 1972, the pickguard was redesigned, peghead nameplate was removed.
In 1978, tunomatic stop tailpiece and covered humbucker DiMarzio pickups replaced original items.

ROUNDUP — Les Paul style routed mahogany body, bound knotty pine top, raised tortoise shell pickguard with engraved steershead, G brand on lower bout, tooled leather side trim, maple neck, 22 fret bound rosewood fingerboard with pearl block inlay with engraved western motif, adjustable bridge/G logo trapeze tailpiece with western motif belt buckle, bound peghead with pine veneer and pearl steershead/logo inlay, 3 per side tuners, gold hardware, 2 exposed DeArmond pickups, control on cutaway bout, 2 volume/tone controls, 3 position switch. Available in Orange Stain finish. Mfd. 1954-1960.

	$4,250	$2,975	$2,550	$2,125	$1,700	$1,530	$1,400

This model is also available with mahogany and maple tops.
This model was originally issued with a jewelled Western styled strap.

SILVER JET — Les Paul style routed mahogany body, bound Nitron plastic top, raised white pickguard with logo, mahogany neck, 22 fret bound rosewood fingerboard with pearloid block inlay, adjustable bridge/G logo trapeze tailpiece, bound black face peghead with logo, 3 per side tuners, chrome hardware, 2 exposed pickups, master volume on cutaway bout, 2 volume/1 tone control, 3 position switch. Available in Silver Sparkle finish. Mfd. 1955-1963.

	100%	98%	95%	90%	80%	70%	60%
1955-1959	$8,500	$5,950	$5,100	$4,250	$3,400	$3,060	$2,805
1960-1964	$4,000	$2,800	$2,400	$2,000	$1,600	$1,440	$1,320

Any models with Silver Sparkle finish found after 1963 are Duo Jets with Sparkle finish (see Duo Jet earlier in this section).

Grading	100%	98%	95%	90%	80%	70%	60%

WHITE PENGUIN — Les Paul style mahogany body, bound arched top, raised gold pickguard with penguin/logo, mahogany neck, 22 fret bound ebony fingerboard with pearl "feather engraved" humptop block inlay, adjustable bridge/G logo tubular trapeze tailpiece, bound V styled white face peghead with vertical Gold Sparkle wings/logo, 3 per side Grover Imperial tuners, gold hardware, 2 exposed DeArmond pickups, master volume on cutaway bout, 2 volume/1 tone control, 3 position switch. Available in White finish. Mfd. 1955-1963.

	$40,000	$28,000	$24,000	$20,000	$16,000	$14,400	$13,200

Originally released with banjo armrest attached to bass lower bout.

This guitar is ultra rare, with approximately less than 100 made.

This instrument has gold sparkle binding and jewelled control knobs.

In 1958, thumbnail fingerboard inlay and roller bridge replaced the respective items,
   3 position switch replaced tone control and was placed by the other switch.

In 1959, horizontal logo and metal nameplate were applied to peghead.

In 1961, double cutaway body became available.

ELECTRIC BASS

BIKINI — double cutaway slide-and-lock poplar body with detachable poplar center block, bolt-on maple neck, 17 fret maple fingerboard with black dot inlay, adjustable ebony bridge/stop tailpiece, black face peghead with logo, 2 per side tuners, chrome hardware, humbucker pickup, volume/tone control. Available in Black finish. Mfd. 1961-1963.

	$500	$350	$300	$250	$200	$180	$165

The slide-and-lock body is called a "Butterfly" back and is interchangeable with 6 string or bass shafts. There was also a "double Butterfly", able to accommodate both necks. Controls for this instrument are located on top of detachable center block.

BROADKASTER — precision style maple body, white pickguard, bolt-on maple neck, 20 fret maple fingerboard with black dot inlay, fixed bridge with cover, 2 per side tuners, chrome hardware, exposed pickup, volume/tone control. Available in Natural and Sunburst finish. Mfd. 1975-1979.

	$525	$370	$315	$260	$210	$190	$170

COMMITTEE — double cutaway walnut body, clear pickguard, thru body maple/walnut neck, 22 fret rosewood fingerboard with pearl dot inlay, fixed bridge, bound peghead with burl walnut veneer and pearl logo inlay, 2 per side tuners, chrome hardware, exposed pickup, volume/tone control. Available in Natural finish. Mfd. 1977-1981.

	$425	$295	$250	$210	$170	$150	$135

Grading	100%	98%	95%	90%	80%	70%	60%

MODEL 6070 — double round cutaway hollow bound maple body, arched top with painted bound f holes, finger rests, maple neck, 20 fret rosewood fingerboard with white dot inlay, string mute with switch, roller bridge/G logo trapeze tailpiece, bound blackface peghead with metal nameplate, 2 per side tuners, gold hardware, covered pickup, volume control, tone/standby switches, padded back. Available in Amber Red and Sunburst finish. Mfd. 1962-1972.

	$500	$350	$300	$250	$200	$180	$165

This instrument is also called the Country Gentleman Bass.

MODEL 6071 — single round cutaway hollow bound maple body, painted bound f holes, finger rests, maple neck, 21 fret rosewood fingerboard with white dot inlay, string mute with switch, roller bridge/G logo trapeze tailpiece, blackface peghead with logo, 4 on one side tuners, gold hardware, covered pickup, volume control, tone/standby switches. Available in Mahogany finish. Mfd. 1964-1972.

	$400	$280	$240	$200	$160	$145	$130

In 1967, gold hardware was replaced with chrome hardware.

MODEL 6072 — double round cutaway hollow bound maple body, arched top with painted bound f holes, finger rests, maple neck, 20 fret rosewood fingerboard with white dot inlay, string mute with switch, roller bridge/G logo trapeze tailpiece, bound blackface peghead with metal nameplate, 2 per side tuners, gold hardware, 2 covered pickups, master volume control on upper treble bout, 2 volume controls, pickup selector/tone/standby switches, padded back. Available in Sunburst finish. Mfd. 1964-1972.

	$650	$455	$390	$325	$260	$235	$215

MODEL 6073 — single round cutaway hollow bound maple body, painted bound f holes, finger rests, maple neck, 21 fret rosewood fingerboard with white dot inlay, string mute with switch, roller bridge/G logo trapeze tailpiece, blackface peghead with logo, 4 on one side tuners, gold hardware, 2 covered pickups, master volume control on upper treble bout, 2 volume controls, pickup selector/tone/standby switches. Available in Mahogany finish. Mfd. 1964-1972.

	$450	$315	$270	$225	$180	$160	$150

In 1967, gold hardware was replaced with chrome hardware.

MODEL 7615 — offset double cutaway asymmetrical mahogany body treble bout cutout, rosewood pickguard with finger rests, mahogany neck, 22 fret bound rosewood fingerboard with white dot inlay, fixed bridge, bound peghead with logo, 2 per side tuners, chrome hardware, 2 exposed pickups, 2 controls, 3 position switch. Available in Mahogany finish. Mfd. 1972-1975.

	$275	$195	$165	$140	$110	$100	$90

Grading	100%	98%	95%	90%	80%	70%	60%

TK 300 7626 — offset double cutaway maple body with divit in bottom, white pickguard, bolt-on maple neck, 20 fret rosewood fingerboard, fixed bridge with cover, 4 on one side tuners, chrome hardware, 4 on one side tuners, exposed pickup, volume/tone control. Available in Autumn Red Stain and Natural finish. Mfd. 1977-1981.

	$300	$210	$180	$150	$120	$110	$100

GRETSCH - CURRENT PRODUCTION

Responding to the popularity of Gretsch guitars with vintage collectors, Gretsch has re-issued their classic instruments with technological improvements and updates, manufactured in Japan.

ACOUSTIC

CRIMSON FLYER — single round cutaway dreadnought style, solid spruce top, triangle soundhole, multi bound body, floral pattern rosette, chestnut back/sides, 2 piece mahogany neck, 22 fret rosewood fingerboard with pearl dot inlay, pearl scroll inlay at 12th fret, rosewood bridge with black pearl pins, pearl floral bridge wing inlay, bound body matching peghead with pearl logo inlay, 3 per side gold tuners, active ceramic pickup, volume/tone control. Available in Cherry Sunburst finish. Mfd. 1991 to date.

Mfr.'s Sug. Retail	$1,350	$945	$810	$675	$540	$485	$445	$405

 Crimson Flyer V — similar to Crimson Flyer, except has rosewood/metal tunomatic bridge/Bigsby vibrato.

Mfr.'s Sug. Retail	$1,650	$1,155	$990	$825	$660	$595	$545	$495

RANCHER — jumbo style, spruce top with "G" brand, bound triangle soundhole, tortoise shell pickguard with engraved steerhead, 3 stripe bound body, maple back/sides/neck, 14/21 fret bound rosewood fingerboard with western motif engraved pearl block inlays, rosewood bridge with black white dot pins, bound peghead with pearl steerhead/logo inlay, 3 per side gold tuners. Available in Transparent Orange finish. Mfd. 1991 to date.

Mfr.'s Sug. Retail	$1,050	$735	$630	$525	$420	$380	$345	$315

 Rancher C — similar to Rancher, except has single round cutaway, single coil pickup, volume/tone control.

Mfr.'s Sug. Retail	$1,500	$1,050	$900	$750	$600	$540	$495	$450

 Rancher CV — similar to Rancher, except has single round cutaway, no pickguard, rosewood/metal tunomatic bridge/Bigsby vibrato, single coil pickup, volume/tone control.

Mfr.'s Sug. Retail	$1,750	$1,225	$1,050	$875	$700	$630	$575	$525

Grading	100%	98%	95%	90%	80%	70%	60%

Rancher 12 — similar to Rancher, except has 12 strings, 6 per side tuners.

Mfr.'s Sug. Retail	$1,500	$1,050	$900	$750	$600	$540	$495	$450

Rancher C12 — similar to Rancher, except has 12 strings, single round cutaway, 6 per side tuners, single coil pickup, volume/tone control.

Mfr.'s Sug. Retail	$1,600	$1,120	$960	$800	$640	$575	$530	$480

SUN VALLEY — dreadnought style, solid spruce top, triangle soundhole, 3 stripe bound body, floral pattern rosette, rosewood back/sides, mahogany neck, 14/20 fret bound rosewood fingerboard with pearl diamond inlay, pearl scroll inlay at 12th fret, rosewood bridge with black pearl dot pins, pearl floral bridge wing inlay, bound blackface peghead with pearl floral/logo inlay, 3 per side gold tuners. Available in Natural finish. Mfd. 1991 to date.

Mfr.'s Sug. Retail	$1,250	$875	$750	$625	$500	$450	$415	$375

SYNCHROMATIC — jumbo style, arched spruce top, bound fang soundholes, raised bound tortoise shell pickguard, 3 stripe bound body, arched maple back, maple sides/neck, 14/20 fret bound rosewood fingerboard with pearl split humpblock inlay, adjustable stylized ebony bridge/step trapeze tailpiece, bound blackface peghead with pearl model name/logo inlay, 3 per side gold tuners. Available in Sunburst finish. Mfd. 1991 to date.

Mfr.'s Sug. Retail	$1,500	$1,050	$900	$750	$600	$540	$495	$450

Synchromatic C — similar to Synchromatic, except has single round cutaway.

Mfr.'s Sug. Retail	$1,750	$1,225	$1,050	$875	$700	$630	$575	$525

Add $100 for Natural finish.

ACOUSTIC ELECTRIC

NIGHTBIRD — single round cutaway jumbo style, solid spruce top, triangle soundhole, 3 stripe bound body, floral pattern rosette, maple back/sides, 2 piece mahogany neck, 21 fret bound rosewood fingerboard with pearl dot inlay, pearl scroll inlay at 12th fret, rosewood bridge with black pearl dot pins, pearl floral pattern bridge wing inlay, bound blackface peghead with pearl logo inlay, 3 per side gold tuners, active ceramic pickup, volume/tone control. Available in Ebony finish. Curr. mfr.

Mfr.'s Sug. Retail	$1,200	$840	$720	$600	$480	$430	$395	$360

Nightbird V — similar to Nightbird, except has rosewood/metal tunomatic bridge/Bigsby vibrato tailpiece.

Mfr.'s Sug. Retail	$1,500	$1,050	$900	$750	$600	$540	$495	$450

Grading	100%	98%	95%	90%	80%	70%	60%

ACOUSTIC ELECTRIC BASS

ACOUSTIC BASS — single round cutaway jumbo style, spruce top, triangle soundhole, 3 stripe bound body, floral pattern rosette, maple back/sides/neck, 23 fret bound rosewood fingerboard with pearl dot inlay, pearl scroll inlay at 12th fret, rosewood strings thru bridge, bound blackface peghead with pearl logo inlay, 2 per side gold tuners, active ceramic pickup, volume/tone control. Available in Transparent Orange finish. Curr. mfr.

Mfr.'s Sug. Retail	$1,400	$980	$840	$700	$560	$505	$460	$420

This model also available with fretless fingerboard.

ELECTRIC

BLACK FALCON 1955 SINGLE CUTAWAY — single round cutaway semi hollow bound maple body, raised gold pickguard with flying falcon, bound f holes, maple neck, 22 fret bound rosewood fingerboard with pearl block inlay, ebony/metal tunomatic bridge/Cadillac tailpiece, bound peghead with pearl gold sparkle logo inlay, 3 per side tuners, gold hardware, 2 humbucker pickups, master volume on upper treble bout, 2 volume/1 tone controls, selector switch. Available in Black finish. Curr. mfr.

Mfr.'s Sug. Retail	$3,250	$2,275	$1,950	$1,625	$1,300	$1,170	$1,070	$975

Black Falcon I — similar to Black Falcon, except has a Bigsby vibrato tailpiece.

Mfr.'s Sug. Retail	$3,000	$2,095	$1,800	$1,500	$1,200	$1,080	$990	$900

This model also available in double round cutaway body (Black Falcon II).

COUNTRY CLASSIC I — single round cutaway semi hollow bound maple body, raised gold pickguard with model name/logo, bound f holes, 3 piece maple neck, 22 fret bound ebony fingerboard with pearl thumbnail inlay, ebony/metal tunomatic bridge/Bigsby vibrato tailpiece, bound blackface peghead with pearl logo inlay, peghead mounted metal nameplate, 3 per side tuners, gold hardware, 2 humbucker pickups, master volume on upper treble bout, 2 volume/1 tone controls, selector switch. Available in Walnut Stain finish. Curr. mfr.

Mfr.'s Sug. Retail	$2,100	$1,475	$1,260	$1,050	$840	$755	$690	$630

This model also available with double round cutaway (Country Classic II).

DUO JET — single round cutaway mahogany body, bound arched maple top, raised white pickguard with logo, mahogany neck, 22 fret bound rosewood fingerboard with pearl humpblock inlay, tunomatic bridge/G logo trapeze tailpiece, bound blackface peghead with pearl horseshoe/logo inlay, 3 per side tuners, chrome hardware, 2 humbucker pickups, master volume control on upper treble bout, 2 volume/1 tone controls, selector switch. Available in Jet Black top finish. Mfd. 1990 to date.

Mfr.'s Sug. Retail	$1,500	$1,050	$900	$750	$600	$540	$495	$450

Grading	100%	98%	95%	90%	80%	70%	60%

JET FIREBIRD — similar to Duo Jet, except has gold pickguard, gold hardware. Available in Cherry Red top finish.

Mfr.'s Sug. Retail	$1,600	$1,120	$960	$800	$640	$575	$530	$480

NASHVILLE — single round cutaway semi hollow bound maple body, raised gold pickguard with logo, bound f holes, 3 piece maple neck, 22 fret bound ebony fingerboard with pearl block inlay, ebony/metal tunomatic bridge/Bigsby vibrato tailpiece, bound blackface peghead with pearl horseshoe/logo inlay, 3 per side tuners, gold hardware, 2 humbucker pickups, master volume on upper treble bout, 2 volume/1 tone controls, selector switch. Available in Transparent Orange finish. Mfd. 1991 to date.

Mfr.'s Sug. Retail	$1,750	$1,225	$1,050	$875	$700	$630	$575	$525

Add $225 for Blue Sunburst finish.

⚡ **Nashville Western** — similar to Nashville, except has stylized "G" brand on lower bass bout, model name in fence post on pickguard, engraved western motif fingerboard inlay.

Mfr.'s Sug. Retail	$1,875	$1,315	$1,125	$940	$750	$675	$615	$560

⚡ **Nashville Tiger Maple** — similar to Nashville, except has figured maple body/neck.

Mfr.'s Sug. Retail	$2,200	$1,540	$1,320	$1,100	$880	$790	$725	$660

ROUNDUP — single round cutaway mahogany body, bound arched maple top, raised gold pickguard with logo, stylized "G" brand on lower bass bout, mahogany neck, 22 fret bound rosewood fingerboard with pearl engraved western motif block inlay, ebony/metal tunomatic bridge/Bigsby vibrato tailpiece, bound peghead with pearl horseshoe/logo inlay, 3 per side tuners, gold hardware, 2 humbucker pickups, master volume control on upper treble bout, 2 volume/1 tone controls, selector switch. Available in Transparent Orange top finish. Curr. mfr.

Mfr.'s Sug. Retail	$1,750	$1,225	$1,050	$875	$700	$630	$575	$525

SILVER JET — single round cutaway mahogany body, bound arched maple top, raised silver pickguard with logo, mahogany neck, 22 fret bound rosewood fingerboard with pearl humpblock inlay, tunomatic bridge/G logo trapeze tailpiece, bound blackface peghead with pearl horseshoe/logo inlay, 3 per side tuners, chrome hardware, 2 humbucker pickups, master volume control on upper treble bout, 2 volume/1 tone controls, selector switch. Available in Sparkle Silver top finish. Curr. mfr.

Mfr.'s Sug. Retail	$1,600	$1,120	$960	$800	$640	$575	$530	$480

Grading	100%	98%	95%	90%	80%	70%	60%

SYNCHROMATIC — single round cutaway jumbo style, arched maple top, bound fang soundholes, raised bound tortoise shell pickguard, 3 stripe bound body, arched maple back, maple sides/neck, 14/20 fret bound rosewood fingerboard with pearl split humpblock inlay, ebony/metal tunomatic bridge/Bigsby vibrato tailpiece, bound blackface peghead with pearl model name/logo inlay, 3 per side tuners, gold hardware, humbucker pickup, volume/tone control, pickguard mounted pickup/controls. Available in Natural finish. Mfd. 1991 to date.

Mfr.'s Sug. Retail	$2,500	$1,750	$1,500	$1,250	$1,000	$900	$825	$750

SYNCHROMATIC JAZZ — single round cutaway multi-bound auditorium style, carved spruce top, raised bound flame maple pickguard, f holes, flame maple back/sides/neck, 20 fret multi-bound ebony fingerboard with pearl split hump block inlay, adjustable ebony stairstep bridge/trapeze tailpiece, multi-bound blackface peghead with pearl logo inlay, 3 per side Imperial tuners, gold hardware, humbucker pickup, volume control, pickguard mounted pickup/control. Available in Natural and Shaded finish. Mfd. in USA. New 1993.

Mfr.'s Sug. Retail	$5,700	$3,990	$3,420	$2,850	$2,280	$2,050	$1,880	$1,710

TENNESSEE ROSE 6119 — single round cutaway semi hollow bound maple body, raised silver pickguard with model name/logo, bound f holes, maple neck, 22 fret bound rosewood fingerboard with pearl thumbnail inlay, ebony/metal tunomatic bridge/Bigsby vibrato tailpiece, black face peghead with pearl logo inlay, 3 per side tuners, chrome hardware, 2 humbucker pickups, master volume on upper treble bout, 2 volume/1 tone controls, selector switch. Available in Dark Cherry Red Stain finish. Curr. mfr.

Mfr.'s Sug. Retail	$1,495	$1,045	$895	$750	$600	$540	$495	$450

WHITE FALCON 1955 SINGLE CUTAWAY — single round cutaway semi hollow bound maple body, raised gold pickguard with flying falcon, bound f holes, maple neck, 22 fret bound rosewood fingerboard with pearl block inlay, ebony/metal tunomatic bridge/Cadillac tailpiece, bound peghead with pearl gold sparkle logo inlay, 3 per side tuners, gold hardware, 2 humbucker pickups, master volume on upper treble bout, 2 volume/1 tone controls, selector switch. Available in White finish. Mfd. 1991 to date.

Mfr.'s Sug. Retail	$3,250	$2,275	$1,950	$1,625	$1,300	$1,170	$1,070	$975

White Falcon I — similar to White Falcon, except has a Bigsby vibrato tailpiece.

Mfr.'s Sug. Retail	$3,000	$2,095	$1,800	$1,500	$1,200	$1,080	$990	$900

This model also available in double round cutaway body (White Falcon II).

Grading	100%	98%	95%	90%	80%	70%	60%

ELECTRIC BASS

BROADKASTER — single round cutaway semi hollow bound maple body, bound f holes, maple neck, 20 fret bound rosewood fingerboard with pearl thumbnail inlay, ebony/metal tunomatic bridge/trapeze tailpiece, blackface peghead with pearl logo inlay, 2 per side tuners, chrome hardware, 2 humbucker pickups, 2 volume/1 tone controls, selector switch. Available in Natural and Transparent Orange finish. Curr. mfr.

Mfr.'s Sug. Retail	$1,875	$1,315	$1,125	$940	$750	$675	$615	$560

GUDELSKY MUSICAL INSTRUMENTS

Currently manufactured and distributed by Gudelsky Musical Instruments located in Vista, CA since 1985

A former student of James L. D'Aquisto, Paul Gudelsky has been building and selling stringed instruments since 1985. He offers a small line of instruments on a customer order only basis that include hollow body archtops (acoustic and electric/acoustic), ranging between $4,290 and $5,500; semi hollow bodies ranging from $4,235 to $4,400; and solid bodies ranging from $2,450 to $3,500. The preceding prices are approximate values. Mr. Gudelsky is flexible on shapes and options but does not build bolt-on necks.

GUILD

Manufactured by Guild Guitars, located in Westerly, RI. Distributed by U.S. Music Corp., located in New Berlin, WI.

Manufacturer currently located in Westerly, RI since 1969. Previously located in Hoboken, NJ from 1956 to 1969. Originally located in New York, NY from 1952 to 1956.

Guild was founded in 1952 by Alfred Dronge. In 1966, Guild was purchased by Avnet. Guild instruments have always been of exceptional quality and are rather desirable in the vintage marketplace.

ACOUSTIC

Add $100 for transducer pickup.

Add $295 for transducer pickup and preamp system on all currently manufactured acoustic models.

Add 15% for left handed version of all currently manufactured models (except Artist Award model).

Grading	100%	98%	95%	90%	80%	70%	60%

Dreadnought Series

All models in this series have dreadnought style bodies.

D-4 — solid spruce top, round soundhole, tortoise shell pickguard, 3 stripe bound body/rosette, mahogany back/sides/neck, 14/20 fret rosewood fingerboard with pearl dot inlay, rosewood bridge with white black dot pins, 3 per side chrome tuners. Available in Natural finish. Curr. mfr.

Mfr.'s Sug. Retail	$650	$455	$390	$325	$260	$235	$215	$195

Add $245 for high gloss finish (D-4HG).

D4-12 — similar to D-4, except has 12 strings, 6 per side tuners.

Mfr.'s Sug. Retail	$750	$525	$450	$375	$300	$270	$245	$225

D-6 — similar to D-4, except has gold hardware. Available in Natural finish. Curr. mfr.

Mfr.'s Sug. Retail	$795	$555	$475	$395	$315	$280	$260	$235

Add $200 for high gloss Natural or Sunburst finish (D-6HG).

D-15 — mahogany top/back/sides/neck, round soundhole, tortoise shell pickguard, 3 stripe rosette, 14/20 fret rosewood fingerboard with pearl dot inlay, rosewood bridge with white black dot pins, 3 per side chrome tuners. Available in Black, Natural and Woodgrain Red finish. Mfd. 1987 to date.

Mfr.'s Sug. Retail	$850	$595	$510	$425	$340	$305	$280	$255

D-25 — solid spruce top, round soundhole, tortoise shell pickguard, black bound body, 3 stripe rosette, mahogany back/sides/neck, 14/20 fret rosewood fingerboard with pearl dot inlay, rosewood bridge with white black dot pins, 3 per side chrome tuners. Available in Black, Natural and Sunburst finish. Curr. mfr.

Mfr.'s Sug. Retail	$995	$695	$595	$500	$400	$360	$330	$300

D25-12 — similar to D-25 except has 12 strings.

Mfr.'s Sug. Retail	$1,095	$765	$655	$545	$435	$395	$360	$330

D-30 — solid spruce top, round soundhole, tortoise shell pickguard, bound body, 3 stripe rosette, maple back/sides/neck, 14/20 fret rosewood fingerboard with pearl dot inlay, rosewood bridge with white black dot pins, pearl Chesterfield/logo peghead inlay, 3 per side gold tuners. Available in Black, Natural and Sunburst finish. Mfd. 1987 to date.

Mfr.'s Sug. Retail	$1,295	$905	$775	$645	$515	$465	$425	$385

D-40 — solid spruce top, round soundhole, tortoise shell pickguard, bound body, 3 stripe rosette, mahogany back/sides/neck, 14/20 fret rosewood fingerboard with pearl dot inlay, rosewood bridge with white black dot pins, pearl Chesterfield/logo peghead inlay, 3 per side gold tuners. Available in Natural finish. Disc. 1991.

	$1,295	$905	$775	$645	$515	$465	$425

This model also available with single sharp cutaway (D-4C).

Grading	100%	98%	95%	90%	80%	70%	60%

D-50 — solid spruce top, round soundhole, tortoise shell pickguard, 5 stripe bound body/rosette, rosewood back/sides, mahogany neck, 14/20 fret ebony fingerboard with pearl dot inlay, ebony bridge with white black dot pins, pearl Chesterfield/logo peghead inlay, 3 per side gold tuners. Available in Natural and Sunburst finish. Curr. mfr.

Mfr.'s Sug. Retail	$1,395	$975	$835	$700	$560	$505	$460	$420

D-55 — solid spruce top, round soundhole, tortoise shell pickguard, 3 stripe bound body/rosette, rosewood back/sides, 3 piece mahogany neck, 14/20 fret bound ebony fingerboard with pearl block/abalone wedge inlay, ebony bridge with white abalone dot pins, maple endpin wedge, bound peghead with pearl shield/logo inlay, 3 per side gold tuners. Available in Natural and Sunburst finish. Curr. mfr.

Mfr.'s Sug. Retail	$1,795	$1,255	$1,075	$895	$715	$645	$590	$540

D-100 — spruce top, round soundhole, black pickguard, maple bound body, abalone purfling/rosette, rosewood back/sides, 3 piece mahogany/maple neck, 14/20 fret maple bound ebony fingerboard with abalone crown inlay, ebony bridge with white abalone dot pins, maple endpin wedge, maple bound peghead with abalone shield/logo inlay, 3 per side gold tuners. Available in Natural and Sunburst finish. Curr. mfr.

Mfr.'s Sug. Retail	$3,595	$2,515	$2,155	$1,795	$1,435	$1,290	$1,185	$1,075

⇥ **D-100C** — similar to D-100, except has handcarved heel.

Mfr.'s Sug. Retail	$3,895	$2,725	$2,335	$1,950	$1,555	$1,395	$1,280	$1,165

DV-52S — solid spruce top, round soundhole, tortoise shell pickguard, 3 stripe bound body, herringbone rosette, rosewood back/sides, mahogany neck, 14/20 fret ebony fingerboard with pearl dot inlay, ebony bridge with white black dot pins, pearl Chesterfield/logo peghead inlay, 3 per side gold tuners. Available in Natural and Sunburst finish. Curr. mfr.

Mfr.'s Sug. Retail	$1,095	$765	$655	$545	$435	$395	$360	$330

Add $200 for high gloss finish (DV-52HG).

Jumbo Series

All models in this series have jumbo style bodies, round soundholes and tortoise shell pickguards.

JF-4 — solid spruce top, bound body, 3 stripe rosette, mahogany back/sides/neck, 14/20 fret rosewood fingerboard with pearl dot inlay, rosewood bridge with white black dot pins, 3 per side chrome tuners. Available in Natural finish. Curr. mfr.

Mfr.'s Sug. Retail	$795	$555	$475	$395	$315	$280	$260	$235

Add $200 for high gloss finish (JF4-HG).

⇥ **JF4-12S** — similar to JF-4, except has 12 strings, 6 per side tuners.

Mfr.'s Sug. Retail	$995	$695	$595	$500	$400	$360	$330	$300

Add $200 for high gloss finish (JF4-12HG).

Grading	100%	98%	95%	90%	80%	70%	60%

JF-30 — solid spruce top, bound body, 3 stripe rosette, maple back/sides/neck, 14/20 fret rosewood fingerboard with pearl dot inlay, rosewood bridge with white black dot pins, pearl Chesterfield/logo peghead inlay, 3 per side gold tuners. Available in Natural and Sunburst finish. Curr. mfr.

Mfr.'s Sug. Retail	$1,295	$905	$775	$645	$515	$465	$425	$385

JF30-12 — similar to JF-30, except has 12 strings, 6 per side tuners.

Mfr.'s Sug. Retail	$1,395	$975	$835	$700	$560	$505	$460	$420

JF-55 — solid spruce top, 3 stripe bound body/rosette, rosewood back/sides, mahogany neck, 14/20 fret bound ebony fingerboard with pearl block/abalone wedge inlay, ebony bridge with white abalone dot pins, maple endpin wedge, bound peghead with pearl shield/logo inlay, 3 per side gold tuners. Available in Natural finish. Curr. mfr.

Mfr.'s Sug. Retail	$1,895	$1,325	$1,135	$950	$760	$685	$625	$570

This model also available in 12 string version (JF55-12) with Natural and Sunburst finish.

JF65-12 — solid spruce top, 3 stripe bound body/rosette, maple back/sides/neck, 14/20 fret bound ebony fingerboard with pearl block/abalone wedge inlay, ebony bridge with white abalone dot pins, maple endpin wedge, bound peghead with pearl shield/logo inlay, 6 per side gold tuners. Available in Blonde and Sunburst finish. Curr. mfr.

Mfr.'s Sug. Retail	$1,895	$1,325	$1,135	$950	$760	$685	$625	$570

JF-100 — solid spruce top, maple bound body, abalone purfling/rosette, rosewood back/sides, 3 piece mahogany neck with maple center strip, 14/20 fret maple bound ebony fingerboard with abalone crown inlay, ebony bridge with white abalone pins, maple endpin wedge, ebony endpin, maple bound peghead with abalone shield/logo inlay, 3 per side tuners. Available in Natural finish. Curr. mfr.

Mfr.'s Sug. Retail	$3,995	$2,795	$2,395	$1,995	$1,595	$1,435	$1,315	$1,195

This model also available in 12 string version (JF100-12).

ACOUSTIC BASS

B30 — grand concert style, spruce top, round soundhole, tortoise shell pickguard, 3 stripe bound body/rosette, mahogany back/sides/neck, 14/20 fret rosewood fingerboard with pearl dot inlay, rosewood bridge with white pins, pearl Chesterfield/logo peghead inlay, 2 per side chrome tuners. Available in Natural and Sunburst finish. Mfd. 1987 to date.

Mfr.'s Sug. Retail	$1,395	$975	$835	$700	$560	$505	$460	$420

B500C — similar to B30, except has single round cutaway, maple back/sides, transducer bridge pickup, volume/concentric treble/bass control, preamp. Available in Natural and Sunburst finish. Curr. mfr.

Mfr.'s Sug. Retail	$1,695	$1,185	$1,015	$845	$675	$605	$555	$505

Grading	100%	98%	95%	90%	80%	70%	60%

ACOUSTIC ELECTRIC

CCE-100 — single round cutaway classic style, oval soundhole, bound body, wood inlay rosette, mahogany back/sides/neck, 24 fret rosewood fingerboard, rosewood bridge, 3 per side gold tuners, transducer pickup, 4 band EQ with preamp. Available in Natural finish. Curr. mfr.

Mfr.'s Sug. Retail	$1,395	$975	$835	$700	$560	$505	$460	$420

F Series

All models in this series have single round cutaway folk style body, oval soundhole, tortoise shell pickguard, 3 stripe bound body/rosette, transducer pickup, volume/4 band EQ preamp system with built in phase reversal, unless otherwise listed.

F4-CE — solid spruce top, mahogany back/sides/neck, 24 fret rosewood fingerboard with pearl dot inlay, rosewood bridge with white black dot pins, 3 per side chrome tuners. Available in Natural finish. Curr. mfr.

Mfr.'s Sug. Retail	$895	$625	$535	$445	$360	$325	$300	$275

Add $55 for mahogany top (F4-CEMH). Available in Amber and Natural finish.

F5-CE — solid spruce top, rosewood back/sides, mahogany neck, 24 fret rosewood fingerboard with pearl dot inlay, rosewood bridge with white black dot pins, 3 per side chrome Grover tuners. Available in Black, Natural and Sunburst finish. Curr. mfr.

Mfr.'s Sug. Retail	$1,195	$835	$715	$600	$480	$430	$395	$360

Add $100 for deep body version of this model (FF5-CE).

F25-CE — solid spruce top, mahogany back/sides/neck, 24 fret rosewood fingerboard with pearl dot inlay, rosewood bridge with white black dot pins, 3 per side chrome Grover tuners, volume control, concentric treble/bass control, active preamp. Available in Black, Natural and Sunburst finish. Disc. 1992.

	$835	$715	$600	$480	$430	$395	$360

Last Mfr.'s Sug. Retail was $1,195.

F30-CE — solid spruce top, flame maple back/sides, mahogany neck, 24 fret rosewood fingerboard with pearl dot inlay, rosewood bridge with white black dot pins, pearl Chesterfield/logo peghead inlay, 3 per side gold Grover tuners. Available in Black, Blonde, Natural and Sunburst finish. Curr. mfr.

Mfr.'s Sug. Retail	$1,495	$1,045	$895	$750	$600	$540	$495	$450

F65-CE — solid spruce top, flame maple back/sides, mahogany neck, 24 fret bound ebony fingerboard with pearl block/abalone wedge inlay, ebony bridge with white abalone dot pins, bound peghead with pearl shield/logo inlay, 3 per side gold Grover tuners. Available in Natural and Sunburst finish. Curr. mfr.

Mfr.'s Sug. Retail	$1,895	$1,325	$1,135	$950	$760	$685	$625	$570

Grading	100%	98%	95%	90%	80%	70%	60%

Songbird Series

S-4CE — routed out Les Paul style mahogany body, solid spruce top, round soundhole, tortoise shell pickguard, 3 stripe bound body/rosette, mahogany neck, 22 fret rosewood fingerboard with pearl dot inlay, rosewood bridge with white black dot pins, 3 per side chrome tuners, transducer bridge pickup, volume/concentric treble/bass control, preamp. Available in Natural finish. Curr. mfr.

Mfr.'s Sug. Retail	$995	$695	$595	$500	$400	$360	$330	$300

SONGBIRD — similar S-4CE, except has pearl Chesterfield/logo peghead inlay, gold tuners. Available in Black, Natural and White finish. Curr. mfr.

Mfr.'s Sug. Retail	$1,295	$905	$775	$645	$515	$465	$425	$385

ACOUSTIC ELECTRIC BASS

B4E — single round cutaway folk style, spruce top, oval soundhole, tortoise shell pickguard, 3 stripe bound body/rosette, mahogany back/sides/neck, 22 fret rosewood fingerboard with pearl dot inlay, rosewood bridge with white black dot pins, 2 per side chrome tuners, transducer pickups, volume/4 band EQ control with preamp. Available in Natural finish. Curr. mfr.

Mfr.'s Sug. Retail	$995	$695	$595	$500	$400	$360	$330	$300

B30E — grand concert style, spruce top, round soundhole, tortoise shell pickguard, 3 stripe bound body/rosette, mahogany back/sides/neck, 14/20 fret rosewood fingerboard with pearl dot inlay, rosewood bridge with white pins, pearl Chesterfield/logo peghead inlay, 2 per side chrome tuners, transducer bridge pickup, volume/concentric treble/bass control, preamp. Available in Natural and Sunburst finish. Curr. mfr.

Mfr.'s Sug. Retail	$1,595	$1,115	$955	$795	$635	$575	$525	$475

B30ET - thinline version of B30E. Disc. 1992. Last Mfr.'s Sug. Retail was $1,595.

ELECTRIC

ARTIST AWARD — single round cutaway hollow style, bound solid spruce archtop, 2 bound f holes, bound tortoise shell pickguard, German maple back/sides, 5 piece maple neck, 20 fret bound ebony fingerboard with pearl block/abalone wedge inlay, adjustable ebony bridge, stylized trapeze tailpiece, bound peghead with pearl/abalone inscribed block/logo inlay, 3 per side Imperial tuners, gold hardware, special design pickup. Available in Blonde and Sunburst finish. Mfd. 1991 to date.

Mfr.'s Sug. Retail	$5,495	$3,845	$3,295	$2,745	$2,195	$1,975	$1,810	$1,645

DUANE EDDY 400 — single round cutaway semi hollow body, arched bound spruce top, f holes, raised black pickguard with Duane Eddy's signature, maple back/sides, mahogany neck, 20 fret bound rosewood fingerboard with pearl block inlay, adjustable bridge/Bigsby vibrato, bound peghead with pearl Chesterfield/logo inlay, 3 per side tuners, chrome hardware, 2 covered humbuckers, 2 volume/2 tone controls, 3 position switch, mix control. Available in Natural finish. Mfd. 1963-1969.

	$1,500	$1,050	$900	$750	$600	$540	$495

Grading	100%	98%	95%	90%	80%	70%	60%

DUANE EDDY 500 — similar to Duane Eddy 400, except has figured maple back/sides/neck, ebony fingerboard, gold hardware.

	$2,100	$1,475	$1,260	$1,050	$840	$755	$690

F-112 (Starfire IV) — 335 style bound maple body, black pickguard, 2 f holes, 3 piece maple neck, 22 fret bound ebony fingerboard with pearl dot inlay, tunomatic bridge/stop tailpiece, pearl Chesterfield/logo peghead inlay, 3 per side tuners, gold hardware, 2 humbucker pickups, 2 volume/2 tone controls, 3 position switch. Available in Black, Blonde, Blue, Green, Red and Walnut finish. Curr. mfr.

Mfr.'s Sug. Retail	$1,895	$1,325	$1,135	$950	$760	$685	$625	$570

GEORGE BARNES ACOUSTI-LECTRIC — single round cutaway hollow style, arched bound spruce top, raised bound black pickguard, figured maple back/sides/neck, 20 fret bound rosewood fingerboard with pearl block inlay, adjustable rosewood bridge/harp style tailpiece, bound peghead with pearl shield/logo inlay, 3 per side tuners with pearl buttons, chrome hardware, 2 covered humbucker pickups, 2 volume/2 tone controls, 3 position switch, pickguard mounted controls. Available in Natural finish. Mfd. 1964-1967.

	$2,200	$1,540	$1,320	$1,100	$880	$790	$725

Bound slots were placed into the top of this instrument so that the pickups would not touch it.

MANHATTAN (X-170) — single round cutaway hollow style, bound curly maple archtop, 2 f holes, bound black pickguard, curly maple back/sides/neck, 20 fret bound rosewood fingerboard with pearl block inlay, adjustable rosewood bridge, stylized trapeze tailpiece, pearl Chesterfield/logo peghead inlay, 3 per side tuners, gold hardware, 2 humbucker pickups, 2 volume/2 tone controls, 3 position switch. Available in Blonde and Sunburst finish. Mfd. 1988 to date.

Mfr.'s Sug. Retail	$1,795	$1,255	$1,075	$895	$715	$645	$590	$540

SAVOY (X-160) — similar to Manhattan, except has unbound rosewood fingerboard with pearl dot inlay, Bigsby vibrato trapeze tailpiece, chrome hardware. Available in Black, Blonde and Sunburst finish. Mfd. 1991 to date.

Mfr.'s Sug. Retail	$1,595	$1,115	$955	$795	$635	$575	$525	$475

STUART (X-500) — single round cutaway hollow style, bound solid spruce archtop, 2 bound f holes, bound tortoise shell pickguard, German maple back/sides, 5 piece maple neck, 20 fret bound ebony fingerboard with pearl block/abalone wedge inlay, adjustable ebony bridge, stylized trapeze tailpiece, bound peghead with pearl shield/logo inlay, 3 per side Imperial tuners, gold hardware, 2 humbucker pickups, 2 volume/2 tone controls, 3 position switch. Available in Blonde and Sunburst finish. Mfd. 1988 to date.

Mfr.'s Sug. Retail	$2,495	$1,745	$1,495	$1,250	$1,000	$900	$825	$750

Grading	100%	98%	95%	90%	80%	70%	60%

X-2000 (Nightbird) — routed out Les Paul style mahogany body, bound figured maple top, bound tortoise shell pickguard, mahogany neck, 22 fret bound ebony fingerboard with pearl block/abalone wedge inlay, tunomatic bridge/stop tailpiece, bound peghead with pearl shield/logo inlay, 3 per side tuners, gold hardware, 2 humbucker pickups, volume/tone control, 3 position/single coil switches. Available in Amberburst, Black, Cherry Sunburst and Natural finish. Curr. mfr.

Mfr.'s Sug. Retail	$1,995	$1,395	$1,195	$995	$795	$720	$660	$600

X-3000 (Nightingale) — similar to X-2000, except has 2 f holes.

Mfr.'s Sug. Retail	$1,995	$1,395	$1,195	$995	$795	$720	$660	$600

ELECTRIC BASS

Pilot Series

All models in this series are available fretless at no extra cost.

PRO4 — offset double cutaway asymmetrical maple body, bolt on maple neck, 22 fret rosewood fingerboard with pearl dot inlay, fixed bridge, 4 on one side tuners, black hardware, 2 J-style active EMG pickups, 2 volume/tone controls, active preamp. Available in Amber, Black, Natural and White finish. Curr. mfr.

Mfr.'s Sug. Retail	$995	$695	$595	$500	$400	$360	$330	$300

PRO5 — similar to Pro4, except has 5 strings, 4/1 per side tuners.

Mfr.'s Sug. Retail	$1,095	$765	$655	$545	$435	$395	$360	$330

ST4 — offset double cutaway asymmetrical poplar body, bolt on maple neck, 22 fret rosewood fingerboard with pearl dot inlay, fixed bridge, 4 on one side tuners, black hardware, P-style/J-style pickups, 2 volume/tone controls. Available in Black, Natural and White finish. Curr. mfr.

Mfr.'s Sug. Retail	$795	$555	$475	$395	$315	$280	$260	$235

Also available with mahogany body.

ST5 — similar to ST4, except has 5 strings, 4/1 per side tuners.

Mfr.'s Sug. Retail	$895	$625	$535	$445	$360	$325	$300	$275

HAMBURGUITAR

Manufacturer located in Westland, MI.

These guitars are custom built by Bernie Hamburger of Westland, MI. They are available in 4 different body configurations with virtually every kind of option imaginable. The base price is $1,490 with prices increasing, depending upon options.

HAMER

Manufacturer located in Arlington Heights, IL and also has overseas manufacture. Imported and distributed by Kaman Music Corporation located in Bloomfield, CT.

Cofounded by Paul Hamer and Jol Dantzig.

Hamer USA Series

All instruments are made in Arlington Heights, IL and display the USA logo on the headstock.

ELECTRIC

Grading	100%	98%	95%	90%	80%	70%	60%

CALIFORNIAN DELUXE — strat style alder body, bolt-on maple neck, 27 fret ebony fingerboard with offset pearl dot inlay, pearl boomerang inlay at 3rd and 12th fret, double locking vibrato, 6 on one side tuners, gold hardware, stacked coil/humbucker EMG pickups, 3 position switch, volume/tone control, coil split in volume control, active electronics. Curr. mfr.

Mfr.'s Sug. Retail	$1,800	$1,260	$1,080	$900	$720	$650	$595	$540

⊰ **Californian Elite** — similar to Californian Deluxe, except has mahogany body, all fingerboard inlay are pearl boomerangs, 2 humbucker Seymour Duncan pickups and no tone control or active electronics.

Mfr.'s Sug. Retail	$1,700	$1,190	$1,020	$850	$680	$610	$560	$510

This model is available with figured maple body.
This model is also available with 12 strings.

Grading	100%	98%	95%	90%	80%	70%	60%

Californian Doubleneck — similar to Californian Elite, except has doubleneck construction with a variety of configurations, 12/6 strings are the most popular. The necks on this model are glued in rather than bolt on. The base price is $2,700.

CENTAURA — strat style ash body, bolt-on maple neck, 24 fret pau ferro fingerboard with pearl offset inlay, double locking vibrato, 6 on one side Schaller tuners, black hardware, Duncan 2 single coil/1 humbucker pickups, volume/tone control, 5-position switch, active electronics with bypass switch. Mfd. 1992 to date.

Mfr.'s Sug. Retail	$1,500	$1,050	$900	$750	$600	$540	$495	$450

Centaura Deluxe — similar to Centaura, except has alder body, ebony fingerboard, pearl boomerang inlay at 3rd and 12th fret, chrome hardware and EMG pickups.

Mfr.'s Sug. Retail	$1,800	$1,260	$1,080	$900	$720	$650	$595	$540

SUNBURST ARCHTOP CUSTOM — double cutaway arched bound mahogany body, mahogany neck, 22 fret bound rosewood fingerboard with abalone crown inlay, tunomatic bridge/stop tailpiece, 3 per side tuners, gold hardware, 2 humbucker Seymour Duncan pickups, 1 volume/2 tone controls, 3 position switch. Mfd. 1992 to date.

Mfr.'s Sug. Retail	$1,900	$1,330	$1,140	$950	$760	$685	$625	$570

Add $200 for figured maple top.

Sunburst Archtop Standard — similar to Sunburst Archtop Custom, except has unbound fingerboard with pearl dot inlay and chrome hardware.

Mfr.'s Sug. Retail	$1,700	$1,190	$1,020	$850	$680	$610	$560	$510

Add $200 for figured maple top.

T-62 — strat style alder body, white pickguard, bolt-on bird's eye maple neck, 22 fret pau ferro fingerboard with pearl dot inlay, standard vibrato, Lubritrak nut, 6 on one side locking Sperzel tuners, 3 single coil Alnico pickups, volume control, 5-position switch, 3 band EQ with bypass switch. Available in Seafoam Green, 3-tone Sunburst and Vintage White finish. Mfd. 1992 to date.

Mfr.'s Sug. Retail	$1,700	$1,190	$1,020	$850	$680	$610	$560	$510

VINTAGE S — similar to T-62, except has figured maple body, no pickguard, and tone control. Available in Amberburst, Cherry Sunburst, 3-tone Sunburst and '59 Burst finish.

Mfr.'s Sug. Retail	$2,050	$1,435	$1,230	$1,025	$820	$745	$675	$615

Grading	100%	98%	95%	90%	80%	70%	60%

ELECTRIC BASS

CHAPARRAL BASS — offset double cutaway alder body, bolt-on maple neck, 21 fret rosewood fingerboard with pearl dot inlay, fixed bridge, 4 on one side tuners, chrome hardware, EMG P-style/J-style pickups, 1 volume/2 tone controls, active electronics. Mfd. 1992 to date.

Mfr.'s Sug. Retail	$1,500	$1,050	$900	$750	$600	$540	$495	$450

Add $100 for set in neck construction.

Chaparral 5-String Bass — similar to Chaparral Bass, except has set in 5 string neck, reverse headstock, 2 EMG pickups and mix control.

Mfr.'s Sug. Retail	$1,700	$1,190	$1,020	$850	$680	$610	$560	$510

IMPACT BASS — offset double cutaway rosewood body, African sapelle/purpleheart thru body 5 string neck, 24 fret pau ferro fingerboard with abalone boomerang inlay, fixed bridge, 2/3 per side tuners, gold hardware, 2 EMG/1 transducer bridge pickups, 2 volume/1 treble/1 bass controls, active electronics. Mfd. 1991 to date.

Mfr.'s Sug. Retail	$2,500	$1,750	$1,500	$1,250	$1,000	$900	$825	$750

TWELVE STRING BASS (Short Scale) — double cutaway figured maple body, set in maple neck, 21 fret rosewood fingerboard with pearl dot inlay, fixed bridge, 6 per side tuners, chrome hardware, 2 EMG pickups, 2 volume/1 tone controls, active electronics. Mfd. 1991 to date.

Mfr.'s Sug. Retail	$2,200	$1,540	$1,320	$1,100	$880	$790	$725	$660

Hamer Slammer Series

All instruments in this series are manufactured overseas and distributed by Hamer located in Arlington Heights, IL. The specifics on these models are the same as those featured in the USA Series (see above) with corresponding names, but the materials and components are not of the same quality.

ELECTRIC

CALIFORNIAN— locking vibrato. Available in Natural finish. Curr. mfr.

Mfr.'s Sug. Retail	$650	$455	$390	$325	$260	$235	$215	$195

CENTAURA — maple fingerboard, standard vibrato, reverse headstock. Available in Black, Blood Red and 3 Tone Sunburst finish. Curr. mfr.

Mfr.'s Sug. Retail	$500	$350	$300	$250	$200	$180	$165	$150

CENTAURA — locking vibrato, reverse headstock. Available in Amber Burst, Candy Red, Black Metalflake, Black Pearl, Cherry Metalflake, Transparent Cherry, Vintage White and 3 Tone Sunburst finish. Curr. mfr.

Mfr.'s Sug. Retail	$600	$420	$360	$300	$240	$215	$195	$180

Grading	100%	98%	95%	90%	80%	70%	60%

CENTAURA — locking vibrato, regular headstock. Available in Transparent Cherry finish. Curr. mfr.

Mfr.'s Sug. Retail	$650	$455	$390	$325	$260	$235	$215	$195

DIABLO — locking vibrato. Available in Light Brown Sunburst. Curr. mfr.

Mfr.'s Sug. Retail	$650	$455	$390	$325	$260	$235	$215	$195

SUNBURST ARCH TOP — Available in Black finish. Curr. mfr.

Mfr.'s Sug. Retail	$700	$490	$420	$350	$280	$250	$230	$210

SUNBURST FLAT TOP — Available in Cherry Sunburst finish. Curr. mfr.

Mfr.'s Sug. Retail	$700	$490	$420	$350	$280	$250	$230	$210

ELECTRIC BASS

CENTAURA — bolt-on neck. Available in Black, Blood Red and 3 Tone Sunburst finish. Curr. mfr.

Mfr.'s Sug. Retail	$600	$420	$360	$300	$240	$215	$195	$180

CENTAURA 5 — bolt-on neck. Available in Black Metalflake, Black Pearl, Blue Metalflake, Candy Red and Vintage White finish. Curr. mfr.

Mfr.'s Sug. Retail	$700	$490	$420	$350	$280	$250	$230	$210

CHAPARRAL — Available in 3 Tone Sunburst finish. Curr. mfr.

Mfr.'s Sug. Retail	$700	$490	$420	$350	$280	$250	$230	$210

HEARTFIELD

Manufacturer located in Japan. Distributed by Fender Musical Instruments Corp., located in Scottsdale, AZ.

ELECTRIC

Elan Series

In 1991 - 1992, this series featured ivoroid bound figured maple top, bound fingerboard with triangle inlay, humbucker/single coil/humbucker pickups. The below descriptions are for currently manufactured instruments.

ELAN I — strat style mahogany body, bookmatched figured maple top, mahogany neck, 22 fret ebony fingerboard with pearl dot inlay, fixed bridge, 3 per side tuners with pearl buttons, gold hardware, 2 humbucker pickups, volume/tone control, 5 position switch. Finish information unavailable at this time. Curr. mfr.

Mfr.'s Sug. Retail	$1,120	$785	$670	$560	$450	$405	$370	$335

Grading	100%	98%	95%	90%	80%	70%	60%

⚔ **Elan II** — similar to Elan I, except has locking Floyd Rose vibrato, locking tuners, chrome hardware.

Mfr.'s Sug. Retail	$1,190	$835	$715	$595	$475	$430	$390	$360

⚔ **Elan III** — similar to Elan I, except has double locking Floyd Rose vibrato, black hardware, humbucker/single coil/humbucker pickups.

Mfr.'s Sug. Retail	$1,400	$980	$840	$700	$560	$505	$460	$420

RR Series

RR 8 — offset double shorthorn cutaway alder body, white pickguard, mahogany neck, 22 fret rosewood fingerboard with pearl dot inlay, fixed bridge, 3 per side tuners, chrome hardware, humbucker pickup, volume/tone control, 3 mini switches with LED's, active electronics. Finish information unavailable at this time. Curr. mfr.

Mfr.'s Sug. Retail	$490	$345	$295	$245	$195	$175	$160	$150

⚔ **RR 9** — similar to RR 8, except has standard vibrato.

Mfr.'s Sug. Retail	$540	$380	$325	$270	$215	$195	$180	$165

RR 58 — offset double shorthorn cutaway mahognay body, black pickguard, mahognay neck, 22 fret rosewood fingerboard with abalone dot inlay, fixed bridge, 3 per side tuners, chrome hardware, 2 humbucker pickups, volume/tone control, 5 position switch. Finish information unavailable at this time. Curr. mfr.

Mfr.'s Sug. Retail	$700	$490	$420	$350	$280	$250	$230	$210

⚔ **RR 59** — similar to RR 8, except has standard vibrato, locking tuners, 2 humbucker pickups.

Mfr.'s Sug. Retail	$770	$540	$460	$385	$310	$280	$255	$230

Talon Series

TALON — strat style basswood body, black pickguard, bolt-on maple neck, 22 fret rosewood fingerboard with pearl dot inlay, double locking Floyd Rose vibrato, 6 on one side tuners, black hardware, 2 single coil/1 humbucker pickups, volume/tone control, 5 position switch. Finish information unavailable at this time. Curr. mfr.

Mfr.'s Sug. Retail	$480	$335	$290	$240	$190	$170	$155	$145

⚔ **Talon I** — similar to Talon, except has humbucker/single coil/humbucker pickups.

Mfr.'s Sug. Retail	$600	$420	$360	$300	$240	$215	$195	$180

⚔ **Talon II** — similar to Talon, except has 24 fret fingerboard, 2 humbucker DiMarzio pickups.

Mfr.'s Sug. Retail	$650	$455	$390	$325	$260	$235	$215	$195

⚔ **Talon III** — similar to Talon, except has humbucker/single coil/humbucker pickups.

Mfr.'s Sug. Retail	$800	$560	$480	$400	$320	$290	$265	$240

This model is also available with no pickguard, reverse headstock (Talon IIIR).

Grading	100%	98%	95%	90%	80%	70%	60%

TALON IV — strat style basswood body, black pickguard, bolt-on maple neck, 24 fret rosewood fingerboard with triangle inlay, 12th and 24th frets have additional red triangle inlay, double locking Floyd Rose vibrato, 6 on one side tuners, black hardware, humbucker/single coil/humbucker pickups, volume/tone control, 5 position switch. Finish information is unavailable at this time. Curr. mfr.

Mfr.'s Sug. Retail	$930	$650	$555	$465	$370	$335	$305	$280

This model is available with reverse headstock (Talon V).

ELECTRIC BASS

DR Series

This series has offset double cutaway alder body, bolt-on 3 piece maple/graphite neck, rosewood fingerboard with offset pearl dot inlay, fixed bridge, 2 J-style pickups, volume/tone/balance controls, 2 position switch, active electronics. Finish information is unavailable at this time. Curr. mfr.

DR 4 — 22 fret fingerboard, 2 per side tuners, chrome hardware.

Mfr.'s Sug. Retail	$1,000	$700	$600	$500	$400	$360	$330	$300

DR 5 — 5 strings, 24 fret fingerboard, 2/3 per side tuners, chrome hardware.

Mfr.'s Sug. Retail	$1,100	$770	$660	$550	$440	$395	$365	$330

DR 6 — 6 strings, 24 fret fingerboard, 3 per side tuners, gold hardware, 2 humbucker pickups.

Mfr.'s Sug. Retail	$1,380	$965	$830	$690	$550	$495	$455	$415

DR C Series

This series has offset double cutaway figured hardwood body, thru body 3 piece maple/graphite neck, 24 fret rosewood fingerboard with offset pearl dot inlay, fixed bridge, gold hardware, 2 J-style pickups, volume/tone/balance controls, 2 position switch, active electronics. This series is custom made. Finish information is unavailable at this time. Curr. mfr.

DR 4C — 2 per side tuners.

Mfr.'s Sug. Retail	$1,700	$1,190	$1,020	$850	$680	$610	$560	$510

DR 5C — 5 strings, 2/3 per side tuners.

Mfr.'s Sug. Retail	$1,800	$1,260	$1,080	$900	$720	$650	$595	$540

DR 6C — 6 strings, 3 per side tuners.

Mfr.'s Sug. Retail	$2,100	$1,475	$1,260	$1,050	$840	$755	$690	$630

Grading	100%	98%	95%	90%	80%	70%	60%

Prophecy Series

PR I — double cutaway basswood body, bolt-on maple neck, 22 fret rosewood finger-board with pearl dot inlay, fixed bridge, graphite nut, 4 on one side tuners, chrome hardware, P-style/J-style pickups, volume/balance control. Finish information is unavailable at this time. Curr. mfr.

Mfr.'s Sug. Retail	$650	$455	$390	$325	$260	$235	$215	$195

⚡ Pr II — similar to Prophecy I, except has ash body, gold hardware, volume/treble/bass controls, active electronics.

Mfr.'s Sug. Retail	$750	$525	$450	$375	$300	$270	$245	$225

⚡ Pr III — similar to Prophecy I, except has laminated ash body, thru body laminated maple neck, gold hardware, volume/treble/bass controls, active electronics.

Mfr.'s Sug. Retail	$1,150	$805	$690	$575	$460	$415	$380	$345

HERITAGE

This trademark was established in 1985 and is currently manufactured and distributed worldwide, with corporate offices located in Kalamazoo, MI.

This company was established by previous employees from the Gibson Guitar Corporation when Gibson moved from Kalamazoo, MI to Nashville, TN.

ACOUSTIC

HFT-445 (formerly H-445) — dreadnought style, solid spruce top, round soundhole, white bound body and wooden inlay rosette, black pickguard, mahogany back/sides, maple neck, 14/20 fret rosewood fingerboard with pearl dot inlay, rosewood bridge with white pins, 3 per side chrome tuners. Available in Antique Sunburst and Natural finish. Mfd. 1989 to date.

Mfr.'s Sug. Retail	$995	$695	$595	$500	$400	$360	$330	$300

HFT-475 — single sharp cutaway jumbo style, solid spruce top, round soundhole, 5 stripe bound body and rosette, black pickguard, mahogany back/sides/neck, 20 fret bound rosewood fingerboard with pearl block inlay, rosewood bridge with white pins, bound peghead, 3 per side chrome tuners. Available in Antique Sunburst and Natural finish. Curr. mfr.

Mfr.'s Sug. Retail	$1,600	$1,120	$960	$800	$640	$575	$530	$480

Add $150 for DeArmond pickup.

Grading	100%	98%	95%	90%	80%	70%	60%

HFT-485 — jumbo style, solid spruce top, round soundhole, 3 stripe bound body/rosette, rosewood pickguard, rosewood back/sides, mahogany neck, 14/21 fret bound rosewood fingerboard with pearl block inlay, rosewood bridge with white pins, bound peghead, 3 per side chrome tuners. Available in Antique Sunburst and Natural finish. Curr. mfr.

Mfr.'s Sug. Retail	$1,800	$1,260	$1,080	$900	$720	$650	$595	$540

    Add $150 for DeArmond pickup.

ACOUSTIC ELECTRIC

SAE CUSTOM — single cutaway mahogany body with carved maple top, f holes, bound body, mahogany neck, 22 fret bound rosewood with pearl dot inlay, tunomatic bridge/stop tailpiece, 3 per side tuners, chrome hardware, 2 humbucker/1 transducer bridge pickups, 2 volume/1 tone controls, 3 mini toggle switches. Available in Antique, Transparent Almond, Transparent Amber, Transparent Blue, Transparent Cherry and Transparent Emerald Green finish. Mfd. 1992 to date.

Mfr.'s Sug. Retail	$1,230	$865	$740	$615	$490	$440	$405	$370

   ⅜ **SAE Cutaway** — similar to SAE Custom, except electronics consist of transducer bridge pickup and volume/tone control.

Mfr.'s Sug. Retail	$965	$670	$575	$480	$385	$350	$320	$290

ELECTRIC

ACADEMY CUSTOM — single rounded cutaway thin style, bound curly maple top/back/sides, f holes, bound maple pickguard, mahogany neck, 22 fret bound rosewood fingerboard with pearl crown inlay, tunomatic bridge/stop tailpiece, bound peghead, 3 per side tuners, gold hardware, 2 humbuckers, 2 volume/tone controls, 3 position switch. Available in Almond Sunburst and Antique Sunburst finish. Mfd. 1992 to date.

Mfr.'s Sug. Retail	$1,555	$1,085	$930	$775	$620	$560	$515	$465

    Add $100 for Natural or Transparent Colors finish.

ALVIN LEE MODEL — 335 style, bound curly maple top/back/sides, f holes, black pickguard, mahogany neck, 22 fret bound ebony fingerboard with pearl dot inlay, tunomatic bridge/stop tailpiece, 3 per side tuners, chrome hardware, humbucker/single coil/humbucker pickup, 3 volume/2 tone control, 3 position switch. Available in Transparent Cherry finish. Curr. mfr.

Mfr.'s Sug. Retail	$1,630	$1,140	$980	$815	$650	$585	$535	$490

H-127 CUSTOM — tele style mahogany body, bound arch maple top, maple neck, 22 fret maple fingerboard with pearl dot inlay, tunomatic bridge/stop tailpiece, 6 on one side tuners, chrome hardware, 2 single coil pickups, volume/tone control, 3 position switch. Available in Antique Sunburst and Sunsetburst finish. Mfd. 1992 to date.

Mfr.'s Sug. Retail	$1,190	$835	$715	$595	$475	$430	$390	$360

Grading	100%	98%	95%	90%	80%	70%	60%

⚲ **H-127 Standard** — similar to H-127 Custom, except has solid mahogany body. Disc. 1992.

| Mfr.'s Sug. Retail | $1,010 | $705 | $605 | $505 | $405 | $365 | $335 | $305 |

H-140CM — les paul style mahogany body, bound curly maple top, white pickguard, mahogany neck, 22 fret rosewood fingerboard with pearl dot inlay, tunomatic bridge/stop tailpiece, 3 per side tuners, chrome hardware, 2 volume/ tone controls, 3 position switch. Available in Antique Sunburst and Antique Cherry Sunburst finish. Mfd. 1989 to date.

| Mfr.'s Sug. Retail | $940 | $660 | $565 | $470 | $375 | $340 | $310 | $280 |

> Add $50 for Natural or Transparent Colors finish.
> Add $50 for Var-i-phase electronics (H-140CMV).
> Also available with plain maple top in a Gold finish (H-140 Gold Top).

H-147 — similar to H-140CM, except has plain maple top, bound ebony fingerboard with pearl block inlay, bound peghead and gold hardware. Mfd. 1989-92.

| | | $855 | $730 | $605 | $485 | $435 | $400 | $365 |

> Last Mfr.'s Sug. Retail was $1,215.

H-150CM — les paul style mahogany body, bound arch curly maple top, white pickguard, mahogany neck, 22 fret bound rosewood fingerboard with pearl crown inlay, tunomatic bridge/stop tailpiece, 3 per side tuners, chrome hardware, 2 humbucker pickups, 2 volume/2 tone controls, 3 position switch. Available in Antique Sunburst and Antique Cherry Sunburst finish. Mfd. 1989 to date.

| Mfr.'s Sug. Retail | $1,210 | $850 | $725 | $605 | $485 | $435 | $400 | $365 |

> Add $50 for Natural or Transparent Colors finish.
> Add $170 for Seymour Duncan or EMG pickups (H-150CM Classic).

⚲ **H-150CM Deluxe** — similar to H-150CM, except has bound body matching peghead and gold hardware. Available in Almond Sunburst, Antique Sunburst and Antique Cherry Sunburst finish. Mfd. 1992 only.

| | $1,290 | $1,105 | $920 | $735 | $665 | $605 | $550 |

> This is a limited edition model, there are no options available.
> Last Mfr.'s Sug. Retail was $1,835.

⚲ **H-150P** — similar to H-150CM, except has solid hardwood body. Available in Blue, Red and White finish. Mfd. 1992 to date.

| Mfr.'s Sug. Retail | $825 | $580 | $495 | $415 | $330 | $300 | $275 | $250 |

> Add $100 for Gold finish.

H-157 — similar to H-150CM, except has black pickguard, bound ebony fingerboard with pearl block inlay, bound peghead with diamond and logo inlay and gold hardware. Available in Black and White finish.

| | | $960 | $820 | $685 | $550 | $495 | $450 | $410 |

> Add $100 for Natural or Transparent Colors finish.
> Last Mfr.'s Sug. Retail was $1,370.

Grading	100%	98%	95%	90%	80%	70%	60%

H-357 — firebird style mahogany body, white pickguard, thru body mahogany neck, 22 fret rosewood fingerboard with pearl dot inlay, tunomatic bridge/stop tailpiece, 6 on one side tuners, chrome hardware, 2 humbucker pickups, 2 volume/2 tone controls, 3 position switch. Available in Antique Sunburst, Black, Blue, Red and White finish. Mfd. 1989 to date.

Mfr.'s Sug. Retail	$1,250	$875	$750	$625	$500	$450	$415	$375

Also available with black pickguard and reverse headstock.

LITTLE-001 — small size asymmetrical double cutaway curly maple body/neck, 22 fret bound rosewood fingerboard with pearl dot inlay, tunomatic bridge/stop tailpiece, 3 per side tuners, chrome hardware, humbucker pickup, volume control. Available in Transparent Amber, Transparent Black and Transparent Cherry finish. Mfd. 1992 to date.

Mfr.'s Sug. Retail	$910	$635	$545	$455	$365	$330	$300	$275

MARK SLAUGHTER ROCK — radical single cutaway mahogany body/neck, 22 fret rosewood fingerboard with pearl dot inlay, tunomatic bridge/stop tailpiece, reverse headstock, 6 on one side tuners, chrome hardware, 2 single coil/1 humbucker pickups, volume/tone control, 5 position switch. Available in Black, Red and White finish. Mfd. 1989 to date.

Mfr.'s Sug. Retail	$1,080	$755	$650	$540	$430	$390	$355	$325

Add $200 for double locking Kahler vibrato.

PARSONS STREET — asymmetrical double cutaway solid mahogany body, curly maple top, mahogany neck, 22 fret bound rosewood fingerboard with pearl block inlay, tunomatic bridge/stop tailpiece, 3 per side tuners, chrome hardware, 2 single coil/1 humbucker pickups, volume/tone control, 5 position and Var-i-phase switch. Available in Antique Sunburst, Antique Cherry Sunburst and Natural finish. Mfd. 1989-92.

	$945	$810	$670	$535	$480	$440	$400

Last Mfr.'s Sug. Retail was $1,345.

PROSPECT STANDARD — 335 style, bound curly maple top/back/sides, f holes, white pickguard, mahogany neck, 20 fret bound rosewood fingerboard with pearl dot inlay, tunomatic bridge/stop tailpiece, 3 per side tuners, chrome hardware, 2 humbucker pickups, 2 volume/tone controls, 3 position switch. Available in Almond Sunburst and Antique Sunburst finish. Mfd. 1992 to date.

Mfr.'s Sug. Retail	$1,240	$870	$745	$620	$495	$445	$410	$370

Add $100 for Natural or Transparent Colors finish.

Grading	100%	98%	95%	90%	80%	70%	60%

ROY CLARK MODEL — single rounded cutaway thin style, bound curly maple top/back/sides, bound f holes, bound maple pickguard, mahogany neck, 22 fret bound rosewood fingerboard with split block inlay, tunomatic bridge/stop tailpiece, bound peghead, 3 per side tuners, gold hardware, 2 humbuckers, 2 volume/tone controls, 3 position switch. Available in Almond Sunburst and Antique Sunburst finish. Mfd. 1992 to date.

Mfr.'s Sug. Retail	$1,780	$1,245	$1,070	$890	$710	$640	$585	$535

Add $100 for Natural or Transparent Colors finish.

JOHNNY SMITH — single rounded cutaway hollow style, solid spruce top, bound body and f holes, bound curly maple pickguard, curly maple back/sides/neck, 20 fret ebony fingerboard with abalone block inlay, ebony bridge, trapeze tailpiece, bound peghead with abalone/pearl rose inlay, 3 per side tuners, black hardware, pickguard mounted humbucker pickup, pickguard mounted volume control. Available in Antique Sunburst finish. Mfd. 1992 to date.

Mfr.'s Sug. Retail	$4,180	$2,925	$2,510	$2,090	$1,670	$1,505	$1,380	$1,255

Add $300 for Natural or Transparent Colors finish.
Personally signed by Johnny Smith.

STAT — strat style bound curly maple/mahogany body, mahogany neck, 22 fret rosewood fingerboard with pearl dot inlay, tunomatic bridge/stop tailpiece, 6 on one side tuners, chrome hardware, 2 single coil/1 humbucker pickups, volume/tone control, 3 mini toggle and coil split switch. Available in Antique Sunburst, Antique Cherry Sunburst and Cherry finish. Mfd. 1989 to 1991.

		$545	$470	$390	$315	$280	$260	$235

Last Mfr.'s Sug. Retail was $785.

SWEET 16 — single sharp cutaway hollow style, solid spruce top, bound body and f holes, bound curly maple pickguard, curly maple back/sides/neck, 20 fret ebony fingerboard with pearl split block inlay, ebony bridge with pearl 16 inlay, trapeze tailpiece, bound peghead with pearl Sweet 16 and logo inlay, 3 per side tuners, gold hardware, pickguard mounted humbucker pickup, pickguard mounted volume control. Available in Almond Sunburst and Antique Sunburst finish. Mfd. 1989 to date.

Mfr.'s Sug. Retail	$2,800	$1,960	$1,680	$1,400	$1,120	$1,010	$925	$840

Add $300 for Natural or Transparent Colors finish.

Heritage , cont.

Grading	100%	98%	95%	90%	80%	70%	60%

ELECTRIC BASS

CHUCK JACOBS MODEL — offset double cutaway asymmetrical maple body, thru body maple neck, 24 fret bound rosewood fingerboard with pearl dot inlay, fixed bridge, bound peghead, 2 per side tuners, black hardware, 2 J-style active EMG pickups, 2 volume/2 tone controls. Available in Black, Red and White finish. Curr. mfr.

Mfr.'s Sug. Retail	$2,040	$1,430	$1,225	$1,025	$815	$735	$675	$615

Add $100 for flame maple top. Available in Sunsetburst, Transparent Black, and Transparent Cherry finish (Chuck Jacobs CM Model).

HB-IV — offset double cutaway maple body, thru body maple neck, 24 fret rosewood fingerboard with pearl dot inlay, fixed bridge, 2 per side tuners, black hardware, 2 active EMG pickups, 2 volume/2 tone/bass expander controls. Available in Black, Red and White finish. Curr. mfr.

Mfr.'s Sug. Retail	$1,570	$1,100	$940	$785	$630	$565	$515	$470

Add $100 for curly maple top. Available in Antique Sunburst, Transparent Black and Transparent Cherry finish.

⅗ **HB-V** — similar to HB-IV, except has 5 strings, 3/2 per side tuners.

Mfr.'s Sug. Retail	$1,670	$1,170	$1,000	$835	$670	$600	$550	$500

Eagle Series

AMERICAN EAGLE — single rounded cutaway hollow style, solid spruce top, bound body and f holes, bound flame maple pickguard with pearl space shuttle inlay, solid figured maple back/sides, 5 piece figured maple neck, 20 fret bound ebony fingerboard with pearl/abalone American heritage inlay, ebony/rosewood bridge with pearl star inlay, Liberty Bell shaped trapeze tailpiece, bound peghead with pearl eagle, stars, American Flag and Heritage logo inlay, pearl truss rod cover with engraved owner's name, 3 per side Kluson tuners, gold hardware, pickguard mounted Heritage pickup with 3 star inlay on cover, volume control on pickguard. Available in Natural finish. Mfd. 1989 to date.

Mfr.'s Sug. Retail	$8,330	$5,830	$5,000	$4,165	$3,330	$3,000	$2,750	$2,500

All binding on this model is red, white and blue.

EAGLE — single rounded cutaway hollow style, solid mahogany top/pickguard, f holes, bound body, mahogany back/sides/neck, 20 fret rosewood fingerboard with pearl dot inlay, rosewood bridge/trapeze tailpiece block, 3 per side tuners, chrome hardware, pickguard mounted Heritage pickup, volume control on pickguard. Available in Antique Sunburst finish. Mfd. 1989 to date.

Mfr.'s Sug. Retail	$1,780	$1,245	$1,070	$890	$710	$640	$585	$535

Add $200 for Natural or Transparent Colors finish.
Add $100 for gold hardware.

Grading	100%	98%	95%	90%	80%	70%	60%

⊰ **Eagle Classic** — single rounded cutaway hollow style, solid spruce top, f holes, bound maple pickguard, bound body, solid curly maple back/sides, 5 piece maple neck, 20 fret bound ebony fingerboard, ebony/metal bridge/trapeze tailpiece, bound peghead, 3 per side tuners, gold hardware, 2 humbucker pickups, 2 volume/tone controls, 3 position switch. Available in Almond Sunburst and Antique Sunburst finish. Mfd. 1992 to date.

Mfr.'s Sug. Retail	$2,680	$1,875	$1,610	$1,340	$1,070	$965	$885	$805

Add $300 for Natural or Transparent Colors finish.
Subtract $100 for Black or White finish.

⊰ **Eagle TDC** — similar to Eagle, except has thin body style, tunomatic bridge, 2 humbucker pickups, 2 volume/tone controls and 3 position switch.

Mfr.'s Sug. Retail	$1,890	$1,325	$1,135	$945	$755	$680	$620	$565

GOLDEN EAGLE — single rounded cutaway hollow style, solid spruce top, bound body and f holes, bound maple pickguard, curly maple back/sides/neck, 20 fret bound ebony fingerboard with pearl cloud inlay, ebony bridge with pearl V inlay, trapeze tailpiece, bound peghead with pearl eagle on tree and logo inlay, pearl truss rod cover with owner's name, 3 per side Kluson tuners, gold hardware, pickguard mounted humbucker pickup, pickguard mounted volume control. Available in Antique Sunburst finish. Mfd. 1989 to date.

Mfr.'s Sug. Retail	$3,350	$2,345	$2,010	$1,675	$1,340	$1,200	$1,100	$1,000

Add $300 for Natural or Transparent Colors finish.

SUPER EAGLE — similar to Golden Eagle, except has pearl split block fingerboard inlay, 2 humbucker pickups, 2 volume/tone controls and 3 position switch.

Mfr.'s Sug. Retail	$3,790	$2,655	$2,275	$1,895	$1,515	$1,365	$1,250	$1,135

500 Series

H-535 — 335 style, bound curly maple top/back/sides, f holes, bound curly maple pickguard, mahogany neck, 22 fret bound rosewood fingerboard with pearl dot inlay, tunomatic bridge/stop tailpiece, 3 per side tuners, chrome hardware, 2 humbucker pickups, 2 volume/tone controls, 3 position switch. Available in Antique Sunburst finish. Mfd. 1989 to date.

Mfr.'s Sug. Retail	$1,240	$870	$745	$620	$495	$445	$410	$370

Add $100 for Natural or Transparent Colors finish.
Add $50 for Var-i-phase and coil split.

⊰ **H-535 Custom** — similar to H-535, except has pearl diagonal inlay and bound peghead with pearl logo inlay. Available in Antique Sunburst and Transparent Black finish. Mfd. 1991-92.

	$1,040	$890	$745	$595	$535	$490	$445

Last Mfr.'s Sug. Retail was $1,490.

Grading	100%	98%	95%	90%	80%	70%	60%

H-550 — single rounded cutaway hollow style, bound curly maple top/back/sides, bound f holes, bound curly maple pickguard, curly maple neck, 20 fret bound ebony fingerboard with pearl split block inlay, tunomatic bridge/trapeze tailpiece, bound peghead with pearl split block and logo inlay, 3 per side tuners, chrome hardware, 2 humbucker pickups, 2 volume/tone controls, 3 position switch. Available in Antique Sunburst finish. Mfd. 1989 to 1991.

	$1,210	$1,040	$865	$690	$620	$570	$520

Add $100 for Natural or Transparent Colors finish.
Last Mfr.'s Sug. Retail was $1,725.

H-555 — similar to H-535, except has bound f holes, curly maple neck, ebony fingerboard with abalone/pearl diamond/arrow inlay with block after 17th fret, bound peghead with abalone/pearl diamond/arrow and logo inlay, gold hardware. Available in Almond Sunburst and Antique Sunburst finish.

Mfr.'s Sug. Retail	$1,730	$1,210	$1,040	$865	$690	$625	$570	$520

Add $100 for Natural or Transparent Colors finish.

H-574 — single rounded cutaway hollow style, bound curly maple top/back/sides, f holes, white pickguard, mahogany neck, 20 fret rosewood fingerboard with pearl dot inlay, tunomatic bridge/stop tailpiece, 3 per side tuners, chrome hardware, 2 humbuckers, 2 volume/tone controls, 3 position switch. Available in Antique Sunburst finish. Mfd. 1989 to 1991.

	$875	$750	$625	$500	$450	$415	$375

Add $50 for Natural finish.
Last Mfr.'s Sug. Retail was $1,250.

H-575 — similar to H-574, except has sharp cutaway, maple pickguard and rosewood bridge/trapeze tailpiece. Available in Antique Sunburst finish. Mfd. 1989 to date.

Mfr.'s Sug. Retail	$1,445	$1,010	$865	$720	$575	$515	$470	$430

Add $200 for Natural or Transparent Colors finish.

H-575 Custom — similar to H-575, except has bound fingerboard with pearl diagonal inlay, bound peghead with pearl logo inlay and gold hardware. Available in Sunsetburst finish.

Mfr.'s Sug. Retail	$1,855	$1,295	$1,110	$925	$740	$670	$610	$555

Add $200 for Natural or Transparent Colors finish.
Subtract $100 for Black or White finish.

H-576 — similar to H-574, except has bound maple pickguard, bound fingerboard with pearl block inlay and bound peghead with curly maple veneer. Available in Antique Sunburst finish. Mfd. 1989 to date.

Mfr.'s Sug. Retail	$1,580	$1,105	$950	$790	$630	$570	$520	$475

Add $100 for Natural or Transparent Colors finish.

HOHNER

The Hohner trademark was established approximately 1858 and the current primary manufacturer is located in Korea. Currently distributed in the U.S. by HSS, A Division of Hohner, Inc., located in Richmond, VA.

Grading	100%	98%	95%	90%	80%	70%	60%

ACOUSTIC

HAG294 — small body, spruce top, round soundhole, bound body, 5 stripe rosette, black pickguard, mahogany back/sides/neck, 12/18 fret ebonized fingerboard with white dot inlay, ebonized bridge, 3 per side die cast tuners. Available in Natural finish. Mfd. 1991 to date.

Mfr.'s Sug. Retail	$110	$75	$65	$55	$45	$40	$35	$30

⚹ **HAG294C** — similar to HAG294, except has classical body styling.

Mfr.'s Sug. Retail	$110	$75	$65	$55	$45	$40	$35	$30

HMC10 — classical style, spruce top, round soundhole, bound body, wooden inlay rosette, mahogany back/sides/neck, 14/19 fret ebonized fingerboard/bridge, 3 per side die cast tuners. Available in Natural finish. Mfd. 1991 to date.

Mfr.'s Sug. Retail	$220	$155	$130	$110	$90	$80	$70	$65

⚹ **HMC40** — similar to HMC10, except has rosewood back/sides.

Mfr.'s Sug. Retail	$300	$210	$180	$150	$120	$110	$100	$90

HMW400 — dreadnought style, spruce top, round soundhole, bound body, 5 stripe rosette, black pickguard, mahogany back/sides/neck, 14/20 fret ebonized fingerboard with white dot inlay, ebonized bridge with white pins, 3 per side die cast tuners. Available in Natural and Sunburst finish. Mfd. 1990 to date.

Mfr.'s Sug. Retail	$200	$140	$120	$100	$80	$70	$65	$60

This model has turquoise pickguard with Sunburst finish.

HMW600 — similar to HMW400, except has herringbone binding and rosette and enclosed chrome tuners. Available in Black and Natural finish.

Mfr.'s Sug. Retail	$265	$185	$160	$130	$105	$95	$85	$80

HMW1200 — similar to HMW400, except has 12 strings.

Mfr.'s Sug. Retail	$300	$210	$180	$150	$120	$110	$100	$90

Grading	100%	98%	95%	90%	80%	70%	60%

ACOUSTIC ELECTRIC

HAG21 — single rounded cutaway classic style, solid maple body, spruce top, round soundhole, bound body, wooden inlay rosette, mahogany neck, 20 fret rosewood fingerboard with white dot inlay, rosewood bridge with white pins, 3 per side chrome tuners, piezo bridge pickup, volume/tone control. Available in Natural finish. Mfd. 1990-92.

	$350	$300	$250	$200	$180	$165	$150

Last Mfr.'s Sug. Retail was $500.

HAG22 — similar to HAG21, except has dreadnought styling. Available in Sunburst finish.

	$350	$300	$250	$200	$180	$165	$150

Last Mfr.'s Sug. Retail was $500.

TWP600 — single flat cutaway dreadnought style, spruce top, triangle soundhole, bound body, 3 stripe rosette, mahogany back/sides/neck, 20 fret rosewood fingerboard with white dot inlay, rosewood bridge with white pins, 3 per side chrome tuners, piezo bridge pickup, 3 band EQ system. Available in Blue Sunburst (disc. 1992), Natural and Pumpkin Burst finish. Mfd. 1992 to date.

Mfr.'s Sug. Retail	$500	$350	$300	$250	$200	$180	$165	$150

ACOUSTIC ELECTRIC BASS

TWP600B — single flat cutaway dreadnought style, spruce top, triangle soundhole, bound body, 3 stripe rosette, mahogany back/sides/neck, 20 fret rosewood fingerboard with white dot inlay, strings thru rosewood bridge, 2 per side chrome tuners, piezo electric bridge pickup, 3 band EQ system. Available in Blue Sunburst (disc. 1992), Natural and Pumpkin Burst finish. Mfd. 1992 to date.

Mfr.'s Sug. Retail	$595	$415	$360	$300	$240	$215	$195	$180

ELECTRIC

G3T — steinberger style maple body, thru body maple neck, 24 fret rosewood fingerboard with white dot inlay, Steinberger vibrato, black hardware, 2 single coil/1 humbucker EMG pickups, volume/tone control, 3 mini switches, passive filter in tone control. Available in Black and White finish. Mfd. 1990 to date.

Mfr.'s Sug. Retail	$650	$455	$390	$325	$260	$235	$215	$195

Add $35 for left handed version.

JACK GUITAR — similar to G3T, except has asymmetrical double cutaway body. Available in Black and Metallic Red finish.

Mfr.'s Sug. Retail	$765	$530	$455	$380	$305	$275	$250	$230

Grading	100%	98%	95%	90%	80%	70%	60%

JT60— offset double cutaway maple body, tortoise shell pickguard, bolt on maple neck, 22 fret rosewood fingerboard with pearl dot inlay, standard vibrato, 6 on one side tuners, chrome hardware, 3 single coil pickups, 2 volume/1 tone controls, 5 position switch, advance tone passive electronics. Available in Ivory finish. Mfd. 1992 to date.

Mfr.'s Sug. Retail	$400	$280	$240	$200	$160	$145	$130	$120

L59 — les paul style solid maple body, bound figured maple top, black pickguard, mahogany neck, 22 fret bound rosewood fingerboard with pearl crown inlay, tunomatic bridge/stop tailpiece, bound peghead with pearl pineapple/logo inlay, 3 per side tuners, chrome hardware, 2 humbucker pickups, 2 volume/tone controls, 3 position switch. Available in Black, Gold Top, Ivory and Violin finish. Mfd. 1990 to date.

Mfr.'s Sug. Retail	$575	$405	$345	$285	$230	$205	$190	$175

Add $25 for left handed version (Cherry Sunburst finish only).
This model is available with gold hardware.

LP75 — similar to LP59, except has white pickguard, bolt-on neck, diamond peghead inlay. Available in Antique Sunburst and Black finish. Mfd. 1990 to 1991.

	$260	$220	$185	$150	$135	$120	$110

Last Mfr.'s Sug. Retail was $375.

L90 — les paul style bound maple/mahogany body, white pickguard, mahogany neck, 22 fret bound rosewood fingerboard with pearl crown inlay, tunomatic bridge/stop tailpiece, bound peghead with pearl diamond/logo inlay, 3 per side tuners, chrome hardware, 2 PAF pickups, 2 volume/tone controls, 3 position switch. Available in Gold Top finish. Mfd. 1992 to date.

Mfr.'s Sug. Retail	$630	$440	$380	$315	$250	$225	$205	$190

SE35 — 335 style maple bound top/back/sides, black pickguard, mahogany neck, 22 fret rosewood fingerboard with pearl dot inlay, tunomatic bridge/stop tailpiece, pearl pineapple/logo peghead inlay, chrome hardware, 2 humbucker pickups, 2 volume/tone controls, 3 position switch. Available in Black, Natural, Sunburst and White finish. Mfd. 1990 to date.

Mfr.'s Sug. Retail	$550	$385	$330	$275	$220	$200	$180	$165

This model is available with gold hardware.

SE400 — single rounded cutaway hollow body, maple bound top/back/sides, f holes, black pickguard, mahogany neck, 22 fret bound rosewood fingerboard with pearl block inlay, tunomatic bridge/trapeze tailpiece, bound peghead with pearl pineapple/logo inlay, 2 humbucker pickups, 2 volume/tone controls, 3 position switch. Available in Tobacco Sunburst finish. Mfd. 1992 to date.

Mfr.'s Sug. Retail	$700	$490	$420	$350	$280	$250	$230	$210

Grading	100%	98%	95%	90%	80%	70%	60%

ST59 — strat style alder body, white pickguard, bolt-on maple neck, 22 fret maple fingerboard with black dot inlay, standard vibrato, 6 on one side tuners, chrome hardware, 3 single coil pickups, volume/2 tone controls, 5 position switch, active tone electronics. Available in Black, Blue, Red and Twotone Sunburst finish. Mfd. 1990 to date.

Mfr.'s Sug. Retail	$420	$295	$250	$210	$170	$150	$135	$125

Subtract $10 for left handed version without advance tone electronics.

ST CUSTOM — strat style flame maple body, bolt-on maple neck, 22 fret rosewood fingerboard with abalone dot inlay, double locking vibrato, 6 on one side tuners, black hardware, 2 single coil/1 humbucker EMG pickups, volume/tone control, 3 mini switches. Available in Cherry Sunburst finish. Mfd. 1990-91.

	$735	$630	$525	$420	$380	$345	$315

Last Mfr.'s Sug. Retail was $1,050.

ST LYNX — strat style maple body, bolt-on maple neck, 24 fret rosewood fingerboard with white dot inlay, double locking vibrato, 6 on one side tuners, black hardware, single coil/humbucker EMG pickups, volume/tone control, 3 position switch. Available in Metallic Blue and Metallic Red finish. Mfd. 1990 to date.

Mfr.'s Sug. Retail	$700	$490	$420	$350	$280	$250	$230	$210

Add $25 for left handed version.

ST METAL S — similar to ST Custom, except has non-figured maple body, white sharktooth fingerboard inlay. Available in Black, Black Crackle and Pearl White finish.

	$440	$380	$315	$250	$225	$205	$190

Add $30 for left handed version.
Last Mfr.'s Sug. Retail was $630.

ST VICTORY — strat style maple body, black pickguard, bolt-on maple neck, 22 fret rosewood fingerboard with white dot inlay, reverse headstock, double locking vibrato, 6 on one side tuners, black hardware, humbucker pickup, volume/tone control. Available in Metallic Dark Purple and Metallic Red finish. Mfd. 1990-91.

	$405	$345	$285	$230	$205	$190	$175

Last Mfr.'s Sug. Retail was $575.

TE CUSTOM — tele style bound maple body, white pickguard, bolt-on maple neck, 21 fret rosewood fingerboard with white dot inlay, fixed bridge, 6 on one side tuners, chrome hardware, 2 single coil pickups, volume/tone control, 3 position switch. Available in Threetone Sunburst finish. Mfd. 1992 to date.

Mfr.'s Sug. Retail	$450	$315	$270	$225	$180	$160	$150	$135

TE Custom XII — similar to TE Custom, except has 12 strings, black pickguard and 2 humbucker pickups. Available in Black finish. Mfd. 1990 to date.

Mfr.'s Sug. Retail	$550	$385	$330	$275	$220	$200	$180	$165

Grading	100%	98%	95%	90%	80%	70%	60%

TE PRINZ — tele style bound flamed maple body, tortoise shell pickguard, bolt-on maple neck, 21 fret maple fingerboard with black dot inlay, fixed bridge, 6 on one side tuners, chrome hardware, pickups, volume/tone control, 3 position switch. Available in Natural finish. Mfd. 1990 to date.

Mfr.'s Sug. Retail	$515	$350	$300	$250	$200	$180	$165	$150

Revelation Series

RTS — offset double cutaway asymmetrical poplar body, black pickguard, bolt-on maple neck, 24 fret rosewood fingerboard with offset pearl dot inlay, locking Wilkinson vibrato, roller nut, 6 on one side Schaller tuners, chrome hardware, 3 single coil pickups, volume/2 tone controls, 5 position switch. Available in Black, Marble Red, Marble White, Red, Sunburst, Transparent Blue, Transparent Honey and Transparent Red finish. Curr. mfr.

Mfr.'s Sug. Retail	$900	$630	$540	$450	$360	$325	$300	$275

RTX — similar to RTS, except has middle and bridge pickups in humbucker configuration and has active tone electronics.

Mfr.'s Sug. Retail	$900	$630	$540	$450	$360	$325	$300	$275

Rockwood Series

LX100G — strat style maple body, black pickguard, bolt-on maple neck, 22 fret rosewood fingerboard with pearl dot inlay, standard vibrato, 6 on one side tuners, chrome hardware, 3 single coil pickups, 2 volume/1 tone controls, 5 position switch. Available in Black and Red finish. Mfd. 1992 to date.

Mfr.'s Sug. Retail	$250	$175	$150	$125	$100	$90	$80	$75

LX200G — similar to LX100G, except has white pickguard, 2 single coil/1 humbucker pickups, volume/tone control, coil split switch. Available in White finish. Mfd. 1992 to date.

Mfr.'s Sug. Retail	$330	$230	$195	$165	$130	$120	$110	$100

LX250G — Les Paul style bound maple body, white pickguard, mahogany neck, 22 fret bound rosewood fingerboard with pearl crown inlay, tunomatic bridge/stop tailpiece, 3 per side tuners, chrome hardware, 2 humbucker pickups, 2 volume/2 tone controls, 3 position switch. Available in Antique Sunburst and Black finish. Mfd. 1992 to date.

Mfr.'s Sug. Retail	$345	$240	$205	$175	$140	$125	$115	$105

Grading	100%	98%	95%	90%	80%	70%	60%

ELECTRIC BASS

B2 — steinberger style maple body, thru body maple neck, 24 fret rosewood fingerboard with white dot inlay, Steinberger bridge, black hardware, 2 humbucker pickups, 2 volume/1 tone controls. Available in Black and Red finish. Mfd. 1990-92.

	$385	$330	$275	$220	$200	$180	$165

Last Mfr.'s Sug. Retail was $550.

B2A — similar to B2, except has active tone electronics with switch and LED. Mfd. 1990-92.

	$440	$375	$310	$250	$225	$205	$190

Add $35 for left handed version.
Last Mfr.'s Sug. Retail was $625.

B2ADB — similar to B2A, except has Steinberger DB bridge. Available in Black and Metallic Red finish. Mfd. 1992 to date.

Mfr.'s Sug. Retail	$770	$540	$460	$385	$310	$280	$255	$230

B2AFL — similar to B2A, except is fretless with an ebonol fingerboard.

	$485	$415	$350	$280	$250	$230	$210

Last Mfr.'s Sug. Retail was $695.

B2B — similar to B2, except has bolt-on neck and P-style/J-style pickups. Available in Black finish. Mfd. 1992 to date.

Mfr.'s Sug. Retail	$490	$345	$295	$245	$195	$175	$160	$150

B2V — similar to B2, except is a 5 string. Available in Black finish.

	$475	$405	$340	$270	$245	$225	$205

Last Mfr.'s Sug. Retail was $675.

BBASS — offset double cutaway maple body, thru body maple neck, 24 fret rosewood fingerboard with white dot inlay, Steinberger DB bridge, 2 per side tuners, black hardware, 2 J-style pickups, 2 volume/1 tone controls, active tone electronics with switch and LED. Available in Black, Natural and Transparent Red finish. Mfd. 1990 to date.

Mfr.'s Sug. Retail	$750	$525	$450	$375	$300	$270	$245	$225

This model is available in 5 string at no additional cost (BBASSV).

HP — offset double cutaway hardwood body, white pickguard, bolt on maple neck, 20 fret maple fingerboard with black dot inlay, fixed bridge, 4 on one side tuners, chrome hardware, P-style pickup, volume/tone control. Available in Black and Red finish. Mfd. 1990-92.

	$260	$220	$185	$150	$135	$120	$110

Last Mfr.'s Sug. Retail was $370.

Grading	100%	98%	95%	90%	80%	70%	60%

JACK BASS CUSTOM — steinberger style offset double cutaway maple body, thru body maple neck, 24 fret rosewood fingerboard with white dot inlay, Steinberger bridge, black hardware, 2 J-style pickups, 2 volume/1 tone controls, active tone electronics with switch and LED. Available in Black, Metallic Red and Natural finish. Mfd. 1990 to date.

Mfr.'s Sug. Retail	$830	$580	$500	$415	$330	$300	$275	$250

Add $70 for 5 string (Jack Bass Custom 5) version.

JJ — offset double cutaway asymmetrical maple body, bolt-on maple neck, 20 fret rosewood fingerboard with white dot inlay, fixed bridge, 4 on one side tuners, chrome hardware, 2 volume/1 tone controls, active tone electronics with switch and LED. Available in Black and Vintage Sunburst finish. Mfd. 1990-92.

		$385	$330	$275	$220	$200	$180	$165

Last Mfr.'s Sug. Retail was $550.

JJFL — similar to JJ, except has tortoise shell pickguard and no frets. Mfd. 1992 to date.

Mfr.'s Sug. Retail	$440	$310	$265	$220	$175	$160	$145	$135

PJB — offset double cutaway maple body, white pickguard, bolt on maple neck, 20 fret maple fingerboard with black dot inlay, fixed bridge, 4 on one side tuners, chrome hardware, P-style/J-style pickups, 2 volume/1 tone controls. Available in Black and White finish. Mfd. 1990-92.

		$295	$250	$210	$170	$150	$135	$125

Last Mfr.'s Sug. Retail was $425.

PJFL — similar to PJB, except has fretless ebonol fingerboard. Available in Black finish.

		$310	$265	$220	$175	$160	$145	$135

Last Mfr.'s Sug. Retail was $440.

PJSX — similar to PJB, except has rosewood fingerboard with white dot inlay. Available in Black and Metallic Red finish.

		$295	$250	$210	$170	$150	$135	$125

Subtract $35 for left handed version (Black finish only).
Last Mfr.'s Sug. Retail was $425.

Rockwood Series

LX100B — offset double cutaway hardwood body, bolt-on maple neck, 21 fret rosewood fingerboard with white dot inlay, fixed bridge, 4 on one side tuners, chrome hardware, P-style pickup, volume/tone control. Available in Black and Red finish. Mfd. 1992 to date.

Mfr.'s Sug. Retail	$300	$210	$180	$150	$120	$110	$100	$90

LX200B — similar to LX100B, except has short scale neck.

Mfr.'s Sug. Retail	$270	$190	$160	$135	$110	$100	$90	$80

HOHNER, cont.

LX300B — similar to LX100B, except has white pickguard, P-style/2 J-style pickups and 2 volume/1 tone control.

Mfr.'s Sug. Retail	$370		$260	$220	$185	$150	$135	$120	$110

I

IBANEZ

Manufactured at the Fuji plant in Matsumoto, Japan since the early 1960s. Currently distributed since 1972 by Ibanez U.S.A., located in Bensalem, PA.

Manufacture in Japan and worldwide distribution began in the early 1960s, utilizing only the "Ibanez" logo. Since 1972, guitars exported to the U.S. can be identified by the definitive "Ibanez U.S.A." logo.

Grading	100%	98%	95%	90%	80%	70%	60%

ACOUSTIC

Performance Series

PF5 — dreadnought style, spruce top, round soundhole, bound body, 5 stripe rosette, mahogany back/sides, nato neck, 14/20 fret rosewood fingerboard with pearl dot inlay, rosewood bridge with white black dot pins, 3 per side chrome tuners. Available in Natural matte finish. Mfd. 1992 to date.

Mfr.'s Sug. Retail	$200	$140	$120	$100	$80	$70	$65	$60

PF10 — dreadnought style, spruce top, round soundhole, bound body, 5 stripe rosette, mahogany back/sides/neck, 14/20 fret rosewood fingerboard with pearl dot inlay, rosewood bridge with black white dot pins, 3 per side chrome tuners. Available in Natural finish. Mfd. 1991 to date.

Mfr.'s Sug. Retail	$240	$170	$145	$120	$95	$85	$80	$75

Add $30 for Black finish.

PF10-12 — similar to PF10, except has twelve strings, 6 per side tuners.

Mfr.'s Sug. Retail	$270	$190	$160	$135	$110	$100	$90	$80

PF10CE — similar to PF10, except has single cutaway, 3 per side chrome die cast tuners, piezo electric pickup, volume/tone control. Mfd. 1992 to date.

Mfr.'s Sug. Retail	$370	$260	$220	$185	$150	$135	$120	$110

PF18S — dreadnought style, solid spruce top, round soundhole, bound body, 5 stripe rosette, mahogany back/sides/neck, 14/20 fret rosewood fingerboard with pearl dot inlays, rosewood bridge with black white dot pins, 3 per side chrome die cast tuners. Available in Natural gloss finish. Mfd. 1992 to date.

Mfr.'s Sug. Retail	$370	$260	$220	$185	$150	$135	$120	$110

Grading	100%	98%	95%	90%	80%	70%	60%

PF20TV — dreadnought style, flame maple top, round soundhole, bound body, 5 stripe rosette, mahogany back/sides/neck, 14/20 fret rosewood fingerboard with pearl dot inlay, rosewood bridge with black white dot pins, 3 per side chrome enclosed tuners. Available in Traditional Violin finish. Mfd. 1991 to date.

Mfr.'s Sug. Retail	$300	$210	$180	$150	$120	$110	$100	$90

PF30 — dreadnought style, cedar top, bound body, 5 stripe rosette, mahogany back/sides/neck, 14/20 fret rosewood fingerboard with pearl dot inlay, rosewood bridge with black white dot pins, 3 per side chrome enclosed tuners. Available in Natural finish. Mfd. 1991-92.

		$205	$175	$145	$115	$105	$95	$85

Last Mfr.'s Sug. Retail was $290.

PF40 — dreadnought style, flame maple top, round soundhole, bound body, 5 stripe rosette, mahogany back/sides/neck, 14/20 fret rosewood fingerboard with pearl dot inlay, rosewood bridge with white black dot pins, 3 per side chrome die cast tuners. Available in Natural finish. Mfd. 1991 to date.

Mfr.'s Sug. Retail	$350	$245	$210	$175	$140	$125	$115	$105

PF50 — dreadnought style, spruce top, round soundhole, herringbone bound body and rosette, rosewood back/sides, mahogany neck, 14/20 fret bound rosewood fingerboard with abalone dot inlay, rosewood bridge with black abalone dot pins, bound peghead, 3 per side chrome die cast tuners. Available in Natural finish. Mfd. 1991 to date.

Mfr.'s Sug. Retail	$430	$300	$260	$215	$175	$155	$140	$130

PF5012 — similar to PF50, except has 12 strings.

Mfr.'s Sug. Retail	$480	$335	$290	$240	$190	$170	$155	$145

PF50S — similar to PF50, except has solid spruce top.

Mfr.'s Sug. Retail	$550	$385	$330	$275	$220	$200	$180	$165

PF75M — dreadnought style, spruce top, round soundhole, herringbone bound body and rosette, flame maple back/sides, maple neck, 14/20 fret bound maple fingerboard with black dot inlays, rosewood bridge with white abalone dot pins, bound peghead with abalone Ibanez logo inlay, 3 per side chrome die cast tuners. Available in Natural finish. Mfd. 1992 to date.

Mfr.'s Sug. Retail	$550	$385	$330	$275	$220	$200	$180	$165

Ragtime Series

R001 — parlor style, solid spruce top, round soundhole, wooden inlay binding and rosette, rosewood back/sides/neck, 14/20 fret rosewood fingerboard, rosewood bridge with white black dot pins, 3 per side gold die cast tuners. Available in Natural finish. Mfd. 1992 to date.

Mfr.'s Sug. Retail	$600	$420	$360	$300	$240	$215	$195	$180

Grading	100%	98%	95%	90%	80%	70%	60%

R300 — parlor style, cedar top, round soundhole, wooden inlay binding and rosette, mahogany back/sides/neck, 14/20 fret rosewood fingerboard, rosewood bridge with white black dot pins, 3 per side chrome die cast tuners. Available in Natural finish. Mfd. 1992 to date.

Mfr.'s Sug. Retail	$400	$280	$240	$200	$160	$145	$130	$120

R302 — similar to R300, except has 12 strings.

Mfr.'s Sug. Retail	$450	$315	$270	$225	$180	$160	$150	$135

R350 — similar to R300, except for ovankol back/sides.

Mfr.'s Sug. Retail	$450	$315	$270	$225	$180	$160	$150	$135

Nomad Series

N600 — single cutaway classical style, cedar top, round soundhole, 5 stripe bound body, wooden inlay rosette, mahogany back/sides/neck, 21 fret rosewood fingerboard with pearl dot inlays, rosewood bridge with white black dot pins, 3 per side chrome die cast tuners, piezo electric pickup with 3-band EQ. Available in Natural finish. Mfd. 1992 to date.

Mfr.'s Sug. Retail	$600	$420	$360	$300	$240	$215	$195	$180

Add $50 for Black finish.

N601N — single cutaway classic style, cedar top, round soundhole, 5 stripe bound body, wooden inlay rosette, mahogany back/sides/neck, 21 fret rosewood fingerboard/tied bridge, classical style peghead, 3 per side open classic gold tuners, piezo electric pickup with 3-band graphic equalizer. Available in Natural finish. Mfd. 1992 to date.

Mfr.'s Sug. Retail	$680	$475	$405	$340	$270	$245	$225	$205

N700D — single cutaway deeper dreadnought style, spruce top, round soundhole, 5 stripe bound body, wooden inlay rosette, ovankol back/sides, mahogany neck, 21 fret rosewood fingerboard with snowflake inlays, rosewood bridge with white black dot pins, 3 per side gold die cast tuners, piezo pickup, 3 band graphic equalizer. Available in Natural finish. Mfd. 1992 to date.

Mfr.'s Sug. Retail	$700	$490	$420	$350	$280	$250	$230	$210

N800 — single cutaway jumbo style, flame maple top, round soundhole, abalone bound body and rosette, flame maple back/sides, mahogany neck, 21 fret bound rosewood fingerboard with abalone block inlays, rosewood bridge with black white dot pins, bound peghead, 3 per side chrome die cast tuners, piezo pickup, Matrix 4 band EQ. Available in Transparent Blue and Transparent Violin finish. Mfd. 1992 to date.

Mfr.'s Sug. Retail	$850	$595	$510	$425	$340	$305	$280	$255

N900S — similar to N800, except has solid spruce top and gold die cast tuners.

Mfr.'s Sug. Retail	$1,100	$770	$660	$550	$440	$395	$365	$330

Grading	100%	98%	95%	90%	80%	70%	60%

ACOUSTIC-ELECTRIC

ATL10 — telecaster thinline style, spruce top, oval soundhole, bound body, 3 stripe rosette, maple back/sides/neck, 22 fret rosewood fingerboard with pearl dot inlays, rosewood bridge with white pearl dot pins, 6 per side black die cast tuners, piezo pickup, 3 band equalizer. Available in Black and Blue Night finish. Mfd. 1992 to date.

Mfr.'s Sug. Retail	$500	$350	$300	$250	$200	$180	$165	$150

ELECTRIC

Artstar Series

AF200 — single rounded cutaway semi-hollow style, spruce top with bound body and f holes, raised pickguard, spruce back/sides, mahogany/maple 3 piece neck, 20 fret bound rosewood fingerboard with pearl/abalone rectangle inlays, ebony bridge with trapeze tailpiece, bound peghead, 3 per side nylon head tuners, gold hardware, 2 Super 58 humbuckers, volume/tone control, 3 position selector switch. Available in Antique Violin finish. Mfd. 1991 to date.

Mfr.'s Sug. Retail	$1,400	$980	$840	$700	$560	$505	$460	$420

AM200 — double cutaway semi-hollow style, burl mahogany top with bound body and f holes, raised pickguard, burl mahogany back/sides, mahogany/maple 3 piece neck, 20 fret bound rosewood fingerboard with pearl abalone rectangle inlay, tunomatic bridge stop tailpiece, bound peghead, 3 per side nylon head tuners, gold hardware, 2 Super 58 humbuckers, volume/tone control, 3 position selector switch. Available in Antique Violin finish. Mfd. 1991 to date.

Mfr.'s Sug. Retail	$1,400	$980	$840	$700	$560	$505	$460	$420

AS200 — similar to AM200, except has flame maple top/back/sides.

Mfr.'s Sug. Retail	$1,400	$980	$840	$700	$560	$505	$460	$420

EX Series

EX160 — strat style maple body, bolt-on maple neck, 22 fret rosewood fingerboard with pearl dot inlay, standard vibrato, 6 on one side tuners, chrome hardware, 2 single coil/1 humbucker pickups, volume/tone control, 5 position switch. Available in Black and Matte Stain finish. Curr. mfr.

Mfr.'s Sug. Retail	$330	$230	$195	$165	$130	$120	$110	$100

Grading	100%	98%	95%	90%	80%	70%	60%

EX170 — strat style maple body, bolt-on maple neck, 22 fret maple fingerboard with black dot inlay, standard vibrato, 6 on one side tuners, chrome hardware, humbucker/single coil/humbucker pickups, volume/tone control, 5 position switch. Available in Black, Blue Night and Matte Violin finish. Curr. mfr.

Mfr.'s Sug. Retail	$350	$245	$210	$175	$140	$125	$115	$105

Add $50 for left handed version (EX170L).

EX270 — similar to EX170, except has single locking vibrato and black hardware. Available in Black, Blue Night and Candy Apple finish. Curr. mfr.

Mfr.'s Sug. Retail	$470	$330	$280	$235	$190	$170	$155	$140

EX350 — strat style basswood body, bolt-on maple neck, 22 fret bound rosewood fingerboard with triangle inlay, double locking vibrato, 6 on one side tuners, chrome hardware, humbucker/single coil/humbucker Ibanez pickups, volume/tone control, 5 position switch. Available in Black, Burgundy Red, Desert Yellow and Laser Blue finish. Curr. mfr.

Mfr.'s Sug. Retail	$570	$400	$340	$285	$230	$205	$190	$170

EX360 — similar to EX350, except has 2 single coil/1 humbucker Ibanez pickups. Available in Black, Dark Grey, Jewel Blue and Purple Pearl finish. Disc. 1992.

	$350	$300	$250	$200	$180	$165	$150

Last Mfr.'s Sug. Retail was $500.

EX365 — similar to EX350, except has reverse headstock, single coil/humbucker Ibanez pickups. Available in Black, Laser Blue and Ultra Violet finish. Disc. 1992.

	$335	$290	$240	$190	$170	$155	$145

Last Mfr.'s Sug. Retail was $480.

EX370 — similar to EX350. Available in Black, Burgundy Red, Jewel Blue and Ultra Violet finish.

Mfr.'s Sug. Retail	$570	$400	$340	$285	$230	$205	$190	$170

Add $80 for flame maple top, gold hardware (EX370FM). Available in Antique Violin, Cherry Sunburst and Wine Burst finish.

EX1500 — strat style maple body, tortoise shell pickguard, bolt-on maple neck, 22 fret maple fingerboard with black dot inlay, standard vibrato, 6 on one side tuners, gold hardware, humbucker/single coil/humbucker pickups, volume/tone control, 5 position switch. Available in Antique Violin and Black finish. Mfd. 1993 to date.

Mfr.'s Sug. Retail	$430	$300	$260	$215	$175	$155	$140	$130

EX1700 — similar to EX1500, except has bound body, no pickguard, chrome hardware. Available in Cherry Sunburst and Transparent Turquoise finish. Mfd. 1993 to date.

Mfr.'s Sug. Retail	$430	$300	$260	$215	$175	$155	$140	$130

Grading	100%	98%	95%	90%	80%	70%	60%

EX3700 — strat style basswood body, bound flame maple top, bolt-on maple neck, 24 fret maple fingerboard with black dot inlay, double locking vibrato, 6 on one side tuners, gold hardware, humbucker/single coil/humbucker Ibanez pickups, volume/tone control, 5 position switch. Available in Transparent Purple, Transparent Red and Transparent Turquoise finish. Mfd. 1993 to date.

Mfr.'s Sug. Retail	$650	$455	$390	$325	$260	$235	$215	$195

FGM Series

The FGM Series was co-designed by Frank Gambale.

FGM100 — sculpted thin strat style mahogany body, one piece maple neck, 22 fret bound rosewood fingerboard with matched color sharktooth inlay, double locking vibrato, 6 on one side tuners, black hardware, humbucker/DiMarzio single coil/DiMarzio Ibanez humbucker pickups, volume/tone control, 5 position selector switch. Available in Black, Desert Sun Yellow, Pink Salmon and Sky Blue finish. Mfd. 1991 to date.

Mfr.'s Sug. Retail	$1,300	$910	$780	$650	$520	$470	$430	$390

GB Series

The GB Series was co-designed by George Benson.

GB10 — single rounded cutaway hollow style, arched spruce top, bound body and f holes, raised pickguard, maple back/sides, maple 3 piece neck, 22 fret bound ebony fingerboard with pearl/abalone rectangle inlay, ebony bridge with pearl arrow inlays, ebony/metal tailpiece, bound peghead with abalone logo and George Benson standard Ibanez inlays, 3 per side nylon head tuners, gold hardware, 2 humbucker Ibanez pickups, two volume/tone controls, 3 position switch. Available in Brown Sunburst or Natural finish. Mfd. 1978 to date.

Mfr.'s Sug. Retail	$1,600	$1,120	$960	$800	$640	$575	$530	$480

The 21st fret has a George Benson signature block inlay.

GB12 — single rounded cutaway hollow style, arched flame maple top/back/sides, abalone and plastic bound body and f holes, raised matched pickguard, 22 fret ebony fingerboard with special GB 12 inlay, ebony bridge with flower inlay, gold and ebony tailpiece with vine inlay, bound peghead with abalone logo and George Benson 12th Anniversary Ibanez inlays, 3 per side nylon head tuners, gold hardware, 2 humbucker Ibanez pickups, two volume/tone controls, 3 position switch. Available in Brown Sunburst finish. Mfd. 1990-92.

	$1,400	$1,200	$1,000	$800	$720	$660	$600

The 21st fret has a George Benson signature scroll inlay.
This is a limited edition 12th Anniversary George Benson model guitar.
Last Mfr.'s Sug. Retail was $2,000.

Grading	100%	98%	95%	90%	80%	70%	60%

GB30 — single rounded cutaway hollow style, arched maple top/back/sides, bound body and f holes, raised black pickguard, mahogany neck, 22 fret bound ebony fingerboard with offset pearl dot inlay, tunomatic bridge/stop tailpiece, bound peghead with abalone logo and George Benson standard Ibanez inlay, 3 per side nylon head tuners, black hardware, 2 Ibanez humbuckers, two volume/tone controls, 3 position switch. Available in Black or Transparent Red finish. Mfd. 1991-92.

	$910	$780	$650	$520	$470	$430	$390

The 21st fret has a George Benson signature block inlay.
Last Mfr.'s Sug. Retail was $1,300.

GB100 — similar to GB12, except does not have George Benson 12th Anniversary inlay on peghead. Mfd. 1993 to date.

Mfr.'s Sug. Retail	$2,300	$1,610	$1,380	$1,150	$920	$830	$760	$690

JEM Series

The JEM Series was co-designed by Steve Vai. All models in this series have a hand slot routed into the bodies.

JEM7V — strat style alder body, pearloid pickguard, bolt-on maple neck, 24 fret ebony fingerboard with pearl vine inlay, double locking vibrato, 6 on one side tuners, gold hardware, humbucker/single coil/humbucker Ibanez pickups, volume/tone control, 5 position switch. Available in White finish. Mfd. 1993 to date.

Mfr.'s Sug. Retail	$2,000	$1,400	$1,200	$1,000	$800	$720	$660	$600

JEM77GMC — strat style basswood body, transparent pickguard, bolt-on maple neck, 24 fret rosewood fingerboard with fluorescent vine inlay, double locking vibrato, 6 on one side tuners, charcoal hardware, humbucker/single coil/humbucker DiMarzio pickups, volume/tone control, 5 position switch. Available in Green Multi Color finish. Mfd. 1992 to date.

Mfr.'s Sug. Retail	$2,100	$1,475	$1,260	$1,050	$840	$755	$690	$630

JEM77BFP — similar to JEM77GMC, except has a maple fingerboard with Blue vine inlay and Blue Flower Pattern finish.

Mfr.'s Sug. Retail	$1,800	$1,260	$1,080	$900	$720	$650	$595	$540

JEM77FP — similar to JEM77GMC, except has a floral pattern finish.

Mfr.'s Sug. Retail	$1,800	$1,260	$1,080	$900	$720	$650	$595	$540

JEM77PMC — similar to JEM77GMC, except has a maple fingerboard with 3 color pyramid inlays and Purple Multi color finish. Mfd. 1991-92.

	$1,475	$1,260	$1,050	$840	$755	$690	$630

Last Mfr.'s Sug. Retail was $2,100.

Grading	100%	98%	95%	90%	80%	70%	60%

⚐ **JEM777** — similar to JEM77GMC, except has a maple fingerboard with 3 color pyramid inlay, black pickguard. Available in Desert Sun Yellow finish.

Mfr.'s Sug. Retail	$1,600	$1,120	$960	$800	$640	$575	$530	$480

⚐ **JEM777V** — similar to JEM77GMC, except has Black finish.

Mfr.'s Sug. Retail	$1,700	$1,190	$1,020	$850	$680	$610	$560	$510

JS Series

The JS Series was co-designed by Joe Satriani.

JS1 — strat style basswood contoured body, bolt-on maple neck, 22 fret rosewood fingerboard with pearl dot inlay, double locking vibrato, 6 on one side tuners, chrome hardware, humbucker/single coil/humbucker DiMarzio pickups, volume/tone control, 5 position switch. Available in Black, Inferno Red and White finish. Mfd. 1991 to date.

Mfr.'s Sug. Retail	$1,200	$840	$720	$600	$480	$430	$395	$360

JS3 — similar to JS1, except has 2 humbucker DiMarzio pickups, 3 position switch and Custom Graphic finish.

Mfr.'s Sug. Retail	$2,300	$1,610	$1,380	$1,150	$920	$830	$760	$690

JS4 — similar to JS3, except has Electric Rainbow finish.

Mfr.'s Sug. Retail	$2,300	$1,610	$1,380	$1,150	$920	$830	$760	$690

JS5 — similar to JS3, except has Rainforest finish.

Mfr.'s Sug. Retail	$2,300	$1,610	$1,380	$1,150	$920	$830	$760	$690

JS6 — similar to JS3, except has mahogany body, fixed bridge and Oil finish.

Mfr.'s Sug. Retail	$2,300	$1,610	$1,380	$1,150	$920	$830	$760	$690

VOYAGER Series

The VOYAGER Series was co-designed by Reb Beach.

RBM1 — strat style mahogany body with vibrato wedge cutaway, metal pickguard, bolt-on maple neck, 22 fret rosewood fingerboard with pearl dot inlay, double locking vibrato, 6 on one side tuners, gold hardware, 2 single coil/1 humbucker pickups, volume control, 5 position switch. Available in Black, Blue or Candy Apple finish. Mfd. 1991 to date.

Mfr.'s Sug. Retail	$1,200	$840	$720	$600	$480	$430	$395	$360

Grading	100%	98%	95%	90%	80%	70%	60%

RBM2 — similar to RBM1, except has koa top, Bolivian rosewood neck/fingerboard. Available in Natural finish.

Mfr.'s Sug. Retail	$2,100	$1,475	$1,260	$1,050	$840	$755	$690	$630

R Series

R442 — strat style alder body, bolt-on maple neck, 22 fret maple fingerboard with black dot inlay, locking vibrato, 6 on one side locking tuners, black hardware, 2 single coil/1 humbucker Ibanez pickups, volume/tone control, 5 position switch. Available in Transparent Blue, Transparent Cherry and Transparent Sunburst finish. Mfd. 1992 only.

		$490	$420	$350	$280	$250	$230	$210

Last Mfr.'s Sug. Retail was $700.

R540LTD — strat style basswood body, bolt-on maple neck, 22 fret bound rosewood fingerboard with sharktooth inlay, double locking vibrato, 6 on one side tuners, black hardware, humbucker/single coil/humbucker Ibanez pickups, volume/tone control, 5 position switch. Available in Black, Candy Apple and Jewel Blue finish. Mfd. 1992 to date.

Mfr.'s Sug. Retail	$1,000	$700	$600	$500	$400	$360	$330	$300

R540 — similar to R540LTD, except has pearl dot inlay, 2 single coil/1 humbucker Ibanez pickups. Available in Blue Burst finish. Mfd. 1992 only.

		$665	$570	$475	$380	$345	$315	$285

Last Mfr.'s Sug. Retail was $950.

R540HH — similar to R540, except has 2 humbucker Ibanez pickups. Available in White finish.

		$650	$555	$465	$370	$335	$305	$280

Last Mfr.'s Sug. Retail was $930.

R542 — strat style stand body, bolt-on maple neck, 22 fret rosewood fingerboard with abalone oval inlay, locking vibrato, 6 on one side locking tuners, black hardware, 3 single coil Ibanez pickups, volume/tone control, 5 position switch. Available in Blue, Candy Apple or White finish. Mfd. 1992 only.

		$560	$480	$400	$320	$290	$265	$240

Last Mfr.'s Sug. Retail was $800.

RV470 — strat style alder body, gravure top, transparent pickguard, bolt-on maple neck, 22 fret rosewood fingerboard with pearl dot inlay, standard vibrato, 6 on one side locking tuners, gold hardware, volume/tone control, 5 position switch. Available in Purpleburst and Tobaccoburst finish. Mfd. 1993 to date.

Mfr.'s Sug. Retail	$850	$595	$510	$425	$340	$305	$280	$255

Grading	100%	98%	95%	90%	80%	70%	60%

RG Series

RG470 — strat style basswood body, bolt-on maple neck, 24 fret rosewood fingerboard with pearl dot inlay, double locking vibrato, 6 on one side tuners, black hardware, humbucker/single coil/humbucker Ibanez pickups, volume/tone control, 5 position switch. Available in Black, Emerald Green and Jewel Blue finish. Mfd. 1993 to date.

Mfr.'s Sug. Retail	$750	$525	$450	$375	$300	$270	$245	$225

Add $150 for left handed version (RG470L). Available in Black finish.

RG550 — strat style basswood body, black pickguard, bolt-on maple neck, 24 fret maple fingerboard with black dot inlay, double locking vibrato, 6 on one side tuners, black hardware, humbucker/single coil/humbucker Ibanez pickups, volume/tone control, 5 position switch. Available in Black, Candy Apple and Desert Sun Yellow finish. Mfd. 1991 to date.

Mfr.'s Sug. Retail	$800	$560	$480	$400	$320	$290	$265	$240

Add $100 for left handed version. Available in Black finish. Mfd. 1992 only.

RG550DX — similar to RG550, except has body-color-matched mirror pickguard. Available in Laser Blue and Purple Neon finish.

Mfr.'s Sug. Retail	$850	$595	$510	$425	$340	$305	$280	$255

RG560 — similar to RG550, except has rosewood fingerboard with pearl dot inlay, 2 single coil/1 humbucker Ibanez pickups. Available in Black, Candy Apple and Jewel Blue finish. Mfd. 1992 only.

		$525	$450	$375	$300	$270	$245	$225

Last Mfr.'s Sug. Retail was $750.

RG565 — similar to RG550, except has body-color matched fingerboard inlay, reverse headstock, single coil/humbucker Ibanez pickups. Available in Candy Apple, Emerald Green and Laser Blue finish. Mfd. 1992 only.

		$560	$480	$400	$320	$290	$265	$240

Last Mfr.'s Sug. Retail was $800.

RG570 — strat style basswood body, bolt-on maple neck, 24 fret rosewood fingerboard with pearl dot inlay, double locking vibrato, 6 on one side tuners, black hardware, humbucker/single coil/humbucker Ibanez pickups, volume/tone control, 5 position switch. Available in Black, Candy Apple, Emerald Green, Jewel Blue and Purple Neon finish. Mfd. 1992 only.

		$525	$450	$375	$300	$270	$245	$225

Add $150 for left handed version (RG570L). Available in Jewel Blue finish.
Last Mfr.'s Sug. Retail was $750.

RG570FM — similar to RG570, except has flame maple top. Available in Amber, Transparent Blue and Transparent Cherry finish. Mfd. 1992 only.

		$595	$510	$425	$340	$305	$280	$255

Last Mfr.'s Sug. Retail was $850.

Grading	100%	98%	95%	90%	80%	70%	60%

RG750 — strat style basswood body, bolt-on maple neck, 24 fret bound maple fingerboard with sharktooth inlay, double locking vibrato, bound peghead, 6 on one side tuners, black hardware, humbucker/single coil/humbucker Ibanez pickups, volume/tone control, 5 position switch. Available in Black and Candy Apple finish. Mfd. 1992 only.

		$700	$600	$500	$400	$360	$330	$300

Last Mfr.'s Sug. Retail was $1,000.

RG760 — similar to RG750, except has rosewood fingerboard, 2 single coil/1 humbucker Ibanez pickups. Available in Black, Jewel Blue and Emerald Green finish.

		$700	$600	$500	$400	$360	$330	$300

Last Mfr.'s Sug. Retail was $1,000.

RG770 — strat style basswood body, bolt-on maple neck, 24 fret bound rosewood fingerboard with pearl sharktooth inlay, double locking vibrato, bound peghead, 6 on one side tuners, black hardware, humbucker/single coil/humbucker Ibanez pickups, volume/tone control. Available in Black, Emerald Green finish. Mfd. 1991 to date.

Mfr.'s Sug. Retail	$1,000	$700	$600	$500	$400	$360	$330	$300

Available with transparent pickguard, maple fingerboard with body-color-matched sharktooth inlay (RG770DX). Available in Laser Blue and Violet Metallic finish.

RG1200 — strat style basswood flame maple top body, pearloid pickguard, bolt-on maple neck, 24 fret bound rosewood fingerboard with abalone oval inlay, double locking vibrato, bound peghead, 6 on one side tuners, humbucker/Ibanez single coil/DiMarzio humbucker pickups, volume/tone control, 5 position switch. Available in Transparent Red and Transparent Blue finish. Mfd. 1992 only.

Mfr.'s Sug. Retail	$1,350	$945	$810	$675	$540	$485	$445	$405

R Series

RT150 — strat style alder body, white pickguard, bolt-on maple neck, 24 fret rosewood fingerboard with pearl dot inlay, standard vibrato, 6 on one side tuners, chrome hardware, humbucker/single coil/humbucker pickups, volume/tone control, 5 position switch. Available in Black and Deep Red finish. Mfd. 1993 to date.

Mfr.'s Sug. Retail	$400	$280	$240	$200	$160	$145	$130	$120

RT450 — similar to RT150, except has tortoise shell pickguard, locking tuners, Ibanez pickups. Available in Amber, Black and Tobacco Sunburst finish.

Mfr.'s Sug. Retail	$550	$385	$330	$275	$220	$200	$180	$165

RT452 — similar to RT450, except has 12 strings, fixed bridge, 6 per side tuners. Available in Amber finish.

Mfr.'s Sug. Retail	$650	$455	$390	$325	$260	$235	$215	$195

Grading	100%	98%	95%	90%	80%	70%	60%

RT650 — strat style alder body, bound gravure top, pearloid pickguard, bolt-on maple neck, 24 fret bound rosewood fingerboard with pearl dot inlay, standard vibrato, 6 on one side locking tuners, chrome hardware, humbucker/single coil/humbucker Ibanez pickups, volume/tone control, 5 position switch. Available in Transparent Blue and Transparent Red finish. Mfd. 1993 to date.

Mfr.'s Sug. Retail	$750	$525	$450	$375	$300	$270	$245	$225

S Series

S470 — sculpted thin strat style mahogany body, bolt-on maple neck, 22 fret rosewood fingerboard with pearl dot inlay, double locking vibrato, 6 on one side tuners, black hardware, humbucker/single coil/humbucker Ibanez pickups, volume/tone control, 5 position switch. Available in Black, Transparent Blue and Transparent Red finish. Mfd. 1991 to date.

Mfr.'s Sug. Retail	$900	$630	$540	$450	$360	$325	$300	$275

SF470 — similar to S470, except has tunomatic bridge/stop tailpiece.

Mfr.'s Sug. Retail	$750	$525	$450	$375	$300	$270	$245	$225

S540 — strat style mahogany body, bolt-on maple neck, 22 fret maple fingerboard with abalone oval inlay, pearl "Custom Made" inlay at 21st fret, double locking vibrato, 6 on one side tuners, black hardware, humbucker/single coil/humbucker Ibanez pickups, volume/tone control, 5 position switch. Available in Jade Metallic and Oil finish. Mfd. 1991 to date.

Mfr.'s Sug. Retail	$1,050	$735	$630	$525	$420	$380	$345	$315

Add $100 for flame maple top (S540FM). Available in Cherry Wine and Transparent Turquoise finish.

Add $100 for burl mahogany top (S540BM). Available in Antique Violin finish.

S540SLTD — similar to S540, except has bound rosewood fingerboard with sharktooth inlay, bound peghead. Available in Black, Emerald Green, Jewel Blue, Lipstick Red and Purple Neon finish.

Mfr.'s Sug. Retail	$1,000	$700	$600	$500	$400	$360	$330	$300

540S7 — sculpted thin strat style mahogany body, bolt-on maple neck, 22 fret rosewood fingerboard with pearl dot inlay, double locking vibrato, 7 on one side tuners, black hardware, 2 single coil/1 humbucker DiMarzio pickups, volume/tone control, 5 position switch. Available in Black finish. Mfd. 1992 only.

	$910	$780	$650	$520	$470	$430	$390

This model is a 7 string, similar to the Universe series.
Last Mfr.'s Sug. Retail was $1,300.

Grading	100%	98%	95%	90%	80%	70%	60%

USA Custom Exotic Wood Series

UCEWFM — strat style mahogany body, figured maple top, bolt-on birdseye maple neck, 24 fret rosewood fingerboard with pearl dot inlay, double locking vibrato, 6 on one side tuners, black hardware, humbucker/Ibanez single coil/DiMarzio humbucker pickups, volume/tone control, 5 position switch. Available in Natural, Transparent Blue, Transparent Ebony and Transparent Purple finish. Mfd. 1992 only.

	$1,190	$1,020	$850	$680	$610	$560	$510

Last Mfr.'s Sug. Retail was $1,700.

Universe Series

This series was co-designed by Steve Vai. All are seven string guitars.

UV7 — strat style basswood body, transparent pickguard, bolt-on maple neck, 24 fret rosewood fingerboard with green dot inlay, double locking vibrato, 7 on one side tuners, black hardware, humbucker/single coil/humbucker DiMarzio pickups, volume/tone control, 5 position switch. Available in Black finish. Mfd. 1991 to date.

Mfr.'s Sug. Retail	$1,600	$1,120	$960	$800	$640	$575	$530	$480

UV7P — similar to UV7, except has white pickguard and pearl abalone pyramid inlay. Available in White finish.

Mfr.'s Sug. Retail	$1,700	$1,190	$1,020	$850	$680	$610	$560	$510

UV777 — similar to UV7, except has black pickguard, maple fingerboard with 3 color pyramid inlay. Available in Green finish.

Mfr.'s Sug. Retail	$1,800	$1,260	$1,080	$900	$720	$650	$595	$540

UV77 — similar to UV7, except has 3 color pyramid inlay. Available in Multi-colored finish.

Mfr.'s Sug. Retail	$2,200	$1,540	$1,320	$1,100	$880	$790	$725	$660

USA Custom Graphic Series

This series was produced in 1992 only and prices reflect the 1992 manufacturer's suggested retail.

92UCGR1 — strat style basswood body, bolt-on maple neck, 24 fret bound rosewood fingerboard with sharktooth inlay, double locking vibrato, 6 on one side tuners, bound peghead, black hardware, DiMarzio single coil/Ibanez humbucker pickups, volume/tone control. Available in Ice World finish.

Mfr.'s Sug. Retail	$1,550	$1,085	$930	$775	$620	$560	$515	$465

92UCGR2 — similar to 92UCGR1, except has reverse headstock, DiMarzio humbucker/Ibanez single coil/DiMarzio humbucker pickups. Available in No Bones About It finish.

Mfr.'s Sug. Retail	$1,600	$1,120	$960	$800	$640	$575	$530	$480

Grading	100%	98%	95%	90%	80%	70%	60%

92UCGR3 — similar to 92UCGR1, except has reverse headstock, 2 Ibanez humbucker pickups. Available in Grim Reaper finish.

Mfr.'s Sug. Retail	$1,550	$1,085	$930	$775	$620	$560	$515	$465

92UCGR4 — similar to 92UCGR1, except has unbound fingerboard with pearl dot inlay, DiMarzio humbucker/Ibanez single coil/DiMarzio humbucker pickups. Available in Angel Depart finish.

Mfr.'s Sug. Retail	$1,550	$1,085	$930	$775	$620	$560	$515	$465

92UCGR5 — similar to 92UCGR1, except has unbound maple fingerboard with black dot inlay, DiMarzio single coil/humbucker pickups. Available in Unzipped finish.

Mfr.'s Sug. Retail	$1,500	$1,050	$900	$750	$600	$540	$495	$450

92UCGR6 — similar to 92UCGR1, except has unbound rosewood fingerboard with pearl dot inlay, DiMarzio humbucker/Ibanez single coil/DiMarzio humbucker pickups. Available in Sea Monster finish.

Mfr.'s Sug. Retail	$1,550	$1,085	$930	$775	$620	$560	$515	$465

92UCGR7 — similar to 92UCGR1, except has reverse headstock, DiMarzio humbucker/Ibanez single coil/DiMarzio humbucker pickups. Available in Alien's Revenge finish.

Mfr.'s Sug. Retail	$1,600	$1,120	$960	$800	$640	$575	$530	$480

92UCGR8 — similar to 92UCGR1, except has unbound maple fingerboard with black dot inlay, 2 DiMarzio humbucker pickups. Available in Cosmic Swirl II finish.

Mfr.'s Sug. Retail	$1,500	$1,050	$900	$750	$600	$540	$495	$450

ELECTRIC BASS

Affirma Series

This series was designed by Swiss luthier, Rolf Spuler. His design incorporates a neck that extends half-way through the body with individual bridges for each string. There is a thumb slot and pearl/abalone AFR and pearl block with Ibanez/serial number inscriptions inlaid into the body, located between the single coil pickup and the bridges. All models are available in fretless configuration at no additional charge.

A104 — offset double cutaway asymmetrical saman body, maple neck, 24 fret ebony fingerboard with offset pearl inlay at 12th fret, 4 "Mono Rail" bridges, tuning lever on low string bridge, body matching peghead veneer, 2 per side tuners, black hardware, single coil/4 bridge piezo pickups, volume/concentric treble/bass/mix controls, active electronics. Available in Natural finish. Curr. mfr.

Mfr.'s Sug. Retail	$1,900	$1,330	$1,140	$950	$760	$685	$625	$570

This model is also available with kralo walnut or flame maple body.

Grading	100%	98%	95%	90%	80%	70%	60%

A105 — similar to A104, except has 5 strings, 5 Mono Rail bridges, 3/2 per side tuners.

Mfr.'s Sug. Retail	$2,000	$1,400	$1,200	$1,000	$800	$720	$660	$600

CT Bass Series

CTB1 — precision style maple body, bolt-on maple 3 piece neck, 22 fret rosewood fingerboard with pearl dot inlay, die cast fixed bridge, 2 per side tuners, chrome hardware, P-style/J-style Ibanez pickups, 2 volume/1 tone controls. Available in Black, Blue Night, Red and White finish. Mfd. 1992 only.

	$315	$270	$225	$180	$160	$150	$135

Add $50 for left handed version (CTB1L).
Last Mfr.'s Sug. Retail was $450.

CTB3 — similar to CTB1, except has CT Custom inlay, black hardware, two volume/tone controls. Available in Black, Blue Night, Natural and Transparent Red finish.

	$420	$360	$300	$240	$215	$195	$180

Last Mfr.'s Sug. Retail was $600.

CTB5 — precision style maple body, bolt-on 3 piece maple neck, 22 fret rosewood fingerboard with CT Custom inlay, 5 string die cast fixed bridge, 3/2 per side tuners, black hardware, 2 J-style EMG pickups, 2 volume/tone controls. Available in Black, Natural and Transparent Red finish. Mfd. 1992 only.

	$490	$420	$350	$280	$250	$230	$210

Last Mfr.'s Sug. Retail was $700.

EX Bass Series

EXB404 — precision style maple body, maple 3 piece neck, 22 fret rosewood fingerboard with pearl dot inlay, die cast fixed bridge, 4 on one side tuners, chrome hardware, P-style/J-style pickups, 2 volume/1 tone controls. Available in Black, Burgundy Red and Jewel Blue finish. Curr. mfr.

Mfr.'s Sug. Retail	$430	$300	$260	$215	$175	$155	$140	$130

Add $50 for left handed version (EXB404L).

EXB445 — precision style maple body, bolt-on maple 3 piece neck, 22 fret rosewood fingerboard with pearl dot inlays, 5 string die cast fixed bridge, 4/1 per side tuners, black hardware, 2 J-style EMG pickups, 2 volume/1 tone controls. Available in Black and Burgundy Red finish. Curr. mfr.

Mfr.'s Sug. Retail	$530	$370	$320	$265	$210	$190	$175	$160

S Bass Series

SB1500 — precision style bubinga body, bolt-on bubinga/wenge 5 piece neck, 22 fret ebony fingerboard with abalone oval inlays, AccuCast-B bridge, 4 on one side tuners, chrome hardware, P-style/J-style EMG pickups, 2 volume/tone controls. Available in Natural finish. Mfd. 1992 only.

	$910	$780	$650	$520	$470	$430	$390

Last Mfr.'s Sug. Retail was $1,300.

Grading	100%	98%	95%	90%	80%	70%	60%

Soundgear Bass Series

SR400 — offset double cutaway maple body, bolt-on 3 piece maple neck, 24 fret rosewood fingerboard with pearl dot inlay, fixed bridge, 2 per side tuners, black hardware, P-style/J-style Ibanez pickup, 2 volume/1 tone controls. Available in Black, Jewel Blue and Candy Apple finish. Mfd. 1993 to date.

Mfr.'s Sug. Retail	$500	$350	$300	$250	$200	$180	$165	$150

   Add $50 for left handed version (SR400L).

SR500 — similar to SR400, except has active pickups, volume/treble/bass/mix control. Available in Black, Natural and Transparent Turquoise finish. Mfd. 1993 to date.

Mfr.'s Sug. Retail	$650	$455	$390	$325	$260	$235	$215	$195

SR505 — similar to SR500, except has 5 strings, 3/2 per side tuners, 2 J-style EMG pickups. Available in Black, Transparent Red and Transparent Turquoise finish. Mfd. 1993 to date.

Mfr.'s Sug. Retail	$750	$525	$450	$375	$300	$270	$245	$225

SR800 — offset double cutaway basswood body, bolt-on maple 5 piece neck, 24 fret rosewood fingerboard with pearl dot inlay, AccuCast-B bridge, 2 per side tuners, black hardware, P-style/J-style Ibanez pickups, 2 volume/tone controls. Available in Black, Candy Apple and Jewel Blue finish. Curr. mfr.

Mfr.'s Sug. Retail	$700	$490	$420	$350	$280	$250	$230	$210

   Add $150 for left handed version (SR800L).
   Add $100 for fretless fingerboard version (SR800F). Mfd. 1992 only.

SR885 — offset double cutaway basswood body, maple 3 piece neck, 24 fret rosewood fingerboard with pearl dot inlay, 5 string Gotoh bridge, 3/2 per side tuners, black hardware, 2 J-style Ibanez pickups, 2 volume/tone controls. Available in Black, Candy Apple and Laser Blue finish. Mfd. 1991 to date.

Mfr.'s Sug. Retail	$850	$595	$510	$425	$340	$305	$280	$255

SR886 — similar to SR885, except has 6 strings. Available in Black and Candy Apple finish. Mfd. 1992 only.

	$980	$840	$700	$560	$505	$460	$420

   Last Mfr.'s Sug. Retail was $1,400.

SR890 — offset double cutaway ash body, bolt-on 3 piece maple neck, 24 fret rosewood fingerboard with pearl dot inlay, fixed bridge, 2 per side tuners, gold hardware, P-style/J-style active Ibanez pickup, volume/treble/2 mid/bass/mix controls. Available in Transparent Cherry and Transparent Turquoise finish. Mfd. 1993 to date.

Mfr.'s Sug. Retail	$1,000	$700	$600	$500	$400	$360	$330	$300

   Add $200 for 5 string version (SR895).

Grading	100%	98%	95%	90%	80%	70%	60%

SR900 — offset double cutaway ash body, bolt-on maple 3 piece neck, 24 fret rosewood fingerboard with pearl dot inlay, AccuCast-B bridge, 2 per side tuners, black hardware, P-style/J-style Ibanez pickups, 2 volume/tone controls. Available in Emerald Green and Purple Neon finish. Mfd. 1992 only.

		$630	$540	$450	$360	$325	$300	$275

Last Mfr.'s Sug. Retail was $900.

SR950 — similar to SR900, except has ebony fingerboard with abalone oval inlay, gold hardware. Available in Transparent Cherry and Transparent Turquoise finish.

		$700	$600	$500	$400	$360	$330	$300

Last Mfr.'s Sug. Retail was $1,000.

SR1300 — offset double cutaway padauk body, bolt-on 5 piece bubinga/wenge neck, 24 fret wenge fingerboard with pearl dot inlay, fixed bridge, 2 per side tuners, black hardware, P-style/J-style Ibanez pickup, volume/treble/2 mid/bass/mix controls. Available in Oil finish. Curr mfr.

Mfr.'s Sug. Retail	$1,300	$910	$780	$650	$520	$470	$430	$390

SR1305 — similar to SR1300, except has 5 strings, 3/2 per side tuners, 2 J-style pickups.

Mfr.'s Sug. Retail	$1,500	$1,050	$900	$750	$600	$540	$495	$450

SR1306 — similar to SR1300, except has 6 strings, 3 per side tuners, 2 J-style pickups.

Mfr.'s Sug. Retail	$1,700	$1,190	$1,020	$850	$680	$610	$560	$510

SR1500 — offset double cutaway bubinga or padauk body, bubinga/wenge 5 piece neck, 22 fret ebony fingerboard with pearl dot inlay, fixed bridge, 2 per side tuners, black hardware, P-style/J-style EMG pickups, 2 volume/tone controls. Available in Natural finish. Mfd. 1991-92.

		$980	$840	$700	$560	$505	$460	$420

Last Mfr.'s Sug. Retail was $1,400.

SR2000 — offset double cutaway maple body, thru body 5 piece maple/walnut neck, 24 fret wenge fingerboard with abalone oval inlay, fixed bridge, 2 per side tuners, gold hardware, P-style/J-style Ibanez pickups, volume/treble/2 mid/bass/mix controls. Available in Oil and Transparent Purple finish. Mfd. 1993 to date.

Mfr.'s Sug. Retail	$1,600	$1,120	$960	$800	$640	$575	$530	$480

SR2005 — similar to SR2000, except has 5 strings, 3/2 per side tuners, 2 J-style pickups.

Mfr.'s Sug. Retail	$1,900	$1,330	$1,140	$950	$760	$685	$625	$570

Ibanez , cont.

Grading	100%	98%	95%	90%	80%	70%	60%

TR Bass Series

TRB1 — offset double cutaway alder body, bolt-on maple neck, 22 fret rosewood fingerboard with pearl dot inlay, die cast fixed bridge, 4 on one side tuners, black hardware, P-style/J-style pickups, 2 volume/1 tone controls. Available in Black, Candy Apple, Jewel Blue and Transparent Blue finish. Mfd. 1991 to date.

Mfr.'s Sug. Retail	$430	$300	$260	$215	$175	$155	$140	$130

Add $50 for left handed version (TRB1L). Available in Black finish only.

TRB2 — similar to TRB1, except has ash body, gold hardware. Available in Lavender Stain and Walnut Stain finish. Mfd. 1993 to date.

Mfr.'s Sug. Retail	$530	$370	$320	$265	$210	$190	$175	$160

TRB3 — similar to TRB1, except has basswood body, P-style/J-style Ibanez pickups, 2 volume/tone controls. Available in Black, Blue and Lipstick Red finish. Mfd. 1992 only.

		$455	$390	$325	$260	$235	$215	$195

Last Mfr.'s Sug. Retail was $650.

TRB15 — similar to TRB1, except has 5 strings, 4/1 per side tuners, 2 J- style pickups. Available in Black and Transparent Red finish. Mfd. 1993 to date.

Mfr.'s Sug. Retail	$530	$370	$320	$265	$210	$190	$175	$160

USA Custom American Master Bass Series

MAB4FM — offset double cutaway mahogany body, figured maple top, maple/purple heart 3 piece thru body neck, 24 fret rosewood fingerboard with pearl dot inlay, Wilkinson fixed bridge, 2 per side tuners, black hardware, P-style/J-style EMG pickups, 2 volume/tone controls. Available in Natural finish. Disc. 1992.

		$1,820	$1,560	$1,300	$1,040	$935	$860	$780

Last Mfr.'s Sug. Retail was $2,600.

MAB5BE — similar to MAB4FM, except has birdseye maple top and 5 strings.

		$1,960	$1,680	$1,400	$1,120	$1,010	$925	$840

Last Mfr.'s Sug. Retail was $2,800.

J

J.B. PLAYER

Various manufacturers worldwide are contracted by J.B. Player International, a division of MBT Distribution, Inc., located in Charleston, SC, to produce this trademark.

J.B.Player®

ACOUSTIC

Grading	100%	98%	95%	90%	80%	70%	60%

JB-402 — dreadnought style, spruce top, round soundhole, black pickguard, bound body, 5 stripe rosette, nato back/sides/neck, 14/20 fret bound rosewood fingerboard with pearl dot inlay, rosewood bridge with white black dot pins, 3 per side chrome die cast tuners. Available in Natural finish. Curr. mfr.

Mfr.'s Sug. Retail	$225	$160	$135	$115	$90	$80	$70	$65

JB-403 — similar to JB-402, except has different binding color.

Mfr.'s Sug. Retail	$250	$175	$150	$125	$100	$90	$80	$75

JB-405-12 — dreadnought style 12 string, spruce top, round soundhole, black pickguard, stripe bound body/rosette, ash back/sides, bound mahogany neck, 14/20 fret bound rosewood fingerboard with pearl dot inlay, rosewood bridge with white black dot pins, 6 per side chrome die cast tuners. Available in Natural finish. Curr. mfr.

Mfr.'s Sug. Retail	$255	$180	$155	$130	$100	$90	$80	$75

JB-407 — dreadnought style, ash top, round soundhole, black pickguard, bound body, 5 stripe rosette, ash back/sides, mahogany neck, 14/20 fret bound fingerboard with pearl dot inlay, rosewood bridge with white black dot pins, 3 per side chrome die cast tuners. Available in Tobacco Sunburst finish. Curr. mfr.

Mfr.'s Sug. Retail	$290	$205	$175	$145	$115	$105	$95	$85

 Add \$55 for acoustic pickup, volume/3 band EQ and active electronics (JB-407E).

JB-450 — dreadnought style, spruce top, round soundhole, black pickguard, imitation abalone bound body/rosette, ash back/sides, mahogany neck, 14/20 fret bound rosewood fingerboard with hexagon imitation abalone inlay, rosewood bridge with white black dot pins, 3 per side chrome die cast tuners. Available in Natural finish. Curr. mfr.

Mfr.'s Sug. Retail	$295	$205	$175	$145	$115	$105	$95	$85

Grading	100%	98%	95%	90%	80%	70%	60%

JB-505 — classical style, spruce top, round soundhole, herringbone bound body, wooden inlay rosette, ash back/sides, mahogany neck, 12/18 fret rosewood fingerboard, rosewood bridge, 3 per side chrome tuners with nylon buttons. Available in Natural finish. Curr. mfr.

Mfr.'s Sug. Retail	$260	$180	$155	$130	$100	$90	$80	$75

JB-1000 — dreadnought style, spruce top, oval soundhole, black pickguard, 3 stripe bound body/rosette, mahogany back/sides/neck, 14/20 fret bound rosewood fingerboard with pearl dot inlay, rosewood bridge with white black dot pins, 3 per side chrome tuners. Available in Black and White finish. Curr. mfr.

Mfr.'s Sug. Retail	$325	$225	$195	$160	$130	$115	$105	$95

Add $70 for flame maple top and jacaranda back/sides. Available in Natural finish.

The White finish model has black chrome tuners.

JB-5000 — classical style, spruce top, round soundhole, bound body, wooden inlay rosette, mahogany back/sides/neck, 12/18 fret rosewood fingerboard, rosewood bridge, 3 per side gold tuners with pearloid buttons. Available in Natural finish. Curr. mfr.

Mfr.'s Sug. Retail	$350	$245	$210	$175	$140	$125	$115	$105

JB-8000 — dreadnought style, spruce top, round soundhole, black pickguard, bound body, 5 stripe rosette, rosewood back/sides, mahogany neck, 14/20 fret rosewood fingerboard with pearl dot inlay, rosewood bridge with white black dot pins, 3 per side chrome tuners. Available in Natural finish. Curr. mfr.

Mfr.'s Sug. Retail	$425	$295	$250	$210	$170	$150	$135	$125

JB-9000 — dreadnought style, spruce top, round soundhole, black pickguard, bound body, 5 stripe rosette, mahogany back/sides/neck, 14/20 fret rosewood fingerboard with pearl dot inlay, rosewood bridge with white black dot pins, 3 per side chrome tuners. Available in Tobacco Sunburst finish. Curr. mfr.

Mfr.'s Sug. Retail	$395	$275	$235	$195	$155	$140	$125	$115

JB-9000-12 — similar to JB-9000, except has 12 strings, black white dot pins, 6 per side tuners. Available in Natural finish.

Mfr.'s Sug. Retail	$410	$285	$245	$205	$165	$145	$135	$125

KMD-905PU — single venetian cutaway dreadnought style, spruce top, round soundhole, 3 stripe bound body/rosette, mahogany back/sides/neck, 20 fret rosewood fingerboard with pearl dot inlay, rosewood bridge with white black dot pins, 3 per side chrome tuners, acoustic pickup, volume/3 band EQ, active electronics. Available in Tobacco Sunburst finish. Curr. mfr.

Mfr.'s Sug. Retail	$495	$345	$295	$245	$195	$175	$160	$150

Grading	100%	98%	95%	90%	80%	70%	60%

ACOUSTIC ELECTRIC

JB-400AM — les paul style semi hollow style, bound flame maple top, bound fang style soundhole, mahogany back/sides/neck, 22 fret bound ebonized rosewood fingerboard with pearl dot inlay, tunomatic bridge/stop tailpiece, bound peghead, 3 per side tuners, gold hardware, 2 humbucker pickups, volume/tone control, 3 position switch. Available in Natural finish. Curr. mfr.

Mfr.'s Sug. Retail	$1,900	$1,330	$1,140	$950	$760	$685	$625	$570

JB-AL — strat style semi hollow body, black bound maple top, fang style soundhole, basswood back/sides, bolt-on maple neck, 24 fret rosewood fingerboard with pearl dot inlay, tunomatic bridge/stop tailpiece, 3 per side tuners, gold hardware, single coil/humbucker pickup, volume/tone control, 3 position switch. Available in White finish. Curr. mfr.

Mfr.'s Sug. Retail	$1,475	$1,035	$885	$735	$590	$525	$480	$440

KJ-609WPU — single venetian cutaway jumbo style, spruce top, round soundhole, bound body, pearl inlay rosette, birdseye maple back/sides/neck, 21 fret rosewood fingerboard with pearl dot inlay, stylized pearl inlay at 12th fret, rosewood bridge with white black dot pins, 3 per side chrome tuners, acoustic pickup, volume/3 band EQ, active electronics. Available in Natural and Transparent Antique Brown finish. Curr. mfr.

Mfr.'s Sug. Retail	$560	$390	$335	$280	$225	$205	$190	$170

⚡ **KJ-705WPU** — similar to KJ-609WPU, except has mahogany back/sides/neck, 6 on one side tuners. Available in Black and White finish.

Mfr.'s Sug. Retail	$525	$370	$315	$260	$210	$190	$170	$160

ELECTRIC

PG111 — strat style hardwood body, black pickguard, bolt-on maple neck, 22 fret rosewood fingerboard with pearl dot inlay, double locking vibrato, 6 on one side tuners, black hardware, 2 single coil/1 humbucker pickups, volume/2 tone controls, 5 position switch. Available in Black Pearl, Red Pearl and White Pearl finish. Curr. mfr.

Mfr.'s Sug. Retail	$500	$350	$300	$250	$200	$180	$165	$150

⚡ **PG121** — similar to PG111, except has no pickguard, volume/tone control, 3 mini switches instead of 5 position switch, coil split in tone control. Available in Black Pearl, Black/White Crackle, Fluorescent Pink, Fluorescent Yellow, Red/White Crackle and White Pearl finish. Curr. mfr.

Mfr.'s Sug. Retail	$600	$420	$360	$300	$240	$215	$195	$180

Grading	100%	98%	95%	90%	80%	70%	60%

PGP111 — similar to PG 111, except has neck thru construct, maple body/neck, EMG pickups. Available in Black, Black/White Crackle, Fluorescent Yellow, Red, Red/White Crackle, Red/Yellow Crackle, White and White Pearl finish. Curr. mfr.

Mfr.'s Sug. Retail	$550	$385	$330	$275	$220	$200	$180	$165

Add $100 for wireless system with mini switch and LED (PVW111).

⚟ **PGP120** — sharkfin style maple body, maple neck, 22 fret rosewood fingerboard with pearl triangle inlay, double locking vibrato, 6 on one side tuners, black hardware, 2 single coil/1 humbucker EMG pickups, volume/tone control, 5 position switch. Available in Black, Black Pearl and Black/White Crackle finish. Curr. mfr.

Mfr.'s Sug. Retail	$800	$560	$480	$400	$320	$290	$265	$240

⚟ **PGP121** — similar to PG 121, except has neck thru construct, maple body/neck, EMG pickups. Available in Black, Black Pearl, Fluorescent Pink, Fluorescent Pink/Blue Crackle, Fluorescent Yellow Crackle, Ultra Violet and White Pearl finish. Curr. mfr.

Mfr.'s Sug. Retail	$650	$455	$390	$325	$260	$235	$215	$195

Add $25 for wireless system with mini switch and LED (PVW121).

SHG111 — strat style hardwood body, white pickguard, bolt-on maple neck, 22 fret maple fingerboard with black dot inlay, standard vibrato, 6 on one side tuners, chrome hardware, 3 single coil pickups, volume/2 tone controls, 5 position switch. Available in Black, Gun Metal Grey, Pink, Phantom Blue, Red, Red/White Crackle, Terminator Red, Ultra Violet, White, 2 Tone Sunburst and 3 Tone Sunburst finish. Curr. mfr.

Mfr.'s Sug. Retail	$360	$250	$215	$180	$145	$130	$120	$110

This model also available with rosewood fingerboard with pearl dot inlay.

⚟ **SHG112-2S** — tele style hardwood body, black pickguard, bolt-on maple neck, 22 fret maple fingerboard with black dot inlay, fixed bridge, 6 on one side tuners, chrome hardware, 2 single coil pickups, 3 position switch. Available in Aged Blonde and Black finish. Curr. mfr.

Mfr.'s Sug. Retail	$400	$280	$240	$200	$160	$145	$130	$120

Add $30 for 2 single coil/1 humbucker pickup (SHG112-HSS).

ELECTRIC BASS

PGP113 — precision style maple body, black pickguard, bolt-on maple neck, 20 fret rosewood fingerboard with pearl dot inlay, fixed bridge, 4 on one side tuners, black hardware, P-style/J-style EMG pickups, volume/tone control, 3 position switch. Available in Black, Black Pearl, Red, Red Pearl and White Pearl finish. Curr. mfr.

Mfr.'s Sug. Retail	$425	$295	$250	$210	$170	$150	$135	$125

SHB113 — precision style hardwood body, black pickguard, bolt-on maple neck, 20 fret rosewood fingerboard with pearl dot inlay, fixed bridge, black hardware, P-style pickup, volume/tone control. Available in Black, Red and White finish. Curr. mfr.

Mfr.'s Sug. Retail	$400	$280	$240	$200	$160	$145	$130	$120

JACKSON

Manufactured and distributed by Jackson/Charvel Guitar Company located in Fort Worth, TX since 1980.

What began as the custom shop for the Jackson/Charvel Guitar Company has since developed into a complete line of instruments with original custom options as standard features. These instruments have the same level of craftsmanship and quality as if they were actual custom shop orders.

Grading	100%	98%	95%	90%	80%	70%	60%

ELECTRIC

Player's Choice Series

This new series was released in 1993 and incorporates many of the most requested options from the Jackson Custom Shop. Standardization has yielded lower prices.

EXOTIC DINKY — strat style koa body, bound quilted maple top, bolt-on maple neck, 24 fret bound pao ferro fingerboard with offset pearl dot inlay, double locking vibrato, bound peghead with pearl logo inlay, 6 on one side tuners, gold hardware, 2 stacked coil/1 humbucker Seymour Duncan pickups, volume/tone control, 5 position switch. Available in Tobacco Sunburst, Transparent Blue, Transparent Purple and Transparent Red finish. New 1993.

Mfr.'s Sug. Retail	$2,400	$1,680	$1,440	$1,200	$960	$860	$790	$720

Flamed Dinky — similar to Exotic Dinky, except has flame maple body, bound ebony fingerboard with pearl sharkfin inlay, black hardware, Jackson pickups. Available in Transparent Black, Transparent Blue and Transparent Purple finish. New 1993.

Mfr.'s Sug. Retail	$2,200	$1,540	$1,320	$1,100	$880	$790	$725	$660

KING V — V style poplar body, thru body maple neck, 22 fret bound ebony fingerboard with pearl sharkfin inlay, fixed locking bridge, bound peghead with pearl logo inlay, 6 on one side tuners, black hardware, 2 volume/1 tone controls, 5 position switch with opposite switching. Available in Black finish. New 1993.

Mfr.'s Sug. Retail	$2,200	$1,540	$1,320	$1,100	$880	$790	$725	$660

Grading	100%	98%	95%	90%	80%	70%	60%

ORIGINAL RHOADS — sharkfin style poplar body, gold pickguard, thru body maple neck, 22 fret bound ebony fingerboard with pearl sharkfin inlay, tunomatic bridge, strings thru tailpiece with gold V plate, 2 humbucker Seymour Duncan pickups, 2 volume/1 tone controls, 3 position switch. Available in Black finish. New 1993.

Mfr.'s Sug. Retail	$2,500	$1,750	$1,500	$1,250	$1,000	$900	$825	$750

PHIL COLLEN — offset double cutaway maple body, thru body maple neck, 24 fret bound ebony fingerboard with pearl sharkfin inlay, double locking vibrato, bound peghead with pearl Jackson logo inlay, 6 on one side Gotoh tuners, black hardware, single coil/ humbucker Jackson pickups, volume control, 3-position switch. Available in Metallic Black and Pearl White finish. New 1993.

Mfr.'s Sug. Retail	$2,300	$1,610	$1,380	$1,150	$920	$830	$760	$690

RHOADS 10 STRING — sharkfin style quilted maple body, thru body maple, 22 fret bound ebony fingerboard with pearl sharkfin inlay, double locking vibrato, bound peghead with pearl Jackson inlay, double R truss rod cover, 6 on one side tuners, 4 tuners located on bridge end of instrument, gold hardware, volume control, 3 position switch. Available in Transparent Black finish. New 1993.

Mfr.'s Sug. Retail	$2,500	$1,750	$1,500	$1,250	$1,000	$900	$825	$750

Co-designed by Dan Spitz.

Professional Series

DINKY EX — strat style basswood body, black pickguard, bolt-on maple neck, 22 fret rosewood fingerboard with pearl dot inlay, double locking vibrato, 6 on one side tuners, black hardware, humbucker/single coil/humbucker Jackson pickups, volume/tone control, 5 position switch. Available in Black, Deep Metallic Blue, Deep Metallic Red and Snow White finish. New 1993.

Mfr.'s Sug. Retail	$795	$555	$475	$395	$315	$280	$260	$235

Dinky Reverse — strat style basswood body, bolt-on maple neck, 24 fret maple fingerboard with offset black dot inlay, reverse headstock, double locking vibrato, 6 on one side tuners, black hardware, 2 humbucker Jackson pickups, volume/tone control, 3-position switch. Available in Black, Candy Blue, Metallic Violet and Stone finish. Mfd. 1992 to date.

Mfr.'s Sug. Retail	$795	$555	$475	$395	$315	$280	$260	$235

This model also available with rosewood fingerboard with pearl dot inlay.

Grading	100%	98%	95%	90%	80%	70%	60%

◁ **Dinky Std** — strat style basswood body, transparent pickguard, bolt-on maple neck, 24 fret rosewood fingerboard with colored dot inlay, double locking vibrato, 6 on one side tuners, black hardware, 2 stacked coil/1 humbucker Jackson pickups, volume/tone control, 5-position switch. Available in Black, Candy Blue, Dark Metallic Red and Snow White finish. Mfd. 1991 to date.

Mfr.'s Sug. Retail	$895	$625	$535	$445	$360	$325	$300	$275

◁ **Dinky XL** — similar to Dinky Standard, except has no pickguard, bound fingerboard with pearl sharkfin inlay. Available in Deep Metallic Blue, Metallic Black and Pearl White finish. Mfd. 1992 to date.

Mfr.'s Sug. Retail	$995	$695	$595	$500	$400	$360	$330	$300

◁ **Dinky XL (Trans)** — similar to Dinky XL, except has flame maple top. Available in Cherry Sunburst, Transparent Blue, Transparent Red and Transparent Violet finish.

Mfr.'s Sug. Retail	$1,095	$765	$655	$545	$435	$395	$360	$330

FUSION EX — strat style basswood body, black pickguard, bolt-on maple neck, 24 fret rosewood fingerboard with offset white dot inlay, double locking vibrato, 6 on one side tuners, black hardware, 2 single coil/1 humbucker Jackson pickups, volume/tone control, 5-position switch. Available in Black, Deep Metallic Blue, Dark Metallic Red and Snow White finish. Mfd. 1992 to date.

Mfr.'s Sug. Retail	$695	$485	$415	$350	$280	$250	$230	$210

◁ **Fusion HH** — strat style basswood body, bolt-on maple neck, 24 fret bound rosewood fingerboard with offset pearl dot inlay, double locking vibrato, 6 on one side tuners, black hardware, 2 humbucker Jackson pickups, 3-position switch. Available in Black finish. Mfd. 1992 to date.

Mfr.'s Sug. Retail	$895	$625	$535	$445	$360	$325	$300	$275

This model also available with mahogany body in Transparent Red finish.

FUSION PRO — strat style basswood body, bolt-on maple neck, 24 fret bound ebony fingerboard with pearl sharkfin inlay, double locking vibrato, bound peghead with pearl Jackson logo inlay, 6 on one side tuners, black hardware, 2 stacked coil/1 humbucker Jackson pickups, volume/tone control, 5-position and bypass switches, active electronics. Available in Bright Red, Candy Blue, Metallic Black and Pearl White finish. Mfd. 1992 to date.

Mfr.'s Sug. Retail	$1,295	$905	$775	$645	$515	$465	$425	$385

◁ **Fusion Pro (Trans)** — similar to Fusion Pro, except has flame maple top. Available in Cherry Sunburst, Transparent Amber, Transparent Blue and Transparent Red finish.

Mfr.'s Sug. Retail	$1,395	$975	$835	$700	$560	$505	$460	$420

FUSION STANDARD — similar to Fusion Pro, except has unbound rosewood fingerboard with offset pearl dot inlay and no active electronics. Available in Black, Candy Blue, Dark Metallic Red and Snow White finish. Mfd. 1992 to date.

Mfr.'s Sug. Retail	$795	$555	$475	$395	$315	$280	$260	$235

Grading	100%	98%	95%	90%	80%	70%	60%

FUSION XL — similar to Fusion Pro, except has no active electronics. Available in Deep Metallic Blue, Dark Metallic Red, Metallic Black and Snow White finish. Mfd. 1992 to date.

Mfr.'s Sug. Retail	$995	$695	$595	$500	$400	$360	$330	$300

⚐ **Fusion XL (Trans)** — similar to Fusion Pro (Trans), except has no active electronics. Available in Cherry Sunburst, Transparent Blue, Transparent Red and Transparent Violet finish. Mfd. 1992 to date.

Mfr.'s Sug. Retail	$1,095	$765	$655	$545	$435	$395	$360	$330

INFINITY PRO — double cutaway asymmetrical mahogany body, bound figured maple top, set in mahogany neck, 22 fret bound rosewood fingerboard with pearl diamond/abalone dot inlay, double locking vibrato, bound peghead with pearl Jackson logo inlay, 6 on one side tuners, chrome hardware, 2 humbucker Jackson pickups, volume/tone control, 3-position switch. Available in Cherry Sunburst, Star Glo, Transparent Blue, Transparent Red and Transparent Violet finish. Mfd. 1992 to date.

Mfr.'s Sug. Retail	$1,495	$1,045	$895	$750	$600	$540	$495	$450

⚐ **Infinity XL** — double cutaway asymmetrical bound basswood body, bolt-on maple neck, 22 fret rosewood fingerboard with abalone dot inlay, double locking vibrato, 6 on one side tuners, black hardware, 2 humbucker Jackson pickups, volume/tone control, 3-position switch. Available in Black, Deep Metallic Blue, Dark Metallic Red and Magenta finish. Mfd. 1992 to date.

Mfr.'s Sug. Retail	$995	$695	$595	$500	$400	$360	$330	$300

JTX — tele style basswood body, pearloid pickguard, bolt-on maple neck, 24 fret maple fingerboard with black dot inlay, double locking Floyd Rose vibrato, 6 on one side tuners, chrome hardware, single coil/humbucker Jackson pickup, volume control, 3 position/mini switches. Available in Black, Deep Metallic Blue, Deep Metallic Red and Magenta finish. New 1993.

Mfr.'s Sug. Retail	$595	$415	$360	$300	$240	$215	$195	$180

⚐ **JTX (Trans)** — similar to JTX, except has ash body. Available in Transparent Black, Transparent Blue, Transparent Pearl Purple and Transparent Red finish.

Mfr.'s Sug. Retail	$645	$450	$385	$320	$260	$235	$215	$195

KING V PRO-MUSTAINE — V style poplar body, thru body maple neck, 24 fret bound ebony fingerboard with pearl sharkfin inlay, fixed locking Kahler bridge, bound peghead, 6 on one side tuners, black hardware, 2 humbucker pickups, 2 volume/1 tone controls, 3 position switch. Available in Black and Sparkle Silver finish. New 1993.

Mfr.'s Sug. Retail	$1,495	$1,045	$895	$750	$600	$540	$495	$450

Grading	100%	98%	95%	90%	80%	70%	60%

King V Std — V style poplar body, bolt-on maple neck, 22 fret rosewood fingerboard with pearl dot inlay, double locking Floyd Rose vibrato, 2 humbucker Jackson pickups, volume control, 3 position switch. Available in Black, Bright Red, Candy Blue and Snow White finish. New 1993.

Mfr.'s Sug. Retail	$745	$520	$445	$370	$300	$270	$245	$225

KELLY STD — radical explorer style poplar body, bolt-on maple neck, 24 fret rosewood fingerboard with pearl dot inlay, double locking Floyd Rose vibrato, 6 on one side tuners, black hardware, 2 humbucker Jackson pickups, volume control, 3 position switch. Available in Black, Deep Metallic Blue, Deep Metallic Red and Deep Metallic Violet finish. New 1993.

Mfr.'s Sug. Retail	$795	$555	$475	$395	$315	$280	$260	$235

PHIL COLLEN — unbalanced double cutaway poplar body, thru body maple neck, 24 fret bound ebony fingerboard with pearl sharkfin inlay, double locking vibrato, bound peghead with pearl Jackson logo inlay, 6 on one side Gotoh tuners, black hardware, single coil/ humbucker Jackson pickups, volume control, 3-position switch. Available in Metallic Black, Pearl White and Radiant Red Pearl finish. Mfd. 1991 only.

	$1,185	$1,015	$845	$675	$605	$555	$505

Last Mfr.'s Sug. Retail was $1,695.

RANDY RHOADS LIMITED EDITION — sharkfin style maple body, thru body maple neck, 22 fret bound ebony fingerboard with pearl block inlay, standard vibrato, bound peghead, truss rod cover with overlapping RR stamped into it, 6 on one side tuners, gold hardware, 2 humbucker Jackson pickups, 2 volume/tone controls, 3-position switch located on top side of body. Available in White finish with Black pinstriping around body edge. Mfd. 1992 only.

	$1,745	$1,495	$1,250	$1,000	$900	$825	$750

Add $100 for double locking vibrato.

This is a reproduction of the original series that was co-designed by Randy Rhoads. 200 reproductions were mfd.

Last Mfr.'s Sug. Retail was $2,495.

RHOADS EX — sharkfin style poplar body, thru body maple neck, 22 fret rosewood fingerboard with pearl dot inlay, double locking vibrato, 6 on one side tuners, black hardware, 2 humbucker Jackson pickups, volume control, 3-position switch. Available in Black, Bright Red, Candy Blue and Stone finish. Mfd. 1992 to date.

Mfr.'s Sug. Retail	$695	$485	$415	$350	$280	$250	$230	$210

Grading	100%	98%	95%	90%	80%	70%	60%

Rhoads Pro — similar to Rhoads EX except has black pickguard, bound ebony fingerboard with pearl sharkfin inlay, bound peghead with pearl Jackson logo inlay, volume/tone and mid controls, active electronics. Available in Black, Deep Metallic Blue and Snow White finish. Mfd. 1987 to date.

Mfr.'s Sug. Retail	$1,495	$1,045	$895	$750	$600	$540	$495	$450

Rhoads Std — similar to Rhoads Pro, except has dot fingerboard inlay and no fingerboard/peghead binding. New 1993.

Mfr.'s Sug. Retail	$995	$695	$595	$500	$400	$360	$330	$300

SOLOIST ARCHTOP
— strat style mahogany body, arched flame maple top, thru body maple neck, 24 fret bound ebony fingerboard with pearl sharkfin inlay, tunomatic bridge with thru body string holders, bound peghead with pearl Jackson logo inlay, 6 on one side Gotoh tuners, black hardware, 2 humbucker Jackson pickups, volume/tone control, 3-position switch. Available in Cherry Sunburst, Transparent Amber, Transparent Blue and Transparent Red finish. Mfd. 1991 only.

	$1,045	$895	$750	$600	$540	$495	$450

Add $200 for double locking vibrato.
Last Mfr.'s Sug. Retail was $1,495.

Soloist Pro — strat style poplar body, thru body maple neck, 24 fret bound ebony fingerboard with pearl sharkfin inlay, double locking vibrato, bound peghead with pearl Jackson logo inlay, 6 on one side tuners, black hardware, 2 stacked coil/1 humbucker Jackson pickups, volume/tone/mid boost controls, 5 position switch, active electronics. Available in Bright Red, Deep Metallic Blue, Metallic Blue and Pearl White finish. Mfd. 1991 to date.

Mfr.'s Sug. Retail	$1,495	$1,045	$895	$750	$600	$540	$495	$450

Soloist STD — similar to Soloist Pro, except has dot fingerboard inlay and no fingerboard/peghead inlay or mid boost control. New 1993.

Mfr.'s Sug. Retail	$995	$695	$595	$500	$400	$360	$330	$300

Soloist XL — similar to Soloist Pro, except has rosewood fingerboard and no active electronics. Available in Deep Metallic Blue, Dark Metallic Red, Metallic Black and Pearl White finish.

Mfr.'s Sug. Retail	$1,295	$905	$775	$645	$515	$465	$425	$385

STEALTH EX
— strat style basswood body, bolt-on maple neck, 22 fret rosewood fingerboard with offset pearl dot inlay, double locking vibrato, 6 on one side tuners, black hardware, 2 single coil/1 humbucker Jackson pickups, volume/tone control, 5-position switch. Available in Black, Deep Metallic Blue, Dark Metallic Red and Stone finish. Mfd. 1991 to date.

Mfr.'s Sug. Retail	$695	$485	$415	$350	$280	$250	$230	$210

Add $100 for left version of this model.

Grading	100%	98%	95%	90%	80%	70%	60%

Stealth HX — similar to Stealth EX, except has tunomatic bridge, thru body ring and ball holder tailpiece, 3 humbucker Jackson pickups. Available in Black, Deep Metallic Blue, Deep Metallic Red and Deep Metallic Violet finish. New 1993.

Mfr.'s Sug. Retail	$595	$415	$360	$300	$240	$215	$195	$180

STEALTH PRO — similar to Stealth EX, except has ebony fingerboard and pearl Jackson logo peghead inlay. Available in Metallic Blue finish.

Mfr.'s Sug. Retail	$1,195	$835	$715	$600	$480	$430	$395	$360

Stealth Pro (Trans) — similar to Stealth Pro, except has ash body and body matching headstock without pearl inlay. Available in Transparent Amber finish.

Mfr.'s Sug. Retail	$1,295	$905	$775	$645	$515	$465	$425	$385

> This model is available with figured maple top in Transparent Blue and Transparent Violet finish.

STEALTH XL — similar to Stealth EX, except has ash body. Available in Transparent Amber, Transparent Blue, Transparent Red and Transparent Violet finish.

Mfr.'s Sug. Retail	$895	$625	$535	$445	$360	$325	$300	$275

WARRIOR PRO — radically X-shaped offset poplar body, thru body maple neck, 24 fret bound ebony fingerboard with pearl sharkfin inlay, double locking vibrato, bound peghead with pearl Jackson logo inlay, 6 on one side Gotoh tuners, black hardware, 3 single coil Jackson pickups, volume/tone control, 5-position and mid-range sweep switches. Available in Candy Blue, Ferrari Red, Midnight Black, Pearl Yellow and Snow White Pearl finish. Mfd. 1991 only.

	$1,185	$1,015	$845	$675	$605	$555	$505

Last Mfr.'s Sug. Retail was $1,695.

Jackson U.S.A. Series

The standard features on these models are the same as those in the Professional Series, with the addition of custom graphic finishes. The models in this series are the Dinky, Fusion, Rhoads, Soloist and Warrior, and prices usually are an additional $300-$500 over those listed on the corresponding models in the Professional Series.

Grading	100%	98%	95%	90%	80%	70%	60%

ELECTRIC BASS

Professional Series

CONCERT EX — precision style poplar body, bolt-on maple neck, 22 fret rosewood fingerboard with white dot inlay, fixed bridge, 4 on one side tuners, black hardware, Jackson P-style/J-style pickups, volume/tone/mix control. Available in Black, Bright Red, Candy Blue, Snow White and Stone finish. Mfd. 1992 to date.

Mfr.'s Sug. Retail	$595	$415	$360	$300	$240	$215	$195	$180

CONCERT XL — similar to Concert EX, except has bound fingerboard with pearl sharkfin inlay. Available in Deep Metallic Blue, Dark Metallic Red, Metallic Black and Pearl White finish. Mfd. 1992 to date.

Mfr.'s Sug. Retail	$895	$625	$535	$445	$360	$325	$300	$275

⅜ **Concert V** — similar to Concert XL, except has 5 strings, Kramer fixed bridge, volume/treble/bass and mix controls, active electronics.

Mfr.'s Sug. Retail	$995	$695	$595	$500	$400	$360	$330	$300

FUTURA EX (formerly the WINGER BASS) — double cutaway asymmetrical off-set poplar body, bolt-on maple neck, 22 fret rosewood fingerboard with pearl dot inlay, fixed bridge, 4 on one side tuners, black hardware, P-style/J-style Jackson pickups, volume/tone/mix control. Available in Black, Deep Metallic Blue, Magenta and Snow White finish. Mfd. 1992 to date.

Mfr.'s Sug. Retail	$795	$555	$475	$395	$315	$280	$260	$235

The Winger Bass was co-designed by Kip Winger.

FUTURA PRO (formerly the WINGER BASS) — double cutaway asymmetrical offset maple body, thru body maple neck, 21 fret ebony fingerboard with pearl dot inlay, Kahler fixed bridge, 4 on one side tuners, black hardware, 2 EMG pickups, volume/treble/bass/mix control, active electronics. Available in Candy Red, Metallic Black and Pearl White finish. Mfd. 1992 to date.

Mfr.'s Sug. Retail	$1,795	$1,255	$1,075	$895	$715	$645	$590	$540

⅜ **Futura Pro (Trans)** — similar to Futura Pro, except has lacewood body/neck and has body color matching bound peghead. Available in Carmel Lace, Cinnibar and Natural finish.

Mfr.'s Sug. Retail	$1,895	$1,325	$1,135	$950	$760	$685	$625	$570

⅜ **Futura XL** — similar to Futura Pro, except has Jackson fixed bridge and P-style/J-style pickups. Available in Dark Metallic Red, Metallic Black and Pearl White finish.

Mfr.'s Sug. Retail	$1,295	$905	$775	$645	$515	$465	$425	$385

Grading	100%	98%	95%	90%	80%	70%	60%

‡ **Futura XL (Trans)** — similar to Futura Pro (Trans), except has Jackson fixed bridge and P-style/J-style pickups.

Mfr.'s Sug. Retail	$1,395	$975	$835	$700	$560	$505	$460	$420

JERRY JONES

Manufactured and distributed by Jerry Jones Guitars, located in Nashville, TN, since 1981.

This company specializes in popular 1950s instrument/styling and component reproductions.

ELECTRIC

All instruments in this series are available in: Almond, Black, Copper, Red and Turquoise finish.

Add $50 for below models if with a Neptune bridge (fixed bridge with metal saddles).

BARITONE — single cutaway poplar body, transparent pickguard, bolt-on poplar neck, 23 fret rosewood fingerboard with pearl dot inlay, fixed bridge with rosewood saddle, 3 per side tuners, chrome hardware, 2 lipstick pickups, volume/tone control, 3 position switch. Curr. mfr.

Mfr.'s Sug. Retail	$795	$555	$475	$395	$315	$280	$260	$235

ELECTRIC SITAR — single cutaway poplar body, transparent pickguard, 13 sympathetic strings with own nut/bridge/lipstick pickup, bolt-on poplar neck, 21 fret rosewood fingerboard with white dot inlay, fixed buzz bridge/thru body tailpiece, 6 on one side tuners, chrome hardware, 2 lipstick pickups, 3 volume/tone controls. Curr. mfr.

Mfr.'s Sug. Retail	$1,195	$835	$715	$600	$480	$430	$395	$360

GUITARLIN — deep double cutaway poplar body with hollow sound channels, masonite top/back, transparent pickguard, bolt-on poplar neck, 31 fret rosewood fingerboard with white dot inlay, fixed bridge with rosewood saddle, 3 per side tuners, chrome hardware, 2 lipstick pickups, volume/tone control, 3 position switch. Curr. mfr.

Mfr.'s Sug. Retail	$795	$555	$475	$395	$315	$280	$260	$235

LONGHORN DOUBLENECK — similar to Guitarlin, except has 2 necks, 4 pickups and any combination of guitar/bass necks.

Mfr.'s Sug. Retail	$1,270	$890	$760	$635	$510	$460	$420	$380

Grading	100%	98%	95%	90%	80%	70%	60%

SHORTHORN — double cutaway poplar body, white pickguard, bolt-on poplar neck, 21 fret rosewood fingerboard with pearl dot inlay, fixed bridge with rosewood saddle, 3 per side tuners, chrome hardware, 3 lipstick pickups, volume/tone control, 5 position switch. Curr. mfr.

Mfr.'s Sug. Retail	$870	$610	$520	$435	$350	$315	$290	$265

SINGLE CUTAWAY — similar to Shorthorn, except has single rounded cutaway style body.

Mfr.'s Sug. Retail	$870	$610	$520	$435	$350	$315	$290	$265

TWELVE STRING — similar to Single Cutaway, except has 12 strings, fixed bridge with metal saddles, 6 per side tuners, 2 pickups. Curr. mfr.

Mfr.'s Sug. Retail	$895	$625	$535	$445	$360	$325	$300	$275

ELECTRIC BASS

LONGHORN 4 — double deep cutaway bound poplar body with hollow sound chambers, transparent pickguard, bolt-on poplar neck, 24 fret rosewood fingerboard with white dot inlay, fixed bridge with rosewood saddle, 2 per side tuners, chrome hardware, 2 lipstick pickups, volume/tone control, 3 position switch. Curr. mfr.

Mfr.'s Sug. Retail	$795	$555	$475	$395	$315	$280	$260	$235

Longhorn 6 — similar to Longhorn 4, except has 6 strings.

Mfr.'s Sug. Retail	$795	$555	$475	$395	$315	$280	$260	$235

SINGLE CUTAWAY 4 — similar to Longhorn 4, except has single cutaway style body. Disc. 1992.

	$415	$360	$300	$240	$215	$195	$180

Last Mfr.'s Sug. Retail was $595.

Single Cutaway 6 — similar to Longhorn 4, except has single cutaway style body, 6 strings. Disc. 1992.

	$415	$360	$300	$240	$215	$195	$180

Last Mfr.'s Sug. Retail was $595.
Add $50 for 5 pickups.

KALAMAZOO

As this edition goes to press, more research is being performed on this line of instruments. These guitars were manufactured at the Gibson factory in Kalamazoo, MI, hence the name. The Kalamazoo line was created during the Great Depression, approximately 1927, and were Gibson's lowest priced line of production instruments. Look for more information on these instruments in the second edition of the *Blue Book of Guitar Values*.

KAY

The Kay Musical Instrument Co. was founded in 1931 by Henry Kay Kuhrmeyer, who at that time was president of the Stromberg-Voisinet Co. The Stromberg-Voisinet Co. was established in the late 1800's, producing several different lines of instruments - the Kay-Kraft line of guitars being the most popular. Henry Kuhrmeyer decided to start a new company using that line as its basis and used the existing facilities at 316 Union Park Court in Chicago, IL, to manufacture and distribute the instruments. The company grew very rapidly with the guitar boom of the late 1950s-early 1960s, offering acoustic and electric guitars and basses with an initial price tag ranging from $24.50 to $400. With the waning of the guitar boom and the quality of Kay's instruments, the Kay trademark was eventually purchased by an importer of overseas produced instruments. While not extremely desirable from a quality-made-instruments viewpoint, these instruments are experiencing some collectability as a novelty item due to their quirky designs and features, with a few models reaching as high as $900-$1,000.

L

LADO

Manufacturer located in Scarborough, Ontario, Canada. Lado Musical, Inc. can be contacted for dealer information (see Trademark Index).

The Lado company was founded by Croatian luthier, Joe Kovacic, who arrived in North America in 1971. These instruments are crafted by hand.

ELECTRIC

Pro Series

Grading	100%	98%	95%	90%	80%	70%	60%

CLASSIC — strat style curly maple body, thru body maple neck, 24 fret maple fingerboard with black pearl dot inlay, double locking vibrato, 6 on one side Schaller tuners, black hardware, rail/humbucker Seymour Duncan pickups, volume/tone control, 3 position switch. Available in Cobalt Blue, Deep Purple, Oriental Blue, Red and Transparent Black finish. Curr. mfr.

Mfr.'s Sug. Retail	$1,995	$1,395	$1,195	$995	$795	$720	$660	$600

This model is also available with Bartolini, DiMarzio, EMG and LADO pickups.

GOLDEN WING — strat style curly maple body, maple body outline inlay, thru body maple neck, 24 fret ebony fingerboard with brass sharktooth inlay, double locking vibrato, bound reverse headstock, 6 on one side tuners, gold hardware, 2 humbucker Seymour Duncan pickups, volume/tone control, 3 position switch. Available in Cobalt Blue, Deep Purple, Oriental Blue, Red and Transparent Black finish. Curr. mfr.

Mfr.'s Sug. Retail	$2,595	$1,815	$1,555	$1,295	$1,035	$930	$855	$780

This model is also available with Bartolini, DiMarzio, EMG and LADO pickups.

ROCKER — similar to Classic, except has 7 piece maple/mahogany body/neck construct, 24 fret ebony fingerboard with pearl sharktooth inlay, 2 single coil/1 humbucker pickup.

Mfr.'s Sug. Retail	$2,495	$1,745	$1,495	$1,250	$1,000	$900	$825	$750

This model is also available with Bartolini, DiMarzio, EMG and LADO pickups.

Grading	100%	98%	95%	90%	80%	70%	60%

ELECTRIC BASS

Custom Series

STUDIO 604-P — offset double cutaway maple body, carved padauk top, thru body maple/padauk laminated neck, 24 fret ebony fingerboard with pearl dot inlay, fixed bridge, bone nut, padauk veneer on peghead, 2 per side Schaller tuners, black hardware, 2 Bartolini pickups, volume/balance/3 band EQ controls, active electronics. Available in Natural finish. Curr. mfr.

Mfr.'s Sug. Retail	$2,195	$1,540	$1,320	$1,100	$880	$790	$725	$660

Studio 605-B — similar to Studio 604-P, except has 5 strings, bubinga wood instead of padauk wood, abalone hexagon fingerboard inlay.

Mfr.'s Sug. Retail	$2,395	$1,675	$1,435	$1,195	$955	$855	$785	$715

Studio 606-Z — similar to Studio 604-P, except has 6 strings, zebra wood top, 7 piece maple/zebra/ebony neck, abalone hexagon fingerboard inlay.

Mfr.'s Sug. Retail	$2,595	$1,815	$1,555	$1,295	$1,035	$930	$855	$780

Legend Series

LEGEND 304 — offset double cutaway maple body, thru body maple/wenge neck, 24 fret ebony fingerboard with pearl dot inlay, fixed bridge, 2 per side Schaller tuners, black hardware, 2 EMG pickups, volume/treble/bass/balance controls. Available in Cobalt Blue, Deep Purple, Oriental Blue, Red and Transparent Black finish. Curr. mfr.

Mfr.'s Sug. Retail	$1,895	$1,325	$1,135	$950	$760	$685	$625	$570

This model is also available with Gotoh tuners and Bartolini pickups.

Legend 305 — similar to Legend 304, except has 5 strings.

Mfr.'s Sug. Retail	$2,195	$1,540	$1,320	$1,100	$880	$790	$725	$660

Legend 306 — similar to Legend 304, except has 6 strings.

Mfr.'s Sug. Retail	$2,395	$1,675	$1,435	$1,195	$955	$855	$785	$715

Medallion Series

MEDALLION 404 — offset double cutaway maple body, thru body maple neck, 22 fret ebony fingerboard with pearl dot inlay, fixed bridge, 2 per side Schaller or Gotoh tuners, chrome hardware, P-style/J-style EMG pickups, volume/tone/balance controls. Available in Cobalt Blue, Deep Purple, Oriental Blue, Red and Transparent Black finish. Curr. mfr.

Mfr.'s Sug. Retail	$1,895	$1,325	$1,135	$950	$760	$685	$625	$570

Add $300 for black hardware.

Grading	100%	98%	95%	90%	80%	70%	60%

Medallion 405 — similar to Medallion 404, except has 5 strings, brass diamond fingerboard inlay and 2 J-style pickups.

Mfr.'s Sug. Retail	$2,395	$1,675	$1,435	$1,195	$955	$855	$785	$715

Add $100 for gold hardware.

Signature Series

504 — offset double cutaway asymmetrical maple body, thru body 5 piece rosewood/maple neck, 24 fret ebony fingerboard with pearl dot inlay, fixed bridge, rosewood veneered peghead with pearl dove/logo inlay, 2 per side Schaller tuners, chrome hardware, P-style/J-style Bartolini pickups, volume/treble/bass/balance controls. Available in Cobalt Blue, Deep Purple, Oriental Blue, Red and Transparent Black finish. Curr. mfr.

Mfr.'s Sug. Retail	$2,095	$1,465	$1,255	$1,045	$840	$755	$685	$625

Add $400 for stylized pearl fingerboard inlay and black hardware.
Add $500 for stylized abalone fingerboard inlay and gold hardware.

Standard Series

204 — precision style ash body, thru body maple/ash neck, 22 fret maple fingerboard with black pearl inlay, fixed bridge, 4 on one side Schaller tuners, chrome hardware, P-style/J-style LADO pickups, volume/tone/balance controls. Available in Natural finish. Curr. mfr.

Mfr.'s Sug. Retail	$1,495	$1,045	$895	$750	$600	$540	$495	$450

Add $100 for ebony fingerboard with brass dot inlay.
Add $200 for ebony fingerboard with brass dot inlay and Transparent Black finish.
This model is also available with Bartolini pickups.

LADY LUCK INDUSTRIES, INC.

This company is an importer/exporter and distributor located in Cary, IL.

The instruments offered within this trademark are inexpensive replicas of Ovation acoustic, Les Paul, Paul Reed Smith, Stratocaster and Telecaster electric and Series 10 electric bass guitars whose values are mostly determined by their playability. Prices range from $100-$205.

LAG GUITARS

Handmade instruments from France. No distribution information is available at this time.

Grading		100%	98%	95%	90%	80%	70%	60%

All Lag models, guitars and basses, have several groups of standardized finishes. Refer to the following lists to determine color options.

Standard — Anthracite, Black, Electric Blue, Ferrari Red, Foam Green, Ivory, Salmon Pink and Vintage Yellow finish.

Classic — Cherry, Green, Light Blue, Purple, Sunburst and Tobacco finish.

DeLuxe — Aqua Blue, Black Shadow, Brandy Red, Emerald Green, Purple Haze and Sunburst finish.

Heavy Metal — Craqued Blue, Craqued Green, Craqued Red, Laser Blue, Laser Green, Laser Red, Panther, Smoke and Snake finish.

ELECTRIC

90 COLLECTION — offset double cutaway semi hollow mahogany body, arched curly maple top, bolt-on maple neck, 24 fret ebony fingerboard with offset abalone dot inlay, standard vibrato, roller nut , 3 per side locking Sperzel tuners, gold hardware, 2 humbucker Seymour Duncan pickups, volume/tone/EQ control, 3 position switch, coil split in controls, active electronics. Available in Classic, DeLuxe, and Standard finish. Curr. mfr.

Mfr.'s Sug. Retail	$1,885	$1,325	$1,135	$945	$755	$680	$620	$565

Soundholes and body binding are optional.

CUSTOM — strat style alder body, curly maple top, transparent pickguard, bolt-on maple neck, 24 fret maple fingerboard with offset abalone inlay, double locking vibrato, reverse headstock, 6 on one side tuners, black hardware, 2 single coil/1 humbucker Seymour Duncan pickups, volume/tone/EQ control, 5 position switch, coil split in volume control, active electronics. Available in Classic, DeLuxe, Heavy Metal and Standard finish. Curr. mfr.

Mfr.'s Sug. Retail	$1,800	$1,260	$1,080	$900	$720	$650	$595	$540

This model is also available with birdseye neck, strat style headstock and humbucker/single coil/humbucker pickups.

Rockline Series

This series is available with reverse headstock.

RME — strat style alder body, bolt-on maple neck, 24 fret rosewood fingerboard with offset abalone dot inlay, double locking vibrato, 6 on one side tuners, black hardware, single coil/trembucker Seymour Duncan pickups, volume control, 3 position switch. Available in Classic, DeLuxe, Heavy Metal and Standard finish. Curr. mfr.

Mfr.'s Sug. Retail	$1,605	$1,125	$965	$805	$645	$575	$530	$480

RMV — similar to RME, except has 2 single coil/1 trembucker pickups, tone control, 5 position switch.

Mfr.'s Sug. Retail	$1,715	$1,205	$1,030	$860	$685	$615	$565	$515

Grading	100%	98%	95%	90%	80%	70%	60%

VRL — sharkfin style alder body, bolt-on maple neck, 24 fret rosewood fingerboard with offset abalone dot inlay, double locking vibrato, 6 on one side tuners, black hardware, humbucker Seymour Duncan pickup, volume control. Available in Heavy Metal and Standard finish. Curr. mfr.

Mfr.'s Sug. Retail	$1,800	$1,260	$1,080	$900	$720	$650	$595	$540

This model also available with trembucker pickup.

ELECTRIC BASS

The Natural finish models have a walnut, wenge or bubinga body.
Add $390 for 5 string version.
Add $510 for 6 string version.

90 Bass Collection

BC90 — precision style walnut body, bolt-on maple neck, 24 fret rosewood fingerboard with offset abalone dot inlay, tunomatic bridge/stop tailpiece, 2 per side tuners, black hardware, 2 J-style Bartolini pickups, 2 volume/tone/EQ controls, active electronics. Available in DeLuxe, Natural and Standard finish. Curr. mfr.

Mfr.'s Sug. Retail	$1,650	$1,155	$990	$825	$660	$595	$545	$495

BC90 THL — precision style semi hollow alder body, figured maple top, bolt on maple neck, 24 fret ebony fingerboard with offset abalone dot inlay, tunomatic bridge/stop tailpiece, 2 per side tuners, gold hardware, 2 J-style Bartolini pickups, 2 volume/tone/EQ controls, active electronics. Available in DeLuxe, Natural and Standard finish. Curr. mfr.

Mfr.'s Sug. Retail	$1,750	$1,225	$1,050	$875	$700	$630	$575	$525

This model is also available with soundholes and binding as options.

LARRIVEE

Manufactured and distributed by Larrivee Guitars, Ltd., located in Vancouver, British Columbia, Canada since 1968.

Larrivee guitars have always incorporated top-shelf materials and excellent craftsmanship.

ACOUSTIC

Unless otherwise noted, all Larrivee models are constructed with the same standard materials: spruce top, round soundhole, wood body binding, wooden inlay rosette, transparent pickguard, rosewood or figured maple back/sides, mahogany neck, bound ebony fingerboard, ebony bridge with black pearl dot pins, and 3 per side chrome tuners. All instruments are available in left handed versions at no additional charge.

(more information on the next page)

Grading	100%	98%	95%	90%	80%	70%	60%

In addition, the instruments are available in standard body styles with their own distinct features. Again, variances will be listed.

Numerical suffixes listed below indicate individualized features per model suffix.

05 Mahogany Standard - mahogany back/sides.

09 Standard - pearl logo headstock inlay.

19 Special - abalone/pearl fingerboard inlay, hand-engraved Eagle, Gryphon, Pelican or Seahorse on headstock.

10 Deluxe - abalone purfling on top, abalone/pearl fingerboard inlay, headstock bordered by inlaid silver, hand-engraved Eagle, Gryphon, Pelican or Seahorse on headstock.

72 Presentation - abalone purfling on all bound edges, abalone rosette, abalone/pearl fingerboard inlay, headstock bordered by inlaid silver, hand-engraved Dancing Ladies, Genies, Jester, Mermaid on Seahorse or Tamborine Lady inlay on headstock, bridge wing inlays.

All instruments are also available with following options:

A 12 string variation is available in the following models for an additional $190: Cutaway, Cutaway Jumbo, Dreadnought, Jumbo, Larrivee and Larrivee Jumbo Series.

Add $140 for Fishman Matrix pickup.

Add $280 for Fishman pickup with preamp.

Add $1,000 for Brazilian rosewood (when available).

Classic Series

L-35 — classic style body, unbound fingerboard, tied bridge, 3 per side gold tuners with pearl buttons. Curr. mfr.

	100%	98%	95%	90%	80%	70%	60%
Mfr.'s Sug. Retail	$2,295	$1,605	$1,375	$1,150	$920	$825	$755	$690

Add $300 for cutaway version (L-38).

Cutaway Series

The instruments in this series have the Larrivee body style with a single sharp cutaway. Curr. mfr.

C-05 — Mahogany Standard

	100%	98%	95%	90%	80%	70%	60%
Mfr.'s Sug. Retail	$1,490	$1,040	$890	$745	$595	$535	$490	$445

C-09 — Standard

	100%	98%	95%	90%	80%	70%	60%
Mfr.'s Sug. Retail	$1,830	$1,280	$1,095	$915	$730	$660	$605	$550

C-10 — DeLuxe

	100%	98%	95%	90%	80%	70%	60%
Mfr.'s Sug. Retail	$2,430	$1,700	$1,460	$1,215	$970	$870	$800	$730

C-19 — Special

	100%	98%	95%	90%	80%	70%	60%
Mfr.'s Sug. Retail	$2,110	$1,475	$1,265	$1,055	$845	$760	$690	$635

Grading	100%	98%	95%	90%	80%	70%	60%
⚔ **C-72** – Presentation							
Mfr.'s Sug. Retail	$4,970	$3,475	$2,980	$2,480	$1,985	$1,785	$1,640	$1,490

Cutaway Jumbo Series

All the instruments in this series have jumbo Larrivee body styles with a single sharp cutaway. Curr. mfr.

LCJ-05 – Mahogany Standard

	100%	98%	95%	90%	80%	70%	60%
Mfr.'s Sug. Retail	$1,590	$1,110	$955	$795	$635	$575	$525	$475
⚔ **LCJ-09** – Standard							
Mfr.'s Sug. Retail	$1,930	$1,355	$1,160	$965	$770	$690	$630	$575
⚔ **LCJ-10** – DeLuxe							
Mfr.'s Sug. Retail	$2,530	$1,770	$1,520	$1,265	$1,010	$910	$835	$760
⚔ **LCJ-19** – Special							
Mfr.'s Sug. Retail	$2,210	$1,545	$1,325	$1,105	$885	$795	$730	$665
⚔ **LCJ-72** – Presentation							
Mfr.'s Sug. Retail	$5,170	$3,615	$3,100	$2,580	$2,065	$1,860	$1,700	$1,545

Cutaway Small Body Series

Fashioned after the Larrivee small body style, these instruments have a single sharp cutaway. Curr. mfr.

CS-05 – Mahogany Standard

	100%	98%	95%	90%	80%	70%	60%
Mfr.'s Sug. Retail	$1,490	$1,040	$890	$745	$595	$535	$490	$445
⚔ **CS-09** – Standard							
Mfr.'s Sug. Retail	$1,830	$1,280	$1,095	$915	$730	$660	$605	$550
⚔ **CS-10** – Deluxe							
Mfr.'s Sug. Retail	$2,430	$1,700	$1,460	$1,215	$970	$870	$800	$730
⚔ **CS-19** – Special							
Mfr.'s Sug. Retail	$2,110	$1,475	$1,265	$1,055	$845	$760	$690	$635
⚔ **CS-72** – Presentation							
Mfr.'s Sug. Retail	$4,970	$3,475	$2,980	$2,480	$1,985	$1,785	$1,640	$1,490

Grading	100%	98%	95%	90%	80%	70%	60%

Dreadnought Series

All instruments in this series have dreadnought style bodies. Curr. mfr.

D-05 — Mahogany Standard

	100%	98%	95%	90%	80%	70%	60%
Mfr.'s Sug. Retail	$1,190	$835	$715	$595	$475	$430	$390	$360

D-09 — Standard

Mfr.'s Sug. Retail	$1,540	$1,080	$925	$770	$615	$555	$510	$460

D-10 — DeLuxe

Mfr.'s Sug. Retail	$2,110	$1,475	$1,265	$1,055	$845	$760	$690	$635

D-19 — Special

Mfr.'s Sug. Retail	$1,825	$1,280	$1,095	$915	$730	$660	$605	$550

D-72 — Presentation

Mfr.'s Sug. Retail	$4,480	$3,135	$2,685	$2,240	$1,790	$1,610	$1,480	$1,345

Koa Series

All instruments in this series have single sharp cutaway style bodies, koa top/back/sides, seashell fingerboard/bridge wing inlay, dolphin peghead inlay. Curr. mfr.

C-20 — Larrivee style body.

Mfr.'s Sug. Retail	$2,110	$1,475	$1,265	$1,055	$845	$760	$690	$635

CJ-20 — Larrivee jumbo style body.

Mfr.'s Sug. Retail	$2,210	$1,545	$1,325	$1,105	$885	$795	$730	$665

CS-20 — Larrivee small style body.

Mfr.'s Sug. Retail	$2,110	$1,475	$1,265	$1,055	$845	$760	$690	$635

Larrivee Series

All instruments in this series have Larrivee style bodies. Curr. mfr.

L-05 — Mahogany Standard

Mfr.'s Sug. Retail	$1,190	$835	$715	$595	$475	$430	$390	$360

L-09 — Standard

Mfr.'s Sug. Retail	$1,540	$1,080	$925	$770	$615	$555	$510	$460

Grading	100%	98%	95%	90%	80%	70%	60%
L-10 — Deluxe							
Mfr.'s Sug. Retail	$2,110	$1,475	$1,265	$1,055	$845	$760	$690	$635
L-19 — Special							
Mfr.'s Sug. Retail	$1,825	$1,280	$1,095	$915	$730	$660	$605	$550
L-72 — Presentation							
Mfr.'s Sug. Retail	$4,480	$3,135	$2,685	$2,240	$1,790	$1,610	$1,480	$1,345

Larrivee Jumbo Series

All instruments in this series have Larrivee Jumbo style bodies. Curr. mfr.

	100%	98%	95%	90%	80%	70%	60%
LJ-05 — Mahogany Standard							
Mfr.'s Sug. Retail	$1,295	$905	$775	$645	$515	$465	$425	$385
LJ-09 — Standard							
Mfr.'s Sug. Retail	$1,645	$1,155	$985	$825	$660	$595	$545	$495
LJ-10 — Deluxe							
Mfr.'s Sug. Retail	$2,220	$1,550	$1,325	$1,105	$885	$795	$730	$665
LJ-19 — Special							
Mfr.'s Sug. Retail	$1,930	$1,355	$1,160	$965	$770	$690	$630	$575
LJ-72 — Presentation							
Mfr.'s Sug. Retail	$4,590	$3,215	$2,755	$2,295	$1,835	$1,650	$1,515	$1,375

Larrivee OM Series

All instruments in this series have Larrivee OM style bodies. Curr. mfr.

	100%	98%	95%	90%	80%	70%	60%
OM-05 — Mahogany Standard							
Mfr.'s Sug. Retail	$1,190	$835	$715	$595	$475	$430	$390	$360
OM-09 — Standard							
Mfr.'s Sug. Retail	$1,540	$1,080	$925	$770	$615	$555	$510	$460
OM-10 — Deluxe							
Mfr.'s Sug. Retail	$2,110	$1,475	$1,265	$1,055	$845	$760	$690	$635
OM-19 — Special							
Mfr.'s Sug. Retail	$1,825	$1,280	$1,095	$915	$730	$660	$605	$550
OM-72 — Presentation							
Mfr.'s Sug. Retail	$4,480	$3,135	$2,685	$2,240	$1,790	$1,610	$1,480	$1,345

Grading	100%	98%	95%	90%	80%	70%	60%

Larrivee Small Series

All instruments in this series have Larrivee Small style bodies. Curr. mfr.

LS-05 — Mahogany Standard

Mfr.'s Sug. Retail	$1,190	$835	$715	$595	$475	$430	$390	$360

⚮ LS-09 — Standard

Mfr.'s Sug. Retail	$1,540	$1,080	$925	$770	$615	$555	$510	$460

⚮ LS-10 — Deluxe

Mfr.'s Sug. Retail	$2,110	$1,475	$1,265	$1,055	$845	$760	$690	$635

⚮ LS-19 — Special

Mfr.'s Sug. Retail	$1,825	$1,280	$1,095	$915	$730	$660	$605	$550

⚮ LS-72 — Presentation

Mfr.'s Sug. Retail	$4,480	$3,135	$2,685	$2,240	$1,790	$1,610	$1,480	$1,345

Larrivee 00 Series

All instruments in this series have Larrivee 00 style bodies. Curr. mfr.

00-05 — Mahogany Standard

Mfr.'s Sug. Retail	$1,190	$835	$715	$595	$475	$430	$390	$360

⚮ 00-09 — Standard

Mfr.'s Sug. Retail	$1,540	$1,080	$925	$770	$615	$555	$510	$460

⚮ 00-10 — Deluxe

Mfr.'s Sug. Retail	$2,110	$1,475	$1,265	$1,055	$845	$760	$690	$635

⚮ 00-19 — Special

Mfr.'s Sug. Retail	$1,825	$1,280	$1,095	$915	$730	$660	$605	$550

⚮ 00-72 — Presentation

Mfr.'s Sug. Retail	$4,480	$3,135	$2,685	$2,240	$1,790	$1,610	$1,480	$1,345

Traditional Jumbo Series

All instruments in this series have Jumbo style bodies. Curr. mfr.

J-05 — Mahogany Standard

Mfr.'s Sug. Retail	$1,295	$905	$775	$645	$515	$465	$425	$385

⚮ J-09 — Standard

Mfr.'s Sug. Retail	$1,645	$1,155	$985	$825	$660	$595	$545	$495

⚮ J-10 — Deluxe

Mfr.'s Sug. Retail	$2,220	$1,550	$1,325	$1,105	$885	$795	$730	$665

Grading	100%	98%	95%	90%	80%	70%	60%

J-19 — Special

Mfr.'s Sug. Retail	$1,930	$1,355	$1,160	$965	$770	$690	$630	$575

J-72 — Presentation

Mfr.'s Sug. Retail	$4,590	$3,215	$2,755	$2,295	$1,835	$1,650	$1,515	$1,375

LOWDEN

Lowden instruments are hand built in Ireland. The U.S. distributor is located in Lake Luzerne, NY.

In 1973, George Lowden began designing and manufacturing hand built guitars in Ireland. Demand outgrew a one person effort and luthiers in Japan were contracted in 1981 to collaborate output of hand built Lowden instruments. Since 1985, all production has been in Ireland.

ACOUSTIC

F Series

F-22 — folk style, cedar top, round soundhole, wood bound body, wood inlay rosette, mahogany back/sides, mahogany/rosewood 5 piece neck, 14/20 fret ebony fingerboard with pearl dot inlay, rosewood bridge, pearl logo inlay and rosewood veneer on peghead, 3 per side gold tuners with pearl buttons. Available in Natural finish. Curr. mfr.

Mfr.'s Sug. Retail	$2,145	$1,500	$1,290	$1,075	$860	$775	$710	$645

F-32 — similar to F22, except has spruce top, rosewood back/sides.

Mfr.'s Sug. Retail	$2,745	$1,925	$1,650	$1,375	$1,100	$990	$905	$825

F-38 — similar to F22, except has abalone/wood bound body/rosette, Brazilian rosewood back/sides, abalone leaf fingerboard inlay.

Mfr.'s Sug. Retail	$4,565	$3,195	$2,740	$2,285	$1,830	$1,645	$1,505	$1,370

LSE Series

LSE-I — venetian cutaway folk style, spruce top, round soundhole, wood bound body, wood inlay rosette, mahogany 2 piece neck, 20 fret ebony fingerboard, rosewood bridge, pearl logo inlay and rosewood veneer on peghead, 3 per side gold tuners with pearl buttons, transducer bridge pickup. Available in Natural finish. Curr. mfr.

Mfr.'s Sug. Retail	$2,195	$1,540	$1,320	$1,100	$880	$790	$725	$660

LSE-II — similar to LSE-I, except has Indian rosewood back/sides.

Mfr.'s Sug. Retail	$2,495	$1,745	$1,495	$1,250	$1,000	$900	$825	$750

Grading	100%	98%	95%	90%	80%	70%	60%

O Series

O-10 — jumbo style, cedar top, round soundhole, wood bound body, wood inlay rosette, mahogany back/sides, mahogany 2 piece neck, 14/20 fret ebony fingerboard, rosewood bridge, pearl logo inlay and rosewood veneer on peghead, 3 per side gold tuners with amber buttons. Available in Natural finish. Curr. mfr.

Mfr.'s Sug. Retail	$1,795	$1,255	$1,075	$895	$715	$645	$590	$540

O-12 — similar to O-10, except has spruce top.

Mfr.'s Sug. Retail	$1,875	$1,315	$1,125	$940	$750	$675	$615	$560

O-22 — similar to O-10, except has different woods for binding, purfling and rosette, mahogany/sycamore 5 piece neck.

Mfr.'s Sug. Retail	$2,145	$1,500	$1,290	$1,075	$860	$775	$710	$645

O-22/12 — similar to O-22, except has 12 strings, 6 per side tuners.

Mfr.'s Sug. Retail	$2,445	$1,715	$1,470	$1,220	$975	$875	$805	$730

O-23 — similar to O-10, except has abalone/wood inlay rosette, walnut back/sides, mahogany/sycamore 5 piece neck.

Mfr.'s Sug. Retail	$2,195	$1,540	$1,320	$1,100	$880	$790	$725	$660

O-25 — jumbo style, cedar top, round soundhole, wood bound body, wood inlay rosette, Indian rosewood back/sides, mahogany/rosewood 5 piece neck, 14/20 fret ebony fingerboard, rosewood bridge, pearl logo inlay and rosewood veneer on peghead, 3 per side gold tuners with amber buttons. Available in Natural finish. Curr. mfr.

Mfr.'s Sug. Retail	$2,445	$1,715	$1,470	$1,225	$980	$875	$805	$735

O-25/12 — similar to O-25, except has 12 strings, 6 per side tuners.

Mfr.'s Sug. Retail	$2,745	$1,930	$1,650	$1,370	$1,095	$985	$900	$820

O-32 — similar to O-25, except has spruce top, pearl tuner buttons.

Mfr.'s Sug. Retail	$2,745	$1,925	$1,650	$1,375	$1,100	$990	$905	$825

O-38 — jumbo style, black cedar top, round soundhole, abalone/wood bound body/rosette, Brazilian rosewood back/sides, 14/20 fret ebony fingerboard with abalone leaf inlay, rosewood bridge, pearl logo inlay and rosewood veneer on peghead, 3 per side gold tuners with amber buttons. Available in Natural finish. Curr. mfr.

Mfr.'s Sug. Retail	$4,845	$3,395	$2,910	$2,425	$1,940	$1,745	$1,600	$1,455

MARTIN

Manufacturer located in Nazareth, Pennsylvania, since 1833. Dealer sales only.

Martin is best known for their high quality flattop acoustics. Remarkably, Martin has been in the same location for 160 years and serialization has remained intact and consistent since their first instrument.

When trying to determine the year of an instrument's construction some quick notes about features can be helpful. The few notes contained herein are for readily identifying the instrument upon sight and are by no means meant to be used for truly accurate dating of an instrument. All items discussed are for flat top steel string guitars and involve instruments that are standard production models.

The earliest dreadnoughts, and indeed just about all instruments produced with a neck that joins the body at the 12th fret, have bodies that are bell shaped on the top, as opposed to the more square shouldered styles of most dreadnoughts. Between 1929 to 1934, Martin began placing 14 fret necks on most of their instruments and this brought about the square shouldered body style. A few models maintained 12 fret necks into the late 1940's and one model had a 12 fret neck until the late 1980's.

Turn of the century instruments have square slotted pegheads with an intricate pearl fern inlay that runs vertically up the peghead. This was replaced by a vertical inlay known as the "flowerpot" or the "torch" inlay, in approximately 1905. By approximately 1934, a solid peghead with a vertical pearl "C.F. Martin" inlay had replaced the former peghead design. In 1932, the "C.F. Martin & Co. Est. 1833" scroll logo began appearing on certain models' pegheads. Bridges from the 1900's are rectangular with "pyramid" wings. In approximately 1929, the "belly" bridge replaced the rectangle bridge. This bridge has a straight slot cut across the entire length of the bridge. In 1965, the straight cut saddle slot was changed to a routed slot. It was in approximately 1936, that Martin began using the "tied" bridge on their instruments.

Pickguards were not standard features on instruments until approximately 1933 when tortoise shell pickguards were introduced. In 1966, black pickguards became standard. In approximately 1970, Martin stopped using Brazilian rosewood for its regular production instruments, and as a result, premiums are being asked for instruments manufactured from this exotic wood.

 , cont.

ACOUSTIC

BACKPACKER — paddle style body, solid spruce top, round soundhole, one-piece mahogany body/neck with hollowed out sound cavity, 15 fret hardwood fingerboard with white dot inlay, hardwood bridge with white black dot pins, 3 per side chrome mini tuners. Available in Natural finish. Curr. mfr.

Mfr.'s Sug. Retail	$210	$145	$125	$100	$80	$70	$65	$60

Add $125 for acoustic pickup.

Arch Tops

Tailpiece variations were common on all arch and carved top instruments.

Grading	90%	80%	70%	60%	50%	40%	20%

C-1 — auditorium style body, carved spruce top, round soundhole, raised black pickguard, bound top/rosette, mahogany back/sides/neck, 14/20 fret rosewood fingerboard with white dot inlay, rosewood bridge/trapeze tailpiece, vertical pearl logo inlay on headstock, 3 per side nickel tuners. Available in Sunburst finish. Mfd. 1931-1942.

	$1,025	$720	$615	$510	$410	$370	$340

In 1934 f holes replaced the soundhole.

C-2 — similar to C-1, except has stripe bound body/rosette, rosewood back/sides, ebony fingerboard with pearl snowflake inlay, ebony bridge. Available in Dark Laquer finish. Mfd. 1931-1942.

	$1,500	$1,050	$900	$750	$600	$540	$495

In 1934 f holes replaced soundhole and Golden Brown top finish became standard.
Bound fingerboard and pickguard added in 1935.
Hexagon fingerboard inlay added in 1939.

C-3 — similar to C-1, except has 2 stripe bound body/rosette, pearl bound pickguard, rosewood back/sides, bound ebony fingerboard with pearl snowflake inlay, ebony bridge, gold tailpiece, bound peghaed, gold single unit tuners. Available in Laquer finish. Mfd. 1932-1935.

	$2,250	$1,575	$1,345	$1,125	$900	$810	$740

In 1934 Black and white binding added to pickguard, f holes replaced soundhole stained top became standard.

F-1 — concert style body, carved spruce top, f holes, raised black pickguard, stripe bound top, mahogany back/sides/neck, 14/20 fret ebony fingerboard with white dot inlay, adjustable ebony bridge/trapeze tailpiece, logo decal on headstock, 3 per side nickel tuners. Available in Sunburst finish. Mfd. 1940-1942.

	$1,525	$1,070	$915	$765	$610	$550	$505

F-2 — similar to F-1, except has rosewood back/sides.

	$1,725	$1,210	$1,040	$865	$690	$620	$570

Grading	90%	80%	70%	60%	50%	40%	20%

F-7 — similar to F-1, except has bound pickguard, rosewood back/sides, bound fingerboard with ivoroid hexagon inlay, bound peghead with pearl vertical logo inlay, chrome hardware. Available in Sunburst finish. Mfd. 1935-1942.

	$1,250	$875	$750	$625	$500	$450	$415

In 1937 fingerboard inlay changed to pearloid.

F-9 — similar to F-1, except has stripe bound pickguard, rosewood back/sides, bound fingerboard with pearl hexagon inlay, bound peghead with pearl vertical logo inlay, gold hardware. Available in Golden Brown Sunburst finish. Mfd. 1935-1942.

	$2,475	$1,730	$1,485	$1,235	$985	$880	$810

R-17 — grand concert style body, arched mahogany top, f holes, raised black pickguard, bound body, mahogany back/sides/neck, 14/20 fret rosewood fingerboard,rosewood bridge/trapeze tailpiece, logo decal on peghead, 3 per side nickel single unit tuners. Available in Sunburst finish. Mfd. 1934-1942.

	$675	$475	$405	$340	$270	$245	$225

R-18 — similar to R-17, except has arched spruce top, 3 stripe bound body/rosette, white dot fingerboard inlay. Mfd. 1932-1941.

	$875	$615	$525	$435	$350	$315	$290

In 1933, f holes replace the soundhole.

Auditorium Series

Grading	100%	98%	95%	90%	80%	70%	60%

000-16 — auditorium style, solid spruce top, round soundhole, tortoise shell pickguard, bound body, 3 stripe rosette, mahogany back/sides/neck, 14/20 fret rosewood fingerboard with pearl snowflake inlay, rosewood bridge with black white dot pins, rosewood peghead veneer, 3 per side chrome tuners. Available in Natural finish. Mfd. 1990 to date.

Mfr.'s Sug. Retail	$1,520	$1,065	$910	$760	$610	$550	$505	$455

000C-16 — similar to 000-16, except has single round cutaway, oval soundhole, 22 fret fingerboard.

Mfr.'s Sug. Retail	$1,690	$1,185	$1,015	$845	$675	$605	$555	$505

000-18 — similar to 000-16, except has black pickguard, round dot fingerboard inlay. Curr. mfr.

Mfr.'s Sug. Retail	$2,200	$1,540	$1,320	$1,100	$880	$790	$725	$660

000-28 — auditorium style, solid spruce top, round soundhole, black pickguard, 5 stripe bound body/rosette, rosewood back/sides, mahogany neck, 14/20 fret ebony fingerboard with pearl dot inlay, ebony bridge with white black dot pins, rosewood peghead veneer, 3 per side chrome tuners. Available in Natural finish. Curr. mfr.

Mfr.'s Sug. Retail	$2,490	$1,740	$1,495	$1,245	$995	$890	$820	$745

 , cont.

Grading	100%	98%	95%	90%	80%	70%	60%

000-28C — similar to 000-28, except has classical style body. Mfd. 1962-1966.

	$725	$505	$435	$360	$290	$260	$240

000-45 — similar to 000-28, except has abalone bound body/rosette, bound fingerboard with abalone hexagon inlay, abalone dot bridge pins, bound peghead with abalone logo inlay, gold tuners. Curr. mfr.

Mfr.'s Sug. Retail	$6,530	$4,570	$3,920	$3,265	$2,610	$2,350	$2,155	$1,960

Post-war production of this model has been on a special order basis.

Classic Series

Unless indicated otherwise, all instruments in this series have classic style bodies, solid spruce top, bound body, mahogany neck, 12/19 fret fingerboard, tied bridge, slotted peghead, 3 per side gold pearl button tuners. Available in Natural finishes.

N-10 — wooden inlay rosette, mahogany back/sides, rosewood fingerboard/bridge. Mfd. 1969-1985.

	$450	$315	$270	$225	$180	$160	$150

N-10, Current Manufacture — this model is a special order instrument.

Mfr.'s Sug. Retail	$2,620	$1,830	$1,570	$1,310	$1,045	$940	$865	$785

N-20 — wooden inlay rosette, rosewood back/sides, ebony fingerboard/bridge. Mfd. 1968 to date.

Mfr.'s Sug. Retail	$2,900	$2,030	$1,740	$1,450	$1,160	$1,040	$955	$870

In 1970, a rounded peak peghead became standard.

0-16NY — concert style, spruce top, round soundhole, 3 stripe bound body/rosette, mahogany back/sides/neck, 12/19 fret rosewood fingerboard, rosewood bridge with black white dot pins, slotted peghead 3 per side tuners with plastic buttons. Available in Natural finish. Mfd. 1961 to date.

1961-1969		$725	$505	$435	$360	$290	$260	$240
1970-1992		$575	$405	$345	$285	$230	$205	$190
Curr. Mfr.'s Sug. Retail	$2,180	$1,530	$1,310	$1,090	$870	$785	$720	$655

This instrument is currently a special order instrument.

the current production of this instrument features a solid peghead with tuners runnig parallel to the body.

00-16C — 3 stripe rosette, mahogany back/sides, rosewood fingerboard/bridge. Curr. mfr.

Mfr.'s Sug. Retail	$2,330	$1,630	$1,400	$1,165	$930	$840	$770	$700

Above instrument is a special order model.

Original instrument mfd. 1962-1975, re-introduced 1976-1981 with sparse production. More research is being done on earlier models as this edition goes to press.

Grading	100%	98%	95%	90%	80%	70%	60%

00-18C — 3 stripe rosette, mahogany back/sides, rosewood fingerboard/bridge. Mfd. 1962 to date.

Mfr.'s Sug. Retail	$2,480	$1,735	$1,490	$1,240	$990	$885	$820	$745

This instrument is a special order model today.

00-18G — mahogany back/sides, ebony fingerboard/bridge. Available in polished Lacquer finish. Mfd. 1936-1962.

	$1,100	$770	$660	$550	$440	$395	$365

After the 1940's, these models came with a rosewood fingerboard/bridge.

00-21NY — grand concert style, spruce top, round soundhole, tortoise shell bound body, herringbone rosette, rosewood back/sides, mahogany neck, 12/19 fret ebony fingerboard, ebony bridge with black white dot pins, slotted peghead with logo decal, 3 per side tuners. Available in Natural finish. Mfd. 1961-1965.

	$1,300	$910	$780	$650	$520	$470	$430

00-28C — 3 stripe rosette, rosewood back/sides, ebony fingerboard/bridge. Mfd. 1966 to date.

Mfr.'s Sug. Retail	$2,760	$1,930	$1,655	$1,380	$1,105	$995	$910	$825

This instrument is a special order model.

00-28G — rosewood back/sides, 12/20 fret ebony fingerboard. Mfd. 1936-1962.

	$1,100	$770	$660	$550	$440	$395	$365

Dreadnought Series

All instruments in this series have dreadnought style bodies.

D-1 — spruce top, round soundhole, black pickguard, bound body, 3 stripe rosette, mahogany back/sides/neck, 14/20 fret rosewood fingerboard with pearl dot inlay, rosewood bridge with brown white dot pins, mahogany peghead veneer, 3 per side chrome tuners. Available in Natural finish. New 1993.

Mfr.'s Sug. Retail	$995	$695	$595	$500	$400	$360	$330	$300
Grading		**90%**	**80%**	**70%**	**60%**	**50%**	**40%**	**20%**

STYLE 15, PRE-WAR — mahogany top, round soundhole, 2 stripe rosette, mahogany back/sides/neck, 14/19 fret rosewood fingerboard with dot inlay, rosewood bridge with white pins, 3 per side nickel tuners with plastic buttons. Available in Natural finish. Mfd. 1935-1944.

	$1,200	$840	$720	$600	$480	$430	$395

Early models are found with birch or maple bodies.

Grading	100%	98%	95%	90%	80%	70%	60%

Style 15, Post-war — similar to style 15, Pre-war. Mfd. 1948-1961.

	$700	$490	$420	$350	$280	$250	$230

Grading	100%	98%	95%	90%	80%	70%	60%

D-16 — spruce top, round soundhole, black pickguard, 3 stripe bound body/rosette, mahogany back/sides/neck, 14/20 fret rosewood fingerboad with pearl dot inlay, rosewood bridge with black pins, rosewood peghead veneer, 3 per side chrome tuners. Available in Natural finish. Mfd. 1986 to date.

Mfr.'s Sug. Retail	$1,550	$1,085	$930	$775	$620	$560	$515	$465

Koa back/sides offered in limited quantities (D-16K).

In 1987, ash or walnut back/sides were offered in limited quantities (D-16A/D-16W).

5-16 — tenor style, spruce top, round soundhole, 3 stripe bound body/rosette, mahogany back/sides/neck, 12/19 fret rosewood fingerboard, rosewood bridge with black white dot pins, 3 per side chrome tuners. Available in Natural finish. Mfd. 1962-1963.

	$925	$650	$555	$465	$370	$335	$305

Grading	90%	80%	70%	60%	50%	40%	20%

STYLE 17 — pre-war folk style, spruce top, round soundhole, rosewood bound body, mahogany back/sides, cedar neck, 12/19 fret ebony fingerboard with pearl dot inlay, ebony bridge with black pins, slotted peghead with 3 per side die cast tuners with plastic buttons. Available in Natural finish. Mfd. 1909-1937.

1909-1913	$1,025	$720	$615	$510	$410	$370	$340
1914-1921	$1,250	$875	$750	$625	$500	$450	$415
1922-1928	$850	$595	$510	$425	$340	$305	$280
1929-1937	$750	$525	$450	$375	$300	$270	$245

In 1914, 3 stripe rosette was added.

In 1922, mahogany top, 1 stripe rosette, ebony nut, pointed bridge replace respective items.

In 1927, rosewood fingerboard/bridge replace respective items.

Between 1929 and 1930, this instrument was also referred to as the Style 25 on the production tables.

In 1931, a pickguard became optional.

In 1934, a 14 fret model was introduced in sizes 0-17 and 00-17.

In 1935, Dark finish replaces Natural finish.

In 1936, this model was made with nickel plated tuner buttons.

Available in sizes 2-17, 0-17 and 00-17.

5-17 — tenor style, mahogany top, round soundhole, mahogany back/sides/neck, 12/19 fret rosewood fingerboard, rosewood bridge with black pins, 3 per side die cast tuners with nickel buttons. Available in Dark finish. Mfd. 1938-1945.

	$550	$385	$330	$275	$220	$200	$180

STYLE 18 — pre-war dreadnought style, spruce top, round soundhole, wood bound body, rope patterned wood inlay rosette, rosewood back/sides, cedar neck, 12 fret ebony fingerboard, pointed ebony bridge with ebony pearl dot pins, 3 per side brass tuners with ivory buttons.

1898-1928	$1,200	$840	$720	$600	$480	$430	$395

(prices for later models on next page)

Grading	100%	98%	95%	90%	80%	70%	60%
1929-1955	$5,500	$3,850	$3,300	$2,750	$2,200	$1,980	$1,815
1956-1966	$3,800	$2,660	$2,280	$1,900	$1,520	$1,365	$1,255

In 1901, 3 stripe rosette replaces original item.

In 1909, fingerboard inlay was added.

In 1917, this model became available in a 19 fret version, with mahogany back/sides/neck.

In 1919, rosewood bound body became available.

In 1920, 20 fret fingerboard became standard.

In 1923, this model began to come with steel strings, gut strings optional, with a dark top at extra charge, and a regular pointed bridge.

In 1930, a belly bridge with a slanted saddle became available.

In 1931, D style body with 14/20 fret fingerboard was introduced.

In 1932, a pickguard became optional.

In 1934, models were available with 12/20 and 14/20 fret fingerboards, metal hardware, black Fiberloid plastic binding, shaded Sunburst top.

In 1935, 12/20 fret fingerboards were no longer standard production.

By 1956, rosewood fingerboard/bridges were standard.

In 1966, the black Boltaron binding became standard.

Grading	90%	80%	70%	60%	50%	40%	20%

D-18 — solid spruce top, round soundhole, black pickguard, 3 stripe bound body/rosette, mahogany back/sides/neck, 14/20 fret ebony fingerboard with pearl dot inlay, ebony bridge with black white dot pins, 3 per side chrome tuners. Available in Natural finish. Mfd. 1935 to date.

	90%	80%	70%	60%	50%	40%	20%
1935-1945	$6,000	$4,200	$3,600	$3,000	$2,400	$2,160	$1,980

Grading	100%	98%	95%	90%	80%	70%	60%
1946-1949	$4,500	$3,150	$2,700	$2,250	$1,800	$1,620	$1,485
1950-1959	$3,200	$2,240	$1,920	$1,600	$1,280	$1,150	$1,055
1960-1969	$1,900	$1,330	$1,140	$950	$760	$685	$625
1970-1979	$1,200	$840	$720	$600	$480	$430	$395

⚄ **1980 to date.**

Mfr.'s Sug. Retail	$1,800	$1,260	$1,080	$900	$720	$650	$595	$540

During the 1940s, the fingerboard/bridge wood was changed to rosewood.

⚄ **D-18S** — similar to D-18, except has pre-war dreadnought style body, 12/20 fret fingerboard. Mfd. 1968 to date.

Mfr.'s Sug. Retail	$2,330	$1,630	$1,400	$1,165	$930	$840	$770	$700

This model is a special order instrument.

⚄ **D12-18** — similar to D-18, except has 12 strings, 6 per side tuners. Mfd. 1973 to date.

Mfr.'s Sug. Retail	$2,130	$1,495	$1,280	$1,065	$850	$765	$700	$635

 , cont.

Grading	100%	98%	95%	90%	80%	70%	60%

D-19 — spruce top, round soundhole, black pickguard, 3 stripe bound body/rosette, mahogany back/sides/neck, 14/20 fret rosewood fingerboard with pearl dot inlay, rosewood bridge with white black dot pins, rosewood peghead veneer with logo decal, 3 per side chrome tuners. Available in Dark Brown finish. Mfd. 1976-1988.

	100%	98%	95%	90%	80%	70%	60%
	$850	$595	$510	$425	$340	$305	$280

D12-20 — solid spruce top, round soundhole, black pickguard, 3 stripe bound body/rosette, mahogany back/sides/neck, 12/20 fret rosewood fingerboard with pearl dot inlay, rosewood bridge with black white dot pins, 6 per side chrome tuners. Available in Natural finish. Mfd. 1964 to date.

Mfr.'s Sug. Retail	$2,480	$1,735	$1,490	$1,240	$990	$885	$820	$745

Grading	90%	80%	70%	60%	50%	40%	20%

STYLE 21 — pre-war dreadnought style, round soundhole, rosewood bound body, herringbone rosette, rosewood back/sides, cedar neck, 12/19 fret ebony fingerboard, ebony pyramid bridge, slotted peghead, 3 per side brass tuners with ivory buttons. Available in Natural finish. Mfd. 1898-1955.

	90%	80%	70%	60%	50%	40%	20%
1898-1926	$2,500	$1,750	$1,500	$1,250	$1,000	$900	$825
1927-1938	$3,200	$2,240	$1,920	$1,600	$1,280	$1,150	$1,055

Grading	100%	98%	95%	90%	80%	70%	60%
1939-1955	$1,700	$1,190	$1,020	$850	$680	$610	$560

In 1901, pearl diamond fingerboard inlay was added.
By 1917, ebony pearl dot bridge pins were added.
By 1923, mahogany neck replaced original item.
In 1923, 12/20 fret fingerboard replaced original item.
In 1930, belly bridge and slanted saddle were added.
In 1932, a pickguard became optional, black plastic body binding replaced original item.
By 1936, tortoise shell body binding became standard.
In 1944, dot fingerboard inlay became standard.
In 1947, rosewood fingerboard/bridge became standard.

D-21 — spruce top, round soundhole, tortoise shell bound body, herringbone rosette, rosewood back/sides, mahogany neck, 14/20 fret rosewood fingerboard with pearl dot inlay, rosewood bridge with black pins, 3 per side chrome tuners. Mfd. 1955-1969.

$3,200	$2,240	$1,920	$1,600	$1,280	$1,150	$1,055

Grading	90%	80%	70%	60%	50%	40%	20%

STYLE 28 — pre-war dreadnought style, spruce top, round soundhole, ivory/herringbone bound body, pearl rosette, rosewood back/sides, cedar neck, 12/19 fret ebony fingerboard, ebony bridge, 3 per side tuners. Available in Natural finish. Mfd. 1898-1934.

	90%	80%	70%	60%	50%	40%	20%
1898-1922	$2,025	$1,420	$1,215	$1,015	$810	$730	$670
1923-1934	$10,500	$7,350	$6,300	$5,250	$4,200	$3,780	$3,465

In 1901, pearl diamond fingerboard inlay was added.
In 1917, 12/20 fret fingerboard became standard.
In 1919, plastic body binding became standard.
By 1923, mahogany neck became standard.
In 1927, white black dot bridge pins were added.
In 1928, gut strings were replaced with steel.
In 1932, pickguard became optional.

D-28 — solid spruce top, round soundhole, black pickguard, 5 stripe bound body/rosette, rosewood 2 piece back/sides, 14/20 fret ebony fingerboard with pearl dot inlay, ebony bridge with white black dot pins, 3 per side chrome tuners. Available in Natural finish. Mfd. 1935 to date.

	90%	80%	70%	60%	50%	40%	20%
1935-1939	$30,000	$21,000	$18,000	$15,000	$12,000	$10,800	$9,900
1940-1945	$25,500	$17,850	$15,300	$12,750	$10,200	$9,180	$8,415

Grading	100%	98%	95%	90%	80%	70%	60%
1946-1949	$15,000	$10,500	$9,000	$7,500	$6,000	$5,400	$4,950
1950-1959	$5,000	$3,500	$3,000	$2,500	$2,000	$1,800	$1,650
1960-1969	$3,500	$2,450	$2,100	$1,750	$1,400	$1,260	$1,150
1970-1979	$1,500	$1,050	$900	$750	$600	$540	$495
1980-1992	$1,000	$700	$600	$500	$400	$360	$330

Curr. mfr.

Mfr.'s Sug. Retail	$2,060	$1,440	$1,235	$1,030	$825	$740	$680	$620

Add $100 for 12 string version of this model (D12-28).
From 1935-1944, this model had pearl diamond fingerboard inlays.
From 1935-1947, this model had herringbone bound body.

D12-28 — similar to D-28, except has 12 strings. Mfd. 1970 to date.

Mfr.'s Sug. Retail	$2,160	$1,500	$1,295	$1,080	$865	$780	$715	$650

D-28S — similar to D-28, except has a pre-war dreadnought style body, 12/20 fret fingerboard, slotted headstock. Mfd. 1968 to date.

Mfr.'s Sug. Retail	$2,620	$1,830	$1,570	$1,310	$1,045	$940	$865	$785

Current model is a special order instrument.

Grading		90%	80%	70%	60%	50%	40%	20%

D-28V — similar to D-28, fashioned after the original dreadnought design, herringbone bound body, square headstock. Available in Antique Top finish. Mfd. 1983-1985.

		$3,850	$3,080	$2,505	$2,120	$1,375	$1,350	$1,155

Brazilian rosewood is used in place of Indian rosewood.

This was a Vintage Series instrument. 260 instruments were produced. It's original price was $2,600.

Grading		100%	98%	95%	90%	80%	70%	60%

DC-28 — similar to D-28, except has single rounded cutaway, 14/22 fret fingerboard. Mfd. 1981 to date.

Mfr.'s Sug. Retail	$2,550	$1,785	$1,530	$1,275	$1,020	$920	$840	$765

Grading		90%	80%	70%	60%	50%	40%	20%

STYLE 30 — pre-war dreadnought style, spruce top, round soundhole, ivory/herringbone bound body, pearl rosette, rosewood back/sides, cedar neck, 12/19 fret ivory bound ebony fingerboard with pearl diamond inlay, ebony bridge, 3 per side silver tuners with ivory buttons. Available in Natural finish. Mfd. 1901-1917.

		$1,500	$1,050	$900	$750	$600	$540	$495
		$1,800	$1,260	$1,080	$900	$720	$650	$595

Grading		100%	98%	95%	90%	80%	70%	60%

D-35 — solid spruce top, round soundhole, black pickguard, 5 stripe bound body/rosette, rosewood 3 piece back/sides, 14/20 fret bound ebony fingerboard with pearl dot inlay, ebony bridge with white black dot pins, 3 per side chrome tuners. Available in Natural finish. Mfd. 1965 to date.

1965-1969		$1,500	$1,050	$900	$750	$600	$540	$495
1970-1975		$1,250	$875	$750	$625	$500	$450	$415
1976-1986		$1,000	$700	$600	$500	$400	$360	$330
Mfr.'s Sug. Retail	$2,160	$1,500	$1,295	$1,080	$865	$780	$715	$650

The current model is a Special Order instrument.

D-35S — similar to D-35, except has a pre-war dreadnought style body, 12/20 fret fingerboard, slotted headstock. Mfd. 1968 to date.

Mfr.'s Sug. Retail	$2,760	$1,930	$1,655	$1,380	$1,105	$995	$910	$825

D12-35 — similar to D-35S, except has 12 strings. Mfd. 1965 to date.

Mfr.'s Sug. Retail	$2,760	$1,930	$1,655	$1,380	$1,105	$995	$910	$825

Grading	100%	98%	95%	90%	80%	70%	60%

D-37K — spruce top, round soundhole, tortoise shell pickguard, 5 stripe bound body, abalone rosette, figured koa 2 piece back/sides, mahogany neck, 14/20 fret ebony fingerboard with pearl inlay, ebony bridge with white black dot pins, koa peghead veneer with logo decal, 3 per side chrome tuners. Available in Amber Stain finish. Mfd. 1980 to date.

Mfr.'s Sug. Retail	$2,490	$1,740	$1,495	$1,245	$995	$890	$820	$745

This model is currently a special order instrument.

⚔ **D-37K2** — similar to D-37K, except has figured koa top, black pickguard.

Mfr.'s Sug. Retail	$2,650	$1,855	$1,590	$1,325	$1,060	$955	$875	$795

D-41 — solid spruce top, round soundhole, black pickguard, abalone bound body rosette, rosewood back/sides, mahogany neck, 14/20 fret bound ebony fingerboard with abalone hexagon inlay, ebony bridge with white abalone dot pins, rosewood veneer on bound peghead with abalone vertical logo inlay, 3 per side gold tuners. Available in Natural finish. Mfd. 1969 to date.

Mfr.'s Sug. Retail	$3,390	$2,370	$2,035	$1,695	$1,350	$1,215	$1,115	$1,015

In 1987, this model was redesigned with structural changes occurring, more fingerboard inlay was added and downsized, and a tortoise shell pickguard was added, which is still the current style.

⚔ **D12-41** — similar to D-41, except has 12 strings, 12/20 fret fingerboard, 6 per side tuners.

Mfr.'s Sug. Retail	$3,860	$2,700	$2,315	$1,930	$1,540	$1,390	$1,270	$1,155

⚔ **D-41S** — similar to D-41, except has a pre-war dreadnought style body, 12/20 fret fingerboard, slotted headstock. Mfd. 1969 to date.

Mfr.'s Sug. Retail	$3,720	$2,595	$2,230	$1,860	$1,485	$1,335	$1,225	$1,115

This model is a special order instrument.

Grading	90%	80%	70%	60%	50%	40%	20%

STYLE 42 — pre-war dreadnought style, solid spruce top, round soundhole, ivory/pearl bound body, pearl rosette, rosewood back/sides, cedar neck, 12/19 fret ivory bound ebony fingerboard with pearl snowflake inlay, ivory bridge, 3 per side silver tuners with pearl buttons. Available in Natural finish. Mfd. 1875-1942.

	$3,675	$2,570	$2,000	$1,830	$1,465	$1,320	$1,210

 , cont.

Grading	90%	80%	70%	60%	50%	40%	20%

D-45, PRE-WAR — solid spruce top, round soundhole, black pickguard, abalone bound body rosette, rosewood back/sides, mahogany neck, 14/20 fret bound ebony fingerboard with snowflake inlay, ebony bridge with white abalone dot pins, rosewood veneer on bound peghead with abalone vertical logo inlay, 3 per side gold tuners. Available in Natural finish. Mfd. 1938-1942.

	90%	80%	70%	60%	50%	40%	20%
1938-1939	$100,000	$70,000	$60,000	$50,000	$40,000	$36,000	$33,000
1940-1942	$85,000	$59,500	$51,000	$42,500	$34,000	$30,600	$28,050

In 1939, abalone hexagon fingerboard and gold tuners were added.

Grading	100%	98%	95%	90%	80%	70%	60%

D-45 — 1968 to date.

	100%	98%	95%	90%	80%	70%	60%
1968-1969		$16,000	$11,200	$9,600	$8,000	$6,400	$5,760	$5,280
1970-1975		$6,000	$4,200	$3,600	$3,000	$2,400	$2,160	$1,980
1976-1985		$4,500	$3,150	$2,700	$2,250	$1,800	$1,620	$1,485
Mfr.'s Sug. Retail	$6,410	$4,490	$3,845	$3,205	$2,565	$2,305	$2,115	$1,925

In 1968, D-45 brought back by popular demand.

D-45S — similar to D-45, except has a pre-war dreadnought style body, 12/20 fret fingerboard, slotted headstock. Mfd. 1969 to date.

		100%	98%	95%	90%	80%	70%	60%
Mfr.'s Sug. Retail	$6,860	$4,800	$4,115	$3,430	$2,740	$2,475	$2,260	$2,055

This model is a special order instrument.

D12-45 — similar to D-45S, except has 12 strings, 6 per side tuners with pearl buttons.

		100%	98%	95%	90%	80%	70%	60%
Mfr.'s Sug. Retail	$7,020	$4,915	$4,210	$3,510	$2,810	$2,530	$2,320	$2,110

D-60 — solid spruce top, round soundhole, tortoise shell pickguard, 3 stripe bound body/rosette, birdseye maple back/sides, maple neck, 14/20 fret ebony fingerboard with pearl snowflake inlay, ebony bridge with white red dot pins, birdseye maple veneer on ebony bound peghead, 3 per side gold tuners with ebony buttons. Available in Natural finish. Mfd. 1990 to date.

		100%	98%	95%	90%	80%	70%	60%
Mfr.'s Sug. Retail	$2,880	$2,025	$1,730	$1,440	$1,150	$1,035	$950	$860

D-62 — similar to D-60, except has figured maple back/sides, mahogany neck, figured maple peghead veneer, gold tuners with pearl buttons. Mfd. 1988 to date.

		100%	98%	95%	90%	80%	70%	60%
Mfr.'s Sug. Retail	$2,280	$1,595	$1,370	$1,140	$910	$820	$750	$685

Grading	100%	98%	95%	90%	80%	70%	60%

D-76 (BICENTENNIAL LIMITED EDITION) — solid spruce top, round soundhole, black pickguard, herringbone bound body/rosette, rosewood 3 piece back/sides, mahognay neck, 14/20 fret ebony fingerboard with 13 pearl star inlays, ebony bridge with white black dot pins, rosewood peghead veneer with pearl eagle/logo inlay, 3 per side gold tuners. Available in Natural finish. Mfd 1976 only.

	$1,575	$1,100	$945	$785	$630	$565	$515

There were 1,976 models mfd., with an additional 98 (D-45E) exclusively for employees.

HD-28 — solid spruce top, round soundhole, black pickguard, herringbone bound body/rosette, rosewood 2 piece back/sides, 14/20 fret ebony fingerboard with pearl dot inlay, ebony bridge with white black dot pins, 3 per side chrome tuners. Available in Natural finish. Mfd. 1976 to date.

Mfr.'s Sug. Retail	$2,460	$1,720	$1,475	$1,225	$980	$875	$805	$735

Also available with solid red cedar top (CHD-28) and larch top (LHD-28).

☆ HD-28LE — similar to HD-28, except has tortoise shell pickguard, pearl diamond/square fingerboard inlay.

	$2,400	$1,920	$1,560	$1,320	$1,080	$820	$720

This was a Special Edition guitar with a Limited Edition label. This model was Guitar-of-the-Month for December, 1985.

☆ HD-28R — similar to HD-28, except has larger soundhole.

Mfr.'s Sug. Retail	$2,570	$1,795	$1,540	$1,285	$1,025	$925	$845	$770

HD-35 — solid spruce top, round soundhole, black pickguard, herringbone bound body/rosette, rosewood 3 piece back/sides, 14/20 fret bound ebony fingerboard with pearl dot inlay, ebony bridge with white black dot pins, 3 per side chrome tuners. Available in Natural finish. Mfd. 1978 to date.

Mfr.'s Sug. Retail	$2,790	$1,950	$1,670	$1,395	$1,115	$1,005	$920	$835

Also available with solid red cedar top (CHD-35).

CUSTOM 15 — solid spruce top, round soundhole, tortoise shell pickguard, herringbone bound body, 5 stripe rosette, rosewood back/sides, 14/20 fret ebony fingerboard with pearl diamond inlay, ebony bridge with white black dot pins, rosewood peghead veneer, 3 per side chrome tuners. Available in Natural finish. Curr. mfr.

Mfr.'s Sug. Retail	$2,890	$2,025	$1,735	$1,440	$1,150	$1,035	$950	$865

 , cont.

Grading	100%	98%	95%	90%	80%	70%	60%

STYLE 15 — mahogany top, round soundhole, 2 stripe bound body/rosette, black pickguard, mahogany back/sides/neck, 14/20 fret rosewood fingerboard with white dot inlay, rosewood bridge with white pins, black face peghead with logo decal, 3 per side nickel tuners with plastic buttons. Available in Natural finish. Mfd. 1935-1944, re-introduced 1948-1961.

	100%	98%	95%	90%	80%	70%	60%
1935-1944	N/A	N/A	N/A	$1,025	$720	$615	$510
1948-1961	$875	$615	$525	$435	$350	$315	$290

A few early models had maple or birch bodies.
Production of this model was suspended during WWII.

0-15 — similar to Style 15, except has concert style body.

	100%	98%	95%	90%	80%	70%	60%
1935-1944	N/A	N/A	N/A	$1,200	$840	$720	$600
1948-1961	$825	$580	$495	$415	$330	$300	$275

00-17 — grand concert style, mahogany top, round soundhole, 3 stripe bound body/rosette, mahogany back/sides/neck, 14/20 fret rosewood fingerboard, rosewood bridge with black pins, 3 per side tuners. Available in Dark Natural finish. Mfd. 1982-1987.

	100%	98%	95%	90%	80%	70%	60%
	$975	$685	$585	$485	$390	$355	$325

This instrument was a special order item.

Jumbo Series

All instruments in this series have jumbo style bodies.

J-18 — solid spruce top, round soundhole, tortoise shell pickguard, 5 stripe bound body/rosette, mahogany back/sides/neck, 14/20 fret rosewood fingerboard with pearl dot inlay, rosewood bridge with black white dot pins, rosewood peghead veneer, 3 per side chrome tuners with ebony buttons. Available in Natural finish. Mfd. 1988 to date.

	100%	98%	95%	90%	80%	70%	60%
Mfr.'s Sug. Retail	$1,970	$1,380	$1,180	$985	$790	$710	$650	$590

J-21 — spruce top, round soundhole, tortoise shell pickguard, 5 stripe bound body/rosette, rosewood back/sides, mahogany neck, 14/20 fret rosewood fingerboard with pearl dot inlay, rosewood bridge with black white dot pins, rosewood veneer peghead, 3 per side chrome tuners. Available in Natural finish. Mfd. 1985 to date.

	100%	98%	95%	90%	80%	70%	60%
Mfr.'s Sug. Retail	$2,290	$1,600	$1,370	$1,140	$910	$820	$750	$685

This model is a special order instrument.

Grading	100%	98%	95%	90%	80%	70%	60%

J-40 — solid spruce top, round soundhole, black pickguard, 5 stripe bound body/rosette, rosewood back/sides, mahogany neck, 14/20 fret bound ebony fingerboard with abalone hexagon inlay, ebony bridge with white abalone dot pins, rosewood peghead veneer, 3 per side chrome tuners. Available in Natural finish. Mfd. 1985 to date.

Mfr.'s Sug. Retail	$2,440	$1,710	$1,465	$1,220	$975	$875	$805	$730

Add $190 for Black finish (J-40BK).

J C-40 — similar to J-40, except has single rounded cutaway. Mfd. 1987 to date.

Mfr.'s Sug. Retail	$2,560	$1,790	$1,535	$1,280	$1,025	$920	$840	$765

J12-40 — similar to J-40, except has 12 strings, 6 per side gold tuners with ebony buttons.

Mfr.'s Sug. Retail	$2,520	$1,760	$1,510	$1,260	$1,000	$900	$825	$750

J-65 — solid spruce top, round soundhole, tortoise shell pickguard, tortoise shell bound body, 3 stripe rosette, figured maple 2 piece back/sides, maple neck, 14/20 fret bound ebony fingerboard with pearl dot inlay, ebony bridge with white red dot pins, rosewood peghead veneer with logo decal, 3 per side gold tuners with pearl buttons. Available in Natural finish. Mfd. 1985 to date.

Mfr.'s Sug. Retail	$2,370	$1,655	$1,420	$1,180	$945	$850	$780	$710

J12-65 — similar to J-65, except has 12 strings, 6 per side tuners.

Mfr.'s Sug. Retail	$2,460	$1,720	$1,475	$1,225	$980	$875	$805	$735

M Series

M-36 — grand auditorium style, solid spruce top, round soundhole, tortoise shell pickguard, 5 stripe bound body/rosette, rosewood back/sides, mahogany neck, 14/20 fret bound ebony fingerboard with pearl dot inlay, rosewood bridge with white black dot pins, rosewood veneer on bound peghead, 3 per side chrome tuners. Available in Natural finish. Mfd. 1978 to date.

Mfr.'s Sug. Retail	$2,170	$1,520	$1,295	$1,085	$865	$780	$715	$650

Early production models came with an unbound peghead.

M-38 — similar to M-36, except has abalone rosette. Mfd. 1977 to date.

Mfr.'s Sug. Retail	$2,700	$1,890	$1,620	$1,350	$1,080	$970	$890	$810

M-64 — similar to M-36, except has flame maple back/sides/neck, unbound fingerboard/peghead. Mfd. 1985 to date.

Mfr.'s Sug. Retail	$2,290	$1,600	$1,370	$1,140	$910	$820	$750	$685

Martin & Co. EST. 1833 , cont.

Grading		100%	98%	95%	90%	80%	70%	60%

MC-28 — single round cutaway grand auditorium style, solid spruce top, oval soundhole, black pickguard, 3 stripe bound body/rosette, rosewood back/sides, mahogany neck, 22 fret ebony fingerboard with pearl dot inlay, ebony bridge with white black dot pins, rosewood peghead veneer, 3 per side chrome tuners. Available in Natural finish. Mfd. 1981 to date.

Mfr.'s Sug. Retail		$2,500	$1,750	$1,500	$1,250	$1,000	$900	$825	$750

MC-68 — single round cutaway grand auditorium style, solid spruce top, oval soundhole, tortoise shell pickguard, 5 stripe bound body/rosette, flame maple back/sides, maple neck, 22 fret bound ebony fingerboard with abalone dot inlay, ebony bridge with white abalone dot pins, rosewood veneer on bound peghead with abalone inlay, 3 per side gold tuners. Available in Natural and Sunburst finish. Mfd. 1985 to date.

Mfr.'s Sug. Retail		$2,760	$1,930	$1,655	$1,380	$1,105	$995	$910	$825

OM Series

Grading		90%	80%	70%	60%	50%	40%	20%

OM-18 — orchestra style, spruce top, tortoise shell pickguard, round soundhole, wooden bound body, rope pattern rosette, mahogany back/sides/neck, 14/20 fret ebony fingerboard with pearl dot inlay, ebony bridge with black pearl dot pins, 3 per side tuners with ivoroid buttons. Available in Natural finish. Mfd. 1930-1933.

		$4,500	$3,150	$2,700	$2,250	$1,800	$1,620	$1,485

This model has banjo style tuners.

OM-28 — orchestra style, solid spruce top, round soundhole, black pickguard, 5 stripe bound body/rosette, rosewood back/sides, mahogany neck, 14/20 fret ebony fingerboard with pearl dot inlay, ebony bridge with white black dot pins, rosewood peghead veneer, 3 per side chrome tuners. Available in Natural finish. Mfd. 1929-1933.

		$11,750	$8,225	$7,050	$5,875	$4,700	$4,230	$3,880
Grading		100%	98%	95%	90%	80%	70%	60%

OM-28, Current Manufacture — these instruments were re-introduced as special order items.

Mfr.'s Sug. Retail		$2,650	$1,855	$1,590	$1,325	$1,060	$955	$875	$795
Grading			90%	80%	70%	60%	50%	40%	20%

OM-45 — orchestra style, solid spruce top, round soundhole, black pickguard, abalone bound body/rosette, rosewood back/sides, mahogany neck, 14/20 fret bound ebony fingerboard with abalone snowflake inlay, ebony bridge with white abalone dot pins, bound peghead with rosewood veneer and abalone logo inlay, 3 per side gold banjo style tuners with ivoroid buttons. Available in Natural finish. Originally mfd. 1930-1933.

		$22,500	$15,750	$13,500	$11,250	$9,000	$8,100	$7,425

Grading	90%	80%	70%	60%	50%	40%	20%

≵ **OM-45 Deluxe** — similar to OM-45, except has abalone vine pickguard inlay, abalone snowflake bridge wings inlay. Mfd. 1930.

	$27,500	$19,250	$16,500	$13,750	$11,000	$9,900	$9,075

Grading	100%	98%	95%	90%	80%	70%	60%

≵ **OM-45, Current Manufacture** — similar to OM-45, except has abalone hexagon fingerboard inlay, gold enclosed tuners. Mfd. 1977 to date.

Mfr.'s Sug. Retail	$6,530	$4,570	$3,920	$3,265	$2,610	$2,350	$2,155	$1,960

This is a special order instrument.

ACOUSTIC BASS

All models have jumbo style bodies, and are available with fretless fingerboard at no additional charge.

B-40 — jumbo style, solid spruce top, round soundhole, black pickguard, 5 stripe bound body/rosette, rosewood back/sides, mahogany neck, 17/23 fret ebony fingerboard, ebony bridge with white black dot pins, rosewood peghead veneer, 2 per side chrome tuners. Available in Natural finish. Mfd. 1988 to date.

Mfr.'s Sug. Retail	$2,570	$1,795	$1,540	$1,285	$1,025	$925	$845	$770

Add $230 for acoustic pickup, volume/tone controls, active preamp.

≵ **B-540** — similar to B-40, except has 5 strings, striped ebony fingerboard/bridge, 5/2 per side tuners. Mfd. 1992 to date.

Mfr.'s Sug. Retail	$2,630	$1,840	$1,580	$1,320	$1,055	$950	$870	$790

≵ **BC-40** — similar to B-40, except has single rounded cutaway, oval soundhole. Mfd. 1990 to date.

Mfr.'s Sug. Retail	$2,770	$1,940	$1,660	$1,385	$1,110	$1,000	$915	$830

B-65 — similar to B-40, except has tortoise shell pickguard, flame maple back/sides. Mfd. 1987 to date.

Mfr.'s Sug. Retail	$2,460	$1,720	$1,475	$1,225	$980	$875	$805	$735

ELECTRIC

D-28E — dreadnought style, spruce top, round soundhole, black pickguard, 3 stripe bound body/rosette, rosewood back/sides, 14/20 fret ebony fingerboard with pearl dot inlay, ebony bridge with white black dot pins, 3 per side tuners, gold hardware, 2 single coil exposed DeArmond pickups, 2 volume/2 tone pickups, 3 position switch. Available in Natural finish. Mfd. 1959-1965.

	$1,830	$1,280	$1,095	$915	$730	$660	$605

Grading	100%	98%	95%	90%	80%	70%	60%

E Series

These models have offset rounded double cutaway bodies, mahogany necks, rounded wave cresting style headstocks and 3 per side tuners.

E-18 — 9 piece maple/rosewood/walnut body, 22 fret rosewood fingerboard with pearl dot inlay, Leo Quan wrapped bridge, brass nut, rosewood peghead veneer with CFM logo decal, Sperzel tuners, chrome hardware, 2 humbucker covered DiMarzio pickups, 2 volume/2 tone controls, 3 position/phase switches. Available in Natural finish. Mfd. 1979-1983.

	$400	$280	$240	$200	$160	$145	$130

Add $50 for coil tap switch (EM-18).

E-28 — similar to E-18, except has mahogany body, thru body neck, 24 fret ebony fingerboard, single unit tunomatic bridge/stop tailpiece, exposed Seymour Duncan pickups, 2 volume/treble/bass controls, active electronics. Available in Sunburst finish. Mfd. 1980-1983.

	$650	$455	$390	$325	$260	$235	$215

F Series

These guitars have a traditional style Martin headstock.

F-50 — single rounded cutaway semi hollow bound plywood body, f holes, raised black pickguard, mahogany neck, 20 fret rosewood fingerboard with white dot inlay, adjustable plexiglass bridge/trapeze tailpiece, 3 per side tuners, chrome hardware, adjustable exposed pickup, volume/tone control. Available in Sunburst finish. Mfd. 1961-1965.

	$625	$440	$375	$310	$250	$225	$205

F-55 — similar to F-50, except has 2 pickups, 2 volume/2 tone controls, 3 position switch.

	$750	$525	$450	$375	$300	$270	$245

F-65 — similar to F-50, except has double cutaway, Bigsby style vibrato, 2 pickups, 2 volume/2 tone controls, 3 position switch.

	$550	$385	$330	$275	$220	$200	$180

GT Series

These guitars have a non-traditional large headstock, with 2 sharp upper corners scooping down to the center.

GT-70 — single rounded cutaway semi hollow bound plywood body, arch top, f holes, raised white pickguard, mahogany neck, 22 fret bound rosewood fingerboard with white dot inlay, adjustable bridge/Bigsby style vibrato, bound peghead with logo decal, 3 per side tuners, chrome hardware, 2 exposed pickups, 2 volume/2 tone controls, 3 position switch. Available in Black and Burgundy finish. Mfd. 1965-1968.

	$750	$525	$450	$375	$300	$270	$245

Grading	100%	98%	95%	90%	80%	70%	60%

GT-75 — similar to GT-70, except has double rounded cutaways.

		100%	98%	95%	90%	80%	70%	60%
		$775	$540	$460	$385	$310	$280	$255

GT-75-12 — similar to GT-75, except has twelve strings.

		100%	98%	95%	90%	80%	70%	60%
		$600	$420	$360	$300	$240	$215	$195

This model has a traditional style headstock.

ELECTRIC BASS

These models have offset rounded double cutaway bodies, mahogany necks, rounded wave cresting style headstocks and 2 per side tuners.

EB-18 — 9 piece maple/rosewood/walnut body, 22 fret rosewood fingerboard with pearl dot inlay, Leo Quan fixed bridge, brass nut, rosewood peghead veneer with CFM logo decal, Grover tuners, chrome hardware, exposed DiMarzio pickup, volume/tone control, 2 position switch. Available in Natural finish. Mfd. 1979-1983.

		100%	98%	95%	90%	80%	70%	60%
		$425	$295	$250	$210	$170	$150	$135

EB-28 — mahogany body, thru body mahognay neck, 22 fret ebony fingerboard with pearl dot inlay, Schaller tunomatic bridge/stop tailpiece, rosewood peghead veneer with CFM logo decal, Schaller tuners, chrome hardware, P-style/J-style exposed DiMarzio pickups, 2 volume/treble/bass controls, 3 position pickup, phase and bypass switches, active electronics. Available in Sunburst finish. Mfd. 1980-1983.

		100%	98%	95%	90%	80%	70%	60%
		$650	$455	$390	$325	$260	$235	$215

MODULUS GRAPHITE

Manufactured and distributed by Modulus Graphite, Inc., located in San Francisco, CA.

Modulus Graphite was started in 1977 by Geoff Gould. The company began manufacturing replacement necks for other companies and eventually developed its own line of instruments.

All necks are made of a graphite/epoxy composite, all fingerboards are made of a phenolic/ebonol mixture, unless otherwise listed.

All models are available with the following, unless otherwise listed: Standard finishes are Amber, Clear Blue, Clear Green, Clear Red, Deep Black, Monza Red, Pure White, Sea Foam Green, Surf Green and Vintage Pink.

Custom color finishes include: Black Cherry, Blue/Greenburst, Blue/Purpleburst, Blue Velvet, Charcoal Metalflake, Cherryburst, Clear Black, Green Velvet, Honeyburst and Purple Metalflake.

Add $100 for Custom Color finishes.

Grading	100%	98%	95%	90%	80%	70%	60%

ELECTRIC

The following options are available on all models in this series:
Add $75 for black or gold hardware.
Add $100 for body matching colored neck.
Add $200 for double locking or standard vibrato.

Blackknife Series

BOB WEIR SIGNATURE — offset double cutaway alder body, cocobola top, thru body neck, 24 fret fingerboard with white dot inlay, double locking Floyd Rose vibrato, 6 on one side tuners, black hardware, 2 single coil/1 humbucker EMG pickups, volume/tone/active electronics control, 3 mini switches. Curr. mfr.

Mfr.'s Sug. Retail	$3,200	$2,240	$1,920	$1,600	$1,280	$1,150	$1,055	$960

CLASSIC — offset double cutaway alder body, figured maple top, bolt-on neck, 22 fret fingerboard with white dot inlay, fixed bridge, 6 on one side tuners, gold hardware, humbucker/single coil/humbucker EMG pickups, volume/tone/active electronics control, 3 mini switches. Curr. mfr.

Mfr.'s Sug. Retail	$2,495	$1,745	$1,495	$1,250	$1,000	$900	$825	$750

CUSTOM — offset double cutaway alder body, figured maple top, thru body neck, 24 fret fingerboard with white dot inlay, double locking Floyd Rose vibrato, 6 on one side tuners, gold hardware, humbucker/single coil/humbucker EMG pickups, volume/tone/active electronics control, 3 mini switches. Curr. mfr.

Mfr.'s Sug. Retail	$2,995	$2,095	$1,795	$1,495	$1,195	$1,075	$985	$895

MODEL T — tele style alder body, bolt-on neck, 22 fret fingerboard with white dot inlay, strings thru bridge, 6 on one side tuners, chrome hardware, 1 Seymour Duncan/1 Van Zandt single coil pickups, volume/tone control, 3 position switch. Curr. mfr.

Mfr.'s Sug. Retail	$1,695	$1,185	$1,015	$845	$675	$605	$555	$505

⚞ **Model T Custom** — similar to Model T, except has figured maple top, black hardware, active electronics control.

Mfr.'s Sug. Retail	$2,095	$1,465	$1,255	$1,045	$840	$755	$685	$625

SPECIAL 3H — strat style alder body, bolt-on neck, 22 fret fingerboard with white dot inlay, double locking Floyd Rose vibrato, 6 on one side tuners, chrome hardware, 2 single coil/1 humbucker EMG pickups, volume/tone control, 3 mini switches. Curr. mfr.

Mfr.'s Sug. Retail	$1,995	$1,395	$1,195	$995	$795	$720	$660	$600

⚞ **Special 3H Custom** — similar to Special 3H, except has figured maple top, black hardware, active electronics control.

Mfr.'s Sug. Retail	$2,395	$1,675	$1,435	$1,195	$955	$855	$785	$715

Grading	100%	98%	95%	90%	80%	70%	60%

VINTAGE — offset double cutaway alder body, white pickguard, bolt-on neck, 22 fret fingerboard with white dot inlay, 3 single coil Van Zandt pickups, volume/2 tone controls, 5 position switch. Curr. mfr.

Mfr.'s Sug. Retail	$1,895	$1,325	$1,135	$950	$760	$685	$625	$570

Vintage Custom — similar to Vintage, except has figured maple top, black hardware.

Mfr.'s Sug. Retail	$2,295	$1,605	$1,375	$1,150	$920	$825	$755	$690

ELECTRIC BASS

The following options are available on all models in this series:

Add 10% for left handed version.
Add $100 for fretless fingerboard.
Add $100 for Kahler bridge upgrade.
Add $100 for black or gold hardware.
Add $100 for body matching colored neck.
Add $600 for piezo bridge pickup (4-string).
Add $700 for piezo bridge pickup (5-string).
Add $800 for piezo bridge pickup (6-string).
Add $200 for fretless fingerboard with lines.
Add $200 for Bartolini pickups with treble/bass controls.
Add $250 for Bartolini pickups with treble/bass/mix controls.

M92-4 — offset double cutaway alder or poplar body, black pickguard, bolt-on neck, 24 fret fingerboard with white dot inlay, fixed bridge, 2 per side tuners, chrome hardware, humbucker covered pickup, volume/treble/bass controls, active electronics. Available in Black, Monza Red, Natural, Seafoam Green, Transparent Blue, Transparent Green, Transparent Red, Transparent Yellow, Vintage Pink and White finish. New 1993.

Mfr.'s Sug. Retail	$1,795	$1,255	$1,075	$895	$715	$645	$590	$540

M92-5 — similar to M92-4, except has 5 strings, 3/2 per side tuners.

Mfr.'s Sug. Retail	$1,995	$1,395	$1,195	$995	$795	$720	$660	$600

MODULUS PRIME-4 — offset double cutaway ash body, bolt-on neck, 24 fret cocabola fingerboard, fixed bridge, 2 per side tuners, chrome hardware, humbucker pickup, volume/treble/bass controls, active electronics. Available in Natural finish. New 1993.

Mfr.'s Sug. Retail	$1,995	$1,395	$1,195	$995	$795	$720	$660	$600

Add $100 for Transparent Color finishes.

Modulus Prime-5 — similar to Modulus Prime-4, except has 5 strings, 3/2 per side tuners.

Mfr.'s Sug. Retail	$2,195	$1,540	$1,320	$1,100	$880	$790	$725	$660

Modulus Prime-6 — similar to Modulus Prime-4, except has 6 strings, 3 per side tuners.

Mfr.'s Sug. Retail	$2,495	$1,745	$1,495	$1,250	$1,000	$900	$825	$750

Grading	100%	98%	95%	90%	80%	70%	60%

Quantam Series

4 SPi — offset double cutaway alder/poplar body, bolt-on neck, 24 fret fingerboard with white inlay, fixed Modulus/Gotoh bridge, 2 per side tuners, chrome hardware, 2 active EMG pickups, 2 volume/treble/bass controls. Curr. mfr.

Mfr.'s Sug. Retail	$2,195	$1,540	$1,320	$1,100	$880	$790	$725	$660

The treble/bass controls are concentric in some models.

5 SPi — similar to 4 SPi, except has 5 strings, 3/2 per side tuners.

Mfr.'s Sug. Retail	$2,395	$1,675	$1,435	$1,195	$955	$855	$785	$715

6 SPi — similar to 4 SPi, except has 6 strings, 3 per side tuners.

Mfr.'s Sug. Retail	$2,695	$1,885	$1,620	$1,350	$1,080	$970	$890	$810

4 SPi CUSTOM — similar to 4 SPi, except has figured maple top, black hardware.

Mfr.'s Sug. Retail	$2,495	$1,745	$1,495	$1,250	$1,000	$900	$825	$750

5 SPi Custom — similar to 5 SPi, except has figured maple top, black hardware.

Mfr.'s Sug. Retail	$2,695	$1,885	$1,620	$1,350	$1,080	$970	$890	$810

6 SPi Custom — similar to 6 SPi, except has figured maple top, black hardware.

Mfr.'s Sug. Retail	$2,995	$2,095	$1,795	$1,495	$1,195	$1,075	$985	$895

4 TBX — offset double cutaway alder body, figured maple top, thru body neck, 24 fret fingerboard with white dot inlay, fixed Modulus/Gotoh bridge, graphite/epoxy nut, 2 per side Modulus/Gotoh tuners, gold hardware, 2 humbucker EMG pickups, 2 volume/treble/bass controls. Curr. mfr.

Mfr.'s Sug. Retail	$3,395	$2,375	$2,040	$1,695	$1,360	$1,225	$1,120	$1,025

The treble/bass controls are concentric in some models.

5 TBX — similar to 4 TBX, except has 5 strings, Schaller bridge.

Mfr.'s Sug. Retail	$3,695	$2,585	$2,220	$1,845	$1,475	$1,325	$1,215	$1,100

6 TBX — similar to 4 TBX, except has 6 strings, Kahler bridge.

Mfr.'s Sug. Retail	$3,995	$2,795	$2,395	$1,995	$1,595	$1,435	$1,315	$1,195

N

NATIONAL

As this edition went to press, more research is under way on this trademark and the results will be published in the 2nd edition of the Blue Book of Guitar Values.

NEO

Manufacturer located in Buckingham, PA since 1991. Contact the manufacturer for details (see Trademark Index).

Neo guitars were developed to capitalize on the visual effects that neon lighting can provide a musician while performing. Their original concept has been expanded to include gumballs, money or gold fish contained within the instrument's body. Originally, there were four basic instruments in this line which had a price range of $2,800-$3,700. Additionally, the company has expanded this concept to include electric bass guitars and violins.

NORMAN GUITARS

Manufacturer located in Canada. Distributed by MMS, Inc. located in Neptune, NJ.

ACOUSTIC

B Series

All models in this series have the following options:
Add 10% for left handed version.
Add $159 for L R Baggs passive pickup system.
Add $325 for L R Baggs active pickup system with 3 band EQ.

Grading	100%	98%	95%	90%	80%	70%	60%

B15 — dreadnought style, wild cherry top, round soundhole, black pickguard, bound body, black ring rosette, wild cherry back/sides, mahogany neck, 14/21 fret rosewood fingerboard with pearl dot inlay, rosewood bridge with white black dot pins, 3 per side chrome tuners. Available in Natural finish. Mfd. 1991.

	100%	98%	95%	90%	80%	70%	60%
	$360	$250	$215	$180	$145	$130	$120

Add $125 for 12 string version.

Grading	100%	98%	95%	90%	80%	70%	60%

B20 — dreadnought style, solid spruce top, round soundhole, black pickguard, bound body, one ring rosette, cherry back/sides, mahogany neck, 14/21 fret rosewood fingerboard with pearl dot inlay, rosewood bridge with white black dot pins, 3 per side chrome tuners. Available in Natural finish. Mfd. 1991.

	$420	$295	$250	$210	$170	$150	$135

    Add $120 for 12 string version.
This model also available in folk style build.

B50 — dreadnought style, solid spruce top, round soundhole, black pickguard, bound body, 3 ring wooden inlay rosette, maple back/sides, mahogany neck, 14/21 fret rosewood fingerboard with pearl dot inlay, rosewood bridge with white black dot pins, 3 per side chrome tuners. Available in Natural finish. Mfd. 1991.

	$695	$485	$415	$350	$280	$250	$230

    Add $125 for 12 string version.

CUTAWAY — venetian cutaway dreadnought style, solid spruce top, round soundhole, black pickguard, bound body, 3 ring wooden inlay rosette, cherry back/sides, mahogany neck, 14/21 fret rosewood fingerboard with pearl dot inlay, rosewood bridge with white black dot pins, 3 per side chrome tuners. Available in Natural finish. Mfd. 1991.

	$595	$415	$360	$300	$240	$215	$195

Studio Series

All models in this series have the following options:
    Add 10% for left handed version.
    Add $159 for L R Baggs passive pickup system.
    Add $325 for L R Baggs active pickup system with 3 band EQ.

ST40 — dreadnought style, solid cedar top, round soundhole, black pickguard, bound body, 3 stripe rosette, mahogany back/sides/neck, 14/21 fret rosewood fingerboard with pearl dot inlay, rosewood bridge with white black dot pins, 3 per side chrome tuners. Available in Natural finish. Mfd. 1991.

	$520	$365	$310	$260	$210	$190	$170

ST68 — dreadnought style, solid spruce top, round soundhole, black pickguard, bound body, 3 ring wooden inlay rosette, rosewood back/sides, mahogany neck, 14/21 fret ebony fingerboard with pearl dot inlay, ebony bridge with white black dot pins, 3 per side chrome tuners. Available in Natural finish. Mfd. 1991.

	$950	$665	$570	$475	$380	$345	$315

O

OVATION

Manufacturer located in New Hartford, CT since 1967. Distributed by Kaman Music Corp. located in Bloomfield, CT.

Using synthetic materials that he used to build helicopter rotor blades, Charles H. Kaman founded Ovation Instruments, Inc. in 1967, and began constructing acoustic instruments out of the material he used in his aeronautical endeavors. Also known as one of the first companies to make acoustic instruments with pickups built into the bridge.

All Ovation instruments have a synthetic rounded back/sides construct.

ACOUSTIC

Grading	100%	98%	95%	90%	80%	70%	60%

Adamas Series

All Adamas models have a carbon-graphite composite with a birch veneer top and carved fiberglass body binding. There are also 11 various sized soundholes with leaf pattern maple veneer around them, situated around the upper bouts on both sides of the fingerboard. All models have 6 piezo bridge pickups, volume/3 band EQ controls, and active preamp.

ADAMAS 6 — folk style, composite top, mahogany neck, 14/24 fret walnut extended fingerboard with maple/ebony inlay, walnut bridge with carved flower designs, carved flower design on peghead, 3 per side gold tuners. Available in Beige, Black, Blue, Brown and Red finish. Curr. mfr.

Mfr.'s Sug. Retail	$2,800	$1,960	$1,680	$1,400	$1,120	$1,010	$925	$840

⅜ **Adamas Cutaway** — similar to Adamas 6, except has venetian cutaway, no soundholes on cutaway side.

Mfr.'s Sug. Retail	$2,900	$2,030	$1,740	$1,450	$1,160	$1,040	$955	$870

⅜ **Adamas 12** — similar to Adamas 6, except has 12 strings.

Mfr.'s Sug. Retail	$3,000	$2,095	$1,800	$1,500	$1,200	$1,080	$990	$900

ADAMAS II — folk style, composite top, mahogany/maple 5 piece neck, 14/24 fret walnut extended fingerboard with maple/ebony triangle inlay, walnut bridge, walnut veneer on peghead, 3 per side gold tuners. Available in Beige, Black, Blue, Brown and Red finish. Curr. mfr.

Mfr.'s Sug. Retail	$2,100	$1,475	$1,260	$1,050	$840	$755	$690	$630

Grading	100%	98%	95%	90%	80%	70%	60%

Adamas II Cutaway — similar to Adamas II, except has venetian cutaway, no soundholes on cutaway side.

Mfr.'s Sug. Retail	$2,200	$1,540	$1,320	$1,100	$880	$790	$725	$660

Adamas II 12 — similar to Adamas II, except has 12 strings.

Mfr.'s Sug. Retail	$2,300	$1,610	$1,380	$1,150	$920	$830	$760	$690

Celebrity Series

CELEBRITY — folk style, spruce top, round soundhole, 5 stripe bound body, leaf pattern rosette, mahogany neck, 14/20 fret bound rosewood fingerboard with pearl dot inlay, walnut bridge with pearloid dot inlays, rosewood veneer on peghead, 3 per side chrome tuners. Available in Barnboard, Brownburst, Natural and Sunburst finish. Curr. mfr.

Mfr.'s Sug. Retail	$380	$265	$225	$190	$150	$135	$120	$110

Add $90 for pearl diamond/dot inlay, piezo bridge pickups, volume/tone control.

Celebrity 12 — similar to Celebrity, except has 12 strings. Available in Natural and Sunburst finish.

Mfr.'s Sug. Retail	$470	$330	$280	$235	$190	$170	$155	$140

Add $90 for piezo bridge pickups, volume tone control.

CELEBRITY CLASSIC — classic style, spruce top, round soundhole, 5 stripe bound body, leaf pattern rosette, mahogany neck, 12/19 fret bound rosewood fingerboard, walnut bridge, 3 per side gold tuners with pearloid buttons. Available in Natural finish. Curr. mfr.

Mfr.'s Sug. Retail	$380	$265	$225	$190	$150	$135	$120	$110

Add $90 for piezo bridge pickups, volume/tone control.
Add $150 for venetian cutaway, piezo bridge pickups, volume/tone control.

CELEBRITY CUTAWAY — single venetian cutaway folk style, spruce top, round soundhole, 5 stripe bound body, leaf pattern rosette, mahogany neck, 20 fret bound rosewood fingerboard with pearloid diamond/dot inlay, walnut bridge with pearloid dot inlay, walnut veneer on peghead, 3 per side chrome tuners, 6 piezo bridge pickups, volume/tone control. Available in Barnboard, Brownburst, Natural and Sunburst finish. Mfd. 1991 to date.

Mfr.'s Sug. Retail	$500	$350	$300	$250	$200	$180	$165	$150

Celebrity Cutaway Shallow — similar to Celebrity Cutaway, except has super shallow body.

Mfr.'s Sug. Retail	$530	$370	$320	$265	$210	$190	$175	$160

Add $40 for preamp with 3 band EQ.

Grading	100%	98%	95%	90%	80%	70%	60%

Classic Series

CLASSIC — classic style, cedar top, round soundhole, 5 stripe bound body, leaf pattern rosette, 5 piece mahogany/maple neck, 12/19 fret extended ebony fingerboard, walnut bridge, walnut veneer on peghead, 3 per side gold tuners, piezo bridge pickup, volume/3 band EQ control, active preamp. Available in Natural finish. Curr. mfr.

Mfr.'s Sug. Retail	$1,420	$995	$850	$710	$570	$510	$465	$425

⅔ **Classic Cutaway** — similar to Classic, except has venetian cutaway. Available in Natural and White finish.

Mfr.'s Sug. Retail	$1,520	$1,065	$910	$760	$610	$550	$505	$455

This model is also available with super shallow body.

Collector's Series

1993 COLLECTOR'S — single venetian cutaway folk style, solid spruce top, multi upper bout soundholes, 5 stripe bound body, multiple woods veneer around soundholes, mahogany/padauk/ebony 5 piece neck, 22 fret ebony fingerboard, maple "1993" inlay at 12th fret, string thru walnut bridge, maple logo inlay on peghead, 3 per side gold Schaller tuners with ebony buttons, piezo bridge pickup, volume/3 band EQ control, active preamp. Available in Natural finish. Mfd. 1993 only.

Mfr.'s Sug. Retail	$1,500	$1,050	$900	$750	$600	$540	$495	$450

Custom Series

CUSTOM BALLADEER — folk style, spruce top, round soundhole, 5 stripe bound body, leaf pattern rosette, 5 piece mahogany/maple neck, 14/20 fret ebony fingerboard with pearl diamond/dot inlay, walnut bridge with pearl dot inlay, 3 per side nickel tuners, 6 piezo bridge pickups, volume/3 band EQ control, FET preamp. Available in Black, Natural, Sunburst and White finish. Curr. mfr.

Mfr.'s Sug. Retail	$1,050	$735	$630	$525	$420	$380	$345	$315

⅔ **Custom Balladeer Shallow Cutaway** — similar to Custom Balladeer, except has venetian cutaway, super shallow body.

Mfr.'s Sug. Retail	$1,150	$805	$690	$575	$460	$415	$380	$345

⅔ **Custom Balladeer 12** — similar to Custom Balladeer, except has 12 strings, 6 per side chrome tuners with pearloid buttons.

Mfr.'s Sug. Retail	$1,250	$875	$750	$625	$500	$450	$415	$375

Grading	100%	98%	95%	90%	80%	70%	60%

CUSTOM LEGEND — folk style, spruce top, round soundhole, abalone bound body, abalone leaf pattern rosette, 5 piece mahogany/maple neck, 14/20 fret bound ebony fingerboard with abalone diamond/dot inlay, walnut bridge with carved flower designs and pearl dot inlay, walnut veneer on peghead, 3 per side gold tuners with pearloid buttons, 6 piezo bridge pickups, volume/3 band EQ control, active preamp. Available in Black, Natural, Sunburst and White finish. Curr. mfr.

	100%	98%	95%	90%	80%	70%	60%
Mfr.'s Sug. Retail	$1,600	$1,120	$960	$800	$640	$575	$530	$480

Custom Legend Cutaway — similar to Custom Legend, except has venetian cutaway.

	100%	98%	95%	90%	80%	70%	60%
Mfr.'s Sug. Retail	$1,700	$1,190	$1,020	$850	$680	$610	$560	$510

This model is also available with super shallow body.

Custom Legend 12 — similar to Custom Legend, except has 12 strings.

	100%	98%	95%	90%	80%	70%	60%
Mfr.'s Sug. Retail	$1,800	$1,260	$1,080	$900	$720	$650	$595	$540

Elite Series

This series has the same soundhole design/pattern as the Adamas series.

ELITE — folk style, spruce top, 5 stripe bound body, 5 piece mahogany/maple neck, 14/22 fret extended rosewood fingerboard with maple triangle inlay, walnut bridge, 3 per side gold tuners, 6 piezo bridge pickups, volume/3 band EQ control, active preamp. Available in Black, Natural, Sunburst and White finish. Curr. mfr.

	100%	98%	95%	90%	80%	70%	60%
Mfr.'s Sug. Retail	$1,375	$965	$825	$685	$550	$495	$450	$410

Elite Cutaway — similar to Elite, except has venetian cutaway.

	100%	98%	95%	90%	80%	70%	60%
Mfr.'s Sug. Retail	$1,475	$1,035	$885	$735	$590	$525	$480	$440

Elite Shallow Cutaway — similar to Elite, except has super shallow body, venetian cutaway.

	100%	98%	95%	90%	80%	70%	60%
Mfr.'s Sug. Retail	$1,475	$1,035	$885	$735	$590	$525	$480	$440

Add $200 for Angel Step Walnut finish.

Elite 12 — similar to Elite, except has 12 strings.

	100%	98%	95%	90%	80%	70%	60%
Mfr.'s Sug. Retail	$1,575	$1,100	$945	$785	$630	$565	$515	$470

Elite 12 Shallow Cutaway — similar to Elite, except has 12 strings, super shallow body, venetian cutaway.

	100%	98%	95%	90%	80%	70%	60%
Mfr.'s Sug. Retail	$1,675	$1,170	$1,000	$835	$670	$600	$550	$500

Add $200 for Angel Step Walnut finish.

Grading	100%	98%	95%	90%	80%	70%	60%

Legend Series

LEGEND — folk style, spruce top, round soundhole, 5 stripe bound body, leaf pattern rosette, 5 piece mahogany/maple neck, 14/20 fret bound rosewood fingerboard with pearl diamond/dot inlay, walnut bridge, walnut veneer on peghead, 3 per side gold tuners. Available in Black, Natural, Sunburst and White finish. Curr. mfr.

Mfr.'s Sug. Retail	$1,035	$730	$625	$520	$415	$375	$340	$310

Add $225 for volume/3 band EQ control, active preamp.

Legend Cutaway — similar to Legend, except has venetian cutaway, volume/3 band EQ control, active preamp.

Mfr.'s Sug. Retail	$1,360	$950	$815	$680	$545	$490	$445	$405

This model is also available with super shallow body.

Legend 12 — similar to Legend, except has 12 strings, volume/3 band EQ control, active preamp.

Mfr.'s Sug. Retail	$1,460	$1,020	$875	$730	$585	$525	$480	$440

Legend 12 Shallow Cutaway — similar to Legend 12, except has super shallow body, venetian cutaway.

Mfr.'s Sug. Retail	$1,575	$1,100	$945	$785	$630	$565	$515	$470

Pinnacle Series

PINNACLE — folk style, spruce top, 5 stripe bound body, leaf pattern rosette, mahogany neck, 14/20 fret rosewood fingerboard with white dot inlay, rosewood bridge with white dot inlay, rosewood veneer on peghead, 3 per side chrome tuners, 6 piezo bridge pickups, volume/3 band EQ control, FET preamp. Available in Barnboard, Black, Ebony Stain, Natural, Opaque Blue, Sunburst, Transparent Blue Stain and White finish. Mfd. 1991-92.

		$630	$540	$450	$360	$325	$300	$275

Last Mfr.'s Sug. Retail was $900.

Pinnacle Shallow Cutaway — similar to Pinnacle, except has venetian cutaway, super shallow body. Mfd. 1991 to date.

Mfr.'s Sug. Retail	$1,000	$700	$600	$500	$400	$360	$330	$300

Ultra Deluxe Series

ULTRA DELUXE — folk style, spruce top, round soundhole, 5 stripe bound body, leaf pattern rosette, 14/20 fret bound rosewood fingerboard with abalone diamond/dot inlay, walnut bridge with white dot inlay, rosewood veneer on peghead, 3 per side gold tuners. Available in Barnboard, Black, Brownburst, Natural and Sunburst finish. Curr. mfr.

Mfr.'s Sug. Retail	$480	$335	$290	$240	$190	$170	$155	$145

Add $200 for piezo bridge pickups, FET preamp, volume/tone control.

Grading	100%	98%	95%	90%	80%	70%	60%

Ultra Deluxe Cutaway — similar to Ultra Deluxe, except has venetian cutaway, 6 piezo bridge pickups, FET preamp, volume/tone control. Available in Barnboard, Flame Maple Brownburst and Sunburst finish. Curr. mfr.

Mfr.'s Sug. Retail	$730	$510	$440	$365	$290	$260	$240	$220

Ultra Deluxe Shallow Cutaway — similar to Ultra Deluxe Cutaway, except has super shallow body. Available in Barnboard, Black, Flame Maple Brownburst, Flame Maple Redburst, Natural, Sunburst and White finish. Curr. mfr.

Mfr.'s Sug. Retail	$780	$545	$470	$390	$315	$280	$260	$235

Ultra Deluxe 12 — similar to Ultra Deluxe, except has 12 strings.

Mfr.'s Sug. Retail	$530	$370	$320	$265	$210	$190	$175	$160

Add $200 for piezo bridge pickups, volume/tone control, FET preamp.

ACOUSTIC BASS

CELEBRITY — single venetian cutaway folk style, spruce top, round soundhole, 5 stripe bound body, leaf pattern rosette, mahogany neck, 20 fret bound rosewood fingerboard with pearloid diamond/dot inlay, walnut bridge with pearloid dot inlay, walnut veneer on peghead, 2 per side chrome tuners, piezo bridge pickups, volume/tone control, FET preamp. Available in Ebony Stain, Natural and Sunburst finish. Mfd. 1993 to date.

Mfr.'s Sug. Retail	$600	$420	$360	$300	$240	$215	$195	$180

ELITE — single venetian cutaway folk style, spruce top, 5 stripe bound body, multiple soundholes around the top bouts with leaf pattern veneer, 5 piece mahogany/maple neck, 22 fret extended rosewood fingerboard with maple triangle inlay, walnut bridge, 2 per side gold tuners, piezo bridge pickup, volume/3 band EQ control, active preamp. Available in Black, Natural and Sunburst finish. Mfd. 1992 to date.

Mfr.'s Sug. Retail	$2,100	$1,475	$1,260	$1,050	$840	$755	$690	$630

P

PRS GUITARS

Manufactured and distributed by Paul Reed Smith Guitars located in Annapolis, MD.

Paul Reed Smith began building guitars individually circa 1975 and established PRS Guitars during 1985.

ACOUSTIC

This series of instruments was designed and built by Dana Bourgeois and Paul Reed Smith.

Grading	100%	98%	95%	90%	80%	70%	60%

CUSTOM CUTAWAY — single flat cutaway dreadnought style, spruce top, round soundhole, abalone bound body and rosette, figured maple back/sides, mahogany neck, 20 fret Brazilian rosewood fingerboard with abalone bird inlay, Brazilian rosewood bridge with ebony pearl dot pins, 3 per side chrome locking PRS tuners, volume/tone control, preamp system. Available in Antique Natural, Black Cherry and Grayblack finish. Disc. 1992.

Mfr.'s Sug. Retail	$2,590	$1,810	$1,550	$1,295	$1,035	$930	$855	$775

    Add $150 for gold hardware.
    Add $150 for Amber Sunburst and Walnut Sunburst finish.

MAHOGANY CUTAWAY — single flat cutaway dreadnought style, spruce top, round soundhole, wood bound body and rosette, mahogany back/sides/neck, 20 fret rosewood fingerboard, rosewood bridge with ebony pearl dot pins, rosewood veneer on peghead, 3 per side chrome locking PRS tuners, volume/tone control, preamp system. Available in Natural finish. Disc. 1992.

Mfr.'s Sug. Retail	$1,970	$1,380	$1,180	$985	$790	$710	$650	$590

    Add $150 for gold hardware.
    Add $150 for Antique Natural and Black Cherry finish.

ROSEWOOD SIGNATURE — dreadnought style, spruce top, round soundhole, abalone bound body and rosette, rosewood back/sides, mahogany neck, 20 fret Brazilian rosewood fingerboard with abalone bird inlay, Brazilian rosewood bridge with ebony pearl dot pins, 3 per side gold locking PRS tuners, gold endpin, volume/tone control, preamp system. Available in Antique Natural finish. Disc. 1992.

Mfr.'s Sug. Retail	$3,190	$2,225	$1,915	$1,595	$1,275	$1,145	$1,050	$950

    Add $150 for Rosewood Sunburst finish.

Grading	100%	98%	95%	90%	80%	70%	60%

ELECTRIC

ARTIST — offset double cutaway mahogany body, bound carved flame maple top, mahogany neck, 24 fret rosewood fingerboard with abalone bird inlay, standard vibrato, abalone signature headstock inlay, 3 per side locking PRS tuners, chrome hardware, 2 humbucker PRS pickups, volume/tone/5 position control, certificate of authenticity. Available in Amber, Dark Cherry Sunburst, Indigo and Teal Black finish. Mfd. 1990 to 1992.

	$2,645	$2,270	$1,890	$1,510	$1,360	$1,245	$1,135

Last Mfr.'s Sug. Retail was $3,780.

≯ **Artist (1993 revision)** — similar to Artist, except has curly maple top, 22 fret fingerboard, maple bound fingerboard and peghead. Mfd. 1993 to date.

Mfr.'s Sug. Retail	$3,780	$2,645	$2,270	$1,890	$1,510	$1,360	$1,245	$1,135

These models available with semi hollow body, stop tailpiece.

CE BOLT ON — offset double cutaway bound alder body, bolt on maple neck, 24 fret rosewood fingerboard with abalone dot inlay, standard vibrato, 3 per side PRS locking tuners, chrome hardware, 2 humbucker PRS pickups, volume/tone/5 position control. Available in Black and Classic Red finish. Curr. mfr.

Mfr.'s Sug. Retail	$1,290	$905	$775	$645	$515	$465	$425	$385

≯ **CE Bolt On Maple Top** — similar to CE Bolt On, except has figured maple top. Available in Black Sunburst, Cherry Sunburst, Dark Blue, Greyblack, Purple, Royal Blue, Scarlet Red, Scarlet Sunburst, Tobacco Sunburst, Tortoise Shell, Vintage Sunburst and Vintage Yellow finish. Curr. mfr.

Mfr.'s Sug. Retail	$1,590	$1,110	$955	$795	$635	$575	$525	$475

CUSTOM — offset double cutaway mahogany body, bound flame maple top, mahogany neck, 24 fret rosewood fingerboard with abalone/pearl moon inlay, standard vibrato, 6 per side locking PRS tuners, chrome hardware, 2 humbucker PRS pickups, volume/tone/5 position control. Available in Black Cherry, Black Sunburst, Emerald Green, Greyblack, Royal Blue, Scarlet Red, Scarlet Sunburst, Tortoise Shell and Whale Blue finish. Curr. mfr.

Mfr.'s Sug. Retail	$1,890	$1,325	$1,135	$945	$755	$680	$620	$565

This model also available with pearl bird inlay and stop tailpiece.

≯ **Custom 22** — similar to Custom, except has 22 fret fingerboard, stop tailpiece. New 1993.

Mfr.'s Sug. Retail	$1,890	$1,325	$1,135	$945	$755	$680	$620	$565

Grading	100%	98%	95%	90%	80%	70%	60%

DRAGON — offset double cutaway mahogany body, arched bound flame maple top, mahogany neck, 22 fret ebony fingerboard with abalone/pearl/turquoise dragon inlay, stop tailpiece, abalone signature inlay on peghead, 3 per side locking PRS tuners, gold hardware, 2 humbucker PRS pickups, volume/tone/5 position control. Available in Amber, Dark Cherry Sunburst, Indigo and Teal Black finish. Mfd. yearly.

1992 series

	100%	98%	95%	90%	80%	70%	60%
Mfr.'s Sug. Retail	$8,000	$5,600	$4,800	$3,400	$3,200	$2,880	$2,640	$2,400

1993 series — 100 mfd.

Mfr.'s Sug. Retail	$11,000	$7,700	$6,600	$5,500	$4,400	$3,960	$3,650	$3,300

EG BOLT ON — offset double cutaway alder body, white pickguard, bolt on maple neck, 22 fret rosewood fingerboard with pearl dot inlay, standard vibrato, 3 per side locking PRS tuners, chrome hardware, 3 single coil PRS-Fralin pickups, volume/tone control, 5 position switch. Available in Black, Black Sunburst and Classic Red finish. Curr. mfr.

Mfr.'s Sug. Retail	$1,070	$750	$640	$535	$430	$390	$355	$325

This model also available with 2 single coil/1 humbucker and humbucker/single coil/humbucker pickups configurations, push/pull coil split or dual tone in tone control.

EG Bolt On Maple Top — similar to EG Bolt On, except has 3 piece maple top. Available in Black Sunburst and Greyblack Sunburst finish.

Mfr.'s Sug. Retail	$1,320	$925	$790	$660	$530	$475	$435	$395

EG Bolt On LH — similar to EG Bolt On, except is left handed version. Mfd. 1993 to date.

Mfr.'s Sug. Retail	$1,285	$890	$770	$640	$510	$460	$420	$380

EG Bolt On LH Maple Top

Mfr.'s Sug. Retail	$1,585	$1,110	$955	$795	$630	$570	$520	$475

STANDARD — offset double cutaway mahogany body/neck, 24 fret rosewood fingerboard with abalone/pearl moon inlay, standard vibrato, 3 per side locking PRS tuners, chrome hardware, 2 humbucker PRS pickups, volume/tone/5 position controls. Available in Black, Natural Mahogany and Vintage Cherry finish. Curr. mfr.

Mfr.'s Sug. Retail	$1,760	$1,230	$1,055	$880	$705	$635	$580	$530

PEAVEY

Manufactured and distributed by Peavey Electronics Corp. located in Meridian, MS since 1965.

Hartley Peavey began building amplifiers when he was a teenager. By 1965, his senior year in college, he had constructed several amplifiers and formed Peavey Electronics. Though it began as an amplifier company, Hartley realized he would need to diversify and soon he began producing an entire range of equipment for the music industry. Peavey Electronics was the first manufacturer to use computerized equipment to both design and produce guitars.

Grading	100%	98%	95%	90%	80%	70%	60%

ACOUSTIC ELECTRIC

ECOUSTIC — single rounded cutaway dreadnought style, cedar top, oval soundhole, bound body, 5 stripe rosette, mahogany back/sides, maple neck, 22 fret rosewood fingerboard with white dot inlay, rosewood bridge with white pins, 3 per side gold tuners, piezo bridge pickup, 3 band EQ. Available in Black, Natural and Transparent Red finish. Curr. mfr.

Mfr.'s Sug. Retail	$700	$490	$420	$350	$280	$250	$230	$210

ELECTRIC

DESTINY CUSTOM — strat style mahogany body, quilted maple top, thru body figured maple neck, 24 fret bound rosewood fingerboard, pearl oval inlay at 12th fret, double locking vibrato, 6 on one side tuners, gold hardware, 2 stacked coil/1 humbucker pickups, volume/tone control, 5 position and coil tap switches. Available in Honey Burst, Transparent Black, Transparent Blue, Transparent Honey Burst and Transparent Red finish. Curr. mfr.

Mfr.'s Sug. Retail	$1,000	$700	$600	$500	$400	$360	$330	$300

G-NINETY — strat style poplar body, bolt on laminated maple neck, 24 fret bound rosewood fingerboard with pearl dot inlay, double locking vibrato, reverse headstock, 6 on one side tuners, black hardware, 2 single coil/1 humbucker pickups, volume/tone control, 5 position switch. Available in Black, Blue, Eerie Dess Black, Eerie Dess Blue, Eerie Dess Multi, Eerie Dess Red, Pearl White, Raspberry Pearl and Sunfire Red finish. Curr. mfr.

Mfr.'s Sug. Retail	$600	$420	$360	$300	$240	$215	$195	$180

Grading	100%	98%	95%	90%	80%	70%	60%

GENERATION S-1 — tele style mahogany body, figured maple top, bolt on laminated maple neck, 22 fret rosewood fingerboard with pearl dot inlay, fixed brass bridge, graphlon nut, 6 on one side tuners, gold hardware, active single coil/humbucker pickup, volume/tone control, 3 position and filter switches. Available in Transparent Amber, Transparent Black, Transparent Blue and Transparent Red finish. Curr. mfr.

Mfr.'s Sug. Retail	$800	$560	$480	$400	$320	$290	$265	$240

This model also available with double locking vibrato (Generation S-2).

⚡ **Generation S-3** — similar to Generation S-1, except has hollow sound chambers, maple fingerboard with black dot inlay, 3 stacked coil pickups, coil tap in tone control. Available in Transparent Black, Transparent Blue, Transparent Honey Sunburst and Transparent Red finish. Curr. mfr.

Mfr.'s Sug. Retail	$500	$350	$300	$250	$200	$180	$165	$150

ODYSSEY — tele style mahogany body, carved flame maple top, set mahogany neck, 24 fret bound ebony fingerboard with white arrow inlay, tunomatic bridge/stop tailpiece, graphlon nut, bound peghead, 3 per side tuners, gold hardware, 2 humbucker Alnico pickups, 2 volume/2 tone controls, 3 position and coil split switches. Available in '59 Vintage Sunburst, Tobacco Sunburst, Transparent Black, Transparent Blue and Transparent Red finish. Curr. mfr.

Mfr.'s Sug. Retail	$1,000	$700	$600	$500	$400	$360	$330	$300

⚡ **Odyssey Custom** — similar to Odyssey, except has bound top, 2 color pearl 3D block fingerboard inlay, black hardware. Available in Transparent Black finish.

Mfr.'s Sug. Retail	$1,300	$910	$780	$650	$520	$470	$430	$390

PREDATOR — strat style poplar body, white pickguard, bolt on laminated maple neck, 22 fret maple fingerboard with black dot inlay, standard vibrato, 6 on one side tuners, chrome hardware, 3 single coil pickups, volume/2 tone controls, 5 position switch. Available in Black, Red and White finish. Curr. mfr.

Mfr.'s Sug. Retail	$240	$170	$145	$120	$95	$85	$80	$75

TRACER — strat style poplar body, bolt on laminated maple neck, 24 fret maple fingerboard with black dot inlay, standard vibrato, graphlon nut, 6 on one side tuners, chrome hardware, 2 single coil/1 humbucker pickups, volume/tone control, 5 position switch. Available in Black, Red and White finish. Curr. mfr.

Mfr.'s Sug. Retail	$330	$230	$195	$165	$130	$120	$110	$100

⚡ **Tracer LT** — similar to Tracer, except has rosewood fingerboard with white dot inlay, double locking vibrato, black hardware. Available in Black, Metallic Blue, Metallic Red and White finish.

Mfr.'s Sug. Retail	$430	$300	$260	$215	$175	$155	$140	$130

Grading	100%	98%	95%	90%	80%	70%	60%

VANDENBERG QUILT TOP — strat style mahogany body with side slot cuts, set mahogany neck, 24 fret bound rosewood fingerboard with white stripes and arrows inlay, double locking vibrato, reverse headstock, 6 on one side tuners, gold hardware, 2 humbucker pickups, volume/tone control, 3 position switch. Available in Transparent Honey Sunburst, Transparent Pink and Transparent Violet finish. Curr. mfr.

Mfr.'s Sug. Retail	$1,400	$980	$840	$700	$560	$505	$460	$420

VANDENBERG SIGNATURE — strat style poplar body with side slot cuts, bolt on laminated maple neck, 24 fret ebony fingerboard with pearl dot inlay, double locking vibrato, reverse headstock, 6 on one side tuners, black hardware, single coil/humbucker pickup, volume/tone control, 3 position switch. Available in '62 Blue, Black, Pearl White, Raspberry Pearl, Rock-It Pink and Sunfire Red finish. Curr. mfr.

Mfr.'s Sug. Retail	$850	$595	$510	$425	$340	$305	$280	$255

This model comes with a certificate signed by Adrian Vandenberg.

ELECTRIC BASS

B-NINETY — precision style poplar body, bolt on laminated maple neck, 21 fret rosewood fingerboard with white dot inlay, fixed bridge, graphlon nut, 4 on one side tuners, black hardware, P-style/J-style pickup, 2 volume/1 tone controls. Available in '62 Blue, Black, Charcoal Gray, Pearl White, Raspberry Pearl and Sunfire Red finish. Curr. mfr.

Mfr.'s Sug. Retail	$500	$350	$300	$250	$200	$180	$165	$150

This model is also available in left handed version.

B-Ninety Active — similar to B-Ninety, except has active electronics.

Mfr.'s Sug. Retail	$550	$385	$330	$275	$220	$200	$180	$165

DYNA-BASS — precision style poplar body, bolt on laminate maple neck, 21 fret rosewood fingerboard with white dot inlay, fixed bridge, graphlon nut, 4 on one side tuners, gold hardware, 2 humbucker pickups, volume/mix/3 band EQ controls, frequency switch. Available in '62 Blue, Black, Charcoal Gray, Pearl White and Sunfire Red finish. Curr. mfr.

Mfr.'s Sug. Retail	$700	$490	$420	$350	$280	$250	$230	$210

Add $50 for 5 string version.

FOUNDATION — precision style poplar body, bolt on laminate maple neck, 21 fret maple fingerboard with black dot inlay, fixed bridge, graphlon nut, 4 on one side tuners, chrome hardware, 2 single coil pickups, 2 volume/1 tone control. Available in Black, Red and White finish. Curr. mfr.

Mfr.'s Sug. Retail	$330	$230	$195	$165	$130	$120	$110	$100

Add $30 for fretless model.
Add $120 for 5 string version.
Add $30 for rosewood fingerboard with white dot inlay, Sunburst finish.

Grading	100%	98%	95%	90%	80%	70%	60%

FURY — similar to Foundation, except has white pickguard, P-style pickup, volume/tone control.

Mfr.'s Sug. Retail	$300	$210	$180	$150	$120	$110	$100	$90

MIDIBASE — precision style alder body, maple neck, 21 fret rosewood fingerboard with white dot inlay, fixed bridge, graphlon nut, 4 on one side tuners, black hardware, 2 humbucker pickups, 2 volume/tone/mix controls, bypass switch. Available in Pearl White finish. Curr. mfr.

Mfr.'s Sug. Retail	$1,800	$1,260	$1,080	$900	$720	$650	$595	$540

PALAEDIUM — precision style alder body, bolt on maple neck, 21 fret ebony fingerboard with pearl dot inlay, fixed bridge, graphlon nut, 4 on one side tuners, gold hardware, 2 humbucker pickups, volume/tone/mix control. Available in Transparent Amber, Transparent Red and Transparent Violet finish. Curr. mfr.

Mfr.'s Sug. Retail	$800	$560	$480	$400	$320	$290	$265	$240

RJ4 — offset double cutaway maple body, thru body laminated maple neck, 21 fret ebony fingerboard with pearl arrow inlay, fixed bridge, graphlon nut, 4 on one side tuners, black hardware, P-style/J-style pickups, volume/mix/3 band EQ controls, bypass switch, active electronics. Available in Black Pearl Burst, Blue Pearl Burst, Purple Pearl Burst and Red Pearl Burst finish. Curr. mfr.

Mfr.'s Sug. Retail	$1,100	$770	$660	$550	$440	$395	$365	$330

This model is also available with koa body/neck and rosewood fingerboard, Hipshot D'Tuner.

SARZO — offset double cutaway ash body, thru body maple/purpleheart 5 piece neck, 24 fret ebony fingerboard with pearl oval inlay, fixed brass bridge, brass nut, 4 on one side tuners, gold hardware, 2 humbucker pickups, volume/tone/3 band EQ controls, bypass switch, active electronics. Available in Transparent Black, Transparent Red and Transparent Violet finish. Curr. mfr.

Mfr.'s Sug. Retail	$1,100	$770	$660	$550	$440	$395	$365	$330

TL5 — offset double cutaway figured maple body, thru body maple/purpleheart 5 piece neck, 24 fret ebony fingerboard with pearl oval inlay, fixed brass bridge, graphlon nut, 3/2 per side tuners, gold hardware, 2 humbucker pickups, volume/treble/bass/selector controls, active electronics. Available in Honey Sunburst, Transparent Black, Transparent Blue, Transparent Emerald, Transparent Red and Transparent Violet finish. Curr. mfr.

Mfr.'s Sug. Retail	$1,500	$1,050	$900	$750	$600	$540	$495	$450

TL6 — similar to TL5, except has 6 strings, pearl arrow fingerboard inlay, 2 P-style pickups.

Mfr.'s Sug. Retail	$1,900	$1,330	$1,140	$950	$760	$685	$625	$570

Grading	100%	98%	95%	90%	80%	70%	60%

UNITY — precision style poplar body, thru body laminated maple neck, 21 fret rosewood fingerboard with pearl dot inlay, fixed bridge, graphlon nut, 4 on one side tuners, black hardware, P-style/J-style pickups, 2 volume/tone control. Available in '62 Blue, Black, Charcoal Gray, Pearl White and Sunfire Red finish. Curr. mfr.

Mfr.'s Sug. Retail	$700	$490	$420	$350	$280	$250	$230	$210

⚔ **Unity Koa** — similar to Unity, except has koa body/neck, gold hardware. Available in Natural finish.

Mfr.'s Sug. Retail	$750	$525	$450	$375	$300	$270	$245	$225

PEDULLA, M.V.

Manufactured and distributed by M.V. Pedulla Guitars located in Rockland, MA since the late 1970's.

This company was formed in the late 1970's by Michael V. and Ted Pedulla. This new company originally dabbled in acoustic, electric and bass guitar designs until they produced a design that was more specialized for a bass player's particular application.

ELECTRIC BASS

All models in this series are available with the following options:
Add $300 for left handed version.
Add $100 for birdseye maple fingerboard.
Add $225 for active tone filter system (TBIBT).
Add $200 for custom tinted colors: Arctic Night, Charcoal, Emerald Green, Vintage Cherry or Violet.

MVP/Buzz Series

This series consists of 2 models, the MVP and the Buzz. The MVP is a fretted instrument, while the Buzz is fretless - all other aspects are identical. The following are model descriptions and prices in this series:
Add $100 for black or gold hardware; the Deluxe.
Add $200 for flame maple body, black or gold hardware; the Custom (A).
Add $400 for higher quality flame maple body, black or gold hardware; the Custom (AA).
Add $600 for highest quality flame maple body, black or gold hardware; the Signature (AAA).
Add $900 for quilted maple body, black or gold hardware; the Limited Edition.
The Custom (A), Custom (AA), Signature and Limited Edition models are available in Amber Tint, Amber/Cherry Sunburst, Cherry Tint, Gold/Amber Sunburst, Light Gold Tint, Natural and Peacock Blue Tint finish.

Grading	100%	98%	95%	90%	80%	70%	60%

MVP/BUZZ STANDARD — offset double cutaway flame maple body, thru body maple laminate neck, 24 fret ebony fingerboard with pearl dot inlay, fixed bridge, brass nut, 2 per side tuners, chrome hardware, P-style/J-style Bartolini pickups, volume/tone/mix control, active electronics. Available in Champagne, Black, Lime Green, Metallic Midnight Blue, Red and White finish. Curr. mfr.

Mfr.'s Sug. Retail	$1,775	$1,240	$1,065	$885	$710	$640	$585	$535

Also available with 2 J-style or 2 humbucker Bartolini pickups.

MVP5/Pentabuzz Standard — similar to MVP/Buzz Standard, except has 5 strings.

Mfr.'s Sug. Retail	$2,075	$1,450	$1,240	$1,035	$830	$745	$680	$620

MVP6/Hexabuzz Standard — similar to MVP/Buzz Standard, except has 6 strings, 2 J-style or 2 humbucker Bartolini pickups.

Mfr.'s Sug. Retail	$2,275	$1,590	$1,360	$1,135	$905	$815	$745	$680

MVP8/Octabuzz Standard — similar to MVP/Buzz Standard, except has 8 strings.

Mfr.'s Sug. Retail	$2,075	$1,450	$1,240	$1,035	$830	$745	$680	$620

Exotic Series

ES4 CUSTOM — offset double cutaway flame maple body, thru body maple neck, 24 fret ebony fingerboard with pearl dot inlay, fixed bridge, brass nut, 2 per side Gotoh tuners, chrome hardware, 2 humbucker Bartolini pickups, volume/tone/mix controls, active electronics. Available in Amber Sunburst, Amber Tint, Cherry Sunburst, Cherry Tint, Emerald Tint, Green/Emerald Sunburst, Light Gold Tint, Natural and Peacock Blue Tint finish. Curr. mfr.

Mfr.'s Sug. Retail	$2,375	$1,660	$1,425	$1,185	$950	$850	$780	$710

Add $300 for highest quality flame maple body.

ES5 — similar to ES4, except has 5 strings.

Mfr.'s Sug. Retail	$2,675	$1,870	$1,605	$1,335	$1,065	$960	$880	$800

ES6 — similar to ES4, except has 6 strings.

Mfr.'s Sug. Retail	$2,875	$2,000	$1,725	$1,430	$1,145	$1,030	$945	$860

ET4 — offset double cutaway flame maple body, bubinga or zebrawood top, thru body neck, 24 fret ebony fingerboard with pearl dot inlay, fixed bridge, brass nut, 2 per side Gotoh tuners, chrome hardware, 2 humbucker Bartolini pickups, volume/tone/mix controls, active electronics. Available in Natural finish. Curr. mfr.

Mfr.'s Sug. Retail	$2,675	$1,870	$1,605	$1,335	$1,065	$960	$880	$800

ET5 — similar to ET4, except has 5 strings.

Mfr.'s Sug. Retail	$2,975	$2,080	$1,785	$1,480	$1,185	$1,065	$980	$890

ET6 — similar to ET4, except has 6 strings.

Mfr.'s Sug. Retail	$3,175	$2,225	$1,900	$1,590	$1,265	$1,135	$1,045	$950

Pedulla , cont.

Grading	100%	98%	95%	90%	80%	70%	60%

Mark Egan Series

This series is co-designed by Mark Egan.

ME4 — offset double cutaway flame maple body, thru body maple neck, 24 fret ebony fingerboard with pearl dot inlay, ebony thumbrests, fixed bridge, brass nut, 2 per side Gotoh tuners, chrome hardware, 2 J-style pickups, volume/tone/mix controls, active electronics. Available in Amber Sunburst, Amber Tint, Cherry Sunburst, Cherry Tint, Emerald Green Tint, Green/Blue Sunburst, Light Gold Tint, Natural and Peacock Blue Tint finish. Curr. mfr.

Mfr.'s Sug. Retail	$2,675	$1,870	$1,605	$1,335	$1,065	$960	$880	$800

ME5 — similar to ME4, except has 5 strings.

Mfr.'s Sug. Retail	$2,975	$2,080	$1,785	$1,480	$1,185	$1,065	$980	$890

ME6 — similar to ME4, except has 6 strings.

Mfr.'s Sug. Retail	$3,175	$2,225	$1,900	$1,590	$1,265	$1,135	$1,045	$950

ME4F+8 — offset double cutaway flame maple body, double neck construct with all Pedulla neck, bridge, pickup and electronic variations available, one neck is a fretless 4 string, the other is a fretted 8 string. Available in Amber Sunburst, Amber Tint, Cherry Sunburst, Cherry Tint, Emerald Green Tint, Green/Blue Sunburst, Light Gold Tint, Natural and Peacock Blue Tint finish. Curr. mfr.

Mfr.'s Sug. Retail	$6,050	$4,235	$3,630	$3,025	$2,420	$2,180	$1,995	$1,815

Series II

S-II4 — offset double cutaway poplar body, bolt on maple neck, fretless or 22 fret rosewood fingerboard with pearl dot inlay, fixed bridge, brass nut, 2 per side Gotoh tuners, black hardware, P-style/J-style Bartolini pickups, volume/tone/mix controls. Available in Black, Champagne, Lime Green, Midnight Blue, Red, Yellow and White finish. Curr. mfr.

Mfr.'s Sug. Retail	$1,195	$835	$715	$600	$480	$430	$395	$360

Add $200 for flame maple body.
Add $400 for higher quality flame maple body.
Add $200 for humbucker pickups, active electronics.

S-II5 — similar to S-II4, except has 5 strings, maple body, humbucker Bartolini pickups, active electronics.

Mfr.'s Sug. Retail	$1,595	$1,115	$955	$795	$635	$575	$525	$475

S-II6 — similar to S-II5, except has 6 strings.

Mfr.'s Sug. Retail	$1,795	$1,255	$1,075	$895	$715	$645	$590	$540

Grading	100%	98%	95%	90%	80%	70%	60%

ThunderBass Series

This series has 2 variatons - the T and the ET. These instruments have a flame maple body - with the ET model featuring an exotic wood top. The T model is available in two grades of flame maple body, the Custom (AA) and the Signature (AAA). The ET model tops have one of the following woods; bubinga, quilted maple or zebrawood. Prices listed are for the Signature (AAA) and ET models.

Subtract $300 for the Custom (AA) model.

T4/ET4 — offset double cutaway body, thru body maple/bubinga 5 piece neck, 24 fret ebony fingerboard with pearl dot inlay, fixed bridge, 2 per side MVP/Gotoh tuners, black hardware, 2 humbucker Bartolini pickups, volume/tone/pan control. Available in Natural finish. New 1993.

Mfr.'s Sug. Retail	$2,675	$1,870	$1,605	$1,335	$1,065	$960	$880	$805

This model is also available with gold hardware.

T5/ET5 — similar to T4/ET4, except has 5 strings, 3/2 per side tuners.

Mfr.'s Sug. Retail	$2,975	$2,080	$1,785	$1,480	$1,185	$1,065	$980	$890

T6/ET6 — similar to T4/ET4, except has 6 strings, 3 per side tuners.

Mfr.'s Sug. Retail	$3,175	$2,225	$1,900	$1,590	$1,265	$1,135	$1,045	$950

RAINSONG

Manufactured by Kuau Technology Limited located in Maui, HI since 1982. In 1985, they began developing graphite-epoxy instruments with Pimentel & Sons Luthiers from Albuquerque, NM. Composite materials are created in Escondido, CA and sent to Albuquerque for construction. Classical, small body and dreadnought steel string acoustics are the primary body styles. Instruments are custom made and are priced in the $2,500-$3,000 range. Options are available at an additional charge. Custom orders only.

RICKENBACKER

Manufacturer located in Santa Ana, CA.

During the 1930's, Adolf Rickenbacker founded the Electro String Instrument Corp., which primarily produced pickups, lap steels and amplifiers. He is also credited as the inventor of the first electric guitar, although further study has revealed that other people were working on an electric instrument concurrently. The Rickenbacker International, Corp. was founded in 1965 by F.C. Hall, who bought out Adolph and his partners' interest in the Electro String Co. in 1953. Mr. Hall formed Rickenbacker as the sales branch of his company and left Electro String as the manufacturing branch. Rickenbacker International is located in Santa Ana, CA.

Grading	100%	98%	95%	90%	80%	70%	60%

ACOUSTIC

385 — dreadnought style, maple top, round soundhole, pickguard, checkered body/rosette, maple back/sides/neck, 21 fret rosewood fingerboard with pearl triangle inlay, rosewood bridge with white pins. Available in Burst finishes. Mfd. 1958-1972.

	100%	98%	95%	90%	80%	70%	60%
1958-1965	$2,500	$1,750	$1,500	$1,250	$1,000	$900	$825
1965-1972	$1,250	$875	$750	$625	$500	$450	$415

This model was also available in a classic style body (385S).

385-J — similar to 385, except has jumbo style body.

	100%	98%	95%	90%	80%	70%	60%
	$2,750	$1,925	$1,650	$1,375	$1,100	$990	$905

390 — while a few prototypes were made circa 1957, this model was never put into production.

ELECTRIC

Rickenbacker pegheads are generally of the same pattern or design. They have 3 per side tuners and usually have plastic or metal plates with the Rickenbacker logo. Twelve string pegheads are the same size as six string pegheads, with 6 tuners (3 per side) running parallel to the peghead face and 6 tuners running perpendicular with routed slots in the peghead face to accommodate string winding. Necks are mostly maple. However, some are maple/walnut laminates. Pickguards and peghead plates are usually color matched, and controls are usually pickguard mounted. Any differences will be listed where appropriate. Hardware, binding, peghead logo plate and pickguard color is dependent on finish, unless otherwise listed.

In 1964, R style trapeze tailpieces replaced all other trapeze tailpieces.

Grading	90%	80%	70%	60%	50%	40%	20%

ELECTRO SPANISH — folk style, maple top, F holes, bound body, maple back/sides/neck, 14/19 fret rosewood fingerboard with pearl dot inlay, rosewood bridge/trapeze tailpiece, pearl veneer on classic style peghead with metal logo plate, horseshoe pickup. Available in Stained finish. Mfd. 1932-1935.

	$1,000	$700	$600	$500	$400	$360	$330

In 1934, body binding and volume control were added.
This model was replaced by the Ken Roberts model.

Grading	100%	98%	95%	90%	80%	70%	60%

KEN ROBERTS ELECTRO-SPANISH — concert style, laminated bound mahogany top, F holes, laminated mahogany back/sides, mahogany neck, 17/22 fret bound rosewood fingerboard with white dot inlay, compensating bridge/Kauffman vibrato tailpiece, pearloid peghead veneer with brass logo plate, 3 per side tuners, nickel hardware, horseshoe pickup, volume control. Available in Two Tone Brown finish. Mfd. 1935-1940.

	$500	$350	$300	$250	$200	$180	$165

From 1935-1937, the volume control was octagon shaped.
In 1938, round volume control with ridges replaced original item.

200 Series

230 HAMBURG — double cutaway maple body, thru body maple neck, 24 fret rosewood fingerboard with pearloid dot inlay, fixed bridge, 3 per side tuners, 2 humbucker pickups, 2 volume/2 tone controls, 3 position switch. Available in Fireglo, Jetglo, Mapleglo, Midnight Blue, Red and White finish. Mfd. 1987 to date.

Mfr.'s Sug. Retail	$900	$630	$540	$450	$360	$325	$300	$275

250 EL DORADO — similar to 230, except has bound body/fingerboard, gold hardware.

Mfr.'s Sug. Retail	$1,050	$735	$630	$525	$420	$380	$345	$315

Grading	100%	98%	95%	90%	80%	70%	60%

300 Series

This series is also called the Capri Series.

This series utilizes a hollow body, white binding, inlaid fingerboard and Rick-o-Sound jacks. These are available in Fireglo or Natural Grain finish, unless otherwise indicated.

310 — offset pointed double cutaway semi hollow ³⁄₄ size maple body, 21 fret rosewood fingerboard with white dot inlay, tunomatic bridge/trapeze tailpiece, chrome hardware, 2 covered pickups, volume/tone control, 3 position switch. Available in Autumnglo, Fireglo, Mapleglo, Natural or Two-Tone Brown finish. Mfd. 1958-1971. Re-introduced 1981-1988.

	$1,750	$1,225	$1,050	$875	$700	$630	$575

In 1963, a mixer control was added.
Instruments were inconsistently produced with and without F holes in the top.

315 — similar to 310, except has Kauffman vibrato. Mfd. 1958-1975.

	$1,525	$1,070	$915	$765	$610	$550	$505

320 — offset pointed double cutaway semi hollow ³⁄₄ size maple body, bi-level pickguard, thru body maple neck, 21 fret rosewood fingerboard with pearloid dot inlay, tunomatic bridge/R-style trapeze tailpiece, 3 per side tuners, chrome hardware, 3 chrome bar pickups, 2 volume/2 tone/mix controls, 3 position switch. Available in Fireglo, Jetglo, Mapleglo, Midnight Blue, Red and White finish. Mfd. 1958 to date.

Mfr.'s Sug. Retail	$1,000	$700	$600	$500	$400	$360	$330	$300

325 — similar to 320, except has Kauffman vibrato. Available in Fireglo, Mapleglo, Natural or Two-Tone Brown finish. Mfd. 1958-1975.

	$2,400	$1,680	$1,440	$1,200	$960	$860	$790

In 1964, R style trapeze tailpieces replaced all other trapeze tailpieces.

330 — offset double cutaway semi hollow maple body, wedge shaped soundhole, bi-level pickguard, thru body maple neck, 24 fret rosewood fingerboard with pearl dot inlay, tunomatic bridge/R-style trapeze tailpiece, 3 per side tuners, 2 single coil pickups, 2 volume/2 tone/mix controls, 3 position switch. Available in Fireglo, Jetglo, Mapleglo, Midnight Blue, Red and White finish. Mfd. 1958 to date.

Mfr.'s Sug. Retail	$1,200	$840	$720	$600	$480	$430	$395	$360

In 1963, a mixer control was added.

330/12 — similar to 330, except has 12 strings, 6 per side tuners. Mfd. 1965 to date.

Mfr.'s Sug. Retail	$1,300	$910	$780	$650	$520	$470	$430	$390

RIC
Rickenbacker. , cont.

Grading	100%	98%	95%	90%	80%	70%	60%

331 — similar to 330, except has plexi-glass top with frequency controlled flashing lights. Mfd. 1970-1975.

	$4,800	$3,360	$2,880	$2,400	$1,920	$1,730	$1,585

Originally, this model was released with an external power supply box.

This model was also nicknamed Light Show or X-Mas Tree Special.

350 — offset pointed double cutaway semi hollow maple body, bi-level pickguard, thru body maple neck, 24 fret rosewood fingerboard with pearloid dot inlay, tunomatic bridge/R-style trapeze tailpiece, 3 chrome bar pickups, 2 volume/2 tone/mix controls, 3 position switch, stereo output. Available in Fireglo, Jetglo, Mapleglo, Midnight Blue, Red and White finish. Mfd. 1985 to date.

Mfr.'s Sug. Retail	$1,270	$890	$760	$635	$510	$460	$420	$380

This model also referred to as the "350 Liverpool".

360 — offset double cutaway semi hollow maple body, wedge shaped soundhole, pickguard, thru body maple neck, 21 fret bound rosewood fingerboard with pearl triangle inlay, tunomatic bridge/R-style trapeze tailpiece, 2 single pickups, 2 volume/2 tone diamond controls, 3 position switch. Available in Autumnglo, Black, Fireglo, Natural and Two Tone Brown finish. Mfd. 1958-1968.

	$1,320	$925	$790	$660	$530	$475	$435

The above description is referred to as the Old Style which ran from 1958-1968.

In the early 1960's, round control knobs and bi-level pickguards began replacing original items.

In 1964, the 360 New Style was released and featured an unbound, rounded top, bound soundhole and checkered body binding which ran from 1964-1990.

In 1963, a mixer control was added.

In 1960, stereo output became optional.

360/12 — similar to 360, except has 12 strings, 6 per side tuners.

	$1,420	$995	$850	$710	$570	$510	$465

365/360WB — offset double cutaway semi hollow maple body, wedge shaped sound-hole, pickguard, thru body maple neck, 21 fret bound rosewood fingerboard with pearl triangle inlay, tunomatic bridge/vibrato tailpiece, 2 single pickups, 2 volume/2 tone diamond controls, 3 position switch. Available in Autumnglo, Black, Fireglo, Natural and Two Tone Brown finish. Mfd. 1958 to date.

Mfr.'s Sug. Retail	$1,430	$1,000	$855	$715	$570	$510	$465	$425

In 1985, this model was re-introduced as 360VB featuring Old Style body, high gain pickups and R style tailpiece.

In 1991, this model was renamed the 360WB and is still in production.

360/12WB — similar to 360WB, except has 12 strings, 6 per side tuners.

Mfr.'s Sug. Retail	$1,530	$1,070	$915	$765	$610	$550	$505	$455

See 365 description, above this one.

Grading	100%	98%	95%	90%	80%	70%	60%

370 — similar to 360, except has 3 pickups. Mfd. 1958 to date.

Mfr.'s Sug. Retail	$1,445	$1,015	$870	$725	$575	$515	$470	$430

370/12 — similar to 360/12, except has 3 pickups.

Mfr.'s Sug. Retail	$1,545	$1,080	$925	$770	$620	$560	$515	$465

370/12WB — similar to 360/12WB, except has 3 pickups.

Mfr.'s Sug. Retail	$1,655	$1,160	$995	$830	$660	$595	$545	$495

381 — offset sharp double cutaway semi hollow maple body, carved top, white bi-level pickguard, checkered bound body, bound wedge shaped soundhole, thru body maple neck, 21 fret bound rosewood fingerboard with pearl triangle inlay, tunomatic bridge/trapeze tailpiece, chrome hardware, 2 chrome bar pickups, 2 volume/2 tone/mix controls, 3 position switch. Available in Brownburst and Natural finish. Mfd. 1958-early 1960s. Reintroduced late 1960s-1974.

	$1,800	$1,260	$1,080	$900	$720	$650	$595

The original run of this series, 1958-early 1960s, had single pickguards, 2 controls. Fingerboard inlay was both dot and triangle. There are also a number of variations that Rickenbacker produced, some with F shaped soundholes and some with vibratos.

400 Series

The tulip style body shape acquired its nickname from the cutaways radiating out at a 45 degree angle, curving outwards to rounded point, then curving back into a standard.

400 COMBO — tulip style maple body, gold pickguard, thru body maple neck, 21 fret rosewood fingerboard with white dot inlay, covered pickup, volume/tone control, 2 position switch. Available in Blue Green, Golden and Jet Black finish. Mfd. 1956-1958.

	$1,550	$1,085	$930	$775	$620	$560	$515

This was the first thru body neck construct that Rickenbacker manufactured. In 1957, an extra switch was added.

420 — cresting wave style maple body, white pickguard, thru body maple neck, 21 fret rosewood fingerboard with white dot inlay, fixed bridge, chrome hardware, chrome bar pickup, volume/tone control, 2 position switch. Available in Sunburst finish. Mfd. 1965-1984.

	$850	$595	$510	$425	$340	$305	$280

425 — similar to 420, except has vibrato. Mfd. 1958-1973.

	$600	$515	$430	$345	$310	$285	$260

Replaced the 400 Combo.
In 1965, the vibrato was added, at which time the 420 was introduced as the non-vibrato instrument in this style.

Grading	100%	98%	95%	90%	80%	70%	60%

450 COMBO — cresting wave style maple body, white pickguard, thru body maple neck, 21 fret rosewood fingerboard with pearl dot inlay, fixed bridge, chrome hardware, 2 chrome bar pickups, 2 volume/2 tone controls, 3 position switch. Available in Black, Fireglo, Natural and Sunburst finish. Mfd. 1957-1984.

	100%	98%	95%	90%	80%	70%	60%
1957-1958	$1,750	$1,225	$1,050	$875	$700	$630	$575
1959-1984	$1,000	$700	$600	$500	$400	$360	$330

This model was introduced with a tulip style body, metal pickguard, 2 controls and a rotary switch located on the upper treble bout. It was manufactured this way for one year.

In 1958, the cresting wave body style was introduced.

In 1966, the 4 controls were introduced.

From 1962 to 1977, 3 pickups were optional .

450/12 — similar to 450, except has 12 strings, 6 per side tuners. Mfd. 1964-1985.

	100%	98%	95%	90%	80%	70%	60%
	$1,150	$805	$690	$575	$460	$415	$380

460 — similar to 450, except has bound body, bound fingerboard with pearl triangle inlay, mixer control. Available in Black, Fireglo and Natural finish. Mfd. 1961-1985.

	100%	98%	95%	90%	80%	70%	60%
	$1,350	$945	$810	$675	$540	$485	$445

In 1962, stereo output became standard.

470 — while a few prototypes were made circa 1971, this model was never put into production.

480 — cresting wave style maple body, white pickguard, bolt on maple neck, 24 fret bound rosewood fingerboard with white dot inlay, covered tunomatic bridge/R style trapeze taipiece, cresting wave style peghead, chrome hardware, 2 single coil exposed pickups, 2 volume/2 tone controls, 3 position switch. Mfd. 1973-1984.

	100%	98%	95%	90%	80%	70%	60%
	$500	$350	$300	$250	$200	$180	$165

481 — similar to 480, except has bound body, slanted frets, pearl triangle fingerboard inlay, 2 humbucker exposed pickups, phase switch. Mfd. 1973-1984.

	100%	98%	95%	90%	80%	70%	60%
	$450	$315	$270	$225	$180	$160	$150

600 Series

600 COMBO — offset double cutaway maple body, carved top, black pickguard, maple neck, 21 fret rosewood fingerboard with white dot inlay, fixed bridge, chrome hardware, single coil horseshoe pickup, volume/tone control, 2 position switch. Available in Blond finish. Mfd. 1954-1959.

	100%	98%	95%	90%	80%	70%	60%
	$1,350	$945	$810	$675	$540	$485	$445

These instruments have both set and bolt-on necks.

According to Rickenbacker's own records, there are apparently quite a few variations of this model.

These models were on the price lists, as having cresting wave style bodies until 1969, though none were ever produced.

Grading	100%	98%	95%	90%	80%	70%	60%

610 — cresting wave style maple body, bi-level pickguard, thru body maple neck, 21 fret rosewood fingerboard with pearl dot inlay, tunomatic bridge/R-style trapeze tailpiece, 3 per side tuners, 2 single coil pickups, 2 volume/2 tone/mix controls, 3 position switch. Available in Fireglo, Jetglo, Mapleglo, Midnight Blue, Red and White finish. Mfd. 1987 to date.

Mfr.'s Sug. Retail	$1,000	$700	$600	$500	$400	$360	$330	$300

610/12 — similar to 610, except has 12 strings, 6 per side tuners.

Mfr.'s Sug. Retail	$1,100	$770	$660	$550	$440	$395	$365	$330

615 — similar to 610, except has roller bridge/vibrato tailpiece, chrome hardware, 2 chrome bar pickups, 2 volume/2 tone controls. Available in Black, Fireglo and Natural finish. Mfd. 1962-1977.

	$1,025	$720	$615	$510	$410	$370	$340

In 1985, this model was reintroduced as the 610VB.

620 — similar to 610, except has bound body, bound fingerboard with pearl triangle inlay, 2 single coil exposed pickups. Available in Fireglo, Jetglo, Mapleglo, Midnight Blue, Red and White finish. Mfd. 1977 to date.

Mfr.'s Sug. Retail	$1,100	$770	$660	$550	$440	$395	$365	$330

620/12 — similar to 620, except has 12 strings, 6 per side tuners. Mfd. 1981 to date.

Mfr.'s Sug. Retail	$1,200	$840	$720	$600	$480	$430	$395	$360

In 1989, the deluxe trim was replaced by standard trim.

625 — similar to 610, except has bound body, bound fingerboard with pearl triangle inlay, roller bridge/vibrato tailpiece, 2 chrome bar pickups. Available in Fireglo, Jetglo, Mapleglo, Midnight Blue, Red and White finish. Mfd. 1977 to date.

Mfr.'s Sug. Retail	$1,450	$1,015	$870	$725	$580	$520	$475	$435

In 1985, this model was re-introduced as the 620VB.

650 Series

All models in this series have a cresting wave style body, pickguard, maple thru body neck, 24 fret maple fingerboard with black dot inlay, fixed bridge, 3 per side tuners, 2 humbucker pickups, 2 volume/2 tone/mix controls, 3 position switch. Available in Natural finish unless otherwise listed. Mfd. 1992 to date.

650 COMBO — offset double sharp cutaway maple body, carved top, pickguard, maple neck, 21 fret rosewood fingerboard with white dot inlay, fixed bridge, single coil horseshoe pickup, volume control. Available in Natural and Turquoise Blue finish. Mfd. 1957-1960.

	$1,250	$875	$750	$625	$500	$450	$415

In late 1957, a chrome bar pickup replaced the horseshoe pickup.

Grading	100%	98%	95%	90%	80%	70%	60%

ATLANTIS (650A) — maple body, chrome hardware. Available in Vintage Turquoise finish.

Mfr.'s Sug. Retail	$1,100	$770	$660	$550	$440	$395	$365	$330

DAKOTA (650D) — walnut body, walnut peghead laminate, chrome hardware.

Mfr.'s Sug. Retail	$1,000	$700	$600	$500	$400	$360	$330	$300

EXCALIBUR (650E) — African vermillion body, African vermillion peghead laminate, gold hardware.

Mfr.'s Sug. Retail	$1,200	$840	$720	$600	$480	$430	$395	$360

SIERRA (650S) — walnut body, walnut peghead laminate, gold hardware.

Mfr.'s Sug. Retail	$1,100	$770	$660	$550	$440	$395	$365	$330

800 Series

800 (COMBO) — offset double cutaway maple body, carved top, black pickguard, maple neck, 21 fret rosewood fingerboard with white dot inlay, fixed bridge, chrome hardware, double coil horseshoe pickup, 2 volume controls, 2 selector switches. Available in Blond and Turquoise Blue finish. Mfd. 1954-1959.

	$1,150	$805	$690	$575	$460	$415	$380

> In 1957, the pickguard was enlarged and the controls were mounted to it, a chrome bar pickup replaced one of the horseshoe's pickups and Turquoise Blue finish became an option.
>
> This model was on the price list till 1969, though it was no longer available.

850 COMBO — offset double sharp cutaway maple body, carved top, pickguard, maple neck, 21 fret rosewood fingerboard with white dot inlay, fixed bridge, double coil horseshoe pickup, volume/tone controls, 2 switches. Available in Natural and Turquoise Blue finish. Mfd. 1957-1960.

	$1,500	$1,050	$900	$750	$600	$540	$495

> In late 1957, the horseshoe pickup was replaced by a single coil horseshoe and chrome bar pickups. This model was on the price lists till 1967.
>
> There are several variations of this model that were made from 3 pickup designs to thru body neck constructs.

Grading	100%	98%	95%	90%	80%	70%	60%

900 & 1000 Series

900 — tulip style ¾ size maple body, white pickguard, thru body maple neck, 21 fret rosewood fingerboard with white dot inlay, fixed bridge, chrome hardware, single coil pickup, volume/tone control, 2 position switch. Available in Black, Brown, Fireglo, Gray and Natural finish. Mfd. 1957-1980.

	$600	$420	$360	$300	$240	$215	$195

> In 1958, a chrome bar pickup replaced the original pickup.
> In 1961, Fireglo finish became an option.
> By 1974, cresting wave body style became standard.

950 — similar to 900, except has 2 pickups.

	$625	$440	$375	$310	$250	$225	$205

> In 1958, a chrome bar pickup replaced the original pickup.
> In 1961, Fireglo finish became an option.
> By 1974, cresting wave body style became standard.

1000 — similar to 900, except has 18 fret fingerboard. Mfd. 1957-1971.

	$650	$455	$390	$325	$260	$235	$215

> In 1958, a chrome bar pickup replaced the original pickup.
> In 1961, Fireglo finish became an option.

Limited Edition Series

230GF — double cutaway semi hollow maple body, chrome pickguard with Glenn Frey signature, thru body maple neck, 24 fret ebony fingerboard with pearl dot inlay, fixed bridge, chrome peghead logo plate, 3 per side tuners, black hardware, 2 humbucker pickups, chrome volume/tone control, 3 position mini switch. Available in Jetglo finish. Curr. mfr.

Mfr.'s Sug. Retail	$1,000	$700	$600	$500	$400	$360	$330	$300

325JL — offset double cutaway semi hollow 3/4 size maple body, white bi-level pickguard with John Lennon signature and graphic, thru body maple neck, 21 fret rosewood fingerboard with pearl dot inlay, tunomatic bridge/vintage vibrato, white peghead logoplate, 3 per side tuners, chrome hardware, 3 pickups, 2 volume/2 tone/mix controls, 3 position switch. Available in Jetglo finish. Mfd. 1990 to date.

Mfr.'s Sug. Retail	$1,700	$1,190	$1,020	$850	$680	$610	$560	$510

355JL — similar to 325JL, except has full size body, trapeze tailpiece.

Mfr.'s Sug. Retail	$1,730	$1,210	$1,040	$865	$690	$625	$570	$520

> Add $100 for 12 string version of this model (355/12JL).

Grading	100%	98%	95%	90%	80%	70%	60%

370/12RM — offset double cutaway semi hollow bound maple body, bound wedge shaped soundhole, bi-level pickguard with Roger McGuinn's signature, thru body maple neck, 21 fret bound rosewood fingerboard with pearl triangle inlay, tunomatic bridge/R-style trapeze tailpiece, 6 per side tuners, chrome hardware, 3 chrome bar pickups, 2 volume/2 tone/mix controls, 3 position switch. Available in Fireglo finish. Mfd. 1988 only.

	$1,000	$700	$600	$500	$400	$360	$330

Subtract $150 for no signature.

A total of 1,000 of these instruments were made, the first 250 of which were signed by Roger McGuinn.

381JK — double cutaway semi hollow maple body, carved top/back, checkered body binding, bound wedge style soundhole, white bi-level pickguard with John Kay signature and wolf head logo, thru body maple neck, 21 fret bound rosewood fingerboard with pearl triangle inlay, tunomatic bridge/R-style trapeze tailpiece, black peghead logoplate, 3 per side tuners, chrome hardware, 2 humbucker pickups, 2 volume/2 tone/mix controls, 4 position/phase switches, active electronics. Available in Jetglo finish. Mfd. 1988 to date.

Mfr.'s Sug. Retail	$1,800	$1,260	$1,080	$900	$720	$650	$595	$540

660/12TP — cresting wave style bound figured maple body, checkered body binding, gold bi-level pickguard with Tom Petty signature, thru body maple neck, 21 fret bound rosewood fingerboard with pearl triangle inlay, tunomatic bridge/trapeze tailpiece, gold peghead logoplate, 6 per side tuners, chrome hardware, 2 pickups, 2 volume/2 tone/mix controls, 3 position switch. Available in Fireglo and Jetglo finish. Mfd. 1991 to date.

Mfr.'s Sug. Retail	$1,700	$1,190	$1,020	$850	$680	$610	$560	$510

Vintage Reissue Series

The instruments in this series are reproductions from the 1960's, using vintage style pickups, authentic hardware and knobs. The Vintage Re-issue Series is made in small quantities (25-50 annually).

1997 — offset double cutaway semi hollow maple body, F-style soundhole, white bi-level pickguard, thru body maple neck, 21 fret rosewood fingerboard with pearl dot inlay, tunomatic bridge/trapeze tailpiece, 3 per side tuners, chrome hardware, 2 pickups, 2 volume/2 tone/mix controls, 3 position switch. Available in Fireglo, Jetglo, and Mapleglo finish. Curr. mfr.

Mfr.'s Sug. Retail	$1,430	$1,000	$855	$715	$570	$510	$465	$425

Add $125 for 3 pickup version (1997SPC).

Add $70 for R-style trapeze tailpiece (1997VB).

Originally released in 1964 for exclusive United Kingdom distribution.

Grading	100%	98%	95%	90%	80%	70%	60%

1997VB — similar to 1997, except has vibrato tailpiece. Mfd. 1988 to date.

Mfr.'s Sug. Retail	$1,500	$1,050	$900	$750	$600	$540	$495	$450

1997SPC — similar to 1997, except has 3 pickups. New 1993.

Mfr.'s Sug. Retail	$1,555	$1,090	$935	$775	$620	$560	$515	$465

325V59 — offset double cutaway semi hollow 3/4 size maple body, gold bi-level pickguard, thru body maple neck, 21 fret rosewood fingerboard with pearl dot inlay, tunomatic bridge/Bigsby vibrato tailpiece, 3 per side tuners, chrome hardware, 3 pickups, 2 volume/2 tone controls, 3 position switch. Available in Jetglo and Mapleglo finish. Mfd. 1991 to date.

Mfr.'s Sug. Retail	$1,660	$1,160	$995	$830	$665	$595	$545	$495

Reproduction of model released in 1959.

325V63 — similar to 325V59, except has white pickguard, vintage vibrato, 2 volume/2 tone/mix controls. Available in Jetglo finish. Curr. mfr.

Mfr.'s Sug. Retail	$1,660	$1,160	$995	$830	$665	$595	$545	$495

Reproduction of model released in 1963.

360V64 — offset double cutaway semi hollow bound maple body, wedge-style sound-hole, white bi-level pickguard, thru body maple neck, 21 fret rosewood fingerboard with pearl triangle inlay, tunomatic bridge/trapeze tailpiece, 3 per side tuners, chrome hardware, 2 pickups, 2 volume/2 tone/mix controls, 3 position switch. Available in Fireglo finish. Curr. mfr.

Mfr.'s Sug. Retail	$1,560	$1,090	$935	$780	$625	$560	$515	$470

Reproduction of model released in 1964.

360/12V64 — similar to 360V64, except has 12 strings, 6 per side tuners. Available in Fireglo finish. Mfd. 1985 to date.

Mfr.'s Sug. Retail	$1,660	$1,160	$995	$830	$665	$595	$545	$495

381V68 or 381V69 — similar to 360V64, except has carved birdseye maple front/back, checkered binding on body top, bound soundhole/fingerboard, R-style trapeze tailpiece. Available in Fireglo, Jetglo and Mapleglo finish. Mfd. 1987 to date.

Mfr.'s Sug. Retail	$2,190	$1,535	$1,315	$1,095	$875	$785	$720	$655

Reproduction of model released in 1968.
In 1991, model was renamed 381V69.

381/12V69 — similar to 381V69, except has 12 strings, 6 per side tuners. Mfd. 1989 to date.

Mfr.'s Sug. Retail	$2,290	$1,600	$1,370	$1,140	$910	$820	$750	$685

Grading	100%	98%	95%	90%	80%	70%	60%

Double Neck Series

362/12 — offset double cutaway semi hollow checkered bound maple body, bound wedge shaped soundhole, white pickguard, thru body maple/walnut laminate necks, 24 fret bound rosewood fingerboards with pearl triangle inlay, tunomatic bridges/R style tailpieces, 6 per side/3 per side tuners, chrome hardware, 2 single coil exposed pickups per neck, 2 volume/2 tone/mix controls, two 3 position switches, stereo output. Available in Natural finish. Mfd. 1975-1985.

	$2,860	$1,995	$1,715	$1,425	$1,140	$1,025	$940

This was a special order instrument.

ELECTRIC BASS

2000 Series

2030 HAMBURG — double cutaway maple body, thru body maple neck, 20 fret rosewood fingerboard with pearl dot inlay, fixed bridge, 2 per side tuners, 2 single coil pickups, 2 volume/2 tone controls, toggel switch, active electronics. Available in Fireglo, Jetglo, Mapleglo, Midnight Blue, Red, and White finish. Mfd. 1984 to date.

Mfr.'s Sug. Retail	$1,000	$700	$600	$500	$400	$360	$330	$300

2050 EL DORADO — similar to 2030, except has double bound body, bound fingerboard, gold hardware.

Mfr.'s Sug. Retail	$1,200	$840	$720	$600	$480	$430	$395	$360

4000 Series

All models in this series have the following, unless otherwise listed: cresting wave style maple body, pickguard, thru body maple neck, 20 fret rosewood fingerboard, fixed bridge, 2 per side tuners, single coil/horseshoe pickups, 2 volume/2 tone controls, 3 position switch.

4000 — cresting wave style maple body, white pickguard, thru body mahogany neck, 20 fret rosewood fingerboard with white dot inlay, fixed bridge, cresting wave peghead with maple laminate wings, 2 per side tuners, chrome hardware, horseshoe pickup, volume/tone control. Available in Autumnglo, Brownburst, Black, Fireglo, and Natural finish. Mfd. 1957-1987.

1957-1959	$3,250	$2,275	$1,950	$1,625	$1,300	$1,170	$1,070
1960-1964	$2,600	$1,820	$1,560	$1,300	$1,040	$935	$860
1965-1969	$1,000	$700	$600	$500	$400	$360	$330
1970-1987	$500	$350	$300	$250	$200	$180	$165

This is the first production Rickenbacker Bass guitar.

In 1958, a walnut neck replaced the mahogany neck.

In 1960, a maple/walnut laminated neck replaced the walnut neck. Fireglo finish became an option.

In 1963, strings mute was added and Autumnglo and Black finishes became optional.

In 1964, the horseshoe pickup was replaced by a single coil pickup with a metal cover.

Grading	100%	98%	95%	90%	80%	70%	60%

4001 — similar to 4000, except has checkered bound body, maple/walnut laminated neck, bound fingerboard with pearl triangle inlay, chrome bar/horseshoe pickups, 2 volume/2 tone controls, 3 position switch. Available in Fireglo and Natural finish. Mfd. 1961-1986.

	100%	98%	95%	90%	80%	70%	60%
1961-1964	$1,550	$1,085	$930	$775	$620	$560	$515
1965-1969	$1,250	$875	$750	$625	$500	$450	$415
1970-1979	$800	$560	$480	$400	$320	$290	$265
1980-1986	$500	$350	$300	$250	$200	$180	$165

This model was available fretless on special order (4001 FL).

In the early '60s, a few models had ebony fingerboards.

In 1964, the horseshoe pickup was replaced by a single coil pickup with a metal cover.

In 1965, Natural finish became an option.

Stereo output was originally a special order item on the 4001 until 1971 when it became an option.

4002 — similar to 4000, except has checkered bound figured maple body, figured maple/walnut 5 piece neck, bound ebony fingerboard with pearl triangle inlay, 2 humbucker exposed pickups, 2 volume/2 tone controls, 3 position switch, stereo and direct outputs. Available in Mapleglo and Walnut finish. Mfd. 1981 only.

	100%	98%	95%	90%	80%	70%	60%
	$1,000	$700	$600	$500	$400	$360	$330

This was a Limited Edition instrument.

4003 — cresting wave style bound maple body, 2 piece white pickguard, thru body maple neck, 20 fret bound rosewood fingerboard with pearl triangle inlay, fixed bridge, cresting wave style peghead, 2 per side tuners, chrome hardware, 2 single coil exposed pickups (metal cover over bridge pickup), 2 volume/2 tone controls, 3 position switch, stereo output. Available in Natural finish. Mfd. 1973 to date.

	100%	98%	95%	90%	80%	70%	60%
Mfr.'s Sug. Retail	$1,300	$910	$780	$650	$520	$470	$430	$390

This model is also available with fretless fingerboard with pearl dot inlay (4003FL).

In 1985, pickguard was replaced with one piece unit.

4003S — similar to 4003, except has no binding, dot fingerboard inlay, mono output. Available in Red finish. Mfd. 1980 to date.

	100%	98%	95%	90%	80%	70%	60%
Mfr.'s Sug. Retail	$1,200	$840	$720	$600	$480	$430	$395	$360

4003S/5 — similar to 4003, except has 5 strings, no binding, dot fingerboard inlay, 3/2 per side tuners, mono output. Mfd. 1987 to date.

	100%	98%	95%	90%	80%	70%	60%
Mfr.'s Sug. Retail	$1,400	$980	$840	$700	$560	$505	$460	$420

4003S/8 — similar to 4003, except has 8 strings, no binding, dot fingerboard inlay, 4 per side tuners, mono output. Mfd. 1987 to date.

	100%	98%	95%	90%	80%	70%	60%
Mfr.'s Sug. Retail	$1,630	$1,140	$980	$815	$650	$585	$535	$490

Grading	100%	98%	95%	90%	80%	70%	60%

4004 CHEYENNE — cresting wave style walnut body, thru body maple neck, 20 fret maple fingerboard with black dot inlay, fixed bridge, cresting wave style peghead with walnut laminates, 2 per side tuners, gold hardware, 2 humbucker exposed pickups, volume/tone control, 3 position mini switch. Available in Natural finish. New 1993.

Mfr.'s Sug. Retail	$1,430	$1,000	$855	$715	$570	$510	$465	$425

4005 — offset double cutaway semi-hollow maple body, rounded top, bound wedge shaped soundhole, white pickguard, thru body maple/walnut laminate neck, 21 fret bound rosewood fingerboard with pearl triangle inlay, tunomatic bridge/R style trapeze tailpiece, cresting wave style peghead, 2 per side tuners, chrome hardware, 2 single coil exposed pickups, 2 volume/2 tone/mix controls, 3 position switch. Available in Fireglo and Natural finish. Mfd. 1965-1984.

	100%	98%	95%	90%	80%	70%	60%
1965-1969	$1,850	$1,295	$1,110	$925	$740	$670	$610
1970-1979	$750	$525	$450	$375	$300	$270	$245
1980-1984	$650	$455	$390	$325	$260	$235	$215

4008 — cresting wave style bound maple body, white pickguard, thru body maple neck, 21 fret bound rosewood fingerboard with pearl triangle inlay, fixed bridge, cresting wave style peghead, 4 per side tuners, chrome hardware, 2 single coil exposed pickups (metal cover over bridge pickup), 2 volume/2 tone controls, 3 position switch. Available in Fireglo and Natural finish. Mfd. early 1970s-1984.

	$600	$420	$360	$300	$240	$215	$195

This model was available on special order only.

Limited Edition Series

2030GF — double cutaway maple body, chrome pickguard with Glenn Frey signature, thru body maple neck, 20 fret ebony fingerboard with pearl dot inlay, fixed bridge, chrome peghead logoplate, 2 per side tuners, black hardware, 2 humbucker pickups, chrome volume/tone control, 3 position mini switch. Available in Jetglo finish. Curr. mfr.

Mfr.'s Sug. Retail	$1,050	$735	$630	$525	$420	$380	$345	$315

4001CS — cresting wave maple body, white pickguard with Chris Squire signature, thru body maple neck, 20 fret vermilion fingerboard with pearl dot inlay, fixed bridge, white peghead logoplate, 2 per side tuners, chrome hardware, single coil/horseshoe pickups, 2 volume/2 tone controls, 3 position switch. Available in Cream Laquer finish. Curr. mfr.

Mfr.'s Sug. Retail	$1,530	$1,070	$915	$765	$610	$550	$505	$455

The fingerboard and peghead on this model are carved from one piece of African vermilion.

Grading	100%	98%	95%	90%	80%	70%	60%

Vintage Series

4001V63 — cresting wave style maple body, white pickguard, thru body maple neck, 20 fret rosewood fingerboard with pearl dot inlay, fixed bridge, 2 per side tuners, chrome hardware, single coil/horseshoe pickups, 2 volume/2 tone controls, 3 position switch. Available in Fireglo and Mapleglo finish. Mfd. 1984 to date.

Mfr.'s Sug. Retail	$1,660	$1,160	$995	$830	$665	$595	$545	$495

Reproduction of model released in 1963.

ROBIN

Manufacturer located in Houston, TX since 1982.

After several years of collecting, dealing and restoring vintage guitars, the Robin Guitar Company of Houston, TX was formed in 1982. In addition to the standard models listed below, Robin's Custom Shop can assemble virtually anything on a special order basis. Custom graphics and a variety of finishes are also available. Contact manufacturer for prices and designs on custom orders (see Trademark Index). Regular production and distribution done by Robin Guitar Co., Houston, TX.

GUITARS & BASSES

ELECTRIC

Machete Series

All models in this series have reverse single cutaway asymmetrical bodies with terraced cuts on front and back. Headstocks are asymmetrically V-shaped.

MACHETE CUSTOM — figured maple body, thru body maple neck, 24 fret ebony fingerboard with pearl dot inlay, double locking vibrato, 4/2 per side tuners, black hardware, 2 Seymour Duncan blade humbucker pickups, volume/tone control, 3 position switch. Available in Antique Amber and Ruby Red finish. Mfd. 1991 to date.

Mfr.'s Sug. Retail	$2,395	$1,675	$1,435	$1,195	$955	$855	$785	$715

Add $300 for excellent grade figured maple top (Machete Custom Classic).

※ **Machete Deluxe** — similar to Machete Custom, except has mahogany body, thru body mahogany neck and rosewood fingerboard. Available in Cherry finish.

Mfr.'s Sug. Retail	$2,195	$1,540	$1,320	$1,100	$880	$790	$725	$660

※ **Machete Special** — similar to Machete Custom, except has ash body, bolt-on maple neck, rosewood fingerboard and 2 humbucker PJ Marx pickups. Available in Natural oil finish.

Mfr.'s Sug. Retail	$995	$695	$595	$500	$400	$360	$330	$300

Grading	100%	98%	95%	90%	80%	70%	60%

❧ **Machete Standard** — similar to Machete Custom, except has ash body and bolt-on maple neck. Available in Blue and Cherry finish. Mfd. 1991 to date.

Mfr.'s Sug. Retail	$1,650	$1,155	$990	$825	$660	$595	$545	$495

Ranger Series

RANGER CUSTOM — strat style bound ash body, white pickguard, bolt-on figured maple neck, 22 fret rosewood fingerboard with pearl dot inlay, fixed bridge, reverse headstock, 6 on one side tuners, chrome hardware, humbucker/2 single coil pickups, volume/tone control, 5 position switch. Available in Cherry, Orange and Three-tone Sunburst finish. Mfd. 1991 to date.

Mfr.'s Sug. Retail	$1,400	$980	$840	$700	$560	$505	$460	$420

Add $50 for standard vibrato.

❧ **Ranger Special** — similar to Ranger Custom, except has no pickguard, regular maple neck. Available in Natural oil finish.

Mfr.'s Sug. Retail	$995	$695	$595	$500	$400	$360	$330	$300

❧ **Ranger Standard** — similar to Ranger Custom, except has unbound poplar body. Available in Pearl Black, Pearl Red and Pearl White finish.

Mfr.'s Sug. Retail	$1,145	$805	$690	$575	$460	$415	$380	$345

❧ **Ranger Studio** — similar to Ranger Custom, except has unbound body, regular maple neck, standard bridge, locking Sperzel tuners, 3 single coil pickups. Available in Cherry Sunburst, Three Tone Sunburst, Tobacco Sunburst, Two Tone Sunburst, Unburst, Violin Sunburst and the following Transparent finishes: Blue, Bone White, Charcoal Black, Cherry, Green, Honey, Lavender, Natural, Old Blonde, Orange, Purple, Rootbeer, Violet and Yellow.

Mfr.'s Sug. Retail	$1,520	$1,065	$910	$760	$610	$550	$505	$455

Standard Series

MEDLEY SPECIAL — strat style ash body, bolt-on maple neck, 24 fret rosewood fingerboard with pearl dot inlay, double locking vibrato, reverse headstock, 6 on one side tuners, black hardware, single coil/humbucker pickups, volume control, 3 position switch. Available in Natural oil finish. Mfd. 1991 to date.

Mfr.'s Sug. Retail	$995	$695	$595	$500	$400	$360	$330	$300

❧ **Medley Standard II** — similar to Medley Special, except has hardwood body, 2 humbucker Seymour Duncan pickups and tone control. Available in Blue, Cherry, Natural, Pearl Black and Purple finish.

Mfr.'s Sug. Retail	$1,450	$1,015	$870	$725	$580	$520	$475	$435

Add $350 for curly maple top.
Add $400 for quilted maple top.

Grading	100%	98%	95%	90%	80%	70%	60%

⚄ **Medley Standard IV** — similar to Medley Special, except has 2 stacked coil/1 humbucker Seymour Duncan pickups, tone control, 5 position and coil tap switch. Available in Blue, Cherry, Green, Pearl White and Purple finish.

Mfr.'s Sug. Retail	$1,520	$1,065	$910	$760	$610	$550	$505	$455

Add $400 for curly maple body.

⚄ **Medley Standard VI** — similar to Medley Special, except has mahogany body with exotic wood top, Seymour Duncan coil/humbucker pickups and tone control.

Mfr.'s Sug. Retail	$1,750	$1,225	$1,050	$875	$700	$630	$575	$525

Contact manufacturer for availability of colors.

RAIDER STANDARD II — similar to Medley Standard II, except has asymmetrical double cutaway reverse body. Disc. 1992.

Mfr.'s Sug. Retail	$1,450	$1,015	$870	$725	$580	$520	$475	$435

⚄ **Raider Standard IV** — similar to Medley Standard IV, except has asymmetrical double cutaway reverse body. Disc. 1992.

Mfr.'s Sug. Retail	$1,520	$1,065	$910	$760	$610	$550	$505	$455

TEDLEY STANDARD VI — tele style hardwood body, bolt-on maple neck, 24 fret rosewood fingerboard with pearl dot inlay, double locking vibrato, reverse headstock, 6 on one side tuners, black hardware, stacked coil/humbucker Seymour Duncan pickups, volume/tone control, 3 position switch. Available in Cherry, Orange, Pearl Black and Purple finish. Mfd. 1991 to date.

Mfr.'s Sug. Retail	$1,450	$1,015	$870	$725	$580	$520	$475	$435

ELECTRIC BASS

MACHETE 5 STRING — reverse single cutaway asymmetrical ash body, bolt-on maple neck, 24 fret rosewood fingerboard with pearl dot inlay, fixed Schaller bridge, asymmetrical V-shaped headstock, 3/2 per side tuners, black hardware, 2 Bartolini pickups, volume/treble/bass and mix controls, active electronics. Available in Transparent Cherry, Transparent Green and Pearl Black finish. Mfd. 1991 to date.

Mfr.'s Sug. Retail	$1,845	$1,295	$1,110	$925	$740	$670	$610	$555

MEDLEY — precision style ash body, bolt-on maple neck, 24 fret rosewood fingerboard with pearl dot inlay, fixed bridge, asymmetrical V-shaped headstock, 2 per side tuners, black hardware, P-style/J-style pickups, volume/tone control, 3 position switch. Available in Pearl Black, Pearl White, Transparent Blue and Transparent Cherry finish. Mfd. 1991 to date.

Mfr.'s Sug. Retail	$1,145	$805	$690	$575	$460	$415	$380	$345

 **, cont.**

Grading	100%	98%	95%	90%	80%	70%	60%

RANGER — precision style ash body, black pickguard, bolt-on maple neck, 20 fret maple fingerboard with black dot inlay, fixed bridge, reverse headstock, 4 on one side tuners, chrome hardware, P-style/J-style pickups, volume/tone control, 3 position switch. Available in Pearl Black, Pearl Red and Transparent Old Blonde finish. Mfd. 1991 to date.

Mfr.'s Sug. Retail	$1,145	$805	$690	$575	$460	$415	$380	$345

This model available with rosewood fingerboard with pearl dot inlay and fretless.

Ranger Jaybird — similar to Ranger, except has no pickguard, 2 J-style pickups.

Mfr.'s Sug. Retail	$1,145	$805	$690	$575	$460	$415	$380	$345

Ranger Jaywalker — similar to Ranger, except has figured maple top, no pickguard, ebony fingerboard only, 2 active J-style Bartolini pickups, volume/treble/bass/mix controls.

Mfr.'s Sug. Retail	$1,845	$1,290	$1,110	$925	$740	$670	$610	$555

Ranger Special — similar to Ranger, except has no pickguard, rosewood fingerboard only.

Mfr.'s Sug. Retail	$995	$695	$595	$500	$400	$360	$330	$300

S

SAMICK

Manufactured and distributed by Samick Music Corp., located in City of Industry, CA, since 1983.

Grading	100%	98%	95%	90%	80%	70%	60%

ACOUSTIC

ASPEN — dreadnought style, spruce top, round soundhole, black pickguard, 3 stripe bound body/rosette, sapele back/sides, nato neck, 14/20 fret rosewood fingerboard, rosewood bridge with white black dot pins, rosewood veneer on peghead, 3 per side chrome tuners. Available in Natural finish. Curr. mfr.

Mfr.'s Sug. Retail	$250	$175	$150	$125	$100	$90	$80	$75

AUSTIN — single rounded cutaway dreadnought style, solid cedar top, oval soundhole, 5 stripe bound body/rosette, cedar back/sides, maple neck, 14/20 fret bound rosewood fingerboard with pearl dot inlay, stylized pearl inlay at 12th fret, rosewood bridge with white black dot pins, cedar veneer on bound peghead, 3 per side gold tuners, piezo pickup, volume/tone slider control. Available in Natural finish. Curr. mfr.

Mfr.'s Sug. Retail	$450	$315	$270	$225	$180	$160	$150	$135

CHEYENNE — folk style, spruce top, round soundhole, black pickguard, mahogany back/sides, nato neck, 14/20 fret rosewood fingerboard with pearl dot inlay, rosewood bridge with white black dot pins, rosewood veneer on peghead, gold tuners. Available in Natural finish. Curr. mfr.

Mfr.'s Sug. Retail	$360	$250	$215	$180	$145	$130	$120	$110

DEL REY — classical style, solid spruce top, round soundhole, bound body, wooden inlay rosette, rosewood back/sides, nato neck, 12/19 fret rosewood fingerboard, rosewood bridge, rosewood headstock veneer, 3 per side chrome tuners. Available in Pumpkin finish. Curr. mfr.

Mfr.'s Sug. Retail	$300	$210	$180	$150	$120	$110	$100	$90

GALLOWAY — single rounded cutaway dreadnought style, maple top, round soundhole, black pickguard, 3 stripe bound body/rosette, maple back/sides/neck, 14/20 fret bound rosewood fingerboard with pearl dot inlay, rosewood bridge with white black dot pins, 3 per side chrome tuners, piezo pickup, volume/tone slider control. Available in Natural finish. Curr. mfr.

Mfr.'s Sug. Retail	$400	$280	$240	$200	$160	$145	$130	$120

Grading	100%	98%	95%	90%	80%	70%	60%

GRANADA — single rounded cutaway classical style, spruce top, round soundhole, bound body, wooden inlay rosette, rosewood back/sides, nato neck, 12/19 fret rosewood fingerboard, rosewood bridge, rosewood headstock veneer, 3 per side chrome tuners, active piezo pickup, volume/tone slider control. Available in Pumpkin finish. Curr. mfr.

Mfr.'s Sug. Retail	$330	$230	$195	$165	$130	$120	$110	$100

GREENBRIAR — dreadnought style, spruce top, round soundhole, black pickguard, 3 stripe bound body/rosette, mahogany back/sides, nato neck, 14/20 fret rosewood fingerboard with pearl dot inlay, rosewood bridge with black white dot pins, 3 per side chrome tuners. Available in Natural finish. Curr. mfr.

Mfr.'s Sug. Retail	$250	$175	$150	$125	$100	$90	$80	$75

Add $50 for solid spruce top (Bluebird).

Add $80 for single rounded cutaway, piezo pickup, volume/tone slider control (Laredo).

Subtract $10 for left handed design, acoustic pickup, volume/tone control (Beaumont).

This model available with 12 strings, nato back/sides (SW21012 Savannah).

JASMINE — dreadnought style, solid cedar top, round soundhole, tortoise shell pickguard, 3 stripe bound body, herringbone rosette, walnut back/sides, nato neck, 14/20 fret bound rosewood fingerboard with pearl block inlay, rosewood bridge with white pearl dot pins, walnut veneer on bound peghead, 3 per side chrome tuners. Available in Natural finish. Curr. mfr.

Mfr.'s Sug. Retail	$280	$195	$165	$140	$110	$100	$90	$80

LA GRANDE — classical style, cedar top, round soundhole, bound body, wooden inlay rosette, rosewood back/sides, nato neck, 12/19 fret rosewood fingerboard, rosewood bridge, rosewood headstock veneer, 3 per side chrome tuners. Available in Pumpkin finish. Curr. mfr.

Mfr.'s Sug. Retail	$360	$250	$215	$180	$145	$130	$120	$110

LA TOUR — classical style, solid spruce top, round soundhole, bound body, wooden inlay rosette, sapele back/sides, nato neck, 12/19 fret rosewood fingerboard, rosewood bridge, rosewood headstock veneer, 3 per side chrome tuners. Available in Pumpkin finish. Curr. mfr.

Mfr.'s Sug. Retail	$210	$145	$125	$100	$80	$70	$65	$60

LAUREL — dreadnought style, solid spruce top, round soundhole, black pickguard, 3 stripe bound body/rosette, nato neck, 14/20 fret bound rosewood fingerboard with pearl Tree of Life inlay, ebony bridge with white pearl dot pins, bound peghead with pearl logo inlay, 3 per side gold tuners. Available in Natural finish. Curr. mfr.

Mfr.'s Sug. Retail	$400	$280	$240	$200	$160	$145	$130	$120

Grading	100%	98%	95%	90%	80%	70%	60%

MAGNOLIA — jumbo style, sycamore top, round soundhole, black pickguard, 5 stripe bound body/rosette, nato back/sides/neck, 14/20 fret bound rosewood fingerboard with pearl dot inlay, rosewood bridge with white black dot pins, 3 per side black chrome tuners. Available in Black and White finish. Curr. mfr.

Mfr.'s Sug. Retail	$330	$230	$195	$165	$130	$120	$110	$100

NIGHTINGALE — dreadnought style, solid spruce top, round soundhole, black pickguard, 3 stripe bound body/rosette, imitation birdseye back/sides, nato neck, 14/20 fret bound rosewood fingerboard with pearl dot inlay, rosewood bridge with white black dot pins, bound headstock, 3 per side chrome tuners. Available in Transparent Black finish. Curr. mfr.

Mfr.'s Sug. Retail	$350	$245	$210	$175	$140	$125	$115	$105

NIGHTINGALE 12 — dreadnought style, maple top, round soundhole, black pickguard, 3 stripe bound body/rosette, maple back/sides, nato neck, 14/20 fret bound rosewood fingerboard with pearl dot inlay, rosewood bridge with white black dot pins, 6 per side chrome tuners. Available in Transparent Black finish. Curr. mfr.

Mfr.'s Sug. Retail	$300	$210	$180	$150	$120	$110	$100	$90

SANTA FE — dreadnought style, nato top, round soundhole, black pickguard, bound body, 5 stripe rosette, nato back/sides/neck, 14/20 fret nato fingerboard with pearl dot inlay, ebonized maple bridge with black pins, 3 per side chrome tuners. Available in Black, Gloss Brown, and White finish. Curr. mfr.

Mfr.'s Sug. Retail	$180	$125	$110	$90	$70	$65	$60	$50

Add $50 for acoustic pickup, volume/tone control (SW115E1).

SEVILLE — classical style, spruce top, round soundhole, bound body, wooden inlay rosette, mahogany back/sides, nato neck, 12/19 fret rosewood fingerboard, rosewood bridge, 3 per side chrome tuners. Available in Pumpkin finish. Curr. mfr.

Mfr.'s Sug. Retail	$180	$125	$110	$90	$70	$65	$60	$50

SWEETWATER — folk style, spruce top, round soundhole, 3 stripe bound body/rosette, mahogany back/sides, nato neck, 14/20 fret rosewood fingerboard with pearl dot inlay, rosewood bridge with white pins, 3 per side chrome tuners. Available in Natural finish. Curr. mfr.

Mfr.'s Sug. Retail	$220	$155	$130	$110	$90	$80	$70	$65

VICKSBURG — dreadnought style, solid spruce top, round soundhole, black pickguard, herringbone bound body/rosette, rosewood back/sides, nato neck, 14/20 fret bound rosewood fingerboard with pearl diamond inlays, rosewood bridge with white black dot pins, 6 per side gold tuners. Available in Natural finish. Curr. mfr.

Mfr.'s Sug. Retail	$450	$315	$270	$225	$180	$160	$150	$135

Grading	100%	98%	95%	90%	80%	70%	60%

Handcrafted Series

CHAMBRAY — single rounded cutaway folk style, solid cedar top, round soundhole, rosewood pickguard, wooden bound body, wooden inlay rosette, rosewood back/sides, nato neck, 14/20 fret ebony fingerboard with pearl dot inlay, ebony bridge with black white dot pins, rosewood veneer on peghead with pearl logo inlay, 3 per side Schaller gold tuners with pearl buttons, acoustic pickup, volume/tone control, preamp. Available in Natural finish. Curr. mfr.

Mfr.'s Sug. Retail	$1,100	$770	$660	$550	$440	$395	$365	$330

MARSEILLES — folk style, solid spruce top, round soundhole, tortoise shell pickguard, wooden bound body, wooden inlay rosette, ovankol back/sides, nato neck, 14/20 fret bound rosewood fingerboard with pearl dot inlay, ebony bridge with white black dot pins, ovankol veneer on peghead with pearl logo inlay, 3 per side chrome tuners. Available in Natural finish. Curr. mfr.

Mfr.'s Sug. Retail	$460	$320	$275	$230	$185	$165	$150	$140

VERSAILLES — similar to Marseilles, except has solid cedar top, rosewood back/sides, brown white dot bridge pins.

Mfr.'s Sug. Retail	$700	$490	$420	$350	$280	$250	$230	$210

ACOUSTIC BASS

KINGSTON BASS — single rounded cutaway hollow style, maple top, bound body, F holes, maple back/sides/neck, 24 fret bound rosewood fingerboard, thru strings rosewood bridge, 2 per side black chrome tuners, piezo pickup, volume/tone slider control. Available in Black, Natural, Pearl White and Tobacco Sunburst finish. Curr. mfr.

Mfr.'s Sug. Retail	$700	$490	$420	$350	$280	$250	$230	$210

ACOUSTIC ELECTRIC

BLUE RIDGE — single rounded cutaway folk style, figured maple top, oval soundhole, 5 stripe bound body, wooden rosette cap, maple back/sides, nato neck, 22 fret bound rosewood fingerboard with pearl dot inlay, rosewood strings thru bridge, 6 on one side black chrome tuners, active piezo pickup, volume/tone control. Available in Blue Burst, Natural and Tobacco Sunburst finish. Curr. mfr.

Mfr.'s Sug. Retail	$500	$350	$300	$250	$200	$180	$165	$150

Grading	100%	98%	95%	90%	80%	70%	60%

ELECTRIC

Alternative Series

AURORA — strat style alder body, bolt-on maple neck, 24 fret bound rosewood fingerboard with pearl dot inlay, double locking vibrato, 6 on one side tuners, black hardware, single coil/humbucker pickup, volume/tone control, 3 position switch. Available in Aurora finish. Curr. mfr.

Mfr.'s Sug. Retail	$490	$345	$295	$245	$195	$175	$160	$150

HAWK, NIGHTBREED, VIPER — strat style alder body, bolt-on maple neck, 24 fret bound rosewood fingerboard with pearl triangle inlay, double locking vibrato, 6 on one side tuners, black hardware, 2 single coil rail/1 humbucker pickups, volume/2 tone controls, 5 position switch. Curr. mfr.

* **Hawk** — available in Hawk Graphic finish.

Mfr.'s Sug. Retail	$580	$405	$350	$290	$230	$205	$190	$175

* **Nightbreed** — available in Nightbreed Graphic finish.

Mfr.'s Sug. Retail	$650	$455	$390	$325	$260	$235	$215	$195

* **Viper** — available in Viper Graphic finish.

Mfr.'s Sug. Retail	$650	$455	$390	$325	$260	$235	$215	$195

ICE CUBE — strat style acrylic body, bolt-on maple neck, 24 fret rosewood fingerboard with pearl V inlay, double locking vibrato, 6 on one side tuners, gold hardware, 2 single coil/1 humbucker pickups, volume/tone control, 5 position switch. Available in Clear finish. Curr. mfr.

Mfr.'s Sug. Retail	$520	$365	$310	$260	$210	$190	$170	$160

Jazz/Blues Series

BLUENOTE — single round cutaway bound hollow body, arched maple top, raised black pickguard, f holes, maple back/sides/neck, 22 fret bound rosewood fingerboard with abalone/pearl block inlay, adjustable rosewood bridge/trapeze tailpiece, bound blackface peghead with pearl vines/logo inlay, 3 per side tuners, gold hardware, 2 covered humbucker pickups, 2 volume/2 tone controls, 3 position switch. Available in Golden Sunburst, Natural and Tobacco Sunburst finish. Curr. mfr.

Mfr.'s Sug. Retail	$600	$420	$360	$300	$240	$215	$195	$180

KINGSTON — double rounded cutaway semi-hollow style, arched figured maple top, raised black pickguard, bound body, F holes, maple back/sides, nato neck, 22 fret bound rosewood fingerboard with pearl cross inlay, tunomatic bridge/stop tailpiece, bound peghead with pearl vines/logo inlay, 3 per side tuners, chrome hardware, 2 humbucker pickups, 2 volume/2 tone controls, 3 position switch. Available in Black, Cherry Sunburst, Golden Sunburst and Natural finish. Curr. mfr.

Mfr.'s Sug. Retail	$530	$370	$320	$265	$210	$190	$175	$160

Grading	100%	98%	95%	90%	80%	70%	60%

Kingston Classic — similar to Kingston, except has gold hardware. Available in Cherry Sunburst, Golden Sunburst, Natural and Tobacco Sunburst finish.

Mfr.'s Sug. Retail	$560	$390	$335	$280	$225	$205	$190	$170

WABASH — single rounded cutaway hollow style, arched maple top, raised bound black pickguard, bound body, F holes, maple back/sides/neck, 20 fret bound rosewood fingerboard with pearl block inlay, adjustable rosewood bridge/trapeze tailpiece, bound peghead with pearl flower inlay, 3 per side tuners, gold hardware, 2 humbucker pickups, 2 volume/2 tone controls, 3 position switch. Available in Cherry Sunburst, Golden Sunburst and Natural finish. Curr. mfr.

Mfr.'s Sug. Retail	$600	$420	$360	$300	$240	$215	$195	$180

Performance Series

LEGACY — strat style alder body, bolt-on maple neck, 24 fret bound rosewood fingerboard with pearl boomerang inlay, double locking vibrato, 6 on one side tuners, gold hardware, 2 single coil rail/1 humbucker pickups, volume/tone control, 5 position/coil tap switches. Available in Natural finish. Curr. mfr.

Mfr.'s Sug. Retail	$560	$390	$335	$280	$225	$205	$190	$170

PROPHET — similar to Legacy, except has ash body, thru body neck. Available in Transparent Black and Transparent Red finish.

Mfr.'s Sug. Retail	$600	$420	$360	$300	$240	$215	$195	$180

RENEGADE — strat style alder body, bolt-on maple neck, 24 fret maple fingerboard with black dot inlay, standard vibrato, 6 on one side tuners, chrome hardware, 3 single coil pickups, volume/tone control, 5 position switch. Available in Cobalt Blue and Metallic Red finish. Curr. mfr.

Mfr.'s Sug. Retail	$380	$265	$225	$190	$150	$135	$120	$110

SCANDAL — similar to Renegade, except has bound rosewood fingerboard, 2 humbucker pickups, 2 volume/1 tone control, 3 position switch. Available in Fluorescent Green and Metallic Black finish.

Mfr.'s Sug. Retail	$300	$210	$180	$150	$120	$110	$100	$90

SCORPION — strat style alder body, bolt-on maple neck, 24 fret bound rosewood fingerboard with pearl boomerang inlay, double locking vibrato, 6 on one side tuners, gold hardware, 2 single coil/1 humbucker pickups, volume/tone control, 5 position switch, push/pull coil tap in tone control. Available in Black, Metallic Red and Pearl White finish. Curr. mfr.

Mfr.'s Sug. Retail	$520	$365	$310	$260	$210	$190	$170	$160

Scorpion Plus — similar to Scorpion, except has sharktooth fingerboard inlay, direct switch. Available in Black, Blue, Metallic Red and Pearl White finish.

Mfr.'s Sug. Retail	$450	$315	$270	$225	$180	$160	$150	$135

Grading	100%	98%	95%	90%	80%	70%	60%

STINGER — strat style bound alder body, bolt-on maple neck, 24 fret bound rosewood fingerboard with pearl boomerang inlay, double locking vibrato, 6 on one side tuners, gold hardware, 2 single coil rail/1 humbucker pickups, volume/tone control, 5 position/coil tap switches. Available in Antique Red Sunburst and Black finish. Curr. mfr.

Mfr.'s Sug. Retail	$540	$380	$325	$270	$215	$195	$180	$165

Vintage Guitar Series

SOUTHSIDE — strat style laminated body, white pickguard, bolt-on maple neck, 21 fret maple fingerboard with black dot inlay, standard vibrato, 6 on one side tuners, chrome hardware, 3 single coil pickups, volume/2 tone controls, 5 position switch. Curr. mfr.

Mfr.'s Sug. Retail	$220	$155	$130	$110	$90	$80	$70	$65

Southside Classic, Legend — strat style body, white pickguard, bolt-on maple neck, 22 fret rosewood fingerboard pearl dot inlay, standard vibrato, 6 on one side tuners, chrome hardware, 3 single coil pickups, volume/2 tone controls, 5 position switch. Curr. mfr.

Mfr.'s Sug. Retail	$340	$235	$200	$170	$135	$125	$115	$105

Classic — alder body. Available in Antique Orange, Pacific Blue, Candy Apple Red, Seamist Green and Tobacco Sunburst finish.

Mfr.'s Sug. Retail	$320	$225	$195	$160	$130	$115	$105	$95

Legend — ash body. Available in Natural and Transparent Ivory finish.

Mfr.'s Sug. Retail	$340	$235	$200	$170	$135	$125	$115	$105

Southside Heavy — similar to Southside, except has black pickguard, 22 fret rosewood fingerboard with pearl dot inlay, 2 single coil/1 humbucker pickups.

Mfr.'s Sug. Retail	$280	$195	$165	$140	$110	$100	$90	$80

Southside Special — similar to Southside, except has 22 fret rosewood fingerboard with pearl dot inlay.

Mfr.'s Sug. Retail	$270	$190	$160	$135	$110	$100	$90	$80

UPTOWN — tele style laminated body, white pickguard, bolt-on maple neck, 21 fret maple fingerboard with black dot inlay, fixed bridge, 6 on one side tuners, chrome hardware, 2 single coil pickups, volume/tone control, 3 position switch. Available in Butterscotch and Transparent Ivory finish. Curr. mfr.

Mfr.'s Sug. Retail	$290	$205	$175	$145	$115	$105	$95	$85

Uptown Classic — similar to Uptown, except has alder body, gold hardware. Available in Black finish.

Mfr.'s Sug. Retail	$340	$235	$200	$170	$135	$125	$115	$105

Uptown Legend — similar to Uptown, except has ash body, black pickguard. Available in Natural and Transparent Ivory finish.

Mfr.'s Sug. Retail	$340	$235	$200	$170	$135	$125	$115	$105

Grading	100%	98%	95%	90%	80%	70%	60%

ELECTRIC BASS

AURORA — offset double cutaway alder body, maple neck, 24 fret rosewood fingerboard, fixed bridge, 4 on one side tuners, black hardware, P-style/J-style pickup, volume/mid/bass/balance controls. Available in Aurora Multi Palette finish. Curr. mfr.

Mfr.'s Sug. Retail	$520	$365	$310	$260	$210	$190	$170	$160

JAVELIN — offset double cutaway asymmetrical alder body, white pickguard, thumb rest, bolt-on maple neck, 20 fret rosewood fingerboard, fixed bridge, 4 on one side tuners, chrome hardware, 2 J-style pickups, 2 volume/1 tone control. Available in Black, Pearl White, Sunburst finish. Curr. mfr.

Mfr.'s Sug. Retail	$350	$245	$210	$175	$140	$125	$115	$105

PRESTIGE — offset double cutaway laminated body, black pickguard, thumb rest, bolt-on maple neck, 20 fret maple fingerboard with black dot inlay, fixed bridge, 4 on one side tuners, P-style pickup, volume/tone control. Available in Black, Metallic Red and Pearl White finish. Curr. mfr.

Mfr.'s Sug. Retail	$270	$190	$160	$135	$110	$100	$90	$80

⚄ **Prestige GT** — similar to Prestige, except has alder body, no pickguard, 24 fret rosewood fingerboard with pearl dot inlay. Available in Black, Pearl White, Tobacco Sunburst and Transparent Blue finish. Curr. mfr.

Mfr.'s Sug. Retail	$300	$210	$180	$150	$120	$110	$100	$90

PROPHET — offset double cutaway alder body, thru body 3 piece maple neck, 24 fret rosewood fingerboard with pearl dot inlay, fixed bridge, 4 on one side tuners, gold hardware, P-style/J-style pickups, volume/tone control, 3 position switch. Available in Transparent Black, Transparent Blue, and Transparent Red finish. Curr. mfr.

Mfr.'s Sug. Retail	$600	$420	$360	$300	$240	$215	$195	$180

THUNDER — offset double cutaway alder body, bolt-on maple neck, 24 fret rosewood fingerboard with pearl dot inlay, fixed bridge, 4 on one side tuners, gold hardware, P-style/J-style pickups, volume/tone control, 3 position switch. Available in Black Finishing Net, Granite White Sunburst and Pearl White finish. Curr. mfr.

Mfr.'s Sug. Retail	$370	$260	$220	$185	$150	$135	$120	$110

Subtract $20 for fretless version of this model with active pickups (Thunder FL). Available in Black, Grayburst and Pearl White finish.

⚄ **Thunder-5** — similar to Thunder, except has 5 string configuration, 4/1 per side tuners, 2 volume/1 tone controls. Available in Black, Granite Gold, Grayburst, Metallic Red and Pearl White finish.

Mfr.'s Sug. Retail	$500	$350	$300	$250	$200	$180	$165	$150

This model available with active pickups.

Grading	100%	98%	95%	90%	80%	70%	60%

THUNDERBOLT — offset double cutaway alder body, bolt-on maple neck, 24 fret rosewood fingerboard with pearl lightning bolt inlay, fixed bridge, 4 per side tuners, gold hardware, P-style/J-style active pickups, volume/treble/bass/balance controls. Available in Black, Grayburst, Metallic Red and Pearl White finish. Curr. mfr.

Mfr.'s Sug. Retail	$450	$315	$270	$225	$180	$160	$150	$135

SANTA CRUZ

Manufactured and distributed by Santa Cruz Guitar Co., located in Santa Cruz, CA since 1976.

This company was formed in 1976 by Richard Hoover and his instruments are noted for their high quality and select solid wood construction.

ACOUSTIC

All models have round soundholes with wood inlay rosettes. Body trim consists of ivoroid binding with wood purfling, unless otherwise listed. All models are available in Natural finish, unless otherwise indicated. For current option pricing, contact manufacturer directly (see Trademark Index).

MODEL D — dreadnought style, spruce top, koa back/sides, mahogany neck, 14/20 fret bound ebony fingerboard, ebony bridge with black pearl dot pins, ebony veneer on bound peghead with pearl logo inlay, 3 per side gold tuners. Curr. mfr.

Mfr.'s Sug. Retail	$1,975	$1,380	$1,185	$985	$790	$710	$650	$590

This model is also available with rosewood back/sides.

12 Fret D Model — folk style, spruce top, herringbone purfling/rosette, black pickguard, mahogany back/sides, 12/20 fret ebony fingerboard with pearl diamond inlay, ebony bridge with pearl dot pins, ebony veneer on slotted peghead with pearl logo inlay, 3 per side gold tuners. Curr. mfr.

Mfr.'s Sug. Retail	$2,475	$1,730	$1,485	$1,235	$985	$880	$810	$745

MODEL F — jumbo style, spruce top, maple back/sides, maple neck, 14/21 fret bound ebony fingerboard with abalone fan inlay, ebony bridge with black pearl dot pins, ebony veneer on bound peghead with pearl logo inlay, 3 per side gold tuners. Curr. mfr.

Mfr.'s Sug. Retail	$2,400	$1,680	$1,440	$1,200	$960	$860	$790	$720

This model is also available with 12 string or cutaway options.

MODEL FS — single rounded cutaway jumbo style, cedar top, mahogany neck, 21 fret ebony fingerboard, ebony bridge with black pearl dot pins, 3 per side chrome Schaller tuners with ebony buttons. Curr. mfr.

Mfr.'s Sug. Retail	$3,450	$2,415	$2,070	$1,725	$1,380	$1,240	$1,140	$1,035

Grading	100%	98%	95%	90%	80%	70%	60%

MODEL H — folk style, koa top, round soundhole, abalone bound body/rosette, koa back/sides, mahogany neck, 14/20 fret bound ebony fingerboard, ebony bridge with black pearl pins, koa veneer on bound peghead, 3 per side gold tuners with ebony buttons. Curr. mfr.

Mfr.'s Sug. Retail	$2,250	$1,575	$1,345	$1,125	$900	$810	$740	$675

This model is also available with spruce top, rosewood back/sides or cutaway.

⚡ **Model H Acoustic Electric** — folk style, spruce top, mahogany back/sides/neck, 21 fret ebony fingerboard with pearl/gold ring inlay, ebony bridge with black pearl dot pins, 3 per side gold Schaller tuners with ebony buttons, bridge pickup with micro drive preamp. Curr. mfr.

Mfr.'s Sug. Retail	$2,050	$1,435	$1,230	$1,025	$820	$745	$675	$615

MODEL OM (Orchestra Model) — concert grand style, spruce top, tortoise shell pickguard, herringbone rosette, Brazilian rosewood back/sides, mahogany neck, 14/20 fret bound ebony fingerboard with pearl logo inlay at 12th fret, ebony bridge with black pearl dot pins, rosewood peghead veneer, 3 per side gold tuners. Curr. mfr.

Mfr.'s Sug. Retail	$2,525	$1,765	$1,515	$1,265	$1,010	$910	$835	$760

This model may have Indian rosewood back/sides, also.

TONY RICE MODEL — dreadnought style, spruce top, tortoise shell pickguard, herringbone bound body/rosette, rosewood back/sides, mahogany neck, 14/20 fret bound ebony fingerboard with pearl logo inlay at 12th fret, Tony Rice signature at 14th fret, ebony bridge with black pearl dot pins, ebony peghead veneer, 3 per side gold tuners. Curr. mfr.

Mfr.'s Sug. Retail	$2,750	$1,925	$1,650	$1,375	$1,100	$990	$905	$825

This model was co-designed with Tony Rice.

VINTAGE ARTIST — dreadnought style, spruce top, tortoise shell pickguard, herringbone body trim, mahogany back/sides/neck, 14/21 fret bound ebony fingerboard with pearl dot inlay, ebony bridge with black pearl dot pins, Brazilian rosewood veneer on bound peghead with pearl logo inlay, 3 per side chrome tuners. Curr. mfr.

Mfr.'s Sug. Retail	$2,525	$1,765	$1,515	$1,265	$1,010	$910	$835	$760

SANTUCCI

Developed by Sergio Santucci and produced in Rome, ITALY. Distributed in the USA by the Santucci Corp., located in New York, NY.

Grading	100%	98%	95%	90%	80%	70%	60%

ELECTRIC

TREBLEBASS — offset double cutaway alder body, thru body 5 piece maple neck, 24 fret ebony fingerboard with pearl dot inlay, fixed bridge-bass, standard vibrato-guitar, 4/6 per side tuners, chrome hardware, split-bass/single coil/humbucker-guitar EMG pickups, 2 concentric volume/tone controls, 2 mini switches. Available in Black, Blue, Green, Red, White and Yellow finish. Mfd. 1990 to date.

Mfr.'s Sug. Retail	$1,980	$1,385	$1,190	$990	$790	$715	$655	$595

This instrument incorporates both guitar and bass guitar features on one fingerboard, neck and body.

SCHACK

Manufactured by Schack Guitars in Hamersbach, GERMANY. No distributor information at this time.

ELECTRIC

SG665 CUSTOM — offset double cutaway asymmetrical figured maple body, maple neck, 24 fret ebony fingerboard, fixed bridge, 3 per side locking Sperzel tuners, gold hardware, 2 humbucker Seymour Duncan pickups, volume/tone control, 3 position switch. Available in Transparent Stain finish. Curr. mfr.

Mfr.'s Sug. Retail	$2,030	$1,425	$1,220	$1,015	$810	$730	$670	$615

Add $120 for standard vibrato.

ELECTRIC BASS

Unique Series

UNIQUE — offset double cutaway asymmetrical maple body, goncalo alves top, thru body 9 piece maple/bubinga neck, 25 fret ebony fingerboard, fixed bridge, 2 per side tuners, gold hardware, 2 humbucker pickups, 2 volume/treble/mid/bass controls, active electronics. Available in Natural finish. Curr. mfr.

Mfr.'s Sug. Retail	$1,560	$1,090	$935	$780	$625	$560	$515	$470

4 bolt-on — bolt-on neck, J-style pickups.

Mfr.'s Sug. Retail	$1,300	$910	$780	$650	$520	$470	$430	$390

5 bolt-on — bolt-on neck, 2/3 per side tuners, J-style pickups.

Mfr.'s Sug. Retail	$1,395	$975	$835	$700	$560	$505	$460	$420

V - — 2/3 per side tuners.

Mfr.'s Sug. Retail	$1,750	$1,225	$1,050	$875	$700	$630	$575	$525

Schack, cont.

Grading	100%	98%	95%	90%	80%	70%	60%

VI — 3 per side tuners.

Mfr.'s Sug. Retail	$1,960	$1,370	$1,175	$980	$785	$705	$645	$585

Add $65 for parametric EQ.

SCHECTER

SCHECTER GUITAR RESEARCH

Manufacturer and distributor located in Van Nuys, CA since 1976.

Schecter Guitar Research started as a maker of high quality replacement parts and build-your-own instrument kits, which eventually led to their own line of finished instruments.

ELECTRIC

CONTOURED EXOTIC TOP — strat style ash body, figured maple top, bolt-on birdseye maple neck, 22 fret rosewood fingerboard with pearl dot inlay, double locking vibrato, 6 on one side tuners, gold hardware, 2 single coil/1 humbucker pickups, volume/tone control, 5 position switch. Available in Brown Sunburst, Honeyburst, Transparent Turquoise, Vintage Cherry Sunburst, oil and wax finish. Curr. mfr.

Mfr.'s Sug. Retail	$2,300	$1,610	$1,380	$1,150	$920	$830	$760	$690

This model is also available with flame koa or lacewood top.

CUSTOM — strat style figured maple body, bolt-on birdseye maple neck, 22 fret rosewood fingerboard with pearl dot inlay, double locking vibrato, 6 on one side tuners, gold hardware, 2 single coil/1 humbucker pickups, volume/tone control, 5 position switch. Available in Black Cherry, Black Turquoise, Brown Sunburst, Honeyburst, Transparent Turquoise and Vintage Cherry Sunburst. Curr. mfr.

Mfr.'s Sug. Retail	$2,950	$2,065	$1,770	$1,475	$1,180	$1,060	$975	$885

PT CUSTOM — tele style mahogany body, carved bound figured maple top, bolt on birdseye maple neck, 22 fret rosewood fingerboard with pearl dot inlay, tunomatic bridge/stop tailpiece, 6 on one side tuners, gold hardware, volume/tone control, 3 position switch. Available in Cherry Sunburst and Orange Violin finish. Curr. mfr.

Mfr.'s Sug. Retail	$2,400	$1,680	$1,440	$1,200	$960	$860	$790	$720

PT TRADITIONAL — tele style bound alder body, bolt-on birdseye maple neck, 22 fret maple fingerboard with black dot inlay, fixed bridge, 6 on one side tuners, black hardware, 2 humbucker pickups, volume/tone control, 3 position switch. Available in Black finish.

Mfr.'s Sug. Retail	$1,800	$1,260	$1,080	$900	$720	$650	$595	$540

This model is also available with 2 single coil pickups.

Grading	100%	98%	95%	90%	80%	70%	60%

TRADITIONAL — strat style alder body, white pickguard, bolt-on birdseye maple neck, 22 fret rosewood fingerboard with pearl dot inlay, standard vibrato, 6 on one side tuners, gold hardware, 3 single coil pickups, volume/tone control, 5 position switch. Available in Black, Cherry Sunburst, Gold Metallic, Two-Tone Brown Sunburst and Vintage Pure White. Curr. mfr.

Mfr.'s Sug. Retail	$1,800	$1,260	$1,080	$900	$720	$650	$595	$540

This model is also available with maple fingerboard with black dot inlay.

ELECTRIC BASS

BASS/4 — precision style bound ash body, bolt-on birdseye maple neck, 21 fret rosewood fingerboard with pearl dot inlay, fixed bridge, 4 on one side tuners, gold hardware, P-style/J-style pickups, 2 volume/1 tone controls. Available in Black, Honeyburst, Transparent Green, Transparent Purple and White finish. Curr. mfr.

Mfr.'s Sug. Retail	$1,950	$1,365	$1,170	$975	$780	$700	$645	$585

Add $500 for contoured exotic top.
Oil/Wax finish available as option with contoured exotic top.

BASS/5 — jazz style ash body, bolt-on birdseye maple neck, 21 fret rosewood fingerboard with pearl dot inlay, fixed bridge, 5 on one side tuners, gold hardware, 2 volume/1 tone controls. Available in Black, Honeyburst, Transparent Green, Transparent Purple and White finish. Curr. mfr.

Mfr.'s Sug. Retail	$2,150	$1,500	$1,290	$1,075	$860	$775	$710	$645

Add $500 for contoured exotic top.
Oil/Wax finish available as option with contoured exotic top.

SHADOW

Manufacturer located in Germany specializing in reproductions of vintage American guitars.

ELECTRIC

S Series

All S Series models are available in Black, Blue Stain, Blue Thunder, Cognac Stain, Gold, Red Stain, Red Thunder, Tobacco Stain, Violet Stain, White and White Thunder finish.
All S Series models are available with black, chrome or gold hardware.

S 100 — strat style basswood body, bolt-on maple neck, 22 fret rosewood fingerboard with pearl dot inlay, double locking vibrato, 6 on one side tuners, 2 single coil/1 humbucker Shadow pickups, volume/tone control, 5 position switch. Curr. mfr.

Mfr.'s Sug. Retail	$995	$695	$595	$500	$400	$360	$330	$300

Grading	100%	98%	95%	90%	80%	70%	60%

S 110 — similar to S 100, except has active humbucker pickup, on/off switch, tone control, active electronics.

Mfr.'s Sug. Retail	$1,225	$860	$735	$615	$490	$440	$405	$370

S 120 — similar to S 100, except has 2 active humbucker pickups, 2 volume controls and 3 position switch.

Mfr.'s Sug. Retail	$1,315	$925	$790	$660	$530	$475	$435	$395

This model is also available with an alder body (S 121).

S 130 — similar to S 100, except has standard bridge, piezo bridge pickup and 3 band EQ.

Mfr.'s Sug. Retail	$1,125	$790	$675	$565	$455	$405	$370	$335

This model is also available with an alder body (S 131).

S 140 — similar to S 100, except has standard bridge, active humbucker/piezo bridge pickups, 2 volume controls, 3 band EQ and active electronics.

Mfr.'s Sug. Retail	$1,315	$925	$790	$660	$530	$475	$435	$395

This model is also available with an alder body (S 141).

G Series

All G Series models are available in Blue Stain, Cognac Stain and Red Stain finish unless otherwise noted.

G 202 — strat style ash body, bolt-on maple neck, 24 fret rosewood fingerboard with pearl dot inlay, double locking vibrato, 6 on one side tuners, chrome hardware, 2 stacked coil/1 active humbucker Shadow pickups, volume/tone control, coil split switch in volume control, on/off switch in tone control, 5 position switch. Available in Black Stain, Blue Stain, Cognac Stain and Red Stain finish. Curr. mfr.

Mfr.'s Sug. Retail	$1,625	$1,140	$975	$815	$650	$580	$535	$485

This model is also available with black or gold hardware.

G 213 — strat style Brazilian Cedro body, flame maple top/bolt-on neck, 24 fret rosewood fingerboard with pearl dot inlay, double locking vibrato, 6 on one side tuners, gold hardware, 2 stacked coil/1 active humbucker, volume/tone control, coil split switch in volume control, on/off switch in tone control, 5 position switch. Curr. mfr.

Mfr.'s Sug. Retail	$1,995	$1,395	$1,195	$995	$795	$720	$660	$600

G 214 — similar to G 213, except has quilted maple top and birdseye maple neck.

Mfr.'s Sug. Retail	$2,200	$1,540	$1,320	$1,100	$880	$790	$725	$660

Grading	100%	98%	95%	90%	80%	70%	60%

G 233 — similar to G 213, except has standard bridge, piezo bridge pickup, volume control and 3 band EQ.

Mfr.'s Sug. Retail	$1,575	$1,100	$945	$785	$630	$565	$515	$470

This model is also available with quilted maple top and birdseye maple neck (G 234).
This model is also available with birdseye maple top/neck (G 235).

G 243 — strat style Brazilian Cedro body, flame maple top/bolt-on neck, 24 fret rosewood fingerboard with pearl dot inlay, standard bridge, 6 on one side tuners, gold hardware, active humbucker/Piezo bridge pickups, 2 volume controls, 3 band EQ. Curr. mfr.

Mfr.'s Sug. Retail	$1,770	$1,235	$1,060	$880	$705	$635	$580	$530

This model is also available with a quilted maple top and birdseye maple neck (G 244).
This model is also available with birdseye maple top/neck (G 245).

SHENANDOAH

Manufactured and distributed by C. F. Martin & Company.

Shenandoah guitars have acoustic pickups as standard features. This series was discontinued in 1992.

ACOUSTIC

C-20 — classic style, solid spruce top, round soundhole, wooden bound body, wooden inlay rosette, rosewood back/sides, nato neck, 12/19 fret ebonized rosewood fingerboard, ebonized rosewood tied bridge, rosewood peghead veneer, 3 per side gold tuners with pearl buttons. Available in Natural and Yellow Stained Top finish. Disc. 1992.

	$895	$765	$635	$510	$460	$420	$380

Last Mfr.'s Sug. Retail was $1,280.
This model has no factory installed pickup.

D-1832 — dreadnought style, solid spruce top, round soundhole, tortoise shell pickguard, 3 stripe bound body/rosette, mahogany back/sides, nato neck, 14/20 fret rosewood fingerboard with pearl dot inlay, rosewood bridge with black pins, rosewood peghead veneer, 3 per side chrome tuners. Available in Natural finish. Disc. 1992.

	$750	$645	$535	$430	$390	$355	$325

Last Mfr.'s Sug. Retail was $1,075.

D-1932 — similar to D-1832, except has quilted mahogany veneer back/sides. Disc. 1992.

	$925	$790	$660	$530	$475	$435	$395

Add $20 for twelve string version (D12-1932).
Last Mfr.'s Sug. Retail was $1,320.

Grading	100%	98%	95%	90%	80%	70%	60%

D-2832 — dreadnought style, solid spruce top, round soundhole, tortoise shell pickguard, 3 stripe bound body/rosette, rosewood back/sides, nato neck, 14/20 fret ebonized rosewood fingerboard with pearl dot inlay, ebonized rosewood bridge with white black dot pins, rosewood peghead veneer, 3 per side chrome tuners. Available in Natural finish. Disc. 1992.

	$790	$675	$565	$455	$405	$370	$335

Add $75 for 12 string version of this model (D12-2832).
Add $90 for herringbone binding, snowflake fingerboard inlay (HD-2832).
Last Mfr.'s Sug. Retail was $1,125.

D-3532 — similar to D-2832, except has bound fingerboard. Disc. 1992.

	$825	$705	$585	$470	$425	$390	$355

Last Mfr.'s Sug. Retail was $1,175.

D-4132 — similar to D-2832, except has abalone bound body/rosette, bound fingerboard with abalone hexagon inlay, white abalone dot bridge pins, bound peghead, gold tuners. Disc. 1992.

	$1,225	$1,050	$875	$700	$630	$575	$525

Last Mfr.'s Sug. Retail was $1,750.

D-6032 — similar to D-2832, tortoise shell binding, except has birdseye maple back/sides. Disc. 1992.

	$925	$790	$660	$530	$475	$435	$395

Last Mfr.'s Sug. Retail was $1,320.

D-6732 — dreadnought style, solid spruce top, round soundhole, tortoise shell pickguard, tortoise shell binding, 3 stripe rosette, quilted ash back/sides, nato neck, 14/20 fret bound ebonized rosewood neck with pearl dot inlay, pearl vine/diamond inlay at 12th fret, ebonized rosewood bridge with white black dot pins, bound peghead with quilted ash veneer, 3 per side gold tuners with ebony buttons. Available in Natural finish. Disc. 1992.

	$1,040	$890	$745	$595	$535	$490	$445

Last Mfr.'s Sug. Retail was $1,490.

SE-2832 — single rounded cutaway folk style, solid spruce top, round soundhole, 3 stripe bound body/rosette, rosewood back/sides, nato neck, 14/21 fret bound ebonized rosewood fingerboard with pearl diamond inlay, ebonized rosewood bridge with white black dot pins, rosewood veneer peghead, 3 per side chrome tuners, active EQ with volume/treble/mid/bass slider control. Available in Natural and Sunburst Top finish. Disc. 1992.

	$1,030	$880	$735	$590	$525	$480	$440

Last Mfr.'s Sug. Retail was $1,470.

Grading	100%	98%	95%	90%	80%	70%	60%

SE-6032 — similar to SE-2832, except has tortoise shell binding, birdseye maple back/sides/peghead veneer, pearl tuner buttons. Available in Burgundy Burst, Dark Sunburst and Natural finish. Disc. 1992.

	$1,080	$925	$770	$615	$555	$510	$460

Last Mfr.'s Sug. Retail was $1,540.

000-2832 — folk style, solid spruce top, round soundhole, tortoise shell pickguard, 3 stripe bound body/rosette, rosewood back/sides, nato neck, 14/20 fret ebonized rosewood fingerboard with pearl dot inlay, ebonized rosewood bridge with white black dot pins, rosewood peghead veneer with abalone torch inlay, 3 per side chrome tuners. Available in Natural finish. Disc. 1992.

	$850	$725	$605	$485	$435	$400	$365

Last Mfr.'s Sug. Retail was $1,210

SIGMA

Sigma is a division of the C.F. Martin Guitar Company, located in Nazareth, PA since 1970. Initial assembly on Sigma instruments is performed overseas, while the final finishing and inspection is performed in Nazareth, PA.

ACOUSTIC

"1" Series

CS-1 — classic style, spruce top, round soundhole, bound body, wooden inlay rosette, mahogany back/sides/neck, 20/19 fret ebonized fingerboard/tied bridge, 3 per side chrome tuners. Available in Antique Stain finish. Curr. mfr.

Mfr.'s Sug. Retail	$285	$200	$170	$145	$115	$105	$95	$85

DM-1 — dreadnought style, spruce top, round soundhole, black pickguard, bound body, 3 stripe rosette, mahogany back/sides/neck, 14/20 fret ebonized fingerboard with pearl dot inlay, ebonized bridge with black pins, 3 per side chrome tuners. Available in Natural finish. Curr. mfr.

Mfr.'s Sug. Retail	$300	$210	$180	$150	$120	$110	$100	$90

Add $55 for 12 string version (DM12-1).

GCS-1 — similar to DM-1, except has grand concert style body.

Mfr.'s Sug. Retail	$285	$200	$170	$145	$115	$105	$95	$85

SigmaGuitars EST. 1970, cont.

Grading	100%	98%	95%	90%	80%	70%	60%

"2" Series

CS-2 — classic style, spruce top, round soundhole, bound body, wooden inlay rosette, mahogany back/sides/neck, 20/19 fret ebonized fingerboard/tied bridge, 3 per side chrome tuners. Available in Natural finish. Curr. mfr.

Mfr.'s Sug. Retail	$295	$205	$175	$145	$115	$105	$95	$85

DM-2 — dreadnought style, spruce top, round soundhole, tortoise shell pickguard, 3 stripe bound body/rosette, mahogany back/sides/neck, 14/20 fret rosewood fingerboard with pearl dot inlay, rosewood bridge with black white dot pins, 3 per side chrome tuners. Available in Natural finish. Curr. mfr.

Mfr.'s Sug. Retail	$375	$260	$220	$185	$150	$135	$120	$110

Add $10 for Black finish (DM-2B).
Add $45 for 12 string version (DM12-2).

DM-2E/WH — similar to DM-2, except has ebonized fingerboard/bridge, acoustic pickup, 3 band EQ with volume control. Available in White finish.

Mfr.'s Sug. Retail	$630	$440	$380	$315	$250	$225	$205	$190

Add $25 for single rounded cutaway, white black dot bridge pins. Available in Black finish (DM-2CE/B).

DR-2 — similar to DM-2, except has rosewood back/sides, ebonized fingerboard/bridge.

Mfr.'s Sug. Retail	$510	$350	$300	$250	$200	$180	$165	$150

GCS-2 — similar to DM-2, except has grand concert body style.

Mfr.'s Sug. Retail	$420	$295	$250	$210	$170	$150	$135	$125

Generation III Series

CR-8 — classic style, solid spruce top, round soundhole, bound body, wooden inlay rosette, rosewood back/sides, mahogany neck, 12/19 fret ebonized fingerboard/tied bridge, 3 per side gold tuners with pearl buttons. Available in Natural finish. Curr. mfr.

Mfr.'s Sug. Retail	$765	$535	$460	$375	$305	$275	$250	$230

DM-18 — dreadnought style, solid spruce top, round soundhole, tortoise shell pickguard, 3 stripe bound body/rosette, mahogany back/sides/neck, 14/20 fret ebonized fingerboard with pearl dot inlay, ebonized bridge with black white dot pins, abalone logo peghead inlay, 3 per side chrome tuners. Available in Natural finish. Curr. mfr.

Mfr.'s Sug. Retail	$720	$500	$430	$360	$290	$260	$240	$220

DR-28 — similar to DM-18, except has rosewood back/sides, white abalone dot bridge pins, rosewood peghead veneer.

Mfr.'s Sug. Retail	$805	$565	$485	$400	$320	$290	$265	$240

Grading	100%	98%	95%	90%	80%	70%	60%

DR-28H — similar to DR-28, except has herringbone bound body, pearl diamond fingerboard inlay.

| Mfr.'s Sug. Retail | $875 | $615 | $525 | $435 | $350 | $315 | $290 | $265 |

Add $20 for 12 string version (DR12-28H). New 1993.

DR-35 — similar to DR-28, except has 5 stripe bound body, bound fingerboard/peghead.

| Mfr.'s Sug. Retail | $865 | $605 | $520 | $430 | $345 | $310 | $285 | $260 |

DR-41 — similar to DR-28, except has abalone bound body/rosette, bound fingerboard/peghead, abalone hexagon fingerboard inlay.

| Mfr.'s Sug. Retail | $1,010 | $705 | $605 | $505 | $405 | $365 | $335 | $305 |

000-18M — auditorium style, solid spruce top, round soundhole, tortoise shell pickguard, 3 stripe bound body, 5 stripe rosette, mahogany back/sides/neck, 14/20 fret ebonized fingerboard with pearl dot inlay, ebonized bridge with black white dot pins, rosewood peghead veneer with abalone logo inlay, 3 per side chrome tuners. Available in Antique finish. New 1993.

| Mfr.'s Sug. Retail | $710 | $495 | $425 | $355 | $285 | $255 | $235 | $215 |

000-18MC/3B — similar to 000-18M, except has venetian cutaway, acoustic pickup, 3 band EQ with volume control.

| Mfr.'s Sug. Retail | $940 | $660 | $565 | $470 | $375 | $340 | $310 | $280 |

Marquis Series

This series was introduced in 1987.

CS-4 — classical style, spruce top, round soundhole, bound body, wooden inlay rosette, mahogany back/sides/neck, 12/19 fret rosewood fingerboard, rosewood tied bridge, rosewood peghead veneer, 3 per side chrome tuners with pearl buttons. Available in Antique finish. Curr. mfr.

| Mfr.'s Sug. Retail | $445 | $310 | $265 | $220 | $175 | $160 | $145 | $135 |

DM-4 — dreadnought style, spruce top, round soundhole, black pickguard, 3 stripe bound body/rosette, mahogany back/sides/neck, 14/20 fret ebonized fingerboard with pearl dot inlay, pearl horizontal teardrop inlay at 12th fret, ebonized bridge with black white dot pins, rosewood peghead veneer, 3 per side chrome tuners. Available in Black and Natural finish. Curr. mfr.

| Mfr.'s Sug. Retail | $485 | $340 | $290 | $240 | $190 | $170 | $155 | $145 |

Add $15 for mahogany top (DM-4M).
Add $70 for 12 string version (DM12-4).
Add $55 for herringbone bound body/rosette (DM-4H).
Add $30 for Antique and Tobacco Sunburst finish (DM-4Y and DM-4S).
All above DM-4 models are available in left-hand versions.

SigmaGuitars EST.1970 , cont.

Grading	100%	98%	95%	90%	80%	70%	60%

DM-4CV — similar to DM-4, except has venetian cutaway. Available in Violin finish.

Mfr.'s Sug. Retail	$560	$390	$335	$280	$225	$205	$190	$170

※ **DM-4C/3B** — similar to DM-4, except has venetian cutaway, acoustic pickup, 3 band EQ with volume control. Available in Natural finish.

Mfr.'s Sug. Retail	$715	$500	$430	$355	$285	$255	$235	$215

Add $10 for Violin finish (MD-4CV/3B).

DR-4H — similar to DM-4, except has tortoise shell pickguard, herringbone bound body/rosette, rosewood back/sides. Available in Natural finish.

Mfr.'s Sug. Retail	$605	$425	$365	$300	$240	$215	$195	$180

DT-4 — similar to DM-4, except has chestnut back/sides/peghead veneer. Available in Violin finish.

Mfr.'s Sug. Retail	$595	$415	$360	$300	$240	$215	$195	$180

Add $45 for 12 string version (DT12-4).
Subtract $10 for Natural finish (DT-4M).

DV-4 — similar to DM-4, except has ovankol back/sides. Available in Antique finish.

Mfr.'s Sug. Retail	$595	$415	$360	$300	$240	$215	$195	$180

GCS-4 — grand concert style, spruce top, round soundhole, black pickguard, 5 stripe bound body/rosette, mahogany back/sides/neck, 14/20 fret ebonized fingerboard with pearl dot inlay, horizontal teardrop inlay at 12th fret, ebonized bridge with black white dot pins, rosewood peghead veneer, 3 per side chrome tuners. Available in Natural finish. Curr. mfr.

Mfr.'s Sug. Retail	$480	$335	$290	$240	$190	$170	$155	$145

Add $70 for venetian cutaway (GCS-4C).

※ **GCS-4C/3B** — similar to GCS-4, except has Venetian cutaway, acoustic pickup, 3 band EQ with volume control.

Mfr.'s Sug. Retail	$715	$500	$430	$355	$285	$255	$235	$215

ACOUSTIC BASS

STB-M — jumbo style, spruce top, round soundhole, tortoise shell pickguard, 5 stripe bound body/rosette, maple back/sides/neck, 15/21 fret ebonized fingerboard with pearl dot inlay, ebonized strings thru bridge with pearl dot inlay, maple peghead veneer, 2 per side chrome tuners, acoustic pickup, 3 band EQ with volume control. Available in Natural finish. New 1993.

Mfr.'s Sug. Retail	$1,115	$780	$670	$555	$445	$400	$370	$335

Add $10 for black pickguard, rosewood back/sides (STB-R).

Grading	100%	98%	95%	90%	80%	70%	60%

ACOUSTIC ELECTRIC

SE Series

SE-18/2BC — single rounded cutaway folk style, spruce top, round soundhole, 3 stripe bound body/rosette, mahogany back/sides/neck, 22 fret bound ebonized fingerboard with pearl dot inlay, ebonized bridge with white black dot pins, rosewood peghead veneer with abalone logo inlay, 3 per side tuners, acoustic pickup, 2 band EQ with chorus effect and volume control. Available in Black, Natural, Red and Tobacco Sunburst finish. New 1993.

Mfr.'s Sug. Retail	$905	$635	$545	$450	$360	$325	$300	$275

SE-18/3B — similar to SE-18/2BC, except has 3 band EQ with volume control. Available in Natural and Tobacco Sunburst finish.

Mfr.'s Sug. Retail	$860	$600	$515	$430	$345	$310	$285	$260

KEN SMITH BASSES

Manufactured in the U.S. and Japan. Imported and distributed by Ken Smith Basses, Ltd., located in New York, NY.

ELECTRIC BASS

"G" Series

This series has graphite rods lain alongside the truss rod for added strength and durability.

B.T. CUSTOM IV "G" — double cutaway mahogany body with exotic wood top/back, thru body maple/mahogany 5 piece neck, 24 fret ebony fingerboard with pearl dot inlay, fixed bridge, brass nut, ebony veneer on peghead with pearl S inlay, 2 per side tuners, chrome hardware, 2 humbucker pickups, volume/treble/bass/mix controls, active electronics. Available in Natural finish.

Mfr.'s Sug. Retail	$3,300	$2,310	$1,980	$1,650	$1,320	$1,190	$1,090	$990

Add $200 for fretless model.
Add $600 for left handed version.
All models also available with black or gold hardware.
Transparent Charcoal Grey, Transparent Electric Blue and Transparent Scarlet Red finish with maple top/back.

B.T. CUSTOM V "G" — similar to B.T. Custom IV, except has 5 strings.

Mfr.'s Sug. Retail	$3,700	$2,590	$2,220	$1,850	$1,480	$1,330	$1,220	$1,110

Grading	100%	98%	95%	90%	80%	70%	60%

B.T. CUSTOM VI "G" — similar to B.T. Custom IV, except has 6 strings.

Mfr.'s Sug. Retail	$4,000	$2,800	$2,400	$2,000	$1,600	$1,440	$1,320	$1,200

Burner Series

ARTIST — double cutaway mahogany body with exotic wood top/back, bolt-on maple/walnut 5 piece neck, 24 fret rosewood fingerboard with pearl dot inlay, fixed bridge, 2 per side tuners, black hardware, 2 humbucker pickups, volume/treble/bass and mix controls, active electronics. Available in Antique Natural finish. Curr. mfr.

Mfr.'s Sug. Retail	$2,000	$1,400	$1,200	$1,000	$800	$720	$660	$600

   Add $100 for 5 string version.
   Add $300 for 6 string version.

CUSTOM — double cutaway figured maple body, bolt-on maple/walnut 5 piece neck, 24 fret rosewood fingerboard with pearl dot inlay, fixed bridge, 2 per side tuners, black hardware, 2 J-style pickups, volume/treble/bass and mix controls, active electronics. Available in Transparent Antique Natural, Transparent Candy Red and Transparent Cobalt Blue finish. Curr. mfr.

Mfr.'s Sug. Retail	$1,600	$1,120	$960	$800	$640	$575	$530	$480

   Add $100 for 5 string version.
   Add $300 for 6 string version.

Chuck Rainey Series

CR5G — double cutaway mahogany body with exotic wood top and back, thru body maple neck with graphite inlay, 24 fret ebony fingerboard with pearl dot inlay, fixed bridge, 3/2 per side tuners, chrome hardware, 2 humbucker pickups, volume/treble/bass and mix controls, active electronics. Available in Natural finish. Mfd. 1992 to date.

Mfr.'s Sug. Retail	$2,700	$1,890	$1,620	$1,350	$1,080	$970	$890	$810

   Add $200 for fretless model.
   Add $600 for left handed version.

CR6G — similar to CR5G, except has 6 strings.

Mfr.'s Sug. Retail	$2,800	$1,960	$1,680	$1,400	$1,120	$1,010	$925	$840

STARFIELD

Manufactured and distributed by Starfield America, located in North Hollywood, CA.

Grading	100%	98%	95%	90%	80%	70%	60%

ELECTRIC

Altair Series

AMERICAN CLASSIC — offset double cutaway alder body, white pickguard, bolt on maple neck, 22 fret maple fingerboard with offset black dot inlay, standard Wilkinson vibrato, 3 per side locking Magnum tuners, chrome hardware, 3 stacked coil Seymour Duncan pickups, volume/tone control, 5 position switch. Available in Pearl White, Pewter, Popsicle, Sail Blue and Tangerine finish. Curr. mfr.

Mfr.'s Sug. Retail	$1,000	$700	$600	$500	$400	$360	$330	$300

Available with ebony fingerboard with offset pearl dot inlay.

American Custom — similar to American Classic, except has mahogany body, flame maple top, no pickguard, gold hardware, 2 humbucker Seymour Duncan pickups. Available in Tobacco Sunburst, Transparent Cherry, Transparent Green and Transparent Grey finish.

Mfr.'s Sug. Retail	$1,300	$910	$780	$650	$520	$470	$430	$390

American Trad — similar to American Classic, except has mahogany body, black pickguard, fixed bridge, 2 humbucker Seymour Duncan pickups. Available in Transparent Cream, Transparent Green, Transparent Grey, Transparent Mustard and Transparent Red finish.

Mfr.'s Sug. Retail	$1,000	$700	$600	$500	$400	$360	$330	$300

SJ CLASSIC — offset double cutaway alder body, white pickguard, bolt on maple neck, 22 fret rosewood fingerboard with offset pearl dot inlay, standard vibrato, 3 per side tuners, chrome hardware, 3 single coil pickups, volume/tone control, 5 position switch. Available in Black, Blue Mist, Cream, Destroyer Grey, Mint Green and Peach finish. Curr. mfr.

Mfr.'s Sug. Retail	$400	$280	$240	$200	$160	$145	$130	$120

SJ Custom — similar to SJ Classic, except has arched swamp ash body, no pickguard, locking Magnum tuners. Available in Transparent Blue, Transparent Cherry, Transparent Cream, Transparent Green and Transparent Grey finish.

Mfr.'s Sug. Retail	$600	$420	$360	$300	$240	$215	$195	$180

SJ Trad — similar to SJ Classic, except has mahogany body, black pickguard, locking Magnum tuners, 2 single coil/1 humbucker pickups. Available in Transparent Cream, Transparent Green, Transparent Grey, Transparent Mustard and Transparent Red finish.

Mfr.'s Sug. Retail	$600	$420	$360	$300	$240	$215	$195	$180

Cabriolet Series

AMERICAN SPECIAL — single sharp cutaway asymmetrical mahogany body, carved flame maple top, bolt-on maple neck, 22 fret maple fingerboard with offset black dot inlay, fixed Wilkinson bridge, 3 per side tuners, chrome hardware, 2 humbucker Seymour Duncan pickups, volume/tone control, 5 position switch. Available in Tobacco Sunburst, Transparent Cherry, Transparent Green and Transparent Grey finish. Curr. mfr.

| Mfr.'s Sug. Retail | $1,250 | $875 | $750 | $625 | $500 | $450 | $415 | $375 |

Available with ebony fingerboard with offset pearl dot inlay.

American Standard — similar to American Special, except has alder body, standard Wilkinson vibrato, locking Magnum tuners, 3 stacked coil Seymour Duncan pickups. Available in Pearl White, Pewter, Popsicle, Sail Blue and Tangerine finish.

| Mfr.'s Sug. Retail | $950 | $665 | $570 | $475 | $380 | $345 | $315 | $285 |

SJ LIMITED — single sharp cutaway asymmetrical semi-hollow style, bound birdseye maple top, flower petal soundhole, mahogany back, bolt-on maple neck, 22 fret rosewood fingerboard with offset pearl dot inlay, fixed bridge, 3 per side tuners, chrome hardware, 2 humbucker pickups, volume/tone control, 5 position switch. Available in Tobacco Sunburst, Transparent Cherry, Transparent Green and Transparent Grey finish. Curr. mfr.

| Mfr.'s Sug. Retail | $650 | $455 | $390 | $325 | $260 | $235 | $215 | $195 |

STATUS

Manufactured by Status Graphite, located in Essex, England. U.S. distribution is currently pending as this edition goes to press.

ELECTRIC BASS

Empathy Series

H-EM4 — offset double cutaway laminate body, thru body graphite composite neck, 24 fret phenolic fingerboard, fixed bridge, 2 per side tuners, black hardware, 2 Status pickups, volume/treble/mid/bass/mix controls, mini switch, active electronics. Available in Natural finish. Available with Amazaque, Burl Madrone, Figured Maple, Rosewood and Walnut body woods. Curr. mfr.

This is a Custom Order instrument and prices will vary depending on specifications.

This model also available with fretless fingerboard.

H-EM5 — similar to H-EM4, except has 5 strings, 3/2 per side tuners.

This is a Custom Order instrument and prices will vary depending on specifications.

Grading	100%	98%	95%	90%	80%	70%	60%

H-EM6 — similar to H-EM4, except has 6 strings, 3 per side tuners.
This is a Custom Order instrument and prices will vary depending on specifications.

HL-EM4 — offset double cutaway laminate body, thru body graphite composite headless neck, 24 fret phenolic fingerboard, tunomatic bridge/tunable tailpiece, 2 per side tuners, black hardware, 2 Status pickups, volume/treble/mid/bass/mix controls, mini switch, active electronics. Available in Natural finish. Available with Amazaque, Burl Madrone, Figured Maple, Rosewood and Walnut body woods. Curr. mfr.
This is a Custom Order Instrument and prices will vary depending on specifications.
This model also available with fretless fingerboard.

HL-EM5 — similar to HL-EM4, except has 5 strings.
This is a Custom Order instrument and prices will vary depending on specifications.

Energy Series

EN-4 — offset double cutaway ash body, bolt-on maple neck, 24 fret rosewood fingerboard, fixed bridge, 2 per side tuners, black hardware, 2 Status pickups, volume/tone/mix controls. Available in Amber, Black, Green, Natural and Red finish. Curr. mfr.

	100%	98%	95%	90%	80%	70%	60%
Mfr.'s Sug. Retail	$1,395	$975	$835	$700	$560	$505	$460	$420

This model also available with walnut body.
This model also available with fretless fingerboard.

EN-5 — similar to EN-4, except has 5 strings, 3/2 per side tuners.

	100%	98%	95%	90%	80%	70%	60%
Mfr.'s Sug. Retail	$1,595	$1,115	$955	$795	$635	$575	$525	$475

Series 1

S1B-4 — offset double cutaway laminate body, bolt-on maple neck, 24 fret rosewood fingerboard, fixed bridge, 2 per side tuners, black hardware, 2 Status pickups, volume/treble/bass/mix controls, mini switch. Available in Natural finish. Available with Amazaque, Burl Madrone, Maple, Rosewood and Walnut body woods. Curr. mfr.

	100%	98%	95%	90%	80%	70%	60%
Mfr.'s Sug. Retail	$2,195	$1,540	$1,320	$1,100	$880	$790	$725	$660

This model also available with fretless fingerboard.

S1B-5 — similar to S1B-4, except has 5 strings, 3/2 per side tuners.

	100%	98%	95%	90%	80%	70%	60%
Mfr.'s Sug. Retail	$2,395	$1,675	$1,435	$1,195	$955	$855	$785	$715

S1B-6 — similar to S1B-4, except has 6 strings, 3 per side tuners.

	100%	98%	95%	90%	80%	70%	60%
Mfr.'s Sug. Retail	$2,695	$1,885	$1,620	$1,350	$1,080	$970	$890	$810

Grading	100%	98%	95%	90%	80%	70%	60%

S1T-4 — offset double cutaway laminate body, thru body maple neck, 24 fret rosewood fingerboard, fixed bridge, 2 per side tuners, black hardware, 2 Status pickups, volume/treble/bass/mix controls, mini switch. Available in Natural finish. Available with Amazaque, Burl Madrone, Maple, Rosewood and Walnut body woods. Curr. mfr.

Mfr.'s Sug. Retail	$2,395	$1,675	$1,435	$1,195	$955	$855	$785	$715

This model also available with fretless fingerboard.

S1T-5 — similar to S1T-4, except has 5 strings, 3/2 per side tuners.

Mfr.'s Sug. Retail	$2,595	$1,815	$1,555	$1,295	$1,035	$930	$855	$780

S1T-6 — similar to S1T-4, except has 6 strings, 3 per side tuners.

Mfr.'s Sug. Retail	$2,895	$2,025	$1,740	$1,450	$1,160	$1,040	$955	$870

Series 2

H-2-4 — offset double cutaway laminate body, thru body graphite composite neck, 24 fret phenolic fingerboard, fixed bridge, 2 per side tuners, black hardware, 2 Status pickups, volume/treble/mid/bass/mix controls, mini switch, active electronics. Available in Natural finish. Available with Amazaque, Burl Madrone, Maple, Rosewood and Walnut body woods. Curr. mfr.

Mfr.'s Sug. Retail	$3,495	$2,445	$2,095	$1,750	$1,400	$1,260	$1,150	$1,050

This model also available with fretless fingerboard.

H-2-5 — similar to H-2-4, except has 5 strings, 3/2 per side tuners.

Mfr.'s Sug. Retail	$3,695	$2,585	$2,220	$1,845	$1,475	$1,325	$1,215	$1,100

H-2-6 — similar to H-2-4, except has 6 strings, 3 per side tuners.

Mfr.'s Sug. Retail	$3,895	$2,725	$2,335	$1,950	$1,555	$1,395	$1,280	$1,165

HL-2-4 — offset double cutaway laminate body, thru body graphite composite headless neck, 24 fret phenolic fingerboard, tunomatic bridge/tunable tailpiece, 2 per side tuners, black hardware, 2 Status pickups, volume/treble/mid/bass/mix controls, mini switch, active electronics. Available in Natural finish. Available with Amazaque, Burl Madrone, Maple, Rosewood and Walnut body woods. Curr. mfr.

Mfr.'s Sug. Retail	$3,595	$2,515	$2,155	$1,795	$1,435	$1,290	$1,185	$1,075

This model also available with fretless fingerboard.

HL-2-5 — similar to HL-2-4, except has 5 strings.

Mfr.'s Sug. Retail	$3,795	$2,655	$2,275	$1,895	$1,515	$1,365	$1,250	$1,135

STEINBERGER

Manufactured and distributed by Steinberger Sound, located in Nashville, TN, since 1979.

Grading	100%	98%	95%	90%	80%	70%	60%

In 1979, Ned Steinberger introduced the Steinberger Bass, constructed of advanced composite materials referred to as the Steinberger Blend. This new design featured a headless neck and compact body style. Due to the success of this first model, another was introduced in 1982, the Steinberger Guitar. Since then, the line of Steinberger products has expanded with new innovations including hardware and electronic improvements.

ELECTRIC

K Series

This series was co-designed by Steve Klein.

GK4S — radical ergonomic style basswood body, black pickguard, bolt-on Steinberger Blend neck, 24 fret phenolic fingerboard with white dot inlay, Steinberger vibrato, black hardware, 2 single coil/1 humbucker EMG pickups, volume/tone control, 5 position switch. Available in Black and White finish. Mfd. 1990 to date.

Mfr.'s Sug. Retail	$1,800	$1,260	$1,080	$900	$720	$650	$595	$540

Add $250 for active electronics.
This model has Klein's autograph on body.

GK4T — similar to GK4S, except has TransTrem vibrato.

Mfr.'s Sug. Retail	$2,250	$1,575	$1,345	$1,125	$900	$810	$740	$675

L Series

GL2S — one piece body/neck construct, rectangle body, 24 fret phenolic fingerboard with white dot inlay, Steinberger vibrato, black hardware, 2 humbucker EMG pickups, volume/tone control, 3 position switch. Available in Black finish. Mfd. 1989 to date.

Mfr.'s Sug. Retail	$2,150	$1,500	$1,290	$1,075	$860	$775	$710	$645

Add $200 for White finish.
Add $300 for left handed version.
Add $500 for 12 string version, no vibrato available.

GL2T — similar to GL2S, except has TransTrem vibrato.

Mfr.'s Sug. Retail	$2,600	$1,820	$1,560	$1,300	$1,040	$935	$860	$780

GL4S — similar to GL2S, except has 2 single coil/1 humbucker EMG pickups, 5 position switch.

Mfr.'s Sug. Retail	$2,350	$1,645	$1,410	$1,175	$940	$845	$775	$705

GL4T — similar to GL2T, except has 2 single coil/1 humbucker EMG pickups, 5 position switch.

Mfr.'s Sug. Retail	$2,800	$1,960	$1,680	$1,400	$1,120	$1,010	$925	$840

Grading	100%	98%	95%	90%	80%	70%	60%

GL4TA ELITE — similar to GL4T, except has coil split switches, active electronics, gold engraving, signed certificate.

Mfr.'s Sug. Retail	$3,050	$2,135	$1,830	$1,525	$1,220	$1,095	$1,000	$910

GL7TA ELITE — similar to GL4TA Elite, except has humbucker/single coil/ humbucker EMG pickups.

Mfr.'s Sug. Retail	$3,200	$2,240	$1,920	$1,600	$1,280	$1,150	$1,055	$960

M Series

GM2S — double cutaway maple body, bolt-on Steinberger Blend neck, 24 fret phenolic fingerboard with white dot inlay, Steinberger vibrato, black hardware, 2 humbucker EMG pickups, volume/tone control, 3 position switch. Available in Black, Candy Apple Red, Electric Blue and White finish. Curr. mfr.

Mfr.'s Sug. Retail	$1,800	$1,260	$1,080	$900	$720	$650	$595	$540

Add $500 for 12 string version, no vibrato.

GM2T — similar to GM2S, except has TransTrem vibrato.

Mfr.'s Sug. Retail	$2,250	$1,575	$1,345	$1,125	$900	$810	$740	$675

GM4S — similar to GM2S, except has 2 single coil/1 humbucker EMG pickups, 5 position switch.

Mfr.'s Sug. Retail	$1,900	$1,330	$1,140	$950	$760	$685	$625	$570

GM4TA — similar to GM2T, except has 2 single coil/1 humbucker EMG pickups, 5 position switch, active electronics.

Mfr.'s Sug. Retail	$2,450	$1,715	$1,470	$1,225	$980	$875	$805	$735

GM7TA — similar to GM2T except has humbucker/single coil/humbucker EMG pickups, 5 position and coil split switches, active electronics.

Mfr.'s Sug. Retail	$2,600	$1,820	$1,560	$1,300	$1,040	$935	$860	$780

R Series

GR4 — offset double cutaway maple body, bolt-on Steinberger Blend neck, 24 fret phenolic fingerboard with white dot inlay, R Trem vibrato, black hardware, 2 single coil rails/1 humbucker Seymour Duncan pickups, volume/tone control, 5 position switch. Available in Black, Candy Apple Red, Electric Blue and White finish. Curr. mfr.

Mfr.'s Sug. Retail	$1,390	$975	$835	$695	$555	$495	$455	$415

Grading	100%	98%	95%	90%	80%	70%	60%

S Series

S STANDARD — offset double cutaway poplar body with bottom bout cutaway, bolt-on Steinberger Blend neck, 24 fret phenolic fingerboard with white dot inlay, standard vibrato, reverse peghead, 6 on one side gearless tuners, humbucker/single coil/humbucker exposed pickups, volume/tone control, 5 position/coil split switches. Available in Black and White finish. Curr. mfr.

Mfr.'s Sug. Retail	$2,250	$1,575	$1,345	$1,125	$900	$810	$740	$675

S Pro — similar to S Standard, except has mahogany body, bound maple top, TransTrem vibrato, active electronics. Available in Black, Cherry Sunburst, Fireburst and White finish. Curr. mfr.

Mfr.'s Sug. Retail	$2,600	$1,820	$1,560	$1,300	$1,040	$935	$860	$780

GS7ZA — offset double cutaway hardwood body, bolt-on Steinberger Blend neck, 24 fret phenolic fingerboard with white dot inlay, standard vibrato, reverse headstock, Knife Edge Knut, 6 on one side gearless tuners, black hardware, humbucker/single coil/humbucker pickups, volume/tone control, 5 position and coil split switches, active electronics. Available in Black, Candy Apple Red, Electric Blue, Purple and White finish. Disc. 1992.

		$1,715	$1,470	$1,225	$980	$875	$805	$735

Last Mfr.'s Sug. Retail was $2,450.

GS7TA — similar to GS7ZA, except has TransTrem vibrato.

		$1,960	$1,680	$1,400	$1,120	$1,010	$925	$840

Last Mfr.'s Sug. Retail was $2,800.

ELECTRIC BASS

L Series

XL2 — one piece molded body/neck construct, rectangle body, 24 fret phenolic fingerboard with white dot inlay, Steinberger bridge, black hardware, 2 humbucker EMG pickups, 2 volume/1 tone controls. Available in Black finish. Mfd. 1979 to date.

Mfr.'s Sug. Retail	$2,100	$1,475	$1,260	$1,050	$840	$755	$690	$630

Add $200 for White finish.
Add $300 for left handed version.
Add $100 for fretless fingerboard.

XL2DB — similar to XL2, except has Steinberger DB bridge.

Mfr.'s Sug. Retail	$2,400	$1,680	$1,440	$1,200	$960	$860	$790	$720

XL2-5 — similar to XL2, except has 5 strings.

Mfr.'s Sug. Retail	$2,400	$1,680	$1,440	$1,200	$960	$860	$790	$720

XL2DBA ELITE — similar to XL2, except has Steinberger DB bridge, active electronics, gold engraving, signed certificate.

Mfr.'s Sug. Retail	$2,900	$2,030	$1,740	$1,450	$1,160	$1,040	$955	$870

Grading	100%	98%	95%	90%	80%	70%	60%

✄ **XL2-5A ELITE** — similar to XL2, except has 5 strings, active electronics, gold engraving, signed certificate.

Mfr.'s Sug. Retail	$2,900	$2,030	$1,740	$1,450	$1,160	$1,040	$955	$870

✄ **XL2TA ELITE** — similar to XL2, except has TransTrem vibrato, active electronics, gold engraving, signed certificate.

Mfr.'s Sug. Retail	$3,000	$2,095	$1,800	$1,500	$1,200	$1,080	$990	$900

M Series

XM2 — double cutaway maple body, bolt-on Steinberger Blend neck, 24 fret phenolic fingerboard with white dot inlay, Steinberger bridge, black hardware, 2 humbucker EMG pickups, 2 volume/1 tone control. Available in Black, Candy Apple Red, Electric Blue and White finish. Curr. mfr.

Mfr.'s Sug. Retail	$1,600	$1,120	$960	$800	$640	$575	$530	$480

Add $250 for active electronics.
Add $100 for fretless fingerboard.

✄ **XM2DB** — similar to XM2, except has Steinberger DB bridge.

Mfr.'s Sug. Retail	$1,700	$1,190	$1,020	$850	$680	$610	$560	$510

✄ **XM2-5** — similar to XM2, except has 5 strings.

Mfr.'s Sug. Retail	$1,800	$1,260	$1,080	$900	$720	$650	$595	$540

✄ **XM2T** — similar to XM2, except has TransTrem vibrato.

Mfr.'s Sug. Retail	$2,200	$1,540	$1,320	$1,100	$880	$790	$725	$660

Q Series

XQ2 — offset double cutaway maple body, bolt-on Steinberger Blend neck, 24 fret phenolic fingerboard with white dot inlay, Steinberger bridge, black hardware, 2 humbucker EMG pickups, 2 volume/1 tone controls. Available in Black, Candy Apple Red, Electric Blue and White finish. Curr. mfr.

Mfr.'s Sug. Retail	$1,700	$1,190	$1,020	$850	$680	$610	$560	$510

Add $100 for fretless fingerboard.

✄ **XQ2DB** — similar to XQ2, except has Steinberger DB bridge.

Mfr.'s Sug. Retail	$1,800	$1,260	$1,080	$900	$720	$650	$595	$540

✄ **XQ2-5** — similar to XQ2, except has 5 strings.

Mfr.'s Sug. Retail	$2,050	$1,435	$1,230	$1,025	$820	$745	$675	$615

✄ **XQ2T** — similar to XQ2, except has TransTrem vibrato.

Mfr.'s Sug. Retail	$2,300	$1,610	$1,380	$1,150	$920	$830	$760	$690

Grading	100%	98%	95%	90%	80%	70%	60%

Double Neck

GM4S/GM42 — refer to model GM4S, in 6 and 12 string versions, in this section for details.

Mfr.'s Sug. Retail	$4,100	$2,870	$2,460	$2,050	$1,640	$1,475	$1,350	$1,230

⅃ GM4T/GM42 — refer to model GM4T, in 6 and 12 string versions, in this section for details.

Mfr.'s Sug. Retail	$4,600	$3,220	$2,760	$2,300	$1,840	$1,655	$1,520	$1,380

⅃ GM4S/XM2 — refer to models GM4S and XM2, in 6 string guitar and 4 string bass models, in this section for details.

Mfr.'s Sug. Retail	$4,000	$2,800	$2,400	$2,000	$1,600	$1,440	$1,320	$1,200

⅃ GM4T/XM2 — refer to models GM4T and XM2, in 6 string guitar and 4 string bass models, in this section for details.

Mfr.'s Sug. Retail	$4,500	$3,150	$2,700	$2,250	$1,800	$1,620	$1,485	$1,350

STEPHEN'S

Manufactured and distributed by Stephen's Stringed Instruments, located in Seattle, WA.

Stephen's guitars are vintage-styled instruments that offer the patented Stephen's Extended Cutaway neck.

ELECTRIC

Stephen's

S-22EC — strat style alder body, bolt-on maple neck, 22 fret ebony fingerboard with pearl dot inlay, double locking vibrato, 6 on one side tuners, black hardware, 2 single coil/1 humbucker Seymour Duncan pickups, volume/tone control, 5 position switch. Available in Raw finish. Curr. mfr.

Mfr.'s Sug. Retail	$1,575	$1,100	$945	$785	$630	$565	$515	$470

Add $20 for maple fingerboard.
Add $170 for figured maple top.
Subtract $20 for rosewood fingerboard.
Black, Cherry Sunburst, Natural and Tobacco Sunburst finishes are available at $70 - $100 additional cost.

T-22EC — tele style ash body, black pickguard, bolt-on maple neck, 22 fret rosewood fingerboard with pearl dot inlay, strings thru body bridge, 6 on one side tuners, chrome hardware, 2 single coil Seymour Duncan pickups, volume/tone control, 3 position switch. Available in Black and Natural finish. Curr. mfr.

Mfr.'s Sug. Retail	$1,595	$1,115	$955	$795	$635	$575	$525	$475

Add $20 for maple fingerboard.
Add $30 for ebony fingerboard.
Add $200 for figured maple top.
Add $30 for Butterscotch, Cherry Sunburst and Tobacco Sunburst finish.

TAKAMINE

This trademark is manufactured in Japan and distributed by the Kaman Music Corp. of Bloomfield, CT.

ACOUSTIC

Grading	100%	98%	95%	90%	80%	70%	60%

300 Series

307-F — folk style, spruce top, round soundhole, black pickguard, bound body, 3 stripe rosette, mahogany back/sides/neck, 14/20 fret rosewood fingerboard with white dot inlay, rosewood bridge with white pins, 3 per side chrome tuners. Available in Natural finish. Curr. mfr.

Mfr.'s Sug. Retail	$590	$410	$355	$295	$235	$210	$195	$180

330-G — dreadnought style, spruce top, round soundhole, black pickguard, 3 stripe bound body and rosette, mahogany back/sides/neck, 14/20 fret rosewood fingerboard with white dot inlay, rosewood bridge with white pins, 3 per side chrome tuners. Available in Natural finish. Curr. mfr.

Mfr.'s Sug. Retail	$350	$245	$210	$175	$140	$125	$115	$105

    Add $50 for Red Stain finish. New 1993.

332-G — similar to 330-G.

Mfr.'s Sug. Retail	$400	$280	$240	$200	$160	$145	$130	$120

334-G — dreadnought style, spruce top, round soundhole, black pickguard, wood bound body and rosette, rosewood back/sides, mahogany neck, 14/20 fret bound rosewood fingerboard with pearl dot inlay, rosewood bridge with white black dot pins, 3 per side gold tuners. Available in Natural finish. Curr. mfr.

Mfr.'s Sug. Retail	$500	$350	$300	$250	$200	$180	$165	$150

    Add $50 for Black finish.

340-F — dreadnought style, spruce top, round soundhole, black pickguard, 3 stripe bound body and rosette, mahogany back/sides/neck, 14/20 fret rosewood fingerboard with pearl dot inlay, rosewood bridge with black white dot pins, 3 per side chrome tuners. Available in Natural finish. Curr. mfr.

Mfr.'s Sug. Retail	$650	$455	$390	$325	$260	$235	$215	$195

    Add $130 for solid spruce top (340S-F).

Grading	100%	98%	95%	90%	80%	70%	60%

340-EF — similar to 340-F, except has crystal bridge pickups, 3 band EQ.

Mfr.'s Sug. Retail	$850	$595	$510	$425	$340	$305	$280	$255

Add $230 for solid spruce top (340S-EF).

341-F — dreadnought style, spruce top, round soundhole, black pickguard, 5 stripe bound body and rosette, campnosparma back/sides, mahogany neck, 14/20 fret bound rosewood fingerboard with pearl dot inlay, rosewood bridge with white black dot pins, bound peghead, 3 per side chrome tuners. Available in Black finish. Curr. mfr.

Mfr.'s Sug. Retail	$780	$545	$470	$390	$315	$280	$260	$235

341-EF — similar to 341-F, except has crystal bridge pickups, 3 band EQ.

Mfr.'s Sug. Retail	$980	$685	$585	$485	$390	$355	$325	$295

Add $90 for rounded cutaway (341C-EF).

349-F — dreadnought style, mahogany top/back/sides/neck, round soundhole, black pickguard, 3 stripe bound body and rosette, 14/20 fret rosewood fingerboard with pearl dot inlay, rosewood bridge with black white dot pins, 3 per side chrome tuners. Available in Natural finish. Curr. mfr.

Mfr.'s Sug. Retail	$660	$460	$395	$330	$265	$240	$220	$200

349-EF — similar to 349-F, except has crystal bridge pickup, 3 band EQ.

Mfr.'s Sug. Retail	$860	$600	$515	$430	$345	$310	$285	$260

381C-EF — rounded cutaway 12 string dreadnought style, spruce top, round soundhole, black pickguard, 5 stripe bound body and rosette, campnosparma back/sides, mahogany neck, 14/20 fret rosewood fingerboard with pearl diamond/dot inlay, rosewood bridge with white black dot pins, 6 per side chrome tuners, crystal bridge pickups, 3 band EQ. Available in Black finish. Curr. mfr.

Mfr.'s Sug. Retail	$1,190	$835	$715	$595	$475	$430	$390	$360

385-F — 12 string dreadnought style, spruce top, round soundhole, black pickguard, 5 stripe bound body and rosette, mahogany back/sides/neck, 14/20 fret rosewood fingerboard with pearl dot inlay, rosewood bridge with black white dot pins, 6 per side chrome tuners. Available in Natural finish. Curr. mfr.

Mfr.'s Sug. Retail	$750	$525	$450	$375	$300	$270	$245	$225

385-EF — similar to 385-F, except has crystal bridge pickup, 3 band EQ.

Mfr.'s Sug. Retail	$950	$665	$570	$475	$380	$345	$315	$285

360 Series

360S-F — dreadnought style, solid spruce top, round soundhole, black pickguard, 5 stripe bound body and rosette, rosewood back/sides, 14/20 fret bound rosewood fingerboard with pearl dot inlay, rosewood bridge with white black dot pins, 3 per side chrome tuners. Available in Natural finish. Curr. mfr.

Mfr.'s Sug. Retail	$940	$660	$565	$470	$375	$340	$310	$280

Add $130 for left handed version of this model (360SLH-F).

Grading	100%	98%	95%	90%	80%	70%	60%

360C-EF — similar to 360S-F, except has single rounded cutaway, crystal bridge pickups, 3 band EQ.

Mfr.'s Sug. Retail	$1,120	$785	$670	$560	$450	$405	$370	$335

360S-FP — similar to 360S-F, except has crystal bridge pickups, 3 band EQ.

Mfr.'s Sug. Retail	$1,240	$870	$745	$620	$495	$445	$410	$370

Add $90 for round cutaway (360SC-FP).

361EC-EF — rounded cutaway dreadnought style, spruce top, round soundhole, black pickguard, 5 stripe bound body, abalone rosette, campnosparma back/sides, mahogany neck, 14/20 fret bound rosewood fingerboard with pearl dot inlay, rosewood bridge with white black dot pins, 3 per side chrome tuners, crystal bridge pickups, 3 band EQ. Available in Ebony Stain finish. Curr. mfr.

Mfr.'s Sug. Retail	$1,050	$735	$630	$525	$420	$380	$345	$315

361SECA-FP — similar to 361EC-EF, except has solid spruce top, parametric EQ, abalone logo inlay on peghead.

Mfr.'s Sug. Retail	$1,400	$980	$840	$700	$560	$505	$460	$420

400S-F — 12 string dreadnought style, solid spruce top, round soundhole, black pickguard, 5 stripe bound body and rosette, rosewood back/sides, mahogany neck, 14/20 fret bound rosewood fingerboard with pearl dot inlay, rosewood bridge with white black dot pins, 6 per side gold tuners. Available in Natural finish. Curr. mfr.

Mfr.'s Sug. Retail	$1,030	$720	$615	$510	$410	$370	$340	$310

400S-FP — similar to 400S-F, except has crystal bridge pickup, parametric EQ.

Mfr.'s Sug. Retail	$1,330	$930	$795	$660	$530	$475	$435	$395

Classic Series

128-C — classic style, spruce top, round soundhole, 5 stripe bound body, wooden rosette, rosewood back/sides, mahogany neck, 12/19 fret rosewood fingerboard, rosewood bridge, 3 per side gold tuners with nylon buttons. Available in Natural finish. Curr. mfr.

Mfr.'s Sug. Retail	$550	$385	$330	$275	$220	$200	$180	$165

128-EC — similar to 128-C, except has mahogany back/sides, crystal bridge pickups, 3 band EQ.

Mfr.'s Sug. Retail	$750	$525	$450	$375	$300	$270	$245	$225

132S-C — classic style, solid cedar top, round soundhole, 5 stripe bound body, wooden rosette, rosewood back/sides, mahogany neck, 12/19 fret rosewood fingerboard, rosewood bridge, 3 per side gold tuners with nylon buttons. Available in Natural finish. Curr. mfr.

Mfr.'s Sug. Retail	$750	$525	$450	$375	$300	$270	$245	$225

Grading	100%	98%	95%	90%	80%	70%	60%

132C-EC — similar to 132S-C, except has single rounded cutaway, spruce top, crystal bridge pickups, 3 band EQ.

Mfr.'s Sug. Retail	$900	$630	$540	$450	$360	$325	$300	$275

132SC-CP — similar to 132S-C, except single round cutaway, crystal bridge pickup, parametric EQ.

Mfr.'s Sug. Retail	$1,150	$805	$690	$575	$460	$415	$380	$345

Hirade Series

This series was designed by Mass Hirade, Takamine founder.

5-H — classic style, solid cedar top, round soundhole, 5 stripe wood bound body, wooden rosette, rosewood back/sides, mahogany neck, 12/19 fret ebony fingerboard, ebony bridge, 3 per side gold tuners with pearl buttons. Available in Natural finish. Curr. mfr.

Mfr.'s Sug. Retail	$1,300	$910	$780	$650	$520	$470	$430	$390

7-HP — similar to 5-H, except has crystal bridge pickups, parametric EQ.

Mfr.'s Sug. Retail	$1,950	$1,365	$1,170	$975	$780	$700	$645	$585

8-H — similar to 5-H, except has solid spruce top.

Mfr.'s Sug. Retail	$1,800	$1,260	$1,080	$900	$720	$650	$595	$540

15-H — classic style, solid spruce top, round soundhole, wood bound body, wooden rosette, rosewood back/sides, mahogany neck, 12/19 fret ebony fingerboard, ebony bridge with rosette matching inlay, 3 per side gold tuners with pearl buttons. Available in Natural finish. Curr. mfr.

Mfr.'s Sug. Retail	$3,380	$2,365	$2,030	$1,690	$1,350	$1,215	$1,115	$1,015

90-HP — rounded cutaway classic style, solid spruce top, oval soundhole, wood bound body, wooden rosette, rosewood back/sides, mahogany neck, 20 fret extended ebony fingerboard, ebony bridge, 3 per side gold tuners with pearl buttons, crystal bridge pickups, parametric EQ. Available in Natural finish. Curr. mfr.

Mfr.'s Sug. Retail	$2,300	$1,610	$1,380	$1,150	$920	$830	$760	$690

Jasmine Series

26-C — classic style, spruce top, round soundhole, 3 stripe bound body, wood inlay rosette, mahogany back/sides, nato neck, 12/19 fret rosewood fingerboard/bridge, 3 per side gold tuners with pearloid buttons. Available in Natural finish. Curr. mfr.

Mfr.'s Sug. Retail	$280	$195	$165	$140	$110	$100	$90	$80

28-C — similar to 26-C, except has rosewood back/sides. Disc. 1992.

		$245	$210	$175	$140	$125	$115	$105

Add $140 for rounded cutaway, crystal bridge pickups, 4 band volume/EQ control (28C-TC). Curr. mfr.

Last Mfr.'s Sug. Retail was $350.

Grading	100%	98%	95%	90%	80%	70%	60%

33-S — dreadnought style, spruce top, round soundhole, black pickguard, stripe bound body/rosette, mahogany back/sides, nato neck, 14/20 fret rosewood fingerboard with pearl dot inlay, rosewood bridge with white black dot pins, 3 per side chrome die cast tuners. Available in Natural finish. Curr. mfr.

| Mfr.'s Sug. Retail | $260 | $180 | $155 | $130 | $100 | $90 | $80 | $75 |

Add $120 for rounded cutaway, crystal bridge pickups, 4 band volume/EQ control (33C-TS).

312-S — dreadnought style, spruce top, round soundhole, black pickguard, 5 stripe bound body/rosette, mahogany back/sides, nato neck, 14/20 fret rosewood fingerboard with pearl dot inlay, rosewood bridge with white black dot pins, 6 per side chrome tuners. Available in Natural finish. Curr. mfr.

| Mfr.'s Sug. Retail | $330 | $230 | $195 | $165 | $130 | $120 | $110 | $100 |

40-S — dreadnought style, round soundhole, black pickguard, 3 stripe bound body/rosette, nato neck, 14/20 fret bound rosewood fingerboard with pearl dot inlay, rosewood bridge with white black dot pins, bound peghead, 3 per side chrome die cast tuners. Available in Natural finish. Disc. 1992.

| Mfr.'s Sug. Retail | $350 | $245 | $210 | $175 | $140 | $125 | $115 | $105 |

Add $40 for rounded cutaway, crystal bridge pickups, 4 band volume/EQ (40C-TS). Curr. mfr.

41-S — dreadnought style, spruce top, round soundhole, black pickguard with white outline, 3 stripe bound body/rosette, daowood back/sides, nato neck, 14/20 fret bound rosewood fingerboard with pearl dot inlay, rosewood bridge with white black dot pins, 3 per side chrome die cast tuners. Available in Black finish. Curr. mfr.

| Mfr.'s Sug. Retail | $360 | $250 | $215 | $180 | $145 | $130 | $120 | $110 |

Add $90 for rounded cutaway, crystal bridge pickups, 4 band volume/ EQ control (41C-TS).

46-S — similar to 41-S, except has black binding. Available in White finish. Disc. 1992.

| | | $250 | $215 | $180 | $145 | $130 | $120 | $110 |

Add $90 for rounded cutaway, crystal bridge pickups, 4 band volume/EQ control (46C-TS).

Last Mfr.'s Sug. Retail was $360.

49-S — dreadnought style, mahogany top, round soundhole, black pickguard, 3 stripe bound body/rosette, mahogany back/sides, nato neck, 14/20 fret bound rosewood fingerboard with pearl dot inlay, rosewood bridge with white black dot pins, bound peghead, 3 per side chrome die cast tuners. Available in Natural finish. Disc. 1992.

| | | $250 | $215 | $180 | $145 | $130 | $120 | $110 |

Add $90 for rounded cutaway, crystal bridge pickups, 4 band volume/EQ control (49C-TS).

Last Mfr.'s Sug. Retail was $360.

Grading	100%	98%	95%	90%	80%	70%	60%

50C-TS — rounded cutaway dreadnought style, spruce top, round soundhole, black pickguard, 3 stripe bound body/rosette, flame maple back/sides, maple neck, 20 fret bound rosewood fingerboard with pearl dot inlay, rosewood bridge with white black dot pins, body matching peghead, 3 per side chrome die cast tuners, crystal bridge pickups, 4 band volume/EQ control. Available in Blue Stain, Ebony Stain and Red Stain finish. Curr. mfr.

Mfr.'s Sug. Retail	$600	$420	$360	$300	$240	$215	$195	$180

58-TS — jumbo style, cedar top, round soundhole, tortoise shell pickguard, 3 stripe bound body, wood inlay rosette, daowood back/sides, nato neck, 14/20 fret bound rosewood fingerboard with pearl diamond dot inlay, rosewood bridge with white black dot pins, bound peghead, 3 per side gold die cast tuners, crystal bridge pickups, 4 band volume/EQ control. Available in Natural finish. Curr. mfr.

Mfr.'s Sug. Retail	$650	$455	$390	$325	$260	$235	$215	$195

60-S — dreadnought style , spruce top, round soundhole, black pickguard, 3 stripe bound body/rosette, rosewood back/sides, nato neck, 14/20 fret fingerboard with pearl dot inlay, rosewood bridge with white black dot pins, 3 per side chrome die cast tuners. Available in Natural finish. Disc. 1992.

	$275	$235	$195	$155	$140	$125	$115

Add $110 for crystal bridge pickups, 4 band volume/EQ control (60-TS).
Add $160 for rounded cutaway, crystal bridge pickups, 4 band volume/EQ control (60C-TS). Curr. mfr.
Last Mfr.'s Sug. Retail was $390.

70-S — dreadnought style, spruce top, round soundhole, black pickguard, 3 stripe bound body/rosette, Hawaiian koa back/sides, nato neck, 14/20 fret rosewood fingerboard with pearl dot inlay, rosewood bridge with white black dot pins, 3 per side chrome die cast tuners. Available in Natural finish. Curr. mfr.

Mfr.'s Sug. Retail	$400	$280	$240	$200	$160	$145	$130	$120

80S-S — dreadnought style, solid spruce top, round soundhole, black pickguard, 3 stripe bound body/rosette, jacaranda back/sides, nato neck, 14/20 fret bound rosewood fingerboard with pearl dot inlay, rosewood bridge with white black dot pins, bound peghead, 3 per side gold die cast tuners. Available in Natural finish. Curr. mfr.

Mfr.'s Sug. Retail	$540	$380	$325	$270	$215	$195	$180	$165

612-TS — dreadnought style, spruce top, round soundhole, black pickguard, 3 stripe bound body/rosette, rosewood back/sides, nato neck, 14/20 fret bound rosewood fingerboard with pearl dot inlay, rosewood bridge with white black dot pins, 6 per side chrome die cast tuners, crystal bridge pickups, 4 band volume/EQ. Available in Natural finish. Curr. mfr.

Mfr.'s Sug. Retail	$560	$390	$335	$280	$225	$205	$190	$170

Grading	100%	98%	95%	90%	80%	70%	60%

Natural Series

10-N — dreadnought style, solid cedar top, round soundhole, 3 stripe bound body, 5 stripe rosette, mahogany back/sides/neck, 14/20 fret rosewood fingerboard, rosewood strings thru bridge, 3 per side gold tuners with amber buttons. Available in Natural finish. Curr. mfr.

Mfr.'s Sug. Retail	$820	$575	$490	$410	$325	$295	$270	$245

10-EN — similar to 10-N, except has crystal bridge pickup, 3 band EQ.

Mfr.'s Sug. Retail	$1,000	$700	$600	$500	$400	$360	$330	$300

Add $90 for rounded cutaway (10C-EN).

15-N — dreadnought style, solid cedar top, round soundhole, 3 stripe bound body, 5 stripe rosette, rosewood back/sides, mahogany neck, 14/20 rosewood fingerboard, rosewood strings thru bridge, 3 per side gold tuners with amber buttons. Available in Natural finish. Curr. mfr.

Mfr.'s Sug. Retail	$930	$650	$555	$465	$370	$335	$305	$280

15C-NP — similar to 15-N, except has rounded cutaway, crystal bridge pickups, parametric EQ.

Mfr.'s Sug. Retail	$1,330	$930	$795	$660	$530	$475	$435	$395

18C-NP — similar to 15C-NP, except has solid spruce top, abalone bound body and rosette, ebony fingerboard/bridge, abalone logo inlay on peghead.

Mfr.'s Sug. Retail	$1,690	$1,185	$1,015	$845	$675	$605	$555	$505

20-N — jumbo style, solid cedar top, round soundhole, 3 stripe bound body, 5 stripe rosette, mahogany back/sides/neck, 14/20 fret rosewood fingerboard, rosewood strings thru bridge, 3 per side gold tuners with amber buttons. Available in Natural finish. Curr. mfr.

Mfr.'s Sug. Retail	$940	$660	$565	$470	$375	$340	$310	$280

20-EN — similar to 20-N, except has crystal bridge pickup, 3 band EQ.

Mfr.'s Sug. Retail	$1,100	$770	$660	$550	$440	$395	$365	$330

65C-NP — rounded cutaway artist style, solid cedar top, round soundhole, 3 stripe bound body, wooden rosette, rosewood back/sides, mahogany neck, 20 fret ebony fingerboard, classic style ebony bridge, classic style peghead, 3 per side gold tuners with amber buttons, crystal bridge pickups, parametric EQ. Available in Natural finish. Curr. mfr.

Mfr.'s Sug. Retail	$1,290	$905	$775	$645	$515	$465	$425	$385

Takamine GUITARS , cont.

Grading	100%	98%	95%	90%	80%	70%	60%

Santa Fe Series

40-SF — folk style, solid cedar top, round soundhole, 3 stripe bound body/rosette, mahogany back/sides/neck, 20 fret ebony fingerboard, turquoise eagle inay at 12th fret, ebony strings thru bridge, rosewood veneered peghead, 3 per side gold tuners with amber buttons. Available in Natural finish. New 1993.

Mfr.'s Sug. Retail	$850	$595	$510	$425	$340	$305	$280	$255

☆ **40C-ESF** — similar to 40-SF, except has single round cutaway, crystal bridge pickup, 4 band EQ.

Mfr.'s Sug. Retail	$1,200	$840	$720	$600	$480	$430	$395	$360

45C-PSF — single round cutaway folk style, solid cedar top, round soundhole, 3 stripe bound body/rosette, rosewood back/sides, mahogany neck, 20 fret ebony fingerboard with turquoise dot inlay, turquoise eagle inay at 12th fret, ebony strings thru bridge, rosewood veneered peghead, 3 per side gold tuners with amber buttons, crystal bridge pickup, parametric EQ. Available in Natural finish. New 1993.

Mfr.'s Sug. Retail	$1,500	$1,050	$900	$750	$600	$540	$495	$450

48C-PSF — single rounded cutaway folk style, solid spruce top, round soundhole, multi bound body, wood inlay rosette, rosewood back/sides, mahogany neck, 21 fret ebony fingerboard with abalone eagle inlay, strings thru ebony bridge, rosewood peghead veneer with abalone dot/logo inlay, 3 per side gold tuners with amber buttons, piezo bridge pickups, parametric EQ, active electronics. Available in Natural finish. New 1993.

Mfr.'s Sug. Retail	$1,800	$1,260	$1,080	$900	$720	$650	$595	$540

93-ESF — single rounded cutaway folk style, solid cedar top, round soundhole, multi bound, wood inlay rosette, silky oak back/sides, mahogany neck, 21 fret ebony fingerboard with turquoise eagle inlay, ebony bridge with white black dot pins, silky oak peghead veneer with turquoise dot/abalone logo inlay, 3 per side gold tuners with amber buttons, piezo bridge pickups, parametric EQ, active electronics. Available in Natural finish. New 1993.

Mfr.'s Sug. Retail	$1,500	$1,050	$900	$750	$600	$540	$495	$450

Specials Series

26-ST — artist style, solid spruce top, round soundhole, abalone bound body and rosette, campnosparma back/sides, mahogany neck, 14/20 fret bound rosewood fingerboard with pearl diamond inlay, rosewood bridge with white black dot pins, bound peghead with abalone logo inlay, 3 per side gold tuners, crystal bridge pickups, parametric EQ. Available in White finish. Curr. mfr.

Mfr.'s Sug. Retail	$1,580	$1,105	$950	$790	$630	$570	$520	$475

212-ST — similar to 26-ST, except has 12 strings, 6 per side tuners.

Mfr.'s Sug. Retail	$1,680	$1,175	$1,005	$840	$675	$605	$555	$505

Grading	100%	98%	95%	90%	80%	70%	60%

325SRC-EF — rounded cutaway dreadnought style, solid spruce top, round soundhole, black pickguard, 5 stripe bound body and rosette, bubinga back/sides, mahogany neck, 14/20 fret bound rosewood fingerboard with pearl dot inlay, rosewood bridge with white black dot pins, 3 per side chrome tuners, crystal bridge pickups, 3 band EQ. Available in Clear Red finish. Curr. mfr.

Mfr.'s Sug. Retail	$1,150	$805	$690	$575	$460	$415	$380	$345

⚹ **325SRCA-FP** — similar to 325SRC-EF, except has abalone rosette, parametric EQ.

Mfr.'s Sug. Retail	$1,400	$980	$840	$700	$560	$505	$460	$420

350M-F — dreadnought style, spruce top, round soundhole, black pickguard, 5 stripe bound body and rosette, maple back/sides/neck, 14/20 fret rosewood fingerboard with pearl dot inlay, rosewood bridge with white black dot pins, 3 per side chrome tuners. Available in Natural finish. Curr. mfr.

Mfr.'s Sug. Retail	$780	$545	$470	$390	$315	$280	$260	$235

⚹ **350MC-EF** — similar to 350M-F, except has rounded cutaway, crystal bridge pickups, 3 band EQ.

Mfr.'s Sug. Retail	$1,100	$770	$660	$550	$440	$395	$365	$330

592ME-FP — dreadnought style, arched flame maple top, round soundhole, 5 stripe bound body and rosette, flame maple back/sides/neck, 14/20 bound rosewood fingerboard with pearl dot inlay, rosewood bridge with white black pins, bound peghead with pearl logo inlay, 3 per side chrome tuners, crystal bridge pickups, parametric EQ. Available in Ebony Stain finish. Curr. mfr.

Mfr.'s Sug. Retail	$1,480	$1,035	$885	$740	$595	$530	$485	$445

ACOUSTIC ELECTRIC

Jasmine Series

All models in this series have the following features: single rounded cutaway folk style, round soundhole, 3 stripe bound body/rosette, 21 fret bound rosewood fingerboard with pearl dot inlay, rosewood bridge with white black dot pins, body matching bound peghead, 3 per side chrome diecast tuners, crystal bridge pickups, volume/treble/bass control, unless otherwise listed. Curr. mfr.

91C-TS — daowood top/back/sides, nato neck. Available in Black finish.

Mfr.'s Sug. Retail	$480	$335	$290	$240	$190	$170	$155	$145

92C-TS — flame maple top/back/sides, maple neck. Available in Red Stain finish.

Mfr.'s Sug. Retail	$520	$365	$310	$260	$210	$190	$170	$160

95C-TS — flame maple top/back/sides, maple neck. Available in Ebony Stain finish.

Mfr.'s Sug. Retail	$520	$365	$310	$260	$210	$190	$170	$160

Grading	100%	98%	95%	90%	80%	70%	60%

96C-TS — daowood top/back/sides, nato neck, black white dot bridge pins. Available in White finish.

Mfr.'s Sug. Retail	$480	$335	$290	$240	$190	$170	$155	$145

97C-TS — cedar top, daowood back/sides, nato neck, pearl diamond fingerboard inlay, gold die cast tuners. Available in Natural finish.

Mfr.'s Sug. Retail	$600	$420	$360	$300	$240	$215	$195	$180

98C-TS — flame maple top/back/sides, maple neck. Available in Blue Stain finish.

Mfr.'s Sug. Retail	$520	$365	$310	$260	$210	$190	$170	$160

99C-TS — daowood top/back/sides, nato neck. Available in Walnut Sunburst finish.

Mfr.'s Sug. Retail	$480	$335	$290	$240	$190	$170	$155	$145

TAYLOR

Manufacturer located in Santee, CA, since 1974. Distributed by Taylor-Listug, Inc., located in El Cajon, CA. Previously located in Lemon Grove, CA.

ACOUSTIC

400 Series

410 — dreadnought style, solid spruce top, round soundhole, tortoise shell pickguard, 3 stripe bound body and rosette, solid mahogany back/sides/neck, 14/20 fret rosewood fingerboard with pearl dot inlay, rosewood bridge, rosewood veneer on peghead, 3 per side chrome Grover tuners. Available in Natural finish. Curr. mfr.

Mfr.'s Sug. Retail	$1,100	$770	$660	$550	$440	$395	$365	$330

    Add $200 for acoustic pickup system, slide control preamp.

412 — similar to 410, except has grand concert style body.

Mfr.'s Sug. Retail	$1,100	$770	$660	$550	$440	$395	$365	$330

420 — similar to 410, except has rosewood back/sides.

Mfr.'s Sug. Retail	$1,300	$910	$780	$650	$520	$470	$430	$390

500 Series

510 — dreadnought style, solid spruce top, round soundhole, tortoise shell pickguard, 3 stripe bound body and rosette, solid mahogany back/sides/neck, 14/20 fret ebony fingerboard with pearl dot inlay, ebony bridge with black pins, rosewood veneer on peghead, 3 per side gold tuners. Curr. mfr.

Mfr.'s Sug. Retail	$1,600	$1,120	$960	$800	$640	$575	$530	$480

Grading	100%	98%	95%	90%	80%	70%	60%

512 — similar to 510, except has grand concert style body.

Mfr.'s Sug. Retail	$1,700	$1,190	$1,020	$850	$680	$610	$560	$510

555 — similar to 510, except has jumbo style body and 12 strings.

Mfr.'s Sug. Retail	$2,000	$1,400	$1,200	$1,000	$800	$720	$660	$600

600 Series

610 — dreadnought style, solid spruce top, round soundhole, tortoise shell pickguard, 3 stripe bound body and rosette, solid maple back/sides, mahogany neck, 14/20 fret bound rosewood fingerboard with pearl dot inlay, rosewood bridge with black pins, rosewood veneer on peghead, 3 per side gold tuners. Curr. mfr.

Mfr.'s Sug. Retail	$1,900	$1,330	$1,140	$950	$760	$685	$625	$570

612 — similar to 610, except has grand concert style body. Disc. 1992.

	$1,290	$1,105	$920	$735	$665	$605	$550

Last Mfr.'s Sug. Retail was $1,840.

612-C — similar to 612, except has single sharp cutaway. New 1993.

Mfr.'s Sug. Retail	$2,200	$1,540	$1,320	$1,100	$880	$790	$725	$660

615 — similar to 610, except has jumbo style body.

Mfr.'s Sug. Retail	$2,100	$1,475	$1,260	$1,050	$840	$755	$690	$630

700 Series

710 — dreadnought style, solid spruce top, round soundhole, tortoise shell pickguard, 3 stripe bound body and rosette, rosewood back/sides, mahogany neck, 14/20 fret ebony fingerboard with pearl dot inlay, ebony bridge with black pins, rosewood veneer on peghead, 3 per side gold tuners. Curr. mfr.

Mfr.'s Sug. Retail	$1,800	$1,260	$1,080	$900	$720	$650	$595	$540

712 — similar to 710, except has grand concert body.

Mfr.'s Sug. Retail	$1,900	$1,330	$1,140	$950	$760	$685	$625	$570

800 Series

810 — dreadnought style, solid spruce top, round soundhole, tortoise shell pickguard, 3 stripe bound body, abalone rosette, rosewood back/sides, mahogany neck, 14/20 fret bound rosewood fingerboard with pearl snowflake inlay, rosewood bridge with black abalone dot pins, rosewood veneer on bound peghead with pearl logo inlay, 3 per side gold tuners. Curr. mfr.

Mfr.'s Sug. Retail	$1,880	$1,320	$1,130	$940	$750	$675	$615	$560

812 — similar to 810, except has grand concert style body. Disc. 1992.

	$1,370	$1,175	$980	$785	$705	$645	$585

Last Mfr.'s Sug. Retail was $1,960.

Taylor , cont.

Grading	100%	98%	95%	90%	80%	70%	60%

812-C — similar to 812, except has single sharp cutaway. New 1993.

Mfr.'s Sug. Retail	$2,300	$1,610	$1,380	$1,150	$920	$830	$760	$690

815-C — similar to 810, except has single sharp cutaway jumbo style body. New 1993.

Mfr.'s Sug. Retail	$2,400	$1,680	$1,440	$1,200	$960	$860	$790	$720

855 — similar to 810, except has jumbo style body and 12 strings.

Mfr.'s Sug. Retail	$2,400	$1,680	$1,440	$1,200	$960	$860	$790	$720

900 Series

910 — dreadnought style, solid spruce top, round soundhole, tortoise shell pickguard, wood bound body, abalone rosette, maple back/sides/neck, 14/20 fret ebony fingerboard with abalone stylized inlay, ebony bridge with black abalone dot pins, rosewood veneer with abalone stylized T and logo inlay on peghead, 3 per side gold tuners. Curr. mfr.

Mfr.'s Sug. Retail	$3,700	$2,590	$2,220	$1,850	$1,480	$1,330	$1,220	$1,110

This model also available with rosewood back/sides and mahogany neck.

912 — similar to 910, except has grand concert style body. Disc. 1992.

	$1,890	$1,630	$1,360	$1,085	$975	$895	$815

Last Mfr.'s Sug. Retail was $2,715.

912-C — similar to 912, except has single sharp cutaway. New 1993.

Mfr.'s Sug. Retail	$4,000	$2,800	$2,400	$2,000	$1,600	$1,440	$1,320	$1,200

915 — similar to 910, except has jumbo style body. Disc. 1992.

	$1,975	$1,690	$1,410	$1,125	$1,015	$930	$845

Last Mfr.'s Sug. Retail was $2,815.

955 — similar to 910, except has jumbo style body and 12 strings. Disc 1992.

	$2,270	$1,945	$1,625	$1,300	$1,170	$1,070	$975

Last Mfr.'s Sug. Retail was $3,235.

Koa Series

K-20 — dreadnought style, koa top/back/sides/neck, round soundhole, tortoise shell pickguard, 3 stripe bound body, abalone rosette, 14/20 fret rosewood fingerboard with pearl diamond inlay, rosewood bridge with black abalone dot pins, ebony veneer with abalone logo inlay on peghead, 3 per side gold tuners. Disc. 1992.

	$1,480	$1,270	$1,060	$845	$760	$690	$630

This model is also available with solid spruce top.
Last Mfr.'s Sug. Retail was $2,115.

K-22 — similar to K-20, except has grand concert style body.

	$1,535	$1,315	$1,095	$875	$785	$720	$655

Last Mfr.'s Sug. Retail was $2,190.

Grading	100%	98%	95%	90%	80%	70%	60%

Signature Series

DCSM — dreadnought style, spruce top, round soundhole, tortoise shell pickguard, 5 stripe bound body and rosette, rosewood back/sides, mahogany neck, 14/20 fret ebony bound fingerboard with pearl diamond inlay, ebony bridge with black abalone dot pins, rosewood veneer with pearl logo inlay on bound peghead, 3 per side gold tuners. Curr. mfr.

Mfr.'s Sug. Retail	$2,300	$1,610	$1,380	$1,150	$920	$830	$760	$690

This model was co-designed by Dan Crary.

LKSM — 12 string jumbo style, spruce top, round soundhole, wood bound body and wooden rosette, mahogany back/sides/neck, 14/20 fret ebony fingerboard, pearl Leo Kottke inlay at 12th fret, ebony bridge with black pins, rosewood veneer with pearl logo inlay on peghead, 6 per side gold tuners. Curr. mfr.

Mfr.'s Sug. Retail	$2,700	$1,890	$1,620	$1,350	$1,080	$970	$890	$810

This model was co-designed by Leo Kottke.

TOBIAS

Manufacturer located in Burbank, CA. This company was started by Mike Tobias in 1978, and acquired by the Gibson Corp. in 1990.

ELECTRIC BASS

Basic Series

B4 — offset double cutaway asymmetrical alder body, thru body maple/ bubinga neck, 24 fret rosewood fingerboard, fixed bridge, 2 per side tuners, chrome hardware, 2 Bartolini pickups, 2 volume/treble/midrange/bass controls, bypass switch, active electronics. Available in Amber, Blue, Green, Orange, Purple and Red finish. Curr. mfr.

Mfr.'s Sug. Retail	$2,910	$2,035	$1,745	$1,450	$1,160	$1,040	$955	$870

Finishes on this model are transparent.

This model available with black hardware.

This model is also available with bubinga, figured maple, koa, lacewood, walnut or zebra body. Neck laminate may also be maple/purpleheart.

B5 — similar to B4, except has 5 strings.

Mfr.'s Sug. Retail	$3,140	$2,195	$1,885	$1,570	$1,255	$1,125	$1,035	$940

TOBIAS GUITARS , cont.

Grading	100%	98%	95%	90%	80%	70%	60%

⚴ **B6** — similar to B4, except has 6 strings and pau ferro fingerboard.

Mfr.'s Sug. Retail	$3,360	$2,350	$2,015	$1,675	$1,340	$1,200	$1,100	$1,000

Classic Series

C4 — offset double cutaway asymmetrical laminated body, thru body walnut/wenge neck, 24 fret pau ferro fingerboard, fixed bridge, 2 per side tuners, chrome hardware, 2 Bartolini pickups, 2 volume/treble/midrange/bass controls, bypass switch, active electronics. Available in Natural finish. Curr. mfr.

Mfr.'s Sug. Retail	$3,250	$2,275	$1,950	$1,625	$1,300	$1,170	$1,070	$975

This model may have black hardware.

Neck may have walnut/purpleheart or walnut/bubinga laminate, maple may replace walnut in some configurations.

This model also available in birdseye maple/walnut, bubinga/wenge/alder, flame maple/wenge/walnut, goncalo alves/walnut, lacewood/wenge/alder, purpleheart/walnut, walnut/wenge/alder, walnut/wenge/walnut, zebra/walnut or zebra/wenge/alder laminate body.

⚴ **C5** — similar to C4, except has 5 strings.

Mfr.'s Sug. Retail	$3,470	$2,425	$2,080	$1,730	$1,385	$1,245	$1,145	$1,040

⚴ **C6** — similar to C4, except has 6 strings.

Mfr.'s Sug. Retail	$3,700	$2,590	$2,220	$1,850	$1,480	$1,330	$1,220	$1,110

Killer "B" Series

⚴ **KB4** — offset double cutaway asymmetrical ash body, bolt-on maple/purpleheart 5 piece neck, 24 fret pau ferro fingerboard, fixed bridge, 2 per side tuners, black hardware, 2 Bartolini pickups, 2 volume/treble/midrange/bass controls, bypass switch, active electronics. Available in Oil finish. Curr. mfr.

Mfr.'s Sug. Retail	$2,400	$1,680	$1,440	$1,200	$960	$860	$790	$720

Add $200 for Candy Colors finish.
Add $60 for fretless fingerboard.
Add $175 for left handed version.
Add $125 for Clear or Solid Colors finish.
This model also available with alder, maple or lacewood body.

⚴ **KB5** — similar to KB4, except has 5 strings.

Mfr.'s Sug. Retail	$2,500	$1,750	$1,500	$1,250	$1,000	$900	$825	$750

⚴ **KB6** — similar to KB4, except has 6 strings.

Mfr.'s Sug. Retail	$2,600	$1,820	$1,560	$1,300	$1,040	$935	$860	$780

Grading	100%	98%	95%	90%	80%	70%	60%

Signature Series

S4 — offset double cutaway asymmetrical laminate body, thru body laminate neck, 24 fret pau ferro fingerboard, fixed bridge, 2 per side tuners, chrome hardware, 2 Bartolini pickups, 2 volume/treble/midrange/ bass controls, bypass switch, active electronics. Available in Natural finish. Curr. mfr.

Mfr.'s Sug. Retail	$3,810	$2,665	$2,285	$1,900	$1,520	$1,365	$1,255	$1,140

This model may have black hardware.

Neck may have walnut/wenge, walnut/purpleheart or walnut/bubinga laminate. Maple may replace walnut in these laminates.

This model also available in bubinga/wenge/bubinga, figured maple/ mahogany/figured maple, goncalo alves/walnut/goncalo alves, koa/wenge/koa, lacewood/wenge/lacewood, pau ferro/mahogany/pau ferro, zebra/walnut/zebra or zebra/wenge/zebra laminate body.

S5 — similar to S4, except has 5 strings.

Mfr.'s Sug. Retail	$4,030	$2,820	$2,420	$2,015	$1,610	$1,450	$1,330	$1,210

S6 — similar to S4, except has 6 strings.

Mfr.'s Sug. Retail	$4,260	$2,980	$2,555	$2,125	$1,700	$1,530	$1,400	$1,275

Standard Series

ST4 — offset double cutaway asymmetrical ash body, thru body maple/ bubinga 5 piece neck, 24 fret rosewood fingerboard, fixed bridge, 2 per side tuners, black hardware, 2 Bartolini pickups, volume/mix and 3 band EQ controls, active electronics. Available in Black, Natural, Transparent Candy Amber, Transparent Candy Blue, Transparent Candy Red and White finish. Curr. mfr.

Mfr.'s Sug. Retail	$1,900	$1,330	$1,140	$950	$760	$685	$625	$570

This model available in fretless fingerboard at no additional cost.

ST5 — similar to ST4, except has 5 strings.

Mfr.'s Sug. Retail	$2,000	$1,400	$1,200	$1,000	$800	$720	$660	$600

ST6 — similar to ST4, except has 6 strings.

Mfr.'s Sug. Retail	$2,300	$1,610	$1,380	$1,150	$920	$830	$760	$690

TRIGGS GUITARS

Manufactured by Nashville luthier, Jim Triggs.

Triggs Guitars are archtop instruments built by Nashville luthier, Jim Triggs, and incorporate features of older pre-WWII archtop guitars. After a term of apprenticeship with several other guitar manufacturers, Mr. Triggs decided to start his own business specializing in old-world craftsmanship techniques.

TURTLETONE

Manufacturer located in Tempe, AZ.

The Turtletone company produces a line of five solid body instruments (4 guitars, 1 bass) that are Computer Aided Design/Computer Aided Manufacturing (CAD/CAM) instruments. These guitars feature maple bodies and necks, ebony fingerboard, DiMarzio pickups, and Kahler and Grover hardware. List price for the standard instrument is $1,600, and many special orders/options are available per customer order.

VALLEY ARTS

Manufacturer located in City of Industry, CA since 1993. Previously manufactured in N. Hollywood, CA between 1979-1993.

Valley Arts originally began as a retail store in N. Hollywood during 1967. In 1992, Samick was involved in a joint venture with Valley Arts, and in June 1993, Samick acquired Valley Arts entirely.

Grading	100%	98%	95%	90%	80%	70%	60%

ELECTRIC

CUSTOM PRO — strat style ash body, white pickguard, bolt-on birdseye maple neck, 24 fret rosewood fingerboard with pearl dot inlay, double locking vibrato, 6 on one side tuners, gold hardware, 2 single coil/1 humbucker EMG pickups, volume/tone control, 5 position switch. Available in Burnt Amber, Fireburst, Sunset Gold, Transparent Blue, Transparent, Cream, Transparent Green and Transparent Red finish. Curr. mfr.

Mfr.'s Sug. Retail	$1,995	$1,395	$1,195	$995	$795	$720	$660	$600

Add $300 for quilted maple body with ebony fingerboard.
Pickguards are also black depending on color of finish.

STANDARD PRO — strat style maple body, black pickguard, bolt-on maple neck, 24 fret rosewood fingerboard with pearl dot inlay, double locking vibrato, 6 on one side tuners, chrome hardware, 2 single coil/1 humbucker EMG pickups, volume/tone control, 5 position switch. Available in Black, Candy Red, Metallic Teal and White finish. Curr. mfr.

Mfr.'s Sug. Retail	$1,995	$1,395	$1,195	$995	$795	$720	$660	$600

This model is also available with black hardware.

STEVE LUKATHER SIGNATURE — strat style ash body, black pickguard, bolt-on birdseye maple neck, 24 fret rosewood fingerboard with pearl dot inlay, double locking vibrato, 6 on one side tuners, gold hardware, 2 single coil/1 humbucker EMG pickups, volume/tone control, 5 position switch. Available in Fireburst finish. Curr. mfr.

Mfr.'s Sug. Retail	$2,075	$1,450	$1,240	$1,035	$830	$745	$680	$620

This model was co-designed by Steve Lukather and has his signature on the back of the headstock.
Also available with ebony fingerboard.

Grading	100%	98%	95%	90%	80%	70%	60%

ELECTRIC BASS

CUSTOM PRO BASS — precision style carved herringbone bound figured maple body, bolt-on birdseye maple neck, 21 fret rosewood fingerboard with pearl dot inlay, fixed bridge, herringbone bound peghead, 4 on one side tuners, black hardware, P-style/J-style EMG pickups, 2 volume/1 tone controls. Available in Burnt Amber, Fireburst, Sunset Gold, Transparent Blue, Transparent Cream, Transparent Green and Transparent Red finish. Curr. mfr.

Mfr.'s Sug. Retail	$2,675	$1,870	$1,605	$1,335	$1,065	$960	$880	$800

> This model is also available with ebony fingerboard, gold hardware, Bartolini pickups, 2 P-style or 2 J-style pickup configurations and active electronics.

VANTAGE

This trademark was established circa 1977 in Matsumoto, Japan. Currently manufactured in Korea since 1990. Distributed by Music Industries Corp., located in Floral Park, NY, since 1987.

ACOUSTIC

Classic Series

VSC-10 — classic style, spruce top, round soundhole, bound body, wooden inlay rosette, nato back/sides/neck, 12/19 fret rosewood fingerboard/tied bridge, rosewood peghead veneer, 3 per side chrome tuners with plastic buttons. Available in Light Pumpkin finish. Curr. mfr.

Mfr.'s Sug. Retail	$200	$140	$120	$100	$80	$70	$65	$60

VSC-20 — classic style, cedar top, round soundhole, bound body, wooden inlay rosette, ovankol back/sides, nato neck, 12/19 fret rosewood fingerboard/tied bridge, ovankol peghead veneer, 3 per side gold tuners with plastic buttons. Available in Natural finish. Curr. mfr.

Mfr.'s Sug. Retail	$240	$170	$145	$120	$95	$85	$80	$75

VSC-20CE — similar to VSC-20, except has single rounded cutaway, piezo bridge pickup, 3 band EQ with volume slide control.

Mfr.'s Sug. Retail	$390	$275	$235	$195	$155	$140	$125	$115

VSC-30 — similar to VSC-20, except has rosewood back/sides. Available in Light Pumpkin finish.

Mfr.'s Sug. Retail	$320	$225	$195	$160	$130	$115	$105	$95

Grading	100%	98%	95%	90%	80%	70%	60%

Dreadnought Series

VS-5 — dreadnought style, spruce top, round soundhole, black pickguard, bound body, 3 stripe rosette, nato back/sides/neck, 14/20 fret nato fingerboard with white dot inlay, ebonized maple bridge with white black dot pins, 3 per side chrome tuners. Available in Natural finish. Curr. mfr.

Mfr.'s Sug. Retail	$200	$140	$120	$100	$80	$70	$65	$60

Add $10 for left hand version (VS-5/LH).

VS-10 — similar to VS-5, except has 3 stripe bound body.

Mfr.'s Sug. Retail	$220	$155	$130	$110	$90	$80	$70	$65

VS-12 — similar to VS-10, except has 12 strings, 6 per side tuners.

Mfr.'s Sug. Retail	$290	$205	$175	$145	$115	$105	$95	$85

Add $10 for Black finish (VS-12B).

VS-15 — dreadnought style, spruce top, round soundhole, black pickguard, 3 stripe bound body/rosette, nato back/sides/neck, 14/20 fret rosewood fingerboard with white dot inlay, rosewood bridge with black white dot pins, 3 per side chrome tuners. Available in Natural finish. Curr. mfr.

Mfr.'s Sug. Retail	$250	$175	$150	$125	$100	$90	$80	$75

VS-20 — dreadnought style, nato top, round soundhole, black pickguard, 3 stripe bound body/rosette, nato back/sides/neck, 14/20 fret bound rosewood fingerboard with white dot inlay, rosewood bridge with white black dot pins, bound peghead, 3 per side chrome tuners. Available in Black, Natural and Tobacco Sunburst finish. Curr. mfr.

Mfr.'s Sug. Retail	$270	$190	$160	$135	$110	$100	$90	$80

VS-25 — dreadnought style, cedar top, round soundhole, black pickguard, herringbone bound body/rosette, ovankol back/sides, mahogany neck, 14/20 fret rosewood fingerboard with white dot inlay, rosewood bridge with white black dot pins, 3 per side tuners. Available in Natural finish. Curr. mfr.

Mfr.'s Sug. Retail	$280	$195	$165	$140	$110	$100	$90	$80

Add $50 for solid cedar top (VS-25S).
Add $60 for left handed version with solid cedar top (VS-25S/LH).

VS-25CE — similar to VS-25, except has single sharp cutaway, solid cedar top, piezo bridge pickup, 3 band EQ with volume slide control.

Mfr.'s Sug. Retail	$480	$335	$290	$240	$190	$170	$155	$145

VS-25CE-12 — similar to VS-25CE, except has 12 strings, 6 per side tuners.

Mfr.'s Sug. Retail	$530	$370	$320	$265	$210	$190	$175	$160

Grading	100%	98%	95%	90%	80%	70%	60%

VS-30 — dreadnought style, maple top, round soundhole, black pickguard, 3 stripe bound body/rosette, maple back/sides/neck, 14/20 fret bound rosewood fingerboard with white dot inlay, rosewood bridge with white black dot pins, bound peghead, 3 per side chrome tuners. Available in Natural finish. Curr. mfr.

Mfr.'s Sug. Retail	$290	$205	$175	$145	$115	$105	$95	$85

VS-33 — dreadnought style, spruce top, round soundhole, black pickguard, 5 stripe bound body/rosette, oak back/sides, mahogany neck, 14/20 fret bound rosewood fingerboard, rosewood bridge with white black dot pins, bound peghead, 3 per side chrome tuners. Available in Transparent Black, Transparent Blue and Transparent Red finish. Curr. mfr.

Mfr.'s Sug. Retail	$300	$210	$180	$150	$120	$110	$100	$90

VS-35CE — single sharp cutaway dreadnought style, nato top, oval soundhole, 3 stripe bound body/rosette, nato back/sides/neck, 20 fret bound rosewood fingerboard with white dot inlay, rosewood bridge with white black dot pins, bound peghead, 3 per side chrome tuners, piezo bridge pickup, 3 band EQ with volume slide control. Available in Black and Tobacco Sunburst finish. Curr. mfr.

Mfr.'s Sug. Retail	$430	$300	$260	$215	$175	$155	$140	$130

Add $10 for left handed version of this model (VS-35CE/LH).

VS-50S — dreadnought style, solid spruce top, round soundhole, black pickguard, herringbone bound body/rosette, nato back/sides/neck, 14/20 fret rosewood fingerboard with white dot inlay, rosewood bridge with white black dot pins, bound peghead, 3 per side gold tuners. Available in Natural finish. Curr. mfr.

Mfr.'s Sug. Retail	$350	$245	$210	$175	$140	$125	$115	$105

Add $10 for left handed version of this model (VS-50S/LH).

ACOUSTIC ELECTRIC

VS-40CE — single sharp cutaway dreadnought style, nato top, oval soundhole, 3 stripe bound body/rosette, nato back/sides/neck, 20 fret bound rosewood fingerboard with white dot inlay, rosewood bridge with white black dot pins, bound peghead, 3 per side chrome tuners, piezo bridge pickup, 3 band EQ with volume slide control. Available in Black and White finish. Curr. mfr.

Mfr.'s Sug. Retail	$440	$310	$265	$220	$175	$160	$145	$135

VS-40CEM — similar to VS-40CE, except has maple back/sides.

Mfr.'s Sug. Retail	$450	$315	$270	$225	$180	$160	$150	$135

Add $10 for left handed version of this model (VS-40CEM/LH).
Add $10 for 12 string version of this model (VS-40CEM-12).

Grading	100%	98%	95%	90%	80%	70%	60%

VST-40SCE — single sharp cutaway dreadnought style, solid spruce top, round soundhole, 3 stripe bound body, herringbone rosette, nato back/sides/neck, 20 fret rosewood fingerboard with white dot inlay, rosewood bridge with white black dot pins, bound peghead, 3 per side gold tuners, piezo bridge pickup, 3 band EQ with volume slide control. Available in Natural finish. Curr. mfr.

Mfr.'s Sug. Retail	$500	$350	$300	$250	$200	$180	$165	$150

ELECTRIC

100 Series

All models in this series have strat style laminated body, bolt-on maple neck, 24 fret maple fingerboard with offset black dot inlay, standard vibrato, and 6 on one side tuners, unless otherwise listed.

111T — chrome hardware, single coil/humbucker pickup, volume/tone control, 3 position switch. Available in Black, Cherry Sunburst, Red and Tobacco Sunburst finish. Curr. mfr.

Mfr.'s Sug. Retail	$300	$210	$180	$150	$120	$110	$100	$90

Add $10 for left handed version of this model (111T/LH).

118DT — double locking vibrato, black hardware, 2 single coil/1 humbucker pickups, volume/2 tone controls, 5 position switch. Available in Gold Granite, Marble Stone, Metallic Black and Red Granite finish. Curr. mfr.

Mfr.'s Sug. Retail	$400	$280	$240	$200	$160	$145	$130	$120

118T — chrome hardware, 2 single coil/1 humbucker pickups, volume/2 tone controls, 5 position switch. Available in Black, Cherry Sunburst and Tobacco Sunburst finish. Curr. mfr.

Mfr.'s Sug. Retail	$330	$230	$195	$165	$130	$120	$110	$100

200 Series

All models in this series have strat style alder body, bolt-on maple necks, 24 fret maple fingerboard with offset black dot inlay, standard vibrato, 6 on one side tuners, black hardware, volume/2 tone controls, 5 position switch.

213T — 3 single coil pickups. Available in Tobacco Sunburst and Transparent Blue finish. Curr. mfr.

Mfr.'s Sug. Retail	$360	$250	$215	$180	$145	$130	$120	$110

218T — 2 single coil/1 humbucker pickups. Available in Transparent Black, Transparent Blue and Transparent Red finish. Curr. mfr.

Mfr.'s Sug. Retail	$370	$260	$220	$185	$150	$135	$120	$110

300 Series

This series is the same as the 200 Series, except has rosewood fingerboards.

Grading	100%	98%	95%	90%	80%	70%	60%

311T — single coil/humbucker pickup. Available in Metallic Black Cherry and Metallic Blue finish. Curr. mfr.

Mfr.'s Sug. Retail	$380	$265	$225	$190	$150	$135	$120	$110

320T — humbucker/single coil/humbucker pickups. Available in Metallic Black, Metallic Black Cherry and Pearl White finish. Curr. mfr.

Mfr.'s Sug. Retail	$390	$275	$235	$195	$155	$140	$125	$115

400 Series

This series is the same as the 300 Series, except has double locking vibrato.

418DT — 2 single coil/1 humbucker pickups. Available in Black Fishnet, Black Sandstone, Metallic Black and Red Sandstone finish. Curr. mfr.

Mfr.'s Sug. Retail	$480	$335	$290	$240	$190	$170	$155	$145

600 Series

635V — double cutaway semi-hollow style nato body, bound body/F-holes, raised black pickguard, nato neck, 22 fret rosewood fingerboard with offset pearl dot inlay, tunomatic/stop tailpiece, 3 per side tuners, chrome hardware, 2 humbucker pickups, 2 volume/2 tone controls, 3 position switch. Available in Black, Cherry Sunburst and Walnut finish. Curr. mfr.

Mfr.'s Sug. Retail	$450	$315	$270	$225	$180	$160	$150	$135

Add $40 for gold hardware with Natural finish.

700 Series

All models in this series have strat style alder body, bolt-on maple neck, 24 fret rosewood fingerboard with offset pearl dot inlay, double locking vibrato, 6 on one side tuners, black hardware, volume/2 tone controls, 5 position switch, unless otherwise noted.

718DT — 2 single coil/1 humbucker pickups, coil tap. Available in Burgundy, Dark Marble Stone, Transparent Black and Transparent Red finish. Curr. mfr.

Mfr.'s Sug. Retail	$500	$350	$300	$250	$200	$180	$165	$150

720DT — humbucker/single coil/humbucker pickups, coil tap. Available in Dark Marble Stone, Multicolor and Red Granite finish. Curr. mfr.

Mfr.'s Sug. Retail	$550	$385	$330	$275	$220	$200	$180	$165

728GDT — figured maple top, bound fingerboard, gold hardware, 2 single coil/1 humbucker pickups, coil tap. Available in Antique Violin finish. Curr. mfr.

Mfr.'s Sug. Retail	$630	$440	$380	$315	$250	$225	$205	$190

Grading	100%	98%	95%	90%	80%	70%	60%

800 Series

All models in this series have strat style alder body, bound figured maple top, bolt-on maple neck, bound rosewood fingerboard with offset pearl dot inlay, double locking vibrato, body matching bound peghead, 6 on one side tuners, volume/2 tone controls, 5 position switch.

818DT— black hardware, 2 single coil/1 humbucker pickups, coil tap. Available in Transparent Black, Transparent Blue and Transparent Red finish. Curr. mfr.

Mfr.'s Sug. Retail	$500	$350	$300	$250	$200	$180	$165	$150

Add $30 for gold hardware (818GDT).

820GDT — gold hardware, humbucker/single coil/humbucker pickups, coil tap. Available in Transparent Blue and Transparent Burgundy finish. Curr. mfr.

Mfr.'s Sug. Retail	$550	$385	$330	$275	$220	$200	$180	$165

900 Series

928GDT — strat style ash body, thru body 7 piece maple rosewood neck, 24 fret rosewood fingerboard with offset pearl dot inlay, double locking vibrato, 6 on one side tuners, gold hardware, 2 single coil/1 humbucker pickups, volume/2 tone controls, 5 position/coil tap switches. Available in Transparent Burgundy finish. Curr. mfr.

Mfr.'s Sug. Retail	$850	$595	$510	$425	$340	$305	$280	$255

ELECTRIC BASS

225B — precision style alder body, bolt-on maple neck, 20 fret maple fingerboard with offset black dot inlay, fixed bridge, 2 per side tuners, chrome hardware, P-style pickup, volume/tone control. Available in Black, Dark Blue Sunburst and Red finish. Curr. mfr.

Mfr.'s Sug. Retail	$330	$230	$195	$165	$130	$120	$110	$100

330B — similar to 225B, except has rosewood fingerboard with offset pearl inlay, black hardware, P-style/J-style pickups, 2 volume/1 tone controls. Available in Transparent Black, Transparent Blue and Transparent Red finish. Curr. mfr.

Mfr.'s Sug. Retail	$400	$280	$240	$200	$160	$145	$130	$120

Also available with fretless fingerboard.

525B — similar to 330B, except has higher quality bridge. Available in Black Fishnet and Red Granite finish. Curr. mfr.

Mfr.'s Sug. Retail	$420	$295	$250	$210	$170	$150	$135	$125

Grading	100%	98%	95%	90%	80%	70%	60%

725B — offset double cutaway asymmetrical alder body, bolt-on maple neck, 24 fret rosewood fingerboard with offset pearl dot inlay, fixed bridge, 2 per side tuners, black hardware, P-style/J-style pickups, 2 volume/2 tone controls. Available in Black, Dark Marble Stone, Metallic Black, Pearl White, Red and Transparent Red finish. Curr. mfr.

Mfr.'s Sug. Retail	$450	$315	$270	$225	$180	$160	$150	$135

Add $10 for left handed version of this model.
Also available with fretless fingerboard.

750B — similar to 725B, except has 5 strings, 3/2 per side tuners. Available in Blue Marble Stone and Pearl White finish.

Mfr.'s Sug. Retail	$500	$350	$300	$250	$200	$180	$165	$150

Add $50 for active electronics.

930B — offset double cutaway asymmetrical ash body, thru body 7 piece maple/rosewood neck, 24 fret rosewood fingerboard with offset pearl dot inlay, fixed bridge, 2 per side tuners, gold hardware, P-style/J-style pickups, 2 volume/2 tone controls. Available in Transparent Burgundy and Transparent Purple finish. Curr. mfr.

Mfr.'s Sug. Retail	$750	$525	$450	$375	$300	$270	$245	$225

VESTER

Trademark established in 1990 and manufactured in Korea. Distributed by Midco International, Effingham, IL.

ELECTRIC

JAR 1370 — strat style carved alder body, bolt-on maple neck, 24 fret rosewood fingerboard with pearl sharktooth inlay, double locking vibrato, 6 on one side Gotoh tuners, black hardware, 2 single coil/1 humbucker alnico pickups, volume/tone and preamp controls, 5 position switch. Available in Metallic Ice Blue, Metallic Red and Pearl White finish. Curr. mfr.

Mfr.'s Sug. Retail	$600	$420	$360	$300	$240	$215	$195	$180

JAR 1380 — strat style mahogany body, carved bound figured maple top, bolt on maple neck, 24 fret rosewood fingerboard with mixed sharktooth/dot inlay, block "Vester" inlay at 24th fret, double locking vibrato, 6 on one side tuners, black hardware, 2 active humbucker pickups, volume/tone control, 3 position switch. Available in Cherry Burst, Transparent Black and Transparent Green finish. Curr. mfr.

Mfr.'s Sug. Retail	$700	$490	$420	$350	$280	$250	$230	$210

Grading	100%	98%	95%	90%	80%	70%	60%

JAR 1400 — strat style alder body, bolt-on maple neck, 22 fret rosewood fingerboard with mixed pearl sharktooth/dot inlay, double locking vibrato, 6 on one side Gotoh tuners, black hardware, 2 single coil/1 humbucker pickups, volume/tone control, 5 position and coil tap switches. Available in Fluorescent Yellow, Metallic Dark Blue, Metallic Red and Pearl White finish. Curr. mfr.

Mfr.'s Sug. Retail	$600	$420	$360	$300	$240	$215	$195	$180

JAR 1412 — strat style alder body, bolt-on maple neck, 24 fret rosewood fingerboard with pearl dot inlay, fixed bridge, 12 string headstock, 6 per side Gotoh tuners, black hardware, 2 humbucker pickups, volume/tone control, 3 position switch. Available in Metallic Dark Blue, Metallic Red and Pearl White finish. Curr. mfr.

Mfr.'s Sug. Retail	$600	$420	$360	$300	$240	$215	$195	$180

JFA 500 — semi hollow strat style, alder body, bound spruce top, lightning bolt soundhole, maple neck, 22 fret rosewood fingerboard with pearl dot inlay, tunomatic bridge/stop tailpiece, 6 on one side tuners, chrome hardware, single coil/humbucker pickups, volume/tone control, 3 position switch, coil split in tone control. Available in Red, Tobacco Sunburst and White finish. Curr. mfr.

Mfr.'s Sug. Retail	$400	$280	$240	$200	$160	$145	$130	$120

JJM 1010 — strat style alder body, black pickguard, bolt-on maple neck, 22 fret maple fingerboard with black dot inlay, standard vibrato, 6 on one side tuners, chrome hardware, 2 single coil/1 humbucker pickups, volume/tone control, 5 position switch. Available in Black, Red and White finish. Curr. mfr.

Mfr.'s Sug. Retail	$300	$210	$180	$150	$120	$110	$100	$90

JJM 1020 — similar to JJM 1010, except has 24 frets, double locking vibrato, humbucker/single coil/humbucker pickups. Available in Black, Fluorescent Yellow, Red and White finish. Curr. mfr.

Mfr.'s Sug. Retail	$500	$350	$300	$250	$200	$180	$165	$150

JJR 550 — strat style alder body, bolt-on maple neck, 22 fret rosewood fingerboard with pearl dot inlay, double locking vibrato, 6 on one side tuners, chrome hardware, single coil/humbucker pickups, volume control, 3 position switch. Available in Blue Green, Metallic Gold and Rubine Red finish. Curr. mfr.

Mfr.'s Sug. Retail	$340	$235	$200	$170	$135	$125	$115	$105

Add $30 for graphic designs.

JJR 1070 — strat style alder body, bolt-on maple neck, 24 fret rosewood bound fingerboard with pearl inverted V inlay, double locking vibrato, 6 on one side tuners, black hardware, humbucker/single coil/humbucker pickups, 3 mini switches. Available in Pearl White finish. Curr. mfr.

Mfr.'s Sug. Retail	$460	$320	$275	$230	$185	$165	$150	$140

Add $40 for Graphic Designs finish.

Grading	100%	98%	95%	90%	80%	70%	60%

JJR 1170 — strat style alder body, set maple neck, 24 fret rosewood fingerboard with pearl sharktooth inlay, double locking vibrato, 6 on one side tuners, black hardware, 2 single coil/1 humbucker alnico pickups, volume/tone and preamp controls, 3 mini switches, active electronics. Available in Black finish. Curr. mfr.

Mfr.'s Sug. Retail	$440	$310	$265	$220	$175	$160	$145	$135

JJR 1175 — similar to JJR 1170, except has 2 humbucker pickups, no preamp control or mini switches, 5 position switch. Available in Metallic Charcoal Grey and Pearl White finish. Curr. mfr.

Mfr.'s Sug. Retail	$440	$310	$265	$220	$175	$160	$145	$135

Subtract $40 for Crackle Blue/Green/Red/Yellow, Crackle Silver/Blue and Crackle Yellow/Blue finish.

JJR 1290 — strat style alder body, bound figured maple top, bolt-on maple neck, 24 fret bound rosewood fingerboard with pearl dot inlay, double locking vibrato, 6 on one side Gotoh tuners, black hardware, 2 single coil/1 humbucker pickups, volume/tone control, 5 position switch. Available in Cherry Sunburst, Transparent Blue, Transparent Green and Transparent Red finish. Curr. mfr.

Mfr.'s Sug. Retail	$470	$330	$280	$235	$190	$170	$155	$140

Models with the Transparent Red finish have reverse headstocks.

JJR 1462 — this is a double neck construct with one side being similar to JAR 1412 and the other being similar to JJR 1030. Both necks have 22 fret rosewood fingerboards with pearl dot inlay, 3 position neck selector switch included. Available in White finish. Curr. mfr.

Mfr.'s Sug. Retail	$1,200	$840	$720	$600	$480	$430	$395	$360

OAR 1500 — offset double cutaway asymmetrical mahogany body, carved maple top, set mahogany neck, 24 fret rosewood fingerboard with pearl dot inlay, standard vibrato, 3 per side Gotoh locking tuners, chrome hardware, 2 humbucker pickups, volume tone control, 3 position and coil split mini switches. Available in Metallic Red, Pearl Blue and Pearl White finish. Curr. mfr.

Mfr.'s Sug. Retail	$600	$420	$360	$300	$240	$215	$195	$180

ELECTRIC BASS

OPR 436 — offset double cutaway asymmetrical maple body, bolt-on maple neck, 24 fret rosewood fingerboard with pearl dot inlay, fixed bridge, 2 per side tuners, chrome hardware, P-style/J-style pickups, 2 volume/1 tone controls. Available in Black and Metallic Red finish. Curr. mfr.

Mfr.'s Sug. Retail	$380	$265	$225	$190	$150	$135	$120	$110

Grading	100%	98%	95%	90%	80%	70%	60%

OPR 935 — similar to OPR 436, except has alder body and black hardware. Available in Black, Blue and Metallic Red finish. Curr. mfr.

Mfr.'s Sug. Retail	$400	$280	$240	$200	$160	$145	$130	$120

OPR 935EQ — similar to OPR 935, except has volume/treble/bass and mix controls and active electronics. Available in Black and Metallic Red finish.

Mfr.'s Sug. Retail	$420	$295	$250	$210	$170	$150	$135	$125

OPR 1135 — offset double cutaway asymmetrical alder body, bolt-on maple neck, 24 fret rosewood fingerboard with pearl dot inlay, fixed bridge, 2 per side tuners, black hardware, 2 humbucker pickups, 2 volume/1 tone controls. Available in Black and White finish. Curr. mfr.

Mfr.'s Sug. Retail	$450	$315	$270	$225	$180	$160	$150	$135

OPR 1135EQ — similar to OPR 1135, except has volume/treble/bass and mix controls and active electronics.

Mfr.'s Sug. Retail	$500	$350	$300	$250	$200	$180	$165	$150

OPR 1235 — similar to OPR 1135, except has 5 strings, 3/2 per side tuners, P-style/J-style pickups, 1 volume/2 tone controls, 3 position mini switch. Available in Black and Metallic Red finish. Curr. mfr.

Mfr.'s Sug. Retail	$500	$350	$300	$250	$200	$180	$165	$150

OPR 1335EQ — similar to OPR 1235, except has 2 humbucker pickups, volume/treble/bass and mix controls and active electronics. Available in Black and Pearl White finish.

Mfr.'s Sug. Retail	$550	$385	$330	$275	$220	$200	$180	$165

OPR 1435EQ — precision style carved alder body, bolt-on 5 piece maple/mahogany neck, 24 fret rosewood fingerboard with pearl dot inlay, fixed bridge, 2 per side tuners, black hardware, P-style/J-style pickups, volume/treble/bass and mix controls, active electronics. Available in Fluorescent Blue, Metallic Charcoal Grey and Pearl White finish. Curr. mfr.

Mfr.'s Sug. Retail	$530	$370	$320	$265	$210	$190	$175	$160

VIGIER

Manufactured and distributed by Vigier Guitars, located in Evry, FRANCE.

Grading	100%	98%	95%	90%	80%	70%	60%

ELECTRIC

ARPEGE III — offset double cutaway asymmetrical flame maple body, thru body maple neck, 22 fret phenowood fingerboard, double locking vibrato, 3 per side tuners, black hardware, 2 humbucker pickups, volume/tone/mix controls, 3 position and memory switches, coil split in volume control. Available in Antique Violin, Ash, Aquatic Blue, Burgundy, Emerald Green, French Kiss, Honey, Night Blue and Red finish. Curr. mfr.

Mfr.'s Sug. Retail	$3,770	$2,635	$2,260	$1,880	$1,500	$1,350	$1,235	$1,125

All finishes are transparent.

EXCALIBUR — strat style ash body, mirrored pickguard, bolt-on maple neck, 24 fret maple fingerboard with black dot inlay, double locking vibrato, 6 on one side Gotoh tuners, chrome hardware, 3 single coil Seymour Duncan pickups, volume/tone control, 5 position switch. Available in Black, Honey, Natural Malt, Ocean Blue and Wine Fire finish. Curr. mfr.

Mfr.'s Sug. Retail	$1,730	$1,210	$1,040	$865	$690	$625	$570	$520

Add $40 for 2 single coil/1 humbucker pickup configuration.
Add $65 for humbucker/single coil/humbucker pickup configuration.

Excalibur Custom — similar to Excalibur, except has bound flame maple top, body color matching head stock.

Mfr.'s Sug. Retail	$2,045	$1,430	$1,225	$1,025	$820	$745	$675	$615

Add $40 for 2 single coil/1 humbucker pickup configuration.
Add $65 for humbucker/single coil/humbucker pickup configuration.

PASSION III — offset double cutaway asymmetrical alder body, half thru body carbon fiber weave neck, 24 fret Phenowood fingerboard, double locking vibrato, pearl logo inlay on peghead, 3 per side tuners with quick winders, chrome hardware, 2 single coil/1 humbucker Seymour Duncan pickups, push/pull volume control with active electronics switch, 6 position rotary tone control with parametric EQ, 3 position switch. Available in Antique Violin, Black, Burnt Metal, Devil Burnt Metal, Ferrari Red, Flip Flop Blue, Fuschia, Lemon, Natural, Night Blue, Pearl White, Peppermint, Silver Black, Sunburst Grey and Transparent Red finish. Curr. mfr.

Mfr.'s Sug. Retail	$3,150	$2,200	$1,890	$1,575	$1,260	$1,130	$1,040	$945

Grading	100%	98%	95%	90%	80%	70%	60%

ELECTRIC BASS

ARPEGE III — offset double cutaway asymmetrical flame maple body, thru body maple neck, 21 fret phenowood fingerboard, fixed bridge, 2 per side tuners, black hardware, 2 single coil pickups, volume/tone/mix/bypass controls, memory switch. Available in Antique Violin, Ash, Aquatic Blue, Burgundy, Devil Burnt, Emerald Green, French Kiss, Honey, Night Blue and Red finish. Curr. mfr.

Mfr.'s Sug. Retail	$3,685	$2,580	$2,215	$1,840	$1,470	$1,325	$1,215	$1,100

All finishes are transparent.
Add $295 for 5-string version of this model.
Add $690 for 6-string version of this model.

PASSION III — double offset cutaway asymmetrical alder body, half thru carbon fiber weave neck, 21 fret Phenowood fingerboard, fixed bridge, 2 per side tuners, black hardware, 2 single coil pickups, volume/tone/mix controls, parametric EQ/active electronic switches. Available in Antique Violin, Black, Devil Burnt Metal, Ferrari Red, Flip Flop Blue, Fuschia, Lemon, Natural, Night Blue, Pearl White, Peppermint, Silver Black, Sunburst Grey and Transparent Red finish. Curr. mfr.

Mfr.'s Sug. Retail	$2,960	$2,070	$1,775	$1,475	$1,180	$1,060	$975	$885

Passion III Custom — similar to Passion III, except has flame maple body, chrome hardware. Available in Antique Violin, Aquatic Blue, Ash, Burgundy, Devil Burnt, Emerald Green, French Kiss, Honey, Night Blue and Red finish.

Mfr.'s Sug. Retail	$3,240	$2,270	$1,945	$1,625	$1,300	$1,170	$1,070	$975

Add $285 for 5-string version of this model.
Add $580 for 6-string version of this model.

WARWICK

Manufacturer located in Germany (established 1982) and distributed exclusively in the U.S. Dana B. Goods, a subsidiary of Seymour Duncan, located in Goleta, CA.

Grading	100%	98%	95%	90%	80%	70%	60%

ACOUSTIC BASS

ALIEN — single sharp cutaway concert style, spruce top, asymmetrical soundhole located in upper bout, rosewood thumb rest, wood bound body, ovankol soundhole cap, ovankol back/sides, 2 piece mahogany neck with wenge center strip, 24 fret wenge fingerboard, wenge/metal bridge, ebony peghead veneer with pearl W inlay, 2 per side chrome tuners, piezo pickup, 4 band EQ, active electronics. Available in Natural finish. Curr. mfr.

Mfr.'s Sug. Retail	$3,000	$2,095	$1,800	$1,500	$1,200	$1,080	$990	$900

ELECTRIC BASS

All models in this group of instruments have tunomatic bridge/stop tailpiece, ebony peghead veneer with pearl W inlay and slanted tuners.

DOLPHIN PRO I — offset double cutaway asymmetrical boire body, half thru body 7 piece wenge/zebrano neck, 24 fret wenge fingerboard with pearl dolphin inlay, 2 per side tuners, chrome hardware, J-style/humbucker MEC pickups, concentric volume-balance/concentric treble-bass control, active electronics, push/pull electronics switch in volume control, push/pull coil split switch in tone control. Available in Natural finish. Curr. mfr.

Mfr.'s Sug. Retail	$3,400	$2,380	$2,040	$1,700	$1,360	$1,225	$1,120	$1,025

Add $500 for 5 string version of this model.
Available with fretless fingerboard at no additional cost.

Dolphin Pro II — offset double cutaway asymmetrical ash body, bolt-on 3 piece maple neck, 24 fret wenge fingerboard, 2 per side tuners, chrome hardware, 2 J-style MEC pickups, volume/concentric treble-bass/balance controls, active electronics, push/pull electronics switch in volume control. Available in Black, Black Stain, Blue, Blue Stain, Red Stain and Wine Red finish. Curr. mfr.

Mfr.'s Sug. Retail	$2,050	$1,435	$1,230	$1,025	$820	$745	$675	$615

Also available with Bartolini or EMG pickups.

Warwick, cont.

Grading	100%	98%	95%	90%	80%	70%	60%

FORTRESS — offset double cutaway swamp maple body, bolt-on 3 piece wenge neck, 24 fret wenge fingerboard, 2 per side tuners, chrome hardware, P-style/J-style MEC pickup, volume/treble/bass/balance control. Available in Black Stain, Blue Stain, Red Stain and White finish. Curr. mfr.

Mfr.'s Sug. Retail	$1,200	$840	$720	$600	$480	$430	$395	$360

STREAMER — offset double cutaway contoured ash body, bolt-on cherry neck, 24 fret maple fingerboard with pearl dot inlay, 2 per side tuners, chrome hardware, P-style/J-style MEC pickups, 2 volume/2 tone controls. Available in Natural finish. Curr. mfr.

Mfr.'s Sug. Retail	$2,100	$1,475	$1,260	$1,050	$840	$755	$690	$630

Add $500 for 5 string version of this model, available with 2 J-style pickups.

Streamer Stage I — offset double cutaway contoured flame maple body, thru body 5 piece maple/wenge neck, 24 fret wenge fingerboard with pearl dot inlay, 2 per side tuners, gold hardware, P-style/J-style MEC pickups, volume/treble/bass/balance control, active electronics, push/pull electronics switch in volume control. Available in Natural finish. Curr. mfr.

Mfr.'s Sug. Retail	$2,650	$1,855	$1,590	$1,325	$1,060	$955	$875	$795

Available with fretless fingerboard at no additional cost.

Streamer Stage I-V — similar to Streamer Stage I, except has 5 strings, 7 piece maple/wenge neck, 3/2 per side tuners, 2 humbucker Bartolini pickups.

Mfr.'s Sug. Retail	$3,700	$2,590	$2,220	$1,850	$1,480	$1,330	$1,220	$1,110

Streamer Stage I-VI — similar to Streamer Stage I, except has 6 strings, 7 piece maple/wenge neck, 3 per side tuners, 2 humbucker Bartolini pickups.

Mfr.'s Sug. Retail	$4,600	$3,220	$2,760	$2,300	$1,840	$1,655	$1,520	$1,380

STREAMER STAGE II — offset double cutaway contoured afzelia body, half thru 7 piece wenge/afzelia neck, 24 fret ebony fingerboard with pearl/abalone Tao inlay, abalone W peghead inlay, 2 per side tuners, gold hardware, 2 J-style MEC pickups, volume/concentric treble-bass/mid/balance control, active electronics, push/pull electronics switch in volume control. Available in Natural finish. Curr. mfr.

Mfr.'s Sug. Retail	$3,100	$2,170	$1,860	$1,550	$1,240	$1,115	$1,025	$930

Add $300 for 5 string version of this model.
Also available with Bartolini or EMG pickups.

Grading	100%	98%	95%	90%	80%	70%	60%

THUMB BASS — offset double cutaway asymmetrical contoured bubinga body, half thru body 7 piece wenge/bubinga neck, 24 fret wenge fingerboard, 2 per side tuners, black hardware, 2 J-style MEC pickups, volume/concentric treble-bass/ concentric mid-balance control, active electronics. Available in Natural finish. Curr. mfr.

Mfr.'s Sug. Retail	$2,900	$2,030	$1,740	$1,450	$1,160	$1,040	$955	$870

This model is available with fretless fingerboard at no additional cost.

Thumb Bass 5 — similar to Thumb Bass, except has 5 strings, 3/2 per side tuners.

Mfr.'s Sug. Retail	$3,300	$2,310	$1,980	$1,650	$1,320	$1,190	$1,090	$990

Thumb Bass 6 — similar to Thumb Bass, except has 6 strings, 3 per side tuners, 2 humbucker Bartolini pickups.

Mfr.'s Sug. Retail	$4,050	$2,835	$2,430	$2,025	$1,620	$1,460	$1,335	$1,215

WASHBURN

Trademark established 1864 with current manufacture in both the U.S. and overseas. Distributed by Washburn International, located in Vernon Hills, IL.

Washburn began as the distribution house for Lyon & Healy instruments. Lyon and Healy was a large manfacturer at the turn of the century (100,000 instruments annually) located in Chicago and was named after George Washburn Lyon and P.J. Healy. It was originally started in 1864 by Oliver Ditson. The Chicago plant was virtually destroyed by fire circa 1920 and many of their instruments thereafter were built by other companies. The Washburn name was picked up by the Tonk Brothers Co. in 1929 and was eventually purchased by an importer of Asian-built instruments during the 1970's. A new line of instruments was introduced in 1993 that are hand-built in Chicago, IL, U.S.A., bringing the Washburn trademark back to the United States.

ACOUSTIC

Classic Guitar Series

C40 CADIZ — classical style, spruce top, round soundhole, 3 stripe bound body, wooden inlay rosette, mahogany back/sides/neck, 12/19 fret rosewood fingerboard, rosewood bridge, 3 per side nylon head chrome tuners. Available in Natural finish. Curr. mfr.

Mfr.'s Sug. Retail	$260	$180	$155	$130	$100	$90	$80	$75

C60 Zarazoga — similar to C40, except has rosewood back/sides, rosewood veneer on peghead, gold tuners.

Mfr.'s Sug. Retail	$370	$260	$220	$185	$150	$135	$120	$110

Grading	100%	98%	95%	90%	80%	70%	60%

C80S Madrid — similar to C40, except has solid spruce top, rosewood back/sides, rosewood veneer on peghead, gold tuners.

Mfr.'s Sug. Retail	$460	$320	$275	$230	$185	$165	$150	$140

C84CE — similar to C40, except has single rounded cutaway, solid spruce top, rosewood back/sides, rosewood veneer on peghead, gold tuners, EQUIS II preamp system.

Mfr.'s Sug. Retail	$730	$510	$440	$365	$290	$260	$240	$220

C100SW VALENCIA — classical style, solid cedar top, round soundhole, 3 stripe bound body, wooden inlay rosette, rosewood back/sides, mahogany neck, 12/19 fret ebony fingerboard, jacaranda bridge with bone saddle, rosewood veneer on peghead, 3 per side pearl head gold tuners. Available in Natural finish. Disc. 1991.

	$1,050	$900	$750	$600	$540	$495	$450

Last Mfr.'s Sug. Retail was $1,500.

C200SW Sevilla — similar to C100SW, except has ebony reinforcement in the neck.

	$1,330	$1,140	$950	$760	$685	$625	$570

Last Mfr.'s Sug. Retail was $1,900.

Steel String Guitar Series

D10 — dreadnought style, spruce top, round soundhole, black pickguard, 3 stripe bound body and rosette, mahogany back/sides/neck, 14/20 fret rosewood fingerboard with pearl dot inlay, rosewood bridge with pearl dot black pins, 3 per side chrome die cast tuners. Available in Natural and Mahogany finishes. Curr. mfr.

Mfr.'s Sug. Retail	$260	$180	$155	$130	$100	$90	$80	$75

D10CE — similar to D10, except has EQ300 preamp system.

Mfr.'s Sug. Retail	$440	$310	$265	$220	$175	$160	$145	$135

D12 — similar to D10, except available in Natural, Brown, Black and White finishes.

Mfr.'s Sug. Retail	$340	$235	$200	$170	$135	$125	$115	$105

Add $30 for Woodstone Brown and Woodstone Blue finish.
Add $40 for left handed version of this model (D12LH).
Black finish comes with pearl dot white pins.

D1212 — similar to D12, except has 12 strings. Available in Natural and Tobacco Sunburst finish.

Mfr.'s Sug. Retail	$390	$275	$235	$195	$155	$140	$125	$115

D12CE — similar to D12, except has single rounded cutaway, pearl W inlay at 12th fret, EQUIS II preamp system. Available in Natural, Black, White, Tobacco Sunburst and Woodstone Brown finish.

Mfr.'s Sug. Retail	$630	$440	$380	$315	$250	$225	$205	$190

Grading	100%	98%	95%	90%	80%	70%	60%

D1212CE — similar to D1212, except has single rounded cutaway, EQUIS II preamp system. Available in Natural and Tobacco Sunburst finish.

Mfr.'s Sug. Retail	$680	$475	$405	$340	$270	$245	$225	$205

D13 — dreadnought style, spruce top, round soundhole, black pickguard, 3 stripe bound body and rosette, ovankol back/sides, mahogany neck, 14/20 fret rosewood fingerboard with pearl dot inlay, rosewood bridge with pearl dot F white pins, 3 per side chrome die cast tuners. Available in Natural finish. Curr. mfr.

Mfr.'s Sug. Retail	$380	$265	$225	$190	$150	$135	$120	$110

D1312 — similar to D13, except has 12 strings.

Mfr.'s Sug. Retail	$430	$300	$260	$215	$175	$155	$140	$130

D14 — dreadnought style, spruce top, round soundhole, tortoise shell pickguard, 3 stripe bound body and rosette, rosewood back/sides, mahogany neck, 14/20 fret rosewood fingerboard with pearl dot inlay, rosewood bridge with pearl dot white pins, 3 per side chrome die cast tuners. Available in Natural and Tobacco finish. Disc. 1992.

		$245	$210	$175	$140	$125	$115	$105

Add $35 for left handed version of this model (D14LH).
Last Mfr.'s Sug. Retail was $350.

D17SCE — single rounded cutaway dreadnought style, solid spruce top, round soundhole, black pickguard, 3 stripe bound body/rosette, mahogany back/sides/neck, 20 fret bound rosewood fingerboard with pearl diamond inlay, stylized W inlay at 12th fret, rosewood bridge with black white dot pins, pearl diamond inlay on bridge wings, bound peghead, 3 per side gold tuners with pearl buttons, EQUIS II preamp system, 1/4 and XLR output jack. Available in Black and Natural finish. Curr. mfr.

Mfr.'s Sug. Retail	$790	$555	$475	$395	$315	$280	$260	$235

Add $50 for 12 string version of this model (D17SCE12). **Available in Natural finish only.**

D17CE — similar to D17SCE, except has flamed sycamore top/back/sides.

Mfr.'s Sug. Retail	$830	$580	$500	$415	$330	$300	$275	$250

Add $50 for 12 string version of this model (D17CE12).

D20S — dreadnought style, solid spruce top, round soundhole, tortoise shell pickguard, 3 stripe bound body and rosette, flame maple back/sides, mahogany neck, 14/20 fret rosewood fingerboard with pearl diamond/12th fret W inlay, rosewood bridge with pearl dot white pins, rosewood veneer on peghead, 3 per side chrome die cast tuners. Available in Natural finish. Curr. mfr.

Mfr.'s Sug. Retail	$530	$370	$320	$265	$210	$190	$175	$160

D21S — similar to D20S, except has rosewood back/sides, gold tuners. Available in Natural and Tobacco Sunburst finish.

Mfr.'s Sug. Retail	$560	$390	$335	$280	$225	$205	$190	$170

Grading	100%	98%	95%	90%	80%	70%	60%

D21SE — similar to D21S, except has EQUIS II preamp system. Available in Natural finish. Disc. 1992.

	$400	$340	$285	$230	$205	$190	$170

Last Mfr.'s Sug. Retail was $570.

D21SLH — similar to D21S, except is left handed. Available in Natural finish. Disc. 1992.

	$350	$300	$250	$200	$180	$165	$150

Last Mfr.'s Sug. Retail was $510.

D25S — jumbo style, solid spruce top, round soundhole, tortoise shell pickguard, 3 stripe bound body and rosette, ovankol back/sides, 5 piece mahogany/rosewood neck, 14/20 fret rosewood fingerboard with pearl diamond/12th fret W inlay, rosewood bridge with pearl dot white pins, 3 per side gold die cast tuners. Available in Natural finish. Curr. mfr.

Mfr.'s Sug. Retail	$550	$385	$330	$275	$220	$200	$180	$165

D25S12 — similar to D25S, except has 12 strings. Disc. 1992.

	$350	$300	$250	$200	$180	$165	$150

Last Mfr.'s Sug. Retail was $500.

D28S — dreadnought style, solid spruce top, round soundhole, black pickguard, 3 stripe bound body and rosette, 3 piece rosewood back/sides, mahogany neck, 14/20 fret bound rosewood fingerboard with snowflake inlay, rosewood bridge with pearl dot white pins, bound peghead, 3 per side gold die cast tuners. Available in Natural finish. Curr. mfr.

Mfr.'s Sug. Retail	$600	$420	$360	$300	$240	$215	$195	$180

D28SLH — similar to D28S, except is left handed. Disc. 1992.

	$405	$350	$290	$230	$205	$190	$175

Last Mfr.'s Sug. Retail was $580.

D28S12 — similar to D28S, except has 12 strings.

Mfr.'s Sug. Retail	$650	$455	$390	$325	$260	$235	$215	$195

D2812LH — similar to D28S, except is left handed, has 12 strings. Disc. 1992.

	$435	$370	$310	$250	$225	$205	$190

Last Mfr.'s Sug. Retail was $620.

D29S — dreadnought style, solid cedar top, round soundhole, tortoise shell pickguard, 3 stripe bound body and rosette, rosewood back/sides, 5 piece mahogany/rosewood neck, 14/20 fret rosewood fingerboard with diamond/12th fret W inlay, rosewood bridge with pearl dot white pins, 3 per side gold die cast tuners. Available in Natural finish. Curr. mfr.

Mfr.'s Sug. Retail	$550	$385	$330	$275	$220	$200	$180	$165

Grading	100%	98%	95%	90%	80%	70%	60%

D30S — jumbo style, solid cedar top, round soundhole, tortoise shell pickguard, 3 stripe bound body, 5 stripe rosette, birdseye maple back/sides, mahogany neck, 14/20 fret rosewood fingerboard with pearl dot inlay, rosewood bridge with pearl dot white pins and bone saddle, birdseye maple veneer on peghead, 3 per side chrome die cast tuners. Available in Natural finish. Curr. mfr.

Mfr.'s Sug. Retail	$750	$525	$450	$375	$300	$270	$245	$225

D32S — similar to D30S, except has Makassar back/sides, bound fingerboard/peghead, Makassar veneer on peghead.

Mfr.'s Sug. Retail	$800	$560	$480	$400	$320	$290	$265	$240

D32S12 — similar to D32S, except has 12 strings. Disc. 1992.

	$545	$470	$390	$315	$280	$260	$235

Last Mfr.'s Sug. Retail was $780.

D61SW PRAIRIE SONG — dreadnought style, solid spruce top, round soundhole, rosewood pickguard, 3 stripe bound body, 5 stripe rosette, rosewood back/sides, mahogany neck, 14/20 fret rosewood fingerboard with pearl dot inlay, rosewood bridge with pearl dot black pins, rosewood veneer on peghead, 3 per side chrome die cast tuners. Available in Natural finish. Curr. mfr.

Mfr.'s Sug. Retail	$1,000	$700	$600	$500	$400	$360	$330	$300

Add $250 for EQUIS II preamp system.

D61SW12 — similar to D61SW, except has 12 strings. Disc. 1992.

	$660	$565	$470	$375	$340	$310	$280

Last Mfr.'s Sug. Retail was $940.

D68SW HARVEST — dreadnought style, solid spruce top, round soundhole, rosewood pickguard, maple/rosewood binding and rosette, rosewood back/sides, 5 piece mahogany/rosewood neck, 14/20 fret rosewood fingerboard with pearl dot inlay, ebony bridge with pearl dot black pins, rosewood veneered maple bound peghead with abalone Washburn inlay, 3 per side pearloid head chrome die cast tuners. Available in Natural finish. Curr. mfr.

Mfr.'s Sug. Retail	$1,500	$1,050	$900	$750	$600	$540	$495	$450

Add $250 for EQUIS II preamp system.

D70SW HARVEST DELUXE — dreadnought style, solid spruce top, round sound-hole, rosewood pickguard, maple/rosewood bound body, abalone inlay rosette, 3 piece rosewood back/sides, 5 piece mahogany/rosewood neck, 14/20 fret ebony fingerboard with abalone eye inlay, ebony bridge with abalone box inlay and pearl dot black pins, rosewood veneered maple bound peghead with abalone Washburn inlay, 3 per side pearloid head chrome die cast tuners. Available in Natural finish. Mfd. 1990 to date.

Mfr.'s Sug. Retail	$2,000	$1,400	$1,200	$1,000	$800	$720	$660	$600

Add $250 for EQUIS II preamp system.

Grading	100%	98%	95%	90%	80%	70%	60%

D90SW GOLDEN HARVEST — similar to D70SW, except has abalone bound body, tree of life abalone inlay on fingerboard, unbound peghead and pearloid head gold die cast tuners.

Mfr.'s Sug. Retail	$4,000	$2,800	$2,400	$2,000	$1,600	$1,440	$1,320	$1,200

Stephen's Extended Cutaway Series

This series has a patented neck to body joint that allows full access to all 24 frets and is called the patented Stephen's Extended Cutaway, designed by Stephen Davies.

DC60 LEXINGTON — single rounded cutaway dreadnought style, solid spruce top, oval soundhole, 3 stripe bound body and rosette, ovankol back/sides, mahogany neck, 24 fret bound rosewood fingerboard with pearl dot inlay, rosewood bridge with black dot pins, 3 per side pearloid chrome die cast tuners. Available in Natural finish. Disc. 1992.

	$580	$500	$415	$330	$300	$275	$250

Last Mfr.'s Sug. Retail was $830.

❉ **DC60E** — similar to DC60, except has the EQUIS II preamp system. Curr. mfr.

Mfr.'s Sug. Retail	$1,400	$980	$840	$700	$560	$505	$460	$420

DC80 CHARLESTON — single rounded cutaway dreadnought style, solid cedar top, oval soundhole, 3 stripe bound body and rosette, rosewood back/sides, mahogany neck, 24 fret bound rosewood fingerboard with diamond inlay, rosewood bridge with pearl dot white pins, rosewood veneer on bound peghead, 3 per side pearloid head gold die cast tuners. Available in Natural finish. Disc. 1992.

	$630	$540	$450	$360	$325	$300	$275

Last Mfr.'s Sug. Retail was $900.

❉ **DC80E** — similar to DC80, except has EQUIS II preamp system. Curr. mfr.

Mfr.'s Sug. Retail	$1,500	$1,050	$900	$750	$600	$540	$495	$450

J20S — jumbo style, solid cedar top, oval soundhole, bound body, 5 stripe rosette, walnut back/sides, mahogany neck, 21 fret rosewood fingerboard with pearl snowflake inlay at 12th fret, rosewood bridge with pearl dot white pins and bone saddle, walnut veneer on peghead, 3 per side chrome die cast tuners. Available in Natural finish. Curr. mfr.

Mfr.'s Sug. Retail	$900	$630	$540	$450	$360	$325	$300	$275

J50S — jumbo style, solid spruce top, oval soundhole, bound body, 5 stripe rosette, birds eye maple back/sides, mahogany neck, 21 fret bound rosewood fingerboard with pearl snowflake inlay at the 12th fret, rosewood bridge with pearl dot white pins and bone saddle, birds eye maple veneer on bound peghead, 3 per side pearl button gold die cast tuners. Available in Natural finish. Curr. mfr.

Mfr.'s Sug. Retail	$1,150	$805	$690	$575	$460	$415	$380	$345

Add $250 for EQUIS II preamp system.

Grading	100%	98%	95%	90%	80%	70%	60%

ACOUSTIC BASS

AB20 — single sharp cutaway dreadnought style, spruce top, diagonal sound channels, bound body, mahogany back/sides, maple neck, 23 fret rosewood fingerboard with pearl dot inlay, rosewood bridge with brass insert, 2 per side tuners, chrome hardware, EQUIS II bass preamp system. Available in Black, Natural and Tobacco Sunburst finish. Curr. mfr.

	100%	98%	95%	90%	80%	70%	60%
Mfr.'s Sug. Retail	$900	$630	$540	$450	$360	$325	$300	$275

This model is also available with hardwood top/back/sides and fretless.

AB25 — similar to AB20, except has 5 strings. Available in Black and Tobacco Sunburst finish.

	100%	98%	95%	90%	80%	70%	60%
Mfr.'s Sug. Retail	$1,000	$700	$600	$500	$400	$360	$330	$300

AB40 — single rounded cutaway jumbo style, arched spruce top, diagonal sound channels, bound body, quilted ash back/sides, multi layer maple neck, 24 fret bound ebony fingerboard with pearl dot inlay, ebonized rosewood bridge with brass insert, bound peghead with pearl Washburn logo and stylized inlay, 2 per side tuners, gold hardware, active electronics, 1 volume/2 tone controls, EQUIS II bass preamp system. Available in Natural and Tobacco Sunburst finish. Curr. mfr.

	100%	98%	95%	90%	80%	70%	60%
Mfr.'s Sug. Retail	$2,250	$1,575	$1,345	$1,125	$900	$810	$740	$675

Subtract $150 for fretless fingerboard (AB40FL).

AB42 — similar to AB40, except has humbucker pickup. Available in Tobacco Sunburst. Curr. mfr.

	100%	98%	95%	90%	80%	70%	60%
Mfr.'s Sug. Retail	$2,500	$1,750	$1,500	$1,250	$1,000	$900	$825	$750

AB45 — similar to AB40, except has 5 strings, 3/2 per side tuners. Available in Tobacco Sunburst finish. Disc. 1991.

	98%	95%	90%	80%	70%	60%
	$1,610	$1,380	$1,150	$920	$830	$760	$690

Last Mfr.'s Sug. Retail was $2,300.

ACOUSTIC ELECTRIC

Festival Series

EA20 NEWPORT — single sharp cutaway parlor style, mahogany top, oval soundhole, bound body, 3 stripe rosette, mahogany back/sides/neck, 21 fret rosewood fingerboard with pearl dot inlay, rosewood bridge with pearl dot white pins, 3 per side chrome die cast tuners, EQUIS II preamp system. Available in Black, White and Tobacco Sunburst finish. Curr. mfr.

	100%	98%	95%	90%	80%	70%	60%
Mfr.'s Sug. Retail	$850	$595	$510	$425	$340	$305	$280	$255

Add $50 for 12 string version of this model (EA2012). Available in Black and Natural finish.

The White finish model has pearl dot black pins.

Grading	100%	98%	95%	90%	80%	70%	60%

EA30 MONTEREY — single sharp cutaway dreadnought style, spruce top, oval soundhole, 3 stripe bound body, 5 stripe rosette, flame maple back/sides, mahogany neck, 21 fret rosewood fingerboard, rosewood bridge with pearl dot white pins, 3 per side chrome die cast tuners, EQUIS II preamp system. Available in Natural, Transparent Red, Transparent Blue and Transparent Black finish. Disc. 1992.

	$510	$440	$365	$290	$260	$240	$220

Add $100 for left handed version of this model (EA30LH).
Add $40 for 12 string version of this model (EA3012). Available in Natural finish.
Last Mfr.'s Sug. Retail was $730.

EA36 MARQUEE (formerly EA46) — single cutaway dreadnought style, figured maple top, 3 stripe bound body, diagonal sound channels, figured maple back/sides, mahogany neck, 23 fret rosewood bound fingerboard with pearl diamond inlay, rosewood bridge with pearl dot black pins, flame maple veneer on bound peghead, 3 per side pearl button gold die cast tuners, EQUIS II preamp system. Available in Natural and Tobacco Sunburst finish. Curr. mfr.

Mfr.'s Sug. Retail	$1,000	$700	$600	$500	$400	$360	$330	$300

Add $50 for 12 string version of this model (EA3612).

EA40 WOODSTOCK — single sharp cutaway dreadnought style, arched spruce top, oval soundhole, abalone bound body and rosette, mahogany back/sides/neck, 21 fret bound rosewood fingerboard, rosewood bridge with pearl dot black pins, 3 per side chrome die cast tuners, EQUIS II preamp system. Available in Black and White finish. Disc. 1992.

	$770	$660	$550	$440	$395	$365	$330

Add $40 for string version of this model (EA4012). Disc. 1992
Also available with birdseye maple back/sides. Available in Natural finish.
Last Mfr.'s Sug. Retail was $1,100.

EA44 — single sharp cutaway dreadnought style, solid cedar top, oval soundhole, 3 stripe bound body/rosette, rosewood back/sides, mahogany neck, 20 fret bound rosewood fingerboard with pearl diamond inlay, rosewood bridge with white black pins, bound peghead with rosewood veneer, 3 per side chrome tuners with pearl buttons. Available in Black, Natural and Tobacco Sunburst finish. Curr. mfr.

Mfr.'s Sug. Retail	$1,100	$770	$660	$550	$440	$395	$365	$330

EA45 — similar to EA44, except has a deeper body. Available in Natural and Tobacco Sunburst finish. Curr. mfr.

Mfr.'s Sug. Retail	$1,150	$805	$690	$575	$460	$415	$380	$345

Grading	100%	98%	95%	90%	80%	70%	60%

EC41 TANGLEWOOD — classical style, spruce top, oval soundhole, 5 stripe bound body/rosette, ovankol back/sides, mahogany neck, 21 fret bound rosewood fingerboard with pearl dot inlay, rosewood bridge, ovankol veneer on bound peghead, 3 per side pearl button gold tuners, EQUIS II preamp system. Available in Natural finish. Disc 1992.

	$490	$420	$350	$280	$250	$230	$210

Last Mfr.'s Sug. Retail was $700.

Solid Body Series

This series has solid bodies with the soundhole area routed out for a resonance cavity.

SBC20 — single rounded cutaway classical style, spruce top, round soundhole, bound body, wooden inlay rosette, mahogany body/neck, 22 fret rosewood fingerboard with pearl dot inlay, rosewood bridge, 3 per side chrome die cast tuners, Sensor pickups, volume/tone control. Available in Natural finish. Disc. 1992.

	$385	$330	$275	$220	$200	$180	$165

Last Mfr.'s Sug. Retail was $550.

SBF24 — similar to SBC20, except has dreadnought style, pearl dot white pins and active electronics. Available in Natural, Pearl White and Black finish. Disc. 1992.

	$400	$340	$285	$230	$205	$190	$170

Last Mfr.'s Sug. Retail was $570.

ELECTRIC

Classic Series

HB35 — double cutaway semi hollow style, arched maple top/back/sides, bound body and F holes, raised black pickguard, 20 fret bound rosewood fingerboard with pearl split rectangle inlay, tunomatic bridge/stop tailpiece, bound peghead with pearl Washburn logo and stylized inlay, 3 per side tuners, gold hardware, 2 humbucker Washburn pickups, 2 volume/tone controls, 3 position switch. Available in Natural, Tobacco Sunburst and Wine Red finish. Curr. mfr.

Mfr.'s Sug. Retail	$800	$560	$480	$400	$320	$290	$265	$240

J6 — single cutaway hollow style, arched maple top/back/sides, bound body and F holes, raised black pickguard, 5 piece maple/rosewood neck, 20 fret bound rosewood fingerboard with split rectangle abalone inlay, ebony bridge, trapeze tailpiece, bound peghead with abalone Washburn logo and stylized inlay, 3 per side tuners, gold hardware, 2 humbucker pickups, 2 volume/tone controls, 3 position switch. Available in Natural and Tobacco Sunburst finish. Curr. mfr.

Mfr.'s Sug. Retail	$900	$630	$540	$450	$360	$325	$300	$275

Grading	100%	98%	95%	90%	80%	70%	60%

J10 — single cutaway hollow style, arched solid spruce top, bound body and F holes, raised bound tortoise shell pickguard, flame maple back/sides, multi layer maple neck, 20 fret bound ebony fingerboard with pearl/abalone split rectangle inlay, ebony bridge, trapeze tailpiece, bound peghead with abalone Washburn logo and stylized inlay, 3 per side pearl button tuners, gold hardware, 2 humbucker pickups, 2 volume/tone controls, 3 position switch. Available in Natural and Tobacco Sunburst finish. Disc. 1992.

	$1,260	$1,080	$900	$720	$650	$595	$540

Last Mfr.'s Sug. Retail was $1,800.

WP50 — Les Paul style, carved bound flame maple top, mahogany body/neck, raised white pickguard, 22 fret bound rosewood fingerboard with pearl trapezoid inlay, tunomatic bridge/stop tailpiece, 3 per side pearl button tuners, chrome hardware, 2 humbucker Washburn pickups, 2 volume/tone controls, 3 position switch. Available in Cherry Sunburst and Tobacco Sunburst finish. Disc. 1992.

	$420	$360	$300	$240	$215	$195	$180

Last Mfr.'s Sug. Retail was $600.

WP80 — similar to WP50, except has carved maple top, black raised pickguard, ebonized fingerboard and gold hardware. Available in Black and White finish. Disc. 1992.

	$475	$405	$340	$270	$245	$225	$205

Last Mfr.'s Sug. Retail was $680.

KC Series

This series was discontinued in 1991.

KC20 — strat style hardwood body, arched top and back, scalloped cutaways, bolt-on maple neck, 22 fret rosewood fingerboard with pearl dot inlay, standard vibrato, 6 on one side tuners, chrome hardware, 2 single coil/1 humbucker Washburn pickups, volume/tone control, 5 position switch. Available in Black and White finish.

	$245	$210	$175	$140	$125	$115	$105

Add $50 for left handed version of this model (KC20LH).
Last Mfr.'s Sug. Retail was $350.

KC40 — similar to KC20, except has solid alder body and double locking vibrato. Available in Black and White finish.

	$330	$280	$235	$190	$170	$155	$140

Add $70 for left handed version of this model (KC40LH).
Last Mfr.'s Sug. Retail was $470.

KC42 — similar to KC40, except has reverse headstock. Available in Black, Woodstone Fluorescent Red and Woodstone Fluorescent Yellow finish.

	$350	$300	$250	$200	$180	$165	$150

Last Mfr.'s Sug. Retail was $500.

Grading	100%	98%	95%	90%	80%	70%	60%

KC44 — similar to KC40, except has humbucker/single coil/humbucker Washburn pickups. Available in Black Rain and White Rain finish.

| | $350 | $300 | $250 | $200 | $180 | $165 | $150 |

Last Mfr.'s Sug. Retail was $500.

KC70 — similar to KC40, except has black hardware, 3 individual pickup selector and coil tap switches. Available in Black, Metallic Black Cherry, White Rain, Woodstone Brown, Woodstone Red and Woodstone Silver finish.

| | $455 | $390 | $325 | $260 | $235 | $215 | $195 |

Add $100 for left handed version of this model (KC70LH).
Last Mfr.'s Sug. Retail was $650.

KC90 — strat style alder body, arched top and back, scalloped cutaways, bolt-on maple neck, 24 fret rosewood fingerboard with pearl dot inlay, double locking vibrato, 6 on one side tuners, black hardware, 2 Seymour Duncan single coil/1 humbucker pickups, 5 position and coil tap switches. Available in Black, Blond, Metallic Red, Natural Gold, Transparent Red and White.

| | $680 | $580 | $485 | $390 | $355 | $325 | $295 |

Last Mfr.'s Sug. Retail was $970.

Mercury Series

MG30 — strat style hardwood body, bolt-on maple neck, 24 fret rosewood fingerboard with offset pearl dot inlay, double locking vibrato, 6 on one side tuners, chrome hardware, 2 single coil/1 humbucker Washburn pickups, volume/tone control, 5 position switch with coil tap. Available in Metallic Red, Pacific Blue Rain and Tobacco Sunburst finish. Curr. mfr.

| Mfr.'s Sug. Retail | $480 | $335 | $290 | $240 | $190 | $170 | $155 | $145 |

MG34 — similar to MG30, except has maple fingerboard with black offset dot inlay, humbucker/single coil/humbucker pickups. Available in Black, Metallic Dark Blue and Purple Rain finish. Curr. mfr.

| Mfr.'s Sug. Retail | $500 | $350 | $300 | $250 | $200 | $180 | $165 | $150 |

MG40 — strat style alder body, white pickguard, bolt-on maple neck, 24 fret rosewood fingerboard with offset pearl dot inlay, double locking vibrato, 6 on one side tuners, black hardware, volume/tone control, 5 position switch with coil tap. Available in Black, Ice Pearl, Metallic Red and Pearl Blue finish. Curr. mfr.

| Mfr.'s Sug. Retail | $570 | $400 | $340 | $285 | $230 | $205 | $190 | $170 |

MG42 — similar to MG40, except has 2 humbucker pickups. Available in Metallic Purple and Midnight Blue Metallic finish.

| Mfr.'s Sug. Retail | $570 | $400 | $340 | $285 | $230 | $205 | $190 | $170 |

MG43 — similar to MG40, except has maple fingerboard with offset black dot inlay, 3 single coil pickups. Available in Black and Metallic Red finish.

| Mfr.'s Sug. Retail | $550 | $385 | $330 | $275 | $220 | $200 | $180 | $165 |

Grading	100%	98%	95%	90%	80%	70%	60%

MG44 — similar to MG40, except has maple fingerboard with offset black dot inlay, humbucker/single coil/humbucker pickups. Available in Black, Black Cherry Metallic, Metallic Red and Midnight Blue Metallic finish.

Mfr.'s Sug. Retail	$590	$410	$355	$295	$235	$210	$195	$180

MG52 — strat style hardwood body, white pickguard, bolt-on maple neck, 24 fret rosewood fingerboard with offset pearl dot inlay, tunomatic bridge/stop tailpiece, 6 on one side tuners, chrome hardware, 2 humbucker Washburn pickups, volume/tone control, 5 way switch with coil tap. Available in Metallic Dark Blue and Tobacco Sunburst finish. Curr. mfr.

Mfr.'s Sug. Retail	$430	$300	$260	$215	$175	$155	$140	$130

MG70 — strat style alder body, flamed maple top, transparent pickguard, bolt-on maple neck, 24 fret rosewood fingerboard with offset pearl dot inlay, double locking vibrato, 6 on one side tuners, gold hardware, volume/tone control, 5 position switch with coil tap. Available in Transparent Blue and Vintage Sunburst finish. Curr. mfr.

Mfr.'s Sug. Retail	$700	$490	$420	$350	$280	$250	$230	$210

MG72 — similar to MG70, except has 2 humbucker pickups. Available in Transparent Purple and Vintage Sunburst finish.

Mfr.'s Sug. Retail	$700	$490	$420	$350	$280	$250	$230	$210

MG74 — similar to MG70, except has maple fingerboard with offset black dot inlay, humbucker/single coil/humbucker pickups. Available in Transparent Purple and Vintage Sunburst finish.

Mfr.'s Sug. Retail	$720	$500	$430	$360	$290	$260	$240	$220

Signature Series

EC26 ATLANTIS — strat style basswood body, bolt-on maple neck, 26 fret rosewood fingerboard with pearl dot inlay, locking vibrato, 6 on one side locking tuners, chrome hardware, single coil/humbucker Seymour Duncan pickup, volume/tone control, 5 position switch. Available in Black, Red and White finish. Disc. 1991.

	$770	$660	$550	$440	$395	$365	$330

This model features the patented Stephen's Extended Cutaway.
Last Mfr.'s Sug. Retail was $1,100.

N2 — strat style alder body, bolt-on maple neck, 22 fret rosewood fingerboard with pearl dot inlay, double locking vibrato, reverse headstock, 6 on one side tuners, chrome hardware, 2 humbucker Washburn pickups, volume control, 3 position switch. Available in Natural and Padauk finish. Curr. mfr.

Mfr.'s Sug. Retail	$700	$490	$420	$350	$280	$250	$230	$210

This model was co-designed with Nuno Bettencourt.

Grading	100%	98%	95%	90%	80%	70%	60%

SB80 — double cutaway mahogany body, arched bound flame maple top, raised white pickguard, mahogany neck, 22 fret bound rosewood fingerboard with pearl stylized V inlay, tunomatic bridge/stop tailpiece, 3 per side tuners, chrome hardware, 2 humbucker Washburn pickups, 2 volume/2 tone controls, 3 position switch. Available in Natural and Vintage Sunburst finish. Curr. mfr.

Mfr.'s Sug. Retail	$800	$560	$480	$400	$320	$290	$265	$240

SS40 — strat style poplar body, bolt-on maple neck, 22 fret maple fingerboard with abalone inlay, double locking vibrato, 6 on one side tuners, gold hardware, 2 angled humbucker Washburn pickups, volume control, 5 position switch. Available in Black finish. Curr. mfr.

Mfr.'s Sug. Retail	$800	$560	$480	$400	$320	$290	$265	$240

This model was co-designed with Steve Stevens.

USA Custom Shop Series

All the instruments in this series are hand built in Chicago. They all feature Seymour Duncan and Bill Lawrence pickups.

Laredo Series

LT82 — tele style alder body, white pickguard, bolt-on maple neck, 22 fret maple fingerboard with black dot inlay, strings thru bridge, 6 on one side tuners, chrome hardware, 2 single coil pickups, volume/tone control, 3 position switch. Available in Black and Tobacco Sunburst finish. Curr. mfr.

Mfr.'s Sug. Retail	$800	$560	$480	$400	$320	$290	$265	$240

This model is available with rosewood fingerboard with pearl dot inlay.

LT92 — similar to LT82, except has ash body, pearloid pickguard. Available in Natural and Tobacco Sunburst finish.

Mfr.'s Sug. Retail	$1,000	$700	$600	$500	$400	$360	$330	$300

This model is available with rosewood fingerboard with pearl dot inlay.

Mercury Series

MG94 — strat style alder body, bolt-on maple neck, 24 fret maple fingerboard with offset black dot inlay, double locking vibrato, 6 on one side tuners, chrome hardware, humbucker/single coil/humbucker pickups, volume/tone control, 5 position switch. Available in Green Iridescent, Iridescent, Midnight Blue Metallic and 3 Tone Sunburst finish. Curr. mfr.

Mfr.'s Sug. Retail	$1,000	$700	$600	$500	$400	$360	$330	$300

This model is available with rosewood fingerboard with pearl dot inlay.

MG104 — similar to MG94, except has quilted maple top. Available in Transparent Red and Vintage Sunburst finish.

Mfr.'s Sug. Retail	$1,100	$770	$660	$550	$440	$395	$365	$330

Grading	100%	98%	95%	90%	80%	70%	60%

MG112 — similar to MG94, except has quilted maple top, rosewood fingerboard with offset pearl dot inlay, tunomatic bridge/stop tailpiece, graphite nut, 2 humbucker pickups. Available in Transparent Red and Vintage Sunburst finish.

Mfr.'s Sug. Retail	$1,000	$700	$600	$500	$400	$360	$330	$300

MG142 — strat style mahogany body, quilted maple top, bolt-on maple neck, 24 fret ebony fingerboard with offset pearl dot inlay, tunomatic bridge/stop tailpiece, graphite nut, 6 on one side tuners, chrome hardware, 2 humbucker pickups, volume/tone control, 5 position switch. Available in Transparent Red and Vintage Sunburst finish. Curr. mfr.

Mfr.'s Sug. Retail	$1,700	$1,190	$1,020	$850	$680	$610	$560	$510

MG154 — similar to MG142, except has double locking vibrato, humbucker/single coil/humbucker pickups.

Mfr.'s Sug. Retail	$1,800	$1,260	$1,080	$900	$720	$650	$595	$540

Nuno Bettencourt Series

This series was co-designed with Nuno Bettencourt and employs the patented Extended Stephen's Cutaway.

N4 — strat style alder body, bolt-on maple neck, 22 fret ebony fingerboard with pearl dot inlay, double locking vibrato, reverse peghead, 6 on one side tuners, chrome hardware, 2 humbucker pickups, volume control, 3 position switch. Available in Natural finish. Curr. mfr.

Mfr.'s Sug. Retail	$1,500	$1,050	$900	$750	$600	$540	$495	$450

Add $100 for padauk body.

Silverado Series

This series employs the patented Stephen's Extended Cutaway. They also have rosewood or maple fingerboards.

LT93 — strat style alder body, pearloid pickguard, bolt-on maple neck, 22 fret fingerboard with black dot inlay, standard vibrato, 6 on one side locking tuners, chrome hardware, 3 single coil pickups, volume/2 tone controls, 5 position switch. Available in Black and Tobacco Sunburst finish. Curr. mfr.

Mfr.'s Sug. Retail	$1,300	$910	$780	$650	$520	$470	$430	$390

LT103 — similar to LT93, except has flame maple or swamp ash body. Available in Natural and Tobacco Sunburst finish.

Mfr.'s Sug. Retail	$1,600	$1,120	$960	$800	$640	$575	$530	$480

Grading	100%	98%	95%	90%	80%	70%	60%

Steve Stevens Signature Series

This series was co-designed with Steve Stevens.

SS80 — strat style poplar body, bolt-on maple neck, 22 fret maple fingerboard with abalone dot inlay, double locking vibrato, 6 on one side tuners, gold hardware, 2 humbucker pickups, volume control, 3 position switch. Available in Black finish. Curr. mfr.

Mfr.'s Sug. Retail	$1,500	$1,050	$900	$750	$600	$540	$495	$450

SS100 — similar to SS80, except has black dot inlay, black hardware. Available in Vintage Frankenstein Graphic finish.

Mfr.'s Sug. Retail	$1,800	$1,260	$1,080	$900	$720	$650	$595	$540

Wings Series

SB50 — double cutaway mahogany body, black pickguard, mahogany neck, 22 fret rosewood fingerboard with pearl dot inlay, tunomatic bridge/stop tailpiece, 3 per side vintage Keystone tuners, chrome hardware, 2 single coil "soapbar" pickups, volume/2 tone controls, 3 position switch. Available in Ivory, Tobacco Sunburst and Wine Red finish. Curr. mfr.

Mfr.'s Sug. Retail	$900	$630	$540	$450	$360	$325	$300	$275

SB100 — similar to SB50, except has bound arched figured maple top, no pickguard, bound fingerboard with pearl stylized V inlay, 2 humbucker pickups. Available in Cherry Sunburst and Vintage Sunburst finish.

Mfr.'s Sug. Retail	$2,500	$1,750	$1,500	$1,250	$1,000	$900	$825	$750

ELECTRIC BASS

Axxess Series

XS2 — precision style hardwood body, maple neck, 24 fret rosewood fingerboard with pearl dot inlay, fixed bridge, 4 on one side tuners, chrome hardware, P-style Washburn pickup, push/pull volume/tone control. Available in Black, Red and White finish. Disc. 1992.

	$280	$240	$200	$160	$145	$130	$120

Add $20 for Pacific Blue Rain and Red Rain finish.
Last Mfr.'s Sug. Retail was $400.

Grading	100%	98%	95%	90%	80%	70%	60%

XS4 — precision style alder body, maple neck, 24 fret rosewood fingerboard with pearl dot inlay, fixed bridge, 4 on one side tuners, chrome hardware, P-style/J-style Washburn pickups, volume/treble/bass controls, active electronics. Available in Black and Red finish. Disc. 1992.

		$335	$290	$240	$190	$170	$155	$145

> **Add $70 for fretless version of this model (XS4FL).**
> Last Mfr.'s Sug. Retail was $480.

XS5 — similar to XS4, except has 5 strings, 4/1 tuners and 2 J-style Washburn pickups. Available in Black, Red and White finish.

		$405	$350	$290	$230	$205	$190	$175

> Last Mfr.'s Sug. Retail was $580.

XS6 — similar to XS4. Available in Metallic Cherry Black and Pearl White finish.

		$420	$360	$300	$240	$215	$195	$180

> Last Mfr.'s Sug. Retail was $600.

XS8 — similar to XS4, except black hardware, 2 single coil Status pickups and active 2 band EQ fader control. Available in Charcoal Rain, Black and White finish.

		$560	$480	$400	$320	$290	$265	$240

> Last Mfr.'s Sug. Retail was $800.

Classic Series

B200 — single cutaway alder body, bound carved maple top, 3 piece maple neck, 22 fret bound rosewood fingerboard with pearl dot inlay, fixed bridge, 2 per side tuners, chrome hardware, 2 Washburn pickups, 2 volume/2 tone controls. Available in Metallic Dark Blue finish. Curr. mfr.

Mfr.'s Sug. Retail		$750	$525	$450	$375	$300	$270	$245	$225

Mercury Series

MB2 — offset double cutaway hardwood body, bolt-on maple neck, 24 fret rosewood fingerboard with offset pearl dot inlay, fixed bridge, 4 on one side tuners, chrome hardware, P-style pickup, volume/tone control. Available in Black, Pacific Blue Rain and White finish. Curr. mfr.

Mfr.'s Sug. Retail		$470	$330	$280	$235	$190	$170	$155	$140

MB4 — offset double cutaway alder body, bolt-on maple neck, 24 fret rosewood fingerboard with offset pearl dot inlay, fixed bridge, 4 on one side tuners, chrome hardware, P-style/J-style Washburn pickups, volume/treble/bass controls, 3 position switch, active electronics. Available in Black, Black Cherry Metallic, Ice Pearl, Midnight Blue Metallic and Natural finish. Curr. mfr.

Mfr.'s Sug. Retail		$550	$385	$330	$275	$220	$200	$180	$165

> This model also available with maple fingerboard with black dot inlay.

Grading	100%	98%	95%	90%	80%	70%	60%

MB5 — similar to MB4, except has 5 strings, 4/1 per side tuners, 2 J-style pickups. Available in Black, Ice Pearl and Natural finish.

Mfr.'s Sug. Retail	$670	$470	$400	$335	$265	$240	$220	$200

MB6 — similar to MB4, except has 6 strings, 4/2 per side tuners, 2 J-style pickups. Available in Natural finish.

Mfr.'s Sug. Retail	$750	$525	$450	$375	$300	$270	$245	$225

MB8 — offset double cutaway alder body, flame maple top, bolt-on maple neck, 24 fret rosewood fingerboard with offset pearl dot inlay, fixed bridge, 4 on one side tuners, gold hardware, 2 humbucker active Status pickups, volume/treble/bass/mix controls, active electronics. Available in Tobacco Sunburst, Transparent Blue and Transparent Purple finish. Curr. mfr.

Mfr.'s Sug. Retail	$800	$560	$480	$400	$320	$290	$265	$240

This model also available with maple fingerboard with black dot inlay.

Status Series 1000

S60 — precision style one piece maple body/neck construction, walnut top/back laminates, 24 fret carbonite fingerboard, no headstock, tunable bridge, brass hardware, 2 single coil Status pickups, volume/tone control, active electronics with fader control. Available in Black and White finish. Disc. 1992.

			$700	$600	$500	$400	$360	$330	$300

Last Mfr.'s Sug. Retail was $1,000.

S70 — similar to S60. Available in Natural, Transparent Blue and Transparent Red finish. Curr. mfr.

Mfr.'s Sug. Retail	$1,200	$840	$720	$600	$480	$430	$395	$360

This model is also available with fretless fingerboard (S70FL).

WRC GUITARS

Manufactured and distributed by WRC Music International, Inc., located in Calimesa, CA, since 1990.

ELECTRIC

Neptune Series

This series, designed by Wayne Richard Charvel, uses Pacific seashells for finish.

Grading	100%	98%	95%	90%	80%	70%	60%

CUSTOM — strat style basswood body, bolt-on figured maple neck, 22 fret ebony fingerboard with pearl block inlay, fixed bridge, 3 per side Schaller tuners, chrome hardware, 3 single coil Seymour Duncan pickups, volume/tone control, 3 mini switches. Curr. mfr.

Mfr.'s Sug. Retail	$3,000	$2,095	$1,800	$1,500	$1,200	$1,080	$990	$900

This model is available with the following options: 24 fret maple or rosewood fingerboard with cloud or dolphin inlay; standard or double locking vibrato; black or gold hardware; humbucker, 2 humbucker, single coil/humbucker or 2 single coil/1 humbucker pickup configurations.

DELUXE — strat style basswood body, bolt-on figured maple neck, 24 fret maple fingerboard with pearl dot inlay, fixed bridge, 3 per side Schaller tuners, chrome hardware, humbucker Seymour Duncan pickup, volume/tone control. Curr. mfr.

Mfr.'s Sug. Retail	$2,400	$1,680	$1,440	$1,200	$960	$860	$790	$720

This model is available with the following options: ebony or rosewood fingerboard with abalone inlay; standard or double locking vibrato; black or gold hardware; 2 humbucker, single coil/humbucker, 2 single coil/1 humbucker or 3 single coil pickup configurations.

STANDARD — strat style alder body, bolt-on figured maple neck, 24 fret rosewood fingerboard with pearl dot inlay, double locking Kahler vibrato, 3 per side Grover tuners, chrome hardware, 2 humbucker Seymour Duncan pickups, volume/tone control, 2 mini switches. Curr. mfr.

Mfr.'s Sug. Retail	$2,000	$1,400	$1,200	$1,000	$800	$720	$660	$600

YAMAHA

Manufactured and distributed in Japan. U.S. distribution is by the Yamaha Corporation of America, located in Buena Park, CA.

The Yamaha Corporation was established over 100 years ago in Japan, and their first guitars were produced in the early 1960s. Original guitar manufacture focused on older vintage American designs. In 1971, production was moved from Japan to Taiwan, and to this date, most of the manufacture remains at the Taiwan location.

ACOUSTIC

Classic Series

Grading	100%	98%	95%	90%	80%	70%	60%

CG40A — classical style, spruce top, round soundhole, bound body, wooden inlay rosette, jelutong back/sides, nato neck, 12/19 fret sonokeling fingerboard/bridge, 3 per side chrome tuners. Available in Natural finish. Curr. mfr.

Mfr.'s Sug. Retail	$150	$105	$90	$75	$60	$55	$50	$45

CG100A — classical style, spruce top, round soundhole, bound body, wooden inlay rosette, nato back/sides/neck, 12/19 fret bubinga fingerboard, nato bridge, 3 per side chrome tuners. Available in Natural finish. Curr. mfr.

Mfr.'s Sug. Retail	$240	$170	$145	$120	$95	$85	$80	$75

CG110A — classical style, spruce top, round soundhole, bound body, wooden inlay rosette, nato back/sides/neck, 12/19 fret bubinga fingerboard, nato bridge, 3 per side chrome tuners. Available in Natural finish. Curr. mfr.

Mfr.'s Sug. Retail	$280	$195	$165	$140	$110	$100	$90	$80

CG120A — similar to 110A, except has different rosette, rosewood fingerboard and bridge.

Mfr.'s Sug. Retail	$310	$215	$185	$155	$125	$110	$100	$90

CG130A — similar to 120A, except has gold hardware.

Mfr.'s Sug. Retail	$340	$235	$200	$170	$135	$125	$115	$105

Grading	100%	98%	95%	90%	80%	70%	60%

CG150SA — classical style, solid spruce top, round soundhole, bound body, wooden inlay rosette, ovankol back/sides, nato neck, 12/19 fret rosewood fingerboard, rosewood bridge, rosewood veneer on peghead, 3 per side gold tuners. Available in Natural finish. Curr. mfr.

Mfr.'s Sug. Retail	$390	$275	$235	$195	$155	$140	$125	$115

This model is also available with solid cedar top (CG150CA).

CG170SA — classical style, solid spruce top, round soundhole, wooden inlay bound body and rosette, rosewood back/sides, nato neck, 12/19 fret rosewood fingerboard, rosewood bridge, rosewood veneer on peghead, 3 per side gold tuners. Available in Natural finish. Curr. mfr.

Mfr.'s Sug. Retail	$520	$365	$310	$260	$210	$190	$170	$160

This model is also available with solid cedar top (CG170CA).

CG180SA — similar to 170SA, except has different binding and rosette and ebony fingerboard.

Mfr.'s Sug. Retail	$630	$440	$380	$315	$250	$225	$205	$190

CS100A — small body classical style, spruce top, round soundhole, bound body, wooden inlay rosette, nato back/sides/neck, 12/19 fret bubinga fingerboard, nato bridge, 3 per side chrome tuners with plastic buttons. Available in Natural finish. Curr. mfr.

Mfr.'s Sug. Retail	$270	$190	$160	$135	$110	$100	$90	$80

FG Series

FG300A — dreadnought style, spruce top, round soundhole, bound body, 3 stripe rosette, black pickguard, jelutong back/sides, nato neck, 14/20 fret sonokeling fingerboard with pearl dot inlay, sonokeling bridge with white pins, 3 per side chrome tuners with plastic buttons. Available in Natural finish. Curr. mfr.

Mfr.'s Sug. Retail	$200	$140	$120	$100	$80	$70	$65	$60

FG400A — dreadnought style, spruce top, round soundhole, bound body, 3 stripe rosette, black pickguard, nato back/sides/neck, 14/20 fret bubinga fingerboard with pearl dot inlay, nato bridge with white pins, 3 per side chrome tuners with plastic buttons. Available in Natural finish. Curr. mfr.

Mfr.'s Sug. Retail	$260	$180	$155	$130	$100	$90	$80	$75

FG410A — similar to 400A, except has 5 stripe rosette and white pearl dot pins in bridge.

Mfr.'s Sug. Retail	$330	$230	$195	$165	$130	$120	$110	$100

Add $30 for 12-string version of this model (FG410-12A).

FG410EA — similar to 410A, except has piezo pickups and volume/2 tone controls.

Mfr.'s Sug. Retail	$520	$365	$310	$260	$210	$190	$170	$160

Grading	100%	98%	95%	90%	80%	70%	60%

FG420A — dreadnought style, spruce top, round soundhole, black pickguard, 3 stripe bound body, abalone rosette, nato back/sides/neck, 14/20 fret bound bubinga fingerboard with pearl dot inlay, rosewood bridge with white pearl dot pins, 3 per side chrome tuners. Available in Natural finish. Curr. mfr.

Mfr.'s Sug. Retail	$380	$265	$225	$190	$150	$135	$120	$110

Add $40 for 12-string version of this model (FG420-12A).

This model is also available in left-handed version (FG420-LA).

⅄ **FG420E-12A** — similar to FG420A, except has 12 strings, piezo electric pickups and volume/2 tone controls.

Mfr.'s Sug. Retail	$530	$370	$320	$265	$210	$190	$175	$160

FG430A — similar to 420A, except has rosewood fingerboard and bound peghead.

Mfr.'s Sug. Retail	$430	$300	$260	$215	$175	$155	$140	$130

FG435A — dreadnought style, spruce top, round soundhole, black pickguard, agathis back/sides, nato neck, 14/20 bound bubinga fingerboard with pearl snowflake inlay, rosewood bridge with white pearl dot pins, bound peghead, 3 per side chrome tuners. Available in Black, Marine Blue, Oriental Blue, Tinted and Tobacco Brown Sunburst finish. Curr. mfr.

Mfr.'s Sug. Retail	$420	$295	$250	$210	$170	$150	$135	$125

FG450SA — dreadnought style, solid spruce top, round soundhole, black pickguard, bound body, abalone rosette, ovankol back/sides, nato neck, 14/20 fret bound rosewood fingerboard with pearl snowflake inlay, rosewood bridge with black pearl dot pins, bound peghead with rosewood veneer, 3 per side chrome tuners. Available in Natural finish. Curr. mfr.

Mfr.'s Sug. Retail	$500	$350	$300	$250	$200	$180	$165	$150

This model is also available in left-handed version (FG450S-LA).

FG460SA — similar to 450SA, except has rosewood back/sides and gold hardware.

Mfr.'s Sug. Retail	$590	$410	$355	$295	$235	$210	$195	$180

Add $30 for 12-string version of this model (FG460S-12A).

FG470SA — similar to 460SA.

Mfr.'s Sug. Retail	$660	$460	$395	$330	$265	$240	$220	$200

FJ645A — jumbo style, spruce top, round soundhole, black pickguard, bound body, abalone rosette, agathis back/sides, nato neck, 14/20 fret bound rosewood fingerboard with pearl pyramid inlay, nato bridge with white pearl dot pins, bound peghead, 3 per side chrome tuners. Available in Black Burst finish. Curr. mfr.

Mfr.'s Sug. Retail	$550	$385	$330	$275	$220	$200	$180	$165

Grading	100%	98%	95%	90%	80%	70%	60%

FS310A — parlor style, spruce top, round soundhole, black pickguard, bound body, 5 stripe rosette, nato back/sides/neck, 14/20 fret bubinga fingerboard with pearl dot inlay, nato bridge with white pins, 3 per side chrome tuners. Available in Natural finish. Curr. mfr.

Mfr.'s Sug. Retail	$330	$230	$195	$165	$130	$120	$110	$100

Hand Crafted Series

GC30 — classical style, solid white spruce top, round soundhole, bound body, wooden inlay rosette, rosewood back/sides, mahogany neck, 12/19 fret ebony fingerboard, jacaranda bridge, rosewood peghead veneer, 3 per side gold tuners. Available in Natural finish. Curr. mfr.

Mfr.'s Sug. Retail	$1,250	$875	$750	$625	$500	$450	$415	$375

This model is also available with solid cedar top (GC30C).

GC40 — classical style, solid white spruce top, round soundhole, bound body, wooden inlay rosette, jacaranda back/sides, mahogany neck, 12/19 fret ebony fingerboard, jacaranda bridge, jacaranda peghead veneer, 3 per side gold tuners. Available in Natural finish. Curr. mfr.

Mfr.'s Sug. Retail	$1,900	$1,330	$1,140	$950	$760	$685	$625	$570

This model is also available with solid cedar top (GC40C).

GC50 — classical style, solid spruce top, round soundhole, bound body, wooden inlay rosette, jacaranda back/sides, mahogany neck, 12/19 fret ebony fingerboard, jacaranda bridge, jacaranda peghead veneer with stylized Y groove, 3 per side gold tuners. Available in Lacquer finish. Curr. mfr.

Mfr.'s Sug. Retail	$3,100	$2,170	$1,860	$1,550	$1,240	$1,115	$1,025	$930

This model is also available with solid cedar top (GC50C).

GC60 — classical style, solid spruce top, round soundhole, bound body, wooden inlay rosette, jacaranda back/sides, mahogany neck, 12/19 fret ebony fingerboard, jacaranda bridge, jacaranda peghead veneer with stylized Y groove, 3 per side gold tuners. Available in Lacquer finish. Curr. mfr.

Mfr.'s Sug. Retail	$4,200	$2,940	$2,520	$2,100	$1,680	$1,510	$1,385	$1,260

This model is also available with solid cedar top (GC60C).

GC70 — classical style, solid spruce top, round soundhole, bound body, wooden inlay rosette, jacaranda back/sides, mahogany neck, 12/19 fret ebony fingerboard, jacaranda bridge, jacaranda peghead veneer with stylized Y groove, 3 per side gold tuners. Available in Shellac finish. Curr. mfr.

Mfr.'s Sug. Retail	$5,300	$3,710	$3,180	$2,650	$2,120	$1,910	$1,750	$1,590

This model is also available with solid cedar top (GC70C).

GC71 — similar to GC70, except has no peghead groove.

Mfr.'s Sug. Retail	$5,300	$3,710	$3,180	$2,650	$2,120	$1,910	$1,750	$1,590

Grading	100%	98%	95%	90%	80%	70%	60%

GD10 — classical style, solid white spruce top, round soundhole, wooden inlay rosette, rosewood back/sides, mahogany neck, 12/19 fret ebony fingerboard, rosewood bridge, rosewood peghead veneer, 3 per side gold tuners. Available in Natural finish. Curr. mfr.

Mfr.'s Sug. Retail	$700	$490	$420	$350	$280	$250	$230	$210

This model is also available with solid cedar top (GD10C).

GD20 — classical style, solid white spruce top, round soundhole, wooden inlay rosette, rosewood back/sides, mahogany neck, 12/19 fret ebony fingerboard, rosewood bridge, rosewood peghead veneer, 3 per side gold tuners. Available in Natural finish. Curr. mfr.

Mfr.'s Sug. Retail	$900	$630	$540	$450	$360	$325	$300	$275

This model is also available with solid cedar top (GD20C).

LA18 — mid size dreadnought style, solid spruce top, round soundhole, bound body, abalone rosette, mahogany back/sides, mahogany neck, 14/20 fret bound ebony fingerboard with pearl dot inlay, ebony bridge with white pearl dot pins, bound peghead with rosewood veneer and pearl/abalone double L inlay, 3 per side gold tuners. Available in Natural finish. Curr. mfr.

Mfr.'s Sug. Retail	$1,050	$735	$630	$525	$420	$380	$345	$315

LA28 — similar to LA18, except has rosewood back/sides and pearl diamond inlay.

Mfr.'s Sug. Retail	$1,400	$980	$840	$700	$560	$505	$460	$420

LD10 — dreadnought style, solid white spruce top, round soundhole, black pickguard, abalone bound body and rosette, rosewood back/sides, mahogany neck, 14/20 fret bound rosewood fingerboard with pearl dot inlay, rosewood bridge with black pearl dot pins, bound peghead with rosewood veneer, 3 per side gold tuners. Available in Natural finish. Curr. mfr.

Mfr.'s Sug. Retail	$700	$490	$420	$350	$280	$250	$230	$210

LD10E — similar to LD10, except has piezo electric pickups and pop up volume/2 tone and mix controls.

Mfr.'s Sug. Retail	$850	$595	$510	$425	$340	$305	$280	$255

LL15 — dreadnought style, solid spruce top, round soundhole, black pickguard, 5 stripe bound body and rosette, mahogany back/sides/neck, 14/20 fret ebony fingerboard with pearl dot inlay, ebony bridge with black pearl dot pins, rosewood veneer on peghead, 3 per side gold tuners. Available in Natural finish. Curr. mfr.

Mfr.'s Sug. Retail	$1,050	$735	$630	$525	$420	$380	$345	$315

Grading	100%	98%	95%	90%	80%	70%	60%

LL35 — dreadnought style, solid white spruce top, round soundhole, black pickguard, 3 stripe bound body, abalone rosette, jacaranda back/sides, mahogany neck, 14/20 fret bound ebony fingerboard with pearl snowflake inlay, ebony bridge with black pearl dot pins, bound peghead with rosewood veneer and pearl/abalone double L inlay, 3 per side gold tuners. Available in Natural finish. Curr. mfr.

Mfr.'s Sug. Retail	$1,750	$1,225	$1,050	$875	$700	$630	$575	$525

ACOUSTIC ELECTRIC

APX Series

APX4 — single venetian cutaway dreadnought style, spruce top, oval soundhole, 5 stripe bound body and rosette, agathis back/sides, nato neck, 22 fret rosewood fingerboard with pearl dot inlay, rosewood bridge with white pearl dot pins, 3 per side chrome tuners, bridge piezo pickup, volume/treble/bass controls. Available in Black, Natural and Violin Sunburst finish. Curr. mfr.

Mfr.'s Sug. Retail	$500	$350	$300	$250	$200	$180	$165	$150

APX6 — single venetian cutaway dreadnought style, spruce top, oval soundhole, 5 stripe bound body, wooden inlay rosette cap, agathis back/sides, nato neck, 24 fret extended rosewood fingerboard with pearl dot inlay, rosewood bridge with white pearl dot pins, 3 per sides chrome tuners, bridge/body piezo pickups, pop up volume/treble/bass/mix controls. Available in Black, Cherry Sunburst and Cream White finish. Curr. mfr.

Mfr.'s Sug. Retail	$730	$510	$440	$365	$290	$260	$240	$220

APX6N — classical style, spruce top, oval soundhole, 5 stripe bound body, wooden inlay rosette, ovankol back/sides, nato neck, 14/22 fret rosewood fingerboard, rosewood bridge, 3 per side gold tuners, bridge/body piezo pickups, volume/treble/bass/mix controls. Available in Natural finish. Curr. mfr.

Mfr.'s Sug. Retail	$730	$510	$440	$365	$290	$260	$240	$220

APX7 — single venetian cutaway dreadnought style, spruce top, oval soundhole, 5 stripe bound body, wooden inlay rosette cap, agathis back/sides, mahogany neck, 24 fret extended bound rosewood fingerboard with pearl dot inlay, rosewood bridge with white pearl dot pins, bound peghead, 3 per side gold tuners, 2 bridge/body piezo pickups, volume/treble/bass/mix controls. Available in Black, Blue Burst and Light Brown Sunburst finish. Curr. mfr.

Mfr.'s Sug. Retail	$850	$595	$510	$425	$340	$305	$280	$255

APX8 — similar to APX7, except has bridge piezo pickup, mode switch. Available in Gray Burst and Light Brown Sunburst finish.

Mfr.'s Sug. Retail	$950	$665	$570	$475	$380	$345	$315	$285

Grading	100%	98%	95%	90%	80%	70%	60%

APX9-12 — similar to APX7, except is a 12 string with chrome tuners, mode switch. Available in Black, Blue Burst and Light Brown Sunburst finish.

Mfr.'s Sug. Retail	$1,150	$805	$690	$575	$460	$415	$380	$345

APX10 — single venetian cutaway dreadnought style, spruce top, oval soundhole, 5 stripe bound body, abalone rosette cap, sycamore back/sides, mahogany neck, 24 fret extended bound ebony fingerboard with pearl diamond inlay, ebony bridge with white pearl dot pins, bound peghead, 3 per side gold tuners, bridge/body piezo pickups, volume/treble/bass/mix controls, mode switch. Available in Antique Stain Sunburst, Black Burst and Burgundy Red finish. Curr. mfr.

Mfr.'s Sug. Retail	$1,400	$980	$840	$700	$560	$505	$460	$420

APX10N — single venetian cutaway classical style, spruce top, oval soundhole, 5 stripe bound body, wooden inlay rosette, rosewood back/sides, mahogany neck, 24 fret ebony fingerboard, rosewood bridge, rosewood veneer on peghead, 3 per side gold tuners, bridge/body piezo pickups, volume/treble/bass/mix controls, mode switch. Available in Natural finish. Curr. mfr.

Mfr.'s Sug. Retail	$1,200	$840	$720	$600	$480	$430	$395	$360

APX20 — similar to APX10, except has abalone bound body and pearl/abalone pyramid inlay. Available in Cream White and Light Brown Sunburst finish. Curr. mfr.

Mfr.'s Sug. Retail	$1,600	$1,120	$960	$800	$640	$575	$530	$480

APX SPECIAL I — single venetian cutaway dreadnought style, tiger stripe sycamore top, oval soundhole, 5 stripe bound body and rosette, agathis back/sides, nato neck, 22 fret rosewood fingerboard with pearl dot inlay, rosewood bridge with white pearl dot pins, bridge piezo pickup, volume/treble/bass controls. Available in Orange Stain and Red Blonde finish. Curr. mfr.

Mfr.'s Sug. Retail	$600	$420	$360	$300	$240	$215	$195	$180

APX SPECIAL II — similar to APX Special I, except has bird's eye maple top. Available in Faded Burst and Purple Burst finish.

Mfr.'s Sug. Retail	$600	$420	$360	$300	$240	$215	$195	$180

ELECTRIC

Image Series

AE1200S — single rounded cutaway hollow body, laminated spruce top, bound body and F holes, raised bound tortoise shell pickguard, beech/birch back/sides, mahogany neck, 20 fret bound ebony fingerboard with abalone split block inlay, metal/grenadilla bridge with trapeze tailpiece, bound peghead, 3 per side tuners, gold hardware, 2 humbucker pickups, 2 volume/tone controls, 3 position switch, coil split in tone controls. Available in Antique Stain and Natural finish. Curr. mfr.

Mfr.'s Sug. Retail	$1,600	$1,120	$960	$800	$640	$575	$530	$480

Grading	100%	98%	95%	90%	80%	70%	60%

AES1500 — single rounded cutaway hollow body, curly maple top, bound body and F holes, raised black pickguard, maple back/sides, 3 piece maple neck, 22 fret bound rosewood fingerboard with pearl dot inlay, bridge/stop tailpiece, abalone Yamaha symbol and scroll inlay on peghead, 3 per side tuners, gold hardware, 2 DiMarzio humbucker pickups, 2 volume/tone controls, 3 position switch, coil split in tone controls. Available in Orange Stain and Pearl Snow White finish. Curr. mfr.

Mfr.'s Sug. Retail	$1,700	$1,190	$1,020	$850	$680	$610	$560	$510

SA1100 — double cutaway semi hollow body, laminated maple top/back/sides, bound body, raised black pickguard, mahogany neck, 22 fret bound rosewood fingerboard with pearl dot inlay, bridge/stop tailpiece, 3 per side tuners, chrome hardware, 2 humbucker pickups, 2 volume/tone controls, 3 position switch, coil split in tone controls. Available in Black, Brown Sunburst, Natural and Orange Sunburst finish. Curr. mfr.

Mfr.'s Sug. Retail	$1,050	$735	$630	$525	$420	$380	$345	$315

SA2200 — similar to SA1100, except has flame maple top, ebony fingerboard with abalone split block inlay, bound peghead with abalone Yamaha logo and stylized inlay and gold hardware. Available in Brown Sunburst and Violin Sunburst finish. Curr. mfr.

Mfr.'s Sug. Retail	$1,500	$1,050	$900	$750	$600	$540	$495	$450

Pacifica Series

812S — tele style alder body, black pickguard, bolt-on maple neck, 24 fret rosewood fingerboard with pearl dot inlay, double locking vibrato, 6 on one side tuners, black hardware, 2 stacked coil/1 humbucker pickups, volume/tone control, 5 position switch with coil split. Available in Black, Dark Red Metallic and Lightning Blue finish. Curr. mfr.

Mfr.'s Sug. Retail	$730	$510	$440	$365	$290	$260	$240	$220

Add $70 for Tangerine Flake finish.

821 — strat style alder body, black pickguard, bolt-on maple neck, 24 fret rosewood fingerboard with pearl dot inlay, double locking vibrato, 6 on one side tuners, black hardware, humbucker/stacked coil/humbucker pickups, volume/tone control, 5 position switch with coil split. Available in Black, Dark Red Metallic and Lightning Blue finish. Curr. mfr.

Mfr.'s Sug. Retail	$730	$510	$440	$365	$290	$260	$240	$220

Add $70 for Silver Flake finish.

This model is also available with reverse headstock (821-R).

Grading	100%	98%	95%	90%	80%	70%	60%

912J — strat style swamp ash body, white pickguard, bolt-on maple neck, 22 fret fingerboard with pearl dot inlay, double locking vibrato, 6 on one side tuners, chrome hardware, 2 stacked coil/1 humbucker DiMarzio pickups, volume/tone control, 5 position switch. Available in Black, Crimson Red, Faded Burst and Translucent Blue finish. Curr. mfr.

Mfr.'s Sug. Retail	$1,060	$740	$635	$530	$425	$385	$350	$320

1212 — strat style basswood body, black pickguard, bolt-on maple neck, 24 fret rosewood fingerboard with pearl slash inlay, double locking vibrato, 6 on one side tuners, black hardware, 2 stacked coil/1 humbucker DiMarzio pickups, volume/tone control, 5 position switch with coil split. Available in Black, Dark Blue Metallic and Dark Red Metallic finish. Curr. mfr.

Mfr.'s Sug. Retail	$1,060	$740	$635	$530	$425	$385	$350	$320

Add $80 for Ruby Red Flake and Silver Flake finish.

1221 — similar to 1212, except has humbucker/stacked coil/humbucker DiMarzio pickups. Available in Black and Dark Blue Metallic Flake finish.

Mfr.'s Sug. Retail	$1,060	$740	$635	$530	$425	$385	$350	$320

Add $80 for Ruby Red Flake and 3 Color Flake finish.

1221M — similar to 1221, except has maple fingerboard with black slash inlay.

Mfr.'s Sug. Retail	$1,060	$740	$635	$530	$425	$385	$350	$320

Add $80 for Silver Flake and Tangerine Flake finish.

1221MS — similar to 1221M, except has tele style body. Available in Black and Yellow Pearl finish.

Mfr.'s Sug. Retail	$1,060	$740	$635	$530	$425	$385	$350	$320

Add $80 for Ruby Red Flake and 3 Color Flake finish.

1230 — similar to 1221, except has 3 humbucker DiMarzio pickups. Available in Black, Dark Red Metallic and Lightning Blue finish.

Mfr.'s Sug. Retail	$1,060	$740	$635	$530	$425	$385	$350	$320

Add $80 for Ruby Red Flake and Silver Flake finish.

1230S — similar to 1230, except has tele style body. Available in Black and Dark Blue Metallic finish.

Mfr.'s Sug. Retail	$1,060	$740	$635	$530	$425	$385	$350	$320

Add $80 for Ruby Red Flake and Silver Flake finish.

1412 — strat style mahogany body with 2 tone chambers, arched flame maple top, 7 piece maple/mahogany thru-body neck, 24 fret bound ebony fingerboard with abalone/pearl block inlay, double locking vibrato, 6 on one side tuners, chrome hardware, 2 stacked coil/1 humbucker DiMarzio pickups, volume/tone control, 5 position switch with coil split. Available in Blonde, Cherry, Faded Burst, Rose Burst and Translucent Black (new 1992) finish. Curr. mfr.

Mfr.'s Sug. Retail	$2,200	$1,540	$1,320	$1,100	$880	$790	$725	$660

Grading	100%	98%	95%	90%	80%	70%	60%

RGZ Series

RGZ112P — strat style alder body, black pickguard, bolt-on maple neck, 22 fret bubinga fingerboard with pearl dot inlay, standard vibrato, 6 on one side tuners, chrome hardware, 2 single coil/1 humbucker pickups , volume/tone control, 5 position switch. Available in Black, Lightning Blue and Vivid Red finish. Curr. mfr.

Mfr.'s Sug. Retail	$300	$210	$180	$150	$120	$110	$100	$90

RGZ121P — similar to RGZ 112P, except has humbucker/single coil/humbucker pickups.

Mfr.'s Sug. Retail	$330	$230	$195	$165	$130	$120	$110	$100

RGZ321P — similar to RGZ 121P, except has double locking vibrato. Available in Black, Lightning Blue and 3D Blue.

Mfr.'s Sug. Retail	$460	$320	$275	$230	$185	$165	$150	$140

RGZ612P — strat style alder body, black pickguard, bolt-on maple neck, 24 fret rosewood fingerboard with pearl dot inlay, double locking vibrato, 6 on one side tuners, black hardware, 2 single coil/1 humbucker pickups, volume/tone control, 5 position switch with coil split. Available in Black, Dark Red Metallic and Lightning Blue. Curr. mfr.

Mfr.'s Sug. Retail	$720	$500	$430	$360	$290	$260	$240	$220

Add $80 for Silver Flake finish.

RGZ612PL — similar to RGZ612P, except is left handed.

Mfr.'s Sug. Retail	$830	$580	$500	$415	$330	$300	$275	$250

Add $90 for Silver Flake finish.

RGZ621P — similar to RGZ612P, except has humbucker/single coil/humbucker pickups. Available in Black, Lightning Blue and Red Metallic.

Mfr.'s Sug. Retail	$720	$500	$430	$360	$290	$260	$240	$220

Add $80 for 3-Color Flake finish.

This model is also available with a reverse headstock (621P-R).

Weddington Series

SPECIAL — Les Paul style mahogany body, set in mahogany neck, 22 fret rosewood fingerboard with pearl dot inlay, adjustable bar bridge/tailpiece, 3 per side tuners, chrome hardware, 2 humbucker DiMarzio pickups, 2 volume/tone controls, 5 position switch with coil spilt. Available in Black, Cherry and Cream White finish. Curr. mfr.

Mfr.'s Sug. Retail	$1,000	$700	$600	$500	$400	$360	$330	$300

Grading	100%	98%	95%	90%	80%	70%	60%

CLASSIC — similar to Standard, except has arched bound maple top, bound fingerboard with pearl split block inlay, pearl Yamaha symbol and stylized oval inlay on peghead and tunomatic bridge/stop tailpiece. Available in Cherry Sunburst, Metallic Black, Metallic Red top/Natural sides finish.

Mfr.'s Sug. Retail	$1,400	$980	$840	$700	$560	$505	$460	$420

CUSTOM — similar to Classic, except has figured maple top, mahogany/maple neck, ebony fingerboard with pearl/abalone inlay, ebony veneer on peghead with pearl Yamaha symbol and stylized scroll inlay. Available in Cherry, Faded Burst and Roseburst finish.

Mfr.'s Sug. Retail	$1,800	$1,260	$1,080	$900	$720	$650	$595	$540

ELECTRIC BASS

Attitude Series

STANDARD — precision style alder body, white pickguard, bolt-on maple neck, 21 fret rosewood fingerboard with pearl dot inlay, fixed bridge, 4 on one side tuners, chrome hardware, P-style/J-style pickups, volume/tone control, 3 position switch. Available in Black Pearl, Crimson Red, Dark Blue Metallic and White finish. Curr. mfr.

Mfr.'s Sug. Retail	$730	$510	$440	$365	$290	$260	$240	$220

STANDARD 5 — similar to Standard, except has 5 strings and 4/1 per side tuners.

Mfr.'s Sug. Retail	$930	$650	$555	$465	$370	$335	$305	$280

DELUXE — similar to Standard, except has Yamaha "Six Pack" pickup and 5 position switch. Available in Metallic Black, Metallic Red, Pacific Blue and White finish.

Mfr.'s Sug. Retail	$900	$630	$540	$450	$360	$325	$300	$275

CUSTOM — precision style alder body, white pickguard, bolt-on maple neck, 21 fret maple fingerboard with offset black slot inlay, solid brass fixed bridge with 4 built in piezo electric pickups, 4 on one side tuners, chrome hardware, woofer/P-style/piezo DiMarzio pickups, volume/tone control, mini toggle pickup select switch, stereo outputs. Available in Crimson Red, Dark Blue Metallic and Light violet Metallic finish. Curr. mfr.

Mfr.'s Sug. Retail	$1,500	$1,050	$900	$750	$600	$540	$495	$450

LIMITED — similar to Custom, except has no piezo electric pickups in brass bridge, "Hipshot" detuning device on E string tuner, separate woofer/P-style pickup volume controls and woofer cut switch. Available in Lightning Red and Thunder Blue finish. Disc. 1992.

		$1,260	$1,080	$900	$720	$650	$595	$540

The Limited was co-designed by Billy Sheehan.
Last Mfr.'s Sug. Retail was $1,800.

Grading	100%	98%	95%	90%	80%	70%	60%

BB Series

BB200 — precision style alder body, bolt-on maple neck, 21 fret rosewood fingerboard with pearl dot tuners, fixed bridge, 4 on one side tuners, chrome hardware, P-style pickup, volume/tone control. Available in Black, Vivid Red and White finish. Curr. mfr.

Mfr.'s Sug. Retail	$370	$260	$220	$185	$150	$135	$120	$110

This model is available with fretless fingerboard (BB200F).

BB300 — similar to BB200, except the bridge is of higher quality.

Mfr.'s Sug. Retail	$430	$300	$260	$215	$175	$155	$140	$130

This model is available in left handed version (BB300L).

BB5000A — precision style alder body, mahogany/maple thru body neck, 24 fret ebony fingerboard with pearl oval inlay, 5 string fixed bridge, 4/1 per side tuners, brass hardware, P-style/J-style pickups, volume/tone/mix controls, active electronics. Available in Cream White, Gunmetal Blue and Purple Pearl finish. Curr. mfr.

Mfr.'s Sug. Retail	$1,700	$1,190	$1,020	$850	$680	$610	$560	$510

This model is available with fretless fingerboard (BB5000AF).

RBX Series

RBX250 — precision style alder body, bolt-on maple neck, 22 fret rosewood fingerboard with pearl dot inlay, fixed bridge, 4 on one side tuners, chrome hardware, P-style pickup, volume/tone control. Available in Black, Crimson Red, Lightning Blue and White finish. Curr. mfr.

Mfr.'s Sug. Retail	$300	$210	$180	$150	$120	$110	$100	$90

This model is available with fretless fingerboard (BB250F).

RBX350 — similar to RBX250, except has P-style/J-style pickups and mix controls.

Mfr.'s Sug. Retail	$400	$280	$240	$200	$160	$145	$130	$120

Add $70 for left handed version (RBX350L).

RBX650 — similar to RBX350, except has black hardware. Available in Black Pearl, Dark Blue Metallic and Dark Red Metallic.

Mfr.'s Sug. Retail	$670	$470	$400	$335	$265	$240	$220	$200

RBX1000 — precision style sculpted ash body, bolt-on maple neck, 24 fret rosewood fingerboard with pearl dot inlay, fixed brass bridge, 4 on one side tuners, chrome hardware, P-style/J-style pickups, volume/2 tone/mix controls, active electronics. Available in Natural Satin, Translucent Black and Translucent Violet. Curr. mfr.

Mfr.'s Sug. Retail	$1,030	$720	$615	$510	$410	$370	$340	$310

Grading	100%	98%	95%	90%	80%	70%	60%

TRB Series

TRB4P — precision style figured maple/rosewood/maple body, maple/mahogany thru body neck, 24 fret ebony fingerboard with pearl dot inlay, solid brass bridge with 4 built in piezo pickups, 2 per side solid brass tuners, P-style/J-style pickups, volume/2 tone/2 mix controls, piezo pickup switch. Available in Red Blonde, Translucent Blue and Translucent Red Sunburst finish. Curr. mfr.

Mfr.'s Sug. Retail	$2,000	$1,400	$1,200	$1,000	$800	$720	$660	$600

TRB5P — similar to TRB4P, except has 5 strings and 3/2 per side tuners.

Mfr.'s Sug. Retail	$2,300	$1,610	$1,380	$1,150	$920	$830	$760	$690

TRB6P — similar to TRB4P, except has 6 strings, 3 per side tuners and 2 J-style pickups.

Mfr.'s Sug. Retail	$2,600	$1,820	$1,560	$1,300	$1,040	$935	$860	$780

YUPS GUITARS

Manufactured by Yups Technologies, Inc. Distributed by BBP located in Minneapolis, MN.

ELECTRIC

O-BOB — double cutaway alder body with a pointed bottom bout, thru body maple neck, 30 fret extended bound ebony fingerboard with pearl block and bow inlay, standard vibrato, 6 on one side locking tuners, black hardware, 2 stacked coil pickups, 3 position switch, 2 coil tap mini switches. Available in Bar Code finish. Curr. mfr.

Mfr.'s Sug. Retail	$1,250	$875	$750	$625	$500	$450	$415	$375

The finish on this model is a simulation of the bar code and it also corresponds to the instrument's serial number. Also known as the Groundtrack guitar.

ZETA

Manufactured and distributed by Zeta Music Systems, Inc., located in Oakland, CA.

Grading	100%	98%	95%	90%	80%	70%	60%

ELECTRIC

MIRROR 6 MIDI GUITAR — radical double cutaway asymmetrical ash body, bolt-on maple neck, 24 fret ebony fingerboard with offset white block inlay, strings thru body bridge, reverse headstock, 6 on one side Gotoh tuners, black hardware, single coil/humbucker/hex EMG pickups, volume/tone/blend/midi controls, 3 position pickup, synth and hex switches. Available in Black, Metallic Grey, Pearl White, Red and Sea Foam Green finish. Mfd. 1989 to date.

Mfr.'s Sug. Retail	$2,995	$2,095	$1,795	$1,495	$1,195	$1,075	$985	$895

Add $800 for double locking vibrato.

ZION

Manufactured and distributed by Zion Guitar Technology, located in Greensboro, NC, since 1980.

ELECTRIC

To date, Zion has specialized in strat styled instruments, but will be producing a new Les Paul and Telecaster style beginning in 1994.

BURNING DESIRE — strat style basswood body, bolt-on maple neck, 22 fret ebony fingerboard with pearl dot inlay, standard Kahler vibrato, graphite nut, 6 on one side locking Sperzel tuners, chrome hardware, 2 stacked coil/1 humbucker Joe Barden pickups, volume/tone control, 3 mini switches. Available in Black with Neon Flames finish. Curr. mfr.

Mfr.'s Sug. Retail	$2,995	$2,095	$1,795	$1,495	$1,195	$1,075	$985	$895

Limited number produced yearly.

Grading	100%	98%	95%	90%	80%	70%	60%

CLASSIC MAPLE — strat style basswood body, arched bound figured maple top, bolt on maple neck, 22 fret ebony fingerboard with pearl dot inlay, locking vibrato, 6 on one side locking tuners, 2 single coil/1 humbucker Zion pickups, volume/tone control, 5 position switch. Available in Amber Top, Black, Transparent Blue Burst, Tobacco Burst and Vintage Burst finish. Curr. mfr.

Mfr.'s Sug. Retail	$1,995	$1,395	$1,195	$995	$795	$720	$660	$600

This model is available with EMG, PJ Marx or Seymour Duncan pickups.
This model available with standard vibrato (RT Classic).
This model also available with maple fingerboard.

GRAPHIC SERIES — similar to Classic Maple, except has basswood body. Available in Frosted Marble, Guilded Frost, Marble Rock and Techno Frost finish.

Mfr.'s Sug. Retail	$1,895	$1,325	$1,135	$950	$760	$685	$625	$570

PICKASSO — similar to Burning Desire, except has black hardware and Zion pickups. Available in Black, Blue/Purple/Pink and Pink/Orange/Yellow finish. Curr. mfr.

Mfr.'s Sug. Retail	$2,495	$1,745	$1,495	$1,250	$1,000	$900	$825	$750

T MODEL — strat style basswood body, pearloid pickguard, bolt-on maple neck, 22 fret ebony fingerboard with pearl dot inlay, standard Gotoh vibrato, graphite nut, 6 on one side locking Sperzel tuners, 3 stacked coil Zion pickups, volume/tone control, 5 position switch. Available in Black, Cream and Tobacco Burst finish. Mfd. 1991 to date.

Mfr.'s Sug. Retail	$1,495	$1,045	$895	$750	$600	$540	$495	$450

This model also available with maple fingerboard.

T Model Maple Top — similar to T Model, except has figured maple top and Zion vibrato. Available in Blue Burst, Tobacco Burst and Vintage Burst finish.

Mfr.'s Sug. Retail	$1,895	$1,325	$1,135	$950	$760	$685	$625	$570

This model is available in left-handed version (Maple Top Left T).

ELECTRIC BASS

RAD BASS — offset double cutaway basswood body, bolt-on maple neck, 20 fret ebony fingerboard, fixed bridge, 4 per side Gotoh tuners, black hardware, P-style/J-style EMG pickups, 2 volume/1 tone controls. Available in Amber Top, Classic Black, Frosted Marble Blue, Frosted Marble Purple, Frosted Marble Red, Purple Burst, Techno-Frost, Tobacco Burst, Transparent Blue Burst, Vintage Burst finish. Curr. mfr.

Mfr.'s Sug. Retail	$1,995	$1,395	$1,195	$995	$795	$720	$660	$600

TRADEMARK INDEX

ALEMBIC, INC.
3077 Wiljan Court Building A
Santa Rosa CA 95407-5702
Phone: 707 523-2611
Fax: 707 523-2935

ALVAREZ
See Saint Louis Music, Inc. for distribution information.

ALVAREZ/YAIRI
See Saint Louis Music, Inc. for distribution information.

TOM ANDERSON GUITARWORKS
2697 Lavery Court Unit 27
Newbury Park CA 91320
Phone: 805 498-1747
Fax: 805 498-0878

ARIA
Distributor - BBE Sound, Inc.
5500 Bolsa Avenue
Huntington Beach CA 92649
Phone: 714 897-6766
Fax: 714 895-6728

BASS COLLECTION
Distributor - Meisel Music, Inc.
32 Commerce Street
PO Box 90
Springfield NJ 07081
Phone: 201 379-5000
Fax: 201 379-5020

BENEDICT GUITAR CO.
3400 Lyndale Avenue South
Minneapolis MN 55408
Phone: 612 822-7335
Fax: 612 822-7335

BLADE GUITARS
Distributor - Solo Professional Products
2870 Technology Drive
Rochester Hills MI 48309
Phone: 313 853-3055
Fax: 313 853-5937

BREEDLOVE GUITAR CO.
19885 8th Street
Tumalo OR 97701
Phone: 503 385-8339
Fax: 503 385-8183

BUSCARINO GUITARS
1250 Seminole Boulevard
Largo FL 34640
Phone: 813 586-4992

CARVIN CORP.
Factory direct only.
Instruments and replacement parts.
1155 Industrial Avenue
Escondido CA 92029
Phone: 619 747-1710
Fax: 619 747-0743

CHANDLER INDUSTRIES, INC.
Instruments and replacement parts.
370 Lang Road
Burlingame CA 94010-2003
Phone: 415 342-1490
Fax: 415 342-9692

CHARVEL
See Jackson/Charvel Guitar, Co. for distribution information.

CHARVETTE (DISCONTINUED)
Distributor was Jackson/Charvel Guitar, Co.

COLLINGS GUITARS
11025 Signal Hill Drive
Austin TX 78737-2834
Phone: 512 288-7776
Fax: 512 288-6045

D'AQUISTO
P.O. Box 259
Greenport NY 11944
Phone: 516 477-2017
Fax: 516 477-0887

EGGLE GUITARS
U.S. Distributor - Dana B. Goods
5427 Hollister Avenue
Santa Barbara CA 93117
Phone: 805 964-9610
Fax: 603 352-8757

EPIPHONE
Distributor - See Gibson Guitar Corp.

ERNIE BALL/MUSIC MAN
151 Suburban Road
PO Box 4117
San Luis Obispo CA 93401
Phone: 805 544-7726
Fax: 805 544-7275

ESP GUITAR CO.
170 West 48th Street 3rd Floor
New York NY 10036
Phone: 212 819-1234
Fax: 212 819-1452

FENDER MUSICAL INSTRUMENTS CORP.
7975 North Hayden Road
Scottsdale AZ 85258
Phone: 602 596-9690
Fax: 602 596-1386

FERNANDES GUITARS USA, INC.
16123 Valerio Street
Van Nuys CA 91406
Phone: 818 988-6790
Fax: 818 988-3094

G & L MUSICAL PRODUCTS
5500 Bolsa Avenue #245
Huntington Beach CA 92649
Phone: 714 897-6766
Fax: 714 895-6728

GIBSON GUITAR CORP.
1818 Elm Hill Park
Nashville TN 37210-3781
Phone: 615 871-4500
Fax: 615 889-5509

GRETSCH
Distributor - Fred Gretsch Enterprises
P.O. Box 2468
Savannah GA 31402
Phone: 912 748-1101
Fax: 912 748-1106

GUDELSKY MUSICAL INSTRUMENTS
2963 Gopher Canyon Road
Vista CA 92084
Phone: 619 726-0610

GUILD
Distributor - U.S. Music Corp.
2885 South James Drive
PO Box 51327
New Berlin WI 53151
Phone: 414 784-8388
Fax: 414 784-9258

HAMBURGUITAR
Distributor - Bernie Hamburger
33467 Fernwood Street
Westland MI 48185
Phone: 313 722-6931

HAMER GUITARS
Custom orders only.
See Kaman Music Corp. for distribution information.
Factory Address
835 West University Drive
Arlington Heights IL 60004
Phone: 708 255-6112

HEARTFIELD
See Fender Musical Instruments Corp. for distribution information.

HERITAGE GUITAR, INC.

225 Parsons Street
Kalamazoo MI 49007
Phone: 616 385-5721
Fax: 616 385-3519

HOHNER, INC.

Distributor - HSS, A Division Of Hohner, Inc.
PO Box 15035
Richmond VA 23227-5035
Phone: 804 550-2700
Fax: 804 550-2670

IBANEZ U.S.A.

1726 Winchester Road
Bensalem PA 19020-0886
Phone: 215 638-8670
Fax: 215 245-8583

J.B. PLAYER

Distributor - J.B. Player International/MBT Distribution
PO Box 30819
Charleston SC 29417
Phone: 803 763-9083
Fax: 803 763-9096

JACKSON

Distributor - Jackson/Charvel Guitar, Co.
1316 East Lancaster Avenue
Fort Worth TX 76102
Phone: 817 336-5114
Fax: 817 870-1271

JERRY JONES GUITARS

913 Church Street
Nashville TN 37203
Phone: 615 255-0088
Fax: 615 255-7742

KAMAN MUSIC CORP.

Distributor for Hamer, Ovation and Takamine
1330 Blue Hills Avenue
PO Box 507
Bloomfield CT 06002-0507
Phone: 203 243-7105
Fax: 203 243-7961

LADO MUSICAL, INC.

689 Warden Avenue Unit 6
Scarborough M1L 3Z5
Ontario CANADA
Phone: 416 690-5010
Fax: 416 690-5022

LADY LUCK INDUSTRIES, INC.

PO Box 195
Cary IL 60013
Phone: 708 639-8907
Fax: 708 639-7010

LARRIVEE GUITARS, LTD.

267 East 1st Street
North Vancouver
British Columbia CANADA V7L 1B4
Phone: 604 985-6520
Fax: 604 985-2169

THE LOWDEN GUITAR CO.

Current Distribution Address
137 Doggett Drive
North Forest City, NC 28043
Phone: 704 245-8904
Fax: 704 245-8965

THE MARTIN GUITAR CO.

(C.F. Martin & Co., Inc.)
510 Sycamore Street
PO Box 329
Nazareth PA 18064
Phone: 215 759-2837
Fax: 215 759-5757

MODULUS GRAPHITE, INC.

575 7th Street
San Francisco CA 94103
Phone: 415 241-8080
Fax: 415 241-8085

NEO PRODUCTS, INC.

4626 Sands Way
PO Box 563
Buckingham PA 18912
Phone: 215 657-1901
Fax: 215 657-1902

OVATION

See Kaman Music Corp. for distribution information.

PRS GUITARS

Distributor - Paul Reed Smith Guitars
1812 Virginia Avenue
Annapolis MD 21401
Phone: 410 263-2701
Fax: 410 280-5068

PEAVEY ELECTRONICS CORP.

711 A Street
Meridian MS 39301
Phone: 601 483-5365
Fax: 601 484-4278

M V PEDULLA GUITARS

83 East Water Street
PO Box 226
Rockland MA 02370
Phone: 617 871-0073
Fax: 617 878-4028

RAINSONG

Distributor - Kuau Technology, Ltd.
PO Box 1031
Puunene HI 96784
Phone: 808 244-9486
Fax: 808 244-9486

RICKENBACKER INTERNATIONAL, CORP.

3895 South Main Street
Santa Ana CA 92707-5710
Phone: 714 545-5574
Fax: 714 754-0135

ROBIN GUITARS

4914 Dickson Unit B
Houston TX 77007
Phone: 713 863-1537
Fax: 713 861-1933

SAINT LOUIS MUSIC, INC.

U.S. Distributor for Alvarez and Alvarez/Yairi
1400 Ferguson Avenue
Saint Louis MO 63133
Phone: 314 727-4512

SAMICK MUSIC CORP.

18521 Railroad Street
City of Industry CA 91748
Phone: 818 964-4700
Fax: 818 965-5224

SANTA CRUZ GUITAR CO.

328 Ingalls Street
Santa Cruz CA 95060
Phone: 408 425-0999
Fax: 408 425-3604

SANTUCCI TREBLEBASS

U.S. Distributor - Santucci Corp.
353 West 57th Street
New York NY 10019
Phone: 212 757-2717
Fax: 212 541-4785

SCHACK GUITARS

No U.S. Distribution available at this time. Factory located at:
W-6451 Hammersbach
Hanauerstr.51
GERMANY

SCHECTER

Distributor - Schecter Guitar Research Instruments & replacement parts
PO Box 80
Van Nuys CA 91408
Phone: 818 787-5334
Fax: 818 787-5425

SHADOW

U.S. Distributor - Chesbro Music Co.
327 Broadway
PO Box 2009
Idaho Dalls ID 83409
Phone: 208 522-8691

SHENANDOAH (DISCONTINUED)
Distributor was The Martin Guitar Co.

SIGMA - DIVISION OF MARTIN
See The Martin Guitar Corp. for distribution informatiion.

KEN SMITH BASSES, LTD.
37 West 20th Street #603
New York NY 10011
Phone: 212 463-8783
Fax: 212 463-9220

STARFIELD AMERICA
7101 Case Avenue
North Hollywood CA 91605
Phone: 215 638-8670
Fax: 215 245-8583

STATUS GRAPHITE
No current U.S. Distributor information available at this time. Manufacturer located:
Coleman's Bridge
Colchester Road
Witham ESSEX CM8 3HP
ENGLAND

STEINBERGER SOUND
1050 Acorn Drive #C
Nashville TN 37210
Phone: 615 872-8420
Fax: 615 872-8475

STEPHENS STRINGED INSTRUMENTS
1733 Westlake Avenue
North Seattle WA 98109
Phone: 206 286-1443
Fax: 206 286-1728

TAKAMINE
See Kaman Music Corp. for distribution information.

TAYLOR GUITARS
Distributor - Taylor-Listug, Inc.
1940 Gillespie Way
El Cajon CA 92020
Phone: 619 258-1207
Fax: 619 258-1623

TOBIAS GUITARS
3087 North California Street
Burbank CA 91504
Phone: 818 567-4476
Fax: 818 567-4573

TRIGGS GUITARS
277 Clovernook Drive
Nashville TN 37210
Phone: 615 391-5844

TURTLETONE
2030 East Broadway #1018
Tempe AZ 85282
Phone: 602 894-1079

VALLEY ARTS
Distributor - Valley Arts Musical Products
18521 Railroad Street
City of Industry CA 91748
Phone: 818 964-4700
Fax: 818 965-5224

VANTAGE
Distributor - Music Industries Corp.
99 Tulip Avenue #101
Floral Park NY 11001
Phone: 516 352-4110
Fax: 516 352-0754

VESTER
Distributor - Midco International
PO Box 748
Effingham IL 62401
Phone: 217 342-9211

VIGIER GUITARS

Distributor - Vigier
27 Z.A. Des Champs Elysees
Evry 91000
FRANCE
Phone: 001-67923
Fax: 001-6497924

WARWICK BASSES

601 Pine Avenue
Goleta CA 93117
Phone: 805 964-9610
Fax: 805 964-9749

WASHBURN

U.S. Distributor - Washburn International
255 Corporate Woods Parkway
Vernon Hills IL 60061
Phone: 708 913-5511
Fax: 708 913-7772

WRC GUITARS

Distributor - WRC Music International, Inc.
Wayne Richard Charvel Guitars
943 Calimesa Boulevard
Calimesa CA 92320
Phone: 714 795-4466
Fax: 714 795-1127

YAMAHA CORP. OF AMERICA

6600 Orangethorpe Avenue
Buena Park CA 90620
Phone: 714 522-9011
Fax: 714 522-9832

ZETA MUSIC SYSTEMS

2230 Livingston Street
Oakland CA 94606
Phone: 510 261-1702
Fax: 510 261-1708

ZION GUITARS

2606-404 Phoenix Drive
Greensboro NC 27406
Phone: 919 852-7603

Fender Serialization

Fender serial numbers are found on the bridgeplate, neckplate, backplate or headstock. From 1950-1954, serial numbers are found on the bridgeplate or vibrato backplate. From 1954-1976, the serial numbers are found on the neckplate, on either the top or bottom. From 1976 to date, the serial number is incorporated in the peghead decal. Vintage Re-issues have their serial number on the neckplate and this method has been used since 1982.

When trying to determine the manufacturing date of an instrument by serialization, it is best to keep in mind that there are no clear cut boundaries between where the numbers began and when they ended. There is constant overlapping of serial numbers between years and models. The following are approximate numbers and dates.

1950	0001-0750
1951	0200-1900
1952	0400-4900
1953	2020-5030
1954	2780-7340
1955	6600-12800
1956	7800-16000
1957	14900-025200
1958	022700-38200
1959	31400-60600
1960	44200-58600
1961	55500-81700
1962	71600-99800
1963	81600-99200

In 1962, as the serialization count neared 100,000, for whatever reason(s), the transition did not occur. Instead, an L preceded a 5-digit sequence. It remained this way circa 1962-1965.

1962	L00400-L13200
1963	L00200-L40300
1964	L20600-L76200
1965	L34980-L69900

In 1965, when CBS bought Fender Musical Instruments, Inc., the serialization has come to be known as the "F Series", due to an "F" being stamped onto the neckplate. This series of numbers was utilized from 1965 to 1973. The approximate numbers and years are as follows:

1965	100001-147400
1966	112170-600200
1967	162165-602550
1968	211480-627740
1969	238945-290835
1970	278910-305415
1971	272500-380020
1972	301395-412360
1973	359415-418360

In late 1976, Fender decided to move to a new numbering system for their serialization. The numbers appeared on the pegheads and for the remainder of 1976, they had a 76 or S6 prefix preceding a 5-digit sequence. In 1977, the serialization went to a letter for the decade (ie, S for the '70s, E for the '80s, N for the '90s), followed by a single digit for the year, and then 5 or 6 additional digits. Examples of this would be:

S8 prefix - 1978	E5 prefix - 1985
E0 prefix - 1980	N1 prefix - 1991

Perhaps it was a great idea, but actuality proved to be otherwise. When instrument production did not meet the levels that matched the already produced decals, there are several overlapping years - sometimes several prefixes can be found within a single year's production. Therefore, dating this period of instruments can only approximate a guitar's actual production date.

Identifying Features on Fender Musical Instruments

Fingerboard Construction

Between 1950-1959, all necks were made out of a solid piece of maple with the frets being driven directly into the neck - this is the standard design for maple necks. Between 1959-1962, the maple neck was planed flat and a rosewood fingerboard with frets and inlay was glued to the top of the neck. This is known as the "slab top" fingerboard variation. Between 1962-1983, the maple necks were rounded to the neck's radius, and a thinner piece of rosewood was glued to the neck. This design is called the "veneer" fingerboard, and can be differentiated from a "slab top" fingerboard by observing the bottom of the neck where the fingerboard is glued to the neck (a radiused lower end of the fingerboard is the veneer, while a rectangular shaped lower end of the fingerboard is the slab board). From 1983 to date, Fender returned to the slab top fingerboard design of the 1959-1962 era.

Neckplate Identification

Between 1950-1971, the neck was attached to the body by means of a 4 screw neckplate. Between 1971-1981, the neckplate was changed to 3 screws, with a micro neck adjustment device being added. In 1981, a transition from the 3 screw design back to the 4 screw design began to occur. By 1983, the 4 screw neckplate was back in standard production, with the micro neck adjuster remaining.

Gibson Serialization

Identifying Gibson instruments by serial number can be a very difficult proposition (in some cases, almost impossible). The best method of identification is by using a combination of the serial number, the factory order number and any features that are definitive to a specific time where changes may have occurred (i.e., logo design change, headstock volutes, etc.). There have been 6 different serial number styles used to date on Gibson instruments. The first started in 1902 and continued until 1947. The serial numbers began with number 100 and continue to 99,999. All numbers are approximations. In most cases, only the better and more expensive models were assigned identification numbers.

YEAR	LAST #
1903	1150
1904	1850
1905	2550
1906	3350
1907	4250
1908	5450
1909	6950
1910	8750
1911	10850
1912	13350
1913	16100
1914	20150
1915	25150
1916	32000
1917	39500
1918	47900
1919	53800
1920	62200
1921	69300
1922	71400
1923	74900
1924	80300
1925	82700
1926	83600
1927	85400
1928	87300
1929	89750
1930	90200
1931	90450
1932	90700
1933	91400
1934	92300
1935	92800
1936	94100
1937	95200
1938	95750
1939	96050
1940	96600
1941	97400
1942	97700
1943	97850
1944	98250
1945	98650
1946	99300
1947	99999

White oval labels were used on instruments from 1902-1954, after which the oval label was changed to an color orange. On instruments with round soundholes, this label is visible directly below the opening. On f hole instruments, it is visible through the upper f hole. The second type of serialization incorporated an "A" prefix which was used between 1947-1961. The first number is A 100.

YEAR	LAST #
1947	A 1305
1948	A 2665
1949	A 4410
1950	A 6595
1951	A 9420
1952	A 12460
1953	A 17435
1954	A 18665
1955	A 21910
1956	A 24755
1957	A 26820
1958	A 28880
1959	A 32285
1960	A 35645
1961	A 36150

When production of solid body guitars began, an entirely new serial number system was developed. Although not used on the earliest instruments (circa 1952), a few have 3 digits stamped on the headstock top. Sometime during 1953, instruments were ink-stamped on the headstock back with 5 or 6 digit numbers, the first designates the last digit of the year, and the following digits are production numbers. The production numbers run in a consecutive order and, aside from a few oddities in the change-over years (1961-1962), it is fairly accurate to identify solid body instruments produced between 1953 and 1961.

Examples of this system:

$$4\ 2205 = 1954$$
$$614562 = 1956$$

In 1961, Gibson started a new serial number system that was used on their instrument line-up. It consisted of numbers that are impressed into the wood. It is also generally known to be the most frustrating and hard to understand system that Gibson has employed. These numbers were used between 1961-1969. There are several instances where batches of numbers are switched in order or duplicated, and not just once, but up to four times. There also seems to be no predictable serialization pattern used during the decade. In general though, the numbers are approximately as follows:

YEAR	APPROXIMATE SERIAL RANGE
1961	100-42440
1962	42441-61180
1963	61450-64220
1964	64240-70500
1962	71180-96600
1963	96601-99999
1967	000001-008010
1967	010000-042900
1967	044000-044100
1967	050000-054400
1967	055000-063999
1967	064000-066010

YEAR	APPROXIMATE SERIAL RANGE
1967	067000-070910
1967	090000-099999
1963, 1967	100000-106099
1963	106100-108900
1963, 1967	109000-109999
1963	110000-111549
1963, 1967	111550-115799
1963	115800-118299
1963, 1967	118300-120999
1963	121000-139999
1963, 1967	140000-140100
1963	140101-144304
1964	144305-144380
1963	144381-145000
1963	147009-149864
1964	149865-149891
1963	149892-152989
1964	152990-174222
1964, 1965	174223-176643
1964	176644-199999
1964	200000-250335
1965	250336-291000
1965	301755-302100
1965	302754-305983
1965, 1967	306000-306100
1965, 1967	307000-307985
1965, 1967	309848-310999
1965	311000-320149
1967	320150-320699
1965	320700-321100
1965	322000-326600
1965	328000-328500
1965	328700-329179
1965, 1967	329180-330199
1965, 1967, 1968	330200-332240
1965	332241-347090
1965	348000-348092
1966	348093-349100
1965	349121-368638
1966	368640-369890
1967	370000-370999
1966	380000-385309
1967	390000-390998
1965, 1966, 1967, 1968	400001-400999
1966	401000-407985
1966	408000-408690
1966	408800-409250
1966	420000-426090
1966	427000-429180
1966	430005-438530
1966	438800-438925
1965, 1966, 1968, 1969	500000-500999
1965	501010-501600
1968	501601-501702
1965, 1968	501703-502706
1968	503010-503110
1965, 1968	503405-520955
1968	520956-530056
1966, 1968, 1969	530061-530850
1968, 1969	530851-530993
1969	530994-539999
1966, 1969	540000-540795
1969	540796-545009

YEAR	APPROXIMATE SERIAL RANGE
1966	550000-556910
1969	558012-567400
1966	570099-570755
1969	580000-580999
1966, 1967, 1968, 1969	600000-600999
1969	601000-601090
1969	605901-606090
1966, 1967	700000-700799
1968, 1969	750000-750999
1966, 1967, 1968, 1969	800000-800999
1966, 1969	801000-812838
1969	812900-814999
1969	817000-819999
1966, 1969	820000-820087
1966	820088-823830
1969	824000-824999
1966, 1969	828002-847488
1966	847499-858999
1967	859001-880089
1967	893401-895038
1968	895039-896999
1967	897000-898999
1968	899000-899999
1968	900000-902250
1968	903000-920899
1968	940000-941009
1968	942001-943000
1968	945000-945450
1968	947415-956000
1968	959000-960909
1968	970000-972864

Between 1970-1975, the method of serializing instruments at Gibson became even more random. All numbers were impressed into the wood and a 6-digit number assigned, although no particular order was given and some instruments have a letter prefix. The orange labels inside hollow bodied instruments were discontinued in 1970, and replaced by white and orange rectangular labels on the acoustics, while a small black, purple and white rectangular label was placed on electric models. Also in 1970, the words "MADE IN USA" were impressed into the back of instrument headstocks, though a few instruments from the 1950's also had "MADE IN USA" impressed into their headstocks.

Year(s)	Approximate Series Manufacture
1970, 1971, and 1972	100000s, 600000s, 700000s, 900000s
1973	000001s, 100000s 200000s, 800000s and a few "A" + 6 digit numbers
1974 and 1975	100000s, 200000s, 300000s, 400000s, 500000s, 600000s, 800000s, and a few "A-B-C-D-E-F" + 6 digit numbers

Between 1975-1977, Gibson used a transfer that utilized 8-digit numbering - the first two indicate the year, 99=1975, 00=1976 and 06=1977, the following 6-digits are in the 100,000-200,000 range. "MADE IN USA" was also included on the transfer and some models also had "LIMITED EDITION" applied. A few bolt-on neck instruments had a date ink-stamped on the heel area.

In 1977, Gibson began using the serialization method that continues to be used today. It utilizes an impressed 8-digit numbering system which includes both serializing and dating instruments. The pattern is as follows: YDDDYPPP - YY is the production year, DDD is the day of the year, PPP is the plant designation and instrument rank. The numbers 001-499 show Kalamazoo production, 500-999 show Nashville production. The Kalamazoo numbers were discontinued in 1984. When acoustic production was begun at the plant built in Bozeman, Montana (1989), the series' numbers were reorganized. Bozeman instruments began using 001-299 designates and, in 1990, Nashville instruments began using 300-999 designates. It should also be noted that the Nashville plant has not reached the 900's since 1977, so these numbers have been reserved for prototypes.

Examples: 70108276 means the instrument was produced on Jan.10, 1978, in Kalamazoo and was the 276th instrument stamped that day.

82765501 means the instrument was produced on Oct. 3,1985, in Nashville and was the 1st instrument stamped that day.

In addition to the above serial number information, Gibson also used Factory Order Numbers (FON) to track batches of instruments being produced at the time. This system is also useful in helping to date and authenticate instruments. There are three separate groupings of numbers that have been identified and are used for their accuracy. The numbers are usually stamped or written on the instrument's back and seen through the lower F hole or round soundhole, or may be impressed on the back of the headstock.

1908-1923 approximate #'s

YEAR		FON
1908		259
1909		309
1910	545,	927
1911	1260,	1295
1912	1408,	1593
1913	1811,	1902
1914	1936,	2152
1915	2209,	3207
1916	2667,	3508
1917	3246,	11010
1918	9823,	11159
1919	11146,	11212
1920	11329,	11367
1921	11375,	11527
1922	11565,	11729
1923	11973	

FON's for the years 1935-1941 usually consisted of the batch number, a letter for the year and the instrument number.

Examples are as follows:
722 A 23, 465 D 58, 863 E 02.

Code Letter and Year

A	1935
B	1936
C	1937
D	1938
E	1939
F	1940
G	1941

From 1952-1961, the FON system followed the pattern of a letter, the batch number and an instrument number - examples are as follows:
Y 2230 21, V 4867 8, R 6785 15.

Code Letter and Year

Z	1952
Y	1953
X	1954
W	1955
V	1956
U	1957
T	1958
S	1959
R	1960
Q	1961

After 1961, the use of FON's was discontinued at Gibson.

There are still variances that Gibson uses on some instruments produced today, but for the most part, the above system can be used for identifying instruments. For the most accurate identification you will need to contact the Gibson Guitar Corporation.

Identifying Features on Gibson Musical Instruments

The most consistent and easily found feature that is consistent through all models of Gibson production is the logo, or lack of one, found on the headstock. The very earliest instruments made are generally found with a star inside a crescent design, or a blank peghead. This lasted until circa 1902. Between 1902 and the late 1920's, "The Gibson" is inlaid in pearl and placed at a slant, and found on the peghead. In the late 1920's, this style of logo was changed to having "The Gibson" read straight across the peghead as opposed to being slanted. Flat top acoustics production began at approximately this same time and generally do not have "The" on the inlay, rather only "Gibson" in script writing. By 1933, this was the established headstock logo for Gibson. Just before WWII, Gibson began making the lettering on the logo thicker and this became standard on most pre-war instruments. Shortly after WWII, the styling of the logo remained but became slanted once again. In 1947, the logo that is still in use today made its debut. This logo has a block styling with the "G" having a tail, the "i" dot is touching the "G", the "b" and "o" are open and the "n" is connected at the bottom. The logo is still slanted. By 1951, the dot on the "i" is no longer connected to the "G".

In 1967, the logo styling became even more squared (pentographed) with the "b" and "o" becoming closed and the "i" dot being removed.

In 1970, Gibson replaced the black tinted piece of wood that had been used on the peghead face with a black fiber, into which both the logo and peghead inlays were placed. With the change in peghead facing came a slightly smaller logo lettering.

By 1972, the "i" dot reappeared on the peghead logo. In 1981, the "n" is connected at the top to the "o". There are a few models through the years that do not follow this timeline, (ie, reissues and limited editions), but most of the production instruments can be found with the above feature changes.

The figuration of the Kluson tuners used on Gibson instruments can be used to date an instrument. Before 1959, all Kluson tuners with plastic buttons had a single ring around the stem end of the button. In 1960, this was changed to a double ring configuration.

Another dating feature of Gibson instruments is the use of a headstock volute found on instruments manufactured 1970-1973. Also in 1965, Gibson switched from a 17-degree angle to a 14-degree angle for the headstock tilt. Before 1950, peghead thickness varied, getting narrower towards the top of the peghead. After 1950, pegheads became one top-to-bottom, uniform thickness.

Gretsch Serialization

Before World War II, serial numbers were penciled onto the inside backs of Gretsch's better quality models. By 1949, small labels bearing "Fred Gretsch Mfg. Co.", and serial/model numbers replaced the penciled numbers inside their instruments. This label, in turn, was replaced by a new style utilizing orange and grey colors circa 1957. A few variations of this system occurred throughout the company's history, the most common being the use of impressed numbers in the headstocks, circa 1949. Serial numbers were also stamped into the headstock nameplate of a few models. The numbers remain consecutive throughout and the following chart gives approximations of the years they occurred.

APPROXIMATE SERIALIZATION RANGE	YEARS
001 - 1000	1939-1945
1001 - 2000	1946-1949
2001 - 3000	1950
3001 - 5000	1951
5001 - 6000	1952
6001 - 8000	1953
8001 - 12000	1954
12001 - 16000	1955
16001 - 21000	1956
21001 - 26000	1957
26001 - 30000	1958
30001 - 34000	1959
34001 - 39000	1960
39001 - 45000	1961
45001 - 52000	1962
52001 - 63000	1963
63001 - 78000	1964
78001 - 85000	1965

In the latter part of 1965, Gretsch decided to begin using a date coded system of serialization. It consists of the first digit, sometimes two, identifying the month, the second or third identifying the year and the following digit (or digits) are the number of the instrument produced that month. Some examples of this system would be:

997 - September, 1969, 7th instrument produced.

11255 - November, 1072, 55th instrument produced.

On solid body instruments, impressed headstock numbers were used with "Made in USA" being added in 1967. Hollow body instruments still made use of a label placed on the inside back of the instrument. About 1973, the label style changed once again, becoming a black and white rectangle with "Gretsch Guitars", incorporating the date-coded serialization. A hyphen was also added between the month and the year to help avoid confusion;

12-4387 - December, 1974, 387th instrument produced.

3-745 - March, 1977, 45th instrument produced.

Martin Serialization

YEAR	LAST #
1898	8348
1899	8716
1900	9128
1901	9310
1902	9528
1903	9810
1904	9988
1905	10120
1906	10329
1907	10727
1908	10883
1909	11018
1910	11203
1911	11413
1912	11565
1913	11821
1914	12047
1915	12209
1916	12390
1917	12988
1918	13450
1919	14512
1920	15848
1921	16758
1922	17839
1923	19891
1924	22008
1925	24116
1926	28689
1927	34435
1928	37568
1929	40843
1930	45317
1931	49589
1932	52590
1933	55084
1934	58679
1935	61947
1936	65176
1937	68865
1938	71866
1939	74061
1940	76734
1941	80013
1942	83107
1943	86724
1944	90149
1945	93623
1946	98158
1947	103468
1948	108269
1949	112961
1950	117961
1951	122799
1952	128436
1953	134501
1954	141345
1955	147328
1956	152775
1957	159061
1958	165576
1959	171047
1960	175689
1961	181297
1962	187384
1963	193327

Year	#
1964	199626
1965	207030
1966	217215
1967	230095
1968	241925
1969	256003
1970	271633
1971	294270
1972	313302
1973	333873
1974	353387
1975	371828
1976	388800
1977	399625
1978	407800
1979	419900
1980	430300
1981	436474
1982	439627
1983	446101
1984	453300
1985	460575
1986	468175
1987	476216
1988	483952
1989	493279
1990	503309
1991	512487

Identifying Features on Martin Musical Instruments

When trying to determine the year of an instrument's construction some quick notes about features can be helpful. The few notes contained herein are for readily identifying the instrument upon sight, and are by no means meant to be used for definitive dating of a particular instrument. All items discussed are for flat top steel string guitars. The earliest dreadnoughts, and indeed just about all instruments produced with a neck joined to the body at the 12th fret, have bodies that are bell shaped on the top, as opposed to the more square shouldered styles of most dreadnoughts. Between 1929-1934, Martin began placing 14 fret necks on most of their instruments, bringing about the square shouldered body style. A few models maintained 12 fret necks into the late 1940's, with one on the market until the late 1980's.

Turn of the century instruments have square slotted headstocks with an intricate pearl fern inlay that runs vertically along the peghead. This was replaced by a vertical inlay known as the "flowerpot" or the "torch" inlay, circa 1905. By approximately 1934, a solid peghead with a vertical pearl "C.F. Martin" inlay had replaced the former peghead design. In 1932, the "C.F. Martin & Co. Est. 1833" scroll logo began appearing on certain models' pegheads. Bridges from the 1900's are rectangular with "pyramid" wings. In approximately 1929, the "belly" bridge replaced the rectangle bridge. This bridge has a straight slot cut across the entire length of the bridge. In 1965, the straight cut saddle slot was changed to a routed slot. Approximately 1936, Martin began using the "tied" bridge on their instruments. Pickguards were not standard features on instruments until circa 1933, when they started using tortoise shell pickguards. In 1966, black pickguards became standard.

Index of Manufacturers

Alembic..93
Alvarez 97
Alvarez Yairi.......................................103
Tom Anderson Guitars.........................107
Aria...109
Bass Collection...................................123
Benedict Guitars 125
Blade...126
Breedlove..128
Buscarino..128
Carvin...129
Chandler..132
Charvel..133
Charvette...141
Collings...142
Coral...144
Danelectro 145
D'Angelico 145
D'Aquisto...146
Eggle...147
Epiphone...149
Ernie Ball/Music Man 153
ESP 155
Fender...157
       Jazz Series......................188
       Precision Series...............190
       Stratocaster Series..........171
       Telecaster Series 179
       Fernandes.......................193
G & L...199
Gibson...202
       ES Series.........................215
       Firebird Series.................223
       Gibson Historical Collection....248
       J Series 205
       Les Paul Series.................227
       SG Series 239
Gretsch - Original U.S. Production........252
Gretsch - Current Production 268
Gudelsky Musical Instruments.............273
Guild...273
Hamburguitar......................................281
Hamer..281
Heartfield...284
Heritage...287
Hohner...295
Ibanez...303
J.B. Player 321

Jackson 325
Jerry Jones 333
Kalamazoo..335
Kay..335
Lado..337
Lady Luck Industries, Inc....................339
Lag Guitars...339
Larrivee...341
Lowden..347
Martin..349
Modulus Graphite................................367
Neo..371
Norman Guitars...................................371
Ovation..373
PRS (Paul Reed Smith) Guitars...........379
Peavey 382
Pedulla, M.V..386
Rainsong...391
Rickenbacker.......................................391
Robin...405
Samick...409
Santa Cruz 417
Santucci...418
Schack...419
Schecter 420
Shadow..421
Shenandoah..423
Sigma..425
Ken Smith Basses 429
Starfield...430
Status..432
Steinberger..434
Stephen's 439
Takamine...441
Taylor..450
Tobias..453
Triggs Guitars 455
Turtletone..456
Valley Arts...457
Vantage 458
Vester..464
Vigier...467
Warwick...471
Washburn...473
WRC Guitars 489
Yamaha..491
Yups...503
Zeta..505
Zion...505